ASIA SMALL AND MEDIUM-SIZED ENTERPRISE MONITOR 2021

VOLUME I—COUNTRY AND REGIONAL REVIEWS

DECEMBER 2021

ASIAN DEVELOPMENT BANK

ADB

6 ADB Avenue, Mandaluyong City, 1550 Metro Manila, Philippines
Tel +63 2 8632 4444; Fax +63 2 8636 2444
www.adb.org

ISBN 978-92-9269-174-5 (print); 978-92-9269-175-2 (electronic); 978-92-9269-176-9 (ebook)
Publication Stock No. SGP210459-2
DOI: http://dx.doi.org/10.22617/SGP210459-2

Notes:
In this publication, "$" refers to United States dollars, "Tk" refers to Bangladesh taka, "₹" refers to Indian rupee, "NRs" refers to Nepalese rupee, "PRs" refers to Pakistan rupees and "SLRs" refers to Sri Lanka rupees.

ADB recognizes "China" as the People's Republic of China, "Ceylon" as Sri Lanka, "Vietnam" as Viet Nam, and "Hanoi" as Ha Noi.

Cover design by Claudette Rodrigo.

Contents

Tables, Figures, and Boxes

Tables

Regional Review

Bangladesh

India

Nepal

Pakistan

Sri Lanka

Figures

Nepal

Pakistan

Sri Lanka

Boxes

Bangladesh

India

Nepal

Foreword

The global economy continued to struggle in 2021 due to the coronavirus disease (COVID-19) pandemic, and developing Asia was no exception. Large government stimulus packages and accommodative monetary policy helped soften the worst of the economic impact and support recovery. Yet with surging new coronavirus variants and consequent lockdowns, the disease remains the main downside risk for short-term economic growth in the region.

The pandemic and nationwide lockdowns severely limited most economic activity, especially for micro, small, and medium-sized enterprises (MSMEs). Including cottage industries, MSMEs are an integral part of the economy in developing Asia. They create jobs, stimulate domestic demand and competition, and are a critical segment for promoting inclusive growth. Yet they were devastated by the pandemic. Revitalizing MSMEs is key to building a resilient economic recovery in the region.

MSME policy design has grown more challenging given the complexity of the MSME business environment and rapidly evolving external environment. Sudden shocks such as the pandemic will require appropriate and timely assistance for MSMEs to survive. Properly designed policy support can help drive business opportunities while shocks are absorbed. Thus, governments need to constantly monitor the evolving business climate to design workable and enforceable policy support for MSME development.

Responding to heightened demand for high-quality multicountry analytical data on MSMEs and regional best practices that support their development, the Asian Development Bank (ADB) successfully launched the *Asia Small and Medium-Sized Enterprise Monitor* in 2020. While the previous issue featured Southeast Asian economies, we turn our focus to South Asia in this new edition. It comprises four volumes: (i) a country and regional review, (ii) a special chapter analyzing the COVID-19 impact on MSMEs in selected economies, (iii) a theme chapter assessing the impact of digitalization on Bangladesh's microfinance industry, and (iv) a technical chapter presenting our Small and Medium-Sized Enterprise Development Index. We hope Volume I continues to support our developing member countries' pursuit of evidence-based policy design on MSME development and access to finance.

Joseph Ernest Zveglich Jr.
Acting Chief Economist
Economic Research and Regional Cooperation Department
Asian Development Bank

Acknowledgments

The *Asia Small and Medium-Sized Enterprise Monitor (ASM) 2021* was prepared by Shigehiro Shinozaki, senior economist, Economic Research and Regional Cooperation Department (ERCD) of the Asian Development Bank (ADB). The work was supervised by Joseph Ernest Zveglich Jr., acting chief economist, and supported by Satoru Yamadera from ERCD's financial cooperation and integration team. The ASM team comprised Shigehiro Shinozaki, team leader; Anuj Chaudhary, ADB consultant for India; Bishal Chalise, ADB consultant for Nepal; Osman Mirza, ADB consultant for Pakistan; Josephine Penaflor Ferre, ADB consultant; and Chona Plete Guatlo, ADB consultant. Administrative support was provided by Richard Supangan and Maria Frederika Bautista.

Shigehiro Shinozaki wrote the Rationale and Methodology, Highlights, Regional Review, and Country Chapters for Bangladesh and Sri Lanka, and provided substantive comments/inputs and initially edited all country papers. Anuj Chaudhary authored the India Chapter. Bishal Chalise authored the Nepal Chapter. Osman Mirza authored the Pakistan Chapter. Josephine Ferre co-authored the Bangladesh Chapter with Shigehiro Shinozaki. Josephine Ferre and Chona Guatlo prepared the ASM 2021 database, guided by Shigehiro Shinozaki.

We thank all data contributors listed for their comprehensive reviews of respective country chapters in this report, despite difficulties working through the COVID-19 pandemic.

Data Contributors in Participating Developing Member Countries of the Asian Development Bank

South Asia

Country	Data Contributors
Bangladesh	Bangladesh Angels; Bangladesh Bank; Bangladesh Bureau of Statistics; Bangladesh Council of Scientific and Industrial Research; Bangladesh Securities and Exchange Commission; Bangladesh Small and Cottage Industries Corporation; BRAC Bank; Chittagong Stock Exchange; Credit Rating Agency of Bangladesh; Dhaka Chamber of Commerce and Industry; Dhaka Stock Exchange; IDLC Finance Limited; National Association of Small Cottage Industries Bangladesh; Metropolitan Chamber of Commerce and Industries; Microcredit Regulatory Authority; Ministry of Commerce; Ministry of Industry; SME Foundation; Palli Karma Sahayak Foundation
India	Bombay Stock Exchange; National Stock Exchange; Ministry of Micro, Small and Medium Enterprises; Reserve Bank of India; Small Industries Development Bank of India; Department of Commerce, Department for Promotion of Industry and Internal Trade, Ministry of Commerce and Industry; Council of Scientific and Industrial Research, Department of Scientific and Industrial Research, Ministry of Science and Technology; The Department of Agriculture, Cooperation and Farmers Welfare, Ministry of Agriculture and Farmers Welfare; Federation of Indian Chambers of Commerce and Industry; Indian Angel Network, Foundation for MSME Clusters; India SME forum; Ministry of Statistics and Program Implementation; Ministry of Skill Development and Entrepreneurship; National Institute for Micro, Small and Medium Enterprises; Securities and Exchange Board of India
Nepal	Central Bureau of Statistics; Deposit and Credit Guarantee Fund; Ministry of Finance; Ministry of Industries Commerce and Supplies; Nepal Planning Commission; Nepal Rastra Bank; Nepal Stock Exchange; Securities Board of Nepal
Pakistan	Federal Board of Revenue; Karandaaz; Ministry of Industries and Production; National Incubation Center, Pakistan Bureau of Statistics; Pakistan Stock Exchange; Securities and Exchange Commission of Pakistan; Small and Medium Enterprise Development Authority; State Bank of Pakistan
Sri Lanka	Central Bank of Sri Lanka; Colombo Stock Exchange; Department of Census and Statistics; Industrial Development Board; Industrial Technological Institute; Ministry of Finance; Ministry of Industries; National Enterprise Development Authority; Securities and Exchange Commission of Sri Lanka

Southeast Asia (Updates)

Country	Data Contributors
Brunei Darussalam	Bank Usahawan; Brunei Darussalam Central Bank; Department of Economic Planning and Statistics; Darussalam Enterprise; Ministry of Energy, Manpower, and Industry; Ministry of Finance and Economy
Cambodia	Cambodia Securities Exchange; General Department of SMEs and Handicraft - Ministry of Industry, Science, Technology and Innovation; Ministry of Commerce; Ministry of Economy and Finance; National Bank of Cambodia; National Institute of Statistics; Securities and Exchange Regulator of Cambodia
Indonesia	Bank Indonesia; Bandan Pusat Statistik; Coordinating Ministry for Economic Affairs; Indonesia Stock Exchange; Ministry of Cooperatives and SMEs; Otoritas Jasa Keuangan
Lao People's Democratic Republic	Bank of the Lao PDR; Lao Securities Commission Office; Lao Securities Exchange; Lao Statistics Bureau; Ministry of Industry and Commerce - Department of SME Promotions; Department of Industry and Handicraft
Malaysia	Bank Negara Malaysia; Bursa Malaysia; Department of Statistics Malaysia; Malaysia Digital Economy Corporation; Ministry of Entrepreneur Development and Cooperatives; Securities Commission Malaysia; SME Corporation Malaysia
Philippines	Bangko Sentral ng Pilipinas; Bureau of Small and Medium Enterprise Development, Department of Trade and Industry; Cooperative Development Authority; Philippine Guarantee Corporation; Philippine Statistics Authority; Philippine Stock Exchange Inc.; Securities and Exchange Commission; Small Business Corporation - Department of Trade and Industry
Singapore	Enterprise Singapore; Singapore Department of Statistics; Ministry of Trade and Industry; Monetary Authority of Singapore; Singapore Exchange
Thailand	Office of Small and Medium Enterprises Promotion; National Statistical Office; Bank of Thailand; Securities and Exchange Commission; The Stock Exchange of Thailand; Thai Credit Guarantee Corporation; The Fiscal Policy Office - Ministry of Finance
Viet Nam	Agency for Business Registration – Ministry of Planning and Investment; Agency for Enterprise Development – Ministry of Planning and Investment; General Statistics Office of Vietnam; Hanoi Stock Exchange; Ho Chi Minh Stock Exchange; Ministry of Finance; Ministry of Science and Technology; State Bank of Vietnam; State Securities Commission of Viet Nam

Abbreviations

ANBC	—	adjusted net bank credit
ADB	—	Asian Development Bank
BCSIR	—	Bangladesh Council of Scientific and Industrial Research
BICM	—	Bangladesh Institute of Capital Market
BFI	—	bank and financial institution
BSE	—	Bombay Stock Exchange
BIGD	—	BRAC Institute of Governance and Development
B2B	—	business-to-business
B2C	—	business-to-commerce
B2P	—	business-to-person
CEE	—	Census of Economic Establishments (Pakistan)
CBSL	—	Central Bank of Sri Lanka
CERSAI	—	Central Registry of Securitization Asset Reconstruction and Security Interest (India)
CCC	—	Ceylon Chamber of Commerce (Sri Lanka)
CPEC	—	China–Pakistan Economic Corridor
CSE	—	Chittagong Stock Exchange (for Bangladesh); Colombo Stock Exchange (for Sri Lanka)
CALL	—	Commercial Agriculture and Livestock Loan (Nepal)
CFC	—	common facility centre (India)
CAGR	—	compound annual growth rate
CMSME	—	cottage, micro, small, and medium-sized enterprise
C2B	—	consumer-to-business
C2C	—	consumer-to-consumer
COVID-19	—	coronavirus disease
CGFMU	—	Credit Guarantee Fund for Micro Unit (India)
CIB	—	credit information bureau
CRIB	—	Credit Information Bureau of Sri Lanka
CIC	—	credit information company
CICRA	—	Credit Information Companies Act
CLCSS	—	Credit Linked Capital Subsidy for Technology Upgradation
CRAB	—	Credit Rating Agency of Bangladesh
DCGF	—	Deposit and Credit Guarantee Fund (Nepal)
DCCI	—	Dhaka Chamber of Commerce and Industry (Bangladesh)
DSE	—	Dhaka Stock Exchange (Bangladesh)
DFS	—	digital financial service
e-CIB	—	electronic Credit Information Bureau
ETF	—	Exchange Traded Fund
EFS	—	Export Finance Scheme; Export Refinance Scheme
FCCISL	—	Federation of Chambers of Commerce and Industry of Sri Lanka

FICCI	—	Federation of Indian Chambers of Commerce and Industry
FNCSI	—	Federation of Nepal Cottage and Small Industries
FNCCI	—	Federation of Nepalese Chamber of Commerce and Industries
FWEAN	—	Federation of Woman Entrepreneurs' Associations of Nepal
FY	—	fiscal year
FDI	—	foreign direct investment
GeM	—	government e-marketplace (India)
G2P	—	government-to-person
GDP	—	gross domestic product
GVA	—	gross value added
GEM	—	Growth Enterprise Market (Pakistan)
IPP	—	Industrial Promotion Policy (Nepal)
ICT	—	information and communication technology
IT	—	information technology
IPO	—	initial public offering
IMF/IFS	—	International Monetary Fund/International Financial Statistics
KW	—	kilowatt
KYC	—	know your customer
LFS	—	Labor Force Survey
LCB	—	licensed commercial bank
LSB	—	licensed specialized bank
LTFF	—	Long-Term Finance Facility (Pakistan)
MLI	—	member lending institution
M&A	—	merger and acquisition
MCCI	—	Metropolitan Chamber of Commerce and Industry (Bangladesh)
MSE	—	micro and small enterprise
MSE-CDP	—	Micro and Small Enterprises Cluster Development Program (India)
MEDEP	—	Micro Enterprise Development Program (Nepal)
MEDPA	—	Micro Enterprise Development Program for Poverty Alleviation (Nepal)
MUDRA	—	Micro Units Development and Refinance Agency (India)
MSMED	—	Micro, Small and Medium Enterprises Development (India)
MSME	—	micro, small, and medium-sized enterprise
MRA	—	Microcredit Regulatory Authority
MF-CIB	—	Microfinance Credit Information Bureau (Bangladesh)
MFI	—	microfinance institution
MOICS	—	Ministry of Industries, Commerce and Supplies (Nepal)
MSDE	—	Ministry of Skill Development and Entrepreneurship (India)
MFS	—	mobile financial services
M&E	—	monitoring and evaluation
NASCIB	—	National Association of Small and Cottage Industries of Bangladesh
NCCSL	—	National Chamber of Commerce of Sri Lanka
NCID	—	National Council for Industrial Development (Bangladesh)
NCGI	—	National Credit Guarantee Institution (Sri Lanka)
NCGTC	—	National Credit Guarantee Trustee Company (India)
NFIS	—	national financial inclusion strategy
NIC	—	National Incubation Center (Pakistan)
NSIC	—	National Small Industries Corporation (India)
NSE	—	National Stock Exchange (India)

NSFI	—	National Strategy for Financial Inclusion (India)
NRB	—	Nepal Rastra Bank
NEPSE	—	Nepal Stock Exchange
NAC	—	NFIS-B Advisory Committee (Bangladesh)
NNC	—	NFIS-B National Council (Bangladesh)
NNS	—	NFIS-B Secretariat (Bangladesh)
NSC	—	NFIS-B Steering Committee (Bangladesh)
NBFC	—	nonbank finance company
NBFI	—	nonbank finance institution
NGO-MFI	—	nongovernment microfinance institution
NGO	—	nongovernment organization
NPF	—	nonperforming financing
NPL	—	nonperforming loan
PBS	—	Pakistan Bureau of Statistics
PCGC	—	Pakistan Credit Guarantee Company
P@SHA	—	Pakistan Software Houses Association
PSX	—	Pakistan Stock Exchange
PKSF	—	Palli Karma-Sahayak Foundation (Bangladesh)
PRC	—	People's Republic of China
P2B	—	person-to-business
P2G	—	person-to-government
P2P	—	person-to-person
R&D	—	research and development
RBI	—	Reserve Bank of India
SFURTI	—	Scheme of Fund for Regeneration of Traditional Industries (India)
STR	—	Secured Transaction Registry (Nepal)
SEBI	—	Securities and Exchange Board of India
SECP	—	Securities and Exchange Commission of Pakistan
SEC	—	Securities and Exchange Commission of Sri Lanka
SEBON	—	Security Board of Nepal
SMEDA	—	Small and Medium Enterprise Development Authority (Pakistan)
SME	—	small and medium-sized enterprise
SIDBI	—	Small Industries Development Bank of India
SMESPD	—	SME and Special Programmes Department (Bangladesh)
SEZ	—	special economic zone
SBP	—	State Bank of Pakistan
UPI	—	unified payments interface (India)
US	—	United States
WEL	—	Women Entrepreneur Loan (Nepal)
WCIC	—	Women's Chamber of Industry and Commerce (Sri Lanka)

Rationale and Methodology

Issues

Micro, small, and medium-sized enterprises (MSMEs) development policy is key to achieving inclusive growth nationally. MSME policy design has grown more challenging given the complexity of the MSME business environment and the rapidly evolving external environment. Liberalized trade and investment brought about by economic integration and expansion, and the advent of advanced technologies, has promoted the structural change needed for the MSME business model to shift from a domestic focus to being globally competitive. This shift requires new policy solutions for emerging growth-oriented MSMEs. A changing external environment accelerated by scientific and technological breakthroughs and foreign direct investment inflows will create more opportunities for MSMEs to do business in developing Asia. Meanwhile, the changing external environment forced by sudden shocks such as the coronavirus disease (COVID-19) pandemic will require appropriate and timely assistance for MSMEs to survive. Properly designed policy support can help these opportunities materialize and for shocks to be absorbed. Thus, governments need to constantly monitor the evolving business climate to design workable and enforceable policy support for MSME development.

Governments in Asian Development Bank (ADB) developing member countries (DMCs) are seeking timely access to high-quality multicountry analytical data and other countries' best practices on MSME development. This is so they can effectively assess and implement enforceable MSME policies. ADB is in the best position to provide data and policy advice, given its long-term expertise and projects supporting MSME development across the region.

Concept

The Asia Small and Medium-Sized Enterprise Monitor (ASM) is a knowledge-sharing product developed as a key resource for MSME development policies in Asia and the Pacific. The ASM, as an annual periodical, reviews financial and nonfinancial conditions of MSMEs at the country and regional level. The ASM has several main objectives: (i) provide in-depth analyses on MSMEs, finance, and policy interventions; (ii) exchange country best practices and experiences on MSME development; and (iii) present timely comparative financial and nonfinancial data on MSMEs. Its target clientele are DMC policymakers responsible for MSME development and access to finance to support their promotion of evidence-based policy design, but also serves additional audiences. The ASM expects that analyzed data on MSME development and access to finance will contribute to increasing analytical outputs on MSMEs from academia; thus, it will promote global and regional dialogue on MSME policies and financial inclusion.

The ASM project continues to follow its phased approach. The Phase 1 project (September 2012–May 2014) designed a feasible framework for a MSME data platform for Asia and the Pacific. As a pilot product, the inaugural ASM 2013 was published in April 2014 with 14 countries from five ADB regions: (i) Kazakhstan in Central Asia; (ii) the People's Republic of China (PRC) and the Republic of Korea (ROK) in East Asia; (iii) Bangladesh, India, and

Sri Lanka in South Asia; (iv) Cambodia, Indonesia, Malaysia, the Philippines, Thailand, and Viet Nam in Southeast Asia; and (v) Papua New Guinea and Solomon Islands in the Pacific.

The Phase 2 project (July 2014–September 2015) improved the ASM platform based on feedback from DMC partner institutions, expanded country coverage, and designed a pilot online ASM database (for internal use only). With the success of the inaugural volume of ASM 2013, ASM 2014 (second edition) was published in September 2015 covering 20 DMCs from five ADB regions: (i) Kazakhstan, the Kyrgyz Republic, and Tajikistan in Central Asia; (ii) the PRC, ROK, and Mongolia in East Asia; (iii) Bangladesh, India, and Sri Lanka in South Asia; (iv) Cambodia, Indonesia, Lao People's Democratic Republic (Lao PDR), Malaysia, Myanmar, the Philippines, Thailand, and Viet Nam in Southeast Asia; and (v) Fiji, Papua New Guinea, and Solomon Islands in the Pacific.

After Phase 2, ADB conducted evaluation surveys for both DMCs and ADB operations, and received positive feedback from both external and internal clients asking to regularize the ASM. In July 2019, after a 4-year interval, the ASM project moved into Phase 3 as a multiyear project, strengthening its global reach and data comparability, and developing a user-friendly online data portal. As the ASM 2013 and 2014 focused specifically on MSME access to finance, ASM 2020 upgraded prior ASM products by extending its analytical coverage to nonfinancial issues on MSME development.

In October 2020, ADB released the four-volume ASM 2020, focusing on 10 Southeast Asian countries.[1] The 2021 edition extended country coverage to five South Asian countries—Bangladesh, India, Nepal, Pakistan, and Sri Lanka, together with data updates from Southeast Asia.

The ASM normally comprises three key components: (i) country and regional reviews, (ii) thematic analysis, and (iii) technical assessments (Figure 1.1). Because of the pandemic, however, ADB added a special chapter to ASM 2020 and ASM 2021.

The Country and Regional Review Volume offers in-depth analyses on financial and nonfinancial issues of a country's MSME development. Each has three review dimensions with 14 subdimensions for analysis: (i) MSME development (scale of MSMEs, employment, business productivity, market access, technology and innovation, and networking and support); (ii) access to finance (bank credit, public financing and guarantees, nonbank financing, digital financial services, capital markets, and financial infrastructure); and (iii) policies and regulations (MSME development and financial inclusion). This component analyzes these dimensions based on data collected from DMC partner institutions by using a standardized ASM data request form. For the ASM 2020 and ASM 2021, one more dimension on the pandemic's impact on MSMEs and policy responses was added. This report is Volume I of the ASM 2021.

As mentioned, for ASM 2021, given the heightened needs of DMC governments, ADB continued to prepare a **Special Chapter** on "How Asia's Small Businesses Survived One Year into the COVID-19 Pandemic." This special study is based on the findings from year-long MSME surveys conducted in March 2020–April 2021 in Indonesia, the Lao PDR, the Philippines, and Thailand. It is Volume II of ASM 2021.

The Thematic Chapter explores each country's best practices related to MSME development by using an impact evaluation approach—an approach that assesses how an intervention affects particular conditions compared with non-intervention. This is a useful analytical tool to evaluate the impact of policy interventions on MSME

1 ADB. Asia Small and Medium-Sized Enterprise Monitor 2020. https://www.adb.org/publications/series/asia-small-medium-sized-enterprise-monitor.

development nationally. The analysis will also be used as a pilot project exercise for MSME development in DMCs. This component is Volume III of the ASM 2021.

The Technical Chapter is a new feature. It aims to design and test a new composite index called the Small and Medium-Sized Enterprise Development Index (SME-DI) to measure two dimensions affecting MSME development, and finance and nonfinance areas, by using multivariate analysis based on country data received in the ASM project. This component is Volume IV of ASM 2021.

Figure 1.1: Key Components of the Asia Small and Medium-Sized Enterprise Monitor

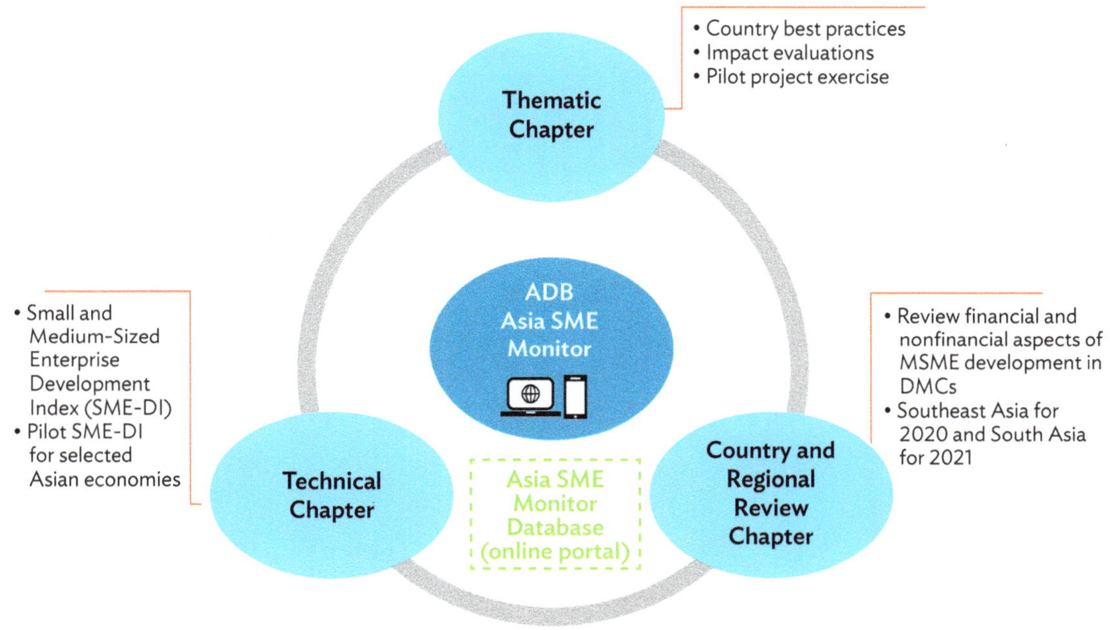

SME = small and medium-sized enterprise.

ADB = Asian Development Bank, DMC = developing member country, MSME = micro, small, and medium-sized enterprise, SME = small and medium-sized enterprise.

Source: ADB. Asia Small and Medium-Sized Enterprise Monitor 2020. https://www.adb.org/publications/series/asia-small-medium-sized-enterprise-monitor.

Evaluation

Figure 1.2 shows the result of an evaluation survey conducted with participating institutions after the launch of ASM 2020. The survey respondents were highly satisfied with the data components and quality of the ASM, with a rating of 4.5 out of 5. Respondents also rated the usefulness of the ASM in designing their MSME development and finance policies, with a rating of 4.7 (Figure 1.2A). The survey respondents expect that the ASM will (i) promote evidence-based policymaking, with a rating of 4.6; and (ii) ensure the timely sharing of other countries' policy practices, with 4.4, suggesting high demand on ASM from DMCs (Figure 1.2B).

Figure 1.2: Evaluation Survey on Asia Small and Medium-Sized Enterprise Monitor 2020

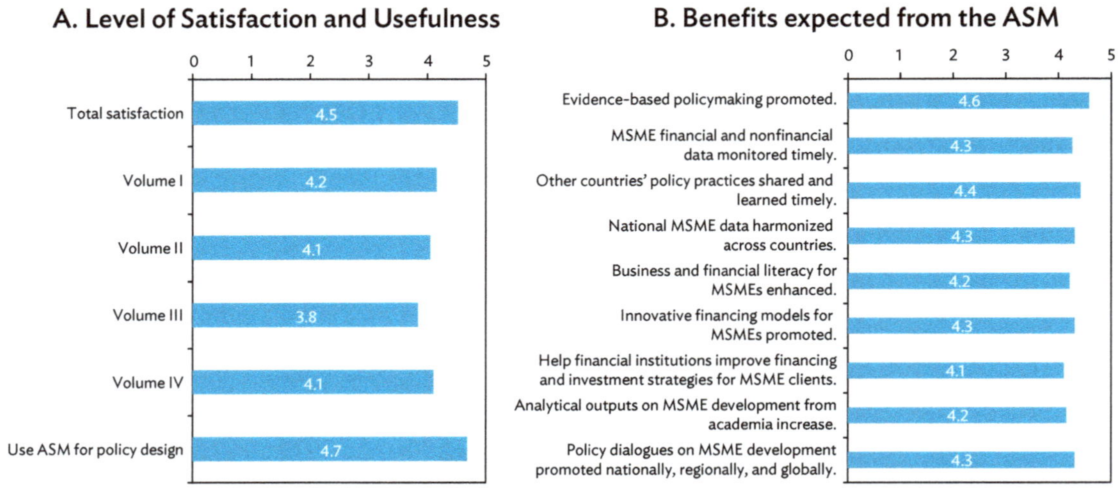

ASM = Asia Small and Medium-Sized Enterprise Monitor; MSME = micro, small, and medium-sized enterprise.5: yes, 4: somewhat yes, 3: neutral, 2: somewhat no, 1: no.

Notes: The survey was conducted from December 2020 to January 2021. Average score of 19 valid responses from participating institutions in developing member countries including Cambodia, the Lao People's Democratic Republic, the Philippines, Singapore, Thailand, and Viet Nam.

Source: Asian Development Bank.

Data Processing

To collect reliable and accurate data with periodic updates, ADB first built up strategic partnerships with key institutions that hold MSME data, including SME agencies, relevant line ministries, statistics offices, central banks, financial authorities, SME banks, and chambers of commerce (Figure 1.3). To systematically compile the data, ADB prepared a Standardized Data Request Form for collecting MSME data from partner institutions, comprising two separate forms on finance and nonfinance. Missing data and information from the data forms were supplemented by surveys, field research, and virtual interviews. For the ASM 2021, virtual missions were conducted in March–April 2021 in Bangladesh, India, Nepal, Pakistan, and Sri Lanka. A total of 88 virtual meetings and interviews were conducted with key stakeholders including central banks, financial authorities, SME agencies, line ministries, and private sector institutions across five South Asian countries, which became the basis for Country Chapter analysis. All data collected were interactively reviewed and finalized by an ADB team and DMC partner institutions. Volume I country and regional data are downloadable from the ADB Asia SME Monitor database (online data portal). The ASM also has a feedback mechanism for participating DMCs through training programs. The training module will be developed based on the ASM findings upon request from DMCs.

Figure 1.3: Data Processing Flow

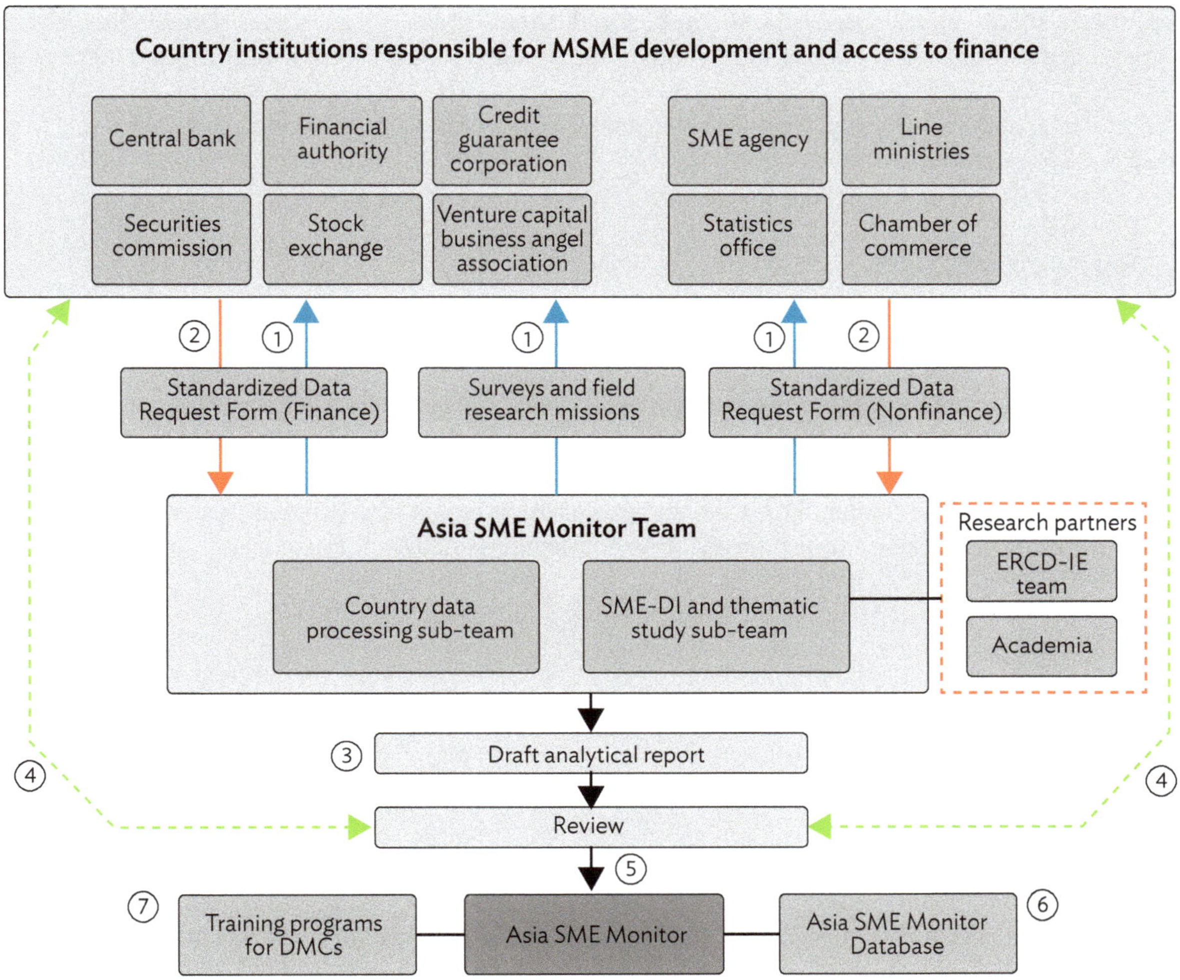

DMC = developing member country; ERCD = Economic Research and Regional Cooperation Department of Asian Development Bank; MSME = micro, small, and medium-sized enterprise; SME = small and medium-sized enterprise; SME-DI = Small and Medium-Sized Enterprise Development Index.

1. The standardized data request forms are delivered to respective counterpart institutions in participating DMCs (one for SME agency, line ministries, statistics office, and chamber of commerce; another for central bank, financial authorities, financial institutions, and finance-/investment-related associations).
2. Country counterpart institutions complete the data forms and return them to the Asia SME Monitor (ASM) team.
3. Based on collected data from counterpart institutions, the ASM team prepares draft country papers.
4. Draft country papers are sent out for review to the counterpart institutions or a focal entity in the participating country. After the necessary revisions reflecting feedback from counterpart institutions, country papers are finalized.
5. All country papers, together with the analytical paper and a thematic study, are consolidated into the single product.
6. Country and regional data under the ASM are downloadable from ADB Asia SME Monitor database (online data portal).
7. ASM is disseminated through the launch seminar at a selected DMC, ADB headquarters, and/or virtual conference. Training programs based on key findings from the ASM are elaborated for requested DMCs as back-to-back events with the dissemination seminar or as standalone events.

Source: Asian Development Bank.

Reading Note

In South Asia, MSME definitions vary by country, using different criteria and categories such as micro and small enterprises (MSEs); small and medium-sized enterprises (SMEs); and cottage, micro, small, and medium-sized enterprises (CMSMEs) following respective country definitions. The ASM relies upon country definitions of MSMEs for comparative analysis as they are a benchmark for their MSME policies, and collectively uses "MSME" throughout, unless otherwise stated.

Moving Forward

The ASM uses a regionally focused approach for analysis. It provides deep analysis of a designated region and countries, with data updates of past analyses of regions and countries each year. Following this, the ASM 2020 focused on Southeast Asia covering 10 countries, and the ASM 2021 did so for South Asia featuring five countries with data updates of Southeast Asian countries. The ASM 2022 will expand country coverage further to Central Asia. Due to the ongoing pandemic and potential outbreaks of new coronavirus variants, data collection and the verification process will be conducted virtually through online missions to designated countries. This approach, however, will be flexible, taking into account COVID-19 conditions in 2022.

Highlights

South Asian economies in 2021 have been recovering well from the COVID-19 pandemic, but risks remain; revitalizing MSMEs will be key to building a resilient economic recovery in the region.

Micro, small, and medium-sized enterprises (MSMEs), including cottage firms, are an integral part of the economy in South Asia. Based on latest available data until 2020 and following national definitions, MSMEs in the region accounted for an average 99.6% of all enterprises, 76.6% of the workforce, and 33.9% of a country's gross domestic product (GDP). They create jobs, stimulate domestic demand and competition, and are critical for inclusive growth. The pandemic hit most MSMEs hard. Economies in the region could recover and boost their resilience to shocks by strengthening MSME growth and dynamics.

MSMEs largely supply domestic markets, with many unregistered and informal; formalizing them and connecting to international markets would boost national productivity.

In Bangladesh, 87% of manufacturers sell their products locally. About 85% of workers in Nepal are informal. The majority of MSMEs are engaged in services and operate in rural areas in the region; only a few cater to international markets, although their impact on exports varies by country. MSMEs in India contribute an average 47% of overall exports (fiscal year [FY]2013–FY2020), higher than the Southeast Asian average of 19.2% (2010–2020). Market access and internationalizing MSMEs are core strategies under national MSME policies in South Asia. Formalizing MSMEs allows their businesses to develop globally and contributes to national productivity.

Growing e-commerce markets have rapidly expanded MSME market reach; fostering technology-based start-ups and youth and women entrepreneurs will further digitize the economy and support inclusive development.

Traditionally, MSMEs are mostly low-tech, with some exceptions—technology-based MSMEs and start-ups have emerged as digital penetration increases and e-commerce markets expand nationally. Their businesses have grown, and are enthusiastic, innovative, and technological adept. Youth and women entrepreneurs have large potential to lead the digital industry at national, regional, and global levels, especially once the pandemic subsides.

The MSME credit market remains small but is growing, supported by government assistance measures; however, high nonperforming MSME loans remain a challenge.

Limited access to financial services is a chronic problem for MSMEs and has become more serious during the pandemic. Across South Asia, bank lending to MSMEs was equivalent to an average 7.0% of a country's GDP (2015–2019) and 14.8% of total bank lending (2015–2020). The MSME credit market is small but growing in Bangladesh, India, and Pakistan. Governments there have offered several financial assistance options to MSMEs using interest rate subsidies, refinancing, credit guarantees, and mandatory lending quotas, contributing to MSME credit growth despite the COVID-19 crisis. However, MSME nonperforming loans (NPLs) remain high, an average 13.6% of total MSME bank loans, above the overall bank average NPL ratio of 8.8% (2015–2020), although ratios have improved over time.

The nonbank finance industry supports MSME working capital needs; microfinance institutions support rural MSMEs and small entrepreneurs, yet their nonperforming loans are rising.

The nonbank finance industry is gradually developing in the region and supports MSME working capital needs, yet it remains small. Nonbank finance institutions (NBFIs) include microfinance institutions (MFIs), credit cooperatives, finance companies, and leasing and factoring companies. Among others, MFIs are critical in improving access to finance for rural MSMEs and small entrepreneurs, yet NPLs are rising. During 2015–2020, NBFI financing accounted for an average 3.2% of a country's GDP and 6.5% of total bank lending. The share of nonperforming financing to total NBFI financing averaged 5.6% and is rising. Public microfinance programs in Bangladesh and Sri Lanka have expanded in rural and poor areas.

Mobile financial services have grown rapidly, supported by national digital infrastructure; but its limited use requires greater digital literacy and skills development.

An interoperable national payment switch contributes to the growth of e-commerce as well as mobile financial services in South Asia. India's digital identification system (*Aadhar*) helps in providing wider digital financial services. Agent banking grew steadily even during the pandemic in Bangladesh, increasingly used in rural and remote areas. Mobile banking has expanded in Nepal and Pakistan. Peer-to-peer lending and equity crowdfunding platforms are being tested through regulatory sandboxes in Pakistan. Meanwhile, digital finance remains the exception, with cash still preferred in Sri Lanka, with digital credit, savings, insurance, and other services a challenge.

Specialized SME equity markets have emerged as growth capital financing venues for eligible MSMEs; yet there are few issuers and investors.

A dedicated SME equity market has been created in Bangladesh (SME platforms formed in 2019), India (BSE SME Exchange and NSE Emerge in 2012), Pakistan (Growth Enterprise Market in 2019), and Sri Lanka (Empower Board in 2018). There is no dedicated SME board in Nepal, but it is being discussed. As SME markets are relatively new to the region, data in these markets are unavailable. But based on existing equity markets that firms including MSMEs can tap, market capitalization averaged 18.2% of a country's GDP (2015–2020). The market size is small, but SME markets in India have grown rapidly since operations started (a compound annual growth rate of 67.4% from 2012 to 2020). Attracting more SME issuers and investors in these new markets is a key challenge.

Governments have comprehensive long-term MSME policies in line with their national development strategies; encouraging the use of a standardized national MSME definition or passing a dedicated MSME law will help effective policy implementation.

National MSME policies support areas like building a conducive business environment; increasing access to markets and finance; skills development; business cluster development; adopting new technologies; and assisting youth and women entrepreneurs, start-ups, agribusiness, and MSME exporters (participation in global value chains). Cottage industries—small manufacturing and home businesses—are also critical. Policies generally provide business infrastructure (business development services and capacity-building training) and financial assistance to MSMEs (through special funds or refinancing, with interest rate subsidies and credit guarantees), following time-bound targets and action plans.

MSMEs are defined by national policy frameworks or stipulated by law, generating a national single definition. However, various MSME definitions are substantially used in statistics office, central banks, and line ministries. India has a dedicated MSME law that guides MSME development. This approach would be worth considering in countries with no legal framework on MSMEs to enhance effective support.

Developing MSME data infrastructure promotes evidence-based MSME assistance and accelerates inclusive growth.

Developing data infrastructure will effectively support MSME development and promote evidence-based economic growth. In South Asia, MSME data infrastructure is not well established. A comprehensive and comparative MSME database covering both financial and nonfinancial conditions with periodic monitoring and evaluation is needed to identify timely assistance needs from MSMEs and provide policy support efficiently. Business registration systems should be strengthened further to monitor MSME development and formalize informal sectors. It is also critical to use granular enterprise data and cloud data through an established system for MSME analysis. Intragovernmental coordination on MSME data sharing between central and local governments should be strengthened as well. Bangladesh stresses the importance of institutionalizing SME statistics under its SME Policy 2019.

Comprehensive national financial inclusion strategies were formulated during 2015–2021; creating robust financial inclusion data is crucial for effective monitoring and policy interventions, while expanding financing options constitutes as a core strategy.

National financial inclusion strategies in the region commonly develop core strategic goals and action plans on digital finance and payments, financial literacy and education, consumer protection, and financial assistance for traditionally unserved and underserved segments, which include MSMEs, women entrepreneurs, and priority sectors such as agriculture. Intragovernmental coordination between central government and financial authorities is well established to implement and fine-tune policies. Robust financial inclusion data would help effectively monitor policy interventions.

The region's financial inclusion strategies are holistic but somewhat bank centric. From a long-term perspective, more attention should be paid to market-based financing via capital markets as a growth capital delivery channel to viable SMEs. Bangladesh's financial inclusion strategy mentions reinforcing SME capital markets.

Large government stimulus packages are supporting businesses and individuals during the pandemic; digitalizing MSME business continues as a policy priority, while more balanced support between firms hurt and benefiting from the pandemic is needed.

South Asia acted quickly to contain COVID-19 infections and curbed its initial impact on economies. Large stimulus packages spending 2%–16% of national GDP went to support businesses and individuals affected by the pandemic and restrictions. Government assistance covers a wide range of financial measures. Following business style changes accelerated by the pandemic, support for digitalizing MSME business continue to be a policy priority post COVID-19. Given the prolonged pandemic, government assistance should consider more balanced support for businesses hit badly by the pandemic (focused group assistance using a phased approach) and those with growth potential that build resilience (entrepreneurship development). This all need to be done without creating excessive budget deficits.

South Asia

Regional Review

Summary

As a region, South Asia is recovering from the impact of the coronavirus disease (COVID-19) pandemic—although speed varies by country given the uncertainty of new variants.[2] The Asian Development Bank (ADB) forecasts an 8.8% rebound in 2021 (led by India) after a 5.6% contraction in 2020.[3]

Like most, South Asian economies were hit hard by the pandemic, containment measures, and lockdowns. Economic growth in Bangladesh slowed to 3.5% in fiscal year (FY) 2020 (ended 30 June 2020) from 8.2% in FY2019. India's economy contracted by 7.3% in FY2021 (ended 31 March 2021) from 4.0% growth in FY2020. Nepal's economy contracted by 2.1% in FY2020 (ended 15 July 2020), well below the 6.7% growth in FY2019. Pakistan suffered a 0.5% contraction in FY2020 (ended 30 June 2020) from 2.1% growth in FY2019, while Sri Lanka's economy contracted by 3.6% in 2020 after growing by 2.3% in 2019. The pandemic and ensuing lockdowns severely limited most economic activities, including micro, small, and medium-sized enterprises (MSMEs).

With large government stimulus packages, recovery began in 2021, although still below pre-pandemic levels. India's gross domestic product (GDP) is forecast to grow by 10.0% in FY2022. Pakistan also expects a strong recovery, with 3.9% growth forecast for FY2021. A resilient Bangladesh economy grew by 5.5% in FY2021. Nepal is expected to grow by 2.3% and Sri Lanka by 3.4% in FY2021. However, the lockdowns and restrictions during the pandemic's second wave remain the main downside risk for these forecasts.

MSMEs, including cottage industries, help drive the region's economies. Based on the latest available data using national MSME definitions, these firms accounted for an average 99.6% of all enterprises, 76.6% of the total workforce, and 33.9% of GDP. They create jobs, stimulate domestic demand, and compete as a critical element of inclusive growth. Devastated by the pandemic, their recovery is critical for the region's revival.

For the most part, MSMEs supplement domestic markets, with few involved in exports or international supply chains, although this varies by country. Many are informal or unregistered. In Bangladesh, 87% of manufacturers exclusively supply local markets. In Nepal, 85% of the workforce are informal workers. The majority of MSMEs are in services and operate in rural areas. Nonetheless, in India, for example, MSMEs contributed an average 47.0% of exports from FY2013 to FY2020, higher than the Southeast Asia average of 19.2% (2010–2020). Increasing market access and internationalizing MSMEs are core strategies under the national MSME development policies across South Asia. Governments are promoting MSME exporters as suppliers or lead firms in global value chains.

2 South Asia comprises Bangladesh, India, Nepal, Pakistan, and Sri Lanka.

3 Asian Development Bank. 2021. *Asian Development Outlook (ADO) 2021 Update*. September.

Traditionally, MSMEs are low-tech, while there are some exceptions. Technology-based MSMEs and start-ups have grown as internet penetration increases and interoperable electronic payment platforms expand. E-commerce has rapidly expanded MSME markets.

Access to finance is a central policy goal for inclusive growth and MSME development. Limited access to financial services is a structural problem that seriously affected MSME operations as the pandemic intensified. Across South Asia, bank lending to MSMEs averaged just 7.0% of a country's GDP during 2015–2019 (a compound annual growth rate [CAGR] of –0.04%) and 14.8% of total bank lending during 2015–2020 (a CAGR of –0.7%). The MSME credit market remains small but growing in Bangladesh (a CAGR of 9.7% in 2015–2020), India (8.6%), and Pakistan (9.6%).

Governments and central banks across the region offer various financial assistance options to MSMEs. These were strengthened further in response to the pandemic—interest rate subsidies, refinancing, credit guarantees, as well as mandatory lending (Nepal) and lending targets to MSMEs (Bangladesh and India). They contributed to MSME credit growth as the COVID-19 crisis developed. However, MSME nonperforming loan (NPL) ratios remain high—an average 13.6%, above the bank average of 8.8% during 2015–2020—if improving (–6.9% CAGR for MSMEs and –2.5% CAGR for gross bank NPLs).

Nonbank finance is gradually developing in the region and helps supply MSME working capital. Yet the industry remains small. Nonbank finance institutions (NBFIs) include microfinance institutions (MFIs), credit cooperatives, finance companies, and leasing and factoring companies. Among others, MFIs play a critical role in improving access to finance for rural MSMEs and small entrepreneurs. Nonetheless, NPLs are rising. During 2015–2020, NBFI financing accounted for an average 3.2% of a country's GDP (4.9% CAGR) and 6.5% of total bank lending (-2.8%). The share of nonperforming financing to total NBFI financing averaged 5.6% and is rising (9.7% CAGR). Public microfinance programs (Bangladesh and Sri Lanka) have expanded in rural and poor areas.

Mobile financial services are rapidly expanding, backed by interoperable online payment platforms. The *Aadhar* digital identification system helps spread digital financial services across India. In Bangladesh, agent banking has grown steadily even during the pandemic and is increasingly popular in rural and remote areas. Mobile banking has also expanded in Nepal and Pakistan. Peer-to-peer lending and equity crowdfunding platforms are being tested through regulatory sandboxes in Pakistan. However, in Sri Lanka, digital finance remains the exception with cash still preferred.

Specialized SME equity markets with concessional listing requirements exist as growth capital financing venues for qualified small firms: in Bangladesh, there are SME platforms in the Chittagong and Dhaka Stock Exchanges; in India, there are the Bombay Stock Exchange's BSE SME Exchange and National Stock Exchange's NSE Emerge; in Pakistan, there is the Growth Enterprise Market (GEM); and in Sri Lanka, there is the Colombo Stock Exchange's Empower Board. There is yet no dedicated SME board in Nepal, but the possibility is being examined. As SME markets remain relatively new in Bangladesh (launched 2019), Pakistan (2019), and Sri Lanka (2018), data on these markets are unavailable. Based on existing equity markets that firms (including MSMEs) can tap, market capitalization averaged 18.2% of a country's GDP during 2015–2020 (–4.2% CAGR). Market size is small, but SME markets in India have grown rapidly since they opened in 2012 (67.4% CAGR in 2012–2020).

Governments have long-term MSME development frameworks, comprehensively covering financial and nonfinancial development in line with their national development strategies. In general, they seek a conducive business environment; access to market and finance; skills development; business clusters; increased use of technology; and offer assistance for groups such as youth and women entrepreneurships, start-ups, agribusiness, and internationalized MSMEs (to join global value chains). Cottage industries—small manufacturing and home businesses—are a critical segment of national MSME policies. They generally provide time-bound goals and action plans for developing appropriate business infrastructure (through business development services and capacity building) and financial assistance to MSMEs (through special funds or refinancing facilities, with interest subsidies and credit guarantees). The COVID-19 pandemic led governments to provide large-scale financial assistance to MSMEs to support them through lockdowns, maintain, and then reopen their businesses.

MSMEs are defined within the national policy frameworks in Bangladesh, Pakistan, and Sri Lanka, while they are stipulated by law in India and Nepal, leaving one national definition. However, there remain various MSME definitions used in statistics office, by central banks and line ministries in Bangladesh, Pakistan, and Sri Lanka. India has a dedicated MSME law that guides MSME development. This could be considered by countries with no legal framework on MSMEs to enhance effective support.

Developing national data infrastructure is key to MSME development and for evaluating evidence-based economic growth. In South Asia, MSME data infrastructure is not well established. A comprehensive, comparative MSME database covers both financial and nonfinancial conditions using periodic monitoring and analysis. It can identify timely assistance needs from MSMEs and better implement policy support. Long-interval census data and financially focused credit bureau and collateral registry data cannot fully capture the current state of MSMEs with any accuracy. To start, business registration must be strengthened to include currently informal MSMEs so their development can be monitored. It is also critical to use granular enterprise and cloud data for analysis. Intragovernmental coordination on MSME data sharing between central and local governments should be strengthened as well. Bangladesh pays attention to institutionalizing SME statistics under the SME Policy 2019.

Each country in this report has a comprehensive national financial inclusion strategy, formulated during 2015–2021. The strategies set core strategic goals and action plans on (i) digital finance and payments, (ii) financial literacy and education, (iii) consumer protection, and (iv) financial assistance for the traditionally unserved and underserved, including MSMEs, women entrepreneurs, and priority sectors such as agriculture. Bangladesh and Sri Lanka plan to create robust financial inclusion data for effective monitoring and for developing policies. Intragovernmental coordination between the central government and financial authorities generally works smoothly to implement and fine-tune policies.

Financial inclusion strategies are generally holistic but bank-centric. From a long-term perspective, more market-based financing (capital market development) is needed to provide qualified SMEs with sufficient growth capital. As mentioned, dedicated SME equity markets exist in Bangladesh, India, Pakistan, and Sri Lanka. But very few, if any, SMEs are listed and thus, few investors. Improving these markets would go a long way toward meeting the goals of national financial inclusion strategies. Bangladesh's financial inclusion strategy mentions reinforcing capital market services for SMEs.

Across the region, each country acted quickly to contain COVID-19 infections and curb the pandemic's impact on the economy. Large government stimulus—with spending from 2% to 16% of GDP—continues to support businesses and individuals affected by pandemic restrictions. The government assistance covers a wide range of measures, including liquidity support to financial institutions; debt restructuring (deferred debt payments); relaxed lending conditions (reduced interest through subsidies and caps); new lending to MSMEs and priority sectors (through refinancing facilities, special funds, and credit guarantees); and temporarily easing regulatory requirements (debt moratoria and NPL reclassifications). In addition, tax relief measures (reduced corporate income taxes) and employee income support (cash transfers) are provided to affected businesses, including MSMEs.

The pandemic accelerated the digital transformation of MSME businesses, and it continues to be a government priority. Formalizing the informal and opening up MSMEs to global are also priorities, along with developing youth and women entrepreneurships. Given the prolonged pandemic, government assistance should consider longer term and more balanced support for businesses hit badly—using more focused group assistance and a phased approach—and for growth-oriented firms and entrepreneurships—by channeling growth capital to them, without putting excessive stress on national budgets.

1. MSME Development

MSMEs in South Asia, 2020

	Percentage share	*Compound annual growth*
• **Number of MSMEs to total enterprises**	***99.6%***	***n/a,***
• **MSME employees to total employees**	***76.6%***	***n/a,***
• **MSME contribution to national GDP**	***33.9%***	***n/a,***
• **MSME export to total export value***	***47.0%***	***2.2%***

GDP = gross domestic product; fiscal year = FY; MSME = micro, small, and medium-sized enterprise.

* India for FY2013–FY2020.

Reporting countries only. Data based on latest available data until 2020.

Scale of MSMEs

MSME definitions vary by country based on different criteria, such as number of employees, fixed assets, annual sales turnover, and paid-up capital (Table 2.1). MSMEs are also classified differently by sector (manufacturing and services in Bangladesh and Sri Lanka). Specific criteria are used in some countries (investment in plant and machinery or equipment in India, use of energy for microenterprises in Nepal, and operating period for start-ups in Pakistan). There are unified national definitions for MSMEs including cottage firms and start-ups stipulated in the national policy frameworks in Bangladesh, Pakistan, and Sri Lanka; or stipulated by law in India and Nepal. Nonetheless, there are other various MSME definitions used in statistics office; by central banks; and within line ministries in Bangladesh, Pakistan, and Sri Lanka. Moreover, national policies categorize MSMEs differently and even differ by institution. As a benchmark, cottage, micro, small, and medium-sized enterprises are categorized separately in Bangladesh and Nepal; micro, small, and medium-sized enterprises are used in India, by Pakistan's central bank, and in Sri Lanka; start-ups, small, and medium-sized enterprises is the national definition used in Pakistan; while there is just one small enterprise category used by Pakistan's Federal Board of Revenue. Obviously, this makes it extremely difficult to compile data, analyze, or even discuss MSMEs across and even within countries due to the lack of a standardized usage of MSME definition. This report nonetheless relies on country-specific definitions of MSMEs for comparative analysis as they are the benchmark for MSME policies. It uses "MSME" throughout, unless otherwise stated.

Regardless of how they are defined, MSMEs—including cottage firms—are an integral part of the region's economy. Based on the latest available data through 2020, and using national firm classifications, MSMEs accounted for an average 99.6% of all enterprises.[4] They dominate businesses even more than in Southeast Asia, which averaged 97.6% during 2010–2020.[5] The number of MSMEs grew by 5.8% in India, 10.7% in Nepal, and 3.3% in Pakistan in terms of CAGR, again higher than in Southeast Asia (average 0.2% CAGR during 2010–2020) (Figure 2.1A).[6]

4 Data refer to 2013 (census) for Bangladesh and Sri Lanka, 2016 (73rd National Sample Survey, July 2015–June 2016) for India, and 2020 (Small and Medium Enterprise Development Authority's estimates) for Pakistan. The share of MSMEs to total enterprise is unavailable for Nepal.

5 Southeast Asia data are based on Asia SME Monitor 2021 database for ASEAN countries.

6 CAGR is calculated based on latest available data: FY2008–FY2018 for India, FY2010–FY2019 for Nepal, and 2005 and 2020 for Pakistan.

Table 2.1: MSME Definitions in South Asia

Country	Category	Definition							Remarks
		Employee	Asset	Turnover	Capital	By Sector	Others	Legal Basis	
Bangladesh	Cottage, micro, small, and medium-sized firm	√	√			√			Defined by the National Industrial Policy 2016.
		√	√	√		√			Utilized by central bank.
India	Micro, small, and medium-sized firm			√			√	√	Micro, Small and Medium Enterprise Development Act, 2006 (amended June 2020).
Nepal	Cottage, micro, small, and medium-sized firm	√	√	√			√	√	Industrial Enterprises Act, 2020
Pakistan	Start-up, small, and medium-sized firm			√			√		Defined by the National SME Policy 2020.
	Micro, small, and medium-sized firm	√		√					Utilized by central bank.
	Small firm	√		√	√		√		Utilized by Federal Board of Revenue.
Sri Lanka	Micro, small, and medium-sized firm	√		√		√			Defined by the National Policy Framework for SME Development (2015).
		√				√			Utilized by statistics office (Economic Census).

MSME = micro, small, and medium-sized enterprise; SME = small and medium-sized enterprise.

Source: Compilation from Country Reviews of Asia Small and Medium-Sized Enterprise Monitor 2021.

By sector, services dominate the MSME sector, especially wholesale and retail trade. An average 44.1% of MSMEs are in wholesale and retail trade, followed by other services such as accommodation and food services (31.2%) and manufacturing (23.8%) (Figure 2.1B).[7] The average share of MSMEs in manufacturing is higher than in Southeast Asia (13.2%). Data from Bangladesh, India, and Sri Lanka refer only to non-agricultural enterprises.

The majority of MSMEs do business outside the capital. An average 77.9% of MSMEs operate in provinces, with the remaining 22.1% based in capital cities, similar to Southeast Asia (88.1% in rural and 18.2% in capitals) (Figure 2.1C).[8] Still, most will likely operate in industrial or urban areas. In Pakistan, 65.2% of MSMEs were in Punjab in 2005, which is home to industrial hubs for both large and small manufacturing. In Nepal, 35.0% in FY2019 were in Bagmati province, which includes the capital Kathmandu.

Comparative country data by firm size are unavailable. But based on what is available, cottage and microenterprises largely dominate businesses in the region. In Bangladesh, cottage industries accounted for 87.5% of all enterprises based on the 2013 census. In Sri Lanka, microenterprises represented 91.8% of enterprises. And in India, microenterprises were estimated to account for 99.5% of unincorporated non-agricultural enterprises in 2018.

With the majority of MSMEs provincial cottage and microenterprises operating in small manufacturing, trade, and services, they are generally low-technology firms supplying relatively static domestic markets with little concern over expanding their business.[9] It would help to strengthen entrepreneurship development; support youth and women entrepreneurs; and foster innovative rural-based businesses, technology-based start-ups, and MSMEs

7 In Nepal "other services" include information and technology and tourism; there is no category for wholesale and retail trade.

8 Capitals include Kathmandu in Nepal, Islamabad in Pakistan, and Colombo in Sri Lanka. For Bangladesh and India, regional classifications refer to urban and rural areas.

9 Based on interviews with government authorities and private institutions in Bangladesh, India, Nepal, Pakistan, and Sri Lanka conducted in March–April 2021.

Figure 2.1: Number of MSMEs

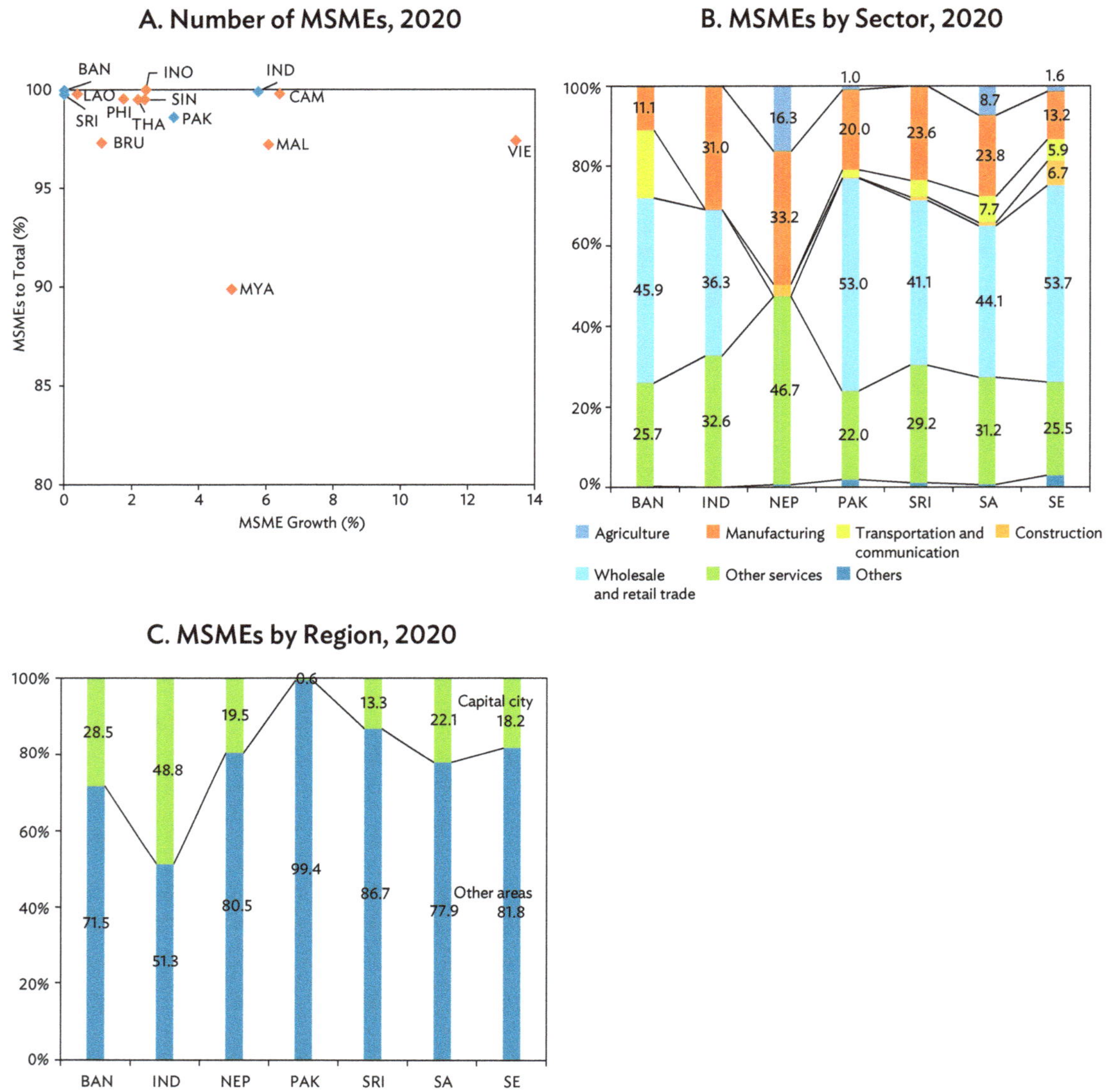

BAN = Bangladesh; BRU = Brunei Darussalam; CAM = Cambodia; IND = India; INO = Indonesia; LAO = Lao People's Democratic Republic; MAL = Malaysia; MSME = micro, small, and medium-sized enterprise; MYA = Myanmar; NEP = Nepal; PAK = Pakistan; PHI = Philippines; SA = South Asia; SE = Southeast Asia; SIN = Singapore; SRI = Sri Lanka; THA = Thailand; VIE = Viet Nam.

Notes: For Figure 2.1A, the share of MSMEs to total refers to the latest available year (end-of-year): 2013 for BAN and SRI; 2014 for CAM; 2016 for IND; 2019 for BRU, INO, MYA (March) and VIE; 2020 for LAO, MAL, PAK, PHI, SIN, and THA. MSME growth (%) refers to compound annual growth during past and latest available data. Data cover: 2005–2020 for PAK; 2006–2019 for MYA (fiscal year); 2006–2020 for LAO and PHI; 2007–2019 for VIE; 2007–2020 for THA; 2008–2018 for IND (fiscal year); 2009–2014 for CAM; 2010–2019 for BRU, INO, and NEP (fiscal year); 2010–2020 for MAL; 2014–2020 for SIN. For Figure 2.1B, data refer to the latest available year (end-of-year): 2005 for PAK; 2013 for BAN and SRI; 2018 for IND (fiscal year); 2019 for NEP (fiscal year). SA refers to average of these 5 countries. SE refers to average of 8 Southeast Asian countries: 2014 for CAM; 2016 for INO; 2019 for BRU and VIE; 2020 for LAO, MAL, PHI, and THA. For Figure 2.1C, SE refers to average of 6 Southeast Asian countries: 2014 for CAM; 2015 for MAL; 2019 for MYA (March); 2020 for LAO, PHI, and THA.

Source: ADB Asia SME Monitor 2021 database.

connected with global value chains. This can be done by providing seed and growth capital through a variety of channels including digital and market-based financing.

Many businesses are unregistered and operate informally. This means they cannot avail of government assistance, access formal financial services, or take advantage of domestic or global developments (foonote 9). MSME registration should be strengthened or reformed. For example, in India, MSMEs are encouraged to obtain a *Udyam* certificate (registered business certificate), which allows them to access government assistance programs.

Employment

Based on available data (until 2020), MSMEs employed an average 76.6% of a country's workforce in South Asia, higher than Southeast Asia average of 67.0% (2010–2020).[10] The number of MSME employees grew by 3.3% in India (CAGR during 2008–2018) and 4.3% in both Nepal (2008–2019) and Pakistan (2015–2018), again more than Southeast Asia's average growth (–0.5% CAGR in 2010–2020) (Figure 2.2A).

By sector, the majority of MSME employees work in services, especially wholesale and retail trade, in line with the sector composition of MSMEs. An average 34.5% of MSME employees work in wholesale and retail trade, followed by other services (27.9%) and manufacturing (25.9%) (Figure 2.2B). The average share of those employed in manufacturing is higher than in Southeast Asia (18.3%), suggesting the relatively large share of cottage industries in South Asia.

Provincial MSMEs employ an average 67.4% of MSME workers, with the remaining 32.6% in capital regions, higher than Southeast Asia (23.0% in capital cities) (Figure 2.2C). In Pakistan, most MSME jobs were in Punjab (60.9% in FY2018). In Nepal, 68.6% were in Bagmati province in FY2020. This suggests MSME workers tend to concentrate in industrial or urban areas.

MSMEs and their employees spread nationwide, but tend to concentrate in industrial or urban areas. Developing MSMEs in rural and remote areas by promoting small manufacturing and innovative rural-based businesses would create many new jobs.

Business Productivity

Regular comparative statistics on MSME contributions to GDP are available only for India. Other countries in the region estimate their contributions to GDP *ad hoc* during MSME policy formulation or as a benchmark for implementing policies or during periodic economic surveys. Based on available data until 2020, MSMEs in South Asia contributed an average 33.9% of a country's GDP, which is slightly below the Southeast Asia average of 40.5% (2010–2020, a 0.5% CAGR).[11] In India, MSMEs' GDP grew by 5.1% CAGR during FY2008–FY2019 (Figure 2.3A). While their share to GDP contracted by 1.4% over the same period, it remained at around 30% (average 29.7% in FY2012–FY2019) (Figure 2.3B).

[10] Data refer to 2013 (census) for Bangladesh and Sri Lanka, FY2018 (Labor Force Survey 2017–2018) for Pakistan, and FY2020 (Industrial Statistics 2019-2020) for Nepal. The share of MSME employees to total is unavailable for India.

[11] Data refer to the SME Policy 2019 for Bangladesh (25.0%), FY2019 for India (30.3%), the 2019 Nepal Rastra Bank (NRB) report for Nepal (22.0%), the Pakistan Economic Survey 2010–2011 (40.0%), and the National SME Policy 2015 for Sri Lanka (52.0%).

Figure 2.2: Employment by MSMEs

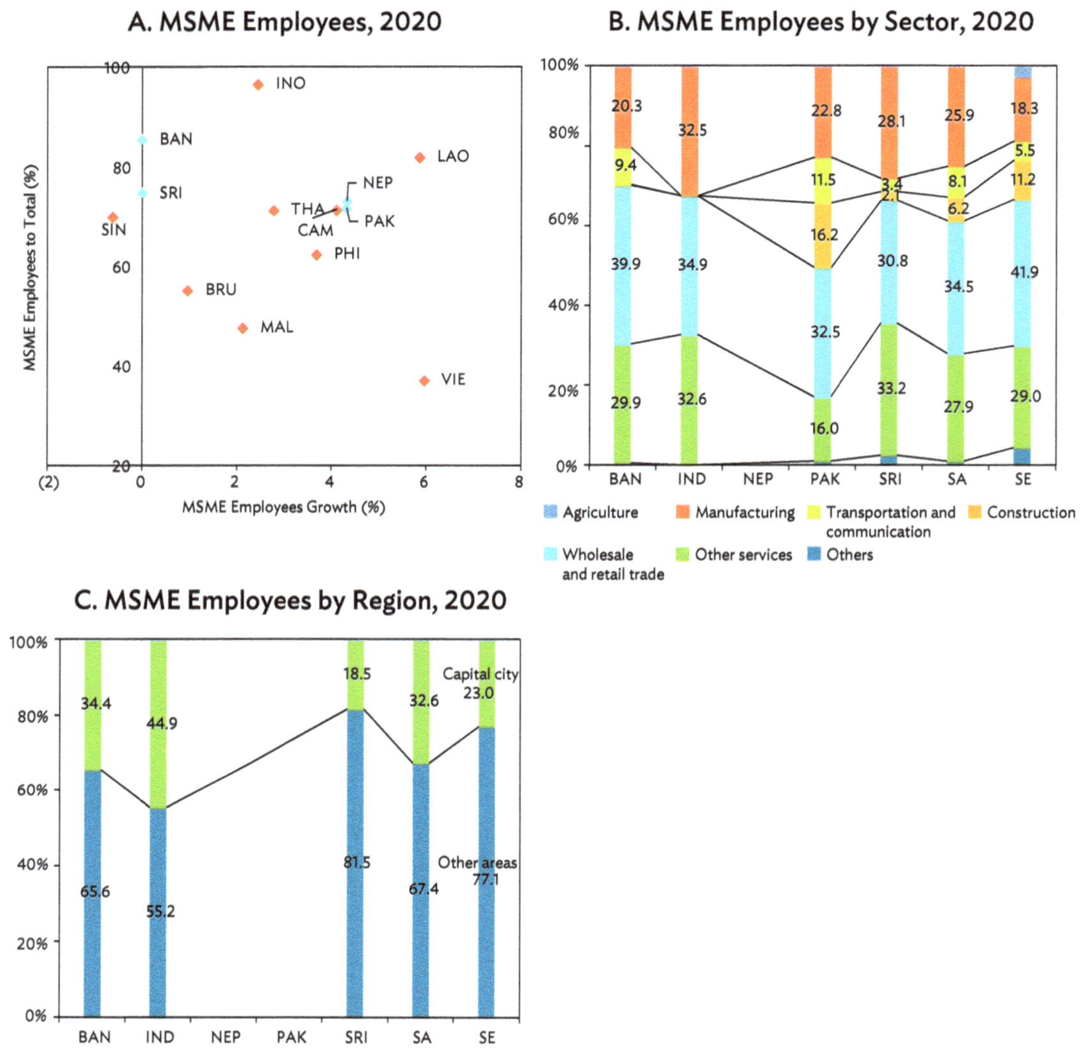

BAN = Bangladesh; BRU = Brunei Darussalam; CAM = Cambodia; IND = India; INO = Indonesia; LAO = Lao PDR; MAL = Malaysia; MSME = micro, small, and medium-sized enterprise; NEP = Nepal; PAK = Pakistan; PHI = Philippines; SA = South Asia; SE = Southeast Asia; SIN = Singapore; SRI = Sri Lanka; THA = Thailand; VIE = Viet Nam.

Notes: For Figure 2.2A, the share of MSME employees to total (%) refers to the latest available year (end-of-year): 2013 for BAN and SRI; 2014 for CAM; 2018 for LAO and PAK; 2019 for BRU, INO, and VIE; 2020 for MAL, NEP, PHI, SIN, and THA. MSME employees growth (%) refers to compound annual growth during past and latest available data. Data covers: 2006–2018 for LAO; 2006–2020 for PHI; 2007–2019 for VIE; 2007–2020 for THA; 2008–2018 for IND (fiscal year); 2008–2019 for NEP (fiscal year); 2009–2014 for CAM; 2010–2019 for BRU and INO; 2014–2020 for SIN; 2015–2018 for PAK (fiscal year); 2015–2020 for MAL. For Figure 2.2B, data refer to the latest available year (end-of-year): 2013 for BAN and SRI; 2018 for IND (fiscal year) and PAK (fiscal year). SA refers to average of these 4 countries. SE refers to average of 8 Southeast Asian countries: 2014 for CAM; 2016 for INO; 2019 for BRU and VIE; 2020 for LAO, MAL, PHI, and THA. For Figure 2.2C, data refer to the latest available year (end-of-year): 2013 for BAN and SRI; 2018 for IND (fiscal year). SA refers to average of these 3 countries. SE refers to average of 4 Southeast Asian countries: 2014 for CAM; 2015 for MAL; 2020 for PHI and THA.

Source: ADB Asia SME Monitor 2021 database.

Data on manufacturing MSMEs, however, are available in Bangladesh, India, and Pakistan. In Bangladesh, the manufacturing gross value added (GVA) of cottage and small enterprises increased by 8.8% CAGR during FY2012–FY2020. Their contribution to manufacturing GVA averaged 17.4% over the same period but contracted by 1.7% CAGR. In India, MSME manufacturing GVA grew by 11.4% CAGR during FY2012–FY2020. Their contribution to manufacturing GVA averaged 32.9% over the same period with a CAGR of 1.1%. In Pakistan, GDP of small manufacturers increased by 15.0% CAGR during 2007–2020. They contributed an average 1.8% of GDP, a 4.3% CAGR over the same period.

In US dollar terms, MSMEs' GDP in India was highest in South Asia ($593.8 billion in FY2019), and when compared with Southeast Asia, second after Indonesia ($689.2 billion in 2019) (Figure 2.3C). South Asian economies are expected to recover strongly from the early pandemic impact, with a forecast 8.8% rebound in 2021, led by India (foonote 3). India's growth foundation has been underpinned by MSMEs. Devastated by the pandemic, revitalizing their dynamics is crucial for building a resilient economic recovery in South Asia.

Figure 2.3: MSME Contribution to Gross Domestic Product

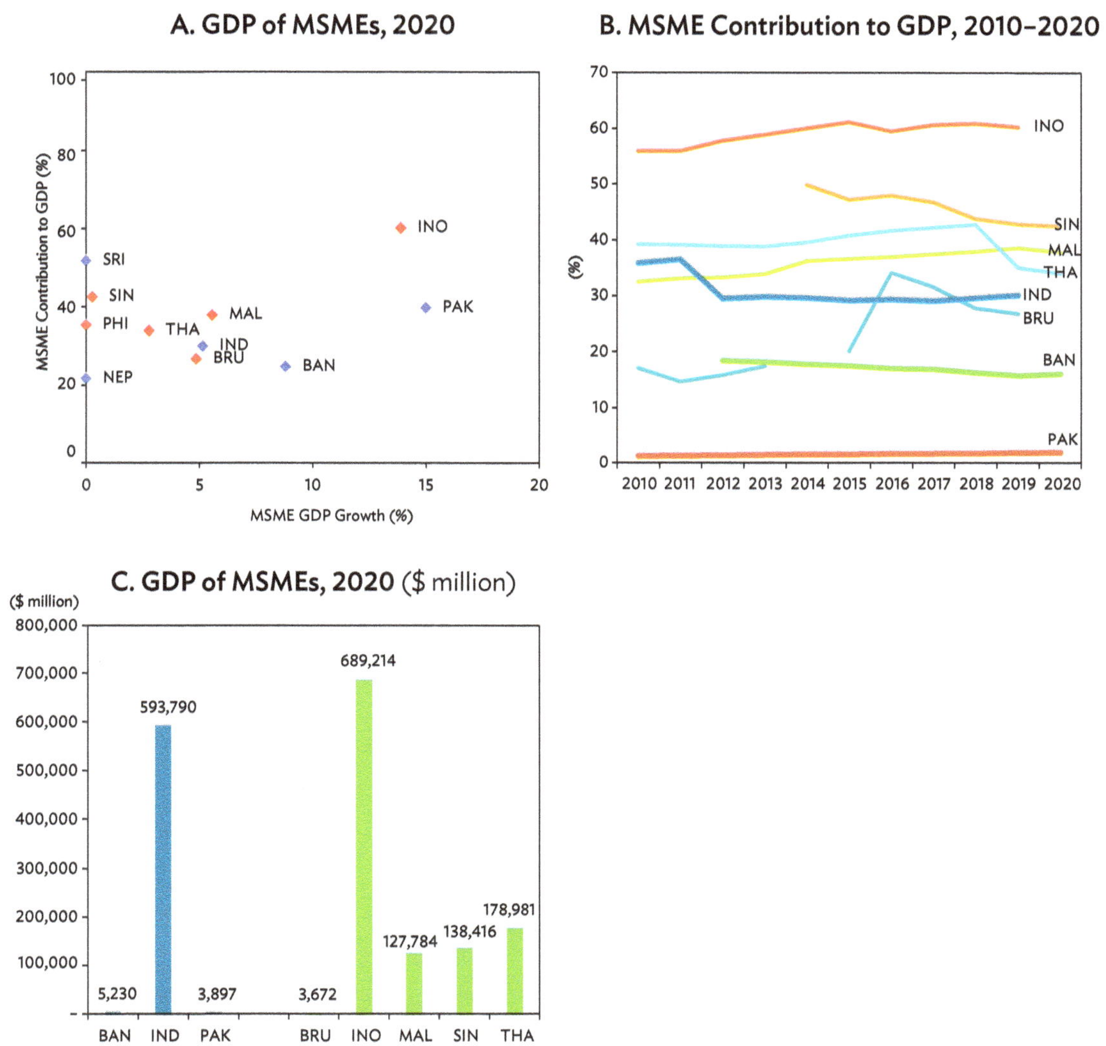

BAN = Bangladesh; BRU = Brunei Darussalam; GDP = gross domestic product; IND = India; INO = Indonesia; MAL = Malaysia; MSME = micro, small, and medium-sized enterprise; NEP = Nepal; PAK = Pakistan; PHI = Philippines; SIN = Singapore; THA = Thailand.

Notes: For Figure 2.3A, MSME contribution to GDP (%) refers to the latest available year (end-of-year): 2006 for PHI; 2019 for BRU and INO; 2020 for MAL, SIN, THA. For BAN, SME Policy 2019; for IND, fiscal year 2019; for NEP, 2019 central bank report; for PAK, Pakistan Economic Survey 2010-2011; for SRI, National SME Policy 2015. MSME GDP growth (%) refers to compound annual growth during past and latest available data. Data covers: 2007–2020 for PAK and THA; 2008–2019 for IND (fiscal year); 2010–2019 for BRU and INO; 2010–2020 for MAL; 2012–2020 for BAN; 2014–2020 for SIN. For Figure 2.3B, data for BRU, IND, and INO are until 2019, and data for other countries are until 2020. For BRU, data in 2014 is not available. For PAK, small manufacturing only. For Figure 2.3C, data refer to 2019 for IND (fiscal year) and INO; 2020 for BAN (fiscal year) and the rest. Exchange rates of local currency to US dollar refer to end-of-year currency rates from the International Monetary Fund (IMF) International Financial Statistics in designated years.

Source: ADB Asia SME Monitor 2021 database.

Market Access

MSMEs in South Asia largely serve domestic markets, with many informal. In Bangladesh, 87% of manufacturers sell their products to local markets. In Nepal, 85% of workers are in the informal sector. Most MSMEs are in services and operate in rural areas; only a few cater to international markets, but their impact on exports varies by country.

There is no country comparative data available on MSME exports, but India regularly monitors MSME exports, which contributed an average 47.0% of country's overall exports at a CAGR of 2.2% from FY2013 to FY2020 (Figure 2.4). MSME export values grew by 5.2% CAGR over the same period. Their contribution to total export

Figure 2.4: MSME Exports

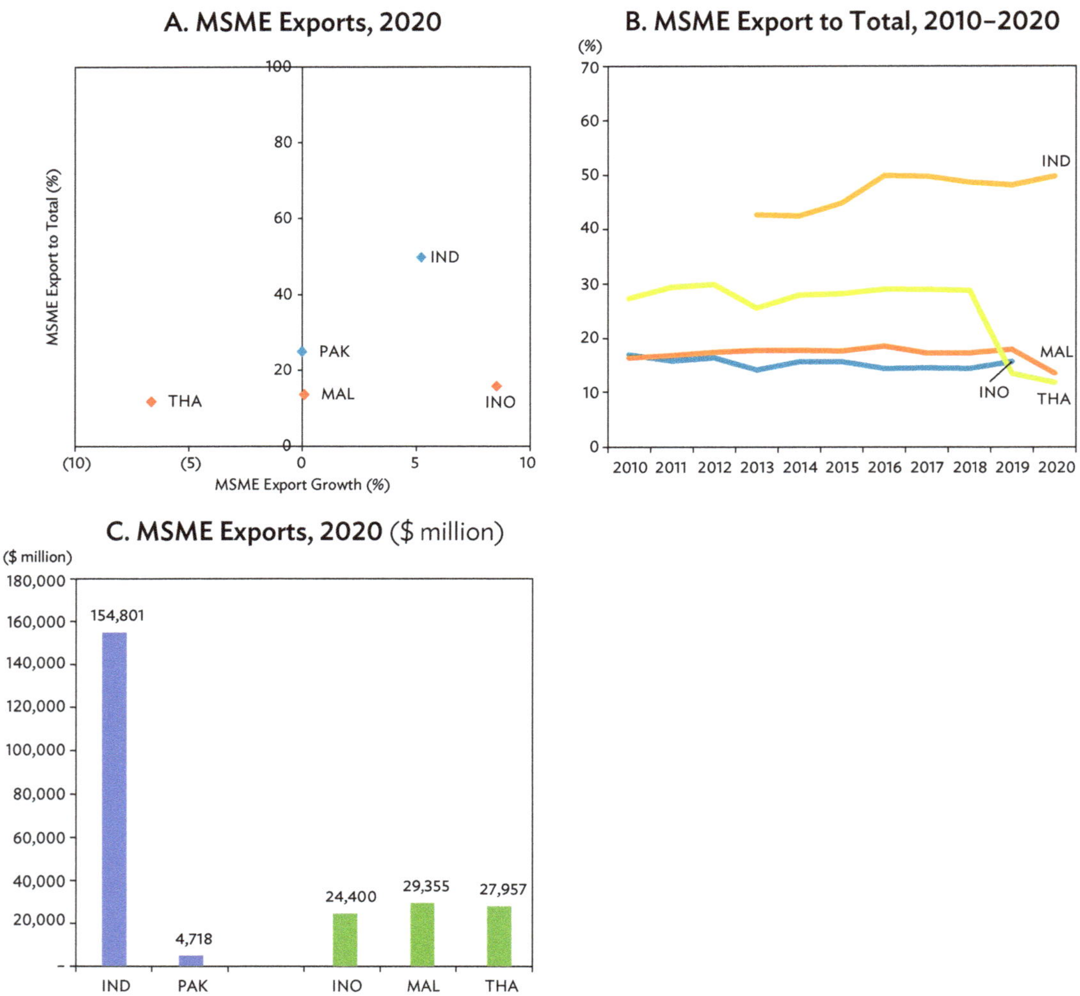

IND = India; INO = Indonesia; MAL = Malaysia; MSME = micro, small, and medium-sized enterprise; THA = Thailand.

Notes: For Figure 2.4A, MSME export to total (%) refers to the latest available year (end-of-year): 2019 for INO and 2020 for IND, MAL, and THA. MSME export growth (%) refers to compound annual growth during past and latest available data. Data cover 2010-2019 for INO, 2010-2020 for MAL and THA, and 2013-2020 for IND. For Figure 2.4C, exchange rates of local currency to US dollar refer to end-of-year currency rates from the International Monetary Fund (IMF) International Financial Statistics in designated years.

Source: ADB Asia SME Monitor 2021 database.

value is higher than the Southeast Asia average of 19.2% (CAGR during 2010–2020) and faster growth of the share (-4.6% CAGR in Southeast Asia). In Pakistan, the Economic Survey 2009–2010 estimated that 25% of total export values come from MSMEs, a higher share than the Southeast Asia average.

Increasing market access and internationalizing MSMEs are core strategies of national MSME development policies in South Asia. Governments in the region want to promote MSME exporters as suppliers or lead firms in global value chains. Bangladesh includes these in its SME Policy 2019. Small industrial parks in Bangladesh also support MSME manufacturing and exports. India offers production-linked incentives to exporters, where the government supports 4%–6% on incremental sales for quality local goods for 5 years. It uses its online portal GeM, a market-based procurement system open to MSMEs and large firms, where start-ups can test selling their products on a trial basis. Pakistan offers a concessional Export Finance Scheme and Long-Term Finance Facility for exporters, including MSMEs. In Sri Lanka, the National SME Policy Framework promotes linking MSMEs with large firms, and assists them to access government procurement, e-commerce, and product development and branding.

Key challenges to internationalizing MSMEs include (i) lack of business linkages with large multinationals; (ii) lack of quality, competitive products, and low investment in research and development (R&D); (iii) lack of business literacy and capacity; (iv) regulatory compliance; and (v) limited access to finance. Every government struggles with these issues. Across South Asia, textiles and ready-made garments remain a promising MSME export opportunity.

Technology and Innovation

MSMEs traditionally are low-tech. Yet there are an increasing number of technology-based MSMEs and start-ups as internet penetration increases across the region. Mobile cellular subscription per 100 people was over 100 in Bangladesh (103 in 2020), Nepal (139 in 2018), and Sri Lanka (139 in 2020), and near 100 in India (84 in 2020) and Pakistan (80 in 2020). Individual internet use remains limited but has been growing, especially since the pandemic began; 13% of the population in Bangladesh (2019), 41% in India (2019), 21% in Nepal (2017), 17% in Pakistan (2019), and 35% in Sri Lanka (2020) (Figure 2.5).

E-commerce has grown rapidly and is highly competitive, supported by national interoperable electronic payment platforms. MSMEs' market reach has expanded just as fast. In Nepal, many e-commerce companies, mostly MSMEs, include online shops such as Food Mandu and Daraz, and ride-sharing apps such as Tootle and Patho. In Sri Lanka, most of the 76 randomly sampled e-commerce providers were MSMEs, nearly 58% of which used new technology for sales and marketing, according to an Export Development Board study in 2020. In Bangladesh, e-wallets for online payments and money transfers such as bKash are helping develop the industry. Low internet connectivity and logistics in rural and remote areas remain challenges (80% of e-commerce transactions are concentrated in urban areas like Dhaka, Chattogram, and Gazipur). More inclusive internet penetration and logistics is needed to further develop domestic e-commerce for rural MSMEs.

Governments promote MSMEs' online business and technology adoption. In India, there is a public recognition program offering income tax and custom duty benefits to MSMEs that establish in-house R&D units. It has also developed an online e-marketplace for MSMEs (MSME Global Mart Web Portal) and a technology incubation program for start-ups. Sri Lanka's Industrial Technology Institute supports MSMEs in technology transfer, adoption, and commercialization through advice and training.

Figure 2.5: Mobile and Internet Penetration, 2020

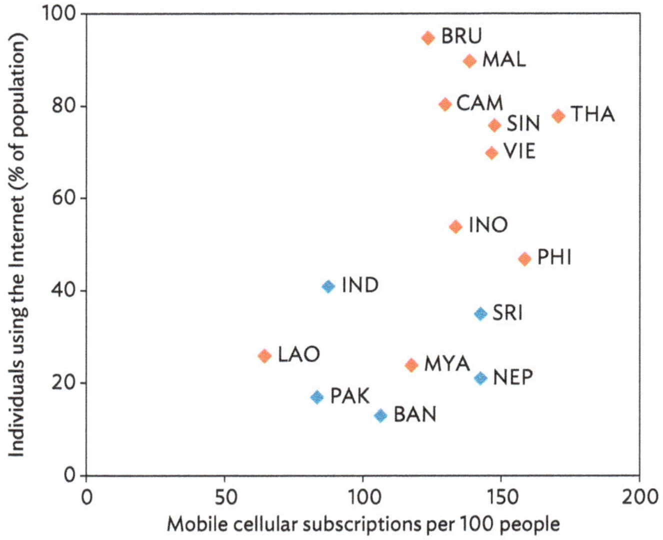

BAN = Bangladesh; BRU = Brunei Darussalam, CAM = Cambodia, IND = India, INO = Indonesia, LAO = Lao People's Democratic Republic, MAL = Malaysia, MYA = Myanmar, NEP = Nepal; PAK = Pakistan; PHI = Philippines, SIN = Singapore, SRI = Sri Lanka; THA = Thailand, VIE = Viet Nam.

Source: World Development Indicators. https://data.worldbank.org/indicator/.

Networking and Support

Private sector chambers of commerce and industry support MSME development through facilitating business linkages, networking, and offering consultation services and skills training. They also lobby with governments on MSME policy formulation and implementation.

There are several business associations and chambers active with MSME support programs across South Asia. In India, there are more than 170 business associations, with the Federation of Indian Chambers of Commerce and Industry (FICCI) leading in MSME support by creating the Confederation of MSMEs that has tie-ups with over 300 industry associations and chambers worldwide. In Bangladesh, the National Association of Small and Cottage Industries (NASCIB) offers skill development programs to cottage industries and MSMEs, organizes trade fairs to expand their international markets, and assists access to banks and nonbank finance institutions. It prioritizes agribusiness, R&D, and women entrepreneurships. In Nepal, the Federation of Women Entrepreneurs' Associations (FWEAN) lobbies with the government for women-led MSMEs, working to provide concessional loans for women entrepreneurs, among others. The Federation of Pakistan Chambers of Commerce and Industry oversees 58 chambers covering around 40% of MSMEs nationwide. They provide support services for MSME members such as a single-window business facilitation center and help desks. In Sri Lanka, the Federation of Chambers of Commerce and Industry (FCCISL) covers 63 chambers, supports MSME trade facilitation, and provides capacity-building programs for start-ups.

Autonomous business communities play a critical role in education, business facilitation, and public-private partnerships for MSME development. There are many independent small business associations duplicating work with less collaboration nationally, suggesting the need for more systematic cooperation of their activities for more effective support in business development (footnote 9).

2. Access to Finance

MSMEs in South Asia, 2015–2020

Bank credit	Percentage share	Compound annual growth
• **MSME loans to national GDP***	***7.0%***	***-0.04%***
• **MSME loans to total bank loans**	***14.8%***	***-0.7%***
• **MSME NPLs to total MSME loans**	***13.6%***	***-6.9%***
Nonbank and market-based finance		
• **NBFI financing to national GDP**	***3.2%***	***+4.9%***
• **NBFI financing to total bank loans**	***6.5%***	***-2.8%***
• **NBFI NPF to total financing**	***5.6%***	***+9.7%***
• **MSME market capitalization to GDP****	***18.2%***	***-4.2%***

GDP = gross domestic product; MSME = micro, small, and medium-sized enterprise; NBFI = nonbank finance institution; NPF = nonperforming financing; NPL = nonperforming loan.

* 2015–2019. ** Data include main market data in case of no MSME market data available.

Reporting countries only. Data based on the latest available data until 2020.

Bank Credit

Increasing access to finance is a central policy for inclusive growth and MSME development. Limited financial access for MSMEs is a structural problem, made worse due to the pandemic. Across South Asia, bank lending to MSMEs averaged 7.0% of a country's GDP during 2015–2019 (CAGR of –0.04%) and 14.8% of total bank lending during 2015–2020 (–0.7%). The South Asia MSME credit market is smaller than Southeast Asia's (14.1% share of GDP and 16.4% of total bank lending during 2010–2020).

NPLs remain high, averaging 13.6% of total MSME bank loans, above the overall bank average NPL ratio of 8.8% during 2015–2020. Yet they have improved (–6.9% CAGR for MSME NPL ratio and –2.5% CAGR for gross bank NPL ratio). The NPL ratio in South Asia is higher than the Southeast Asia average of 4.2% (–0.9% CAGR in 2010–2020), primarily India and Pakistan.

Bank lending to MSMEs was equivalent to 11.7% of India's GDP in 2019, followed by Bangladesh (8.1% in 2020), Sri Lanka (5.0% [2020]), and Pakistan (1.2% [2020]) (Figure 2.6A). The share of MSME bank loans to total bank lending in 2020 was estimated at 20.2% in Bangladesh, followed by India (17.6%), Nepal (11.5% [2017]), Sri Lanka (11.1%), and Pakistan (7.3%). In US dollar terms, India's MSME lending was $256 billion in 2020, followed by Bangladesh ($27 billion), Sri Lanka ($4 billion), and Pakistan ($3 billion) (Figure 2.6B).[12]

Bank loans to MSMEs grew rapidly in South Asia. The CAGR during 2015–2020 was 9.7% in Bangladesh, 9.6% in Pakistan, and 8.6% in India. MSME credit growth in Bangladesh largely followed the central bank's annual lending target. Commercial banks met more than 90% of the targets since they were introduced in 2010. In India, high MSME credit growth was backed by increased banking digitalization, increased registration of MSMEs due to tax incentives introduced in 2017, and in 2020 due to COVID-19 stimulus measures such as the Emergency Credit Line Guarantee Scheme for MSMEs.

12 Exchange rates of local currency to US dollar refer to end-of-year currency rates from the International Monetary Fund/International Financial Statistics (IMF/IFS) in designated years.

Figure 2.6: Bank Credit

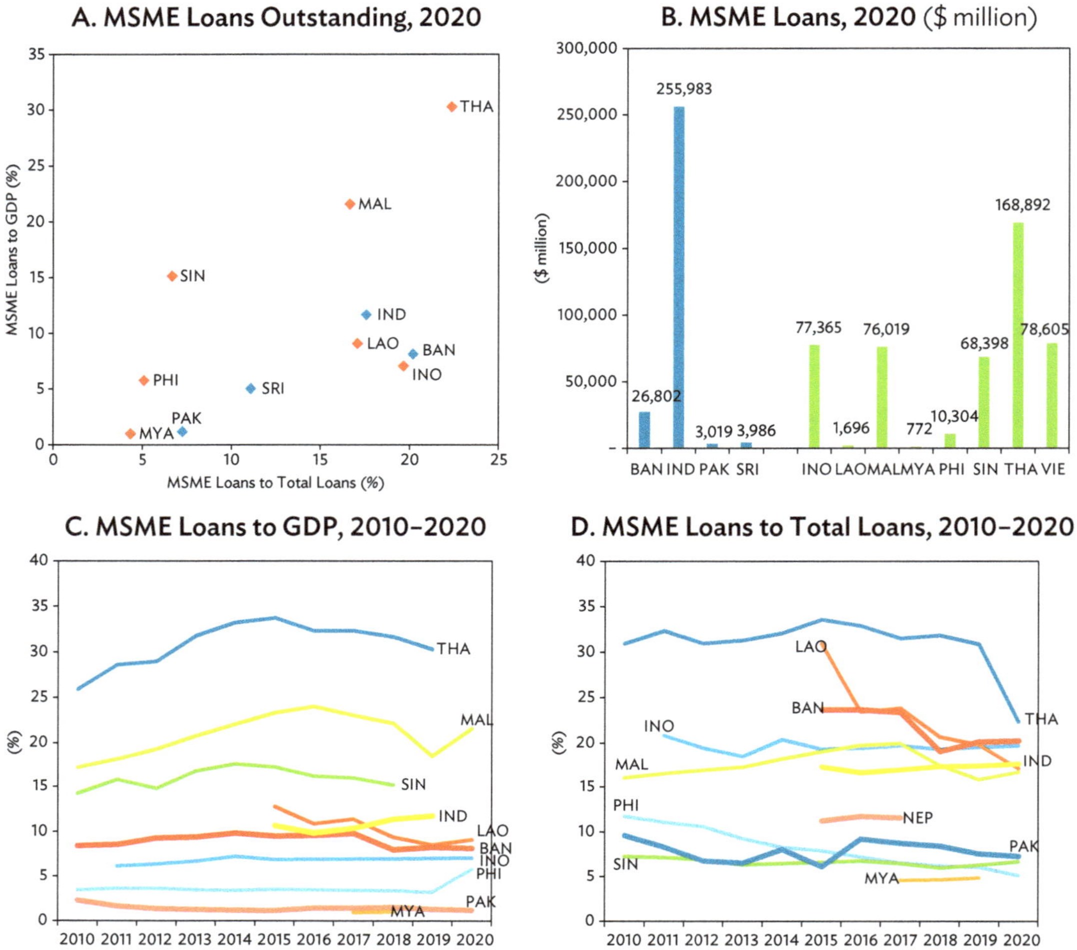

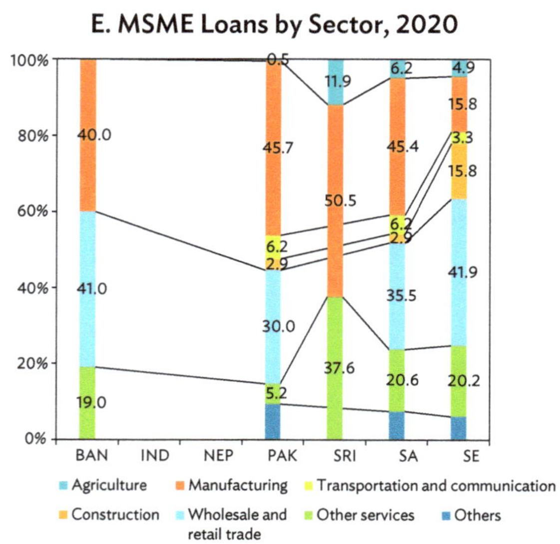

BAN = Bangladesh; BRU = Brunei Darussalam; GDP = gross domestic product; IND = India; INO = Indonesia; LAO = Lao People's Democratic Republic; MAL = Malaysia; MSME = micro, small, and medium-sized enterprise; MYA = Myanmar; PAK = Pakistan; PHI = Philippines; SA = South Asia; SE = Southeast Asia; SIN = Singapore; SRI = Sri Lanka; THA = Thailand; VIE = Viet Nam.

Notes: For Figure 2.6A, MSME loans to GDP (%) refers to the latest available year (end-of-year): 2018 for MYA (fiscal year) and SIN; 2019 for IND and THA; 2020 for the rest. MSME loans to total loans (%) refers to 2017 for NEP (fiscal year); 2019 for MYA (fiscal year); 2020 for the rest. For Figure 2.6B, data refer to 2019 for MYA (fiscal year); end-2020 for the rest. Exchange rates of local currency to US dollar refer to end-of-year currency rates from the International Monetary Fund (IMF) International Financial Statistics in designated years. For Figure 2.6C, data for MYA (fiscal year) and SIN (end-of-year) until 2018; IND (end-of-year) until 2019; the rest (end-of-year) until 2020. For Figure 2.6D, data for NEP (fiscal year) until 2017; MYA (fiscal year) until 2019; the rest (end-of-year) until 2020. For Figure 2.6E, data refer to end-2020 for BAN, PAK, and SRI. SA refers to average of these three countries. SE refers to average of 8 Southeast Asian countries: end-2019 for BRU, LAO, and MYA (fiscal year); end-2020 for the rest.

Source: ADB Asia SME Monitor 2021 database.

Despite this high credit growth, however, the shares of MSME loans to GDP and total bank loans have been shrinking over time in Bangladesh and Pakistan (Figures 2.6C and 2.6D). The share to GDP contracted by 0.3% in Bangladesh and 6.5% in Pakistan with a declining CAGR in 2010–2020. The share of MSME loans to total bank loans contracted by 3.1% with a declining CAGR in 2015–2020 in Bangladesh and 2.7% (2010–2020) in Pakistan. Meanwhile, the shares to GDP and total bank loans have grown at 2.4% CAGR during 2015–2019 and 0.4% during 2015–2020 in India.

In Bangladesh, MSME credit dropped in 2018 due to a change in statistical definition, which has affected the shares to GDP and total loans since. In Pakistan, due to surging NPLs from 2007 to 2012, banks restricted lending to SMEs in 2012.[13] Since the central bank revised regulations to cope with NPLs in 2013, the SME NPL ratio has fallen gradually but remains high at double-digit levels. Due to banks' risk aversion in Pakistan, lending growth to SMEs has decelerated since 2019, affecting shares to GDP and total loans.

The majority of MSME credit went to the manufacturing, followed by services. In 2020, across South Asia, an average 45.4% of a country's MSME bank credit was in manufacturing, followed by wholesale and retail trade (35.5%) and other services (20.6%) (Figure 2.6E). The region's share of MSME credit to manufacturing was higher than Southeast Asia's average of 15.8%, while the share to wholesale and retail trade was lower (41.9%).

In 2020, the share of MSME NPLs to total MSME loans was higher than for non-MSMEs. By country, the MSME NPL ratio was 7.5% in India and 16.9% in Pakistan; all higher than the overall NPL ratio for banks (Figure 2.7A). The spread between the MSME NPL ratio and gross bank NPL ratio was 0.8 percentage points in India and 8.3 percentage points in Pakistan. The NPL ratios in India and Pakistan were also higher than those in Southeast Asia in 2020 (7.0% in Thailand, 6.7% in the Philippines, 4.3% in Singapore, 4.0% in Indonesia, and 3.2% in Malaysia).

MSME NPLs increased by a CAGR of 3.4% in India and 1.1% in Pakistan from 2011 to 2020, lower than the growth in gross bank NPLs (20.7% in India and 3.2% in Pakistan) (Figure 2.7A). The share of MSME NPLs to total MSME loans has been decreasing gradually over time in India (–4.8% CAGR during 2015–2020) and Pakistan (–7.7%) (Figure 2.7B). The MSME NPL ratio increased by a CAGR of 34.6% during 2010–2014 in Bangladesh, but data after 2015 are unavailable.

Increasing MSME access to bank credit remains a challenge. In India, key constraints include MSMEs' inability to repay due to uncertainty and fragile consumer demand amid the pandemic. It is also difficult for lenders to assess the creditworthiness of MSMEs due to a lack of information, business records and plans, especially in rural and remote areas. In Nepal, lenders face the same problem; some say they would not lend to MSMEs unless forced by regulations. In Pakistan, commercial bank credit is skewed toward the public sector—which promises healthy returns with less risk—as many MSMEs are unregistered and cannot supply the documentation required to apply for bank credit.

13 Based on SME loans by commercial banks and specialized banks only. Microenterprise loans are not included.

Figure 2.7: MSME Nonperforming Loans

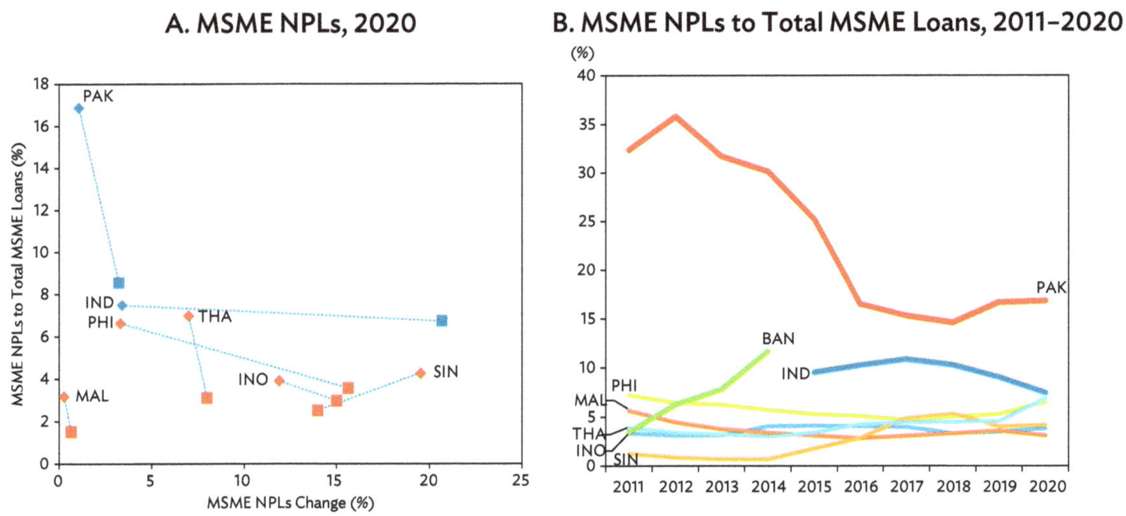

IND = India; INO = Indonesia; MAL = Malaysia; MSME = micro, small, and medium-sized enterprise; NPL = nonperforming loan; PAK = Pakistan; PHI = Philippines; SIN = Singapore; THA = Thailand.

Notes: For Figure 2.7A, ♦ = MSME NPLs, ■ = banks' gross NPLs. MSME NPLs (%) and banks' gross NPLs (%) refer to end-2020. NPL change (%) refers to compound annual change during 2011–2020.

Source: ADB Asia SME Monitor 2021 database.

Public Financing and Guarantees

Governments and central banks in South Asia offer financial assistance to MSMEs to supplement their financing needs. They include mandatory lending, refinancing programs or schemes, special revolving funds, soft-loan programs with interest rate subsidies, and credit guarantees. They have been actively used as emergency assistance tools to MSMEs hurt by financial crises, disasters, and shocks like the COVID-19 pandemic, among others. They expand existing programs or create new ones, providing debt relief, liquidity support for financial institutions, and reducing regulatory requirements. Since the pandemic began, there has been significant financial support to MSMEs, contributing to the MSME credit growth in the region against the COVID-19 crisis (Table 2.2).

a. Mandatory lending

Bangladesh, India, and Nepal set mandatory MSME lending targets. In Bangladesh, the central bank sets an aggregate lending target value for banks to allocate for MSMEs. Started from 2010, it was calculated based on annual loan disbursements, but was changed to net loans outstanding beginning in 2020. The MSME lending target of Tk2,181 billion ($25.7 billion) in 2020 for scheduled banks was met (footnote 12). Conditions include sector allocations (40% of MSME credit for manufacturing, 35% for trade, and 25% for other services); allocation to women entrepreneurs (15%); and a maximum interest rate cap of 9% for women-led firms.

In India, the central bank sets a sub-target of 7.5% of adjusted net bank credit or the credit equivalent of off-balance sheet exposure, whichever is higher, for lending to microenterprises in priority sectors.

Nepal also sets lending targets for priority sectors. Nepal's central bank requires commercial banks to provide 40% of loans to priority sectors by 2024—agriculture (15%), energy and tourism (10%), and MSMEs (15%). Similarly, development banks must lend 20% and finance companies 15% of their loans to priority sectors by 2023. Concessional lending of at least 5% of their portfolio must go to focused groups such as women, small farmers, craftsmen, and ethnic minorities, including microcredits for renewable energy.

b. Refinancing and subsidized loans

In South Asia, refinancing and subsidized loans are the most popular public finance options. In Bangladesh, there are several refinancing schemes for MSMEs, covering women entrepreneurs, cottage industries, MSMEs, and agricultural processing. They are either revolving funds or from donors like the Japan International Cooperation Agency. They come with different loan ceilings, with or without collateral, or have maximum interest rate caps. Amid the pandemic, an emergency revolving refinancing program helps support the working capital requirements of cottage industries and MSMEs.

In India, the Micro Units Development and Refinance Agency (MUDRA), a subsidiary of the Small Industries Development Bank of India (SIDBI), offers collateral free loans up to ₹1 million ($136,886) to eligible MSMEs through a refinancing facility, with loans provided by banks, nonbank finance companies, and MFIs. It has helped 295.6 million MSMEs from FY2016 to FY2021.

In Nepal, the government has 10 concessional loan programs with subsidized interest payments. They vary considerably in loan size, interest concessions, collateral requirements, tenure, credit guarantees, documentation requirements, and target groups. With government interest subsidies of NRs13 billion ($110 million), the Commercial Agriculture and Livestock Loan (CALL) and the Women Entrepreneur Loan (WEL) have been growing rapidly in both loans outstanding and number of borrowers.

In Pakistan, the central bank has set four types of MSME refinancing schemes since 2010, covering financial support for modernizing MSMEs' equipment and factories; women entrepreneurs; and priority sectors such as information technology, furniture, surgical goods, gems, leather, and food processing, with credit guarantees. A refinancing facility was also set up to help MSMEs recover from the pandemic.

In Sri Lanka, the central bank had 13 refinancing programs as of end-2020, including a working capital support facility for MSMEs (*saubagya*), which was renewed as a COVID-19 Renaissance Facility in April 2020. The ADB-funded SME Line of Credit also provides financial intermediation targeting MSMEs and women entrepreneurs in Sri Lanka through participating banks.

c. Credit guarantees

Credit guarantees—either public or private—help fill the MSME financing gap. They are, however, in an early stage of development in South Asia. India, Nepal, and Pakistan have independent credit guarantee institutions, while Bangladesh and Sri Lanka are currently creating one, following the national financial inclusion strategy or a government proposal. Available data show credit guarantee markets remain small compared with Southeast Asia (Figure 2.8).

Figure 2.8: Credit Guarantees, 2020
($ million)

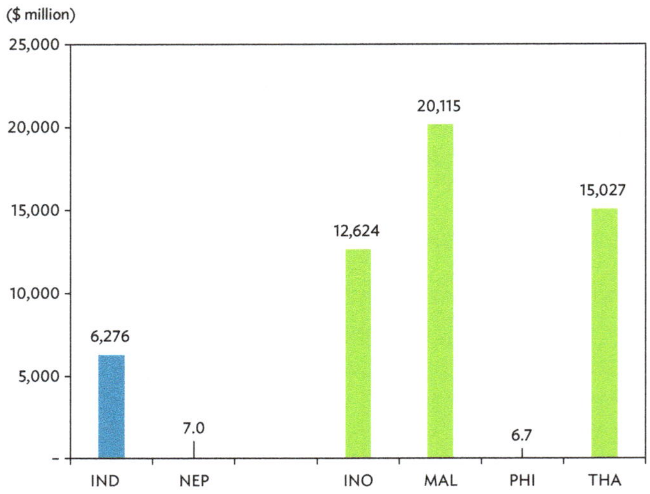

IND = India, INO = Indonesia, MAL = Malaysia, NEP = Nepal, PHI = Philippines, THA = Thailand.

Notes: Data refer to the latest available year: 2018 for NEP (fiscal year), 2020 for IND (fiscal year), and the rest (end-of-year). IND data from Credit Guarantee Fund Trust for Micro and Small Enterprises. INO data from Kredit Usaha Rakyat. MAL data from Credit Guarantee Corporation. NEP data from Deposit and Credit Guarantee Fund. PHI data from PhilGuarantee. THA data from Thai Credit Guarantee Corporation. Exchange rates of local currency to US dollar refer to end-of-year currency rates from the International Monetary Fund (IMF) International Financial Statistics in designated years.

Source: ADB Asia SME Monitor 2021 database.

In India, there are three credit guarantee systems. The Credit Guarantee Fund Trust for Micro and Small Enterprises (CGTMSE), established by the government and SIDBI, provides partial credit guarantees (75%–85% of credit supplied) for micro and small enterprises (collateral-free loans) through member lending institutions, whose approved guarantees jumped over 50% in FY2020. The National Credit Guarantee Trustee Company (NCGTC), institutionalized by the Ministry of Finance, monitors the country's various credit guarantee funds. As of March 2020, it managed six government guarantee funds, including the rapidly growing Credit Guarantee Fund for Micro Units (CGFMU), which offers portfolio guarantees for micro loans up to ₹1 million ($136,886) and up to 50% of the outstanding balance of eligible micro loans.

In Nepal, the Deposit and Credit Guarantee Fund (DCGF), sponsored by the central bank and commercial banks, provides partial credit guarantees (70%–80% of credit supplied) for MSMEs through banks and financial institutions. It automatically guarantees up to NRs10 million ($84,868) disbursed to MSMEs. For loans from NRs10 million to NRs30 million ($254,604), prior DCGF approval is required.

The Pakistan Credit Guarantee Corporation (PCGC) was established in 2019, but was not operational as of April 2021. It will be a partial risk-sharing facility to encourage financial institutions to lend to MSMEs and agribusinesses that lack collateral. In Bangladesh, a new Credit Guarantee Fund is to be created for financing cottage industries and MSMEs under the national financial inclusion strategy for 2024. It plans to provide portfolio guarantees with losses covered by the central bank for up to 30% of the portfolio guarantee limit, and guarantee coverage of up to 80% of the loan principal. In Sri Lanka, the government has proposed the establishment of a National Credit Guarantee Institution (NCGI), with ADB helping provide seed capital and technical assistance for setting it up.

d. Specialized banks and public programs

India and Pakistan have state-owned or sponsored banks dedicated to MSME development. SIDBI, established in 1990, is India's principal institution for promoting and financing MSMEs. It provides direct and indirect lending to MSMEs and institutional finance to small banks, nonbank finance companies, and MFIs. SIDBI also coordinates MSME financing with government and other financial institutions. Indirect credit to MSMEs using other financial institutions covers 94% of its total loans outstanding. Its main borrowers are MSMEs in services, especially wholesale and retail trade (94.5% of loans outstanding in FY2020). Most MSME loans are for capital investments. Around 60% of SIDBI loans are midterm (1–5 years). In Pakistan, SME Bank Limited was established with government sponsorship in 1984. Reorganized in 2002, it operates as a specialized bank catering to MSMEs. In Sri Lanka, the government offers concessional micro-loans to low-income groups—such as smallholder farmers, the self-employed, and owners of micro and small firms—though its own programs or through participating banks. Public microfinance programs such as *Samurdhi* (launched in 1995 to reduce poverty) offer microfinance, skills training, and literacy assistance to low-income families and vulnerable groups, including smallholders and micro and small firm owners producing, for example, handicrafts.

e. Emergency financial assistance

Public finance also provides emergency assistance to MSMEs when unexpected events strike, such as financial crises, disasters, and other shocks like the COVID-19 pandemic.

In Sri Lanka, the central bank introduced a debt relief package in January 2020 to assist MSMEs access bank credit in response to the uncertain economic conditions and a series of droughts. Available to all MSMEs, special concessions include rescheduling existing loans with a 1-year grace period, penalty interest write-offs, doubling loan tenor balances, and working capital loans for re-opening businesses. New loans for investment and working capital and a 1-year capital moratorium are also available for MSMEs who are current on their term loans. After the COVID-19 outbreak in March 2020, the package was extended to cover those self-employed and individuals affected by the pandemic. It also allowed other financial institutions such as licensed finance companies and specialized leasing companies to join.

Emergency financial assistance to MSMEs came relatively soon after the pandemic began. They have continued to expand measures to MSMEs including cottage industries under central bank initiatives and government stimulus throughout 2021. Assistance includes (i) liquidity support for financial institutions to extend MSME financing, including a reduced statutory reserve ratio and capital injection; (ii) debt restructuring and deferred debt payments (principal and interest); (iii) lending rate reduction through policy rate cut, interest subsidies, and interest caps; (iv) new lending to MSMEs and other priorities such as tourism and women entrepreneurs, using extended refinancing facilities, special funds, and credit guarantees; and (v) easing regulations, including debt moratoria and NPL reclassifications (Table 2.2).

Table 2.2: Assistance and Infrastructure for MSME Access to Finance

Item		Bank Credit						Public Finance		
		Refinancing facilities to banks	Credit guarantees/ credir risk sharing	Mandatory lending to MSMEs	Interest rate subsidy	Credit bureaus/ credit information system	Secured transaction legal system	Specialized bank for MSMEs	Direct lending/ special funds/ soft loans	Focused groups financing
Lower-middle-income economies	BAN	√	(CGF planned)	(lending target)	√	√	(Collateral Registry Bureau planned)		√	√
	IND	√ (MUDRA)	√	(lending target)	√	√	√	√ (SIDBI)	√	
	NEP	√	√	√	√	√	√		√	√ (agriculture, women)
	PAK	√	√		√	√	√	√ (SME Bank)	√	√ (women)
	SRI	√	(NCGI planned)		√	√	√		√	√ (youth, women, priority sectors)

Item		Nonbank Finance			Digital Finance			
		MFI development support	NBFI industry development (except MFIs)	Consumer/ client protection policies	Branchless/ agent banking strategy	Peer-to-peer (P2P) lending regulations	Equity crowdfunding (ECF) regulations	National payment system and digital infrastructure
Lower-middle-income economies	BAN	√	√	√	√			√ (NPSB)
	IND	√		√	√	√		√ (UPI, Aadhar)
	NEP	√		√	√			(NPS planned)
	PAK	√	√	√	√	√ (regulatory sandbox)	√ (regulatory sandbox)	√ (Raast)
	SRI	√		√	√			√

Item		Capital Markets					Emergency Assistance (Response to COVID-19)					
		Equity markets that MSMEs can tap	Venture capital and private equity investments	Tax incentive for MSME issuers/ investors	Financial education programs and training	Dedicated financial inclusion strategy	Liquidity support for financial institutions/ capital injection	Debt restructuring/ deferral of debt payments	Relaxed lending conditions/ interest rate reduction	New lending to MSMEs/ emergency refinancing facility	Special credit guarantees	Regulatory forbearance
Lower-middle-income economies	BAN	√ (CSE SME and DSE SME)	√		√	√	√	√	√	√	√	√
	IND	√ (BSE SME Exchange and NSE Emerge)	√		√	√	√	√	√	√	√	√
	NEP	(brainstorming)	√ (limited)		√	√	√	√	√	√		√
	PAK	√ (GEM)	√		√	√	√	√	√	√	√	√
	SRI	√ (Empower Board)	√		√	√	√	√	√	√	√	√

BAN = Bangladesh; BSE = Bombay Stock Exchange; CGF = Credit Guarantee Fund; COVID-19 = coronavirus disease; CSE = Chittagong Stock Exchange; DSE = Dhaka Stock Exchange: GEM = Growth Enterprise Market; IND = India; MSME = micro, small, and medium-sized enterprise; MUDRA = Micro Units Development and Refinance Agency; NCGI = National Credit Guarantee Institution; NEP = Nepal; NPS = National Payment Switch; NPSB = National Payment Switch Bangladesh; NSE = National Stock Exchange; PAK = Pakistan; SRI = Sri Lanka; SIDBI = Small Industries Development Bank of India; SME = small and medium-sized enterprise; UPI = unified payments interface.

Note: World Bank country classification by income (https://datahelpdesk.worldbank.org/knowledgebase/articles/906519-world-bank-country-and-lending-groups).

Source: ADB Asia SME Monitor 2021 database.

Nonbank Financing

The nonbank finance industry is small, yet gradually developing across the region and helps supply MSME working capital. Nonbank finance institutions (NBFIs) include MFIs, credit cooperatives, finance companies, and leasing and factoring companies. Among others, MFIs play a critical role of improving access to finance for rural MSMEs and small entrepreneurs, even as NPLs are rising. During 2015–2020, NBFI financing in South Asia accounted for an average 3.2% of a country's GDP (4.9% CAGR) and 6.5% of total bank lending (–2.8%), lower than the Southeast Asia average (4.0% of GDP and 8.3% of total bank lending from 2010 to 2020). The share of nonperforming financing to total NBFI financing averaged 5.6% over the period, but it is rising (9.7% CAGR). This is much higher than the Southeast Asia average of 0.9% (6.2% CAGR during 2010–2020).

NBFI financing in 2020 was equivalent to 7.8% of GDP in Sri Lanka, followed by Nepal (6.7% [fiscal year]), Bangladesh (2.4%), India (0.8%), and Pakistan (0.3%) (Figure 2.9A).[14] Compared with total bank lending, NBFI financing in 2020 was 12.8% of total bank lending in Sri Lanka, followed by Nepal (8.0% [fiscal year]), Bangladesh (5.9%), India (1.5%), and Pakistan (1.2%). MFIs dominate the nonbank finance industry in Bangladesh, Nepal, and Pakistan, while finance companies dominate the industry in India and Sri Lanka, based on available data.

Nonbank financing has grown rapidly with high CAGRs in Nepal (35.1%; FY2017–FY2020), followed by India (21.2%; 2015–2020), Pakistan (11.7%; 2015–2020), Bangladesh (8.3%; 2015–2020), and Sri Lanka (6.8%; 2015–2020). In US dollar terms, nonbank finance in India reached $20.6 billion in 2020, followed by Bangladesh ($7.9 billion), Sri Lanka ($6.2 billion), Nepal ($2.2 billion), and Pakistan ($0.7 billion) (Figure 2.9B) (footnote 12). Compared with Southeast Asia, India had the second-largest NBFI industry, behind Indonesia.

The share of NBFI financing to GDP increased moderately in Nepal (a CAGR of 24.7%; FY2017–FY2020), India (12.8%; 2015–2020), Pakistan (2.8%; 2015–2020), and Sri Lanka (0.3%; 2015–2020), but contracted in Bangladesh (–4.2%; 2015–2020) (Figure 2.9C). Its growth over time has been slower than bank credit, except in India and Nepal. The share of NBFI financing to total bank loans fell by 6.3% CAGR in Sri Lanka and 4.3% in Bangladesh during 2015–2020 (Figure 2.9D). Pakistan had a CAGR of 0.2% (2015–2020), while 14.6% CAGR (FY2017–FY2020) in Nepal and 12.1% (2015–2020) in India.

The NBFI nonperforming financing to total financing ratio remains high. In 2020, it was 15.0% in Bangladesh, 13.9% in Sri Lanka, 6.0% in Pakistan, 5.8% in India, and 2.3% in Nepal (fiscal year) (Figure 2.10A). Nonperforming financing amounts have increased fast. The CAGR in 2015–2020 was 27.8% in Sri Lanka, followed by Pakistan (24.8%), India (22.1%), and Bangladesh (20.2%) (Figure 2.10A). The share of NBFI nonperforming financing to total financing has sharply increased over time in Bangladesh and Sri Lanka (Figure 2.10B).

[14] NBFI data differs by country: Bangladesh (nonbank finance institutions regulated by Bangladesh Bank); India (nonbank finance institutions regulated by Reserve Bank of India; MSME financing only); Nepal (microfinance institutions); Pakistan (microfinance institutions and leasing companies); and Sri Lanka: (nonbank finance institutions regulated by Central Bank of Sri Lanka).

Figure 2.9: Nonbank Finance

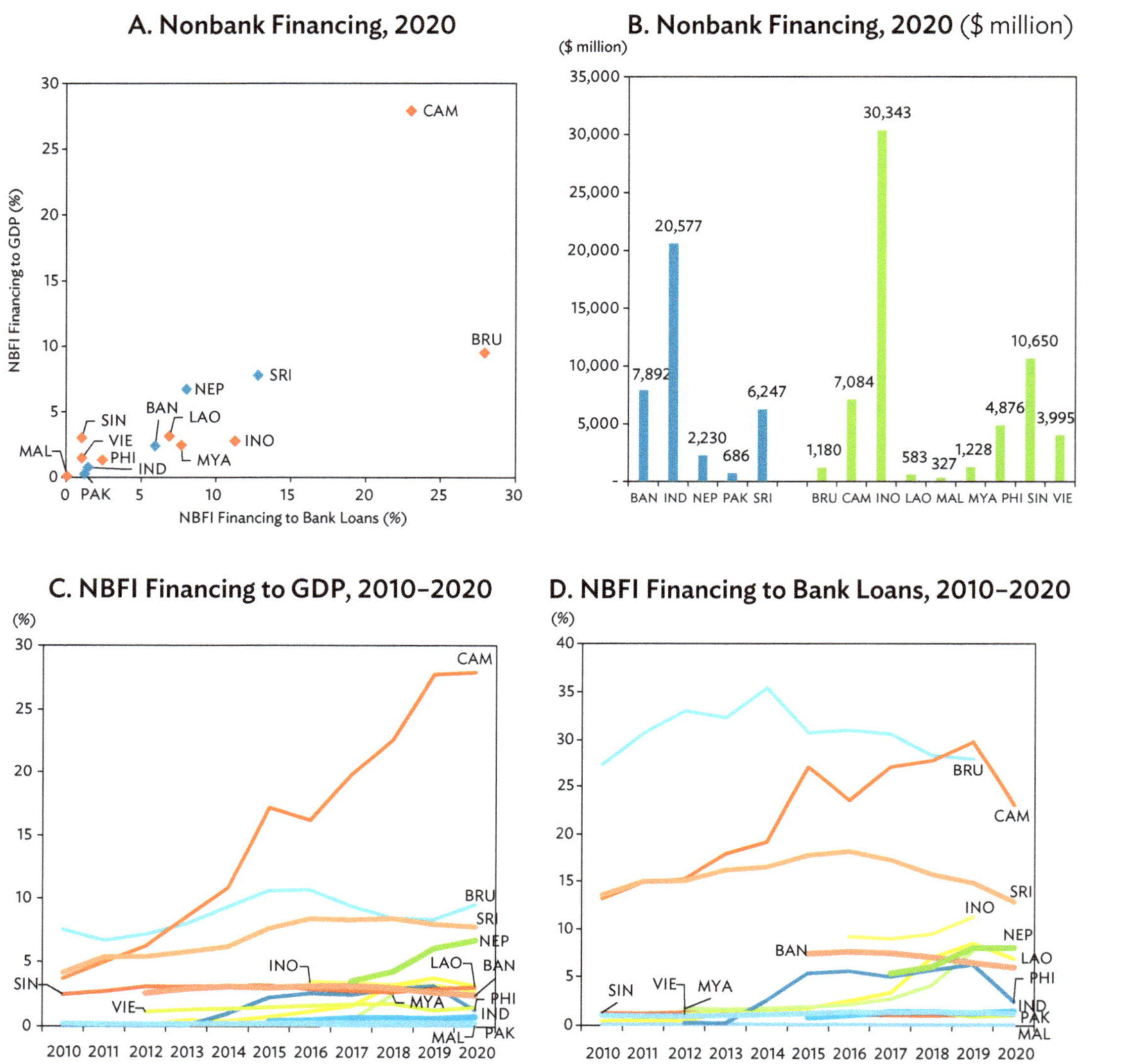

BAN = Bangladesh, BRU = Brunei Darussalam, CAM = Cambodia, GDP = gross domestic product, IND = India, INO = Indonesia, LAO = Lao People's Democratic Republic, MAL = Malaysia, MYA = Myanmar, NBFI = nonbank finance institution, NEP = Nepal, PAK = Pakistan, PHI = Philippines, SIN = Singapore, SRI = Sri Lanka, VIE = Viet Nam.

Notes: NBFI data varies by country: Bangladesh (nonbank finance institutions regulated by Bangladesh Bank); Brunei Darussalam (finance companies and pawnbrokers); Cambodia (microfinance institutions and leasing companies); India (nonbank finance institutions regulated by Reserve Bank of India; MSME financing only); Indonesia (finance companies, microfinance institutions, and government pawnshops); Lao People's Democratic Republic (microfinance institutions, pawnshops, and leasing companies); Malaysia (private equity, venture capital, factoring, and leasing companies); Myanmar (microfinance institutions); Nepal (microfinance institutions); Pakistan (microfinance institutions and leasing companies); Philippines (credit unions and cooperatives [2015–2018], pawnshops [2009–2018], and nonstock savings and loans associations [NSSLAs; 2014–2020]); Singapore (finance companies); Sri Lanka: (nonbank finance institutions regulated by Central Bank of Sri Lanka); Viet Nam (People's Credit Funds and microfinance institutions).

For Figure 2.9A, NBFI financing to GDP (%) refers to the latest available year: 2018 for MYA (fiscal year); 2020 for NEP (fiscal year) and the rest (end-of-year). NBFI financing to bank loans (%) refers to 2019 for BRU, INO, and MYA (fiscal year); 2020 for NEP (fiscal year) and the rest (end-of-year). For Figure 2.9B, data refer to 2019 for MYA (fiscal year); 2020 for NEP (fiscal year) and the rest (end-of-year). Exchange rates of local currency to US dollar refer to end-of-year currency rates from the International Monetary Fund (IMF) International Financial Statistics in designated years. For Figure 2.9C, data for MYA (fiscal year) until 2018; NEP (fiscal year) and the rest (end-of-year) until 2020. For Figure 2.9D, data for BRU, INO, MYA (fiscal year) until 2019; NEP (fiscal year) and the rest (end-of-year) until 2020.

Source: ADB Asia SME Monitor 2021 database.

Figure 2.10: NBFI Nonperforming Financing

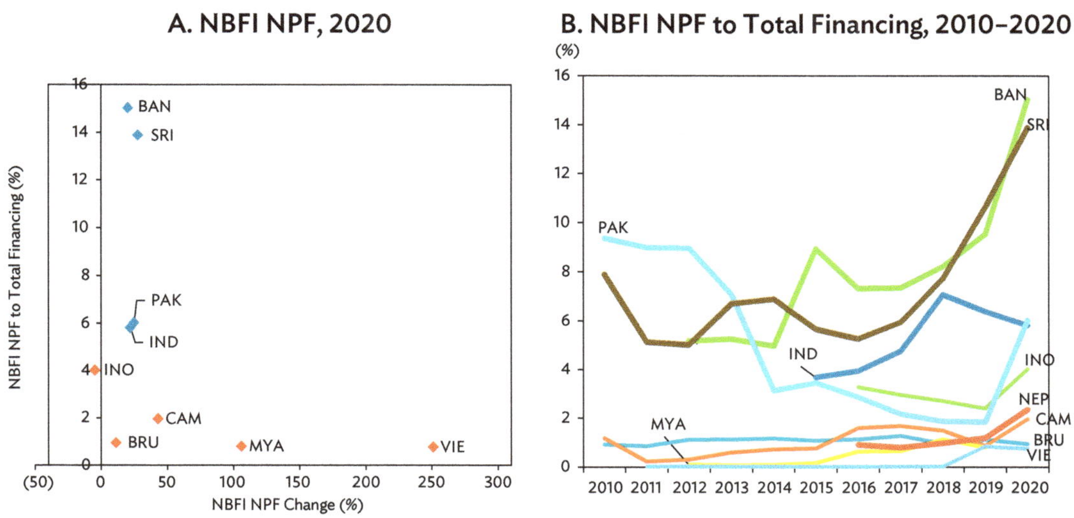

BAN = Bangladesh, BRU = Brunei Darussalam, CAM = Cambodia, IND = India, INO = Indonesia, MYA = Myanmar, NBFI = nonbank finance institution, NEP = Nepal, NPF = nonperforming financing, PAK = Pakistan, SRI = Sri Lanka, VIE = Viet Nam.

Notes: For Figure 2.10A, NBFI NPF to total financing (%) refers to the latest available year: 2019 for MYA (fiscal year); 2020 for the rest (end-of-year). NBFI NPF change (%) refers to compound annual growth during past and latest available data. Data cover 2015–2020 for BAN, BRU, CAM, IND, PAK, and SRI; 2016–2019 for INO and MYA (fiscal year); 2017–2020 for VIE. For Figure 2.10B, data refer to fiscal year for MYA and NEP and end-of-year for the rest.

Source: ADB Asia SME Monitor 2021 database.

Nongovernment (NGO) and private sector MFIs spread nationwide to serve vulnerable segments including agribusinesses and women entrepreneurs in rural and poor areas by offering micro credit, savings, remittances, and insurance, while several government-sponsored microfinance programs (PKSF in Bangladesh, MUDRA in India, and *Samurdhi* in Sri Lanka) have grown and supplemented microfinance markets in the region. Critical challenges to develop the microfinance industry in the region include managing high NPLs while ensuring consumer protection and balancing private and public microfinance programs so as not to trigger market distortions.

Other types of nonbank finance instruments, such as leasing and factoring, have yet to be developed in South Asia. Financial leasing helps cover MSMEs' investment capital needs. Factoring provides short-term liquidity to MSMEs, useful for both domestic and international trade. Venture capital and business angels have increased their presence in the region, investing in technology-based start-ups and early-stage firms, but in the nascent stage of development. Tax and capital controls limit additional investment from them (Pakistan). More diversified financing options with legal support should be strengthened in the region so viable MSMEs can grow further.

Digital Financial Services

Digital financial services (DFS) offer low-cost financing to traditionally unserved and underserved segments, including MSMEs. It is a critical tool for promoting inclusive growth and is a central pillar of mid- to long-term national financial inclusion strategies. Demand for DFS increased sharply in South Asia during the pandemic.

Interoperable online payment platforms for card and internet transactions or a national payment switch are the spine of digital financial infrastructure. It is the basis of e-commerce transactions and mobile financial services.

The National Payment Switch Bangladesh opened in 2012. It processes interbank ATMs, point-of-sale (POS), and internet banking fund transfer (IBFT) transactions. In India, the unified payments interface (UPI), launched in 2016, allows real-time fund transfers between two bank accounts using mobile applications of banks and third parties such as Google Pay. The National Payments Corporation of India runs retail payments and settlements through the UPI. A 12-digit digital identification system *Aadhar* helps operate online payment platforms, verification (e-KYC), , and cloud storage (via Digi Locker). The Nepal Clearing House Limited operates a retail payment system, providing image-based check clearing and electronic fund transfers. An interoperable National Payment Switch (NPS) is planned (as of September 2021). In Pakistan, Raast, launched in 2020, operates as an instant digital payment system. The central bank also launched Roshan Digital Accounts in 2020 using commercial banks to allow overseas Pakistanis to digitally open bank accounts and transfer funds, remittances, make payments, or invest. In Sri Lanka, the central bank uses the Sri Lanka Interbank Payment System (SLIPS) and Common Electronic Fund Transfer Switch (CEFTS) for retail payments and settlement. LankaClear, jointly owned by the central bank and commercial banks, is a clearing house for retail payments.[15]

Agent and mobile banking continues to expand rapidly. In Bangladesh, agent banking has steadily grown even during the pandemic, particularly in rural and remote areas. Based on agreements between the agent and banks, it offers limited banking services for deposits, disbursing credit, and paying remittances. In FY2020, there were 8,764 agents using 12,449 outlets connected with 23 licensed banks in Bangladesh. Mobile banking has expanded in Nepal and Pakistan. There are more than 13 million registered mobile banking users in Nepal, 80% of which are active (as of April 2021). Six million people use debit cards and 0.7 million access internet banking. Low-cost smartphones and expanding internet access help fuel growth in Nepal. In 2020, Pakistan saw mobile banking grow 88%, with internet banking users up 31%.

DFS requires appropriate regulations. In India, the central bank regulates financial technology (fintech) firms directly through licensing or indirectly through banks and associated nonbank finance companies (4,680 fintech firms as of March 2020). The Reserve Bank of India encourages regulatory sandboxes as a way to assess the soundness of new financial services (testing online retail and cross-border payments, for example). Peer-to-peer lending and equity crowdfunding platforms are being tested using regulatory sandboxes in Pakistan.

While DFS is more available, user comfort is an issue. In Sri Lanka, DFS remains the exception, with cash still preferred, according to a national financial inclusion survey 2018–2019. The survey found 85% of respondents used traditional face-to-face transactions with bank cashers, while only 3% used mobile or internet banking. Just 2% owned a mobile money account, most citing "not knowing how to use it" as a reason. Thus, there is a need for strengthening digital finance literacy.

Capital Markets

Specialized SME equity markets have emerged in South Asia to help with growth capital financing for viable small firms.[16] They are organized for qualified and accredited investors, and have either less stringent listing requirements or use a sponsor system for listing.

In Bangladesh, SME platforms were created in 2019 on the Chittagong Stock Exchange (CSE) and Dhaka Stock Exchange (DSE) as dedicated equity markets for high-growth SMEs. Listing requirements such as post-issue paid-up capital are less cumbersome than the main board. Only legally defined qualified investors (high-net-worth

15 Central Bank of Sri Lanka website: https://www.cbsl.gov.lk/en/financial-system/financial-infrastructure/payments-and-settlements-systems

16 In this section, "SME" is used instead of MSME following capital market terminology.

individuals) can invest in the SME platform for newly listed issues. Six firms are listed on the DSE platform and one on the CSE as of end-September 2021.

India's SME equity markets opened in 2012 on the Bombay Stock Exchange (BSE) and National Stock Exchange (NSE). The SME markets—the BSE SME Exchange and NSE Emerge—offer easier listing requirements such as post-issue paid-up capital. During 2012–2020, 93 firms from BSE SME Exchange and 62 firms from NSE Emerge moved onto their respective main boards, which suggests SME markets support MSME growth.

In Pakistan, the Growth Enterprise Market (GEM) was created in 2019. Only accredited investors (institutional investors and high-net-worth individuals) can invest in the GEM. There was no listed company as of June 2021.

Sri Lanka's Empower Board was established in 2018 under the Colombo Stock Exchange, which is a sponsor-driven equity market dedicated to SMEs with easier listing requirements. Under the sponsor system, listing applications must have a sponsor approved by the stock exchange as an individual or organization with market expertise, which should help the listing process run smoothly and ensure quality issuers on the market. As of April 2021, however, there were no listed SMEs. Nepal does not have a dedicated SME board, but authorities are discussing the possibility.

As SME markets are relatively new in Bangladesh, Pakistan, and Sri Lanka, data in these markets are unavailable. Based on existing equity markets that firms, including MSMEs, can tap, market capitalization averaged 18.2% of a country's GDP during 2015–2020 (–4.2% CAGR). Market size is small, but India's SME markets have grown sharply since they opened in 2012 (67.4% CAGR during 2012–2020).

By country, the market capitalization of equity markets was 45.8% of GDP (FY2020) in Nepal, followed by Bangladesh (19.9% for CSE and DSE; FY2020), Sri Lanka (19.8%; 2020), and Pakistan (19.3%; 2020). India's BSE Exchange and NSE Emerge accounted for only 0.1% of GDP in 2020 (Figure 2.11A). By comparison, the share of market capitalization available for SMEs in Southeast Asia averaged 7.7% at a CAGR of 0.5% during 2012–2020. Market capitalization grew at a CAGR of 21.9% in Nepal (FY2012–FY2020), followed by Pakistan (8.3%; 2012–2020), Sri Lanka (4.0%; 2012–2020), and Bangladesh (3.1%; FY2012–FY2020). India's SME markets grew at a 67.4% CAGR, faster than any other markets. In US dollar terms, market capitalization in Bangladesh reached $65.7 billion (FY2020), followed by Pakistan ($50.3 billion; 2020), Sri Lanka ($15.9 billion; 2020), and Nepal ($15.2 billion; FY2020). India's SME markets amounted to $3.7 billion in 2020 (Figure 2.11B) (footnote 12). The growth in market capitalization to GDP increased moderately in Nepal, while remained relatively stable or declined over time in Bangladesh, Pakistan, and Sri Lanka. The share of India's SME markets to GDP is extremely small but growing (Figure 2.11C). The number of listed companies in equity markets increased moderately in Bangladesh, while markets in Nepal, Pakistan, and Sri Lanka have seen relatively stagnant or decreased growth of new issuers. Listed companies in India's SME markets have steadily increased over time (Figure 2.11D).

Regulators and stock exchanges cite several challenges to developing SME capital markets in the region: (i) SME owners do not see any urgency in growing their businesses, (ii) SME owners do not want to dilute their ownership stakes, (iii) high compliance costs of regulations (for example, corporate governance and taxes), (iv) poor accounting, and (v) weak capital market literacy (footnote 9). Thus, it is important to strengthen capital market literacy programs and training to attract SME issuers (including young entrepreneurs and start-ups) and investors (including venture capital firms and business angels). Securities exchange commissions and stock exchanges do offer several literacy and training programs.

Figure 2.11: Equity Markets for MSMEs

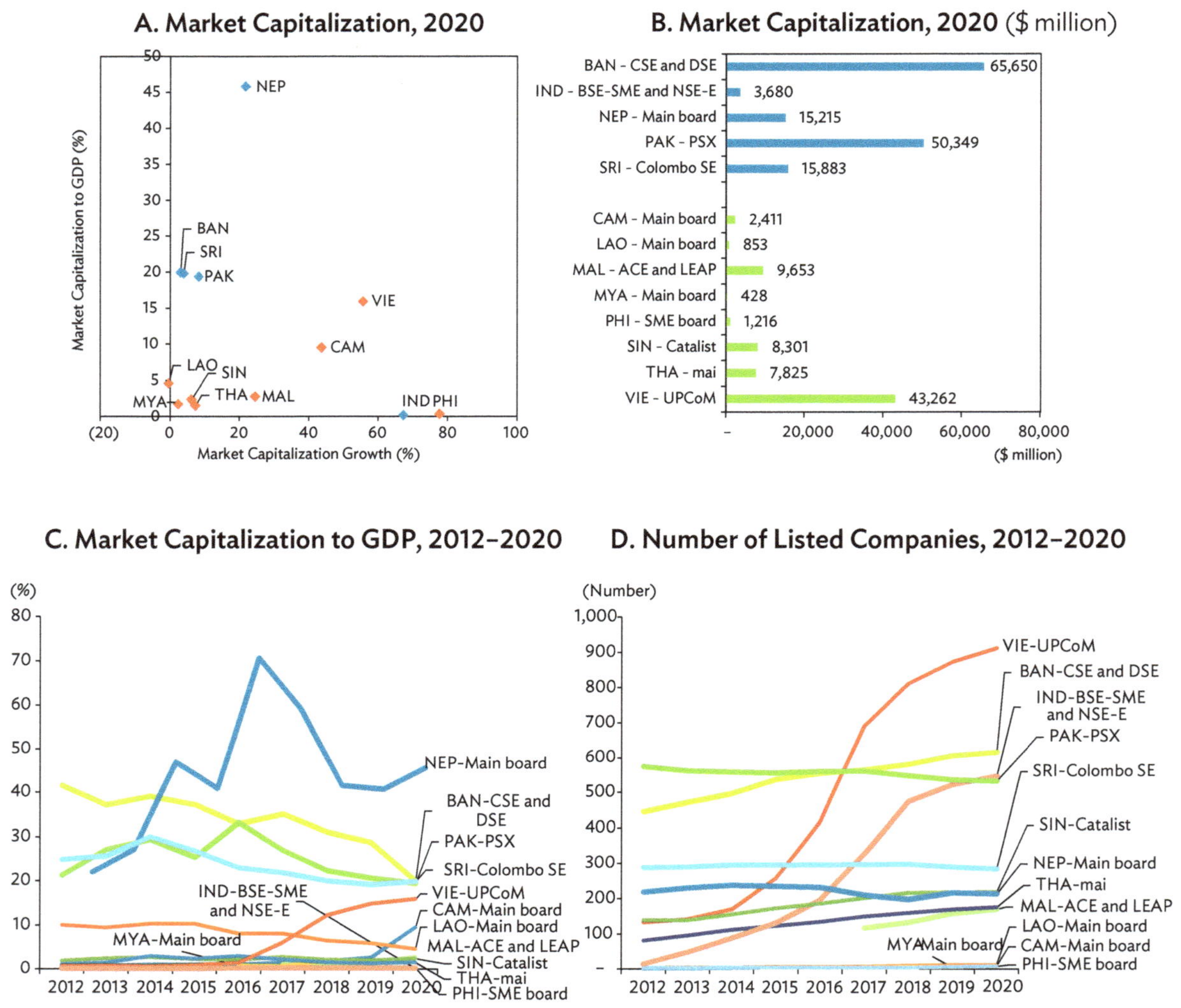

BAN = Bangladesh; BSE = Bombay Stock Exchange; BSE-SME = BSE SME Exchange; CAM = Cambodia; Colombo SE = Colombo Stock Exchange; CSE = Chittagong Stock Exchange; DSE = Dhaka Stock Exchange; GDP = gross domestic product; IND = India; INO = Indonesia; LAO = Lao PDR; MAL = Malaysia; MSME = micro, small, and medium-sized enterprise; MYA = Myanmar; NBFI = nonbank finance institution; NEP = Nepal; NSE = National Stock Exchange; NSE-E =NSE Emerge; PAK = Pakistan; PHI = Philippines; PSX = Pakistan Stock Exchange; SIN = Singapore; SRI = Sri Lanka; THA = Thailand; VIE = Viet Nam.

Notes: For Figure 2.11A, market capitalization to GDP (%) refers to the latest available year: 2018 for MYA, 2020 for BAN (fiscal year), NEP (fiscal year), and the rest (end-of-year). Market capitalization growth (%) refers to compound annual growth during past and latest available data. Data refer to 2016–2019 for MYA; 2012–2020 for the rest. For Figure 2.11B, data refer to 2019 for MYA; 2020 for the rest. Exchange rates of local currency to US dollar refer to end-of-year currency rates from the International Monetary Fund (IMF) International Financial Statistics in designated years. For Figures 2.11C and 2.11D, data refer to fiscal year for BAN and NEP and end-of-year for the rest.

Source: ADB Asia SME Monitor 2021 database.

Financial Infrastructure

A well-organized financial infrastructure—functioning credit bureau, secured lending, and credit enhancement (credit guarantees and rating) systems—is critical to financial inclusion. The countries here all have basic financial infrastructure, including digital infrastructure like interoperable payment systems.

In Bangladesh, there are two credit information bureaus: the Credit Information Bureau established in 1992 under the central bank and, from end-2020, the Microfinance Credit Information Bureau (MF-CIB) under the Microcredit Regulatory Authority as a pilot with 50 selected MFIs. A Collateral Registry Bureau is being established under the national financial inclusion strategy. There are eight credit rating agencies as of end-September 2021, offering SME rating services. These assist financial institutions in reducing loan processing time and costs while mitigating risks associated with lending to MSMEs.

In India, four private credit information companies are regulated by the central bank as of March 2020. They collect credit information sourced from banks, NBFIs, and other lending agencies. A centralized collateral registry (CERSAI) was established in 2011, listing immovable assets for collateral. The central bank also established a Public Credit Registry to maintain a ledger of all borrowers and lenders in the country.

Nepal's Credit Information Bureau was created in 1989, with 140 banks and financial institutions as members as of September 2021. The bureau has also operated a Secured Transaction Registry since FY2017, which is a repository of movable assets of potential borrowers from banks and financial institutions. Two credit rating agencies are operating but do not offer MSME rating services due to low demand and high costs.

Pakistan's central bank established an electronic Credit Information Bureau (e-CIB) in 2005. A digital Secured Transaction Registry has been operating since 2020, with over 85,000 transactions registered as of June 2020. The Credit Information Bureau of Sri Lanka (CRIB) was established in 1990 for credit information management and to offer a secured transaction registry (movable assets).

3. Policies and Regulations

MSME development and financial inclusion are a critical part of national growth strategies toward a more resilient and diversified economy. South Asian countries have a set of policy frameworks covering these areas. If anything, the pandemic accelerated the need to promote MSME digitalization, formalize more businesses, encourage entrepreneurships, diversify market access through internationalization, and increase access to formal financial services for MSMEs. To effectively implement government MSME assistance, using a single national MSME definition is needed as well as strengthening MSME data infrastructure nationally. Table 2.3 summarizes policies and regulations on MSME development and access to finance in South Asia.

MSME Development

a. Medium- and long-term national MSME policies

Governments have long-term MSME development frameworks, which comprehensively cover financial and nonfinancial issues in line with their national development strategies. They all seek a better business environment, access to markets and finance, skills development, business cluster development, use of technology, and special assistance for focused groups such as youth and women entrepreneurships, start-ups, agribusiness, and internationalized MSMEs (participation in global value chains). In South Asia, cottage industries—small manufacturers and home businesses—are an important MSME segment to foster. MSME policies generally aim to boost business infrastructure (through business development services and capacity building) and financial assistance to MSMEs (through special funds or refinancing facilities, with interest rate subsidies and credit guarantees), following time-bound goals and action plans. In South Asia, core lineups of MSME support measures have strengthened over time, which allowed for the quick response and assistance using existing frameworks as the COVID-19 crisis developed.

MSMEs are defined by national policies in Bangladesh, Pakistan, and Sri Lanka, while they are legally stipulated in India and Nepal, creating a single national definition. Nonetheless, various MSME definitions are substantially used by statistics office, central banks, and line ministries (Bangladesh, Pakistan, and Sri Lanka). India has a dedicated MSME law to guide their development, which would be worth considering by governments with no legal MSME framework to enhance effective support. The guiding policies and laws include the following.

- SME Policy 2019, Bangladesh
- Micro, Small and Medium Enterprise Development Act of 2006, India
- Industrial Promotion Policy 2011, Nepal
- National SME Policy Action Plan 2020 (for SME Policy 2019), Pakistan
- National Policy Framework for Small and Medium Enterprise Development 2015, Sri Lanka

Data infrastructure is also critical to effectively support MSME development and to promote evidence-based economic growth. In South Asia, MSME data infrastructure is not well established. There is no comprehensive and comparative MSME database covering both financial and nonfinancial conditions with periodic monitoring and evaluation. This would be crucial for identifying timely assistance needs from MSMEs and to implement policy support measures efficiently and effectively. Long-interval census data and financially focused credit bureau and collateral registry data are not enough to assess or evaluate MSMEs. Business registration should be strengthened further for periodic monitoring, especially for registering informal businesses. It is also critical to use granular enterprise data and cloud data using an established system for MSME analysis. Intragovernmental coordination for sharing MSME data between central and local governments should be strengthened as well. Bangladesh mentions the importance of institutionalizing SME statistics under its SME Policy 2019.

b. Policy coordination, implementation, and monitoring

There are focal government authorities for MSME development policies in the countries here: (i) the Ministry of Industries in Bangladesh; (ii) the Ministry of Micro, Small, and Medium-Sized Enterprises in India; (iii) the Ministry of Industries, Commerce and Supplies in Nepal; (iv) the Ministry of Industries and Production (MOIP) in Pakistan; and (v) the Ministry of Industries (MOI) in Sri Lanka.

Three countries have intragovernmental policy coordination bodies: (i) the National Council for Industrial Development (NCID) in Bangladesh; (ii) the National Board for Micro, Small, and Medium Enterprises in India; and (iii) the Nepal Planning Commission, which designs national development plans including MSME development strategies.

Three countries have specific policy implementing agency for MSMEs: (i) the SME Foundation in Bangladesh, a nonprofit organization established by the government through the Ministry of Industries; (ii) the Small and Medium Enterprise Development Authority under the MOIP in Pakistan; and (iii) the National Enterprise Development Authority under the MOI in Sri Lanka.

Financial Inclusion

a. National financial inclusion strategies

There are comprehensive national financial inclusion strategies, formulated for 2015–2021 in South Asia. They commonly set core strategic goals and action plans on (i) digital finance and payments, (ii) financial literacy and education, (iii) consumer protection, and (iv) financial assistance for traditionally unserved and underserved segments—including MSMEs, women entrepreneurs, and priority sectors such as agriculture. Bangladesh and Sri Lanka are also creating robust financial inclusion data for effective monitoring and policy interventions.

- National Financial Inclusion Strategy of Bangladesh 2020–2024
- National Strategy for Financial Inclusion 2019–2024, India
- Financial Inclusion Roadmap 2017–2022, Nepal
- National Financial Inclusion Strategy 2015, Pakistan
- National Financial Inclusion Strategy for Sri Lanka 2021–2024

Financial inclusion strategies are holistic but remain somewhat bank-centric. From a long-term perspective, more attention should be given to market-based financing (such as capital market development) to provide growth capital to qualified SMEs. Dedicated SME equity markets exist in Bangladesh, India, Pakistan, and Sri Lanka, but attracting more SME issuers and investors in these markets, with an organized liquidity mechanism, is a key challenge for development. They could help national financial inclusion strategies. Bangladesh's financial inclusion strategy mentions reinforcing capital market services for SMEs.

b. Policy coordination, implementation, and monitoring

Central banks coordinate and implement financial inclusion policies in the region: (i) Bangladesh Bank (SME and Special Programmes Department); (ii) Reserve Bank of India; (iii) Nepal Rastra Bank; (iv) State Bank of Pakistan; and (v) Central Bank of Sri Lanka.

There are intragovernmental policy coordination bodies to implement the financial inclusion strategies in Bangladesh, India, and Sri Lanka. In Bangladesh, there are four bodies: (i) the NFIS-B national Council (NNC) to develop strategic directions and oversee implementation of financial inclusion agendas; (ii) the NFIS-B Steering Committee (NSC) to implement NNC strategies; (iii) the NFIS-B Advisory Committee (NAC), a platform for public-private partnerships and advocate for financial inclusion; and (iv) the NFIS-B Secretariat (NNS) for technical administration and research support to the NNC, NSC, and NAC. The Reserve Bank of India established an expert committee on MSMEs in 2019 to conduct a comprehensive MSME review and propose interventions for financial inclusion. In Sri Lanka, several bodies implement its financial inclusion strategy: (i) the National Financial Inclusion Council for policy guidance and strategic direction; (ii) a Management Committee that supervises day-to-day implementation of the strategy; and (iii) Working Groups that consult on digital finance and payments, MSME finance, consumer protection, and financial literacy and capacity building. Sri Lanka's strategy also has a monitoring and evaluation (M&E) system providing (i) a results framework with key performance indicators, (ii) mechanics for coordinating and implementing the M&E system, (iii) financial inclusion data, and (iv) evaluations of key reforms and programs.

In South Asia, intragovernmental coordination between central government authorities and central banks is relatively well established to help implement and fine-tune policy actions under national financial inclusion strategies.

Response to COVID-19

MSMEs were hurt badly by the various waves of COVID-19 infections and the strict quarantines and lockdowns. Bangladesh imposed a nationwide lockdown in March–May 2020. India had several lockdowns in response to the first wave in February–March 2020 and the second wave in March 2021. Nepal introduced a nationwide lockdown in March–July 2020 and strict measures again during the second wave in April 2021. Pakistan had three waves of COVID-19 between March 2020 and May 2021, imposing lockdowns and frequent restrictions. Sri Lanka was in lockdown and strict quarantine measures during March–May 2020.

A series of COVID-19 impact studies in South Asia showed that the lockdowns seriously limited MSMEs' business activities, immediately reducing incomes and profits, especially for micro and small enterprises engaged in personal-contact-based services. There was little or no demand for their products and services and keeping working capital were big challenges to maintain or reopen business. Women-owned firms were more seriously affected in sales, income, and access to funds in each country. Several reports cited low awareness of government MSME assistance programs, suggesting the need for strengthening the dissemination of government assistance programs more effectively to target MSMEs, including youth and women entrepreneurs.

Each country acted quickly to contain infections and limit the pandemic's impact on the economy. Large government stimulus packages with spending from 2% to 16% of a country's GDP helped support affected businesses and individuals.[17] Among others, support for MSMEs thus far has been timely and prompt by using existing frameworks on MSME assistance. Government assistance covers a wide range of financial measures including liquidity support to financial institutions, debt restructuring (deferred debt payments), relaxed lending conditions (interest rate reduction by interest subsidy and caps), new lending to MSMEs and priority sectors (by using refinancing facilities, special funds, and credit guarantees), and regulatory forbearance (debt moratoria and NPL reclassifications). In addition, tax relief measures (corporate income tax reductions) and employment income support (cash transfers) have been provided to affected businesses, especially MSMEs.

Given how the pandemic affected people's daily routines, governments are prioritizing the digital transformation of MSME business, as well as formalizing informal businesses, getting more to join global supply chains (internationalization of MSMEs), and developing youth and women entrepreneurships. Considering the prolonged pandemic, government assistance should consider a more balanced support system between businesses hit badly by the pandemic (focused group assistance with a phased approach) and those with growth potential that can help build economic resilience (entrepreneurship development by channeling growth capital to viable MSMEs). This all needs to be done without excessive strains on national budgets. The MSME business environment requires continuous monitoring through surveys to formulate, fine-tune, and deliver effective and timely assistance to MSMEs, focused groups, and priority sectors.

[17] ADB COVID-19 Policy Database, updated as of 27 September 2021. Total package: $14,453 million or 4.42% of GDP in Bangladesh; $419,025 million or 15.90% of GDP in India; $3,868 million or 11.18% of GDP in Nepal; $21,007 million or 8.35% of GDP in Pakistan; $1,286 million or 1.59% of GDP in Sri Lanka.

Reference–Southeast Asia Update

1. MSME Development

MSMEs in Southeast Asia, 2010–2020

	Percentage share	*Compound annual growth*
• **Number of MSMEs to total enterprises**	***97.6%***	***+0.2%***
• **MSME employees to total employees**	***67.0%***	***–0.5%***
• **MSME contribution to national GDP**	***40.5%***	***+0.5%***
• **MSME export to total export value**	***19.2%***	***–4.6%***

GDP = gross domestic product; MSME = micro, small, and medium-sized enterprise.

Reporting countries only.

Source: ADB Asia SME Monitor 2021 database.

2. Access to Finance

MSMEs in Southeast Asia, 2010–2020

Bank credit	*Percentage share*	*Compound annual growth*
• **MSME loans to national GDP**	***14.1%***	***–3.3%***
• **MSME loans to total bank loans**	***16.4%***	***–0.6%***
• **MSME NPLs to total MSME loans**	***4.2%***	***–0.9%***
Nonbank and market-based finance		
• **NBFI financing to national GDP**	***4.0%***	***+10.2%***
• **NBFI financing to total bank loans**	***8.3%***	***–3.8%***
• **NBFI NPF to total financing**	***0.9%***	***+6.2%***
• **MSME market capitalization to GDP***	***7.7%***	***+0.5%***

GDP = gross domestic product; MSME = micro, small, and medium-sized enterprise; NBFI = nonbank finance institution; NPF = nonperforming financing; NPL = nonperforming loan.

* 2012–2020. Data include primary market data if MSME market data is unavailable; average percentage of available markets. Reporting countries only.

Source: ADB Asia SME Monitor 2021 database.

Table 2.3: Policies and Regulations—South Asia

Country		Regulators and Policymakers	Regulations	Policies
Bangladesh	SME Promotion	Ministry of Industries	Companies Act, 1994	(1) National Industrial Policy 2016
		National Council for Industrial Development		(2) National Innovation and Intellectual Property Policy 2018
		SME Foundation		(3) SME Policy 2019
		Bangladesh Planning Commission, Ministry of Planning	...	(4) Perspective Plan of Bangladesh 2021-2041
	Banking Sector	Bangladesh Bank (SME and Special Programmes Department)	Bank Company Act, 1991	(5) Small and Medium Enterprise Credit Policies and Programmes (2010)
			Prudential Regulations for Small Enterprise Financing	(6) Manual of Credit Guarantee Scheme for Cottage, Micro, and Small Enterprises
	Nonbank Sector		Financial Institution Act, 1993	(7) National Financial Inclusion Strategy of Bangladesh 2020-2024
		Microcredit Regulatory Authority	Microcredit Regulatory Authority Act, 2006	
	Capital Markets	Bangladesh Securities and Exchange Commission	Securities and Exchange Commission Act, 1993	
India	SME Promotion	Ministry of Micro, Small and Medium-Sized Enterprises	Micro, Small and Medium Enterprises Development Act, 2006	(1) National Manufacturing Competitiveness Programme (2005)
				(2) Rajiv Gandhi Udyami Mitra Yojna [support for entrepreneurship development] (2008)
				(3) Scheme of Fund for Regeneration of Traditional Industries (SFURTI) (2005–06)
		National Board of MSMEs		(4) Public Procurement Policy for Goods and Services Produced and Rendered by Micro and Small Enterprises (2012)
		Ministry of Commerce and Industry	Limited Liability Partnership Act, 2008	(5) Interest Equalization Scheme on pre and post shipment rupee export credit (2015)
				(6) Developing District as Export Hub
				(7) Market Access Initiative (MAI) scheme
		Ministry of Skill Development and Entrepreneurship	...	(8) Pradhan Mantri Kaushal Vikas Yojana [skill development scheme]
		Ministry of Agriculture	...	(9) National Agriculture Infrastructure Financing Fund (2020)
	Banking Sector	Reserve Bank of India (Committee on MSMEs)	Banking Regulation Act, 1949	(10) Guidelines for setting up of and operating TReDS (2014)
			Master Circular on Lending to Micro, Small and Medium Enterprises, 2014	(11) National Strategy for Financial Inclusion 2019-2024
			Securitisation and Reconstruction of Financial Assets and Enforcement of Security Interest Act, 2002 [collateral registry]	
	Nonbank Sector		Factoring Regulation Act, 2011	
	Capital Markets	Securities and Exchange Board of India	Alternate Investment Funds Regulations, 2012	
			Issue of Capital and Disclosure Requirements (ICDR) Regulations, 2018	

continued on next page

Table 2.3 *continued*

Country	Regulators and Policymakers		Regulations	Policies
Nepal	SME Promotion	Ministry of Industries, Commerce, and Supplies	Industrial Enterprises Act, 2020	(1) Industrial Promotion Policy 2011
		Nepal Planning Commission		(2) 15th Five Year Plan 2019/20 - 2023/24
		Ministry of Finance		(3) Annual Program and Policies (Budget) [Micro Enterprise Development for Poverty Alleviation Program]
	Banking Sector	Nepal Rastra Bank (NRB)	Bank and Financial Institution Act, 2017	(4) NRB Strategic Plan 2017-2021
			Secured Transaction Act, 2006	(5) Financial Inclusion Roadmap 2017–2022
	Nonbank Sector			(6) Financial Literacy Framework (2020)
	Capital Markets	Security Exchange Board of Nepal	Securities Act, 2007	
Pakistan	SME Promotion	Ministry of Industries and Production	The Companies Act, 2017	(1) SME Policy 2007
		(Small and Medium Enterprise Development Authority)	The Limited Liability Partnership Act, 2017	(2) National SME Policy Action Plan 2020 [for SME Policy 2019]
		Ministry of Finance	...	
		Ministry of Commerce	...	
		Board of Investment	Special Economic Zones Act, 2012	
		Federal Board of Revenue	Sales Tax Act, 1990	
			Income Tax Ordinance, 2001	
			Customs Act, 1969	
		Employees Old Age Benefits Institution (EOBI)	Employees Old Age Benefits Institution (EOBI) Act, 1976	
			Workers Welfare Ordinance, 1971	
			Industrial Relations Act, 2010	
	Banking Sector	State Bank of Pakistan	Banking Companies Ordinance, 1962 (amended 2011)	(3) National Financial Inclusion Strategy 2015
			Microfinance Institutions Ordinance, 2001 (amended 2007)	
			Payment Systems and Electronic Fund Transfer Act, 2007	
			Electronic Transactions Ordinance, 2002	
			Credit Bureau Act, 2015 (Credit Bureaus Amendment Act, 2016)	
			Financial Institutions (Secured Transactions) Act, 2016	
			Prudential Regulations for Small and Medium Enterprises Financing (updated 5 April 2021)	
			Prudential regulations for Micro Finance Banks	
			Various circulars from Agriculture Credit and Microfinance Department (ACMFD) on microcredit and credit guarantees	
	Nonbank Sector	Securities and Exchange Commission of Pakistan	Securities and Exchange Commission of Pakistan Act, 1997	
	Capital Markets			

continued on next page

Table 2.3 *continued*

Country	Regulators and Policymakers		Regulations	Policies
Sri Lanka	SME Promotion	Ministry of Industries	Industrial Promotion Act, No.46 of 1990	(1) Vision 2025: A Country Enriched
		National Enterprise Development Authority	National Enterprise Development Authority Act, No.17 of 2006	(2) Enterprise Sri Lanka (2017)
		Ministry of Trade		(3) National Policy Framework for Small and Medium Enterprise Development (2015)
		Sri Lanka Export Development Board	Sri Lanka Export Development Board Act, No.40 of 1979	
		Co-operative Wholesale Establishment	Co-operative Wholesale Establishment Act, No.44 of 1949	
		Department of Co-operative Development	Co-operative Societies Act, No.5 of 1972	
		Ministry of Agriculture		
		Department of Agrarian Development	Agrarian Development Act, No.46 of 2000	
		Ministry of Plantation		
		Tea Small Holdings Development Authority	Tea Small Holdings Development Act, No.35 of 1975	
		Minister of Education		
		Industrial Technology Institute	Science and Technology Development Act, No.11 of 1994	
		Ministry of Finance		
		Department of Development Finance	...	
		Department of Samurdhi Development	Divineguma Act, No.01 of 2013	
	Banking Sector	Central Bank of Sri Lanka	Banking Act, No.30 of 1988	National Financial Inclusion Strategy for Sri Lanka 2021-2024
			Secured Transactions Act No.49 of 2009	
	Nonbank Sector		Microfinance Act, No.6 of 2016	
	Capital Markets	Security and Exchange Commission of Sri Lanka	Securities and Exchange Commission of Sri Lanka Act, No.36 of 1987	

MSME = micro, small, and medium-sized enterprise.

Source: Compiled from country reviews of Asia Small and Medium-Sized Enterprise Monitor 2021.

Country Review
Bangladesh

Overview

The economy decelerated to 3.5% growth in fiscal year (FY) 2020 (ended 30 June 2020) from 8.2% in FY2019. Nonetheless, it showed resiliency despite the adverse effects of the coronavirus disease (COVID-19) pandemic. Supported by large government stimulus packages to curb the pandemic's impact, the economy quickly shifted to recovery in 2021 with estimated growth of 5.5% in FY2021, although still below its pre-pandemic level. Bangladesh was in nationwide lockdown during March–May 2020, relatively soon after the pandemic started, causing many enterprises to shut down and forcing revenue losses and unemployment. Businesses could reopen after the first lockdown, but the government imposed lockdowns again in July–August 2021 due to the Delta coronavirus variant. The uncertainty surrounding the pandemic remains the main downside risk for short-term economic growth.

Micro, small, and medium-sized enterprises (MSMEs), including cottage industries, are critical to economic growth, covering 99.97% of all enterprises—they absorb around 86% of the labor force. Cottage and small enterprises generate around 16% of manufacturing gross value added, still small but growing. They remain the group most hurt by the pandemic but have shown strong resilience nonetheless. Strengthening MSMEs is key to further boosting the national economy.

Access to finance underpins the growth of MSMEs. With the central bank setting lending targets, commercial bank credit to MSMEs has been steadily rising at a compound annual growth rate (CAGR) of 13.0% from 2010 to 2020, benefitting 0.8 million MSME borrowers by end-2020. As over 80% of MSME credit is for urban establishments, credit to borrowers in rural areas should be strengthened. There are several refinancing schemes for MSMEs to help women and small entrepreneurs continue to access financing.

The nonbank finance industry is an important substitute for bank credit to MSMEs. The growth of lending by central bank-regulated nonbank finance institutions (NBFIs) has been decelerating with increased concentration on manufacturing and rising nonperforming loan (NPL) ratios since 2018. Meanwhile, the microfinance market has grown steadily. The Palli Karma-Sahayak Foundation (PKSF), a wholesale lending institution, offers microenterprise loans in rural and poor areas through partner organizations, increasing sharply since 2018, helping satisfy financing demand from rural MSMEs. The two stock exchanges created a specialized equity market for small and medium-sized enterprises (SMEs) in 2019 with concessional listing requirements.

The SME Policy 2019 is the national framework for MSME development, raising their target contribution to gross domestic product (GDP) to 32% by 2024. The government launched a long-term national development strategy "Perspective Plan of Bangladesh 2021–2041" in 2020 to implement its core national development framework—Vision 2041. It promotes inclusive growth by enhancing MSME dynamism and access to finance. The central bank launched a National Financial Inclusion Strategy for 2020–2024, paying special attention to digitization.

The government sees MSMEs as pivotal for sustainable growth. Thus, MSME development strategies have been formulated to comprehensively cover both financial and nonfinancial agendas with time-bound goals and action plans. Well-organized intragovernmental coordination will be key to successfully implement the strategies. Given the social constraints brought on by the pandemic, MSME digitalization continues to be a policy priority, as well as formalizing informal businesses, opening international markets to MSMEs, and developing youth and women entrepreneurships. From a long-term perspective, more attention should be given to allowing greater capital market access to MSMEs for their growth capital.

1. COVID-19 Impact on MSMEs

The country's high growth momentum was stunted by the COVID-19 pandemic in 2020. The government acted quickly to contain the pandemic, implementing a nationwide lockdown from 26 March to 30 May 2020.[18] It significantly reduced all business activities, including those of MSMEs.

The BRAC Institute of Governance and Development (BIGD), in collaboration with Monash University, conducted a survey to assess the impact of the lockdown on MSMEs before, during, and after the restrictions. The survey interviewed 1,960 MSMEs in July 2020, the majority of which were in light engineering. The initial findings showed sales income dropped sharply—by 76% compared with pre-COVID-19 levels (Figure 3.1). Operating costs fell by 52%, but exceeded sales income by 1.6 times. The result was that profits fell by 96%. After the lockdown was lifted, businesses started reopening, with sales income increasing by 89% and costs up by 15%. This generated a 179% profit increase compared with the lockdown period. However, profitability of the survey respondents remained below pre-lockdown levels.

By sector, services that require physical contact, such as clothing/tailoring shops and beauty parlors, were hardest hit by low sales during the lockdown due to the difficulty in keeping social distancing and low demand for non-essential services. Interestingly, firms holding more capital (Tk2,246,000 [$26,485]) had a smaller drop in sales (25.4% below pre-COVID-19 levels) than firms with less funds (Tk235,000 [$2,771], 48.6%).[19]

The critical challenges for MSMEs during the lockdown was low demand of non-essential products and services (reduced orders), running out of funds (difficulty in paying salaries and maintaining business operations), and no sales/income (due to the shutdown of operations) (BIGD survey). The majority of those surveyed faced a shortage of raw materials, but they responded by raising prices, looking for new procurement channels, and delaying delivery of goods. Despite financial assistance to MSMEs from government stimulus, MSME access to finance remained limited, especially in services. The BIGD survey found the main reason was that many were unaware government assistance was available.

Another survey by the BRAC Bank was conducted by phone in November–December 2020 with 6,030 responses. The survey results showed around 20%–30% had their businesses open, but that 40%–70% had been closed during the lockdown. Once the lockdown was lifted, businesses quickly moved to reopen, with 99% operating on 3 December 2020. Sales dropped by about half during the lockdown (54% in April and 47% in May 2020) compared with pre-pandemic levels. By sector, hardest hit were textiles and accessories (16% in May 2020), auto parts/machineries (16%), steel and sheets (16%), and leather and footwear (21%). After the lockdown, sales recovered gradually, to 73% by November–December 2020. The survey said 60% of SME respondents reduced

[18] The lockdown (public holiday) was announced on 23 March and implemented on 26 March 2020, initially until 4 April, then extended until 30 May 2020. S. Mamun. Coronavirus: Bangladesh declares public holiday from March 26 to April 4. *Dhaka Tribune*. 23 March. https://www.dhakatribune.com/bangladesh/2020/03/23/govt-offices-to-remain-closed-till-april-4.

[19] Exchange rate refers to IMF/IFS, end of 2020.

Figure 3.1: Change in MSME Revenue and Employment (January–May 2019, 2020)

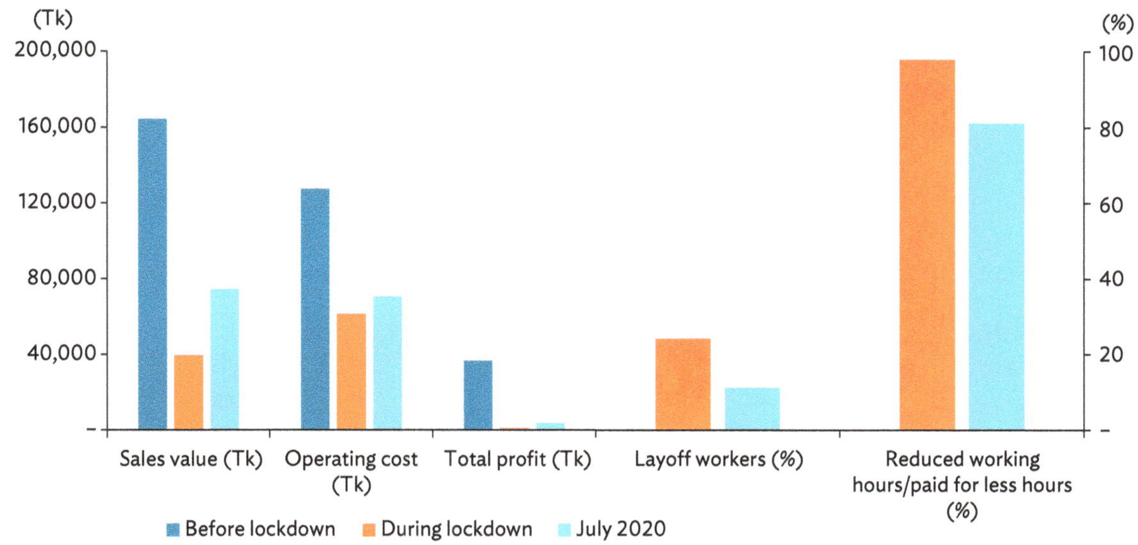

MSME = micro, small and medium-sized enterprise.

Notes: Sales value is the value of goods and services sold in the past month. Operating cost is the total cost of business in the past month. Survey respondents from 1,960 micro and small firms (including light engineering) through interviews. Survey was conducted on 14–23 July 2020.

Source: Recomposed from survey data on BRAC Institute of Governance and Development. 2020. The Impact of COVID-19 Pandemic on Small and Medium Enterprises in Bangladesh. December.

costs, while 20% considered new bank loans to revive their business. Less than 7% considered digitizing their business to e-commerce platforms.

The National Association of Small and Cottage Industries of Bangladesh (NASCIB) focused on women entrepreneurs to assess the pandemic effects.[20] The survey interviewed 55 women entrepreneurs by phone. After the government announced the lockdown in March 2020, 64% of their businesses remained closed for 5 months, 33% had no sales or orders. Another 60% reported a 75% decrease in sales. Some 40% had no income while another 42% reported income fell by 75%. Due to the disruptions, 16% could not pay salaries, while about 80% paid partially. Thus, 71% reported their employees faced financial problems. Women entrepreneurs relied heavily on informal financial sources (71% borrowed from friends) to run or reopen their business during the pandemic. Only 4% of respondents obtained bank loans.

A series of COVID-19 impact studies also suggest the lockdown seriously limited MSMEs' business activities, immediately reducing incomes and profits, especially for smaller firms engaged in personal-contact-based services. Again, among the challenges were no or little demand for their products and services and a lack of funds to maintain or reopen their businesses. Women-owned firms were more seriously affected in sales, income, and funding. Some reports mentioned low awareness of government MSME assistance programs. Thus the government needs to disseminate its programs more effectively to target MSMEs, especially those women-owned.

[20] NASCIB. 2020. Study on Impact of COVID-19 on entrepreneurs and workers especially on women of small and cottage industries. November.

The government launched a Tk200 billion stimulus package in April 2020 to help MSMEs, and has implemented several other measures in response to the COVID-19 crisis.

2. MSME Development

- MSMEs, including cottage industries, are critical to economic growth, comprising 99.97% of all enterprises, with traditional, unskilled distributive trade, their major form of non-agricultural business. Over 70% of MSMEs operate in rural areas.
- MSMEs absorbed 21 million employees, or 86% of the 2013 labor force, the majority of which worked in cottage industries. Most worked in rural MSMEs. Of the total workforce, around 12% were women.
- MSMEs contribute 25% of GDP; the SME policy 2019 expects that to reach 32% by 2024. Cottage and small enterprises generated around 16% of manufacturing gross value added in FY2020; while still small, it has been growing with a CAGR of 8.8% from 2012 to 2020.
- Most MSMEs operate in small domestic markets; a few are involved in international markets. Strong domestic supply chains have helped them survive during the pandemic. Industrial parks support MSME exporters.
- E-commerce has expanded sharply since early 2000, backed by improved infrastructure for online transactions and payment systems. MSMEs have been increasingly active in retail e-commerce. The Bangladesh Council of Scientific and Industrial Research (BCSIR) offers technical support for technology-based MSMEs.
- Business associations and chambers such as the NASCIB, the Dhaka Chamber of Commerce and Industry (DCCI), and the Metropolitan Chamber of Commerce and Industry (MCCI) support MSME industrialization, along with business cluster and infrastructure development through advisory and training services.

Scale of MSMEs

In Bangladesh, cottage industries are defined separately from MSMEs under the national industrial policy, which is updated every 5 years. The National Industrial Policy 2016 describes the current set of cottage, micro, small, and medium-sized enterprise (CMSME) definitions (Table 3.1A). A new industrial policy 2021 is currently under preparation. The 2016 policy defined CMSMEs as either manufacturing or services: (i) a cottage firm (manufacturing) has fixed assets (excluding land and factory buildings with replacement cost) of less than Tk1 million with up to 15 employees including family members; (ii) a manufacturing microenterprise has fixed assets from Tk1 million to less than Tk7.5 million with 16–30 employees; a services microenterprise has less than Tk1 million in fixed assets with up to 15 employees; (iii) a small manufacturing enterprise has fixed assets from Tk7.5 million to less than Tk150 million and 31–120 employees; a small services enterprise has Tk1 million to less than Tk20 million in fixed assets with 16–50 employees; and (iv) a medium-sized manufacturing enterprise has fixed assets from Tk150 million to less than Tk500 million with 121–300 employees; while a medium-sized services enterprise has Tk20 million to less than Tk300 million in fixed assets with 51–120 employees. These definitions came into effect 21 March 2016. CMSME definitions before then followed previous industrial policies.

Latest available CMSME data are based on the Economic Census 2013—the final report was prepared in December 2015. It estimated that 7.8 million nonfarm CMSMEs operated in the country, or 99.97% of all enterprises. By firm size, cottage firms dominated, with 6.8 million firms accounting for 87.5% of enterprises in 2013. This was followed by small enterprises (0.9 million or 11.0%), microenterprises (0.1 million or 1.3%), and medium-sized enterprises (around 7,000 or 0.1%) (Figure 3.2A and Table 3.2). The Census 2013 used the enterprise definition (employment threshold) specified under the National Industrial Policy 2010 (Table 1B).

By sector (excluding agriculture), 45.9% of CMSMEs in 2013 were in wholesale and retail trade (including traditional, unskilled distributive trade), followed by other services such as accommodation and food services (25.7%), transportation and communication (16.9%), and manufacturing (11.1%) (Figure 3.2B). Construction-related CMSMEs held a small share (0.1%).

CMSMEs are spread nationwide. Rural areas dominate, home to 71.5% of CMSMEs in 2013, with the remaining 28.5% in urban areas (Figure 3.2C).[21] Smaller firms operate in rural areas (74.7% of cottage and 60.5% of microenterprises), while relatively larger firms were located in urban areas (52.4% of small and 58.3% of medium-sized enterprises).

Figure 3.2: Number of MSMEs

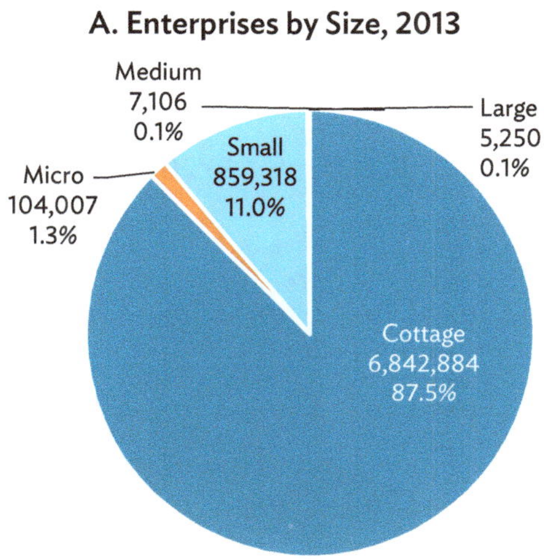

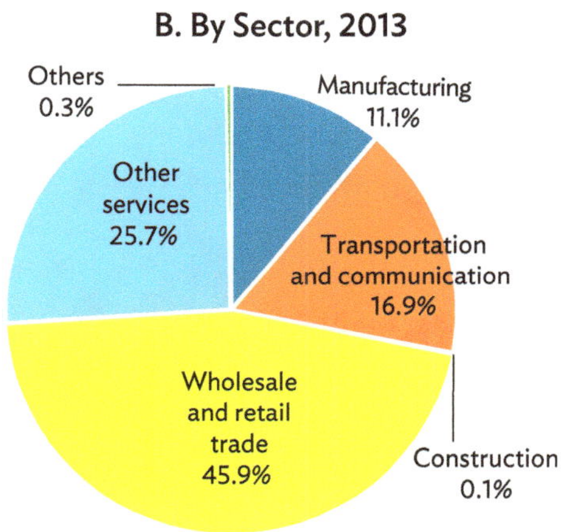

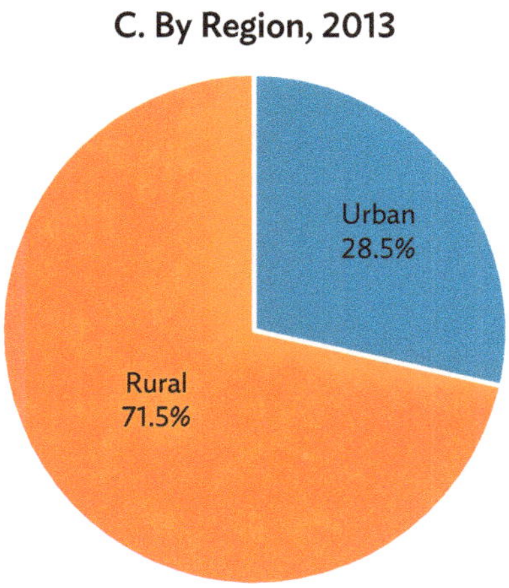

MSME = micro, small, and medium-sized enterprise.

Note: Data refer to permanent and temporary establishments, and economic households. Urban/rural refers to the definitions under the Economic Units Census. Data include cottage industries.

Source: ADB Asia SME Monitor 2021. Data from Bangladesh Bureau of Statistics, Economic Census 2013; Statistical Yearbook Bangladesh 2020; Bangladesh Statistics 2020.

21 The Bangladesh Bureau of Statistics defines "rural" as areas outside the city corporations (metropolis), *paurashava* (municipalities), and *upazila* (subdistricts) headquarters in the country, and "urban" as areas within the jurisdictions of city corporations, *paurashava*, and *upazila* headquarters in the country.

The Bangladesh Bureau of Statistics also compiles statistics on manufacturing MSMEs. Preliminary results from a survey of manufacturing firms from 2012 and 2019 found there were 43,260 manufacturing MSMEs in 2019, or 93.5% of all manufacturing establishments. This was a 10.5% increase from 2012 (a CAGR of 1.4% from 2012 to 2019) and 2 percentage points higher than in 2012 (91.5%) (Table 3.2a). The 2012 survey showed the top five manufacturing MSME sectors accounted for 77.5% of the total: textiles (26.2%), food products (20.1%), ready-made garments (16.7%), other non-metallic mineral products (11.1%), and fabricated metal products except machinery and equipment (3.5%) (Table 3.2b). There was no sector breakdown in the 2019 survey.

Employment

Based on the Economic Census 2013, CMSMEs generated 21 million jobs or 85.9% of the country's labor force (Table 3.2). Cottage industries absorbed 13.2 million workers (53.7% of the total), followed by small enterprises (6.6 million workers or 26.9%), medium-sized enterprises (0.7 million or 2.9%), and microenterprises (0.6 million or 2.3%) (Figure 3.3A).

Figure 3.3: Employment by MSMEs

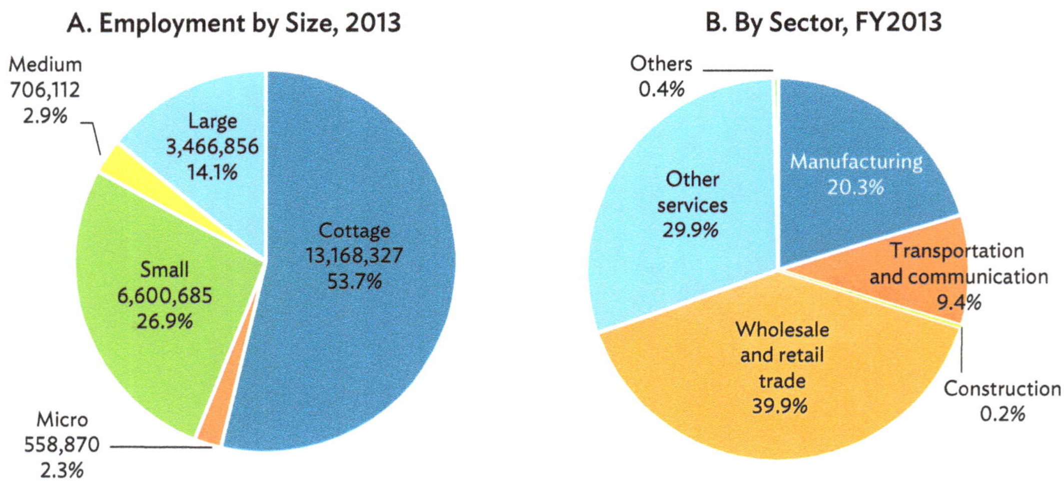

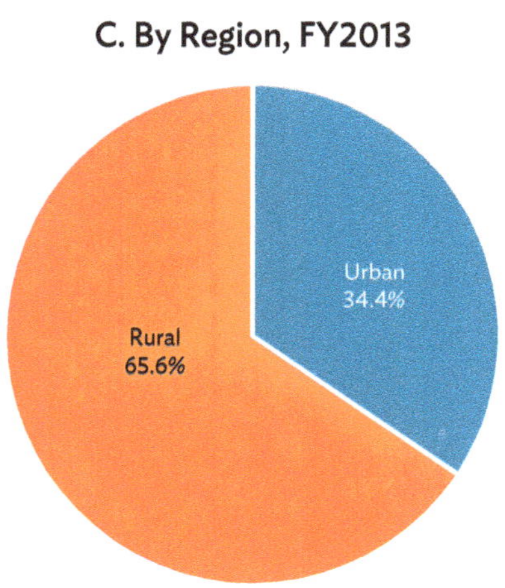

FY = fiscal year; MSME = micro, small, and medium-sized enterprise.

Notes: Data refer to permanent and temporary establishments, and economic households. Urban/rural refers to the definitions under the Economic Units Census. Data include cottage industries.

Source: ADB Asia SME Monitor 2021. Data from Bangladesh Bureau of Statistics, Economic Census 2013; Statistical Yearbook Bangladesh 2020; Bangladesh Statistics 2020.

By sector (excluding agriculture), wholesale and retail trade provided the largest number of jobs, (39.9%), followed by other services (29.9%), manufacturing (20.3%), and transportation and communication (9.4%) (Figure 3.3B). Construction-related CMSMEs absorbed only 0.2% of CMSME workers in 2013.

Rural CMSMEs accounted for the majority of jobs (65.6% in 2013), while the remaining 34.4% worked in urban areas (Figure 3.3C). Similarly, smaller firms created relatively higher employment in rural areas than in urban areas, 72.6% of cottage and 61.2% of microenterprise workers worked in rural areas in 2013, while small and medium-sized enterprises created almost equal shares of jobs in both urban and rural areas.

By gender, the Census 2013 showed female participation in paid economic activities was low at 16.5% of total employment. For CMSMEs, their share was just 11.7%. This suggests more effort is needed to attract women to the job market and to encourage women entrepreneurships.

The Bangladesh Bureau of Statistics manufacturing survey data showed that 1.9 million employees, or 31.5% of total manufacturing jobs, were in MSMEs in 2019, a 9.7% decrease from 2012 (a CAGR of –1.4% from 2012 to 2019), 9.4 percentage points less than 2012 (40.9%) (Table 3.2a).

Business Productivity

Time-bound comparisons of MSME contributions to GDP are unavailable. However, the SME Policy 2019 says they contribute 25% of GDP and targets 32% by 2024. CMSME contributions to manufacturing gross value added (GVA) is tracked annually (FY). The GVA of cottage and small enterprises amounted to Tk443 billion in FY2020, a 7.8% increase from FY2019 (a CGAR of 8.8% from 2012 to 2020), while the GVA of medium-sized and large enterprises was Tk2,267 billion over the same period, a 5.5% increase from FY2019 (a CAGR of 11.1% from 2012 to 2020) (Figure 3.4 and Table 3.2a).

Figure 3.4: Contribution to Gross Value Added

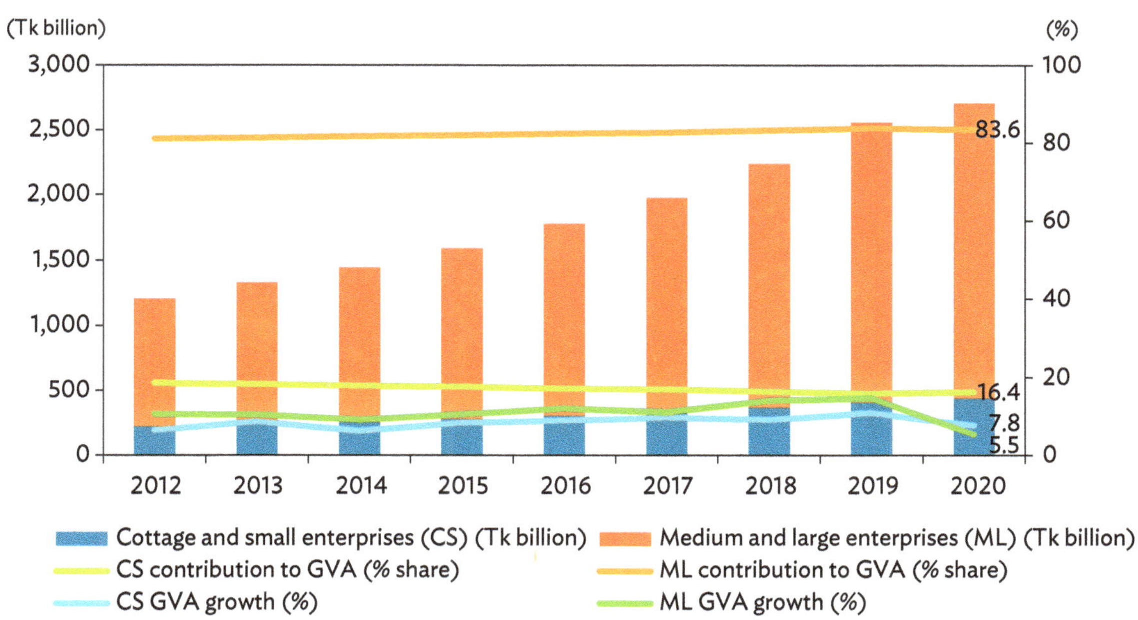

GVA = gross value added.

Notes: Data are presented in fiscal year starting on 1 July of the previous year and ending on 30 June of the reference year. Data refer to GVA of cottage, small, medium-sized, and large manufacturing enterprises. Data at constant prices of 2005–2006.

Source: ADB Asia SME Monitor 2021. Data from Bangladesh Bureau of Statistics.

The COVID-19 pandemic and nationwide lockdown immediately hurt private businesses, but they recovered relatively quickly after the lockdown was lifted, showing moderate growth by end-June 2020 (FY2020). Cottage and small enterprises generated 16.4% of total manufacturing GVA in FY2020 still small compared with 83.6% in medium-sized and large enterprises, but the share has been rising steadily.

Market Access

Most CMSMEs operate in small, stable domestic markets; only a few cater to international markets. According to the Economic Census 2013, 87.4% of manufacturers sell all their products to local markets. With more than 90% of manufacturing classified as CMSMEs (Survey of Manufacturing 2012, 2019), most of the focus is domestic. A strong base of domestic supply chains helped them survive the pandemic thus far.[22] This has helped many avoid the more serious consequences of external shocks. It also allowed many to recover quickly once the lockdown was lifted. However, from a long-term perspective, strengthening competitiveness and promoting participation in global value chains would help the government achieve its goals for inclusive growth.

Market access and internationalizing CMSMEs are part of the core strategies under the SME Policy 2019—as well as the long-term Vision 2041 national development plan and the Perspective Plan of Bangladesh that promotes export-led economic growth. Export values decreased from Tk3,482 billion ($41.4 billion) in FY2019 to Tk2,812 billion ($33.2 billion) in FY2020, a 19.2% decline affected by the pandemic (Figure 3.5 and Table 3.2).[23]

Figure 3.5: Exports and Imports

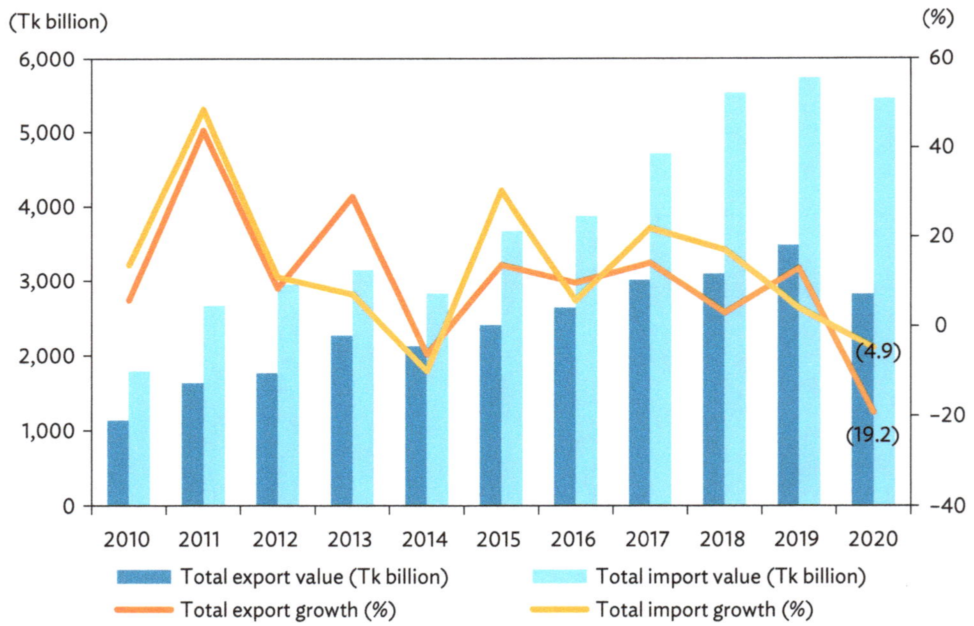

Note: Data are for fiscal years (ending 30 June).

Source: ADB Asia SME Monitor 2021. Data from Foreign Trade Statistics of Bangladesh 2019-2020.

22 Interview with the Ministry of Commerce on 13 April 2021.

23 Amount in US dollars referred to Foreign Trade Statistics of Bangladesh 2019-20. Volume II.

The CAGR from 2010 to 2020, however, grew 9.5%. There is no data available on MSME exports. But given that ready-made garments are a major export commodity and are a major product of MSME manufacturers, there are MSMEs involved in exports.

Import values also fell, from Tk5,723 billion ($68.1 billion) in FY2019 to Tk5,442 billion ($64.2 billion) in FY2020, a 4.9% decline. However, between 2010 and 2020, they had a CAGR of 11.7%. Again, there is no data available on CMSME imports. But given that imported materials like textile and accessories (mainly from the People's Republic of China and India) are used by MSME manufacturers, stable imports are critical for increasing MSME productivity.

There are 76 small industrial parks operating in the country with around 6,000 entrepreneurs—including MSME manufacturers employing about 1 million people. They contribute around 11% of exports and produce 30% of import substitutes.[24] Industrial parks also support MSME exporters.

Technology and Innovation

Access and use of digital devices has grown rapidly in Bangladesh, similar to most of Asia. The number of mobile cellular subscriptions jumped from 2.8 million in 2004 (or 2.0 per 100 people) to 170.1 million in 2020 (103 per 100 people) (World Development Indicators). Nonetheless, individual internet use remains limited at 12.9% of the population in 2019, but continues to grow. Mobile internet subscriptions reached 111.9 million in 2020, yet broadband connections (ISP+PSTN) totaled just 9.5 million.[25]

The e-commerce market has been highly competitive, growing rapidly since the early 2000s, backed by new or improved infrastructure for online transaction and payment systems. According to media reports, there are around 2,000 e-commerce sites and 50,000 Facebook pages offering 30,000 products a day.[26] Many MSMEs use Facebook for marketing and sales. Statista research says sales was $2 billion and served 42.4 million users in 2020. The market is projected to reach $3.6 billion by 2025.[27]

Business-to-business (B2B), business-to-commerce (B2C), consumer-to-consumer (C2C), and business-to-government (B2G) transactions are all used. B2B platforms work for inventory, product distribution, and supplier management. The Bangladesh Garment Manufacturers Exporters Association, a trade association, facilitates ready-made garment orders and procurement using a B2B platform. C2C platforms are peer-to-peer transactions similar to online auctions. B2G platforms are used for government operations and administration, including for business licensing and public procurement. B2C platforms help many MSMEs sell consumer goods and services to customers (for example, ajkerdeal.com, bajna.com, bdbazar.com, and daraz.com). Reports say retail e-commerce has been growing at 72% per month, involving over 35,000 individuals and 25,000 MSMEs (footnote 26).

E-commerce has grown in part due to an interoperable electronic payment platform—National Payment Switch Bangladesh—in operation since end-2012. Emerging e-wallets for online payments and money transfers such as bKash help develop the industry. The challenges to growth include relatively low internet connectivity and infrastructure in rural and remote areas (80% of e-commerce transactions occur in urban areas like Dhaka, Chattogram, and Gazipur). Customer preference for cash-on-delivery also impedes growth. Several business associations support e-commerce development, through advisory and training—including for MSMEs—and

24 Interview with the Bangladesh Small and Cottage Industries Corporation on 6 April 2021.

25 The Bangladesh Telecommunication Regulatory Commission.

26 The United States International Trade Administration. Bangladesh - Country Commercial Guide. eCommerce. Updated 17 September. https://www.trade.gov/country-commercial-guides/bangladesh-ecommerce; The Financial Express. 2020. E-commerce in Bangladesh: Where are we headed? 10 January. https://thefinancialexpress.com.bd/views/views/e-commerce-in-bangladesh-where-are-we-headed-1578666791

27 Statista. eCommerce (Bangladesh). https://www.statista.com/outlook/dmo/ecommerce/bangladesh.

modernizing payment systems. These include the e-Commerce Association of Bangladesh and the Bangladesh Electronic Funds Transfer Network.

The SME Policy 2019 cites the increased use of information and communication technology (ICT) for MSME development. It also aims to expand e-commerce for MSMEs, offer ICT-based support services, promote new technologies for production, and develop incubators. Technology-based MSMEs are expected to boost national productivity and promote export-driven economic growth. The Bangladesh Council of Scientific and Industrial Research (BCSIR) helps develop technology-based MSMEs through research and development (R&D) and new product development and commercialization (Box 3.1).

Box 3.1: The Bangladesh Council of Scientific and Industrial Research Supports Advanced Technology and Innovation of MSMEs during the COVID-19 Pandemic

The Bangladesh Council of Scientific and Industrial Research (BCSIR) is a multidisciplinary research organization under the Ministry of Science and Technology. It was established in 1974. It provides technical and analytical services to national and multinational industries and organizations, including micro, small, and medium-sized enterprises (MSMEs), through research and development (R&D), technology-based product development, and commercialization. It has 13 research laboratories and institutes.

BCSIR's R&D covers various areas such as food science technology, chemical metrology, bio-science/bio-materials, biogas technology, leather technology, microbiology, mining/mineralogy/ metallurgy, nanotechnology, pharmaceutical chemistry, herbal medicine/natural products, fiber and polymer, pulp and paper, renewable energy, glass/ceramics/ building materials, and soil/ environmental science. It has 50 graduate, doctoral, and postdoctoral fellowships for research and analytical work and offers students professional training programs.

By February 2021, BCSIR developed 1,007 technology-based products—food, chemicals for industrial use, cosmetics/ toiletries, aromatic/herbal, fuel/energy-related, glass/ceramics, leather, fiber, and bricks/building materials. It obtained 369 patent rights. Most products developed are based on locally available raw materials and led by MSMEs.

BCSIR is helping MSMEs and entrepreneurs develop products to satisfy specific demand during the pandemic and quarantines. One example is Bright Shine Limited.

Motaher Ahmed Chowdhury owns Bright Shine, a unique enterprise that manufactures shoe-care products in the country. Besides his main business, he ventured into manufacturing COVID-19-related health-care products, in response to research from a BCSIR-sponsored project. BCSIR worked with Bright Shine on product development from the beginning of the pandemic, focusing on water-based liquid sanitizers, herbal and synthetic mouthwashes, and herbal anti-dandruff shampoos.

Source: Interview with BCSIR and presentation during the ADB virtual mission held on 24 February 2021.

Networking and Support

Several business associations and chambers—such as the National Association of Small and Cottage Industries of Bangladesh (NASCIB), the Dhaka Chamber of Commerce and Industry (DCCI), and the Metropolitan Chamber of Commerce and Industry (MCCI)—support industrializing CMSMEs, along with business cluster and infrastructure development directly or indirectly through advisory and training services.

NASCIB, a trade association established in 1984, offers support services for developing CMSMEs through its committees in all 64 districts of the country. It aims to create a self-sustainable and profitable national CMSME ecosystem. With more than 20,000 direct members and 150,000 indirect or associate members, NASCIB provides skill development programs for CMSME entrepreneurs, consultancy and advisory services for expanding operations, business networking through organized national and international trade fairs, and policy advocacy with the government for CMSME development. It has conducted more than 500 capacity-building programs for members since 1991, covering both financial and nonfinancial topics. Given the high demand for access to finance, NASCIB also assists members access banks and NBFIs (recommending them to financial institutions). It prioritizes agribusinesses, R&D, and women entrepreneurships (linking their products to international markets). In response to the COVID-19 pandemic, NASCIB provided free internet connections to members for telemarketing and e-commerce. It monitored the impact on women entrepreneurs offering policy recommendations. It understands the challenges for CMSME development, including limited access to finance, markets, networks, and information, as well as a lack of professional management. Currently, there is no fully functional business development ecosystem.[28]

Established in 1958, DCCI is one of the largest chambers in the country. It focuses on MSME development, with 4,000 active and 16,000 passive members (no membership renewal), with around 78% MSMEs. It set up a special division for MSME development. DCCI has trained more than 25,000 MSME entrepreneurs since its capacity-building programs started in 1991, covering various topics such as international trade and supply chains. During the pandemic, training includes how to set up online platforms and e-commerce portals for marketing and sales. DCCI also prioritizes MSME cluster development and women entrepreneurships. There are 177 MSME clusters active in the country, with agricultural processing a leading type, followed by textiles/garments, leather, and light engineering.[29] It works with relevant government and private organizations such as the SME Foundation, Ministry of Industries, Bangladesh Small and Cottage Industries Corporation and the Bangladesh Bank for MSME development (policy advocacy).

MCCI, founded in 1904, is the oldest chamber for larger industries to promote domestic and international trade. Around half of its members are medium-sized enterprises. It provides consulting services covering taxation, import-export, tariff/nontariff measures, and investments, along with skill development programs. Its services trickle down to small enterprises, given that large enterprises subcontract small firms. Policy advocacy is a major activity, including infrastructure development and labor issues. Challenges to MSME development include lack of information, product quality control, and management capacity to access appropriate markets. Formalizing informal businesses is a critical challenge as it implies increased costs for MSME operations.[30]

28 Interview with NASCIB on 25 February 2021.
29 Interview with DCCI on 8 April 2021.
30 Interview with MCCI on 24 February 2021.

3. Access to Finance

- With the lending target set by the central bank, commercial bank credit to MSMEs steadily increased at a CAGR of 13% from 2010 to 2020. However, the MSME credit market remains small at 8% of GDP, and is concentrated on urban areas (over 80%).
- There are several refinancing programs for MSMEs, particularly for women and CMSME entrepreneurs. A Credit Guarantee Fund for CMSME finance will be established according to the national financial inclusion strategy for 2024.
- While central bank-regulated NBFI market has contracted since 2018 with its focus on manufacturing and increasing NPL ratios, the microfinance market has grown steadily. PKSF, a wholesale lender to microfinance institutions, has contributed to the market growth.
- Mobile financial services have expanded rapidly offering a wider range of payment modalities (cash-in/cash-out, P2P, P2B, B2P, P2G, and G2P). Upscaling digital financial services and the fintech industry is a strategic goal of the national financial inclusion strategy for 2024.
- In 2019, the two stock exchanges (DSE and CSE) opened specialized equity markets for SMEs—the SME platform—with less stringent listing requirements.
- The central bank's Credit Information Bureau has used online services since 2011, while a new Microfinance Credit Information Bureau has been pilot-tested since end-2020. The Collateral Registry Bureau is being prepared as part of the national financial inclusion strategy.

Bank Credit

The banking sector comprises "scheduled" and "non-scheduled" banks. Scheduled banks are defined under the Bangladesh Bank Order of 1972. Non-scheduled banks have specific objectives with their operations limited by various laws and regulations. As of end-2020, there were 61 scheduled banks—6 state-owned commercial banks, 3 state-owned development financial institutions, 43 private commercial banks (including 10 Islamic banks), and 9 foreign commercial banks (Table 3.3). There were 10,578 bank branches as of end-2019. The national financial inclusion strategy aims for all bank branches to run online. There were five non-scheduled banks operating as of end-2020.[31]

Commercial bank credit to MSMEs has been steadily increasing. MSME loans outstanding reached Tk2,273 billion in 2020, an 8.7% increase from 2019 despite the pandemic, with a CAGR of 13.0% from 2010 to 2020 (Figure 3.6A). However, the MSME credit market remains small (8.1% of GDP in 2020, largely unchanged since 2018). The share of MSME loans to total loans was estimated at 20.2%; but this ratio was calculated as commercial bank MSME loans outstanding divided by total loans outstanding of all scheduled banks, which suggests the actual share of MSME loans to all commercial bank loans outstanding would be higher. In 2018, MSME credit dropped sharply due to a change of statistical definition.[32] The MSME NPL ratio has been increasing, but data are available only until 2014 (11.8%). Gross NPLs to total scheduled bank loans was 12.7% in 2020.

Since 2010, the Bangladesh Bank has set an annual target for MSME credit growth. In 2020, it was Tk2,181 billion for scheduled commercial banks (Figure 3.6B and Table 3.3a). It was 90.7% of actual MSME loans disbursed (Tk1,979 billion), but 104.2% of MSME loans outstanding. The lending target was calculated based on loan disbursements through 2019, but was changed to net loans outstanding from 2020, thus, meeting the target.

31 They include Ansar VDP Unnayan Bank, Karmashangosthan Bank, Grameen Bank, Jubilee Bank, and Palli Sanchay Bank.

32 In 2016, Bangladesh Bank issued a circular defining the CMSME sector (cottage, micro, small, and medium-sized enterprises), with the revised definition and disbursement limit made available on 29 June 2017. The circular excluded trade loans to medium-sized and cottage industries from the newly defined CMSMEs, limiting those counted to manufacturing and service sector CMSMEs. This is why there was an overall drop in CMSME credit in 2018.

MSME credit is broadly categorized into three sectors—manufacturing, trade, and other services. In 2020, wholesale and retail trade accounted for 41% of MSME loans outstanding, followed by manufacturing (40%) and other services (19%) (Figure 3.6C). By region, MSME credit is concentrated in urban areas, including the capital, Dhaka (84.2%) (Figure 3.6D). The remaining 15.8% was in rural areas.[33] Given that around 70% of enterprises are CMSMEs, access to credit must be strengthened in rural areas.

Figure 3.6: MSME Loans

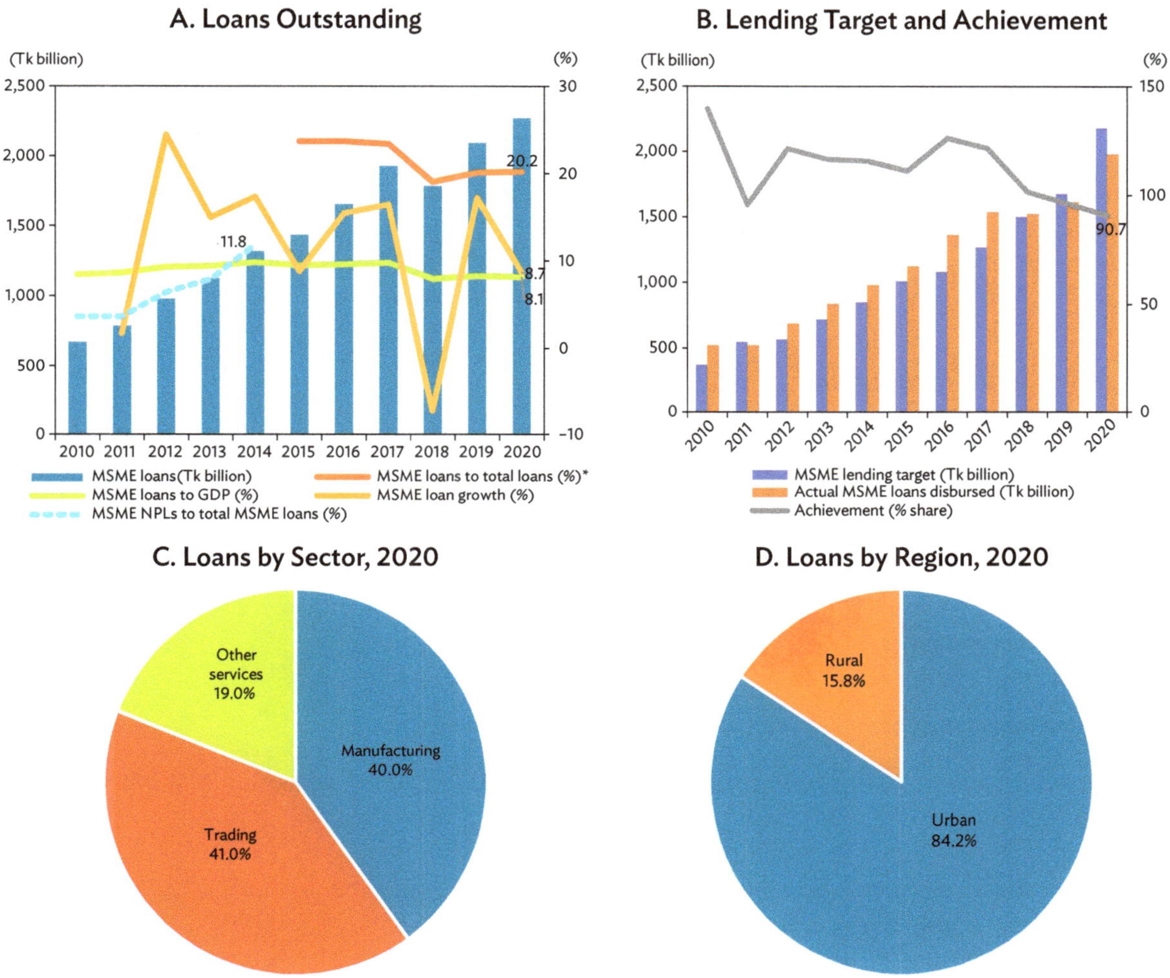

GDP = gross domestic product; MSME = micro, small, and medium-sized enterprise.

Notes: Data for commercial banks only. For Figure 6A, the share of "MSME loans to total loans" was calculated as commercial bank MSME loans outstanding divided by total loans outstanding of all operating banks. Actual percentage share of MSME loans to total loans outstanding in commercial banks would be higher. For Figure 6C, MSMEs were broadly categorized into three sectors: manufacturing, trade, and other services. For Figure 6D, urban/rural classification refers to the definitions under the Economic Census.

Source: ADB Asia SME Monitor 2021. Data from Bangladesh Bank.

---

33 Urban/rural classification refers to the definitions under the Economic Census.

Commercial bank MSME borrowers have increased at a CAGR of 9.8% from 2010 to 2020, reaching 770,150. Non-collateral MSME loans have been increasing as well, reaching Tk206 billion in 2020, although slightly down from Tk211 billion in 2019. The government and central bank support the MSME credit market, particularly during the COVID-19 crisis.

Grameen Bank is a non-scheduled bank (legally under the Grameen Bank Ordinance of 1983) and holds a large share of the microfinance market. It offers group-based micro-loans to the poor in rural areas, based on mutual trust and accountability among borrowers. There are 2,568 branches. As of end-2019, total loans outstanding reached Tk156.7 billion, 2.0% growth from 2018, but down from the previous year's 3.1% growth (Table 3.3b). Total deposits amounted to Tk170.9 billion. There were 9.3 million Grameen bank members in 2019, with 97% of borrowers women. Grameen bank credit does not specially target CMSMEs, but given the large presence of CMSME workers in rural areas, it helps CMSME owners access to finance in rural areas.

Public Financing and Guarantees

The government and central bank play a critical role in supplementing credit markets. Lending targets and refinancing at concessional rates help vulnerable groups including agriculture and CMSMEs access finance. These initiatives are an emergency assistance tool for CMSMEs during crises. While they may risk market distortions in normal times, if balanced, they could be useful during a post-pandemic recovery.

a. Lending targets and cap

To promote credit flows to CMSMEs, the central bank sets an annual lending target with conditions: (i) the credit target for CMSMEs increased to 25% in 2021 with a previous minimum of 1% increment per year; (ii) by sector, manufacturing should receive 40% of the CMSME credit, with 35% for trade, and 25% for other services; (iii) 50% of CMSME loans by financial institutions should go to cottage, micro, and small enterprises in 2021; (iv) a 3-month grace period for short-term (1 year) loans and 3–6 months for mid- to long-term (1–5 years) loans; (v) at least 15% should be disbursed to women entrepreneurs; and (vi) a maximum interest cap of 9% for financing women-led firms for all refinancing programs.[34]

b. Refinancing schemes

There are several Bangladesh Bank refinancing programs for MSMEs, covering women and CMSME entrepreneurs (Table 3.4).

The Small Enterprise Refinance Scheme was introduced in 2004 with initial fund of Tk1 billion, extended to Tk15 billion in response to the large demand from women entrepreneurs. It is a revolving fund, with repayments used for other refinancing. As of end-2020, it refinanced Tk12.3 billion, benefitting 12,725 MSMEs and Tk33.5 billion for 27,697 women entrepreneurs.

The Tk14 billion Refinancing Scheme for Agro-based Industries in Rural Areas, launched in 2001, focuses on agricultural processing for rural CMSMEs. It provides funds to banks and NBFIs at 3% which they relend to CMSMEs at 7%. As of end-2020, it had disbursed Tk19.9 billion to refinance 2,858 CMSMEs.

The Refinancing Scheme for New Entrepreneurs in Cottage, Micro, and Small Enterprise Sector was launched in 2014 with Tk1 billion to provide start-up capital to new entrepreneurs. Entrepreneurs trained by recognized training providers are eligible for a maximum Tk2.5 million loan with collateral and Tk1.0 million loan without collateral.

34 Bangladesh Bank Annual Report 2019/2020.

The central bank, however, instructed financial institutions to approve loans up to Tk2.5 million for women entrepreneurs without collateral but with personal guarantees. Interest is capped at a maximum 7%. As of end-2020, it had refinanced Tk307 million, benefitting 527 new entrepreneurs.

There is another two-step loan refinance facility for MSMEs funded by the Japan International Cooperation Agency. It was launched in 2011 with Tk3.8 billion to provide mid- to long-term financing for CMSMEs. The project was closed in 2016, but a refinancing portion is continuing. As of end-2020, it had refinanced Tk1 billion, benefitting 1,324 CMSMEs.

As an emergency measure to support CMSME working capital during the pandemic, Bangladesh Bank set up a revolving refinance scheme with Tk100 billion for existing and new CMSME entrepreneurs in April 2020. Banks and NBFIs could receive refinancing up to 50% of loans disbursed under the stimulus package at 4% interest. As of end-2020, it had refinanced Tk17.4 billion, benefiting 11,833 CMSME entrepreneurs. The program will run for 3 years.

c. Credit guarantees

There was no independent national credit guarantee corporation as of end-2020. But a new Credit Guarantee Fund will be created to finance CMSMEs according to the national financial inclusion strategy for 2024. Until its establishment, Bangladesh Bank guides financial institutions in implementing credit guarantees for CMSME loans.[35] It instructs participating financial institutions to set a portfolio guarantee limit, guarantee portfolio cap, and guarantee coverage ratio to reduce potential moral hazard risks. The portfolio guarantee limit is the amount of loans and investments approved by Bangladesh Bank, which is set each year. Bangladesh Bank will cover any loss up to 30% of the portfolio guarantee limit of any participating financial institution in case of default (guarantee portfolio cap). Credit guarantees cover a maximum 80% of the loan principal.

Nonbank Financing

The nonbank finance industry is regulated and supervised by Bangladesh Bank and the Microcredit Regulatory Authority (MRA). As of end-2020, Bangladesh Bank, under the Financial Institution Act of 1993, regulated 35 NBFIs, including 3 government-owned, 13 joint-venture, and 19 private institutions (Table 3.5). Their major funding came from term deposits (at least 3 months), other financial institutions' credit facilities, call money, bonds, and securitization.[36] As of FY2019, 724 nongovernment microfinance institutions (NGO-MFIs) with 18,977 branches were regulated by the MRA.

Total NBFI financing regulated by Bangladesh Bank was Tk669 billion in 2020, a slight decline (0.4%) from 2019 (Figure 3.7A). It was equivalent to 2.4% of GDP and has been shrinking since 2018. While the CAGR was 12.1% from 2012 to 2020, growth has been decelerating since 2017, and the ratio of gross NPLs to total loans surged to 15.0% in 2020, triple that in 2012 (5.2%). Total deposit was Tk453 billion in 2020, a CAGR of 11.4% between 2014 and 2020, but slower than financing growth. By sector, manufacturing held the largest share (43.6%) in 2020, followed by construction (18.9%), wholesale and retail trade (13.6%), transportation and communications (3.9%), and agriculture (2.5%) (Figure 3.7B). Those unclassified accounted for the remaining 17.5%.

[35] Bangladesh Bank. 2020. Manual of Credit Guarantee Scheme for Cottage, Micro, and Small Enterprises.

[36] Bangladesh Bank website: https://www.bb.org.bd/en/index.php/financialactivity/bankfi

Figure 3.7: Nonbank Finance

A. Nonbank Finance Institutions Regulated by Bangladesh Bank

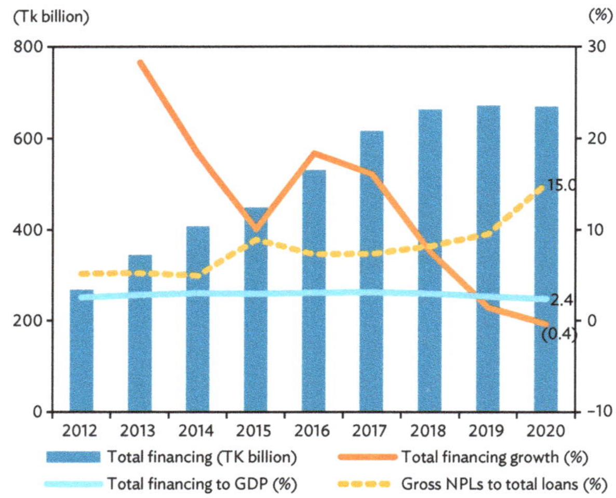

GDP = gross domestic product, NPL = nonperforming loan.

Note: End-of-year data. The "total financing to GDP" was calculated based on GDP in fiscal year (ended 30 June).

Source: ADB Asia SME Monitor 2021 Database. Data from Bangladesh Bank.

B. By Sector, 2020

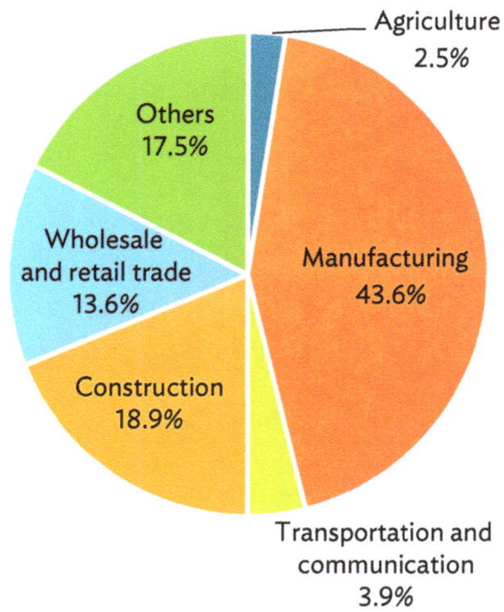

Note: Data based on nonbank finance institutions regulated by Bangladesh Bank.

Source: ADB Asia SME Monitor 2021 Database. Data from Bangladesh Bank.

C. Microfinance Loans

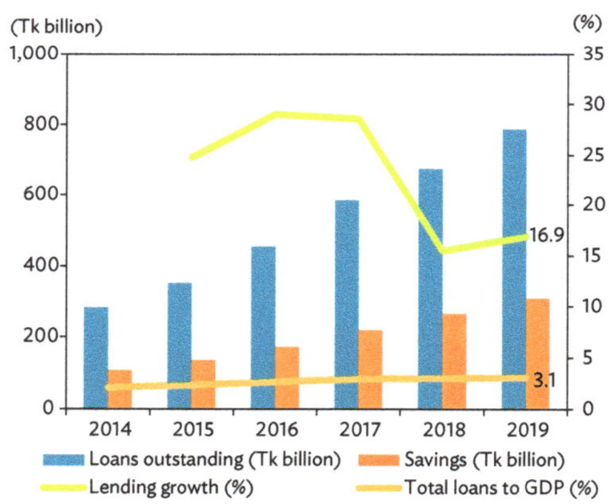

GDP = gross domestic product.

Note: Data are presented in fiscal year (ended 30 June).

Source: ADB Asia SME Monitor 2021. Data from Microcredit Regulatory Authority.

D. Loans by Palli Karma-Sahayak Foundation

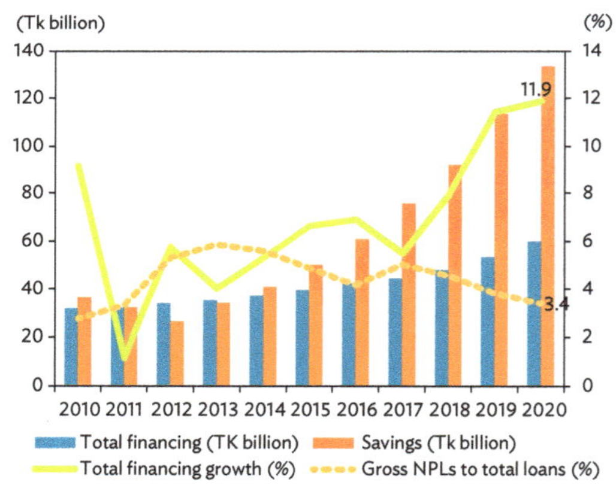

NPL = nonperforming loan.

Notes: Fiscal year (FY) data (ended 30 June). Gross NPLs calculated based on loans with arrears of over 365 days.

Source: ADB Asia SME Monitor 2021. Data from Palli Karma-Sahayak Foundation (PKSF).

Data on microfinance loans include those by NGO-MFIs, Grameen Bank, state-owned and private commercial banks. These are classified into six broad groups of lending: (i) microcredit for small-scale self-employed activities, (ii) microenterprise loans, (iii) loans for the very poor, (iv) agricultural loans, (v) seasonal loans, and (vi) loans for disaster management.[37] In FY2019, outstanding of microfinance loans amounted to Tk787.6 billion, equivalent to 3.1% of GDP, a 16.9% increase from FY2018 and a CAGR of 22.8% from 2014 to 2019 (Figure 3.7C). Total deposits

[37] Microcredit Regulatory Authority website: https://www.mra.gov.bd/images/mra_files/News/mcinbd22072020.pdf

reached Tk306.9 billion in FY2019, a CAGR of 23.5% from 2014 to 2019. There were 25.8 million borrowers, a CAGR of 5.8% over the same period. Microfinance lending has grown steadily.

The NGO-MFI microcredit market has been dominated by two MFIs—BRAC and the Association for Social Advancement (ASA)—each accounting for around 50% of loans outstanding. The top 20 MFIs hold a 75% market share. In FY2019, they disbursed Tk409.5 billion for microenterprise loans, 46.1% of which came from BRAC and 17.4% from ASA. For NGO-MFIs, the average loan size per borrower was Tk30,574 ($360) in FY2019, while average savings per customer was Tk9,481 ($112); both increased at a CAGR of 16.0% for lending and 17.3% for savings from FY2014 to FY2019.[38]

Palli Karma-Sahayak Foundation (PKSF) is a wholesale lending institution to MFIs (partner organizations), set up by the government in 1990 to reduce poverty. It provides various financial services such as credit and insurance for poor households, micro entrepreneurs, and small farmers through 11,147 branches of 278 partner organizations in 64 districts.[39] Its microenterprise loans help improve access to finance for micro entrepreneurs in rural and poor areas. Loans increased sharply since 2018. In FY2020, total PKSF financing reached Tk59.9 billion, backed by deposits of Tk133.3 billion (a CAGR of 13.9%) (Figure 3.7D and Table 3.5a). Its financing grew by 11.9% in FY2020 with a CAGR of 6.6% since 2010, while deposits grew by 17.5% and a CAGR of 13.9%. The NPL ratio has been decreasing since 2018.

Digital Financial Services

As online payment systems improve, the use of digital financial services has been spreading rapidly, especially in mobile banking. Since 2013, scheduled banks have extended their banking services by using cash-in/cash out agents. Agent banking, based on agreements between agents and banks, offers limited banking services like accepting deposits, disbursing credit, and delivering remittances. They are increasingly popular in rural and remote areas. Agent banking continued to grow during the pandemic. As of FY2020, 28 banks held agent banking licenses with 23 actively engaged (footnoted 35). There were 8,764 agents using 12,449 outlets in FY2020. The number of agents grew by 45.8% from FY2019 and outlets increased by 43.6%. There were 7.4 million open accounts holding Tk102 billion in FY2020. Foreign remittances through agent banking totaled Tk173 billion in FY2020, a 196.5% increase from FY2019.

Mobile financial services (MFS) were introduced in 2011, starting from simple cash-in/cash-out services. They and have grown rapidly offering a wider range of payment modalities—including person-to-person (P2P), person-to-business (P2B), business-to-person (B2P), person-to-government (P2G), and government-to-person (G2P). As of June 2021, 15 banks provided MFS using 1.1 million agents nationwide. There were 99.8 million registered clients, 40.9 million active accounts, and 319.8 million transactions (Figure 3.8A and Table 3.6). Transaction value increased by 25.6% CAGR from 2017 to 2020, reaching Tk630 billion in June 2021 (Tk21 billion in average daily transactions). By type of transaction, cash-in/cash-out and P2P transactions were most popular, followed by merchant payments, salary disbursements, utility bill payments, and government payments (Figure 3.8B). Government payments have increased sharply, from Tk414 million at end-2020 to Tk12 billion in June 2021.

Upscaling digital financial services and fintech is a strategic goal of the national financial inclusion strategy for 2024. It promotes greater use of digital finance for utility payments, a feasibility study on distributed ledger technology (blockchains) for the financial sector, and the development of credit/deposit services for MFS account holders, agent banking, along with fintech, regtech (regulation), suptech (supervision), and insurtech (insurance).

[38] Exchange rate refers to IMF/IFS, end of period.

[39] PKSF website: https://pksf-bd.org/web/?page_id=85. Accessed 12 October 2021.

Figure 3.8: Mobile Financial Services

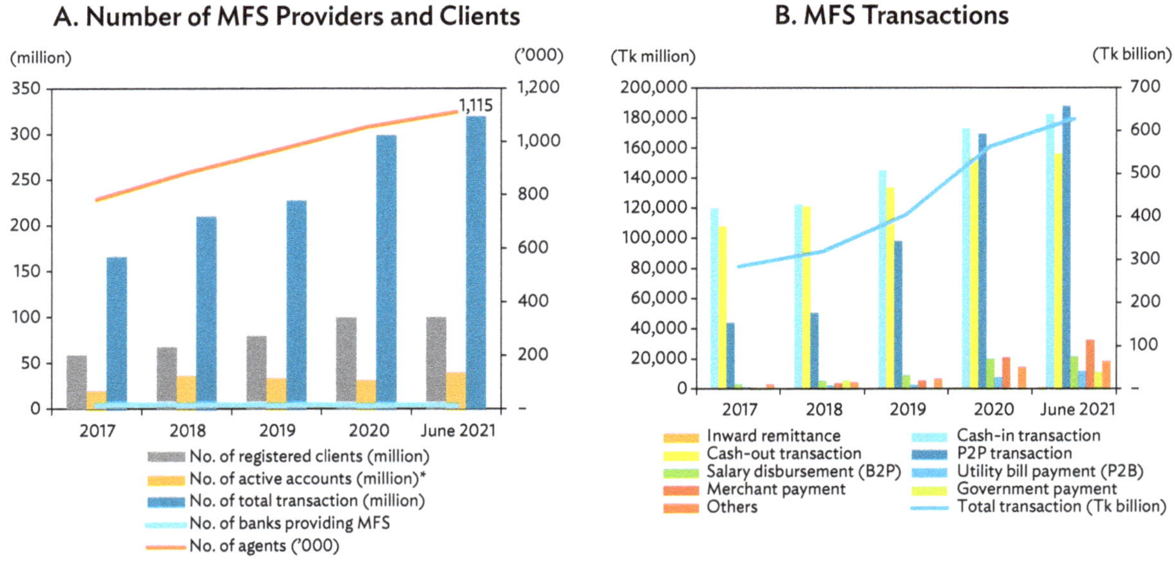

B2P = business-to-person, MFS = mobile financial services, P2B = person-to-business, P2P = person-to-person.

* Actual number of days in month (December for 2017-2020 and June for 2021) has been used for average calculations.

Source: ADB Asia SME Monitor 2021. Data recomposed from Bangladesh Bank. https://www.bb.org.bd/fnansys/paymentsys/mfsdata.php.

Capital Markets

In April 2019, the two stock exchanges—the Chittagong Stock Exchange (CSE) and Dhaka Stock Exchange (DSE)—created a specialized equity market for qualified SMEs. They are called the SME platform and have easier listing requirements.

These SME platforms are dedicated equity markets for SMEs with high growth potential. The listing requirements are concessional compared with the main board. For example, the SME platforms have post-issue paid-up capital requirements of Tk50 million–Tk300 million as opposed to more than Tk500 million for the main board. They also differ by application method; fixed price method and book-building method (Table 3.8). Only qualified investors as defined under the Securities and Exchange Commission Rules of 2018 (Qualified Investor Offer by Small Capital Companies) can invest in the SME platform for newly listed issues.[40] Qualified investors are individuals who register with the Electronic Subscription System of the Exchanges having a minimum investment of Tk10 million in listed securities at market price.

As of end-September 2021, six companies were trading on the DSE SME (two newly listed agribusiness firms and four from the over-the-counter market) and one company in the CSE SME (Nialco Alloys Limited, a bronze and brass producer).[41]

40 All types of investors can participate in the secondary market after the initial public offering (Table 8).

41 DSE SME: https://thefinancialexpress.com.bd/public/stock/bangladesh/dse-sme-platform-to-be-launched-on-september-30-1632537547; CSE SME: https://www.businessinsiderbd.com/markets/news/6616/cse-launches-sme-platform-with-first-listing

Equity markets have been hurt by the pandemic. Market capitalization was Tk3.1 trillion on the DSE and Tk2.4 trillion on the CSE in FY2020, a 22.0% and 25.7% decrease from FY2019, respectively (Figure 3.9 and Table 3.7). However, a CAGR of market capitalization from 2010 to 2020 was up 1.5% for the DSE and 4.8% for the CSE. Annual trading value has been declining by 11.2% CAGR (2010–2020) for the DSE and 13.1% CAGR for the CSE. The number of listed companies was 321 on the DSE and 293 on the CSE in FY2020.

A key challenge for developing the SME capital market is getting SME owners to understand that listing allows their business to grow. Also, young entrepreneurships and start-ups from diverse businesses should be strengthened further. The Securities and Exchange Commission has a series of capital market literacy and training programs to attract potential issuers and investors (including venture capital firms and business angels) through its Financial Literacy Division, the Bangladesh Institute of Capital Market, and the Bangladesh Academy for Securities Market. The DSE and CSE are preparing capacity building training programs to attract issuers and investors to their SME platforms. Agribusiness (rural areas) and technology-oriented firms (urban areas) are potential issuers for the SME platforms.[42]

Figure 3.9: Equity Market

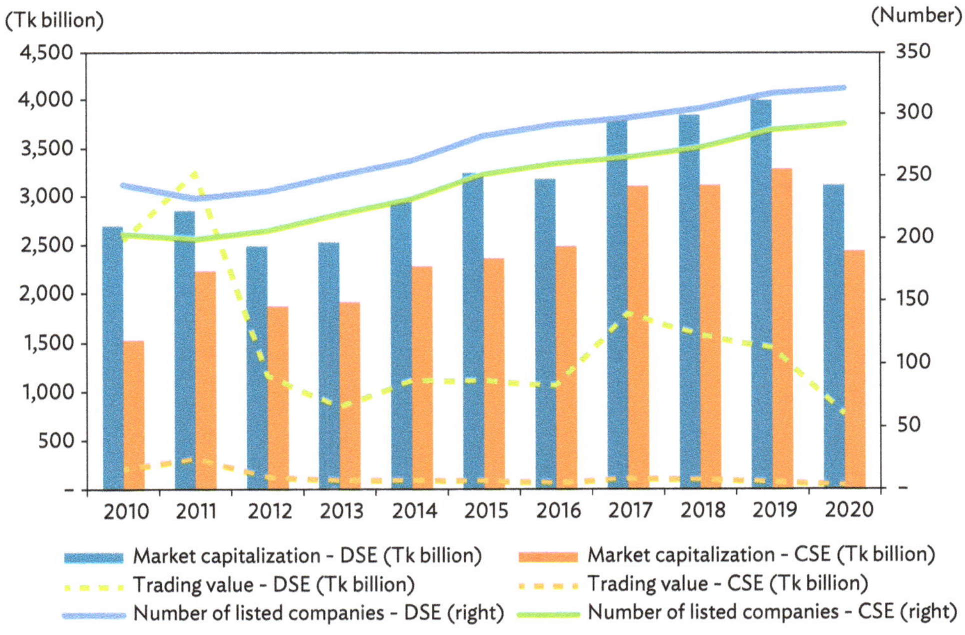

CSE = Chittagong Stock Exchange, DSE = Dhaka Stock Exchange.

Notes: Fiscal year (FY) data (ended 30 June). Data refer to the last trading day of the month. Trading value is total annual turnover.

Source: ADB Asia SME Monitor 2021. Data from various editions of annual reports from Bangladesh Securities and Exchange Commission, Chittagong Stock Exchange, and Dhaka Stock Exchange.

42 Interviews with the Bangladesh Securities and Exchange Commission on 28 April 2021; DSE on 23 February 2021; and CSE on 17 February 2021.

Financial Infrastructure

Well-organized financial infrastructure—a functioning credit bureau, secured lending, and credit enhancement (credit guarantees and rating) systems—is central to boosting financial inclusion. The Credit Information Bureau (CIB), established in 1992 by the Bangladesh Bank, plays a vital role in collecting reliable credit data from banks and NBFIs. It provides credit reports that help financial institutions reduce loan processing time, costs, and mitigate risks associated with MSME loans. Online credit reporting services started in 2011. The CIB database includes detailed borrower information on loan amounts; type of loans (continuous loan, demand loan, fixed-term loan, and short-term agricultural loans and microcredit); past due amounts; collateral; and credit guarantees. Borrowers cannot access their own credit data, but lenders can update incorrect or outdated data.

Following the national financial inclusion strategy, the MRA began operating the Microfinance Credit Information Bureau (MF-CIB) from end-2020 for pilot-testing with 50 selected MFIs. The newly created MF-CIB collects credit histories of microfinance clients from participating MFIs and provides credit reports online to facilitate microcredit to the poor and vulnerable groups, including CMSMEs. To acquaint MFIs and MF-CIB operators with its online software and database management, the MRA provides training sessions (44 training programs for 655 MFI staff members from 290 MFIs as of November 2020).[43] The Collateral Registry Bureau for movable and immovable assets used as loan collateral is being prepared under the national financial inclusion strategy.

There were eight credit rating agencies as of end-September 2021.[44] The Credit Rating Agency of Bangladesh (CRAB) offers several rating services for equity and debt instruments including SMEs. SME rating started in FY2013 for bank loans. Rating fees are shouldered by SMEs due to their high information cost. CRAB analysts assess bankers' credit history data and subjective data through visits to SME clients to check their actual financial and management condition (given the lack of financial and business records in many cases). CRAB uses the Bangladesh Bank definition of SMEs for ratings. SME credit reports are available for banks and NFIs regulated by the central bank (microfinance institutions cannot avail of credit ratings). CRAB rates around 1,800 SMEs annually and has rated about 11,000 SMEs since its services started.[45]

4. Policies and Regulations

- Comprehensive MSME development strategies (SME Policy 2019) cover both financial and nonfinancial agendas with time-bound goals and action plans. Well-organized intragovernmental coordination is key to successfully implement these strategies.
- The national financial inclusion strategy for 2024 uses a holistic approach and coordinates with relevant ministries and financial authorities. In the long term, it will create more value if it emphasizes small-cap market development.
- The government launched a Tk200 billion stimulus package in April 2020 to ease the impact of the pandemic and lockdown on CMSMEs; it has provided several financial assistance measures in response to the COVID-19 crisis.
- The digital transformation of MSME businesses continue as a policy priority, along with formalizing informal businesses, opening foreign markets to MSMEs, and developing youth and women entrepreneurships during the recovery.

[43] About MF-CIB: https://static1.squarespace.com/static/5a84894df14aa1f379d18290/t/5fc24a0fe18c5c478e469553/1606568473443/BFP-B+MF-CIB+2-pager+05.pdf

[44] Bangladesh Securities and Exchange Commission: https://www.sec.gov.bd/home/cragency

[45] Interview with CRAB on 7 April 2021.

MSME Development

The government has a national long-term development framework—Vision 2041. The Perspective Plan of Bangladesh 2021–2041 was launched in March 2020, led by the Bangladesh Planning Commission of the Ministry of Planning. The plan is a national development strategy with growth and poverty targets for FY2041: real GDP growth of 9.9%, extreme poverty ratio of less than 1.0%, and reducing poverty to less than 3.0%. Its strategy includes improving access to finance for the poor. It also aims to (i) help small urban and rural enterprises in manufacturing and services by establishing a Small Business Development Authority as a one-stop shop for promoting small business enterprises; (ii) internationalization of SMEs and individual entrepreneurs (micro-multinationals) through digitalization and well-connected global networks that allow them to compete in the global marketplace; and (iii) integrating SMEs with a national innovation system (Table 3.9).

The Ministry of Industries is responsible for formulating and implementing national industrial policy, including MSME development. The National Industrial Policy 2016 is the third policy after those in 2005 and 2010. As of February 2021, the National Industrial Policy 2021 was being drafted by the Ministry of Industries. The policy created a National Council for Industrial Development (NCID) to implement specific policies. The Executive Committee for NCID is chaired by the Minister of Industries. The policy includes an amended CMSME definition, CMSME development, economic zone/industrial park/high-tech park/cluster development, state-owned industry reform, product quality control/productivity enhancement, intellectual property rights and management, women entrepreneurship development, export industry development, foreign direct investment, industrial technology, environment-friendly industry management, skill development, and monitoring and evaluation. The Ministry of Industries also adopted a National Innovation and Intellectual Property Policy in 2018, which provides a basic framework for innovative and technology-based MSMEs, start-ups, and entrepreneurs.

The SME Policy 2019 is designed to develop CMSMEs, with the Ministry of Industries as implementing agency. The policy uses a generic "SME" that covers CMSMEs. The SME contribution to GDP is targeted to increase from 25% to 32% by 2024. There are 11 strategic goals: (i) improving the investment and business environment and institutional framework; (ii) increasing access to finance for SMEs; (iii) enhancing competition and help SMEs access markets; (iv) providing SME business support services, shortening the time and cost for establishing start-ups; (v) developing and expanding SME cluster-based networks; (vi) increasing the use of information, communications, and other technologies; (vii) expanding skill development, education, and training programs for SME entrepreneurs; (viii) extending programs for women entrepreneur development and offering specialized services; (ix) establishing SMEs links to large industries and protecting SME products; (x) developing capacity for establishing environment-friendly SMEs, including industrial waste management; and (xi) institutionalizing SME statistics and conducting R&D.

The SME Foundation, a nonprofit government organization through the Ministry of Industries, is a key implementing agency for national MSME development strategies. The SME Foundation does policy advocacy for MSME growth, facilitates financial support, and provides skills development and capacity building programs for MSMEs and entrepreneurships (especially technology-based and women entrepreneurs).

The government believes MSMEs are pivotal for sustainable growth. Thus, MSME development strategies have been formulated to cover both financial and nonfinancial aspects with time-bound goals and action plans. Well-organized intragovernmental coordination is essential to successfully implement the strategies, given the array of line ministry initiatives related to CMSME assistance.

Financial Inclusion

Bangladesh Bank formulates and promotes financial inclusion strategies. Early on, it created an internal SME and Special Programmes Department (SMESPD) in 2009 to monitor and promote CMSME access to formal financial services. In 2010, SMESPD created the Small and Medium Enterprise Credit Policies and Programmes for regulated banks and NBFIs, which included indicative targets for MSME loan disbursements.

The SMESPD issued a series of circulars on CMSME financing policies during 2016–2020. They were designed to (i) update targets for CMSME lending for each bank and NBFI; (ii) operate refinance schemes to encourage banks and NBFIs to lend to CMSMEs; (iii) support special policies for women entrepreneurs; (iv) increase the share of manufacturing and services; (v) encourage banks and NBFIs with fewer branches in rural areas to link with MFIs to disburse credit to cottage and microenterprises; (vi) encourage banks and NBFIs to invest in cluster and value chain-related industries centered specific products or services; and (vii) approve or reject in writing CMSME loan applications within 10 working days of receiving the completed application.

In July 2019, Bangladesh Bank launched a new National Financial Inclusion Strategy of Bangladesh 2020–2024, with 12 strategic goals and 65 targets. The goals are to (i) increase financial deepening; (ii) strengthen payment systems and service delivery; (iii) establish a robust data and measurement framework; (iv) promote financial literacy and consumer empowerment; (v) broaden and deepen financial inclusion for women, people affected by climate change, and other underserved segments of the population; (vi) upscale digital financial services and fintech; (vii) strengthen the policy and regulatory environment; (viii) fortify the risk management of financial inclusion initiatives; (ix) strengthen insurance services; (x) reinforce capital market services; (xi) strengthen microfinance; and (xii) strengthen quasi-regulated financial service providers (such as BPO, BHBFC, BMDF, PKSF, Samabay Bank, Ekti Bari Ekti Khamar, and Palli Sanchay Bank) to help provide their financial services by complying to applicable regulations.

There are four bodies to coordinate and implement the national financial inclusion strategy: (i) the NFIS-B national Council (NNC), (ii) NFIS-B Steering Committee (NSC), (iii) NFIS-B Advisory Committee (NAC), and (iv) NFIS-B Secretariat (NNS). NNC develops strategic directions and oversees implementation of financial inclusion agendas (chaired by the Minister of Finance). The NSC is responsible for implementing NNC strategies (chaired by the Bangladesh Bank governor). The NAC is a platform for public-private partnerships and is national advocate for financial inclusion (chaired by the secretary of the Financial Institutions Division of the Ministry of Finance). And NNS, led by Bangladesh Bank, provides technical administration and research support to the NNC, NSC, and NAC.

Overall, the national financial inclusion strategy is holistic and well coordinated with relevant line ministries and financial authorities. Over the long term, capital market development should be seen as a useful growth mechanism for qualified SMEs. The Bangladesh Securities and Exchange Commission regulates capital markets, including the SME platforms under the DSE and CSE. It can help financial inclusion and add value to implementing the strategy.

Response to COVID-19

The government launched a Tk200 billion stimulus package (with a special loan and investment facility for CMSMEs) in April 2020 to ease the impact of the pandemic and lockdown (Table 3.10). The package offers loans (term, working capital, etc.) for affected CMSMEs (for medium-sized firms, working capital loans only). Under the package, banks and NBFIs disburse loans from their own funds to CMSMEs and entrepreneurs at 9% interest (with a government interest rate subsidy of 5%). The loan tenor is for 3 years (1 year for individual entrepreneurs). Of the total loan, 70% is allotted for cottage, micro, and small enterprises (CMS), with the remaining 30% for medium-sized enterprises. Maximum 35% of CMS allocation is for trading, and the rest for services and manufacturing sectors. A Bangladesh Bank circular says 8% of the total should be earmarked to women entrepreneurs. Bangladesh

Bank also has a special refinancing scheme to cover 50% of disbursements under the stimulus package to banks and NBFIs. In addition, a credit guarantee scheme of Tk2,000 crore (Tk20 billion) is formed for loans under the stimulus package for entrepreneurs who cannot provide collateral. The SMESPD issued a circular detailing eligibility, applications, conditions, reporting, and other terms.

A revolving Tk100 billion refinancing scheme for CMSMEs was created in April 2020, providing working capital to CMSME entrepreneurs. Under this scheme, banks and NBFIs can be refinanced by Bangladesh Bank up to 50% of the loan disbursed at 4% interest.

Another Tk15.1 billion stimulus package for CMSMEs, concentrating on marginal entrepreneurs, was also launched in 2020. It supports various activities that improve the living standards of marginalized people. It was allocated to (i) the SME Foundation (Tk3.0 billion for small, cottage, medium industries, and women entrepreneurs); (ii) Bangladesh Small and Cottage Industries Corporation (Tk1.0 billion); (iii) Jayita Foundation (Tk0.5 billion); (iv) NGO Foundation (Tk0.5 billion); (v) Social Development Foundation (Tk3.0 billion); (vi) Rural Poverty Alleviation Foundation (Tk3.0 billion); (vii) Small Farmers Development Foundation (Tk1.0 billion); and Bangladesh Rural Development Board (Tk3.1 billion).

The Livelihood Restoration Loan Program for 2020–2021 aims to improve lives and livelihoods for people in rural areas affected by COVID-19. The program covers all 64 districts of the country except cities and district headquarters. Launched in September 2020, it offers flexible, low-interest-rate loans from PKSF and its partner organizations for micro entrepreneurs, marginal and small farmers, and trained and skilled young entrepreneurs. The program has helped revive and create livelihood opportunities for those affected by the pandemic. It helps restore economic activities and enable entrepreneurs to reinvest in their businesses. As a result, both household income and cash flows in the rural economy have increased.

ADB provided $50.0 million loan and a $0.5 million technical assistance grant for 2021–2022 to the Microenterprise Development Project for the recovery of pandemic-affected microenterprises, increasing liquidity in the rural economy. The project provides working capital to 30,000 micro entrepreneurs.

The International Fund for Agricultural Development also provided additional funding to its Promoting Agricultural Commercialization and Enterprises Project (2021–2022). It included Tk3.14 billion for loan support with Tk2.57 billion and Tk0.57 billion in grants for value chain development of pandemic-affected microenterprises.

The pandemic has accelerated the digital transformation of MSME businesses, which remains a policy priority. The government also hopes to formalize informal businesses and open foreign markets to MSMEs, and encourage youth and women entrepreneurs. Given the long pandemic, the government should consider more balanced support for businesses hit badly by the crisis (focused group assistance with phased approach) and those with growth potential that help build a resilient economic recovery, while avoiding excessive budget deficits.

Data Tables

Table 3.1: MSME Definitions

A. Definition after 21 March 2016

Sector	Item	Cottage	Micro	Small	Medium
Manufacturing	Fixed assets*	Less than Tk1 million	Tk1 million to less than Tk7.5 million	Tk7.5 million to less than Tk150 million	Tk150 million to less than Tk500 million
	Employees	Maximum 15 including family members	16–30	31–120	121–300 (for garments industry maximum 1000)
Service	Fixed assets*		Less than Tk1 million	Tk1 million to less than Tk20 million	Tk20 million to less than Tk300 million
	Employees		Maximum 15	16–50	51–120

*Without land and factory building with replacement costs.

Source: ADB Asia SME Monitor 2021 database. Data from the National Industrial Policy 2016.

B. Definition before 20 March 2016

Sector	Item	Cottage	Micro	Small	Medium
Manufacturing	Fixed assets		Tk0.5 million-Tk5.0 million	Tk5 million-Tk100 million	Tk100 million–Tk300 million
	Employees		10–24	25–99	100–250
Service and Trade	Fixed assets		Less than Tk0.5 million	Tk5 million-Tk10 million	Tk10 million-Tk150 million
	Employees		Fewer than 10	10–25	26–100
	Fixed assets	Less than Tk0.5 million			
	Employees	Fewer than or equal to 10 including family members			

Source: ADB Asia SME Monitor 2021 database. Data from the National Industrial Policy 2010.

C. Definition used by Bangladesh Bank

Sector	Item	Cottage	Micro	Small	Medium
Manufacturing	Fixed assets*	Less than Tk1 million	Tk1 million to less than Tk7.5 million	Tk7.5 million to less than Tk150 million	Tk150 million to less than Tk500 million
	Employees	Maximum 15 including family members	16–30	31–120	121–300 (for garments industry maximum 1000)
Service	Fixed assets*		Less than Tk1 million	Tk1 million to less than Tk20 million	Tk20 million to less than Tk300 million
	Employees		Maximum 15	16–50	51–120
Trade/business	Fixed assets*		Less than Tk1 million	Tk1 million to Tk20 million	
	Employees		Maximum 15	16–50	
	Annual turnover		Maximum Tk20 million	More than Tk20 million to Tk200 million	

MSME = micro, small, and medium-sized enterprise.

*Without land and factory building with replacement costs.

Source: ADB Asia SME Monitor 2021 database. Data from Small and Medium Enterprise Credit Policies and Programmes, Bangladesh Bank.

Table 3.2: MSME Landscape

End-of-year data

Item	2010	2011	2012	2013	2014	2015	2016	2017	2018	2019	2020
NUMBER OF ENTERPRISES1											
Number of enterprises, total	...	...	...	7,818,565	...	...	...	...	...	...	...
Number of MSMEs	...	...	...	7,813,315	...	...	...	...	...	...	...
Cottage	...	...	...	6,842,884	...	...	...	...	...	...	...
Micro	...	...	...	104,007	...	...	...	...	...	...	...
Small	...	...	...	859,318	...	...	...	...	...	...	...
Medium	...	...	...	7,106	...	...	...	...	...	...	...
Number of large enterprises	...	...	...	5,250	...	...	...	...	...	...	...
MSME to total (%)	...	...	...	99.97	...	...	...	...	...	...	...
MSME growth (%)	...	...	...	...	...	...	...	...	...	...	...
MSMEs by sector (% share)											
Agriculture, forestry, and fisheries	...	...	...	...	...	...	...	...	...	...	...
Manufacturing	...	...	...	11.1	...	...	...	...	...	...	...
Transportation and communication	...	...	...	16.9	...	...	...	...	...	...	...
Construction	...	...	...	0.1	...	...	...	...	...	...	...
Wholesale and retail trade	...	...	...	45.9	...	...	...	...	...	...	...
Other services	...	...	...	25.7	...	...	...	...	...	...	...
Others	...	...	...	0.3	...	...	...	...	...	...	...
Number of MSMEs by region (% share)2											
Urban	...	...	...	28.5	...	...	...	...	...	...	...
Rural	...	...	...	71.5	...	...	...	...	...	...	...
EMPLOYMENT											
Number of employment, total	...	...	...	24,500,850	...	...	...	...	...	...	...
Number of employment by MSMEs	...	...	...	21,033,994	...	...	...	...	...	...	...
Cottage	...	...	...	13,168,327	...	...	...	...	...	...	...
Micro	...	...	...	558,870	...	...	...	...	...	...	...
Small	...	...	...	6,600,685	...	...	...	...	...	...	...
Medium	...	...	...	706,112	...	...	...	...	...	...	...
Number of employment by large enterprises	...	...	...	3,466,856	...	...	...	...	...	...	...
MSME employees to total (%)	...	...	...	85.9	...	...	...	...	...	...	...
MSME employees growth (%)	...	...	...	...	...	...	...	...	...	...	...
Share of female employees to total employees (%)	...	...	...	16.5	...	...	...	...	...	...	...
Employment by MSME by sector (% share)											
Agriculture, forestry, and fisheries	...	...	...	...	...	...	...	...	...	...	...
Manufacturing	...	...	...	20.3	...	...	...	...	...	...	...
Transportation and communication	...	...	...	9.4	...	...	...	...	...	...	...
Construction	...	...	...	0.2	...	...	...	...	...	...	...
Wholesale and retail trade	...	...	...	39.9	...	...	...	...	...	...	...
Other services	...	...	...	29.9	...	...	...	...	...	...	...
Others	...	...	...	0.4	...	...	...	...	...	...	...
Employment by MSMEs by region (% share)[2]											
Urban	...	...	...	34.4	...	...	...	...	...	...	...
Rural	...	...	...	65.6	...	...	...	...	...	...	...
CONTRIBUTION TO GDP											
GDP of MSMEs (Tk million)	...	...	...	...	...	...	...	...	...	...	...
MSME contribution to GDP (% share)	...	...	...	...	...	...	...	...	...	...	...
MSME GDP growth (%)	...	...	...	...	...	...	...	...	...	...	...
MSME labor productivity (Tk million)	...	...	...	...	...	...	...	...	...	...	...
MSME GDP by sector (% share)											
Agriculture, forestry, and fisheries	...	...	...	...	...	...	...	...	...	...	...
Manufacturing	...	...	...	...	...	...	...	...	...	...	...
Transportation and communication	...	...	...	...	...	...	...	...	...	...	...
Construction	...	...	...	...	...	...	...	...	...	...	...
Wholesale and retail trade	...	...	...	...	...	...	...	...	...	...	...
Other services	...	...	...	...	...	...	...	...	...	...	...
Others	...	...	...	...	...	...	...	...	...	...	...
MSME GDP by region (% share)2											
Urban	...	...	...	...	...	...	...	...	...	...	...
Rural	...	...	...	...	...	...	...	...	...	...	...
EXPORTS[3]											
Total export value (Tk million)	1,134,589	1,629,733	1,762,288	2,268,607	2,122,602	2,408,850	2,634,668	3,003,837	3,087,936	3,481,620	2,811,668
Total export growth (%)	5.5	43.6	8.1	28.7	(6.4)	13.5	9.4	14.0	2.8	12.7	(19.2)
MSME export value (Tk million)	...	...	...	...	...	...	...	...	...	...	...
MSME export to total export value (%)	...	...	...	...	...	...	...	...	...	...	...
MSME export growth (%)	...	...	...	...	...	...	...	...	...	...	...
IMPORTS[3]											
Total import value (Tk million)	1,794,324	2,659,405	2,942,810	3,144,291	2,822,310	3,670,702	3,869,349	4,712,495	5,511,644	5,722,675	5,441,658
Total import growth (%)	13.5	48.2	10.7	6.8	(10.2)	30.1	5.4	21.8	17.0	3.8	(4.9)
MSME import value (Tk million)	...	...	...	...	...	...	...	...	...	...	...
MSME import to total import value (%)	...	...	...	...	...	...	...	...	...	...	...
MSME import growth (%)	...	...	...	...	...	...	...	...	...	...	...

GDP = gross domestic product; MSME = micro, small, and medium-sized enterprise.

Notes: Aggregate MSME figures include cottage enterprises. Data in 2013 is based on census, except exports/imports.

1 Data refer to permanent and temporary establishments, and economic households.

2 Urban/rural classification refers to the definitions under the Economic Units Census.

3 Data are presented in fiscal year (ended 30 June).

Source: ADB Asia SME Monitor 2021. Data from Bangladesh Bureau of Statistics, Economic Census 2013; Foreign Trade Statistics of Bangladesh 2019-2020.

Table 3.2a: Manufacturing MSMEs

End-of-year data

Item	2012	2013	2014	2015	2016	2017	2018	2019	2020
NUMBER OF ENTERPRISES - MANUFACTURING									
Number of enterprises, total	42,792	...	...	...	...	...	...	46,291	...
Number of MSMEs	39,153	...	...	...	...	...	...	43,260	...
Cottage	...	...	...	...	...	...	...	...	...
Micro	17,384	...	...	...	...	...	...	16,689	...
Small	15,666	...	...	...	...	...	...	23,557	...
Medium	6,103	...	...	...	...	...	...	3,014	...
Number of large enterprises	3,639	...	...	...	...	...	...	3,031	...
MSME to total (%)	91.5	...	...	...	...	...	...	93.5	...
MSME growth (%)*	...	...	...	...	...	...	...	1.4	...
EMPLOYMENT - MANUFACTURING									
Number of employment, total	5,015,937	...	...	...	...	...	...	5,879,844	...
Number of employment by MSMEs	2,051,665	...	...	...	...	...	...	1,852,703	...
Cottage	...	...	...	...	...	...	...	...	...
Micro	271,644	...	...	...	...	...	...	263,720	...
Small	738,801	...	...	...	...	...	...	1,127,841	...
Medium	1,041,220	...	...	...	...	...	...	461,142	...
Number of employment by large enterprises	2,964,272	...	...	...	...	...	...	4,027,141	...
MSME employees to total (%)	40.9	...	...	...	...	...	...	31.5	...
MSME employees growth (%)*	...	...	...	...	...	...	...	(1.4)	...
Share of female employees to total employees (%)	...	...	...	...	...	...	...	...	...
CONTRIBUTION TO GVA**									
Manufacturing gross value added (GVA), total (Tk million)	1,205,674	1,329,941	1,446,534	1,595,680	1,782,229	1,977,653	2,242,701	2,561,179	2,710,672
Cottage and small enterprises (CS) (Tk million)	225,691	245,579	261,131	283,426	309,094	339,458	370,864	411,480	443,476
Medium and large enterprises (ML) (Tk million)	979,983	1,084,362	1,185,403	1,312,254	1,473,135	1,638,195	1,871,837	2,149,699	2,267,196
CS contribution to GVA (% share)	18.7	18.5	18.1	17.8	17.3	17.2	16.5	16.1	16.4
ML contribution to GVA (% share)	81.3	81.5	81.9	82.2	82.7	82.8	83.5	83.9	83.6
CS GVA growth (%)	6.6	8.8	6.3	8.5	9.1	9.8	9.3	11.0	7.8
ML GVA growth (%)	10.8	10.7	9.3	10.7	12.3	11.2	14.3	14.8	5.5

MSME = micro, small, and medium-sized enterprise.

* Compound annual growth between 2012 and 2019.

** Data are presented as fiscal year (ended 30 June). Data refer to gross value added of cottage, small, medium-sized, and large manufacturing enterprises. Data at constant 2005-2006 prices.

Source: ADB Asia SME Monitor 2021. Data from Bangladesh Bureau of Statistics, Survey of Manufacturing 2012, 2019 (preliminary findings).

Table 3.2b: Manufacturing MSMEs by Sector, 2012

End-of-year data

Item	Micro	Small	Medium	Large	MSME	Total
Number of manufacturing enterprises	17,042	15,208	6,074	3,633	38,324	41,957
Food products	5,733	2,416	187	105	8,336	8,441
Beverages	161	187	14	5	362	367
Tobacco products	250	136	53	48	439	487
Textiles	5,424	4,064	1,137	358	10,625	10,983
Wearing apparel (ready-made garments)	764	1,066	2,404	2,752	4,234	6,986
Leather and related products	533	274	100	23	907	930
Wood and products of wood and cork, except furniture; manufacture of articles of straw and plaiting materials	263	31	7	1	301	302
Paper and paper products	214	646	42	0	902	902
Printing and reproduction of recorded media	263	31	7	1	301	302
Coke and refined petroleum products	9	9	0	1	18	19
Chemicals and chemical products	142	328	65	28	535	563
Pharmaceuticals, medicinal chemical and botanical products	15	392	50	37	457	494
Rubber and plastics products	528	460	35	13	1,023	1,036
Other non-metallic mineral products	162	2,782	1,537	173	4,481	4,654
Basic metals	119	689	347	50	1,155	1,205
Fabricated metal products, except machinery and equipment	793	637	19	0	1,449	1,449
Computer, electronic and optical products	78	66	2	3	146	149
Electrical equipment	328	530	14	12	872	884
Machinery and equipment	133	46	12	4	191	195
Motor vehicles, trailers and semi-trailers	76	51	8	2	135	137
Other transport equipment	126	123	19	8	268	276
Furniture	796	235	15	9	1,046	1,055
Repair and installation of machinery and equipment	111	9	0	0	120	120
Recycling	21	0	0	0	21	21
Other manufacturing	187	34	7	7	228	235

Note: Reported data only.

Source: ADB Asia SME Monitor 2021. Data from Bangladesh Bureau of Statistics, Survey of Manufacturing Industries 2012.

Table 3.3: Bank Credit

End-of-year data

Item	2010	2011	2012	2013	2014	2015	2016	2017	2018	2019	2020
OPERATING BANKS											
Number of operating banks, total	47	47	47	56	56	56	57	57	59	59	61
State-owned commercial banks	4	4	4	4	5	6	6	6	6	6	6
State-owned development financial institutions	4	4	4	4	3	2	2	2	3	3	3
Private commercial banks	30	30	30	39	39	39	40	40	41	41	43
Foreign commercial banks	9	9	9	9	9	9	9	9	9	9	9
Credit											
Loans outstanding, total (Tk billion)	...	...	...	...	...	6,055	6,987	8,239	9,388	10,412	11,250
Loans outstanding in domestic currency (Tk billion)	...	...	...	...	...	5,953	6,865	8,106	9,246	10,259	11,096
Loans outstanding in foreign currency (Tk billion)	...	...	...	...	...	102	122	133	142	153	155
Loan growth (%)	...	...	...	...	...	12.6	15.3	18.1	14.1	11.0	8.2
Total bank loans to GDP (%)	...	...	...	...	...	...	...	...	...	...	...
Lending rate (%)	...	...	...	...	...	...	...	...	...	...	...
Gross nonperforming loans (NPLs) (Tk billion)	227	227	427	406	502	594	621	743	3,939	1,124	1,125
Gross NPLs to total loans (%)	7.3	6.1	10.0	8.9	9.7	8.8	9.2	9.3	10.3	11.7	12.7
Deposits											
Deposits, total (Tk billion)	3,722	4,510	5,396	6,273	6,965	7,929	8,934	9,875	11,187	12,564	14,210
Deposits in domestic currency (Tk billion)	...	...	...	...	...	...	...	...	11,165	12,541	14,188
Deposits in foreign currency (Tk billion)	...	...	...	...	...	...	...	...	21.4	22.7	22.1
Deposit rate (%)	...	...	...	...	...	...	...	...	...	...	...
MSME LOANS1											
MSME loans outstanding, total (Tk billion)	671	785	977	1,123	1,318	1,433	1,655	1,926	1,785	2,092	2,273
MSME loans to total loans outstanding (%)2	...	...	...	...	...	23.7	23.7	23.4	19.0	20.1	20.2
MSME loans to GDP (%)	8.4	8.6	9.3	9.4	9.8	9.5	9.5	9.8	7.9	8.2	8.1
MSME loan growth (%)	...	1.7	24.4	14.9	17.3	8.8	15.4	16.4	(7.4)	17.2	8.7
MSME lending rate (%)	...	...	...	...	...	...	...	...	...	...	...
Nonperforming MSME loans (NPLs) (Tk billion)	...	...	...	...	...	...	...	...	...	...	...
MSME NPLs to total MSME loans (%)	3.6	3.6	6.4	7.9	11.8	...	...	...	...	...	...
Number of MSME loan borrowers	301,604	310,871	454,781	738,613	528,656	704,972	606,692	711,986	660,791	751,362	770,150
MSME loan borrowers to total bank borrowers (%)	...	...	...	...	...	...	...	...	...	...	...
MSME loan rejection rate (% of total applications)	...	...	...	...	...	...	...	...	...	...	...
Number of MSME savings account in banks	...	...	...	...	...	...	...	...	...	...	...
Guaranteed MSME loans (Tk billion)	...	...	...	...	...	...	...	...	...	...	...
Non-collateral MSME loans (Tk billion)	...	...	...	...	...	88	104	116	141	211	206
MSME loans outstanding by sector (% share)[3]											
Manufacturing	28.3	29.4	31.4	28.1	30.0	...	...	...	...	...	40.0
Wholesale and retail trade	65.4	64.0	63.4	66.5	62.2	...	...	...	...	...	41.0
Other services	6.3	6.6	5.2	5.4	7.8	...	...	...	...	...	19.0
MSME loans outstanding by region (% share)[4]											
Urban	...	...	...	...	...	...	...	...	82.6	84.4	84.2
Rural	...	...	...	...	...	...	...	...	17.4	15.6	15.8
MSME loans outstanding by type of use (% share)											
For working capital	...	...	...	...	...	...	...	...	...	...	...
For capital investment	...	...	...	...	...	...	...	...	...	...	...
MSME loans outstanding by tenor (% share)											
Less than 1 year	...	...	...	...	...	...	...	...	...	...	...
1-5 years	...	...	...	...	...	...	...	...	...	...	...
More than 5 years	...	...	...	...	...	...	...	...	...	...	...

GDP = gross domestic product; MSME = micro, small, and medium-sized enterprise.

[1] Data for commercial banks only.

[2] Commercial bank MSME loans outstanding divided by total loans outstanding of all operating banks. Actual percentage share of MSME loans to total loans outstanding in commercial banks are thus higher.

[3] MSME is broadly categorized by three sectors: manufacturing, trading, and other services.

[4] Urban/rural classification refers to definitions under the Economic Units Census.

Source: ADB Asia SME Monitor 2021. Data from Bangladesh Bank.

Table 3.3a: MSME Lending Target and Actual Disbursement*

End-of-year data

Item	2010	2011	2012	2013	2014	2015	2016	2017	2018	2019	2020
MSME lending target (Tk million)	371,695	545,343	563,298	717,152	848,260	1,009,609	1,080,448	1,266,807	1,500,787	1,676,901	2,180,608
Total MSME loans disbursed (Tk million)	518,471	520,735	682,625	834,372	980,330	1,121,510	1,361,762	1,537,607	1,523,469	1,612,166	1,978,742
Share of target achievements to total loans (%)	139.5	95.5	121.2	116.3	115.6	111.1	126.0	121.4	101.5	96.1	90.7
MSME loans disbursed by sector											
Manufacturing (Tk million)	145,501	152,633	213,676	233,904	293,630	293,101	335,366	401,146	536,677	565,746	772,521
Wholesale and retail trad (Tk million)	343,631	336,901	435,889	558,612	614,329	717,685	875,264	929,363	635,349	697,034	808,059
Other services (Tk million)	29,340	31,201	33,059	41,856	72,371	110,724	151,132	207,099	351,443	349,387	398,163
Manufacturing (% share to total)	28.1	29.3	31.3	28.0	30.0	26.1	24.6	26.1	35.2	35.1	39.0
Wholesale and retail trad (% share to total)	66.3	64.7	63.9	66.9	62.7	64.0	64.3	60.4	41.7	43.2	40.8
Other services (% share to total)	5.7	6.0	4.8	5.0	7.4	9.9	11.1	13.5	23.1	21.7	20.1

MSME = micro, small, and medium-sized enterprise.

* Data refer to scheduled commercial banks only.

Source: ADB Asia SME Monitor 2021. Data from Bangladesh Bank.

Table 3.3b: Grameen Bank

End-of-year data

Item	2010	2011	2012	2013	2014	2015	2016	2017	2018	2019
Loans outstanding, total (Tk million)	66,434	75,325	80,321	84,385	87,495	96,422	118,244	144,497	153,599	156,721
Growth (%)	21.4	13.4	6.6	5.1	3.7	10.2	22.6	22.2	6.3	2.0
Loans disbursed (Tk million)	96,149	108,539	118,609	133,321	133,321	149,227	187,533	234,715	246,810	254,374
Growth (%)	21.1	12.9	9.3	12.4	...	11.9	25.7	25.2	5.2	3.1
Annual lending rate (%, on average)	...	...	...	...	...	...	...	...	...	...
Gross nonperforming loans (NPLs) (Tk million)	...	...	...	...	...	...	...	...	...	...
Gross NPLs to total loans (%)	...	...	...	...	...	...	...	...	...	...
Deposits (Tk million)*	56,346	66,547	79,162	92,138	105,791	118,792	128,834	140,963	157,137	170,884
Number of members*	8,340,623	8,370,998	8,373,893	8,543,977	8,640,225	8,806,779	8,901,610	8,934,874	9,084,503	9,260,176
Growth (%)	4.6	0.4	0.0	2.0	1.1	1.9	1.1	0.4	1.7	1.9

NPL = nonperforming loan.

* Data for Grameen Bank members only.

Source: ADB Asia SME Monitor 2021. Data from Grameen Bank website (https://grameenbank.org/data-and-report/historical-data-series-in-bdt/).

Table 3.4: Refinancing Schemes for MSMEs

Name of the Fund	Year of the Launch	Fund Size (Tk million)	Taget Beneficiaries	Amount of Refinance (Tk million)*	Number of MSMEs Benefited**	Status
1.Small Enterprise Refinance Scheme (BB Fund)	2004	15,000	General	12,288	12,725	Ongoing
			Women entrepreneurs	33,490	27,697	
2. Refinancing Scheme for Agro-based Industries in Rural Areas	2001	14,000	Rural CMSMEs	19,880	2,858	Ongoing
3. Refinancing Scheme for New Entrepreneurs in Cottage, Micro, and Small Enterprise Sector	2014	1,000	New entrepreneurs	307	527	Ongoing
4. Revolving Refinance Scheme in response to the COVID-19	2020 (April)	100,000	Existing and new CMSME entrepreneurs	17,396	11,833	Ongoing (for 3 years)
5. Financial Sector Project for the Development of Small and Medium-sized Enterprises (FSPDSME) [JICA supported fund]	2011	3,773	CMSME Entrepreneurs	1,033	1,342	Project closed but refinance and recovery activities ongoing.
Grand Total				84,393	56,982	

CMSME = cottage, micro, small, and medium-sized enterprise; JICA = Japan International Cooperation Agency; MSME = micro, small and medium-sized enterprise.

* Data as of end-2020.

Source: ADB Asia SME Monitor 2021. Data from Bangladesh Bank.

Table 3.5: Nonbank Finance

Item	2010	2011	2012	2013	2014	2015	2016	2017	2018	2019	2020
NUMBER OF NONBANK FINANCE INSTITUTIONS											
Nonbank finance institutions regulated by Bangladesh Bank	29	30	31	31	31	31	33	34	34	34	35
Government-owned	1	2	3	3	3	3	3	3	3	3	3
Joint-venture	8	8	10	10	10	10	11	12	12	12	13
Private	20	20	18	18	18	18	19	19	19	19	19
NGO microfinance institutions	516	576	590	649	697	697	680	699	705	724	...
NONBANK FINANCE INSTITUTIONS REGULATED BY BANGLADESH BANK											
Financing outstanding, total (Tk million)	...	...	268,628	344,538	407,375	448,478	530,724	615,962	662,449	671,768	669,232
Growth (%)	...	...	...	28.3	18.2	10.1	18.3	16.1	7.5	1.4	(0.4)
Total financing to GDP (%)*	...	...	2.5	2.9	3.0	3.0	3.1	3.1	2.9	2.6	2.4
Annual lending rate (%, on average)	...	...	...	...	...	...	...	...	...	...	...
Gross nonperforming loans (NPLs) (Tk million)	...	...	13,871	18,064	20,223	40,012	38,693	45,232	54,394	63,988	100,536
Gross NPLs to total loans (%)	...	...	5.2	5.2	5.0	8.9	7.3	7.3	8.2	9.5	15.0
Savings (Tk million)	...	...	...	...	236,644	245,705	382,431	468,003	466,261	449,666	453,431
Number of customers financed, total	...	...	...	...	...	...	...	...	...	...	...
Financing outstanding by sector (% share)											
Agriculture, forestry, and fisheries	...	...	...	1.4	1.4	1.8	2.1	3.1	2.6	2.4	2.5
Manufacturing	...	...	...	40.8	38.8	39.5	41.0	39.4	40.4	42.1	43.6
Transportation and communication	...	...	...	4.4	4.6	3.8	4.2	4.5	4.1	4.3	3.9
Construction	...	...	...	12.2	16.9	17.6	16.8	17.9	19.4	19.3	18.9
Wholesale and retail trade	...	...	...	14.6	15.5	17.2	17.1	16.1	15.0	14.0	13.6
Other services	...	...	...	...	...	...	...	...	...	...	...
Others	...	...	...	26.7	23.5	20.0	18.8	19.0	18.4	18.0	17.5
Financing outstanding by region (% share)											
Urban	...	...	...	...	...	...	...	...	...	...	...
Rural	...	...	...	...	...	...	...	...	...	...	...
MICROFINANCE LOANS**											
Financing outstanding, total (Tk billion)	...	...	...	...	282.2	352.0	454.0	583.6	673.9	787.6	...
Growth (%)	...	...	...	...	...	24.7	29.0	28.5	15.5	16.9	...
Total financing to GDP (%)*	...	...	...	...	2.1	2.3	2.6	3.0	3.0	3.1	...
Annual lending rate (%, on average)	...	...	...	...	...	...	...	...	...	...	...
Gross nonperforming loans (NPLs) (Tk billion)	...	...	...	...	...	...	...	...	...	...	...
Gross NPLs to total loans (%)	...	...	...	...	...	...	...	...	...	...	...
Savings (Tk billion)	...	...	...	...	107.0	135.4	170.7	216.7	263.0	306.9	...
Number of customers financed, total (million)	...	...	...	...	19.4	20.4	23.1	26.0	25.4	25.8	...
Financing outstanding by sector (% share)											
Agriculture, forestry, and fisheries	...	...	...	...	...	...	...	...	...	...	...
Manufacturing	...	...	...	...	...	...	...	...	...	...	...
Transportation and communication	...	...	...	...	...	...	...	...	...	...	...
Construction	...	...	...	...	...	...	...	...	...	...	...
Wholesale and retail trade	...	...	...	...	...	...	...	...	...	...	...
Other services	...	...	...	...	...	...	...	...	...	...	...
Others	...	...	...	...	...	...	...	...	...	...	...
Financing outstanding by region (% share)											
Urban	...	...	...	...	...	...	...	...	...	...	...
Rural	...	...	...	...	...	...	...	...	...	...	...

GDP = gross domestic product; NGO = nongovernment organization; NPL = nonperforming loan.

* Calculated based on gross domestic product in fiscal year (ended 30 June).

** Fiscal year data. Microfinance loans include loans by nongovernment microfinance institutions, Grameen Bank, and commercial banks.

Source: ADB Asia SME Monitor 2021. Data from Bangladesh Bank and Microcredit Regulatory Authority.

Table 3.5a: Nonbank Finance—Palli Karma-Sahayak Foundation

*Fiscal year data (end-June)**

Item	2010	2011	2012	2013	2014	2015	2016	2017	2018	2019	2020
MICROENTERPRISE LOAN PROGRAM - PKSF											
Financing outstanding, total (Tk million)	31,630	31,990	33,820	35,170	37,030	39,481	42,202	44,519	48,038	53,522	59,874
Growth (%)	9.1	1.1	5.7	4.0	5.3	6.6	6.9	5.5	7.9	11.4	11.9
Total financing to GDP (%)	0.2	0.2	0.2	0.2	0.2	0.2	0.2	0.2	0.1	1.5	0.1
Annual lending rate (%, ranges)	1%-7%	1%-7%	1%-8%	1%-8%	1%-8%	1%-8%	1%-7.5%	1%-7.5%	1%-7.5%	1%-7.5%	1%-7.5%
Gross nonperforming loans (NPLs) (Tk million)**	865	1,051	1,790	2,057	2,068	1,923	1,750	2,238	2,187	2,041	2,025
Gross NPLs to total loans (%)	2.7	3.3	5.3	5.8	5.6	4.9	4.1	5.0	4.6	3.8	3.4
Borrower's Savings (Tk million)	36,320	32,028	26,302	34,045	40,686	50,116	60,821	75,578	92,043	113,437	133,310
Number of customers (borrowers) financed, total (million)	8.4	8.2	6.7	7.9	8.1	8.6	9.4	10.0	10.4	10.8	11.0
Number of active partner organizations (POs)	194	200	199	200	199	195	195	198	186	187	187

* Fiscal year (ended 30 June).

** Loans with arrears of over 365 days.

Note: Sector and regional data are not available.

Source: ADB Asia SME Monitor 2021. Data from Palli Karma-Sahayak Foundation (PKSF).

Table 3.6: Mobile Financial Services

End-of-year data

Item	2017	2018	2019	2020	June 2021
Number of banks providing MFS	18	18	16	15	15
Number of agents ('000)	786	886	972	1,059	1,115
Number of registered clients (million)	58.8	67.5	79.5	99.3	99.8
Number of active accounts (million)*	21.0	37.3	34.6	32.3	40.9
Number of total transaction (million)	166.3	210.1	227.4	299.5	319.8
Total transaction (Tk million)	285,710	321,056	406,476	565,569	629,939
Number of daily average transaction (million)	5.4	6.8	7.3	9.7	10.7
Average daily transaction (Tk million)	9,217	10,357	13,112	18,244	20,998
Products (Tk million)					
Inward remittance	46	635	310	1,348	1,770
Cash-in transaction	120,279	122,615	145,627	173,467	183,163
Cash-out transaction	108,947	122,138	134,740	154,442	157,417
P2P transaction	44,252	50,737	98,515	169,822	188,278
Salary disbursement (B2P)	4,055	6,132	10,047	20,937	22,432
Utility bill payment (P2B)	1,847	2,848	3,128	8,341	12,438
Merchant payment	1,300	4,249	6,002	21,472	32,932
Government payment	1,282	6,575	653	414	12,252
Others	3,706	5,127	7,455	15,327	19,258

B2P = business-to-person, MFS = mobile financial services, P2B = person-to-business, P2P = person-to-person.

* Actual number of days in month (December for 2017–2020 and June for 2021) has been used for average calculations.

Source: ADB Asia SME Monitor 2021. Data recomposed from Bangladesh Bank. https://www.bb.org.bd/fnansys/paymentsys/mfsdata.php

Table 3.7: Capital Markets

*Fiscal year data (end-June)**

Item	2010	2011	2012	2013	2014	2015	2016	2017	2018	2019	2020
EQUITY MARKET											
Main Board - DSE											
DSE Broad Index (DGEN/DSEX)[1]	6,154	6,117	4,573	4,105	4,481	4,583	4,508	5,656	5,405	5,422	3,989
Market capitalization (Tk million)[1]	2,700,745	2,853,892	2,491,613	2,530,246	2,943,202	3,247,306	3,185,749	3,801,001	3,847,348	3,998,164	3,119,670
Growth (%)	117.6	5.7	(12.7)	1.6	16.3	10.3	(1.9)	19.3	1.2	3.9	(22.0)
Trading value (Tk million)[2]	2,563,505	3,259,153	1,171,451	857,090	1,125,398	1,123,520	1,072,461	1,805,222	1,590,852	1,459,655	781,625
Trading volume (million shares)[2]	10,133	19,695	18,580	21,556	24,318	26,574	28,959	54,358	45,766	35,893	26,049
Number of listed companies	243	232	238	251	263	283	292	297	305	317	321
Number of IPOs	...	...	...	...	...	...	11	9	11	14	3
Number of delisted companies	...	...	...	...	...	...	...	...	...	...	...
Main Board - CSE											
All-Share Price Index[1]	18,116	17,060	13,736	12,738	13,766	14,097	13,803	17,517	16,558	16,634	11,333
Market capitalization (Tk million)[1]	1,538,393	2,237,585	1,878,171	1,919,891	2,286,679	2,370,421	2,496,849	3,113,243	3,123,522	3,293,303	2,447,567
Growth (%)	57.8	45.4	(16.1)	2.2	19.1	3.7	5.3	24.7	0.3	5.4	(25.7)
Trading value (Tk million)[2]	217,112	321,682	134,855	101,985	102,183	96,480	77,472	118,071	109,851	84,800	53,078
Trading volume (million shares)[2]	1,395	2,721	5,254	2,762	2,700	2,683	2,489	4,032	3,506	2,475	1,675
Number of listed companies	204	200	207	220	232	252	261	266	274	288	293
Number of IPOs	20	17	15	14	16	16	11	9	11	14	4
Number of delisted companies	37	17	1	1	0	0	0	1	0	0	0

CSE = Chittagong Stock Exchange, DSE = Dhaka Stock Exchange, IPO = initial public offering.

* Fiscal year ((ended 30 June).

[1] Data in the last trading day of the month. [2] Total turnover.

Source: ADB Asia SME Monitor 2021. Data from various editions of annual reports from Bangladesh Securities and Exchange Commission, Chittagong Stock Exchange, and Dhaka Stock Exchange.

Table 3.8: Listing Requirements Dhaka Stock Exchange and Chittagong Stock Exchange

Criteria	Stock	
	Main Board	SME Platform
Post-issue paid-up capital	Above Tk500 million.	Tk50 million to Tk300 million.
Reporting requirements	Quarterly and annually (audited).	Annually (audited).
Participants of primary market	Eligible investors (EI) and public.	Only qualified investors (eligible investors, issuers of listed securities, and high net worth individuals having net worth of Tk10 million)
Participants of secondary market	All types of investors.	All types of investors with minimum contract size of Tk0.2 million.
Underwriting	At least 35% underwritten.	The issue shall be at least 50% underwritten.
Credit rating	Credit rating required.	Credit rating is not required for fixed price method but required for book-building method.
SME Platform by Method		
Criteria	Under fixed price method	Book-building method
Pre-issue paid-up capital	No limit.	Tk100 million.
Post-issue paid-up capital	Tk50 million to Tk300 million.	Tk100 million to Tk300 million.
Net profit after tax	No such requirement.	Net profit after tax for immediate preceding two financial years.
Allotment Price	At par.	Alloted at submitted price.
Credit Rating	No credit rating required.	Credit rating required.
Under writing	At least 50% underwritten.	At least 50% underwritten.

SME = small and medium-sized enterprise.

Note: Chittagong Stock Exchange and Dhaka Stock Exchange use the same listing requirements for the main board and SME platform.

Source: ADB Asia SME Monitor 2021. Data from Chittagong Stock Exchange and Dhaka Stock Exchange.

Table 3.9: Policies and Regulations

Regulations	
Name	**Outline**
Companies Act, 1994	Registration and regulation on companies.
Bank Company Act, 1992	Regulation on banking activities.
Prudential Regulations for Small Enterprise Financing (Bangladesh Bank)	Guidelines and regulations for MSME financing by banks and nonbank finance institutions.
Microcredit Regulatory Authority Act, 2006	Regulation on nongovernment microfinance institutions included.
Securities and Exchange Comission Act, 1993	Establishment and regulation on BSEC.

Regulators and Policymakers	
Name	**Responsibility**
Ministry of Industries (MOI)	Industrial policies, including MSME development.
National Council for Industrial Development (NCID)	Implement actionplans under the national industrial policy including MSME development.
Bangladesh Bank (BB)	Regulate and supervise commercial banks and nonbank finance institutions.
Microcredit Regulatory Authority (MRA)	Regulate and supervise nongovernment microfinance institutions (NGO-MFIs).
Bangladesh Securities and Exchange Commission (BSEC)	Regulate and supervise capital markets, including SME platforms.

Policies		
Name	**Responsible Entity**	**Outline**
MSME development		
National Industrial Policy 2016 (March 2016)	MOI	The third policy following the National Industrial Policy 2005 and 2010. The National Industrial Policy 2021 is under drafting by the MOI (As of February 2021). The policy formed the National Council for Industrial Development (NCID) for the effective implementation of policy actions. The Executive Committee for National Council for Industrial Development (ECNCID), chaired by Minister of the MOI, works under the NCID. The policy includes CMSME definition (amendment), CMSME development, economic zone/industrial park/high-tech park/cluster development, state-owned industry reform, product quality control/productivity enhancement, intellectual property creation and management, women entrepreneurship development, export industry development, foreign direct investment, industrial technology, environment-friendly industry management, skill development, and monitoring and evaluation.
National Innovation and Intellectual Property Policy 2018 (November 2018)	MOI	1) Enhance intellectual property (IP) awareness and encourage creativity and innovation. 2) Modernize intellectual property rights (IPR) administration. 3) Create IP and derive economic and commercial benefits. 4) Strengthen the legal framework. 5) Foster respect for IPR. 6) Protect, promote, and manage Traditional Knowledge and Traditional Cultural Expressions (TK&TCEs) and Genetic Resources.
SME Policy 2019 (September 2019)	MOI	Target: SME contribution to GDP to be increased from 25% to 32% by 2024. 11 strategic goals: 1) Improving investment and business environment and institutional framework. 2) Increasing scope of access to finance in SME sector. 3) Enhancing competitive capability and support to access of SME products into the market. 4) SME business support services, support to start-up businesses set up in a short period of time and with low cost. 5) SME cluster-based enterprise network development and expansion. 6) Increasing the use of information, communication, and other technologies. 7) Expansion of skill development, education, and training programs for SME entrepreneurs. 8) Extending programs for women entrepreneurship development and provide specialized services. 9) Establishing SMEs as effective linkage to large industry and protection of SME products. 10) Development of capacity for establishing environment friendly SME industries and industrial waste management. 11) Institutionalizing SME statistics and conduct research and development.

Table 3.2 *continued*

Perspective Plan of Bangladesh 2021-2041 (March 2020)	Bangladesh Planning Commission Ministry of Planning	A long-term national development strategy to implement the Vision 2041 (national development framework). Growth and poverty targets for fiscal year (FY) 2041: real GDP growth of 9.9%; extreme poverty ratio of less than 1.0%; reducing poverty to less than 3.0%. The Plan includes the improvement of access to finance for the poor, addressing: 1) enhanced dynamics of small urban and rural enterprises in manufacturing and services by establishing a Small Business Development Authority (SBDA) as a one stop shop for promoting small business enterprises; 2) internationalization of SMEs and individual entrepreneurs (micro-multinationals) with digitization and tightly connected global networks to compete in the global marketplace. 3) integrating SMEs with the national innovation system.
Access to finance		
Small and Medium Enterprise (SME) Credit Policies & Programmes (2010)	BB	Guidelines formulated by the newly created department (SME and Special Programmes Department [SMESPD] of Bangladesh Bank) for compliance of the banks and financial institutions for the development of SME sector, including an indicative target for SME loan disbursement (the first time in Bangladesh).
CMSME Financing Policies (various issues of SMESPD circulares, 2016-2020)	BB	1) Fixing up the target for CMSME net outstanding for each bank and nonbank finance institution. 2) Operating refinance schemes for encouraging banks and nonbank finance institutions to disburse credit to CMSME sector. 3) Special policy support for women entrepreneurs." 4) Development of manufacturing and services sector emphasized as compared to trade. 5) Encouraging banks and nonbank finance institutions (with less branches in rural areas) to use the linkage with microfinance institutions to disburse credit to cottage and micro sector. 6) Banks and financial institutions encouraged to invest in cluster and value chain based industry that is developed in a certain area centering one or more products or services. 7) Decision relating to the CMSME loan application to be made within 10 working days of receiving the full application (the relevant customer/applicant must be informed in writing about the decision).
National Financial Inclusion Strategy of Bangladesh 2020-2024 (July 2019)	BB	12 strategic goals: 1) Increase financial deepening. 2) Strengthen payment system and service delivery channel. 3) Establish robust data and measurement framework. 4) Promote financial literacy and consumer empowerment. 5) Broaden and deepen financial inclusion of women, population affected by climate change and other underserved segment of population. 6) Upscale digital financial services and fintech. 7) Strengthen the policy and regulatory environment. 8) Fortify risk management of financial inclusion initiatives. 9) Strengthen the insurance services. 10) Reinforce the capital market services. 11) Fortify microfinance services. 12) Strengthen quasi-regulated financial service providers like BPO, BHBFC, BMDF, PKSF, Samabay Bank, Ekti Bari Ekti Khamar and Palli Sanchay Bank to facilitate their financial services by complying applicable regulatory requirements.

( ) = year when the program/initiative was launched.

CMSME = cottage, micro, small, and medium-sized enterprises; MSME = micro, small, and medium-sized enterprise.

Source: ADB Asia SME Monitor 2021 database. Data from SME and Special Programmes Department (SMESPD), Bangladesh Bank; SME Foundation; and Micro Credit Regulatory Authority of Bangladesh.

Table 3.10: COVID-19 Emergency Measures

Name	Fund Size (Tk billion)	Outline
1. Special loan and investment facility for CMSME sector (2020)	200	The package offers working capital loans for cottage, micro, small, and medium-sized enterprises (CMSMEs) affected by COVID-19. Under this package, banks and nonbank finance institutions will disburse loans from their own fund to CMSMEs/entrepreneurs at 9% lending rate (with government interest rate subsidy of 5%, substantially at 4% lending rate to CMSME borrowers). The loan tenor is for 3 years (but 1 year for individual entrepreneurs). 35% of the total package is allocated for trading and services, and the rest is for manufacturing sector. 70% of the total loan is allotted for cottage, micro, and small enterprises, and the remaining 30% goes to the medium-sized enterprises. Per Bangladesh Bank circular, 5% of the total loan should be earmarked to women entrepreneurs, and 15% should be disbursed to rural areas. Bangladesh Bank forms a special refinance scheme to refinance 50% of total disbursements under this stimulus package to banks and nonbank finance institutions. In addition, a credit guarantee scheme of Tk1,000 crore (Tk10 billion) will be implemented to facilitate loans under the stimulus package for entrepreneurs who cannot provide collateral against the loans. To implement this stimulus package, SME and Special Programmes Department (SMESPD) of Bangladesh Bank has issued a circular detailing about eligibility, application, conditions, reporting, and other terms of the package on 13 April 2020.
2. Revolving refinance scheme for CMSME sector (2020)	100	The scheme, established on 26 April 2020, provides working capital facility to CMSME entrepreneurs. Under this scheme, banks and nonbank finance institutions can get refinance from SMESPD up to 50% of the loan disbursed at 4% interest rate (bank rate).
3. Stimulus package for CMSME sector (special attention on marginal entrepreneurs) (2020)	15.1	The package aims to support various activities that improve the living standards of marginalized people and is allocated as follows:
	3.0	Small and Medium Enterprise Foundation (for small, cottage, medium industries, and women entrepreneurs)
	1.0	Bangladesh Small and Cottage Industries Corporation
	0.5	Jayita Foundation
	0.5	NGO Foundation
	3.0	Social Development Foundation
	3.0	Rural Poverty Alleviation Foundation
	1.0	Small Farmers Development Foundation
	3.1	Bangladesh Rural Development Board
4. Livelihood Restoration Loan (LRL) Program (2020-2021)	5	To improve lives and livelihood for the COVID-19-affected people in rural economy, LRL covers all 64 districts of the country excepting city corporation and district headquarters areas. In response to this and to resuming production and compensating for the loss already incurred, the process of necessary support for flexible, low-interest-rate loans from PKSF and its partner organizations (POs) for the micro entrepreneurs, marginal and small farmers, and trained and skilled young entrepreneurs has started from September 2020. The loan program has contributed to the revival and creation of livelihoods opportunities for the victims of the pandemic. It helpes restore economic activities and enable entrepreneurs to invest afresh in their businesses. Both household income and overall cash flow in the rural economy have increased.
5. Microenterprise Development Project (Asian Development Bank) (2021-2022)	4.25	ADB has provided additional funding of $50.0 million loan along with $0.5 million technical assistance grant for restoring the economic activities of the COVID-19-affected microenterprises by increasing liquidity supply in the rural economy. The project aims to provide working capital support to 30,000 micro entrepreneurs badly affected by the pandemic nationwide.
6. Promoting Agricultural Commercialization and Enterprises (PACE) Project (additional financing by IFAD) (2021-2022)	3.14	The additional financing of the PACE project aims to provide loan support with Tk2.57 billion and Tk0.57 billion grant support for value chain development of the COVID-19-affected microenterprises.
Grand Total (Tk billion)	**327.49**	

Source: ADB Asia SME Monitor 2021 database. Data from Central Bank of Sri Lanka website (https://www.cbsl.gov.lk/en/covid-19-measures), Securities and Exchange Commission of Sri Lanka website (https://www.sec.gov.lk/index.php/sec-covid-19-response/), Industrial Development Board, and Department of Development Finance.

Country Review
India

Overview

In fiscal year (FY) 2020 (ended 31 March 2020), gross domestic product (GDP) reached ₹146 trillion, up by 4.0% from the previous year. However, in FY2021, estimates show GDP declined by 7.3% to ₹135 trillion, largely the result of the coronavirus disease (COVID-19) pandemic.[46] With a population of 1.3 billion, the labor force participation rate was 37.5% with a 2018 unemployment rate of 5.8%.[47,48] Micro, small, and medium-sized enterprises (MSMEs) play a crucial role in driving the country's economy. There are an estimated 63 million MSMEs employing 111 million workers. MSMEs contribute 30% of GDP and account for about half of total export values. Access to finance is among the chronic challenges faced by MSMEs in India. The central bank considers MSMEs a priority sector and directs banks to allocate 40% of their lending portfolios to priority sectors including MSMEs. However, MSMEs remain underserved, holding just 17.6% of total commercial bank loans outstanding in 2020. Nonbank finance institutions, including microfinance institutions, provide a viable alternate source of MSME funding, although they remain small in scale. Equity markets dedicated to MSMEs have supported their growth capital funding, but they remain at a nascent stage. Nonetheless, intragovernmental coordination of MSME policy making is well organized within the National Board for MSMEs. The central bank launched a National Strategy for Financial Inclusion in 2020, which promotes increased access to formal financial services for MSMEs.

1. COVID-19 Impact on MSMEs

India experienced its first wave of COVID-19 during February–March 2020. As a result, in March the country imposed a lockdown, its strictest quarantine measure during which only essential establishments such as drug stores, hospitals, vegetable shops, and general provision stores remained open. Other activities such as e-commerce of essential goods and restaurant delivery were allowed. All other economic activities were restricted across the entire country. The restrictions held until 30 May, followed by a phased resumption of economic activity beginning in June through December. Nonetheless, the first wave peaked in September with approximately 100,000 cases daily. Afterward, the number of daily active cases declined gradually. The lockdown significantly affected the economy, leading to significant losses of business income and employment. MSMEs were the most affected, with the highest impact on micro and small industries.

GDP is expected to contract by 7.3% in FY2021 due to the stringent lockdowns. However, it is estimated that the economy will recover FY2022, with the economy rebounding by 10.0%. According to the Centre for Monitoring Indian Economy, the unemployment rate increased from 9.4% in March 2020 to 23.5% in April and 21.7% in May

46 Government of India, National Statistical Office. 2021. Provisional Estimates Of Annual National Income, 2020-21 and Quarterly Estimates (Q4) Of Gross Domestic Product, 2020-21. Press Note. 31 May. https://www.mospi.gov.in/documents/213904/416359/Press%20Note_31-05-2021_m1622547951213.pdf/7140019f-69b7-974b-2d2d-7630c3b0768d.

47 Asian Development Bank (ADB) Key Indicators Database for Asia and the Pacific. https://kidb.adb.org/

48 Labor force participation: http://mospi.nic.in/sites/default/files/publication_reports/Annual_Report_PLFS_2018_19_HL.pdf

(Figure 4.1A). Employment in informal MSME sectors was affected most. The unemployment rate was higher in urban areas (25.0% in April 2020 and 23.1% in May) than rural areas (22.9% and 21.1%). Employment remained stable only in businesses that provided essential services.

There are several COVID-19 impact studies on businesses in India. One survey conducted during 15–31 May 2020 of 14,444 MSMEs by nonbank finance company Magma Fincorp found that around half of MSMEs saw a 20%–50% decrease in earnings.[49] Responses were consistent for both essential and non-essential goods manufacturers. Similarly, a Credit Rating Information Services of India Limited report found that microenterprises, which account for 32% of total MSME debt, had the greatest problems in terms of revenue growth; margins (earnings before interest, taxes, depreciation, and amortization); and working-capital requirements.[50]

An assessment of the COVID-19 impact on MSMEs was also conducted by the National Small Industries Corporation (NSIC) and the Khadi and Village Industries Commission (KVIC)—both under the Ministry of MSMEs, according to a *Rajya Sabha* (upper house) report in August 2021.[51] The NSIC study showed that while 91% of MSMEs were operational, their liquidity (51%) and lack of new orders (17%) were key challenges for continuing operations. The KVIC study reported that 88% of the units set up under the Prime Minister's Employment Generation Programme were negatively affected by the pandemic, while the remaining 12% benefited. Among the MSME units that were negatively affected, 57% had to shut down temporarily with another 30% experiencing reduced production and revenue.

Tamil Nadu, a major state in South India, accounts for 7.8% of India's total MSMEs. A survey conducted in May–June 2020 by the Indian Institute of Technology, a leading technology institution in the state, found that 78% of MSMEs temporarily shut down due to the pandemic, with 79% micro and small enterprises. The survey also found that 74% of MSMEs incurred revenue losses of more than 80%.[52]

A study by the Reserve Bank of India (RBI) found that hospitality and tourism, along with the automotive and aviation sectors, were significantly impacted by the pandemic. According to HVS Anarock, a hospitality consultancy, the industry had an average occupancy rate of 10% in April 2020.[53] This improved to 26% in September due to the gradual reopening of domestic travel. Several hotels were repurposed as quarantine centers and COVID-19 hospitals. The industry was expected to lose ₹900 billion in revenue in 2020, with occupancy and average daily rates returning to pre-pandemic levels only in 2024.

A survey of hoteliers conducted during mid-June and July 2020 by the Federation of Indian Chambers of Commerce and Industry (FICCI), a leading chamber of commerce in India, found that 58.4% of the hoteliers had shut down operations completely due to the lockdown and pandemic (Figure 4.1B).[54] A small proportion remained open as quarantine or residential facilities for COVID-19 front-liners. Indians returning from numerous countries were required to quarantine in these hotels. Approximately 1.7 million passengers were brought back by Air India, the national carrier. A small number of hotels kept their kitchens open for food delivery purposes. The survey was conducted among 248 hotel and tour operators based in 24 cities.

49 The financial impact of COVID-19 on Indian MSMEs and their outlook amid the pandemic. https://magma.co.in/wp-content/uploads/2020/10/MAGMA-SPJIMR-Report-min-1.pdf

50 CRISIL. MSMEs face existential crisis, revenue to fall a fifth. https://www.crisil.com/en/home/newsroom/press-releases/2020/06/msmes-face-existential-crisis-revenue-to-fall-a-fifth.html.

51 Rajya Sabha reply to the question from the Ministry of MSMEs about the impact of COVID-19 pandemic on MSMEs, dated on 3 August 2021.

52 Covid-19 Outbreak and the Micro Small Medium Enterprises: A study of Tamil Nadu.

53 M. Lamba. Hotel occupancy up from 10% in April 2020 to about 26% in September 2020. AnaRock. https://www.anujpuri.com/india-hotel-occupancy-up/.

54 FICCI. Hotels And Tour Operator's Survey on the Impact of Covid-19 on the Travel & Hospitality Industry. https://ficci.in/spdocument/23346/Tour-Survey.pdf.

The country experienced a second wave of COVID-19 infections in March 2021, with the number of daily active cases significantly higher than the first wave. While the central government did not impose a nationwide lockdown, more than 30 affected states/union territories enforced strict lockdowns with similar stringency levels as during the first wave.[55] The second lockdown further damaged the sustainability of MSMEs.

Figure 4.1: COVID-19 Impact on Employment and the Hospitality Industry

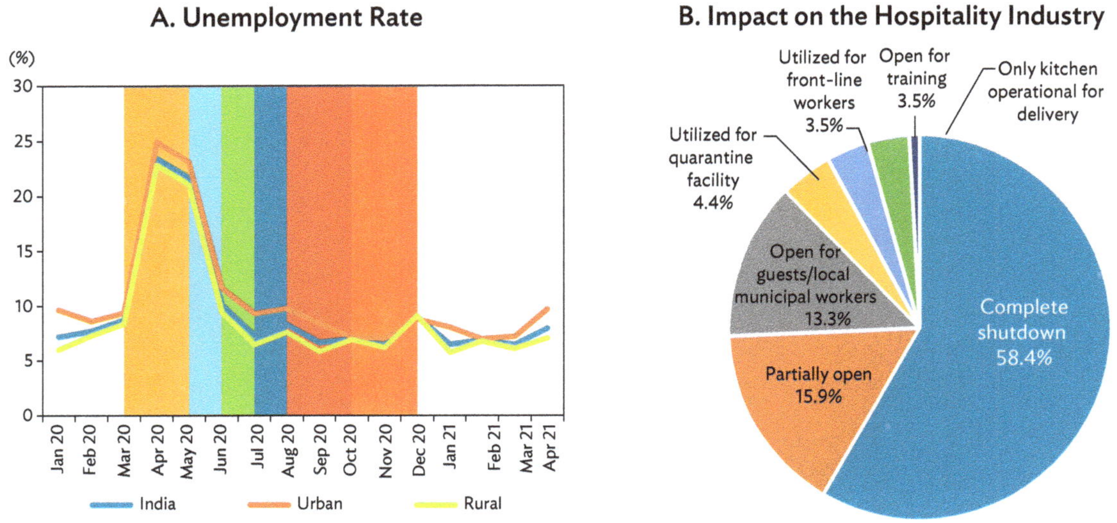

Note: Color bars denote phases of reopening of economic activities from June 2020 onwards.

Source: Centre for Monitoring Indian Economy Unemployment report.

Source: Federation of Indian Chambers of Commerce and Industry. Hotels And Tour Operator's Survey on the Impact of Covid-19 on the Travel & Hospitality Industry. https://ficci.in/spdocument/23346/Tour-Survey.pdf.

2. MSME Development

- The MSME definition was amended in 2020 by size of turnover and investment. Some 63 million MSMEs, or 99%, operate nationwide, with microenterprises and trading firms holding the largest share. Only 4% of MSMEs are registered (2.5 million).
- MSMEs employ 111 million people; one-third of which work in trade with another one-third in manufacturing. Over one-third of MSME employees work in Uttar Pradesh, West Bengal, and Tamil Nadu.
- MSMEs have contributed about 30% of India's GDP since FY2012. Manufacturing gross value added by MSMEs in FY2020 was more than double that in FY2012.
- The majority of MSMEs serve the domestic market. Initiatives such as the One District One Product and Production Linked Incentives focus on increasing MSME participation in exports and integration with global value chains.
- Start-ups and e-commerce firms are actively adopting technology. E-commerce has provided MSMEs with opportunities to access new markets and develop innovative business models, backed by 760 million internet connections in 2020.
- More than 170 business associations and MSME development organizations provide information, knowledge, and network support for MSMEs.

[55] *From Delhi to Kerala: States across India extend lockdowns*, 24 May 2021, accessed via indianexpress.com.

Scale of MSMEs

In India, MSMEs are classified based on turnover and investment in plant and machinery—following the Micro, Small, and Medium Enterprises Development (MSMED) Act of 2006 (Table 4.1). The classification applies to firms in both manufacturing and services. A new MSME classification was introduced on 1 July 2020 as an amendment of the MSMED Act.[56] The previous definition of MSMEs was based only on investment in plant and machinery/ equipment. It also differed for manufacturing and services firms. The financial limits defined under the earlier classification were low compared with the amended classification. The revised definition is expected to cover some 99% of MSMEs. They are classified as: (i) microenterprise: a firm with investment in plant and machinery or equipment not more than ₹10 million and annual turnover not more than ₹50 million; (ii) small enterprise: a firm with investment in plant and machinery or equipment not more than ₹100 million and annual turnover not more than ₹500 million; and (iii) medium-sized enterprise: a firm with investment in plant and machinery or equipment not more than ₹500 million and annual turnover not more than ₹2.5 billion.

MSME data is based on the Survey on Unincorporated Non-Agricultural Enterprises (excluding construction) conducted in the 73rd National Sample Survey from July 2015 to June 2016.[57] The survey was conducted by the Central Statistics Office under the Ministry of Statistics and Programme Implementation. It collected information on original investments in plant and machinery/equipment based on which unincorporated enterprises were classified either as MSMEs or non-MSMEs. The survey identified 99.9% of unincorporated non-agricultural enterprises as MSMEs, mostly microenterprises. The remainder was categorized as other services—including firms involved in wholesale and retail trade of motor vehicles and motorcycles. The government has not updated the data since then. The Ministry of MSMEs does not maintain any database of firms except *Udyam* Registration (MSMEs registered under the MSMED Act).

Data on MSMEs derive from different sources for various years, creating significant variations in the number of units. Data from FY2008 to FY2016 are based on the Fourth All India Census of MSME, conducted with FY2007 as reference. Data collection was done in 2009 with the results published in 2011. Subsequently, the number of MSMEs is estimated based on the 73rd National Sample Survey using 2015–2016 data. The survey estimated that there were 63.4 million MSMEs operating FY2018 (Figure 4.2A and Table 4.2). By sector, MSMEs in trade accounted for 36.3% of MSMEs, followed by other services such as land transport and food services (32.6%) and manufacturing (31.0%) (Figure 4.2B). Rural MSMEs accounted for 51.3% with 48.7% in urban areas.[58]

Male-owned MSMEs accounted for 79.6%, with the remaining 20.4% female-owned. Male-owned MSMEs were more urban (81.6% as compared to 77.8% in rural areas).[59] The top 10 states accounted for 74.0% of MSMEs in FY2018. Uttar Pradesh (14.2%) and West Bengal (14%) held the highest share (Figure 4.2C).

The Ministry of MSMEs introduced the *Udyam* Registration portal on 1 July 2020 for paperless, self-declared registration and classification of enterprises. *Udyam* is Hindi for business or enterprise. Any person setting up an MSME is required to file an *Udyam* Registration at the online portal. All MSMEs are encouraged to obtain an *Udyam* certificate including *Udyog Aadhaar*—a 12-digit unique identification number provided by the Ministry of MSMEs. Those with an *Udyam* certificate are eligible for benefits under numerous government schemes. According to the Ministry, 2,507,112 MSMEs, or only 4% of the total, have registered on the Udyam portal as of March 2021.[60]

56 The Gazette of India. 2020. New MSME definition.https://rbidocs.rbi.org.in/rdocs/content/pdfs/IndianGazzate02072020.pdf.

57 Operational Characteristics of Unincorporated Non-Agricultural Enterprises (Excluding Construction) in India, 73rd National Sample Survey, Ministry of Statistics and Programme Implementation.

58 Urban area is defined as (i) all places with a municipality, corporation, cantonment board or notified town area committee and (ii) all other places that have (a) a minimum population of 5,000, (b) at least 75% of the male main working population engaged in non-agricultural pursuits; and (c) a population density of at least 400 persons per square kilometer.

59 Ministry of MSMEs, Annual Report 2020–2021.

60 Financial Express. 2021. MSME registration crosses 25-lakh mark on Modi govt's Udyam portal; grows 130% in nearly five months. 28 March. https://www.financialexpress.com/industry/sme/msme-tech-msme-registration-crosses-25-lakh-mark-on-modi-govts-udyam-portal-grows-130-in-nearly-five-months/2222324/.

Figure 4.2: Number of MSMEs

A. Overall MSMEs

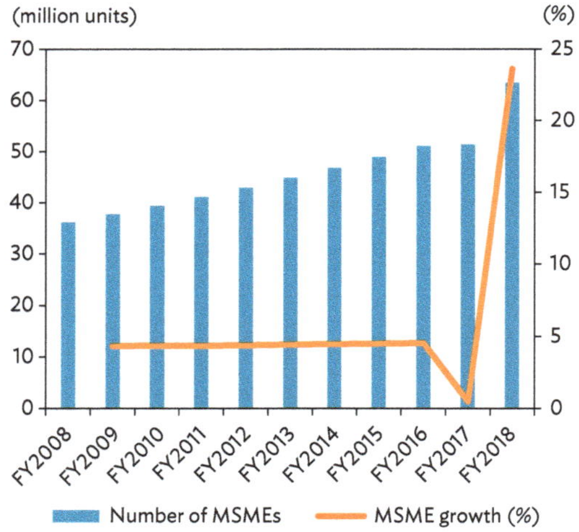

MSME = micro, small, and medium-sized enterprise.

Source: ADB Asia SME Monitor 2021 database. Data from Ministry of MSMEs Annual Reports.

B. By Sector, FY2018

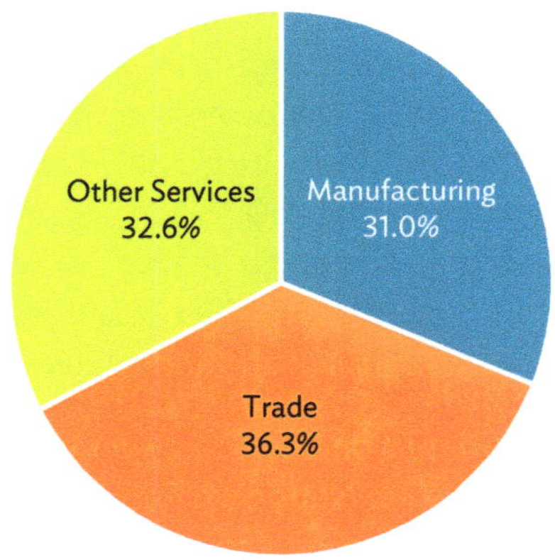

FY = fiscal year.

Note: 3,000 units in non-captive electricity generation and transmission.

Source: ADB Asia SME Monitor 2021 database. Data from estimate based on the 73rd National Sample Survey

C. By Region, FY2018

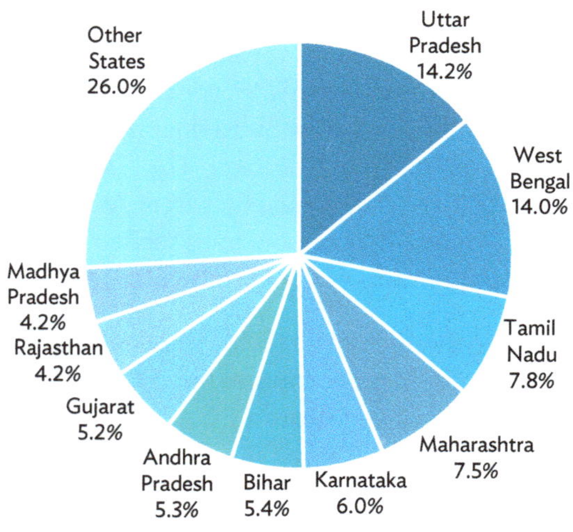

FY = fiscal year.

Source: ADB Asia SME Monitor 2021 database. Data from Ministry of MSMEs Annual Report 2020-21.

Employment

Based on the 2015–2016 data captured by the 73rd National Sample Survey, it was estimated that MSMEs employed approximately 111 million people in FY2018 (Figure 4.3A). MSMEs in manufacturing employed 32.5%, trade employed 34.9%, with the remaining 32.6% employed by MSMEs in other services such as food and land transport (Figure 4.3B). Among the 111 million people employed by MSMEs, 49.8 million people (44.9%) were in urban areas and 61.2 million (55.2%) were rural. Males accounted for 76.1% of MSME employees, with the remaining 23.9% female (footnote 59).

The majority were employed in the micro sector (107.6 million people or 96.9%) in FY2018. Small and medium-sized enterprises accounted for 2.9% and 0.2% of those employed.

Figure 4.3: Employment by MSMEs

A. Overall MSMEs

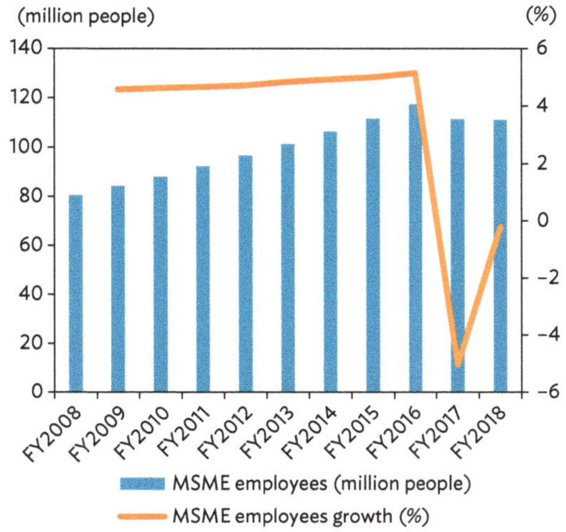

MSME = micro, small, and medium-sized enterprise.

Source: ADB Asia SME Monitor 2021 database. Data from Ministry of MSMEs Annual Reports.

B. By Sector, FY2018

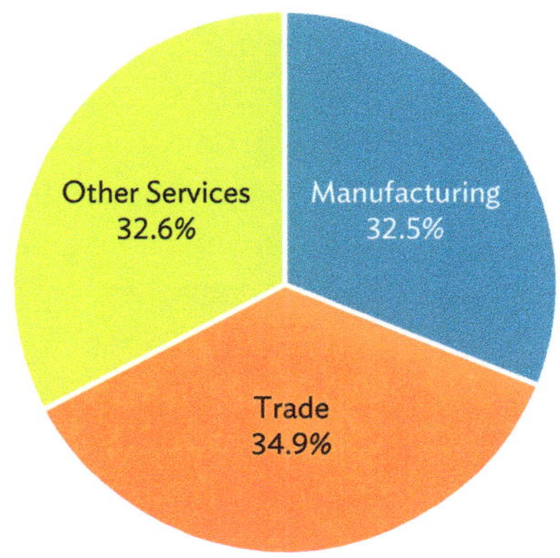

FY = fiscal year.

Note: 7,000 in non-captive electricity generation and transmission.

Source: ADB Asia SME Monitor 2021 database. Data from estimate based on the 73rd National Sample Survey.

C. By Region, FY2018

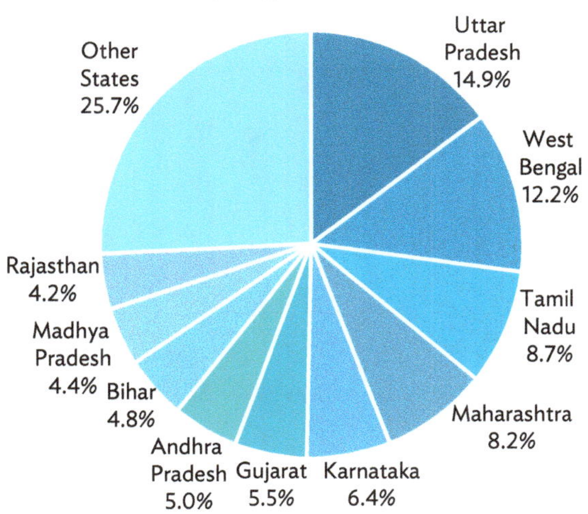

FY = fiscal year.

Source: ADB Asia SME Monitor 2021 database. Data from Ministry of MSMEs Annual Report 2020-2021.

The top 10 states accounted for 74.3% of total MSME employment in FY2018, with the top three: Uttar Pradesh (14.9%), West Bengal (12.2%), and Tamil Nadu (8.7%) (Figure 4.3C). The share of male employees in Uttar Pradesh was 83.5%, West Bengal 67.8%, and Tamil Nadu 66.6%.

Business Productivity

MSMEs contributed ₹24,366 billion to GDP in FY2008. By FY2019, it had increased by 73.7% to ₹42,322 billion (a compounded annual growth rate [CAGR] of 5.1%) (Figure 4.4A). In FY2018, the GDP growth of MSMEs was 8.9%, matching the high of FY2012. Growth fell to a still robust 8.0% in FY2019. The MSME share of national GDP was 30.3% in FY2019, a 5.1% decrease compared with 35.4% in FY2008. From FY2012 to FY2019, however, MSME contributions to India's GDP has been a steady 30%.

The Ministry of MSMEs introduced the Scheme for Micro and Small Enterprises Cluster Development Program, a cluster development approach to augment MSME productivity and competitiveness. The program provides incentives for MSMEs doing similar work to form clusters. It provides funding to establish common facility centres (CFCs) for production/processing, product design, and research and development (R&D). CFCs build and upgrade infrastructure and promote green, sustainable manufacturing technologies. There were 76 CFCs and 169 infrastructure development projects by FY2020.[61]

MSME gross value added (GVA) in manufacturing grew 136.4% from ₹25,833 billion in FY2012 to ₹61,072 billion in FY2020 (13.1% CAGR). In FY2020, the share of MSME GVA to total GVA was 34.8%. MSME GVA growth decelerated from 13.3% in FY2019 to 6.2% in FY2020 (Figure 4.4B).

Figure 4.4: MSME Contribution to Economic Output

A. MSME Contribution to GDP

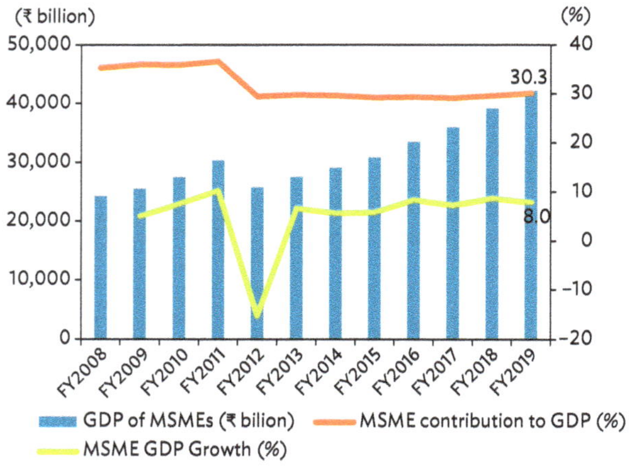

FY = fiscal year; GDP = gross domestic product; MSME = micro, small, and medium-sized enterprise.

Note: FY ends 31 March.

Source: ADB Asia SME Monitor 2021 database. Data from Ministry of MSMEs Annual Reports.

B. MSME Contribution to GVA

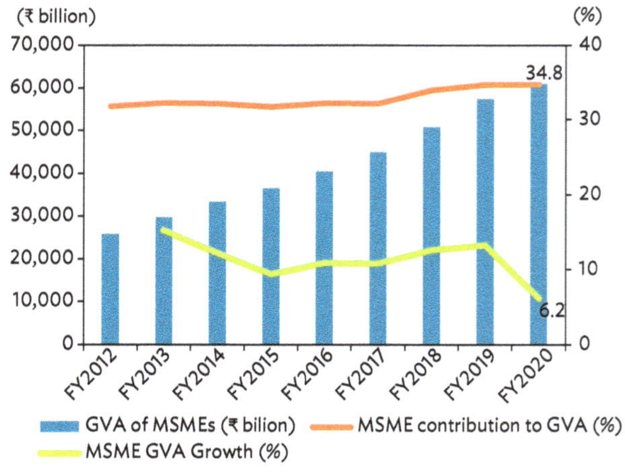

FY = fiscal year; GVA = gross value added; MSME = micro, small, and medium-sized enterprise.

Note: FY ends 31 March.

Source: ADB Asia SME Monitor 2021 database. Data from Ministry of MSMEs Annual Reports.

[61] Ministry of MSMEs, Annual Report 2019-2020.

Market Access

Most MSMEs mainly serve the domestic market. Still, those that export contribute significantly to the country's overall exports. In FY2021, for example, MSME exports were valued at $127,695 million, accounting for 49.8% of the total exports (Figure 4.5A). MSME exports have increased at a CAGR of 2.9% from FY2013 through 2020. However, in FY2021, MSME exports fell sharply by 17.5% due to decreased foreign demand due to the COVID-19 pandemic.

During the FY2013 to FY2021 period, total exports increased the most in FY2018 (10.0%), supported by a 7.5% growth in MSME exports. Export growth began contracting in FY2020, falling 6.0%, with MSME exports down 2.8%. They contracted further in FY2021 (Figure 4.5B).

Pre-pandemic, the largest drop was in FY2016 (-15.5%), with MSME exports falling by 5.9%. One of the main reasons export values fell was global recessionary trends, especially in the United States (US) and the European Union.[62] This reduced global demand, coupled with weaker commodity prices. The value of India's petroleum product exports was hit hard due to the decline in crude prices. In FY2021, total export values decreased by 17.6% due to the pandemic. MSME imports were also affected, declining by 20.4% in FY2021 ($110,465) (Table 4.2).

Figure 4.5: MSME Exports

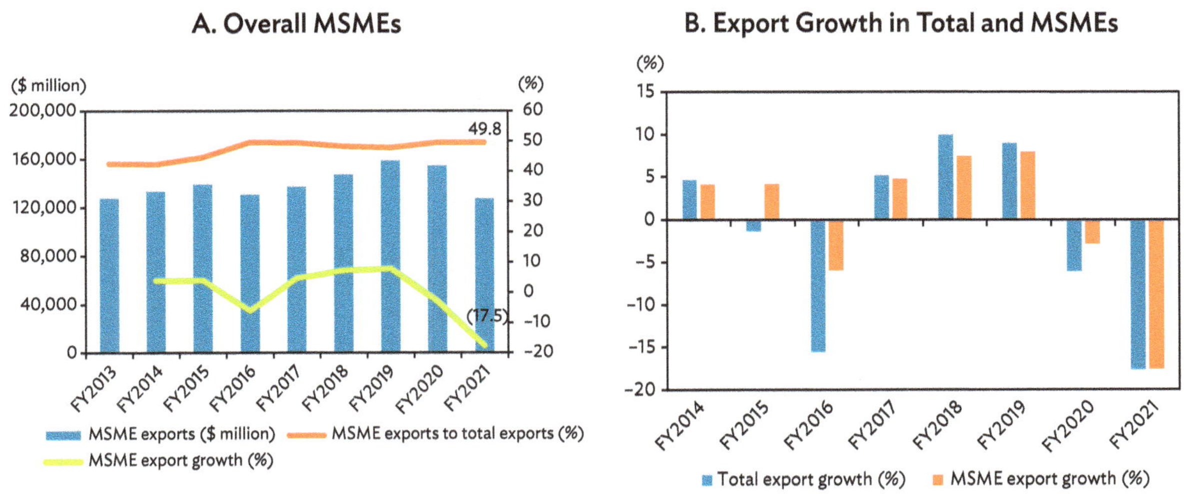

FY = fiscal year; GDP = gross domestic product; MSME = micro, small, and medium-sized enterprise.

Note: FY ends 31 March.

Source: ADB Asia SME Monitor 2021 database. Data from Ministry of MSMEs Annual Reports.

FY = fiscal year; GVA = gross value added; MSME = micro, small, and medium-sized enterprise.

Note: FY ends 31 March.

Source: ADB Asia SME Monitor 2021 database. Data from Ministry of MSMEs Annual Reports.

---

62 Lok Sabha reply on impact of recession on Exports: Government of India, Ministry of Commerce and Industry. Impact of Recession on Exports. http://164.100.24.220/loksabhaquestions/annex/8/AU2506.pdf.

63 Lok Sabha reply on MSME Exports.

In March 2020, India accounted for 80.0% of the world's coir production. Coir is a coarse fiber extracted from husk—the outer coconut shell. It is mainly manufactured by rural micro enterprises. It is a traditional export-oriented industry with exports to the US, the People's Republic of China (PRC), the Netherlands, the Republic of Korea, and the United Kingdom, among others. In FY2020, coir exports were valued at ₹27,579 million, an increase of 45.0% since FY2016. In FY2021, the US accounted for 30.3% of India's total coir exports, followed by the PRC (22.6%) (footnote 59).

To increase exports and global value chain participation, the government introduced a production-linked incentive in November 2020 covering 10 sectors—electronics, pharmaceuticals, food products, textiles, telecoms, specialty steel, white goods (AC and LED), high-efficiency solar modules, automobiles and auto components, and advanced chemistry batteries.[64] Thus, incentives have shifted away from supporting capital expenditures to making them performance-linked. The government will provide companies a production-linked incentive of 4%–6% on incremental sales (over base FY2020) for locally made goods for 5 years.

Box 4.1: One District One Product Initiative to Provide Greater Market Access

In 2018, the state of Uttar Pradesh, among the largest in India, introduced the One District One Product (ODOP) initiative. The concept is part of the state's micro, small, and medium-sized enterprise (MSME) policy. The objective is to improve the quality of products manufactured by MSMEs and craftsmen in each state district. This will enable them to compete and sell their products in domestic and international markets. The initiative also provides a distinct identity to the 75 districts in the state according to identified products. The state government provides both financial and marketing support to the artisans engaged in manufacturing these products. Uttar Pradesh accounts for 44% of India's handicrafts exports, including 39% of carpet and 26% of leather and leather product exports. Overall, Uttar Pradesh's share in total exports is 4.7%.

The Government of Uttar Pradesh launched an annual trade fair to showcase products produced by traditional industries and MSMEs. The initiative is also linked to numerous central government MSME development schemes—such as the Micro Units Development and Refinance Agency (MUDRA) and Prime Minister Employment Guarantee Program. Products selected in Uttar Pradesh are the carpets from Bhadohi, brassware from Moradabad, locks from Aligarh, black pottery from Mirzapur, crockery from Khurja, and leather from Agra and Kanpur. Under the "A Day with MSME" initiative, state government officials spend a day with individual MSME entrepreneurs to understand their work and the problems they face. The Small Industries Development Bank of India implements MSME finance policies in India. It works with 10 districts in Uttar Pradesh to provide credit support and technical expertise to each district's artisans.

The central government has now adopted the ODOP initiative and extended it to the rest of the country. It aims to reach 700 districts across India to promote traditional industries in each district. The Ministry of Commerce and Industry is working with state and central government agencies to promote the ODOP initiative. The objective is to convert each district into an export hub by identifying products with export potential, addressing bottlenecks for exporting these products, and supporting local exporters/manufacturers to scale up production. During its first phase, 106 products have been identified from 103 districts across 27 states. A district export promotion committee has been established in each district, except for those in West Bengal. Draft Export Action Plans have been finalized for 451 districts across the country.

Source: ODOP website, Government of Uttar Pradesh; Press Information Bureau - Ministry of Commerce One District One Product Scheme. Accessed on 2 June 2021.

[64] Production Linked Incentive Scheme: Government of India, Press Information Bureau. Cabinet approves PLI Scheme to 10 key Sectors for Enhancing India's Manufacturing Capabilities and Enhancing Exports – Atmanirbhar Bharat. Press release. https://pib.gov.in/PressReleasePage.aspx?PRID=1671915.

The government also introduced the government e-marketplace (GeM), an online portal for central and state government organizations to procure goods and services. According to Rule 149 of the General Financial Rules-2017, central ministries/departments must use the portal to procure goods and services. GeM is a market-based procurement system open to both MSMEs and large firms. However, there are special initiatives to encourage MSMEs and start-ups to participate. There are provisions that reduce requirements on prior experience/turnover for micro and small enterprises, including start-ups. In addition, the portal allows start-ups to sell their products on a trial basis. As of March 2021, 57.9% of the portal's order value came from MSMEs, with 406,936 MSMEs registered on the site.

Technology and Innovation

Traditionally MSMEs, with few exceptions, use mostly low-level technology. They source their technology through external R&D centers, licensing technology, purchasing existing technology from vendors, and sponsored R&D in universities, among others. Numerous technology development organizations such as the Council of Scientific and Industrial Research and the Biotechnology Industry Research Assistance Council encourage MSMEs to adopt technology and supports them in developing R&D. However, the majority of these initiatives remain in the nascent stage of technology commercialization or adoption. One successful initiative is the Recognition of In-house R&D Units introduced by the Department of Scientific and Industrial Research of the Ministry of Science and Technology. The scheme provides income tax and custom duty benefits to MSMEs that establish in-house R&D units. Approximately 50,000 MSMEs have availed the scheme since its inception in 1973.[65]

The Ministry of MSMEs has introduced several initiatives/schemes to promote the adoption of technology. Three are (i) a Credit Linked Capital Subsidy for Technology Upgradation (CLCSS), (ii) lean manufacturing competitiveness for MSMEs, and (iii) helping manufacturing enterprises become more competitive through quality management standards and quality technology tools. CLCSS offers a 15% subsidy for additional investments up to ₹10 million to upgrade and MSME's technology—normally introducing state-of-the-art or near state-of-the-art technology. The lean manufacturing competitiveness scheme aims to enhance the competitiveness of manufacturing MSMEs by applying various lean manufacturing techniques.[66] The Enabling Manufacturing Sector to be Competitive scheme aims to sensitize and encourage micro and small enterprises to understand and adopt the latest quality management standards and quality technology tools—such as 6 Sigma, Total Productive Maintenance, and Quality Management Standards established by the International Organization for Standardization (ISO).

Expanding internet penetration allows MSMEs to collaborate with e-commerce firms—expediting their use of technology. New internet connections have grown 35.7%, from 560 million in 2018 to 760 million in 2020 (Figure 4.6A). India's e-commerce market is expected to reach $99.1 billion by 2024 (Figure 4.6B). E-commerce has rapidly expanded MSME market reach. Firms such as Amazon and Flipkart are tying up with MSMEs, helping them digitize and sell their products online. Amazon India organizes "Small Business Day," an online sales event that promotes MSME products.

Technology adoption in India is led by numerous start-ups that have emerged in the recent years. The government introduced a start-up action plan in January 2016 to support entrepreneurs and build a robust start-up ecosystem. The government defines a start-up as an entity less than 10 years old (from the date of incorporation/registration) with an annual turnover not exceeding ₹1 billion for any financial year since incorporation/registration.

---

65 Government of India, Department of Scientific and Industrial Research. Directory of Recognized In-House R&D Units. https://cupdf.com/document/directory-rd-2010.html.

66 Lean manufacturing techniques assist in reducing cost and enhancing productivity. A few of the lean manufacturing techniques identified include the 5S System, Total Productive Maintenance (TPM), Just in Time (JIT), and KANBAN System, among others.

Figure 4.6: Internet Connection and E-commerce in India

A. Number of New Internet Connections **B. Size of E-commerce Market**

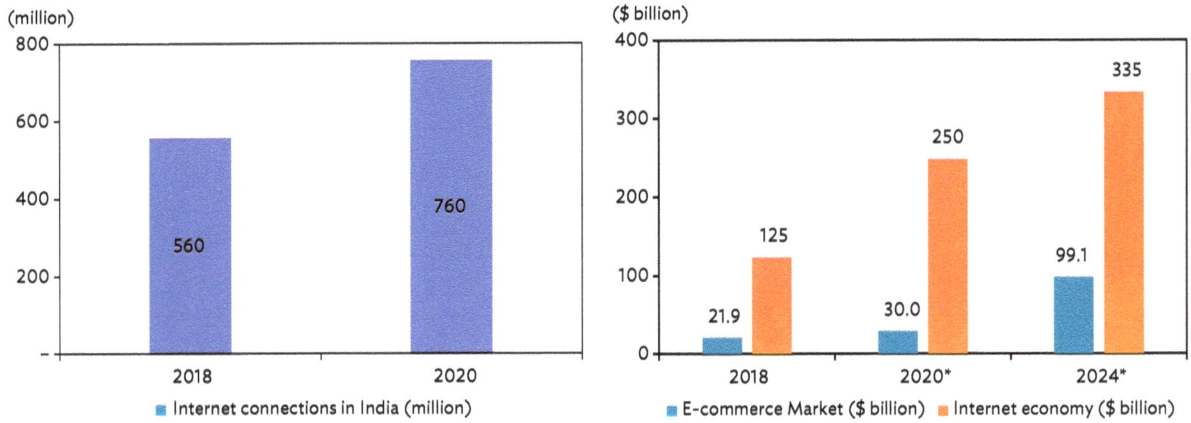

Source: ADB Asia SME Monitor 2021 database. Data from India Brand Equity Foundation.

* estimate.

Source: ADB Asia SME Monitor 2021 database. Data from India Brand Equity Foundation.

As of end-2020, there were 41,317 government-recognized start-ups spread across 601 districts (44% of the recognized start-ups have at least one female director). They employ approximately 500,000 people. More than 30 states/union territories have dedicated policies focused on developing a start-up ecosystem in their states.[67]

Networking and Support

India has more than 170 business associations or chambers of commerce.[68] The Federation of Indian Chambers of Commerce and Industry (FICCI) is among the largest. It has both direct and indirect memberships and, through its regional network, has access to more than 250,000 firms. It provides networking opportunities, business services such as conducting buyer-seller meetings and knowledge products through its numerous policy advocacy papers and newsletters. In end-2013, the FICCI established the Confederation of Micro, Small, and Medium Enterprises.[69] It has tie-ups with over 300 industry associations and chambers worldwide.

There are several MSME development organizations that provide information, knowledge, and network support to MSMEs. For example, the India SME Forum has a network of 87,200 MSME members, including about 7,000 women entrepreneur members, spread across 19 states. It provides development support to MSMEs and has conducted several studies on MSMEs.[70]

Aside from private sector initiatives on business networking and support, several government institutions such as the Ministry of Science and Technology and the Ministry of Commerce and Industry introduced several capacity development programs for MSMEs—either individually or in collaboration with international agencies.

[67] Government of India, Ministry of Commerce and Industry. Evolution of Startup India - Capturing the 5-Year Story. https://www.startupindia.gov.in/content/dam/invest-india/Templates/public/5_years_Achievement_report%20_%20PRINT.pdf.

[68] *The Economic Times.* 2021. Umbrella of 170 associations AICA to address issues of MSME sector. 22 June. https://economictimes.indiatimes.com/small-biz/sme-sector/umbrella-of-170-associations-aica-to-address-issues-of-msme-sector/articleshow/83737208.cms.

[69] FICCI. FICCI-CMSME CONNECT. http://ficci-cmsme.in/connect_cmsme/index.html.

[70] India SME Forum website. https://www.indiasmeforum.org/index.php5

They generally focus on technical and skills development. The Department of Science and Industrial Research of the Ministry of Research and Technology offers a technology incubation program—"Promoting Innovations in Individuals, Start-ups and MSMEs (PRISM)"—that provides fiscal support to individuals and start-ups in priority areas such as green technology, clean energy, industrial-use smart materials, waste-to-wealth, affordable health care, and water and sewage management.

The Ministry of MSMEs has also developed an MSME Global Mart Web Portal, an online e-marketplace for MSMEs.[71] The portal provides opportunities for MSMEs to interact with other firms for business development, subcontracting, and participation in public procurement. During FY2019 and FY2021, 63,227 firms had registered on the site (footnote 59).

3. Access to Finance

- Commercial bank credit to MSMEs increased by more than 150% during 2015–2020, but it remains small with an average 17% share of total loans. Public sector banks are a major provider of MSME loans. The MSME nonperforming loan ratio has gradually improved but remains high at over 7%.
- SIDBI and credit guarantees play vital roles in enhancing MSME access to finance. MUDRA facilitates collateral free loans to MSMEs.
- The nonbank finance industry is increasingly supplementing MSME financing through the growth of microfinance institutions and loan companies. Growing venture capital investments are also contributing to the development of ecosystem for start-ups.
- Financial technology (fintech) and digital finance that leverage public data are making big strides in enhancing MSME access to finance. Digital infrastructure like digital wallets and unified payment interfaces is a key driver in promoting MSME finance.
- Dedicated SME equity markets are expanding as growth capital financing venues for viable MSMEs. However, enhancing capital market literacy and regulatory compliance for potential issuers are key challenges for smaller firms.
- Four private credit bureaus and a centralized collateral registry operate in the country. The government is developing a public credit registry to improve MSME access to credit.

Bank Credit

The Reserve Bank of India (RBI), the central bank, regulates bank and nonbank financing. In India, banks provide loans mainly on the basis of collateral and personal guarantees. Other forms of lending such as cash-flow-based lending remain limited. The number of commercial banks rose from 80 in 2007 to 89 in 2020 (Table 4.3). While the number of public sector banks decreased from 28 in 2007 to 12 in 2020, the number of foreign banks increased significantly from 29 to 45 over the same period. In 2020, there were 22 private sector banks .

Commercial bank credit to MSMEs increased from ₹12.1 trillion in 2015 to ₹18.2 trillion in 2020, an increase of 50.9% (a CAGR of 8.6%) (Figure 4.7A). The year-on-year loan growth was highest in 2018 (16.4%) and lowest in 2016 (0.1%). The loan increase was spurred by the expanding use of digitization in the economy—including access to digital finance and formalizing more MSMEs due to introduction of a Goods and Services Tax in July 2017.[72] Slower growth in commercial bank credit recently—7.4% in 2019 and 7.1% in 2020—is due to a reduction in overall

[71] MSME Mart portal: www.msmemart.com

[72] *The Economic Times*. 2019. MSME lending now fuelled by digitisation and data driven decisions. 28 February. https://economictimes.indiatimes.com/small-biz/sme-sector/msme-lending-now-fuelled-by-digitisation-and-data-driven-decisions/articleshow/68178794.cms.

economic activity and increasing MSME loan defaults, which makes commercial banks more cautious.[73] The 2020 growth was mainly due to COVID-19 stimulus measures such as the Emergency Credit Line Guarantee Scheme (ECLGS), under which loans to MSMEs affected by the pandemic were fully guaranteed by the government.

MSME credit from urban cooperative banks increased from ₹317.4 billion in 2015 to ₹514.1 billion in 2020, an increase of 62.0% (a CAGR of 10.2%) (Figure 4.7B). There were 53 urban cooperative banks operating as of end-2020. From 2015 to 2020, the year-on-year loan growth was highest in 2020 (17.2%), and lowest (–0.7%) in 2016. The 2016 contraction was due to the economic slowdown that year. The high growth in 2020 was due to the numerous government liquidity/credit stimulus measures during the pandemic.

Public banks account for the majority of MSME loans outstanding. In 2020, they accounted for 53.9% of total commercial bank loans outstanding to MSMEs, followed by private banks (41.0%). The remaining loans were provided by foreign, scheduled, and non-scheduled banks.

During 2015–2020, the share of outstanding commercial bank loans to MSMEs averaged 17.2% of total loans outstanding. In 2020, the MSME share was 17.6%, slightly up from 17.4% in 2019. In terms of GDP, the average share of MSME loans to GDP was 10.7% during 2015–2019. It rose from 10.6% in 2015 to 11.7% in 2019. The MSME nonperforming loan (NPL) ratio improved from 9.6% in 2015 to 7.5% in 2020. The highest ratio was in 2017 (10.9%). Still, the MSME NPL ratio remains high compared with the overall commercial bank ratio (6.7% in 2020).

Despite the growth of MSME credit, access to finance remains a key constraint. One reason is the inability of MSMEs to repay due to business uncertainty, such as fragile consumer demand. Moreover, due to a lack of adequate information, lenders find it difficult to assess the creditworthiness of individual MSMEs. While lender coverage is adequate in larger urban areas, credit access is poor in remote urban locations in the country.

Figure 4.7: MSME Loans (1)

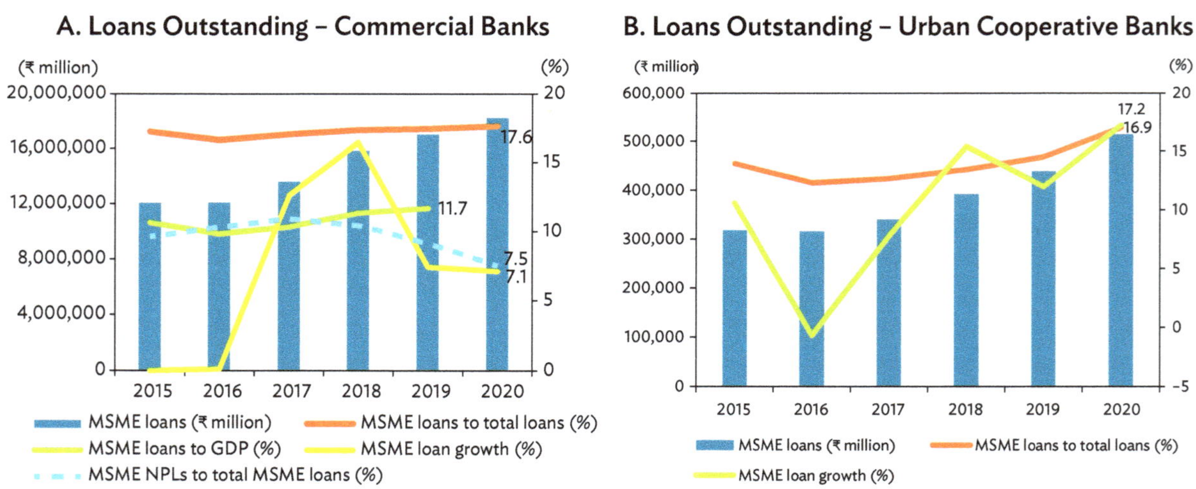

MSME = micro, small, and medium-sized enterprise; NPL = nonperforming loan.

Source: ADB Asia SME Monitor 2021 database. Data from Reserve Bank of India.

---

[73] A. Manikandan. 2020. Banks not keen to lend big to small businesses. The Economic Times. 2 January. https://economictimes.indiatimes.com/small-biz/sme-sector/banks-not-keen-to-lend-big-to-small-businesses/articleshow/73063382.cms.

Public Financing and Guarantees

a. Specialized bank for MSMEs

SIDBI, established in 1990, is India's principal institution for promoting and financing MSMEs. It provides direct and indirect lending to MSMEs and institutional finance to banks, small finance banks, nonbank finance companies (NBFCs), and microfinance institutions (MFIs). It also coordinates other institutions engaged in similar activities. SIDBI's total MSME loans outstanding was ₹1,654 billion in FY2020 (Table 4.3a). Indirect credit accounted for 94.0% of total outstanding loans with direct credit 6.0%. During FY2015 and FY2020, SIDBI loans disbursed to MSMEs increased at a CAGR of 20.8%—from ₹399 billion in FY2015 to ₹1,026 billion in FY2020 (Figure 4.8A). Over the same period, annual average lending rates to MSMEs improved from 9.7% to 6.8%.

MSMEs in services are the largest borrowers of SIDBI loans. They include wholesale and retail trade, with 94.5% of MSME loans outstanding in FY2020, followed by manufacturing (5.2%). Most MSME loans were for capital investments (99.6%). By tenor, 59.3% were midterm (1-5 years).

In 2015, MUDRA was established as a SIDBI subsidiary. MUDRA facilitates collateral free loans up to ₹1 million to eligible MSMEs, provided under the Pradhan Mantri MUDRA Yojana scheme, which coordinates partner member lending institutions (MLIs). MUDRA is a refinance initiative and does not lend directly to MSMEs or entrepreneurs. Loans can come from banks, NBFCs, and MFIs as per the terms and conditions of the lending agency. During FY2016 and FY2021, ₹15.5 trillion credit support was given to 295.6 million MSMEs (Figure 4.8B and Table 4.4).[74]

Figure 4.8: MSME Loans (2)

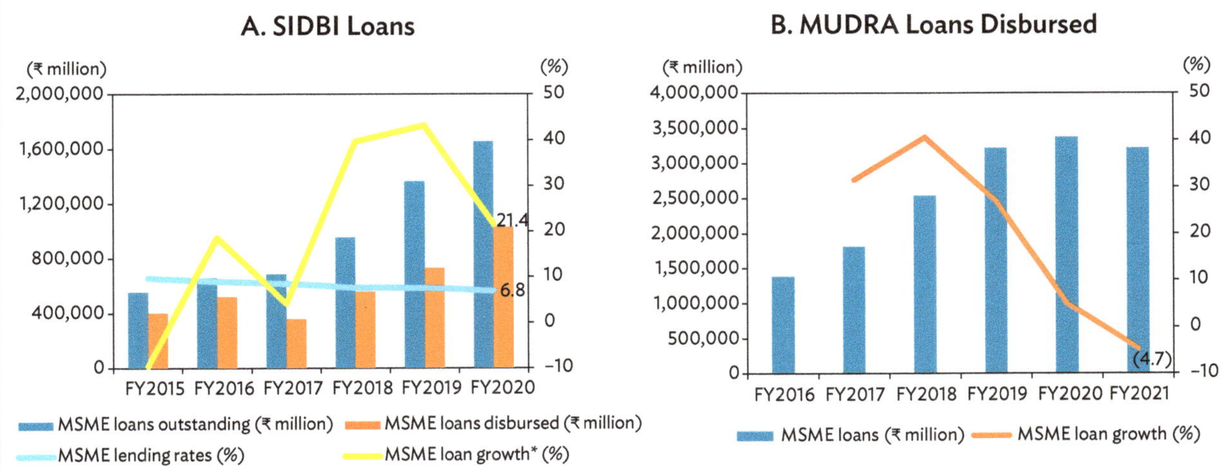

MSME = micro, small, and medium-sized enterprise; SIDBI = Small Industries Development Bank of India.

Source: ADB Asia SME Monitor 2021 database. Data from SIDBI.

MSME = micro, small, and medium-sized enterprise; MUDRA = Micro Units Development and Refinance Agency.

Source: ADB Asia SME Monitor 2021 database. Data from Mudra website.

---

[74] MUDRA 2019-2020 Annual Report.

b. Credit guarantees

Credit guarantees hedge risks associated with MSME lenders. In 2000, the government and SIDBI established the Credit Guarantee Fund Trust for Micro and Small Enterprises (CGTMSE). CGTMSE provides partial credit guarantees to MLIs on micro and small enterprise (MSE) loans up to 75%–85% of credit supplied, so that MSMEs can access collateral-free/third-party guarantee free loans, with a maximum ₹20 million per borrower.

Credit guarantees approved under CGTMSE increased from ₹212.8 billion in FY2015 to ₹458.5 billion in FY2020 (a CAGR of 14.5%) (Figure 4.9A and Table 4.4). Approved credit guarantees grew 52.0% in FY2020, down slightly from 58.2% in FY2019. The overall increase can be attributed to the Retail Trade and Hybrid Security Model, under which CGTMSE provides guarantees for the portion of credit not covered by collateral. In FY2020, 53.4% of the guarantees was provided to public sector units, followed by NBFCs (37.8%). The remaining 8.8% was provided to other MLIs such as private banks, small finance banks, and regional rural banks.

Earlier, in 2014, the National Credit Guarantee Trustee Company (NCGTC) was institutionalized by the Ministry of Finance to regulate and monitor various Credit Guarantee Funds. NCGTC facilitates credit guarantees to MSMEs, education loans, and skill development loans through various central ministry schemes. As of March 2020, NCGTC managed six government guarantee schemes: the (i) Credit Guarantee Fund Scheme for Educational Loans; (ii) Credit Guarantee Fund Scheme for Skill Development; (iii) Credit Guarantee Fund Scheme for Factoring; (iv) Credit Guarantee Fund for Micro Units (CGFMU), (v) Credit Guarantee Fund Scheme for Stand-Up India; and the (vi) ECLGS.

In 2016, CGFMU was created to provide credit guarantees to microenterprises under the Pradhan Mantri MUDRA Yojana. It provides portfolio guarantees for micro loans up to ₹1 million and up to 50% of the outstanding balance of eligible micro loans. The first 5% of the default amount is borne by the lender with up to 50% of the remaining amount settled by CGFMU. MLIs are required to pay a fee for the portfolio of loans covered by guarantees, thereby incentivizing to offer credit as potential losses are protected.

From FY2018 to FY2020, 13.4 million accounts, amounting to ₹2.1 trillion, received guarantee approvals under CGFMU (Figure 4.9B). Credit guarantee loans increased from ₹398.5 billion in FY2018 to ₹942.2 billion in FY2020 (a CAGR of 53.8%). In FY2020, 89.3% of the guarantees were for loan amounts up to ₹500,000.[75] South India accounted for 31.8% of the guarantees, followed by North India (22.6%). As of March 2020, public banks accounted for 93.0% of the guarantees and 95.0% of approved loans under CGFMU. The State Bank of India, Bank of India, Union Bank of India, Punjab National Bank, and Bank of Baroda were the top five public banks involved.

[75] NCGTC Annual Report 2019-2020.

Figure 4.9: Credit Guarantees

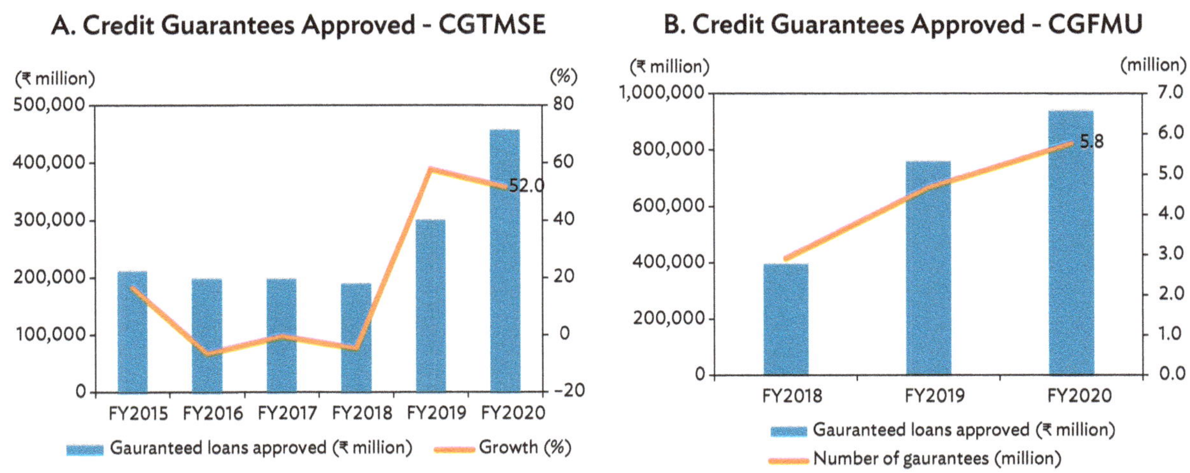

CGTMSE = Credit Guarantee Fund Trust for Micro and Small Enterprises.
Source: ADB Asia SME Monitor 2021 database. Data from CGMTSE Annual Report 2019-20.

CGFMU = Credit Guarantee Fund for Micro Units.
Source: ADB Asia SME Monitor 2021 database. Data from NCGTC Annual Report 2019-20.

Nonbank Financing

NBFCs are playing an increasing role in providing access to finance to MSMEs. They have better reach and are extremely agile compared with India's banks. NBFCs partner with banks to provide MSME loans. They can be classified into 11 broad categories based on activity. All NBFCs are required to hold certificates of registration from RBI and are required to maintain minimum capital. NBFCs obtain their capital largely through bank borrowings and corporate bonds (debentures). In 2020, 41.2% of their capital was obtained through debentures and 31% from bank borrowings.[76] The remainder was obtained from other sources such as commercial paper, inter-corporate borrowings, and financial institution borrowings.

RBI reported 9,533 NBFCs in 2020, including 94 MFIs, 4,115 loan companies, and 7 factoring companies for MSME access (Table 4.5). MSME financing through NBFCs increased 133.8% from ₹575 billion in 2015 to ₹1,503 billion in 2020, a CAGR of 21.2% (Figure 4.10A). MSME borrowings grew by 19.5% in 2020 due to policies such as a 2.0% interest subvention for all goods and services taxes for registered MSMEs. The share of MSME financing to total NBFC financing outstanding was 6.2%. The gross nonperforming financing (NPF) ratio continued to trend downward to 5.8%, lower than the MSME NPL ratio of commercial banks (7.5%) in 2020. By sector, 53.1% of NBFC's financing was MSMEs in services, with the remaining 46.9% going to manufacturing.

MFI loans outstanding grew from ₹92.9 billion in 2015 to ₹229 billion in 2020 (a CAGR of 19.8%) (Figure 4.10B). In 2020, MFI loan growth was 6.8%. MFIs financed 16.5 million MSMEs. NPL ratios in MFIs have decreased, down from 9.5% in 2015 to 4.8% in 2020.

Financing from loan companies amounted to ₹1,258 billion (₹298 billion in 2015), while factoring companies reached ₹13.6 billion (₹3.9 billion in 2015) (Figure 10B). Loan company financing increased sharply by 44.4% in 2020, while factoring fell by 1.4%. Loan companies financed 13 million customers in 2020. The NPL ratio was 6.2%

[76] RBI report on Trend and Progress of Banking in India 2019-2020.

(4.0% in 2015). Factoring provides short-term liquidity to MSMEs and is governed by the Factoring Regulation Act of 2011. Factoring remains largely nascent and has yet to be fully adopted by corporations and public agencies. It is dominated by commercial banks. An amendment to the Factoring Regulation Act in 2020 allows all NBFCs (other than those whose principal business is factoring) to undertake factoring focused on MSMEs.[77]

Figure 4.10: Nonbank Finance

A. MSME Financing by NBFCs Regulated by RBI

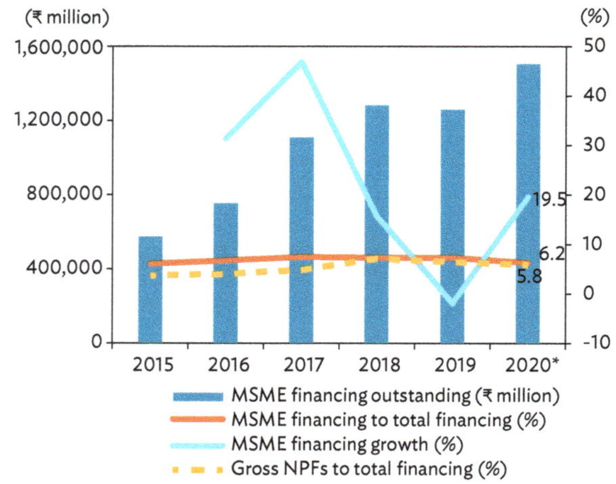

* provisional.

MSME = micro, small, and medium-sized enterprise; NBFC = nonbank finance company; NPF = nonperforming financing; RBI = Reserve Bank of India.

Source: ADB Asia SME Monitor 2021 database. Data from Reserve Bank of India.

B. Microfinance Institutions, Loan Companies, and Factoring Companies

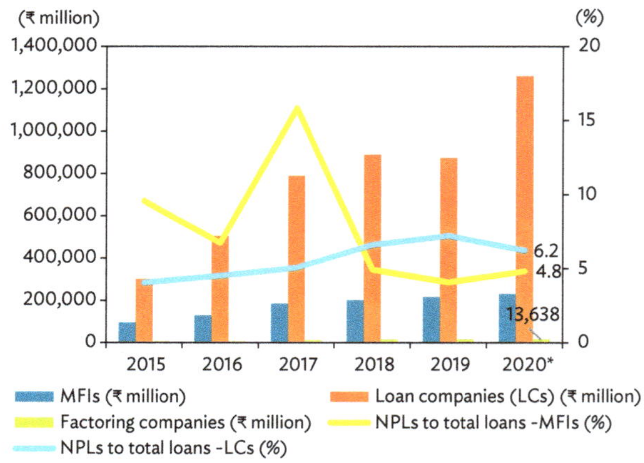

* provisional.

MFI = microfinance institution, NPL = nonperforming loan.

Source: ADB Asia SME Monitor 2021 database. Data from Reserve Bank of India.

In FY2020, NBFC non-food-credit-to-GDP ratio was 11.6%, slightly down from 12.2% in FY2019, but overall it had been growing since FY2013 (8.6%). More than 50% of NBFC credit went toward manufacturing, followed by retail trade (Figure 4.11A). In FY2020, the share of manufacturing in total NBFC credit was 53.6%. Within manufacturing, MSMEs accounted for 7.4% (6.0% for micro and small firms and 1.4% for medium-sized firms) (Figure 4.11B). Large and other industrial sectors accounted for 46.4% and 46.2%, respectively. Infrastructure finance companies, NBFCs, and MFIs together comprised 98.1% of credit extended to manufacturing.

Venture capital has become a key funding source for start-ups. In 2020, total venture capital funding for start-ups reached $9.9 billion, compared with $3.1 billion in 2012 (a CAGR of 15.7%). Despite the COVID-19 pandemic, start-up funding was already $10.1 billion in the first half of 2021. The average deal size increased from $6.7 million in 2012 to $12.4 million in 2020, when 21 start-ups received venture capital investments of more than $100 million.[78] Fintech, Consumer Tech and Software as a Service (SaaS) firms accounted for 75% of venture capital investments in 2020. The India Venture Capital Report 2021 by Bain & Company and Indian Private Equity and Venture Capital

77 The Factoring Regulation (Amendment) Bill, 2020. http://164.100.47.4/BillsTexts/LSBillTexts/Asintroduced 115_2020_LS_Eng.pdf.

78 M. Agarwal and T. Pema. 2021. Indian startup funding in H1 2021 exceeds 2020 levels, expected to touch record levels in 2021. YourStory. 5 July. https://yourstory.com/2021/07/indian-startup-funding-h1-2021-exceeds-2020-level/amp.

Figure 4.11: Nonbank Finance Company Credit by Sector and Borrower

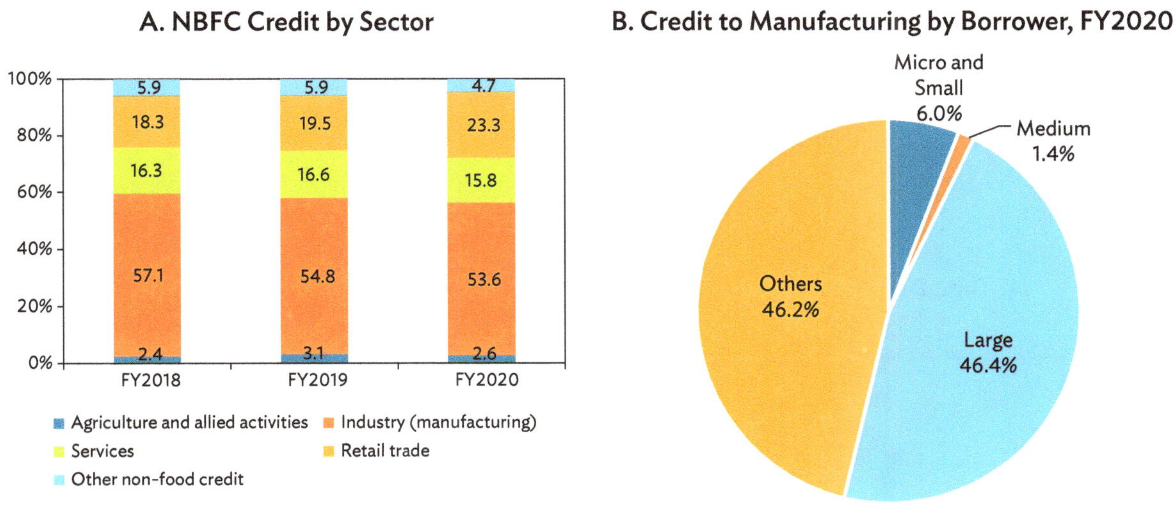

NBFC = nonbank finance company.
Source: ADB Asia SME Monitor 2021 database. Data from Reserve Bank of India.

Association said the number of start-ups in India have increased at a CAGR of 17.0% from 2012 to 2020, by which time there were 37 companies in India with unicorn status, behind only the US and PRC.[79]

Digital Financial Services

As of March 2021, there were 1,2 billion wireless subscribers, comprising 663 million urban and 537 million rural users.[80] This high mobile connectivity, along with declining tariffs, has enabled fintech firms to expand. Several alternative lending models have evolved in recent years, helping MSMEs access finance. Fintech firms are regulated by the RBI either directly by through licenses—such as the "NBFC-P2P" category or through banks and associated NBFCs.

The cornerstone of this digital financial revolution is *Aadhar*, a unique 12-digit identification number issued by the Unique Identification Authority of India for each resident, which can be accessed and verified by fintech firms at marginal cost. As of March 2021, the government issued over 1.3 billion *Aadhar* to residents and was processing up to 30 million authentication requests daily.[81] It has enabled numerous public payment platforms, verification (e-KYC), and cloud storage (Digi Locker), among others.

Digital payments increased from ₹920.4 trillion in FY2016 to ₹1,415 trillion in FY2021, a 53.7% growth (9.0% CAGR) (Figure 4.12A). Their use grew consistently from FY2016 to FY2020 averaging about 20% each year. However, in FY2020, use fell by 0.9% and in FY2021 by 12.8%. In FY2021, retail credit transactions accounted for 72.7% of digital transactions, followed by card payments (13.2%), prepaid payment instruments (11.3%), debit transfers and direct debits (2.4%), and large-value credit transfers (0.4%) (Figure 4.12B).

79 Start-ups with a valuation more than $1 billion.
80 Telecom Regulatory Authority website: https://www.trai.gov.in/sites/default/files/PR_No.33of2021.pdf.
81 Aadhaar website: https://uidai.gov.in/aadhaar_dashboard/

Unified payments interface (UPI) allows real-time fund transfers between two bank accounts using mobile applications of banks and third parties such as Google Pay. It is a pivotal driver for expanding digital finance. The National Payments Corporation of India, an initiative of the RBI and Indian Banks Association, is the umbrella organization operating retail payments and settlement systems. UPI transactions increased from ₹69.6 billion in FY2017 to ₹41.0 trillion in FY2021, a 392.1% CAGR (Figure 4.12C). The number of transactions increased at a CAGR of 493.5%.

Figure 4.12: Digital Transactions in India

A. Total Digital Transaction

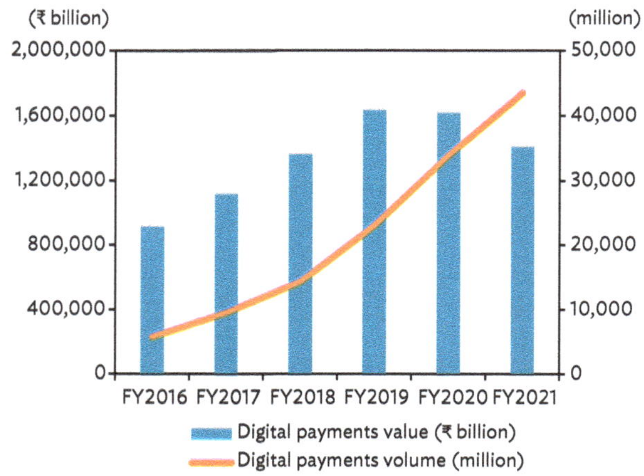

Source: ADB Asia SME Monitor 2021 database. Data from Reserve Bank of India.

B. Digital Transactions by Type, FY2021

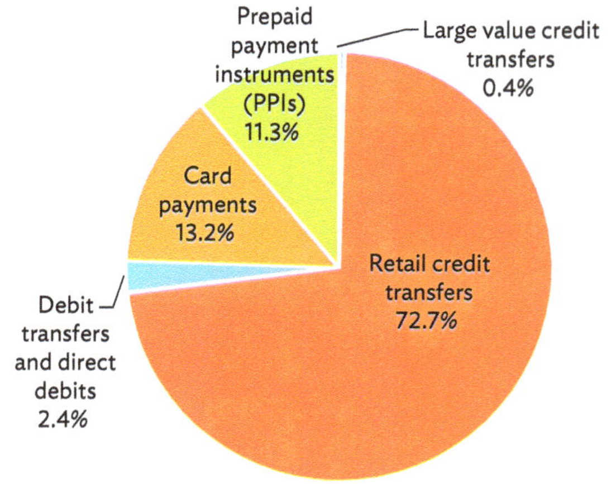

FY = fiscal year.

Source: ADB Asia SME Monitor 2021 database. Data from Reserve Bank of India.

C. Unified Payments Interface Transactions

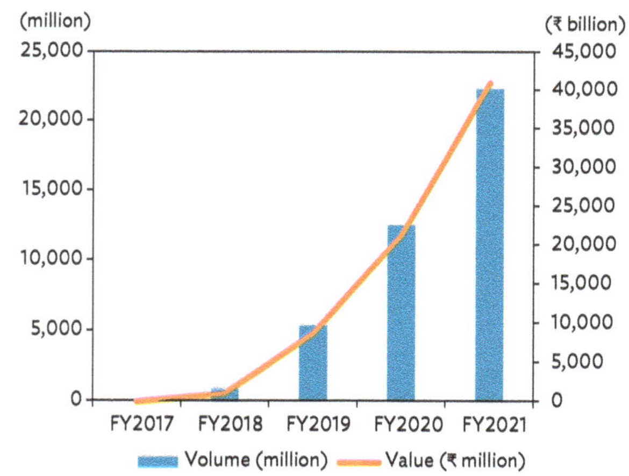

Source: ADB Asia SME Monitor 2021 database. Data from Reserve Bank of India.

As of March 2020, there were 4,680 fintech companies in India.[82] Some 42% were in Tier 1 cities.[83] Fintech lenders fall under several broad categories: (i) marketplace lenders, (ii) balance sheet lenders, (iii) marketplace hybrid models, (iv) invoice-based lending, and (v) supply chain finance. The RBI has adopted a thematic approach to pursue specific policy objectives using a regulatory sandbox initiative. The RBI accepts entities that deal with retail payments (first "cohort") and cross-border payments (second cohort). The third is expected to cover MSME lending. The focus will be on identifying innovations that can leverage technology and reliable data points to enable MSMEs to access credit from the formal financial system faster and more cost-effectively.

The government also introduced an alternate fintech lending platform, where MSMEs can obtain loans from ₹100,000 to ₹50 million with "in-principle" approvals granted within 59 minutes. SIDBI has partnered with the State Bank of India, Bank of Baroda, Punjab National Bank, Vijaya Bank, and Indian Bank to set up the facility.

Capital Markets

The Securities and Exchange Board of India (SEBI) is the capital market regulatory body established under the Ministry of Finance. The SEBI definition for MSMEs for capital markets differs from the one followed by the Ministry of MSMEs. The Bombay Stock Exchange (BSE) and National Stock Exchange (NSE) are the two leading stock exchanges in India. The two have a dedicated board for MSMEs, known as the BSE SME Exchange and NSE Emerge. Listing requirements for both exchanges differ (Table 4.7). MSMEs prefer to list only on one exchange. For MSMEs to list on a stock exchange, their post issue paid-up capital must not be more than ₹250 million.

The BSE market capitalization increased from ₹70,660 billion in 2012 to ₹189,302 billion in 2020 (a CAGR of 13.1%) (Table 4.6). Over the period, the market capitalization of MSMEs listed on the BSE SME Exchange increased at a CAGR of 71.3%. In 2020, the market capitalization of MSMEs listed on the BSE was ₹212,795 million, well above the ₹2,871 million in 2012 (Figure 4.13A). The number of MSMEs listed on the BSE SME Exchange increased from 11 in 2012 to 331 in 2020 (Figure 4.13B). During 2012–2020, 93 firms moved from the BSE SME Exchange to the main board. As of March 2021, there were MSMEs from 17 sectors listed on the exchange with the states of Maharashtra and Gujarat accounting for 65.0% of those listed.[84] The high degree of financial literacy in these two states is a major reason for the large number of MSMEs from these two states.

The overall market capitalization of the NSE has increased from ₹67,636 billion in 2012 to ₹186,412 billion in 2020 (a CAGR of 13.5%). Over the same period, the market capitalization of MSMEs listed on NSE Emerge increased at a CAGR of 57.4% (Figure 4.13A). In 2020, the market capitalization of MSMEs listed on the NSE was ₹56,048 million, well above the ₹1,490 million in 2012. The number of MSMEs listed on NSE Emerge increased from 2 in 2012 to 214 in 2020 (Figure 4.13B). During 2012–2020, 62 firms moved from NSE Emerge to the main board.

82 Reserve Bank of India Bulletin November 2020.

83 Tier 1 cities are those with population of 100,000 and above.

84 Based on discussion with BSE on 1 April 2021.

Figure 4.13: Equity Markets

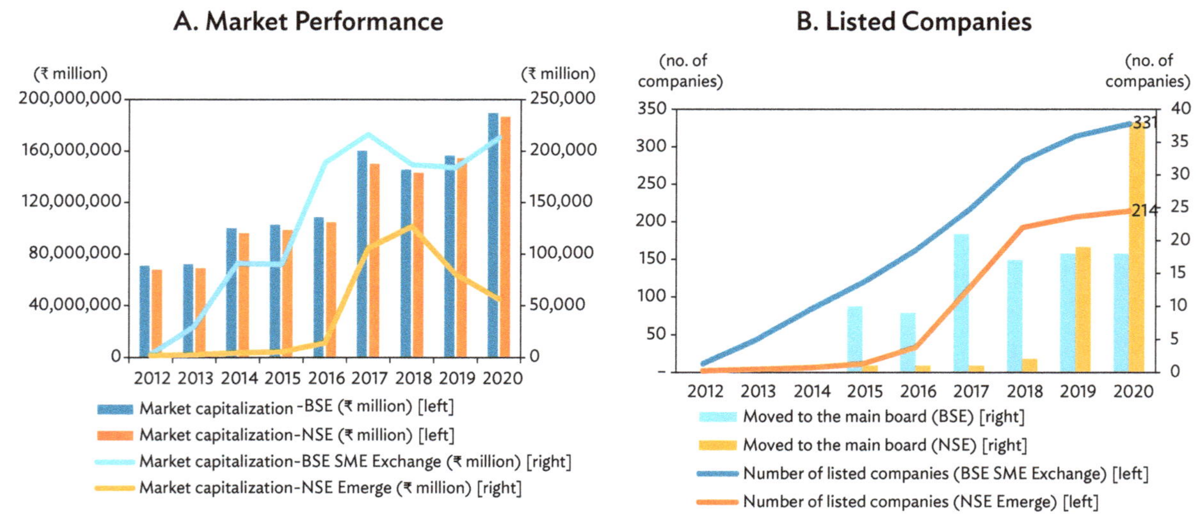

BSE = Bombay Stock Exchange, NSE = National Stock Exchange.

Source: ADB Asia SME Monitor 2021 database. Data from Bombay Stock Exchange and National Stock Exchange.

Critical challenges for capital market development include addressing the low level of financial literacy and MSME owners' fear over diluting their ownership stakes. In addition, high compliance costs, especially related to SEBI regulations, RBI regulations, and Companies Act compliance pose significant financial burdens on MSMEs.

To attract more issuers and investors, the SEBI has relaxed several regulatory requirements for MSMEs. They can file compliance documents every 6 months instead of quarterly (as required for other companies). There is no mandatory requirement for publishing accounts in newspapers by MSMEs. MSME shareholders may be informed once a year through newsletters, the mail, and annual reports, among others. The listing fee for MSMEs is much lower on MSME exchanges than that paid by firms on the main boards.

Financial Infrastructure

As of March 2020, credit information in India is collected through three key agencies: (i) credit information companies (CICs), (ii) the RBI, and (iii) Central Registry of Securitization Asset Reconstruction and Security Interest (CERSAI). There are other sources of credit information as well, such as Information Utilities and data collected by the Ministry of Corporate Affairs—however, their scope is limited.[85] CICs, regulated by RBI under the Credit Information Companies Act 2005, have the largest scope for collecting credit information. CICs source their information from banks, nonbank finance institutions, and other lending agencies.

As of March 2020, there were four private credit bureaus: TransUnion CIBIL, Equifax, Experian, and CRIF High Mark. Each maintains credit history of retail borrowers and provides a credit score, calculated on repayment history, type of credit, age of credit, credit exposure, and credit inquiries.

85 Report of the High Level Task Force on Public Credit Registry for India https://rbi.org.in/scripts/PublicationReportDetails.aspx?ID=895

- TransUnion CIBIL: The Credit Information Bureau Limited (CIBIL) was the first CIC, established in 2000. The agency collects and stores credit-related information from various financial institutions, and prepares a credit report. It also issues a CIBIL Score, a credit score for individuals derived from credit data. A high CIBIL score reflects a higher credit worthiness and vice versa. It also has a CIBIL MSME Rank, which rates MSMEs on a scale of 1 to 10 based on credit history. The scores are accessed by various lending institutions providing credit to individuals or companies. The agency has more than 5,000 members—including banks, financial institutions, nonbank finance companies, and housing finance companies.
- Equifax: The agency was launched in 2010. It established Equifax Credit Information Services Private Limited, a joint venture between Equifax Inc. of the US and seven leading Indian financial institutions—the State Bank of India, Bank of Baroda, Bank of India, Kotak Mahindra Prime Limited, Religare Finvest Limited, Sundaram Finance Limited, and Union Bank of India.
- Experian: Experian Credit Information Company was established in 2006.
- CRIF High Mark Credit Information Services: High Mark was set up in 2010. In 2014, CRIF acquired a majority stake.

In 2011, the government established a centralized collateral registry, the Central Registry of Securitization Asset Reconstruction and Security Interest (CERSAI)—under the Securitization and Reconstruction of Financial Assets and Enforcement of Security Interest Act 2002—to identify immovable assets against which loans are issued.[86] CERSAI aims to minimize fraud and avoid multiple financing by different banks against the same immovable assets. All lending institutions are required to provide details of assets against which the security interest is created on the CERSAI online portal.

Information asymmetry is one major reason MSME access to finance remains restricted. In 2018, the RBI established a Public Credit Registry to maintain a ledger of all borrowers and lenders in the country. The Public Credit Registry is a web-based platform to collect credit details of both individual and corporate borrowers.

4. Policies and Regulations

- The Ministry of MSMEs is the nodal agency for the development of MSMEs in the country. The Micro, Small, and Medium Enterprises Development Act 2006 provides the framework and guidelines for MSME development.
- State (local) governments play a critical role in promoting rural MSME development; central government authorities help these efforts.
- The intra-governmental MSME policy coordinating body (National Board of MSMEs) reviews and recommends national MSME policies and programs; however, several MSME schemes are fragmented across various central government agencies.
- The National Strategy for Financial Inclusion for 2019–2024 was launched in 2020, addressing MSME access to finance as one key pillar.
- After the COVID-19 pandemic started in 2020, the government implemented comprehensive emergency assistance to businesses and households, including various financial assistance programs to MSMEs.

[86] Report of the High Level Task Force on Public Credit Registry for India https://rbi.org.in/scripts/PublicationReportDetails.aspx?ID=895

MSME Development

In 2006, the government introduced the Micro, Small, and Medium Enterprises Development (MSMED) Act to promote and develop MSMEs (Table 4.8). The act also provided a definition of MSMEs. Under the act, a National Board for Micro, Small and Medium Enterprises was constituted. The board, chaired by the minister of MSMEs, reviews MSME policies and programs, and provides strategic directions for MSME development. The Ministry of MSMEs, established in 2007, is the nodal MSME development ministry that provides a policy roadmap and incentives/project schemes to assist MSMEs. The MSME ministry's schemes cover all sectors and apply to firms across all sectors. Priority sectors are identified by the various line ministries.

India has a federal structure. Therefore, state governments are primarily responsible for the development and promotion of MSMEs and implementation of central government schemes. They generally provide feasible business infrastructure and interest subsidies to MSMEs. The central government, through its Ministry of MSMEs, supplements these state efforts to enhance MSME competitiveness.

The central government introduced several schemes to support MSMEs and their cluster development—including an Interest Subsidy Eligibility Certificate (ISEC) Scheme, Scheme of Fund for Regeneration of Traditional Industries (SFURTI), Credit Linked Capital Subsidy for Technology Upgradation (CLCSS), and Micro and Small Enterprises Cluster Development (MSE-CDP):

- **ISEC Scheme:** Introduced in 1977, the scheme finances Khadi institutions and village industries (local artisans) at a concessional rate of 4.0% per annum for capital expenditures and working capital. The difference between the real lending rate and 4.0% is paid by the central government to the banks.
- **SFURTI:** The scheme provides financial assistance up to ₹50 million for a cluster of more than 500 artisans to set up common facility centers, procure machines, raw material banks, and training, among others. From its inception (2005–2006) until 31 March 2021, 88 clusters have received financial assistance.
- **CLCSS:** It provides a 15% subsidy for additional investment up to ₹10 million (up to a ₹1.5 million subsidy) for technology upgrading by micro and small enterprises in pre-identified sectors/subsectors/technologies. The scheme is applicable to both new and existing micro and small enterprises.
- **MSE-CDP:** The scheme offers financial incentives to MSMEs performing similar activities to form clusters. It provides funding support to establish Common Facility Centers (up to 70% of project costs, capped at ₹200 million), infrastructure development (up to 60% of project costs, capped at ₹150 million), marketing hubs (up to 60% of project costs, capped at ₹100 million), and thematic interventions such as exposure visits (up to 50% of project costs, capped at ₹1 million).

The Prime Minister's Employment Generation Programme, launched in 2008, is a central government scheme to create jobs. The scheme, administered by the Ministry of MSMEs, provides a subsidy (up to 25% of project costs) for setting up new non-farm microenterprises.[87] Through December 2020, 640,000 MSMEs were enrolled under the scheme, providing employment to 5.3 million individuals.

There are several line ministries that are involved in MSME and entrepreneurship development. The Ministry of Skill Development and Entrepreneurship (MSDE) offers programs in skill development and entrepreneurship. Most beneficiaries of its skill development programs are self-employed individuals. From 2016 to 2021, the ministry trained 10.7 million individuals under its flagship skill development scheme, Pradhan Mantri Kaushal Vikas Yojana.[88]

[87] Government of India, Ministry of MSMEs. Prime Ministers Employment Generation Programme, PMEGP. https://msme.gov.in/11-prime-ministers-employment-generation-programme-pmegp.

[88] Lok Sabha Reply: https://pqars.nic.in/annex/253/AU2872.pdf

The government covers the entire cost of training and includes a 40-hour module on digital and financial literacy. In April 2020, MSDE launched a pilot project on Entrepreneurship Promotion and Mentoring of Micro and Small Businesses in six "temple" towns: Puri, Varanasi, Haridwar, Kollur, Pandharpur, and Bodh Gaya. The project focuses on harnessing the potential of rural and tribal entrepreneurs.

The export and promotion of goods produced by MSMEs falls under the Ministry of Commerce and Industry. The ministry introduced an Interest Equalization Scheme in 2015 that provides 5% interest subvention to MSME merchandise exporters. Banks provide pre- and post-shipment rupee export credit to eligible MSME exporters at an interest rate that is reduced by 5% per annum. The scheme has enabled MSME exporters to remain competitive in global markets.[89] Additionally, the Ministry of Commerce and Industry is collaborating with state governments to develop districts as export hubs. District export promotion committees institutionalized in each district, prepare a district specific action plan and collaborate with various stakeholders for implementation. District export promotion committees focus on developing an ecosystem of export opportunities for MSMEs. The initiative, introduced in 2019, has identified products with export potential in 725 districts across the country. Traditional toys are considered key products with export potential, and districts such as Krishna (for Kondapalli toys) and Varanasi (for wooden lacquerware and toys) are promoted as export hubs.

Developing agricultural value chains is central to the Ministry of Agriculture. Up to 85% of farm holdings are less than 2 hectares. All government schemes and interventions in the sector are targeted at small farmers. In May 2020, the ministry set up a National Agriculture Infrastructure Financing Fund to support farm-gate infrastructure. Under the scheme, the government is providing interest subvention of 3.0% and credit guarantees up to ₹20 million to eligible farmers for post-harvest management infrastructure and community-farming assets. The ministry also provides direct income support of ₹6,000 per year in three equal installments to small farmers holding less than 2 hectares. Also, the government provides funding support to small farm entrepreneurs identified under the One District One Product scheme of the Ministry of Commerce and Industry.

In 2012, the government introduced the Public Procurement Policy for Micro and Small Enterprises (MSEs). It requires government departments and public sector units to procure 25% of their overall procurement needs from MSEs, including 4% from MSEs owned by scheduled caste/scheduled tribes and 3% from MSEs owned by women.[90] An online procurement marketplace was introduced by the government, monitored through the MSME-SAMBANDH portal, introduced in December 2017. It assists in monitoring procurement activities of central government ministries, departments, and central public sector enterprises. The Ministry of MSMEs has earmarked 358 products reserved for government purchase from micro and small enterprises.[91]

As mentioned, all MSMEs are required to obtain *Udyam Certificates,* including *Udyog Aadhaar,* a 12-digit Unique Identification Number provided by the Ministry of MSMEs. Only those MSMEs that have obtained *Udyam Certificate* are eligible for benefits under the numerous government schemes. Registration is free and completed online at the Udyam' Registration portal.[92] The database is integrated with the Central Board of Direct Taxes and Goods and Service Tax Network agencies in India.

In 2015, the Ministry of MSMEs introduced a Framework for Revival and Rehabilitation of MSMEs. The framework gives banks the necessary guidelines for initiating corrective actions for the revival of distressed MSMEs. The

89 Ministry of Commerce and Industry Annual Report 2020-21.

90 Scheduled caste and scheduled tribe are officially designated groups of individuals defined under India's constitution. These groups have historically faced deprivation, oppression, and social isolation. The list of groups can be found on https://tribal.nic.in/downloads/CLM/CLM_1/3.pdf.

91 Government of India, Ministry of MSMEs. List of 358 Items Reserved for Purchase from Micro and Small Enterprises. http://www.dcmsme.gov.in/schemes/listof358itemsreserved.pdf.

92 Udyam Registration Portal: https://udyamregistration.gov.in

framework suggests that before an MSME loan account becomes nonperforming, the bank or enterprise can seek a Corrective Action Plan with the appropriate authorities in the bank where the enterprise has maximum exposure. The objective is to arrive at an early and feasible solution to preserve the economic value of the assets and allow the enterprise to continue operating.

Financial Inclusion

The RBI introduced priority sector guidelines in 1970 for commercial banks that have been regularly updated.[93] Under the most recent 2018 update, banks are required to allocate 40% of their adjusted net bank credit (ANBC) to priority sectors including MSMEs.[94] Priority sectors are categorized into eight areas—including agriculture, MSMEs, export credit, education, housing, social infrastructure, renewable energy, and others. The guidelines also require banks to allocate 7.5% of their ANBC to microenterprises.

Banks are required to prepare Financial Inclusion Plans (FIPs) and share monthly progress reports with the RBI. FIPs include parameters such as the number of outlets, basic savings bank deposit accounts, overdraft facilities, and communication technology channel, among others. Regular monitoring by the RBI allows for a structural approach to financial inclusion.

In 2014, the RBI introduced the Trade Receivables Discounting System, an electronic bill factoring exchange for MSMEs. The platform facilitates financing/discounting of MSME trade receivables through numerous financiers. MSME sellers, buyers, and financiers join this common platform. Financiers bid on invoices and pay the seller after approval from both the seller and buyer.

In 2019, the RBI established an expert committee on MSMEs to conduct a comprehensive MSME review and propose interventions for financial inclusion.[95] The committee met with various stakeholders—such as central government ministries, state governments, the World Bank and ADB—to prepare a roadmap and offer policy recommendations for MSME development and financial inclusion. The committee identified challenges such as the lack of targeted policies in infrastructure development, low level of technology adoption, limited backward and forward linkages, credit gaps, and delayed payments to MSMEs.

The MSME committee identified 37 broad recommendations including 21 for the RBI. One key recommendation redefined MSMEs, later enacted by the central ministry in 2020. There were several other recommendations on access to finance:

- Establish a National Council for MSMEs under the Chairmanship of the Prime Minister with representation from other line ministries.
- Create a ₹100 billion Fund of Funds to support venture capital/private equity firms investing in MSMEs.
- Increase the collateral security free loans provided to MSMEs to ₹2 million from ₹1 million.
- Adjust Priority Sector Lending to enable banks to specialize in lending to a specific sector.

In November 2020, the RBI introduced a Co-Lending Model scheme to improve credit flow to underserved sectors.[96] Under the scheme, commercial banks are permitted to co-lend with NBFCs that have greater reach. The model provides greater flexibility to lending institutions, and designates NBFCs as the point of contact for customers for loan agreements.

93 Priority Sector Guidelines: https://www.rbi.org.in/Scripts/BS_ViewMasDirections.aspx?id=10497

94 For the purpose of priority sector lending, ANBC denotes the outstanding bank credit in India: https://m.rbi.org.in/Scripts/BS_ViewMasDirections.aspx?id=11959#ANBC

95 RBI Committee on MSMEs: https://www.rbi.org.in/Scripts/PublicationReportDetails.aspx?UrlPage=&ID=924

96 Co-Lending by Banks and NBFCs to Priority Sector: https://www.rbi.org.in/Scripts/NotificationUser.aspx?Id=11991&Mode=0

In January 2021, the RBI allowed banks to deduct credit disbursed to new MSME borrowers (up to ₹2.5 million per borrower) from their net demand and time liability calculation of cash reserve ratio to encourage use idle funds for loans to microenterprises.

The Fund of Funds Scheme for MSMEs, launched in 2020, leverages an equity infusion of ₹500 billion for MSMEs. NSIC Venture Capital Fund Limited, a subsidiary of National Small Industries Corporation, has been incorporated to manage the fund, which increases the MSME size and encourages them to list on domestic exchanges.

In January 2020, the RBI introduced a National Strategy for Financial Inclusion (NSFI) 2019–2024, focusing on increasing access to formal financial services, including MSMEs.[97]

The NSFI recommends using fintech platforms to find innovative ways to increase inclusion while emphasizing customer consent prior to joining a digital platform. A more comprehensive module was developed for entrepreneurs as a part of financial education initiative in line with the NSFI action plan. The NSFI provides the vision and objectives for financial inclusion policies over the 5-year period. The strategy suggests six strategic interventions:

- Universal access to financial services—the strategy proposes to provide banking access to every village within a 5-kilometer radius or cluster of 500 households in hilly areas. It also focusses on promoting financial literacy among customers.
- Providing a basic suite of financial services—individuals enrolled under the Pradhan Mantri Jan Dhan Yojana will be provided insurance and pension coverage. A Public Credit Registry will be operational by March 2022.
- Access to livelihood and skill development—details of account holders interested in skill development will be shared with the skill development agencies and vice versa.
- Financial literacy and education—financial literacy modules will be developed for each target audience—young adults, women, new workers/entrepreneurs, and senior citizens.
- Customer protection and grievance redress—the Internal Grievances Redressal Mechanism for financial service providers will be strengthened through online portals or mobile applications.
- Effective coordination—adoption of geospatial information technology to monitor progress of financial inclusion in underserved regions (such as the Northeastern Region).

Response to COVID-19

The government announced an economic stimulus package to expedite the recovery of MSMEs severely affected by the COVID-19 pandemic. One early intervention was a ₹1.7-trillion economic package for migrant workers affected by the COVID-19 lockdown (Table 4.9). Also, medical insurance coverage up to ₹5 million was introduced for frontline health workers, including doctors, nurses, and paramedics. In May 2020, the government announced a ₹20-trillion package focusing on MSMEs. It included several measures:

- Collateral free and automatic loans worth ₹3 trillion provided to MSMEs with turnover up to ₹2.5 billion or have an outstanding loan up to ₹500 million.
- Stressed MSMEs or MSMEs with nonperforming assets are eligible for a subordinate debt of ₹200 billion. Partial guarantees of ₹40 billion are provided by the government.
- For viable MSMEs, a ₹500 billion fund was set up to assist in their expansion and for listing on a stock exchange.
- Preference given to MSMEs for government procurement up to ₹2 billion.

[97] National Strategy for Financial Inclusion 2019-2024: https://www.rbi.org.in/Scripts/PublicationReportDetails.aspx?UrlPage=&ID=1154

- MSME receivables from the government and central public enterprises to be paid within 45 days.
- Liquidity infusions of ₹300 billion for NBFCs, housing finance companies, and MFIs.
- A ₹450-billion partial guarantee package that provides coverage up to 20% loss to any bank.
- Extension of deadlines for income tax filing for FY2020 from 30 September 2020 to 30 November 2020.

Several states amended their labor laws to reduce the compliance burden. For example, Gujarat amended its Factory Act 1948 to allow maximum daily work hours to 12 hours from 8 hours and weekly hours to 72 hours from 48 hours. The state also said newly established firms would be exempted from labor law compliance for 1,200 days. Maharashtra state increased their maximum daily hours for factory workers from 8 hours to 12 hours and weekly hours from 48 hours to 60 hours. State governments introduced several e-governance initiatives as well, such as establishing online websites for COVID-19 information dissemination. Punjab introduced COVA Punjab—corona.punjab.gov.in. Sikkim, a northeast state, introduced covid19sikkim.org, among others. States also introduced surveillance applications for contact tracing such as "Raksha Serv" in Chhattisgarh, "Corona Mukt Himachal" in Himachal Pradesh, and "Mahakavach" in Maharashtra. This support does not specifically focus on MSMEs, but help them continue operating during the pandemic.

The Securities and Exchange Board of India (SEBI) also eased several regulations and rules on issuing and trading stocks, along with the capital market administrative process in response to the pandemic (Table 9a).

Data Tables

Table 4.1: MSME Definition

A. Until 30 June 2020

Sector	Micro	Small	Medium
Manufacturing	Investment in plant and machinery does not exceed ₹2.5 million	Investment in plant and machinery is more than ₹2.5 million but does not exceed ₹50.0 million	Investment in plant and machinery is more than ₹50 million but does not exceed ₹100 million
Services	Investment in equipment does not exceed ₹1 million	Investment in equipment is more than ₹1 million but does not exceed ₹20 million	Investment in equipment is more than ₹20million but does not exceed ₹50 million

Source: ADB Asia SME Monitor 2021 database. Data from the Micro, Small and Medium Enterprises Development Act of 2006.

B. After 1 July 2020

Sector	Micro	Small	Medium
Investment in plant and machinery or equipment	Not more than ₹10 million	Not more than ₹100 million	Not more than ₹500 million
Annual turnover	Not more than ₹50 million	Not more than ₹500 million	Not more than ₹2.5 billion

MSME = micro, small, and medium-sized enterprise.

Note: Definitions apply to firms engaged in manufacturing and services.

Source: ADB Asia SME Monitor 2021 database. Data from the Micro, Small and Medium Enterprises Development Act of 2006, amendment (1 June 2020).

Table 4.2: MSME Landscape

*Fiscal year data (end-March)**

Item	2008	2009	2010	2011	2012	2013	2014	2015	2016	2017	2018	2019	2020	2021
NUMBER OF ENTERPRISES														
Number of enterprises, total	...	...	...	...	...	...	...	...	...	...	...	...	...	...
Number of MSMEs[a]	36,176,000	37,736,000	39,370,000	41,080,000	42,873,000	44,764,000	46,754,000	48,846,000	51,057,000	51,299,000	63,387,673	...	...	...
Micro	...	...	...	...	...	...	...	...	...	...	63,051,524	...	...	...
Small	...	...	...	...	...	...	...	...	...	...	330,866	...	...	...
Medium	...	...	...	...	...	...	...	...	...	...	5,282	...	...	...
Number of large enterprises	...	...	...	...	...	...	...	...	...	...	...	...	...	...
MSME to total (%)	...	...	...	...	...	...	...	...	99.9	...	...	...	...	...
MSME growth (%)	...	4.3	4.3	4.3	4.4	4.4	4.4	4.5	4.5	0.5	23.6	...	...	...
MSMEs by sector (% share)														
Agriculture, forestry, and fisheries	...	...	...	...	...	...	...	...	...	...	...	...	...	...
Manufacturing	...	...	...	...	...	...	...	...	...	...	31.0	...	...	...
Transportation and communication	...	...	...	...	...	...	...	...	...	...	...	...	...	...
Construction	...	...	...	...	...	...	...	...	...	...	...	...	...	...
Wholesale and retail trade	...	...	...	...	...	...	...	...	...	...	36.3	...	...	...
Other services	...	...	...	...	...	...	...	...	...	...	32.6	...	...	...
Others	...	...	...	...	...	...	...	...	...	...	0.005	...	...	...
Number of MSMEs by region (% share)														
Urban	...	...	...	...	...	...	...	...	...	...	48.8	...	...	...
Rural	...	...	...	...	...	...	...	...	...	...	51.3	...	...	...
EMPLOYMENT														
Number of employment, total	...	...	...	...	...	...	...	...	...	...	...	...	...	...
Number of employment by MSMEs[a]	80,523,000	84,200,000	88,084,000	92,179,000	96,515,000	101,169,000	106,140,000	111,429,000	117,132,000	111,228,000	110,989,000	...	...	...
Micro	...	...	...	...	...	...	...	...	...	...	107,589,900	...	...	...
Small	...	...	...	...	...	...	...	...	...	...	3,195,000	...	...	...
Medium	...	...	...	...	...	...	...	...	...	...	175,000	...	...	...
Number of employment by large enterprises	...	...	...	...	...	...	...	...	...	...	...	...	...	...
MSME employees to total (%)	...	...	...	...	...	...	...	...	...	...	...	...	...	...
MSME employees growth (%)	...	4.6	4.6	4.6	4.7	4.8	4.9	5.0	5.1	(5.0)	(0.2)	...	...	...
Share of female employees to total employees (%)	...	...	...	...	...	...	...	...	...	...	...	...	...	...
Employment by MSME by sector (% share)														
Agriculture, forestry, and fisheries	...	...	...	...	...	...	...	...	...	...	...	...	...	...
Manufacturing	...	...	...	...	...	...	...	...	...	...	32.5	...	...	...
Transportation and communication	...	...	...	...	...	...	...	...	...	...	...	...	...	...
Construction	...	...	...	...	...	...	...	...	...	...	...	...	...	...
Wholesale and retail trade	...	...	...	...	...	...	...	...	...	...	34.9	...	...	...
Other services	...	...	...	...	...	...	...	...	...	...	32.6	...	...	...
Others	...	...	...	...	...	...	...	...	...	...	0.01	...	...	...
Employment by MSMEs by region (% share)														
Urban	...	...	...	...	...	...	...	...	...	...	44.9	...	...	...
Rural	...	...	...	...	...	...	...	...	...	...	55.2	...	...	...
CONTRIBUTION TO GDP														
GDP of MSMEs (Rs bilion)[a]	24,366	25,621	27,582	30,457	25,833	27,584	29,169	30,888	33,517	36,001	39,196	42,322	...	...
MSME contribution to GDP (% share)	35.4	36.1	36.1	36.7	29.6	29.9	29.8	29.3	29.5	29.3	29.8	30.3	...	...
MSME GDP growth (%)	...	5.2	7.7	10.4	(15.2)	6.8	5.7	5.9	8.5	7.4	8.9	8.0	...	...
GVA of MSMEs (Rs bilion)[b]	...	...	...	...	25,833	29,776	33,430	36,582	40,597	45,021	50,743	57,511	61,072	...
MSME contribution to GVA (% share)	...	...	...	...	31.9	32.4	32.3	31.8	32.3	32.2	34.1	34.8	34.8	...
MSME GVA growth (%)	...	...	...	...	...	15.3	12.3	9.4	11.0	10.9	12.7	13.3	6.2	...
MSME labor productivity (Rs)	...	...	...	...	...	...	...	...	...	...	...	...	...	...
MSME GDP by sector (% share)														
Agriculture, forestry, and fisheries	...	...	...	...	...	...	...	...	...	...	...	...	...	...
Manufacturing	...	...	...	...	...	...	...	...	...	...	...	...	...	...
Transportation and communication	...	...	...	...	...	...	...	...	...	...	...	...	...	...
Construction	...	...	...	...	...	...	...	...	...	...	...	...	...	...
Wholesale and retail trade	...	...	...	...	...	...	...	...	...	...	...	...	...	...
Other services	...	...	...	...	...	...	...	...	...	...	...	...	...	...
Others	...	...	...	...	...	...	...	...	...	...	...	...	...	...
MSME GDP by region (% share)														
Urban	...	...	...	...	...	...	...	...	...	...	...	...	...	...
Rural	...	...	...	...	...	...	...	...	...	...	...	...	...	...
EXPORTS														
Total export value ($ million)	163,132	185,295	178,751	249,816	305,964	300,401	314,415	310,352	262,291	275,852	303,526	330,944	311,035	256,350
Total export growth (%)	...	13.6	(3.5)	39.8	22.5	(1.8)	4.7	(1.3)	(15.5)	5.2	10.0	9.0	(6.0)	(17.6)
MSME export value ($ million)	...	...	...	...	...	127,992	133,313	138,896	130,768	137,068	147,390	159,180	154,801	127,695
MSME export to total export value (%)	...	...	...	...	...	42.6	42.4	44.8	49.9	49.7	48.6	48.1	49.8	49.8
MSME export growth (%)	...	...	...	...	...	...	4.2	4.2	(5.9)	4.8	7.5	8.0	(2.8)	(17.5)
IMPORTS														
Total import value ($ million)	251,654	303,696	288,373	369,769	489,319	490,737	450,200	448,033	381,008	384,357	465,581	515,545	470,923	344,960
Total import growth (%)	...	20.7	(5.0)	28.2	32.3	0.3	(8.3)	(0.5)	(15.0)	0.9	21.1	10.7	(8.7)	(26.7)
MSME import value ($ milion)	...	...	...	...	...	...	...	...	...	...	151,221	154,058	138,740	110,465
MSME import to total import value (%)	...	...	...	...	...	...	...	...	...	...	32.5	29.9	29.5	32.0
MSME import growth (%)	...	...	...	...	...	...	...	...	...	...	...	1.9	(9.9)	(20.4)

GDP = gross domestic product; GVA = gross value added; MSME = micro, small, and medium-sized enterprise.

* The fiscal year (FY) of the Government of India ends on 31 March; e.g., FY2021 covers data from 1 April 2020 to 31 March 2021.a From FY2008 to FY2016, data are based on All India Census of MSMEs; FY2017 data are based on the sixth economic census; Data for FY2018 and after are based on the 73rd National Sample Survey.

[b] RBI Report of the Expert Committee on Micro, Small and Medium Enterprises. GVA is estimated by income approach with FY2012 as base year (compensation of employees + operating surplus + consumption for fixed capital).

Source: ADB Asia SME Monitor 2021 database. Data from the Ministry of MSMEs.

Table 4.3: Bank Credit—Commercial and Cooperative Banks

End-of-year data

Item	2007	2008	2009	2010	2011	2012	2013	2014	2015	2016	2017	2018	2019	2020
OPERATING BANKS														
Number of operating banks, total	...	...	...	...	...	...	...	...	...	...	...	...	...	...
Scheduled banks	...	...	...	...	...	...	...	...	...	...	...	...	...	...
Commercial banks	80	77	80	80	84	86	89	90	90	94	93	94	96	89
Public sector banks	28	27	27	26	26	26	26	27	27	27	21	21	18	12
Private sector banks	23	22	22	21	20	20	20	20	20	21	21	21	22	22
Foreign banks	29	28	31	33	38	40	43	43	43	44	45	45	46	45
Small finance bank group	...	...	...	...	...	...	...	...	...	2	6	7	10	10
Regional rural banks	...	...	...	...	...	...	...	...	...	...	...	...	...	...
Cooperative banks	...	...	...	...	...	...	...	...	...	...	...	...	...	...
Rural cooperative banks	...	...	...	...	...	...	...	...	...	...	...	...	...	...
Urban cooperative banks	...	...	...	...	...	...	...	51	50	52	54	54	54	53
Non-scheduled banks	4	4	4	4	4	4	4	4	4	3	10	13	8	8
Non-scheduled urban cooperative banks	...	...	...	...	...	...	...	1,535	1,526	1,519	1,505	1,494	1,487	1,483
CREDIT														
Commercial banks														
Loans outstanding, total (Rs million)	21,291,607	26,379,868	29,942,292	36,816,211	43,311,578	50,068,806	57,266,282	63,253,210	69,888,750	72,673,495	80,125,631	91,248,293	97,644,778	103,391,249
Public sector banks	15,323,385	19,619,289	22,903,786	27,990,655	32,732,203	37,426,862	42,905,350	46,428,178	49,526,140	49,521,160	52,302,454	57,174,454	57,425,166	60,715,174
Private sector banks	4,490,873	5,007,097	5,411,558	6,888,083	8,250,764	10,044,422	11,504,954	13,567,890	16,751,573	19,490,328	23,967,547	29,440,128	35,217,357	37,670,939
Foreign banks	1,474,251	1,749,432	1,622,147	1,931,385	2,321,619	2,589,331	2,846,388	3,245,192	3,595,911	3,586,768	3,501,268	3,994,206	4,123,886	3,984,814
Small finance bank group-scheduled	...	...	...	...	...	...	...	...	...	70,895	296,615	528,313	872,087	1,013,042
Non-scheduled banks	3,098	4,050	4,801	6,088	6,991	8,191	9,590	11,950	15,126	4,344	57,747	111,192	6,282	7,280
Regional rural banks	...	...	...	...	...	...	...	...	...	...	...	...	...	...
Loans outstanding in domestic currency (Rs million)	20,483,637	25,562,006	28,915,017	35,717,537	41,790,307	48,555,497	55,824,901	61,602,041	69,080,779	71,855,633	79,098,356	90,149,619	96,134,087	101,878,057
Loans outstanding in foreign currency (Rs million)	807,970	817,862	1,027,275	1,098,674	1,521,271	1,513,310	1,441,382	1,651,170	807,970	817,862	1,027,275	1,098,674	1,510,691	1,513,193
Loan growth (%)	22.3	23.9	13.5	23.0	17.6	15.6	14.4	10.5	10.5	4.0	10.3	13.9	7.0	5.9
Total commercial bank loans to GDP (%)	30.9	37.2	39.1	44.4	49.6	54.3	58.4	60.1	61.5	59.0	60.8	65.3	67.0	...
Lending rate (%)	...	...	...	...	...	...	...	...	...	...	...	...	...	...
Gross nonperforming loans (NPLs) (Rs million)	544,477	616,501	801,991	926,610	1,285,535	1,847,410	2,518,075	3,024,531	4,369,015	6,880,701	8,322,538	9,222,769	8,889,695	6,975,841
Gross NPLs to total loans (%)	2.6	2.3	2.7	2.5	3.0	3.7	4.4	4.8	6.3	9.5	10.4	10.1	9.1	6.7
Urban cooperative banks (UCBs)														
Loans outstanding, total (Rs million)	629,282	843,937	1,000,931	1,199,650	1,488,444	1,707,603	1,905,426	2,126,958	2,282,701	2,566,055	2,685,282	2,922,257	3,028,238	3,032,837
Scheduled UCBs	369,033	430,554	477,607	584,837	719,026	828,581	921,903	1,027,355	1,133,321	1,201,507	1,308,583	1,410,615	1,410,391	1,391,698
Non-scheduled UCBs	260,249	413,383	523,324	614,813	769,418	879,022	983,523	1,099,603	1,149,380	1,364,548	1,376,700	1,511,643	1,617,847	1,641,139
Loan growth (%)	...	34.1	18.6	19.9	24.1	14.7	11.6	11.6	7.3	12.4	4.6	8.8	3.6	0.2
Gross NPLs (Rs million) - Scheduled UCBs	49,622	57,388	58,005	56,266	59,705	60,832	75,604	82,379	96,314	110,544	118,507	124,886	162,472	156,284
Gross NPLs (Rs million) - Non-scheduled UCBs	47,466	63,238	74,975	70,723	74,902	85,384	97,907	110,445	126,764	165,864	176,652	205,123	240,581	261,603
Gross NPLs to total loans (%) - Scheduled UCBs	13.4	13.3	12.1	9.6	8.3	7.3	8.2	8.0	8.5	9.2	9.1	8.9	11.5	11.2
Gross NPLs to total loans (%) - Non-scheduled UCBs	18.2	15.3	14.3	11.5	9.7	9.7	10.0	10.0	11.0	12.2	12.8	13.6	14.9	15.9
DEPOSITS														
Commercial banks														
Deposits, total (Rs million)	29,833,179	36,232,674	42,361,484	49,269,729	58,034,937	65,723,541	75,796,400	84,300,548	92,268,019	105,029,630	108,385,184	119,205,527	131,089,813	145,207,071
Deposits in domestic currency (Rs million)	29,102,167	35,258,725	41,528,518	47,929,019	57,017,460	64,718,282	72,285,469	81,327,255	89,013,122	103,255,388	106,613,542	117,039,059	128,663,587	142,683,281
Deposits in foreign currency (Rs million)	731,012	973,949	832,966	1,340,710	1,017,477	1,005,259	3,510,930	2,973,293	3,254,897	1,774,243	1,768,464	2,158,688	2,408,624	2,483,798
Deposit rate (%)	...	...	...	...	...	...	...	...	...	...	...	...	...	...
Urban cooperative banks (UCBs)														
Deposits, total (Rs million)	1,003,411	1,326,831	1,668,675	1,920,220	2,241,904	2,607,636	2,977,432	3,383,290	3,669,122	4,721,539	4,350,739	4,611,225	4,900,782	5,116,033
Scheduled UCBs	594,787	674,098	794,762	918,268	1,072,836	1,254,196	1,415,668	1,629,729	1,788,832	2,108,907	2,053,937	2,140,523	2,241,873	2,328,492
Non-scheduled UCBs	408,624	652,733	873,913	1,001,952	1,169,068	1,353,441	1,561,763	1,753,561	1,880,289	2,612,632	2,296,802	2,470,703	2,658,909	2,787,542
MSME LOANS														
Commercial banks														
MSME loans outstanding, total (Rs million)	...	...	...	...	...	...	...	...	12,051,330	12,061,788	13,585,042	15,816,239	16,980,402	18,186,439
Public sector banks	...	...	...	...	...	...	...	...	9,157,455	8,566,109	9,253,114	10,073,669	9,784,895	9,803,718
Private sector banks	...	...	...	...	...	...	...	...	2,574,964	3,113,956	3,897,212	5,079,144	6,313,398	7,452,352
Foreign banks	...	...	...	...	...	...	...	...	314,515	332,373	312,256	437,489	562,902	582,750
Small finance bank group - Scheduled	...	...	...	...	...	...	...	...	...	48,323	112,812	212,420	315,653	344,138
Non-scheduled Banks	...	...	...	...	...	...	...	...	4,396	1,027	9,648	13,517	3,554	3,481
Regional rural banks	...	...	...	...	...	...	...	...	...	...	...	...	...	...
MSME loans to total loans outstanding (%)	...	...	...	...	...	...	...	...	17.2	16.6	17.0	17.3	17.4	17.6
MSME loans to GDP (%)	...	...	...	...	...	...	...	...	10.6	9.8	10.3	11.3	11.7	--
MSME loan growth (%)	...	...	...	...	...	...	...	...	...	0.1	12.6	16.4	7.4	7.1
MSME lending rate (%, annual average)	...	...	...	...	...	...	...	...	...	...	...	...	...	...
Nonperforming MSME loans (Rs million)	...	...	...	...	...	...	...	...	1,156,321	1,246,214	1,482,100	1,637,547	1,545,805	1,366,862
MSME NPLs to total MSME loans (%)	...	...	...	...	...	...	...	...	9.6	10.3	10.9	10.4	9.1	7.5
Number of MSME loan borrowers	...	...	...	...	...	...	...	...	...	...	...	...	...	...
MSME loan borrowers to total bank borrowers (%)	...	...	...	...	...	...	...	...	...	...	...	...	...	...
MSME loan rejection rate (% of total applications)	...	...	...	...	...	...	...	...	...	...	...	...	...	...
Number of MSME savings account in banks	...	...	...	...	...	...	...	...	...	...	...	...	...	...
Guaranteed MSME loans (Rs million)	...	...	...	...	...	...	...	...	...	...	...	...	...	...
Non-collateral MSME loans (Rs million)	...	...	...	...	...	...	...	...	...	...	...	...	...	...
Urban cooperative banks (UCBs)														
MSME loans outstanding, total (Rs million)	52,833	68,723	79,685	170,155	217,022	242,539	269,069	287,208	317,415	315,220	339,759	391,921	438,728	514,054
Scheduled UCBs	46,404	58,476	62,606	148,124	188,412	203,691	227,373	233,293	254,170	245,599	258,431	297,426	330,827	382,123
Non-scheduled UCBs	6,429	10,246	17,080	22,031	28,610	38,847	41,696	53,915	63,245	69,621	81,328	94,495	107,901	131,930
MSME loans to total loans outstanding (%)	8.4	8.1	8.0	14.2	14.6	14.2	14.1	13.5	13.9	12.3	12.7	13.4	14.5	16.9
MSME loan growth (%)	...	30.1	16.0	113.5	27.5	11.8	10.9	6.7	10.5	(0.7)	7.8	15.4	11.9	17.2

MSME = micro, small, and medium-sized enterprise; SIDBI = Small Industries Development Bank of India.

Notes:

1. Non-scheduled banks include local area banks, small finance banks, and payments banks.
2. "Loans outstanding, total" pertains to gross loans and advances reported by scheduled and non-scheduled commercial banks excluding payments banks.
3. "Gross nonperforming loans (NPLs)" pertains to scheduled and non-scheduled commercial banks excluding payments banks.
4. "Deposits, total" pertains to scheduled and non-scheduled commercial banks. The information on deposits held in domestic or foreign currency for payments banks is not included.
5. Information on MSME NPLs is not available for UCBs.
6. Data on MSME loans by sector and region are not available.

Source: ADB Asia SME Monitor 2021 database. Data from Reserve Bank of India.

Table 4.3a: Small Industries Development Bank of India MSME Loans

*Fiscal year data (end-March)**

Item	2008	2009	2010	2011	2012	2013	2014	2015	2016	2017	2018	2019	2020
MSME LOANS													
MSME loans outstanding, total (Rs million)	190,820	293,350	379,020	460,530	537,850	560,597	612,707	553,425	656,321	682,896	952,906	1,362,303	1,654,215
Indirect credit (Rs million)	140,020	242,990	288,720	351,920	424,694	437,946	492,577	437,561	542,347	576,775	856,139	1,268,190	1,554,286
Refinance	140,020	242,990	252,530	324,100	408,936	426,621	480,882	421,532	522,214	553,700	840,342	1,256,475	1,536,076
Microfinance	...	...	36,190	27,820	15,758	11,325	11,695	16,029	20,133	23,075	15,797	11,715	18,210
Others	...	...	...	...	...	...	...	...	...	...	...	...	...
Direct credit (Rs million)	50,800	50,360	90,300	108,610	113,156	122,651	120,129	115,864	113,973	106,120	96,767	94,113	99,929
Refinance	...	...	...	...	...	...	...	...	...	...	...	...	...
Microfinance	...	...	...	...	...	...	...	...	...	...	...	...	...
Others	...	...	...	...	...	...	...	...	...	...	...	...	...
MSME loans disbursed, total (Rs million)	...	212,539	225,815	287,187	297,570	286,405	391,288	399,191	517,779	353,662	553,132	724,298	1,026,040
Indirect credit (Rs million)	...	193,466	195,894	238,815	254,215	268,605	358,320	373,276	491,354	324,190	531,107	698,138	993,877
Refinance	...	179,323	176,402	231,127	246,160	264,716	351,835	362,143	484,711	314,604	523,216	689,098	982,947
Microfinance	...	14,143	19,492	7,688	8,055	3,889	6,485	11,133	6,643	9,586	7,891	9,040	10,930
Others	...	...	...	...	...	...	...	...	...	...	...	...	...
Direct credit (Rs million)	...	19,073	29,921	48,372	43,355	17,800	32,968	25,915	26,425	29,472	22,025	26,160	32,163
Refinance	...	...	...	...	...	...	...	...	...	...	...	...	...
Microfinance	...	...	...	...	...	...	...	...	...	...	...	...	...
Others	...	19,073	29,921	48,372	43,355	17,800	32,968	25,915	26,425	29,472	22,025	26,160	32,163
MSME loans to total SIDBI loans outstanding (%)	100.0	100.0	100.0	100.0	100.0	100.0	100.0	100.0	100.0	100.0	100.0	100.0	100.0
MSME loans to GDP (%)**	0.4	0.7	0.8	0.9	0.6	0.6	0.5	0.4	0.5	0.4	0.6	0.7	0.8
MSME loan growth (%)	33.8	53.7	29.2	21.5	16.8	4.2	9.3	(9.7)	18.6	4.0	39.5	43.0	21.4
MSME lending rate (%, annual average)	...	9.6	8.6	8.9	9.5	9.7	10.0	9.7	9.0	8.4	7.5	7.5	6.8
Nonperforming MSME loans (NPLs) (Rs million)	2,994	317	771	2,790	3,735	5,542	11,531	7,411	10,081	8,232	9,024	8,679	10,408
MSME NPLs to total MSME loans (%)	1.4	0.1	0.2	0.6	0.7	1.0	1.9	1.3	1.5	1.2	0.9	0.6	0.6
Number of MSME loan borrowers	...	4,815	6,493	7,547	8,257	8,198	7,863	7,141	6,489	6,479	5,857	7,244	15,733
MSME loan borrowers to total SIDBI borrowers (%)	100.0	100.0	100.0	100.0	100.0	100.0	100.0	100.0	100.0	100.0	100.0	100.0	100.0
MSME loan rejection rate (% of total applications)	...	...	...	...	...	...	...	...	...	...	...	...	...
Number of MSME savings account in banks	...	...	...	...	...	...	...	...	...	...	...	...	...
Guaranteed MSME loans (Rs million)	...	278,675	339,107	402,283	456,807	413,758	460,773	440,083	527,216	531,892	837,238	1,296,023	1,637,558
Non-collateral MSME loans (Rs million)	...	34,314	53,282	70,868	92,269	147,619	156,312	115,055	133,662	158,350	126,425	77,403	17,154
MSME loans outstanding by sector (% share)													
Manufacturing	...	9.5	11.7	9.8	8.5	5.7	4.7	6.2	6.3	8.1	6.4	5.2	5.2
Construction	...	4.4	3.0	1.6	1.2	0.9	0.7	0.6	0.5	0.3	0.2	0.1	0.0
Services	...	85.4	82.8	85.1	86.3	87.6	87.9	86.0	88.5	88.4	91.9	93.9	94.5
Others	...	0.7	2.6	3.5	4.1	5.8	6.8	7.3	4.8	3.3	1.5	0.7	0.3
MSME loans outstanding by region (% share)													
Urban	...	...	...	...	...	...	...	...	...	...	...	...	...
Rural	...	...	...	...	...	...	...	...	...	...	...	...	...
MSME loans outstanding by type of use (% share)													
For working capital	...	0.3	0.4	0.6	0.7	0.8	0.8	0.9	0.7	0.8	0.6	0.5	0.4
For capital investment	...	99.7	99.6	99.4	99.3	99.2	99.2	99.1	99.3	99.2	99.4	99.6	99.6
MSME loans outstanding by tenor (% share)													
Less than 1 year	...	53.4	44.4	41.9	49.8	67.3	63.8	74.0	50.7	41.9	20.4	32.6	38.9
1-5 years	...	30.8	40.8	46.2	43.1	27.3	31.0	20.7	44.3	53.8	72.8	64.3	59.3
More than 5 years	...	15.9	14.8	11.9	7.1	5.4	5.2	5.2	5.0	4.4	6.8	3.1	1.8

GDP = gross domestic product; MSME = micro, small, and medium-sized enterprise; SIDBI = Small Industries Development Bank of India.

* The fiscal year (FY) of the Government of India ends on 31 March; e.g., FY2020 covers data from 1 April 2019 to 31 March 2020.

** based on real GDP.

Source: ADB Asia SME Monitor 2021 database. Data from SIDBI.

Table 4.4: Public Financing and Guarantees

*Fiscal year data (end-March)**

Item	2008	2009	2010	2011	2012	2013	2014	2015	2016	2017	2018	2019	2020	2021
SUBSIDIZED LOANS TO MSMEs														
Number of funds	...	...	...	...	...	...	...	...	...	...	...	...	...	...
Number of subsidized loans (new approval)	...	...	...	...	...	...	...	...	...	...	...	...	...	...
Outstanding of subsidized loans to MSMEs (Rs million)	...	...	...	...	...	...	...	...	...	...	...	...	...	...
Subsidized loans disbursed to MSMEs (Rs million)	...	...	...	...	...	...	...	...	...	...	...	...	...	...
Number of MSMEs accepted for subsidized loans	...	...	...	...	...	...	...	...	...	...	...	...	...	...
MSME access to subsidized loans (% of total MSMEs)	...	...	...	...	...	...	...	...	...	...	...	...	...	...
CREDIT GUARANTEES - CGTMSE														
Number of guarantee schemes	...	...	...	...	...	...	...	...	...	...	...	...	...	...
Guaranteed loans outstanding to MSMEs (Rs million)	...	...	...	...	...	...	...	...	...	...	...	...	...	...
Guaranteed loans approved to MSMEs (Rs million)	10,560	21,990	68,750	125,890	137,840	160,620	181,880	212,750	199,490	199,310	190,660	301,680	458,510	...
Growth (%)	...	108.2	212.6	83.1	9.5	16.5	13.2	17.0	(6.2)	(0.1)	(4.3)	58.2	52.0	...
Guaranteed loans disbursed to MSMEs (Rs million)	...	...	...	...	...	...	...	...	...	...	...	...	...	...
Number of MSMEs guaranteed	...	...	...	...	...	...	...	...	...	...	...	...	...	...
MSME access to credit guarantees (% of total MSMEs)	...	...	...	...	...	...	...	...	...	...	...	...	...	...
Guaranteed MSME loans to total MSME loans (%)	...	...	...	...	...	...	...	...	...	...	...	...	...	...
Nonperforming guaranteed MSME loans to total guaranteed MSME loans (%)	...	...	...	...	...	...	...	...	...	...	...	...	...	...
CREDIT GUARANTEES - CGFMU														
Number of guarantee schemes	...	...	...	...	...	...	...	...	...	...	...	...	...	...
Guaranteed loans outstanding to MSMEs (Rs million)	...	...	...	...	...	...	...	...	...	...	...	...	...	...
Guaranteed loans approved to MSMEs (Rs million)	...	...	...	...	...	...	...	...	...	...	398,512	762,533	942,168	...
Growth (%)	...	...	...	...	...	...	...	...	...	...	...	91.3	23.6	...
Guaranteed loans disbursed to MSMEs (Rs million)	...	...	...	...	...	...	...	...	...	...	...	...	...	...
Number of MSMEs guaranteed	...	...	...	...	...	...	...	...	...	...	...	...	...	...
MSME access to credit guarantees (% of total MSMEs)	...	...	...	...	...	...	...	...	...	...	...	...	...	...
Guaranteed MSME loans to total MSME loans (%)	...	...	...	...	...	...	...	...	...	...	...	...	...	...
Nonperforming guaranteed MSME loans to total guaranteed MSME loans (%)	...	...	...	...	...	...	...	...	...	...	...	...	...	...
REFINANCING SCHEME - MUDRA LOANS														
Loans disbursed to MSMEs (Rs million)	...	...	...	...	...	...	...	...	1,374,493	1,805,285	2,536,771	3,217,228	3,374,955	3,217,593
Growth (%)	...	...	...	...	...	...	...	...	...	31.3	40.5	26.8	4.9	(4.7)

CGFMU = Credit Guarantee Fund for Micro Unit; CGTMSE = Credit Guarantee Fund Trust for Micro and Small Enterprises; MSME = micro, small, and medium-sized enterprise; MUDRA = Micro Units Development and Refinancing Agency.

* The fiscal year (FY) of the Government of India ends on 31 March; e.g., FY2021 covers data from 1 April 2020 to 31 March 2021.

Source: ADB Asia SME Monitor 2021 database. Data from CGTMSE Annual Reports; National Credit Guarantee Trustee Company (NCGTC) Annual Report; MUDRA Annual Reports.

Table 4.5: Nonbank Finance

End-of-year data

Item	2015	2016	2017	2018	2019	2020*
NUMBER OF NONBANK FINANCE COMPANIES						
Nonbank finance companies (NBFCs) regulated by Reserve Bank of India (RBI)	...	...	...	...	...	9,533
Asset finance companies (AFCs)	...	...	...	...	...	274
Loan companies (LCs)	...	...	...	...	...	4,115
Investment companies (ICs)	...	...	...	...	...	4,964
Infrastructure finance companies (IFCs)	...	...	...	...	...	9
Core investment companies (CICs)	...	...	...	...	...	64
Infrastructure debt funds (IDF-NBFCs)	...	...	...	...	...	4
Microfinance institutions (NBFC-MFIs)	...	...	...	...	...	94
Factoring companies	...	...	...	...	...	7
Mortgage guarantee companies (MGCs)	...	...	...	...	...	1
Residuary nonbank companies (RNBCs)	...	...	...	...	...	1
NONBANK FINANCE COMPANIES REGULATED BY RBI						
MSME financing outstanding, total (Rs million)	574,766	755,150	1,108,210	1,282,338	1,257,732	1,503,208
Growth (%)	...	31.4	46.8	15.7	(1.9)	19.5
MSME financing to total financing outstanding (%)	6.0	6.7	7.4	7.2	7.2	6.2
MSME financing to GDP (%)	...	...	...	...	...	...
Annual financing rate (%, on average)	...	...	...	...	...	...
Gross nonperforming financing (NPFs) (Rs million)	467,032	606,742	867,226	1,530,874	1,540,101	1,265,910
Gross NPFs to total financing (%)	3.7	3.9	4.8	7.1	6.4	5.8
Savings (Rs million)	251,456	298,472	298,127	369,668	473,927	583,590
Number of customers financed, total	...	...	...	...	...	29,626,962
MSME financing outstanding by sector (% share)						
Services	32.7	39.3	43.7	50.2	58.7	53.1
Manufacturing	67.3	60.7	56.3	49.8	41.3	46.9
MSME financing outstanding by region (% share)						
Urban	...	...	...	...	...	...
Rural	...	...	...	...	...	...
MICROFINANCE INSTITUTIONS						
Loans outstanding, total (Rs million)	92,927	127,519	183,270	199,617	214,526	229,032
Growth (%)	...	37.2	43.7	8.9	7.5	6.8
Total loans to GDP (%)	...	...	...	...	...	...
Annual lending rate (%, on average)	...	...	...	...	...	...
Gross nonperforming loans (NPLs) (Rs million)	27,353	25,306	68,950	24,261	21,298	20,357
Gross NPLs to total loans (%)	9.5	6.7	15.8	4.9	4.0	4.8
Savings (Rs million)	...	...	...	...	...	...
Number of customers financed, total	...	...	...	...	...	16,540,758
Financing outstanding by sector (% share)						
Services	24.1	25.0	23.9	28.9	47.4	...
Manufacturing	75.9	75.0	76.1	71.1	52.6	100.0
Financing outstanding by region (% share)						
Urban	...	...	...	...	...	...
Rural	...	...	...	...	...	...
LOAN COMPANIES						
Loans outstanding, total (Rs million)	298,043	502,736	786,312	885,805	871,039	1,257,855
Growth (%)	...	68.7	56.4	12.7	(1.7)	44.4
Total loans to GDP (%)	...	...	...	...	...	...
Annual lending rate (%, on average)	...	...	...	...	...	...
Gross nonperforming loans (NPLs) (Rs million)	153,855	212,092	310,955	463,892	551,125	819,117
Gross NPLs to total loans (%)	4.0	4.5	5.0	6.6	7.2	6.2
Number of customers financed, total	...	...	...	...	...	13,083,528
Financing outstanding by sector (% share)						
Services	22.6	39.3	43.3	54.3	61.2	63.2
Manufacturing	77.4	60.7	56.7	45.7	38.8	36.8
Financing outstanding by region (% share)						
Urban	...	...	...	...	...	...
Rural	...	...	...	...	...	...
FACTORING COMPANIES						
Financing outstanding, total (Rs million)	3,875	3,556	8,949	13,331	13,831	13,638
Growth (%)	...	(8.2)	151.7	49.0	3.8	(1.4)
Total financing to GDP (%)	...	...	...	...	...	...
Annual financing rate (%, on average)	...	...	...	...	...	...
Gross nonperforming financing (NPFs) (Rs million)	8,689	9,217	9,194	8,775	9,765	8,276
Gross NPFs to total financing (%)	28.7	35.4	34.5	28.2	33.1	28.1
Number of customers financed, total	...	...	...	...	...	2,556
Financing outstanding by sector (% share)						
Services	34.9	38.9	14.5	12.3	13.5	13.6
Manufacturing	65.1	61.1	85.5	87.7	86.5	86.4
Financing outstanding by region (% share)						
Urban	...	...	...	...	...	...
Rural	...	...	...	...	...	...

MSME = micro, small, and medium-sized enterprise; GDP = gross domestic product.
* provisional.

Notes:
1. Number of NBFCs registered data cannot be generated for earlier periods and hence, only December 2020 data is available.
2. Data are at December each year, hence it pertains to NBFC Non Deposit (NDSI) and Deposit Taking as NBFCs only submit returns quarterly.
3. Data related to MSMEs are captured from 2015 onward (data for 2014 and before are not captured).
4. MSME data from 2015 to 2019 pertains to NBFC NDSI only as it was not captured for Deposit Taking.
5. MSME data for December 2020 includes NBFC NDSI and Deposit Taking data.
6. Data for Loan Company is not available for 2020 as the classification has been merged to form a new classification Investment and Credit Company (ICC), hence data for ICC has been furnished for 2020, which includes Loan Company, Asset Finance Company and Investment Company data.
7. The gross nonperforming asset data pertains to NBFC NDSI and Deposit Taking. The definition for NDSI was revised from 2015 to exclude companies with asset size below ₹500 crore.
8. Savings data pertains to deposits held by NBFCs.
9. MSME data for 2019 pertains to 30 NBFC-MFIs data while the data for 2020 pertains to 22 NBFC-MFIs.

Source: ADB Asia SME Monitor 2021 database. Data from Reserve Bank of India.

Table 4.6: Capital Markets

End-of-year data

Item	2007	2008	2009	2010	2011	2012	2013	2014	2015	2016	2017	2018	2019	2020
EQUITY MARKETS														
Main Board - BSE														
Index	20,287	9,647	17,465	20,509	15,455	19,427	21,171	27,499	26,118	26,626	34,057	36,068	41,254	47,751
Market capitalization (Rs million)	72,550,752	32,299,475	61,825,516	74,331,359	54,896,096	70,659,730	71,887,381	99,912,882	102,638,153	108,327,186	159,926,986	145,114,711	156,244,669	189,301,957
Growth (%)	...	(55.5)	91.4	20.2	(26.1)	28.7	1.7	39.0	2.7	5.5	47.6	(9.3)	7.7	21.2
Trading value (Rs million)	14,147,234	13,240,524	12,740,647	11,932,558	6,934,064	5,954,647	5,135,594	7,698,099	7,892,643	7,585,677	12,225,145	8,652,792	6,603,331	8,843,711
Trading volume (million shares)	91,572	80,580	105,917	106,199	65,258	59,851	49,120	78,902	78,364	68,029	77,642	59,755	54,986	88,389
Number of listed companies	...	...	4,955	5,034	5,112	5,191	5,294	5,541	5,835	5,820	5,616	5,396	5,519	5,620
Number of IPOs	...	...	...	...	52	57	78	88	80	81	117	104	69	60
Number of delisted companies	...	...	...	43	29	24	21	16	30	284	412	410	9	56
Main Board - NSE														
Index (Nifty 50)	6,139	2,959	5,201	6,135	4,624	5,905	6,304	8,283	7,946	8,186	10,531	10,863	12,168	13,982
Market capitalization (Rs million)	65,432,719	29,167,684	56,996,368	71,393,098	52,322,733	67,636,325	68,838,919	96,000,303	98,311,405	104,382,107	149,717,750	142,664,429	154,239,724	186,411,638
Growth (%)	91.0	(55.4)	95.4	25.3	(26.7)	29.3	1.8	39.5	2.4	6.2	43.4	(4.7)	8.1	20.9
Trading value (Rs million)	30,939,823	31,885,102	38,120,314	36,576,939	27,632,782	28,107,687	28,220,057	38,762,129	43,566,436	46,725,562	66,191,809	79,904,652	83,911,777	135,294,611
Trading volume (million shares)	137,645	142,263	216,033	186,717	149,499	173,233	160,000	215,921	219,526	247,432	343,116	383,822	426,091	674,625
Number of listed companies[1]	1,158	1,428	1,453	1,552	1,640	1,663	1,675	1,702	1,783	1,807	1,786	1,731	1,749	1,748
Number of IPOs	...	...	...	...	33	9	3	5	20	27	36	24	16	12
Number of delisted companies	7	2	7	3	1	8	1	6	4	52	71	91	18	23
Specialized Board for MSMEs														
BSE SME Exchange														
BSE SME Index	...	...	...	...	...	137	452	1,084	802	1,071	2,069	1,790	1,770	1,386
Market capitalization (Rs million)	...	...	...	...	...	2,871	30,124	90,699	89,577	188,444	215,740	186,110	183,489	212,795
Growth (%)	...	...	...	...	...	...	949.2	201.1	(1.2)	110.4	14.5	(13.7)	(1.4)	16.0
Trading value (Rs million)	...	...	...	...	...	327	3,539	28,160	16,197	13,198	24,032	31,318	20,861	13,480
Trading volume (million shares)	...	...	...	...	...	17	71	217	367	342	473	610	479	309
Number of listed companies	...	...	...	...	...	11	43	82	119	162	216	281	314	331
Number of IPOs	...	...	...	...	...	11	32	39	37	43	54	64	33	17
Number of delisted companies	...	...	...	...	...	...	...	...	...	...	...	...	...	...
Moved to the main board	...	...	...	...	...	...	...	...	10	9	21	17	18	18
Moved from the main board	...	...	...	...	...	...	...	...	...	...	...	...	...	...
NSE Emerge														
Index (Nifty NSE Emerge Index)[2]	...	...	...	...	...	...	...	...	...	...	1,819	1,542	1,346	1,688
Market capitalization (Rs million)	...	...	...	...	...	1,490	2,746	4,292	5,174	14,105	105,207	126,396	79,942	56,048
Growth (%)	...	...	...	...	...	...	84.3	56.3	20.5	172.6	645.9	20.1	(36.8)	(29.9)
Trading value (Rs million)	...	...	...	...	...	180	158	705	1,556	3,755	39,296	55,288	16,536	9,556
Trading volume (million shares)	...	...	...	...	...	3.2	2.5	12.4	24.9	69.3	494.5	604.8	298.1	224.5
Number of listed companies	...	...	...	...	...	2	4	6	11	33	111	192	206	214
Number of IPOs	...	...	...	...	...	2	2	2	5	22	78	81	14	8
Number of delisted companies	...	...	...	...	...	...	...	...	...	...	...	...	...	...
Moved to the main board	...	...	...	...	...	...	...	...	1	1	1	2	19	38
Moved from the main board	...	...	...	...	...	...	...	...	...	...	...	...	...	...

BSE = Bombay Stock Exchange; IPO = initial public offering; MSME = micro, small, and medium-sized enterprise; NSE = National Stock Exchange; SME = small and medium-sized enterprise.

Note: Market capitalization and Index closing values are as on last trading date of the calendar year.
[1] This includes equities, debt, institutional trading platform (ITP), and asset management companies.
[2] Nifty SME Emerge index launched in Nov 2017.

Source: ADB Asia SME Monitor 2021 database. Data from Bombay Stock Exchange and National Stock Exchange.

Table 4.7: Listing Requirements - Bombay Stock Exchange and National Stock Exchange

	Bombay Stock Exchange		National Stock Exchange	
Criteria	Main Board	BSE SME Exchange	Main Board	NSE Emerge
Paidup capital	Minimum post issue paid-up capital of ₹10 crores.	Post issue paid-up capital of less then ₹25 crores.	Paid-up equity capital of not less than 10 crores, and capitalization of not less than ₹25 crores.	Paid-up capital of less then ₹25 crores.
Net worth	n/a,	Positive net worth.	Positive net worth (upto issue size of ₹500 crores).	Positive net worth.
Net tangible assets	n/a,	₹1.5 crores.	n/a,	n/a,
Track Record	SEBI's ICDR guidelines needs to be followed by the company.	"The company or the partnership/ proprietorship/limited liability partnership (LLP) firm or the firm which have been converted into the company should have a combined track record of at least 3 years; or In case it has not completed its operation for 3 years, then the company/partnership/ proprietorship/LLP should have been funded by way of loan/equity by banks or financial institutions or central or state government or its undertaking, or its group company should have been listed for at least 2 years either on the Main Board or SME Board of the Nationwide Exchange. The company or the firm or the firm which have been converted into the company should have combined positive cash accruals (earnings before depreciation and tax) in any of the year out of last 3 years and its net worth should be positive."	Track record of at least 3 years.	Track record of at least 3 years.
Munmer of allottees in IPO	Minimum 1,000.	Minimum 50.	Minimum 1,000.	Minimum 50.
IPO underwriting	Not mandatory (under 50% compulsory subscription to QIB's).	Mandatory (100% underwritten with merchant banker underwriting 15%).	Mandatory (Not required if 50% of issue offered for compulsory subscription by QIBs).	Mandatory (100% underwritten with merchant banker underwriting 15%).
Market making	In post issue, market making is not mandatory.	Market making is mandatory to make the securities more liquid.	Not mandatory.	Mandatory.
Observation on DRHP	By SEBI.	By Stock Exchange.	By SEBI.	By Stock Exchange.
IPO grading	Grading of IPO by the rating agencies registered with SEBI is mandatory.	Grading is not mandatory.	Mandatory.	Grading is not mandatory.
IPO application size	₹10,000 - ₹15,000	Minimum ₹ 100,000 (higher than regular IPO)	₹5,000 - ₹ 7,000	Minimum ₹ 100,000 (higher than regular IPO)
IPO timeframe	6 months onwards.	3 - 4 months.	n/a,	n/a,
Reporting requirement	Quarterly.	Biannual.	Quarterly.	Biannual.
Other Details	The minimum issue size shall be ₹10 crores.	The company should mandatorily facilitate trading in demat securities and enter into an agreement with both the depositories.	The company must not be referred to the Board of Industrial and Financial Reconstruction and/or no proceedings have been admitted under Insolvency and Bankruptcy Code against the issuer and promoting companies.	The company must not be referred to erstwhile Board for Industrial and Financial Reconstruction or no proceedings have been admitted under Insolvency and Bankruptcy Code against the issuer and promoting companies.
		The company should mandatorily have website.	The company has not received any winding up petition admitted by a NCLT.	The company has not received any winding up petition admitted by a NCLT/Court.
	The minimum market capitalization of the company shall be ₹25 crores (market capitalization shall be calculated by multiplying the post-issue paid-up number of equity shares with the issue price).	The company should have no change in the promoters in the preceding 1 year from the date of filing its application on BSE for listing on SME Segment.		No material regulatory or disciplinary action by a stock exchange or regulatory authority in the past 3 years against the applicant company.

DRHP = draft red herring prospectus, ICDR = Issue of Capital and Disclosure Requirements, IPO = initial public offering, NCLT = National Company Law Tribunal, QIB = qualified institutional buyer, SEBI = Securities and Exchange Board of India.

Source: ADB Asia SME Monitor 2021 database. Data from Bombay Stock Exchange and National Stock Exchange.

Table 4.8: Policies and Regulations

Regulations	
Name	**Outline**
Micro, Small and Medium Enterprise Development (MSMED) Act 2006	1) Regulatory framework for MSMEs. 2) Concessional public schemes for MSME development. 3) Proposal of a procurement preferential policy. 4) Proposal for closure of business policy to regulate liquidation of weak or stressed units. 5) Compensation for delayed payments in procurement from MSMEs.
Limited Liability Partnership Act 2008	Facilitating the establishment of limited partnership firms.
Banking Regulation Act 1949	Regulation on banking activities.
Securitization and Reconstruction of Financial Assets and Enforcement of Security Interest Act 2002	Establishment of the Central Registry of Securitization Asset Reconstruction and Security Interest (CERSAI).
Factoring Regulation Act 2011	Facilitating alternative financing models for MSMEs.
SEBI Alternate Investment Funds (AIF) Regulations 2012	Regulatory framework for Alternative Investment Funds (AIFs), including SME Funds. AIF Regulations cover three categories: Category I has 4 sub-categories, one of which covers SME Funds. All other categories/sub-categories of AIFs may also invest in SMEs.
SEBI Issue of Capital and Disclosure Requirements (ICDR) Regulations, 2018	Chapter IX of ICDR Regulations pertains to eligibiltiy criteria and various requirements with respect to initial SME public offerings.

Regulators and Policymakers	
Name	**Responsibility**
Ministry of Micro, Small, and Medium-Sized Enterprises (Ministry of MSMEs)	Policies and regulations for the development of MSMEs.
National Board of MSMEs	Reviewing policies/programs of the central government for promotion and development of MSMEs; providing necessary recommendations and advise the central government on the use of funds constituted under the MSMED Act 2006.
Ministry of Commerce and Industry (MCI)	Concessional policies for MSME exporters.
Ministry of Skill Development and Entrepreneurship (MSDE)	Driving programs in skill development and entrepreneurships. MSDE launched a pilot project on Entrepreneurship Promotion and Mentoring of Micro and Small Businesses in six "temple" towns in 2020.
Ministry of Agriculture	Developing agricultural value chains; established a National Agriculture Infrastructure Financing Fund; providing funding support to small farm entrepreneurs identified under One District One Product scheme.
Reserve Bank of India (RBI)	Regulating and supervising banks and nonbanks.
RBI Committee on MSMEs	In 2018–2019, RBI constituted an expert committee on MSMEs to undertake a comprehensive review of the MSME sector. The committee's task force submitted its findings in 2019, addressing long-term recommendations to the central government and the RBI for the economic and financial stability of MSMEs.
Securities and Exchange Board of India (SEBI)	Regulating and supervising capital markets, including SME exchanges.

Policies		
Name	**Responsible Entity**	**Outline**
National Manufacturing Competitiveness Programme (2005)	Ministry of MSMEs	A 10-component program aimed at building the capacity of MSME manufacturers to enable them to compete with multinationals both in domestic and international markets. Components include marketing support, building awareness, and training.
Rajiv Gandhi Udyami Mitra Yojna (2008)	Ministry of MSMEs	Support to potential first-generation entrepreneurs and existing entrepreneurs on legal and procedural issues in completing formalities required for establishing and running an enterprise.
Public Procurement Policy for Goods and Services Produced and Rendered by Micro and Small Enterprises (2012)	Government of India	Mandating central governmental ministries and departments to procure a minimum of 20% of their total purchases of goods and services from MSMEs.
Scheme of Fund for Regeneration of Traditional Industries (SFURTI) (2005–06)	Ministry of MSMEs	Improving the productivity of traditional industries by organizing clusters.
RBI Master Circular—Lending to Micro, Small and Medium Enterprises (2014)	RBI	Compilation of instructions given by the RBI to banks and financial institutions regarding lending to MSMEs.
Guidelines for setting up of and operating TReDS (2014)	RBI	RBI guidelines for setting up and operating the Trade Receivables Discounting System (TReDS).
National Strategy for Financial Inclusion (NSFI) 2019-2024	RBI	NSFI (2019-24) is a document outlining the vision and various action plans to make financial services available, accessible, and affordable to all vulnerable segments and sectors of the economy, including MSMEs, in a safe, transparent manner that supports inclusive and resilient multistakeholder-led growth. It does not yet have segment/sector specific plans.
Interest Equalization Scheme (IES) on pre- and post-shipment rupee export credit (2015)	MCI	Interest equalization at 3% per annum available to eligible exporters, which include manufacturers exporting the 416 four-digit tariff lines and all MSME merchandise exporters. As a part of the MSME package, MSME exporters are given an enhanced interest equalization rate from 3% to 5%under the ongoing IES on pre- and post-shipment rupee export credits. IES has been extended until 30 September 2021 with the same scope and coverage.
Developing District as Export Hub	MCI	The Department of Commerce through the Regional Authorities of Directrate General of Foreign Trade is working with State/Union Territory (UT) Governments to create/promote an Export Hub in districts and enable a phased implementation. One objective is to enable MSMEs, farmers, and small industries to benefit from export opportunities in foreign markets.
Market Access Initiative (MAI) scheme	MCI	The MAI scheme is an export promotion scheme, designed as a catalyst to promote India's exports sustainably. One provision provides financial assistance to Export Promotion Councils and Trade Bodies to organize virtual export promotion events. It encourages articipation in major virtual global events. The digital transformation will allow exporters, particularly MSMEs, to promote and market products to international buyers digitally.

( ) = year when the program/initiative was launched.
MSME = micro, small, and medium-sized enterprise, SME = small and medium-sized enterprise.
Note: In 2009-10, Prime Minister's task force on MSME provided the necessary long term recommendations to be implemented by various central government agencies in India on MSME development, but the task force is not active anymore.
Source: ADB Asia SME Monitor 2021 database. Data from Annual Report of MSMEs for the Financial Year 2012–13 and the Ministry of MSMEs website.

Table 4.9: COVID-19 Emergency Measures

Name	Fund (₹ crores)	Outline
MSME support measures		
Relaxation in statutory and compliance matters	--	Extension in filing income tax returns and Goods and Services Tax (GST).
Access to finance	300,000	Emergency Credit Line Guarantee Scheme (ECLGS): Emergency credit line to MSMEs from banks and nonbank finance companies up to 20% of outstanding credit, with credit guarantees.
	20,000	Credit Guarantee Scheme for Subordinate Debt (CGSSD): Promoters of the MSME will be given subordinate debt by banks, which will be infused by the promoter as equity in the unit.
	50,000	Equity infusion for MSMEs through a Fund of Funds.
Liquidity interventions	--	MSME receivables from the government and central public sector enterprises to be paid within 45 days.
		Payment of 6-month employer and employee contributions to provident funds.
		Reduction in statutory provident fund contribution of both employer and employee for 3 months from 12% to 10%.
Tax measures	--	Due date of income tax returns and audits extended by 4 months.
		Pending income tax refunds upto ₹500,000 credited to taxpayer accounts.
		Reduction of existing rates of Tax Deduction at Source (TDS) and Tax Collection at Source (TCS) by 25%.
Other assistance for MSMEs	--	Suspension of fresh initiation of insolvency proceedings up to 1 year depending upon the pandemic situation.
		One time restructuring of standard MSME loans that were in default without an asset classification downgrade.
		Lenders are allowed to implement a resolution plan under the prudential framework for stressed MSMEs with loans of more than ₹25 crores.
		Preference to MSMEs for government procurement tenders up to ₹200 crores.
		Moratorium on repayment of installments for term loans/overdraft by MSMEs.
		Special liquidity measures for nonbank finance companies, housing finance companies, and microfinance institutions.
		Permissible loan to value ratio (LTV) for loans against pledge of gold ornaments and jewellery for non-agricultural purposes increased from 75% to 90%.
		Central government agencies to provide extension of 6 months to fulfill contractual obligations by contractors and offer partial guarantees to contractors.
Other measures		
Pradhan Mantri Garib Kalyan Package	170,000	Economic relief package to the poor.
		Insurance cover to the health workers upto ₹5 million per worker.
		Free gas, rice or wheat and pulses for 3 months to the poor.
Emergency health response package	15,000	Health package to be given to state governments and Union Territories in three phases until March 2024 to build health infrastructure, including setting up labs, procuring essential medicines, etc.
Relief package for distribution companies (DISCOMs)	90,000	Liquidity support: the state-owned Power Finance Corporation will infuse liquidity to DISCOMs against receivables dues.

MSME = micro, small, and medium-sized enterprise.

Source: ADB Asia SME Monitor 2021 database. Data from Covid-19 Interministerial Notifications (https://covid19.india.gov.in/document-category/ministry-of-finance/).

Table 4.9a: COVID-19 Measures in Capital Markets—SEBI

Name	Outline
Relaxation in Creeping Acquistion under Regulation 3 (2) of SEBI Substantial Acquisition of Shares and Takeovers (SAST) Regulations, 2011	The relaxation provides flexibility for enterprises to raise capital in the wake of developments related to COVID-19: SAST Regulation 3 (2) allows an acquirer along with persons acting in concert (PACs) holding 25 % or more shares in a target company to acquire additional shares in the target company up to 5% within a financial year without making an open offer. This relaxation increases the limit of 5% to 10% for acquisition, only in the form of preferential issue to promoters for FY2021 without requiring an open offer, thereby enabling companies to infuse capital directly from promoters.
Relaxation in Voluntary Open Offer under Regulation 6 (1) of SEBI (SAST) Regulations, 2011	The voluntary open offer can provide temporary support due to falling prices caused by the pandemic. A voluntary open offer can be made by an acquirer who, along with PACs, holds 25% or more shares or voting rights in the company. There is a restriction that if the acquirer/PAC has acquired shares of the company in the preceding 52 weeks, acquirer/PAC shall not be eligible to make a voluntary open offer. However, this restriction has been temporarily relaxed for FY2021 to permit voluntary open offers, even if the acquirer/PAC has purchased shares in the preceding 52 weeks.
Relaxation in regulation 24 (i)(f) of SEBI (buy-back of securities) Regulations, 2018	Regulation 24 (i)(f) provides a restriction that the companies shall not raise further capital for a period of 1 year from the expiry of the buyback period, except in discharge of their subsisting obligations. To enable the company to access capital quicker, SEBI has temporarily relaxed the period of restriction from 1 year to 6 months. This was applicable until 31 December 2020.
Relaxation in filing fees for buy-back of shares	Reduce filing fees for a limited period. The filing fees for buyback of shares were reduced by 50% from June to December 2020. SEBI (buy-back of securities) Regulations of 2018 were amended accordingly.
Relaxations on rights issue	SEBI Circular dated 21 April 2020 introduced the temporary relaxation on rights issue as stipulated in SEBI ICDR Regulations of 2018. These were applicable until 31 March 2021: "i) Eligibility conditions for fast track rights issue: Ease the eligibility requirement of average market capitalization of public shareholding from ₹250 crores to ₹100 crores. The requirement on equzity shares to be listed for at least 3 years was relaxed to 18 months. The condition for no audit qualifications on issuer's audited accounts was replaced with the requirement to disclose the impact of audit qualifications on issuer's financials." "ii) Minimum subscription requirement for rights issue: Minimum subscription requirements for a rights issue was reduced from 90% to 75% of the offer size, subject to certain conditions. " "iii) Minimum threshold requirement for rights issue to file draft offer document: Not requiring the existing threshold to file draft offer document in case of rights issue of ₹10 crores and permitted listed entities raising funds upto ₹25 crores. "
Relaxation on validity of SEBI observations	The validity of SEBI observations expiring between 1 March and 30 September 2020, was extended by 6 months from the date of observation. Those expiring between 1 October and 31 March 2020 were extended until 31 March 2021.
Flexibility on issue size	SEBI permitted an issuer to increase or decrease the fresh issue size by up to 50% of the estimated issue size without requiring to file fresh draft offer document with SEBI. It was effective until 31 March 2021.
Relaxation in eligibility conditions for fast track further public offer	Relax eligibility conditions for fast track public offer opening on or before 31 March 2020. The requirement of average market capitalization of public shareholding of ₹1,000 crores was reduced to ₹500 crores. The condition related to impact of audit qualifications on the audit accounts of the issuer was replaced with the requirement to disclose the impact of audit qualifications on issuer's financials.
Relaxation for procedural matters (issues and listing) on rights issue	One-shot relaxation was granted from strict enforcement of SEBI ICDR Regulations of 2018, pertaining to rights issues, opening up to 31 July 2020. Issuers were permitted to serve the abridged letter of offer and other issue material to shareholders by electronic means. Pursuant to the introduction of dematerialized rights entitlements, SEBI also permitted the physical shareholders to submit their rights application in physical form, in case they had been unable to open a demat account due to lockdowns subject to stipulated conditions. To ensure that all eligible shareholders are able to apply to rights issue during the COVID-19 pandemic, the issuer was mandated to institute an optional mechanism (non-cash mode only) to accept the applications of shareholders subject to ensuring that no third party payments shall be allowed in respect of any application. The aforementioned provisions were further extended for rights issues opening up to 31 December 2020. Additionally, the mandate regarding an optional mechanism was further extended for rights issues opening up to 31 March 2021.
Relaxation in pricing of preferential issues	SEBI granted relaxation and provided an additional option to the existing pricing methodology for preferential issuance. SEBI permitted the issuers to consider the average of weekly high and low of the volume weighted average price (VWAP) of the related equity shares during the 12 weeks preceding the relevant date or the average of weekly high and low of the VWAP of the related equity shares during the 2 weeks preceding the relevant date. This additional pricing option was available in case of allotment by preferential issue made until 31 December 2020.
Relaxation in filing fees for public issue and right issue	The filing fees for all kinds of public issues and rights issues were reduced by 50% from June to December 2020.
Relaxation to ease fund raising from primary market by using non-convertible debentures (NCD)/ non-convertible redeemable preferance shares (NCRPS)/ commercial paper (CP)	"A number of relaxations were introduced to ease raising funds from the primary market by issuing NCD/NCRPS/CP during the COVID-19 pandemic. These were applicable to all entities including MSMEs. 1) listed entities compliant with listing regulations and continuous disclosure requirements could raise funds by issuing NCD/NCRPS/CP until 30 June 2020 while disclosing financial results of 30 September 2019. 2) listed issuers, who have issued NCDs/NCRPS/CPs on or after 1 July 2020 and intend/propose to list such issues NCDs/NCRPS/CPs on or before 31 July 2020 to use available financials as of 31 December 2019."

Source: ADB Asia SME Monitor 2021 database. Data from Securities and Exchange Board of India (SEBI).

Country Review

Nepal

Overview

Nepal's economy contracted by 2.1% in fiscal year (FY) 2020 (ended 15 July 2020), far below the 6.7% growth in FY2019 before the coronavirus disease (COVID-19) pandemic struck.[98] The economy is forecast to recover with 2.3% growth in FY2021.[99] Agriculture contributes 26.4% to the country's gross domestic product (GDP), followed by sluggish manufacturing (12.5%) and robust services sector (61.1%). Value added is often fueled by good monsoons, increased consumption driven by remittances, and private investment. The growth in services is driven by private construction and power generation.

With a population of nearly 30 million, the country has workforce of 20.7 million with a labor participation rate of 38.5% (FY2018). One in five people employed works in non-subsistence agriculture. Almost 85% of workers are in the informal sector.

Micro, small, and medium-sized enterprises (MSMEs) are the key pillar of the country's economy, contributing 22% of GDP and employing 2.8 million people. Between FY2010 and FY2019, micro and small enterprises increased 2.5 times to 390,493 firms. However, the growth rate of MSMEs has been uneven across sectors. The share of manufacturing MSMEs have steadily declined, whereas tourism and agriculture, forestry, and fisheries increased the number of operating MSMEs.

Access to bank credit remains limited for MSMEs, with 16% sourcing funds from banks and financial institutions. Around 11% of outstanding commercial bank loans are with MSMEs. To improve access to finance, the government and central bank provide several soft loan programs, a mandatory lending scheme (5% of loan portfolios are allocated to target groups such as MSMEs), refinancing facilities, and consulting services. A credit guarantee corporation (DCGF), credit information bureau, and secured transaction registry play vital roles in reducing the MSME financing gap. Yet, it remains large with many MSMEs unable to tap the formal financial system.

There is no comprehensive national policy framework for MSMEs. The government's MSME policies are guided by its Industrial Promotion Policy, 5-year plans, annual national budgets, and sector programs from line ministries. The central bank has a Financial Inclusion Roadmap for 2017-2022 and a Financial Literacy Framework to accelerate inclusive growth in the country.

98 Central Bureau of Statistic (2021), National Accounts Statistics of Nepal (2020/21 Annual Estimates), Kathmandu, Nepal.

99 Asian Development Bank. 2021. Asian Development Outlook 2021 Update. September.

1. COVID-19 Impact on MSMEs

COVID-19 posed the unprecedented public health crisis in Nepal. Through 18 July 2021, 667,109 people had been infected and more than 9,550 lives had been lost. The government imposed a strict nationwide lockdown from 24 March to 21 July 2020 to slow the virus spread and adopted health safety measures like social distancing and facemask protocols. This was followed by several rounds of partial or full restrictions on mobility and economic activities.

These steps hurt the economy at macro, firm, and household levels. The lockdown halted economic activities and crippled the economy—with reduced production, job losses, and a likely rise in poverty. As the pandemic continues, the full extent of its economic impact has been fully ascertained. However, initial estimates of the damage following the pandemic's first wave from May 2020 to February 2021—and a second wave still ongoing into July 2021—suggest the impact is severe and will likely continue through 2021 and well into 2022.

In FY2020, the economy contracted by 2.1%, following a streak of high growth the previous 3 years. The Asian Development Bank (ADB) projects the economy to show a modest recovery of 2.3% in FY2021 and 4.1% in FY2022 (footnote 99). The projection is based on the "anticipation of vaccination progress against COVID-19, regional and global economic recovery, assumption of a good monsoon leading to better harvest, and steady inflows of workers' remittance" (ADB 2021).[100] The second-wave resurgence of infections starting in mid-April 2021 and subsequent rounds of economic restrictions lowered earlier forecasts for a 2021 recovery. At the firm level, the lockdowns restricting people's mobility and discouraging in-person contact affected the majority of firms across economic sectors, including MSMEs.

MSMEs are the lynchpin of the economy, contributing 22% of GDP and employing 2.8 million people.[101,102] However, almost half of all business establishments are unregistered, and more than 90% of workers working in MSMEs with fewer than 10 workers have informal employee relationships (Central Bureau of Statistics 2017 and 2018). Thus, MSME contributions to the economy are not recorded in formal statistics and their impact not fully reflected in analyses. Thus, the pandemic's impact on MSMEs hurt the economy well beyond data officially released.

The Nepal Rastra Bank (NRB), the central bank, conducted a snap survey in July 2020 to estimate the COVID-19 impact 1 month after the nationwide lockdown was lifted. The NRB did a follow-up survey in December 2020. These reports are the only nationwide government surveys on the economic impact on MSMEs.

As of July 2020, 61% of the firms surveyed had not reopened whereas only 4% were operating at full capacity.[103] The situation vastly improved 6 months later where more than half of the firms (54%) were operating at full capacity with another 37% operating but below capacity. One in 10 businesses remained closed (Figure 5.1A and Table 5.2).

While large businesses were relatively quick to reopen, a large portion of MSMEs had to overcome several challenges. For example, only 39% of small businesses were in full operation even 6 months after the lockdown

[100] ADB. 2021. Nepal's Economy to Post Modest Recovery in FY2021. News release. 28 April. https://www.adb.org/news/nepal-economy-post-modest-recovery-fy2021.

[101] Nepal Rastra Bank (2019): https://www.nrb.org.np/contents/uploads/2020/04/Study_Reports-नेपालमा साना तथा मझौला उद्धयम वत्तिीय साधन परचािलन-2076.pdf.

[102] Data are from Micro, Cottage and Small Industries Statistics 2018–2019; Department of Industries of the Ministry of Industries, Commerce and Supplies (MOICS). Two employment numbers are from different sources (NRB and MOICS). The NRB says there were 1.7 million SME employees whereas the MOICS report refers to 2.8 million employees from micro, cottage, and small industries. This chapter uses MOICS data.

[103] Nepal Rastra Bank. 2020. Impact of Covid-19 on the economy. https://www.nrb.org.np/contents/uploads/2020/08/Survey-Report-onCOVID-Impact-Final.pdf

compared to 75% of large businesses. Similarly, cottage industries were two times more likely to remain shut than large industries.

In addition, sales transactions were well short of their pre-pandemic level. In July 2020, 96.6% of the firms surveyed reported reduced transaction levels, including cottage industries (97.3%), micro (97.2%), small (95.5%), medium (92.6%), and large firms (86.2%) (Figure 5.1B). A tiny 0.88% of the firms reported higher transaction levels while 2.4% reported no change.

While transaction levels improved in December compared with July 2020, firms were doing only half of the business as conducted before the pandemic. This was true across all types of firms, although medium-sized and large firms performed slightly better than the national average (Figure 1B). This was largely due to subdued demand in the economy, job losses, and lower incomes.

The recovery thus far has been uneven across sectors. Hotels and restaurants, hardest hit by the pandemic, were slowest to recover. Immediately after the lockdown was lifted in July 2020, business was estimated down by 93% compared with the pre-pandemic level. By December 2020, it had recovered modestly (82%). Over the same period, education (37.6%), communications (42.3%), and real estate and rental services (46.4%) were slowest to recover. Electricity, gas, and water (92.5%); agriculture, forest, and fisheries (72.0%); manufacturing (61.9%); and wholesale and retail trade (57.2%) recovered relatively quicker.

The pandemic affected employment and wages as well. In July 2020, firms were operating with 77.5% of the number of pre-pandemic employees (March 2020). This increased by 10 percentage points to 87.5% in December 2020. Similarly, wage costs over the 6-month period increased by 7 percentage points, from 63.4% to 70.4% from pre-pandemic levels (March 2020). Wage costs rose most among large industries (17.2%), followed by medium-sized (10.5%) and cottage (10.3%) industries.

Figure 5.1: COVID-19 Impact on Businesses

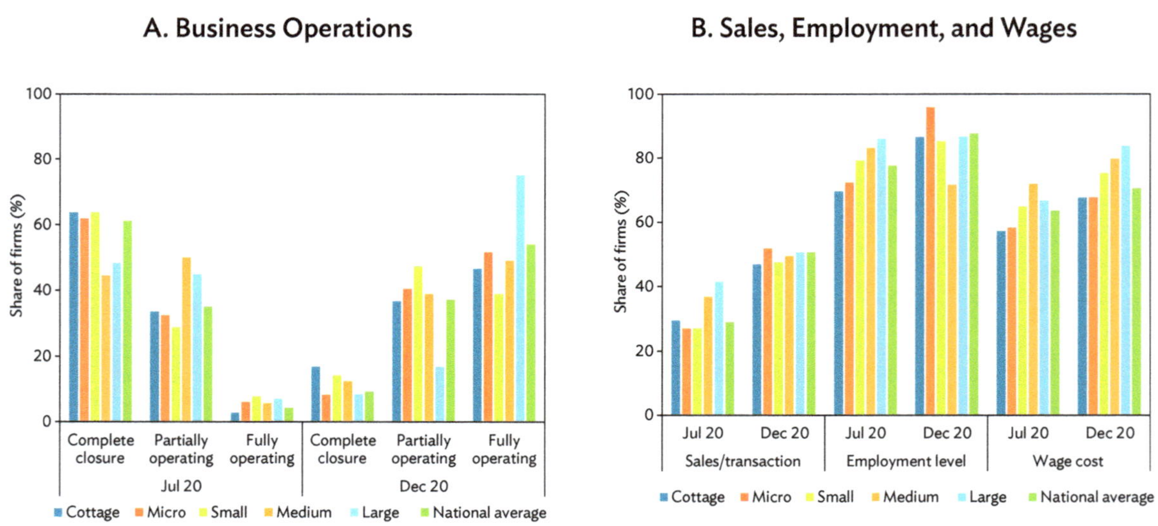

Source: Impact of COVID-19 on Economy First Follow-up July 2020; Second Follow-up Dec 2020; Nepal Rastra Bank.

MSMEs face several challenges due to the COVID-19 pandemic. A decline in sales due to low demand was obvious during the lockdown. This resulted in insufficient revenue to meet even basic operating expenses like wages and salaries, rent, and interest payments. MSMEs also reported difficulties in obtaining additional bank loans given limited liquidity and working capital, according to the NRB survey of firms (NRB 2020).

2. MSME Development

- The number of MSMEs is rising. From FY2010 to FY2019, MSMEs increased 2.5 times, reaching 390,493 as of mid-July 2019. A new definition on micro, cottage, small, and medium-sized enterprises has been effective since February 2020.
- MSMEs employed nearly 2.8 million workers as of mid-July 2019, with an average annual growth rate of 4.3% from FY2009 to FY2019.
- MSMEs contribute 22% of GDP. Their productivity, measured by annual sales per entity, is estimated to be over 4.7 times lower than large firms.
- Market access is one of the major problems MSMEs face. Foreign direct investment has helped them enter and expand both domestic and global markets.
- High mobile phone and internet penetration has contributed to the emergence of a large number of MSMEs engaged in e-commerce.
- There are several business associations such as the Federation of Nepal Cottage and Small Industries (FNCSI), FWEAN, FNCCI, and the Confederation of Nepalese Industries supporting MSME business development through networking, training, and advice.

Scale of MSMEs

The Industrial Enterprises Act 2020 classifies firms in five categories by size: (i) micro, (ii) cottage, (iii) small, (iv) medium, and (v) large. The act defines a microenterprise as one with fewer than nine employees (including the entrepreneur), annual transactions less than NRs10 million, fixed capital of less than NRs2 million, and energy usage less than 20 kilowatts (KW) (Table 5.1). Cottage industries are based on (i) traditional skills and technology; (ii) specific skills or supply of local raw materials, technologies, arts, and culture; and (iii) energy use up to 50 KW.

The other categories are classified solely based on fixed capital. A small firm is one with fixed capital not exceeding NRs150 million. A medium-sized firm has fixed capital from NRs150 million to NRs500 million, while a large firm has fixed capital exceeding NRs500 million.

The Industrial Enterprises Act 2020 replaced the Industrial Enterprises Act 1992, effective 11 February 2020. Thus, most available data are based on the old definition and do not include microenterprises as the 1992 Act did not include them.[104] The term MSME is used throughout this report unless a specific category is cited.

Aside from the national definition, banks and financial institutions use their own definitions to categorize firms. And they differ by bank. Some use borrowing limits of NRs1 million to NRs10 million to define small and medium-sized enterprises, whereas other banks use NRs50 million to NRs200 million. These divergent standards make it difficult to produce consistent MSME data.

[104] The Industrial Enterprises Act 1990 (i) had no category for micro enterprises, (ii) provided a specific industry list for the cottage industries (https://www.lawcommission.gov.np/en/archives/category/documents/prevailing-law/statutes-acts/the-industrial-enterprises-act-2049-1992), (iii) defined small enterprises as a firm with fixed assets up to NRs30 million, and (iv) a medium-sized enterprise as a firm with fixed assets of NRs30 million–NRs100 million.

The number of MSMEs is growing.[105] From FY2010 to FY2019, it expanded 2.5 times—reaching 390,493 by mid-July 2019 (Figure 5.2A and Table 5.3-1). After moderate growth early on, the number of MSMEs has been steadily rising since FY2016. The conclusion of the peace process, promulgation of a new constitution, and local and national elections created conducive, stable environment for entrepreneurs to start new ventures.

The growth of MSMEs have been uneven across sectors. The share of manufacturing MSMEs has steadily declined since FY2010. Then, 49.2% of MSMEs were in manufacturing, while in FY2019, 33.2% came from the sector (Figure 5.2B). Tourism expanded at a compound annual growth rate (CAGR) of 14.4% between FY2010 and FY2019, while agriculture, forestry, and fisheries saw the number of MSMEs grow at a CAGR of 29.5% in 2019, There were very few MSMEs in energy (0.4%), mining and minerals (0.3%), and information and communications technology (ICT) (0.1%). However, it is likely many registered MSMEs are no longer operating, whereas many new MSMEs are not formally registered (Department of Industry 2018).[106]

Also, the geographic spread of MSMEs is quite uneven. In July 2019, 35% were in Bagmati province, where the national capital Kathmandu is situated (Figure 5.2C). Lumbini province has 17% with Province 1 and 2 each having 14%. This is consistent with provincial GDP data.

Data compiled by the Department of Industries (Industrial Statistics 2020) shows that in FY2020, Bagmati had a higher concentration of small firms (79.6% of all small firms) than medium firms (49.4% of all medium firms) or large firms (39.6% of all large firms) (Figure 5.2D).[107] The high concentration of enterprises in Bagmati province is because the Kathmandu Valley is located there. Kathmandu is not only the most populated city in the country but also its main economic center—with a relatively well-developed MSME ecosystem and available technology. It has a more economically active and educated population. People from around the country migrate to Kathmandu in search for job and economic opportunities. Besides being the center for government, Kathmandu is also the headquarters for almost all bank and financial institutions and business houses.

Employment

MSMEs are also one of the largest employers in the country with a workforce of nearly 2.8 million (Figure 5.3A). The average annual growth rate of employment by MSMEs was 4.3% from FY2009 to FY2019. This mimicked the healthy economic growth following the start of the peace process that ended the 1996-2006 civil conflict. GDP growth has been rising since FY2015, peaking at 7.7% in FY2019. The peace and stability provided impetus for heightened economic activity and job creation. The Economic Census 2018 showed that 42.7% of all establishments were in operations in and after 2015 (Central Bureau of Statistics 2018).

Industrial Statistics reported that in FY2020, total employment by registered businesses was 616,502. SMEs held a 73.5% share—46.3% for small enterprises and 27.2% for medium-sized enterprises—with large enterprises at 26.5%.

105 The Department of Industries under the Ministry of Industries, Commerce and Supplies (MOICS) produces two datasets related to MSMEs. The first includes data for "Micro, Cottage and Small Industries" with the second covering "Small, Medium and Large Industries." The first is produced by the Department of Small and Cottage Industries and is based on the firm's registration with department offices around the country (Table 5.3-2). Historical data are published under micro, cottage and small industry statistics 2075—76 (FY2019) booklet. There are several data inconsistencies. The second dataset is produced by the Department of Industries with data covering "small, medium and large industries." The data are sourced from the Industrial Statistics book for each year.

106 Micro, Cottage and Small Industry Statistics 2075-76 (FY2019) booklet, Department of Industry.

107 The data in the 'Industrial Statistics' are based on the information submitted by investor during the firm registration at the Department of Industry, Nepal. Data on industrial capital employed and person engaged are proposed estimates. There may be the variation with actual number after the implementation of the project.

Figure 5.2: Number of MSMEs

A. Overall MSMEs

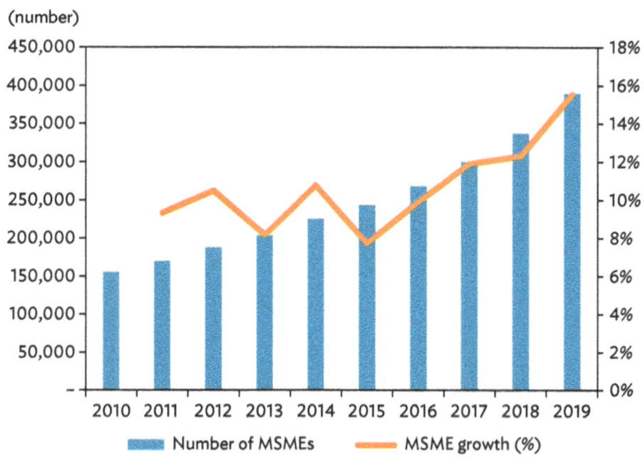

MSME = micro, small, and medium-sized enterprise.

Notes: Fiscal year data. Data refer to micro, cottage, and small industries only.

Source: ADB Asia SME Monitor 2021 database. Data from Department of Industries, MOICS, Nepal 2018-19.

B. By Sector, FY2019

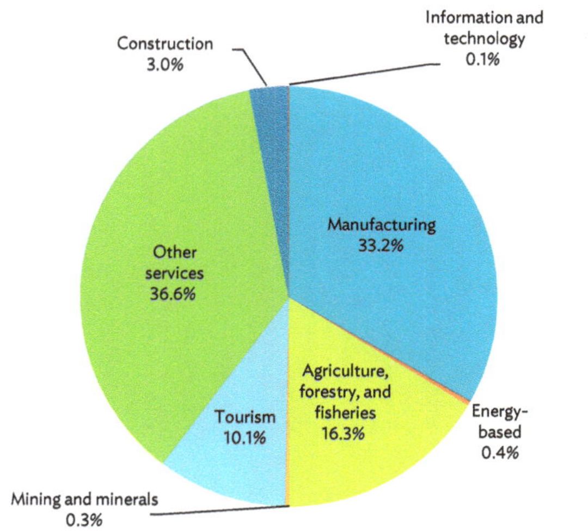

FY = fiscal year.

Note: Data refer to micro, cottage, and small industries only.

Source: ADB Asia SME Monitor 2021 database. Data from Department of Industries, MOICS, Nepal 2018-19.

C. By Region (1), FY2019

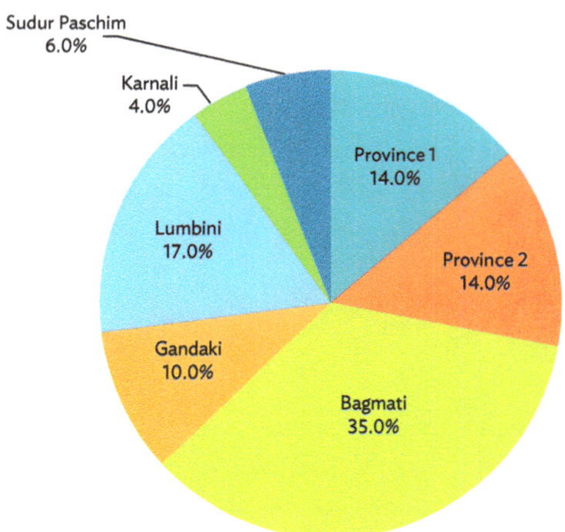

FY = fiscal year.

Note: Data refer to micro, cottage, and small industries only.

Source: ADB Asia SME Monitor 2021 database. Data from Department of Industries, Ministry of Industries, Commerce and Supplies, Nepal 2018-19.

D. By Region (2), FY2020

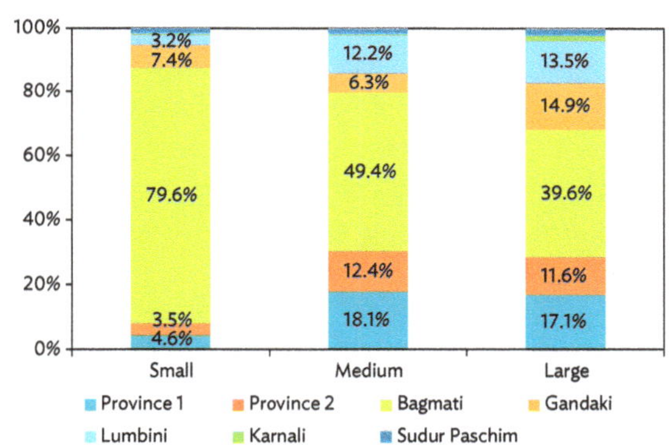

FY = fiscal year.

Note: Data refer to small, medium-sized, and large firms.

Source: ADB Asia SME Monitor 2021 database. Data from Department of Industries, Industrial Statistics 2019-20.

Figure 5.3: Employment by MSMEs

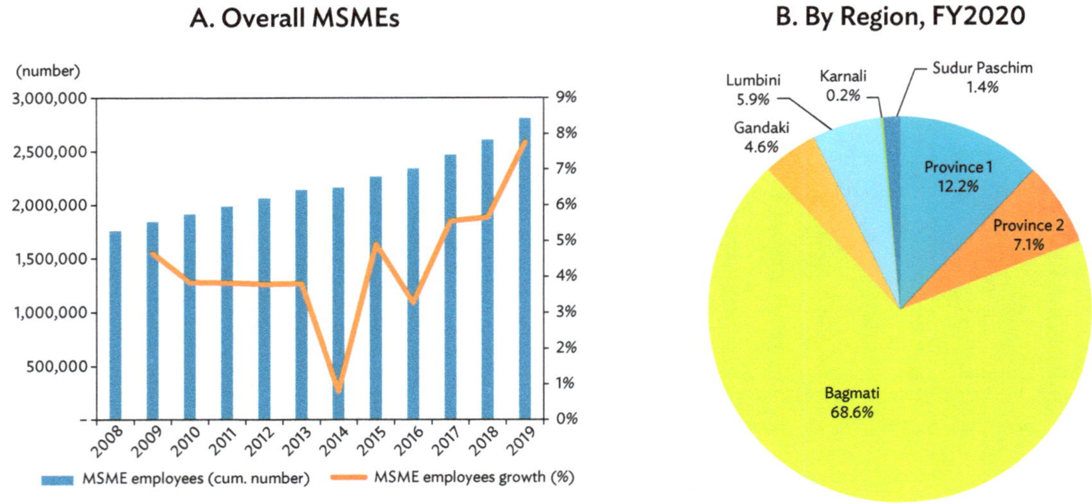

MSME = micro, small and medium enterprise.

Notes: fiscal year data. Data refer to micro, cottage, and small industries only.

Source: ADB Asia SME Monitor 2021 database. Data from Department of Industries, MOICS, Nepal 2018-19.

FY = fiscal year.

Note: Data refer to small and medium-sized enterprises only.

Source: ADB Asia SME Monitor 2021 database. Data from Department of Industries, Industrial Statistics 2019-20.

As with the number of enterprises, SME employment is concentrated in Bagmati province (Figure 5.3B). In FY2020, 68.6% of total SME employment was in Bagmati, followed by Province 1 (12.2%) and Province 2 (7.1%). Karnali, with the smallest provincial economy and lowest concentration of enterprises, held the lowest share of jobs created by SMEs (0.2%). This accents the huge regional disparities in economic opportunities and activities. Data on gender composition are unavailable.

Business Productivity

MSMEs contribute 22% of GDP, as reported in the 2019 NRB report. There are no regular data on whether the MSME contribution to GDP has been rising or falling. The Economic Census (2018) by the Central Bureau of Statistics provides a glimpse on business productivity of MSMEs at the firm level. The census does not categorize enterprises based on the national definition but is based on number of workers employed: (i) micro/cottage enterprises have fewer than 9 employees; (ii) small enterprises have 10-49 employees; (iii) medium-sized enterprises have 50-99 employees; and (iv) large enterprise have 100 or more employees.

There is a wide difference between MSMEs and large enterprises. Annual sales per firm, for example, is 4.7 times lower in medium-sized enterprises than large enterprises (Figure 5.4 and Table 5.3-3). The gap is staggering for small firms (37 times) and microenterprises/cottage industries (239 times). Sales per medium-sized enterprise are nearly 8 times higher than that of small enterprises and 50 times higher than micro/cottage enterprises.

Figure 5.4: Annual Sales Per Firm, 2018

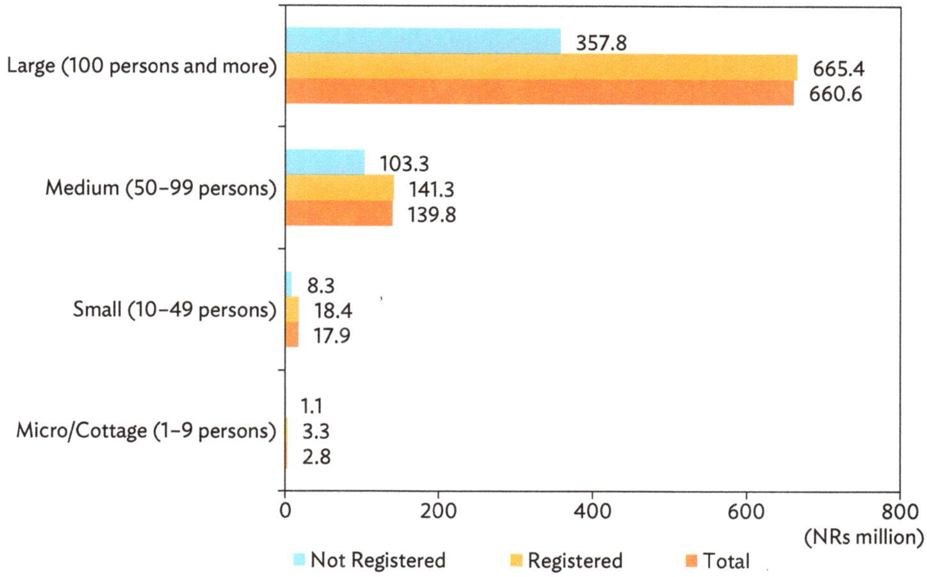

Source: ADB Asia SME Monitor 2021 database. Data from National Report on Revenues/Sales, Expenses, and Profit and Loss, based on National Economic Census 2018, Central Bureau of Statistics.

Market Access

Market access is a major problem for MSMEs, both for domestic and international markets. Nepal had a very high export-to-import ratio of 1:10.9 (NRB 2021)[108]. Total exports amounted to NRs141.1 billion in FY2021, while imports reached NRs1,539.8 billion—exports increased by 44.4% from FY2020 compared to the increment of 0.6% in the previous year whereas imports increased by 28.7% during FY2021 compared to the contraction of 15.6% in FY2020 due to the COVID-19 pandemic. The very low export level also suggests a limited role played by MSMEs in the domestic market. The domestic economy is driven largely by private consumption and investment.

Many SMEs have benefited from foreign investment. As of FY2020, 4,213 small firms received approval for foreign investment, or 83.4% of all firms with foreign investment (Figure 5.5A and Table 5.3-4). Also, 10.4% of medium-sized firms and 6.2% of large enterprises attracted foreign investment. However, the amount of foreign investment per entity is much lower for SMEs than large firms. On average, a large enterprise received NRs661.5 million, a medium-sized firm received NRs98.9 million, and a small enterprise received NRs17.4 million.

Foreign direct investment (FDI) varies widely across sectors. In FY2020, the three largest recipients of FDI were services (33.3%), tourism (31.5%), and manufacturing (23.6%) (Figure 5.5B). Smaller amounts of FDI went to agriculture and forestry-based enterprises (5.7%), followed by ICT (1.9%), energy (1.7%), minerals (1.4%), and infrastructure (0.9%).

108 Current Macroeconomic and Financial Situation of Nepal, (Based on Annual Data of 2020/21), Nepal Rastra Bank, 2021 https://www.nrb.org.np/contents/uploads/2021/08/Current-Macroeconomic-and-Financial-Situation-English-Based-on-Annual-data-of-2020.21-1.pdf

Two neighbors, the People's Republic of China (PRC) and India, are major sources of foreign investment (Figure 5.5C). Together they were involved in half the firms receiving FDI as of mid-July 2020. By total amount, the two provided nearly 74% of inward foreign investment. Despite the relatively large number of SMEs receiving foreign investment, they are mostly domestic market rather than export-oriented.

Figure 5.5: Foreign Investments, FY2020

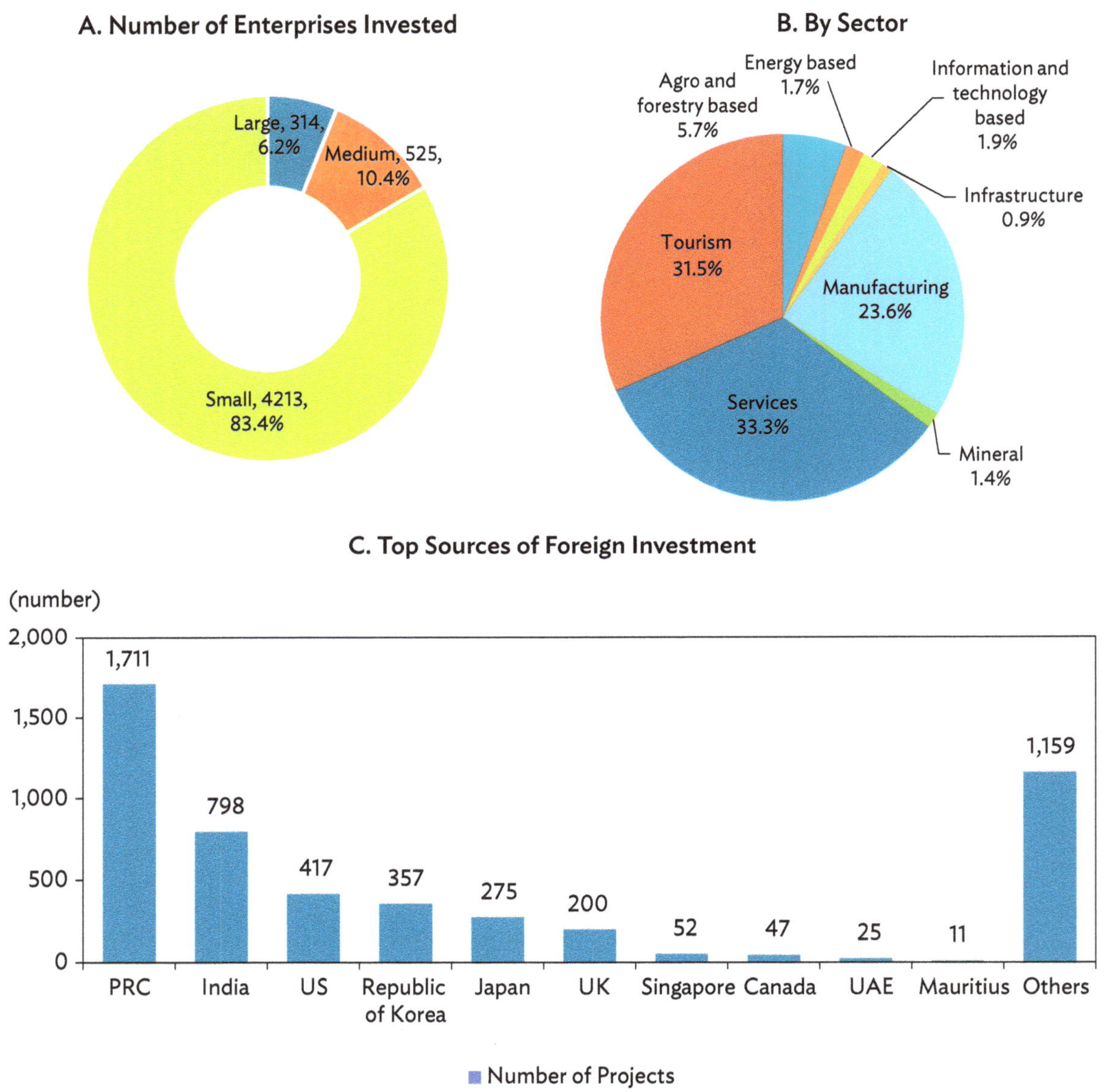

FY = fiscal year, PRC = People's Republic of China, UAE = United Arab Emirates, UK = United Kingdom, US = United States.

Source: ADB Asia SME Monitor 2021 database. Data from Industrial Statistics, Department of Industries, Ministry of Industries, Commerce and Supplies 2019-20.

Technology and Innovation

Since a liberalized economic policy was adopted in the early 1990s, Nepal has made greater strides in expanding access to digital technology, specifically ICT. As of February 2021, mobile penetration was 130.8% of the population with internet penetration reaching 87.2% (Nepal Telecommunication Authority 2021).[109] Using different types of technology depending on territorial suitability has expanded ICT access to even remote areas. This puts Nepal on par with countries like India, the PRC, and other South Asian countries. With costs also declining, the number of people accessing internet content such as social media, video services has also increased (MOCIT 2019).[110] Nepal has 12.3 million Facebook users, or 40.4% of the population.[111]

To support this progress, a National ICT Policy was introduced in 2015 with a vision to transform Nepal into a knowledge and information-based society by harnessing the rapid advances in ICT. This policy recognizes the role of technology in promoting SMEs. It states that "SMEs will be encouraged to apply ICT to develop their business and enhance competitiveness, focusing on ICT for management, production and linkages to buyers" and that "special measures will be taken to ensure that export-oriented SMEs in Nepal are set to increase exports of their goods and services using virtual marketplaces."

One major SMEs sector using ICT is e-commerce. Although it has long history in Nepal, the industry is still in its infancy. The first e-commerce platform was established as early as 2000, with munchahouse.com (munch.com, as of June 2021) used to buy and send gifts. Since then, the industry has expanded tremendously.

As of May 2017, there were 40,000 commercial registered websites (footnote 110). Many e-commerce companies across various industries have started operations. For example, Foodmandu (2010), Sastodeal (2011), Urban Girl/UG Bazaar (2012), and Daraz (2013) are popular online platforms. In 2020, Sastodeal entered into agreement with India's e-commerce giant Flipkart to allow both companies to offer products across borders. This was the first cross-border arrangement of that scale.

Similarly, Nepal has home grown companies offering app-based ridesharing (motorbike and taxi) services. Tootle (2017) and Patho (2018) are two of the most popular. In addition, there are increasing numbers of start-ups on health (Doctor on Call, Hamro Doctor), agriculture (Db2Map, ICT for Agriculture), media (M&S holdings), and mapping (Naxa). However, details of their customer base or transaction levels are not readily available.

With the rising number of e-commerce companies operating, online payment services have also flourished. The first payment gateway was eSewa, launched in 2009. Since then, payment services such as Khalti and IME Pay have become popular. The NRB has licensed 27 commercial banks, 12 development banks, and 7 finance companies to run payment services. The NRB is in the process of establishing a national payment switch to establish an interoperable payment infrastructure that can settle all domestic transactions (NRB 2020).[112] With expanding digital financial services (DFS) for payment—online card payments, internet banking, and mobile banking—it will be easier for SMEs to join e-commerce (see the subsection on DFS for details).

E-commerce activities are concentrated in the Kathmandu valley and other urban centers. As rural users increasingly access the internet through mobile phones, e-commerce operations are expected to expand.

[109] MIS Report, March 2021, Nepal Telecommunication Authority: https://nta.gov.np/wp-content/uploads/2021/05/MIS-Falgun-2077.pdf.

[110] Government of Nepal, Ministry of ICT. 2019 Digital Nepal Framework - Unlocking Nepal's Growth Potential. https://mocit.gov.np/application/resources/admin/uploads/source/EConsultation/EN%20Digital%20Nepal%20Framework%20V8.4%2015%20July%20%202019.pdf.

[111] Napoleoncat. Facebook users in Nepal - January 2021. https://napoleoncat.com/stats/facebook-users-in-nepal/2021/01/.

[112] NRB. Payment Systems Oversight Report. https://www.nrb.org.np/contents/uploads/2020/10/Oversight-Report_2076-77.pdf.

Networking and Support

The Federation of Nepal Cottage and Small Industries (FNCSI) is an umbrella organization for micro, cottage, and small industries with around 40,000 members across the country. Aside from its central federal office, it has chapters in 7 provinces, 77 districts, and municipalities (some 300 out of 700 and expanding). It includes women entrepreneurship committees at the federal office, and in 7 provinces, 60 districts, and 250 municipalities. The FNCSI also includes 27 institutional members, mostly commodity associations with an additional 60,000 members. The FNCSI is the only business network that focusses on MSMEs.

Established in 1990, FNCSI has worked on four broad MSME themes: (i) policy advocacy and specific economic and financial policies and programs; (ii) working with the government to implement MSME-relevant programs; and (iii) capacity building for members through training, workshops, and other interactions that provide specific skills to small and cottage industry owners and staff. These programs focus on (i) improving managerial skills, bookkeeping, financial literacy, and marketing strategies, among others, and (ii) increasing financial and market access by helping members participate in various national and international exhibitions and trade fairs. They also have sales outlets across the country as hubs for entrepreneurs to sell their products.

The Federation of Woman Entrepreneurs' Associations of Nepal (FWEAN), established in July 2003, represents women entrepreneur associations and actively promotes businesses and ventures operated by women. Many MSMEs are women-led. Thus, the FWEAN supports MSME development by enhancing the capacity of women entrepreneurs. It also advocates for women's economic empowerment. The FWEAN was instrumental in lobbying to the government to allow for interest-subsidized, collateral-free loans to women entrepreneurs.

The Federation of Nepalese Chamber of Commerce and Industries (FNCCI), established in 1964, represents private businesses. As of September 2021, its membership spans 114 district and local chambers, 103 commodity and sectoral associations, 935 public and private undertakings, and 20 binational chambers[113]. The FNCCI has committees covering cottage and small industries as well as women entrepreneurship.

The FNCCI runs and Innovation Hub, a business incubator center, that "offers a wide range of resources for entrepreneurs including incubator desks, which give entrepreneurs a workspace and access to a specialized library of books and computer resources."[114] It also supports various sectors through satellite centers or projects such as the Agro Enterprise Centre and Forestry Enterprise Divisions.

The Confederation of Nepalese Industries is a federation, established in April 2002, that represents mainly large and medium-sized manufacturing and service industries. The federation hosts the Women Entrepreneur Forum and Young Entrepreneurs Forum. The two forums hold awareness programs, networking events, and policy training for women and young entrepreneurs. They also help existing entrepreneurs learn about government policies and regulations.

There are also various nonprofit business incubators. For example, Kathmandu University School of Management runs an "Idea Studio" that offers business advisory services, links with potential investors, and offers networking opportunities. It also has a reality show where entrepreneurs pitch their ideas on national television looking for potential investors. However, most incubators are concentrated in urban centers, especially in the Kathmandu valley.

113 FNCCI. Introduction. https://www.fncci.org/introduction-299.html.
114 FNCCI. Innovation Hub. https://www.fncci.org/innovation-hub-159.html

3. Access to Finance

- Family wealth and inheritance, along with private savings, are the two major initial sources of MSME financing. Only 16% of MSMEs source initial financing from banks and financial institutions (BFIs), while 8% rely on informal finance.
- The government and central bank offer several incentives to facilitate MSME lending—concessional loan programs, mandatory lending to MSMEs, and refinancing. A credit guarantee corporation (DCGF) offers partial guarantees (70%–80%) to MSMEs.
- Microfinance institutions target small entrepreneurs, particularly in the remote areas, whose loans outstanding have grown moderately despite the COVID-19 pandemic.
- Mobile banking is popular. From mid-July 2020 to mid-April 2021, there were 358 million DFS transactions valued at NRs26 trillion.
- There is no dedicated SME market. But the Securities Exchange Board is considering a possible SME board.
- The Credit Information Bureau (CIB) has been instrumental in providing timely, accurate, and credible credit information on borrowers, including MSMEs, to BFIs. CIB has been providing a secured transaction registry service since FY2017.
- Financial literacy/education programs help MSMEs access formal financial services, promoted by national and central bank strategies.

Nepal's finance system has five major sectors—banking, insurance, capital market, nonbank finance, and cooperatives. Banking is the largest and holds nearly 89% of total assets, followed by nonbank finance (7.4%) and insurance (3.8%). The capital market is relatively nascent, with market capitalization 84.3% of GDP and trading volume 7.3%.

BFIs (154 as of July 2020) are grouped into four categories: (i) commercial banks, (ii) development banks, (iii) finance companies, and (iv) microfinance institutions (Figure 5.6 and Table 5.4). While commercial banks operate nationwide, other have run specific national and regional operations, as specified in their licensing agreements. There are limited number of other financial institutions—savings and credit cooperatives and nongovernment organizations (NGOs)—that offer limited authorized banking services. In 2020, there were 14 directly supervised by the central bank.

Since 2015, BFIs expanded rapidly as the government decided to expand banking services countrywide to boost access to formal financial services for households and businesses, including MSMEs. There are BFI branches in 700 of 753 municipalities as of June 2021.[115]

MSMEs finance their capital needs from variety of sources. According to NRB (2019), the two major sources of initial financing are family wealth and inheritance (33.1%) and private savings (25.8%) (Figure 5.7 and Table 5.4a). Only 16% source their initial financing from BFIs, while 8% rely on informal finance. Just 0.5% of MSMEs receive investments from venture capital firms, while none issue equity.

[115] NRB. Current Macroeconomic and Financial Situation of Nepal. https://www.nrb.org.np/contents/uploads/2021/07/Current-Macroeconomic-and-Financial-Situation-English-Based-on-Eleven-Months-data-of-2020.21.pdf.

Figure 5.6: Number of Bank and Financial Institutions

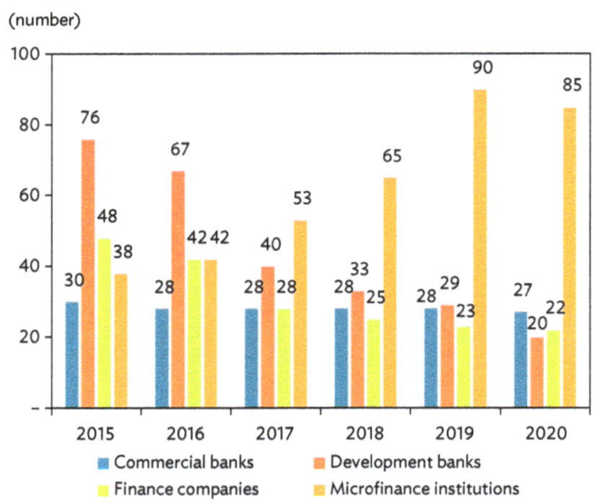

Note: fiscal year data.

Source: ADB Asia SME Monitor 2021 database. Data from Monthly Statistics, Nepal Rastra Bank.

Figure 5.7: Source of Initial Financing for MSMEs, 2019

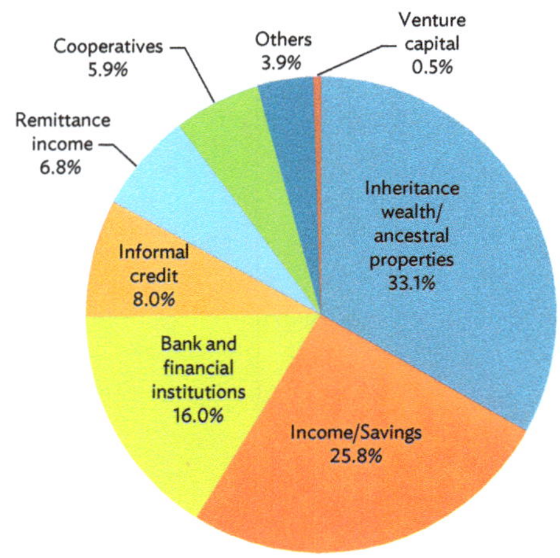

MSME = micro, small, and medium-sized enterprise.

Source: ADB Asia SME Monitor 2021 database. Data from SME Financing in Nepal 2019, Nepal Rastra Bank.

Bank Credit

BFI deposits and credit have grown in tandem, benefiting MSMEs. After growing more than 30% annually prior to FY2008, growth decelerated, hovering between 15%–20% (Figure 5.8A). In July 2020, the credit-to-GDP ratio was 86.9% and total deposits reached 104.4%. Time-series data on credit disbursed to MSMEs is not available.

An NRB survey reported that 11.5% of commercial bank loans outstanding were with SMEs in mid-July 2018, slightly less than 11.7% in mid-July 2017 and slightly more than 11.2% in mid-July 2016. The survey said nearly half of the MSMEs operating at the time of the survey had borrowed from BFIs.

The survey said 84.8% of MSMEs had loans with commercial banks, followed by development bank (8.9%), microfinance institutions (3.8%), and finance companies (2.5%).

Growth by sector has been uneven. In mid-July 2020, most credit was for wholesale and retail trade (20.3%), manufacturing (17.3%), and construction (10.6%) (Figure 5.8B). Mines and minerals (0.2%); metal, machinery, and electrical tools fitting (1.4%); and transportation (3.0%) had the lowest share.

By region, most BFI credit and deposits are concentrated in the Kathmandu valley (Figures 5.8C–D and Tables 5.4b–c). As of September 2021, 49% males and 32% women held active savings accounts.[116]

MSME loans tend to be smaller (NRs1 million or less) and for shorter periods (1 year or less). Interest ranges from 5% to 18% with the average 12.5% (NRB 2019).[117] Low-interest-rate loans are often subsidized by the government or central bank to promote MSMEs.

116 NRB Financial Inclusion Portal (https://emap.nrb.org.np/).

117 SME Financing in Nepal, 2019. NRB.

Figure 5.8: Bank and Financial Institution Credit

A. Loans Outstanding and Deposits

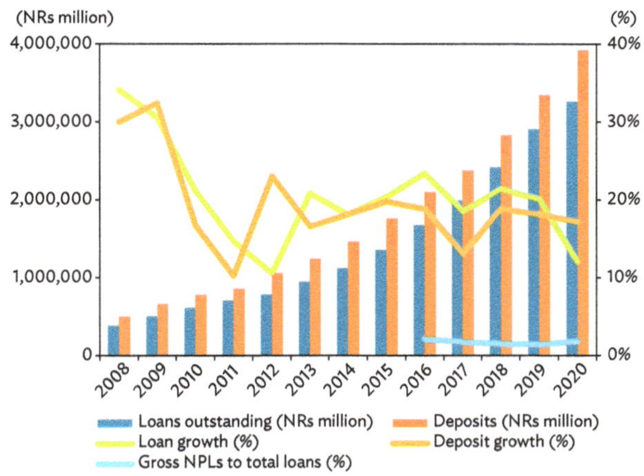

NPL = nonperforming loan.

Source: ADB Asia SME Monitor 2021 database. Data from Monthly Statistics, Nepal Rastra Bank.

B. By Sector, FY2020

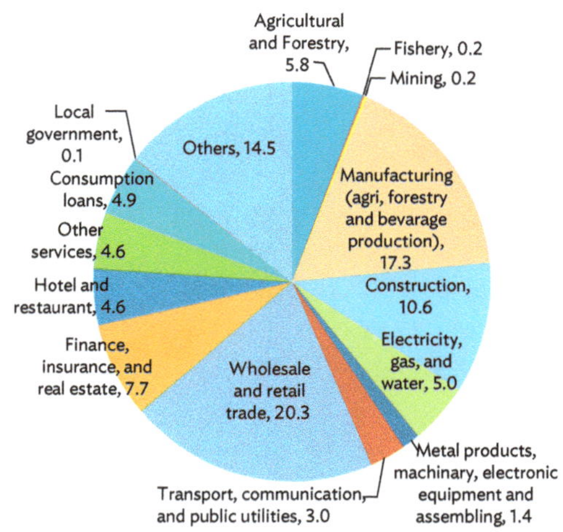

FY = fiscal year.

Source: ADB Asia SME Monitor 2021 database. Data from Monthly Statistics, Nepal Rastra Bank.

C. Loans Outstanding by Region

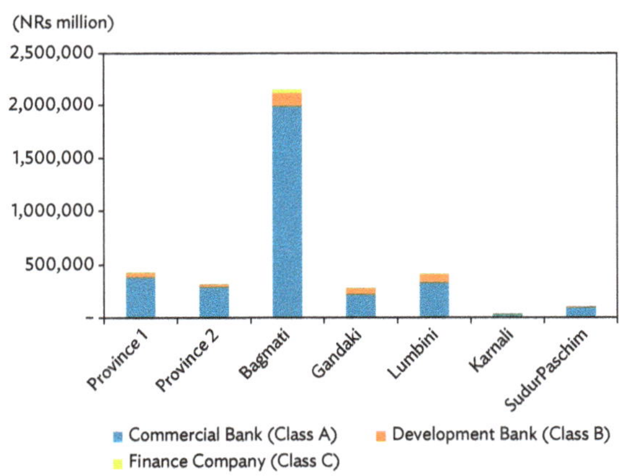

Source: ADB Asia SME Monitor 2021 database. Data from Financial Inclusion Portal, Nepal Rastra Bank (accessed in May 2021).

D. Savings Deposit by Region

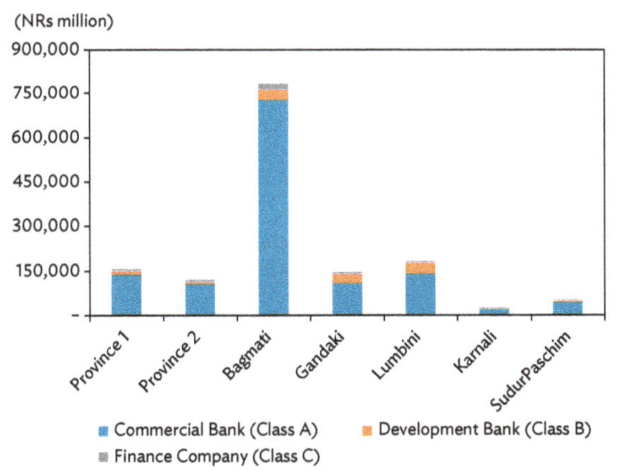

Source: ADB Asia SME Monitor 2021 database. Data from Financial Inclusion Portal, Nepal Rastra Bank (accessed in May 2021).

Based on interviews, the major barrier to MSME access to finance is the information asymmetry between lenders and borrowers.[118] Many MSMEs, particularly those in the informal sector, are unaware about loan assessment procedures. They lack documentation, business records, and proper business plans. This makes it difficult for BFIs to assess a borrower's creditworthiness. Thus, unless forced by NRB regulations, many BFIs do not generally lend to MSMEs or the informal sector. In addition, low economies of scale, use of outdated technologies, and limited market access impede MSME productivity and growth.

[118] Based on the ADB virtual fact-finding mission to Nepal with banks, business associations/federations, and the NRB, conducted in March and April 2021.

Public Financing and Guarantees

a. Soft loan programs

The government and central bank offer several incentives to encourage lending to specific sectors or groups, which have difficulty accessing credit. There are 10 loan schemes the government provides with interest subsidies (Table 5.5a). They vary considerably in terms of loan size, interest concessions, collateral requirements, tenure, credit guarantees, documentation requirements, and target group.

The two most popular are the Commercial Agriculture and Livestock Loan (CALL) and the Women Entrepreneur Loan (WEL). CALL provides up to NRs50 million and offers a discount on insurance premium and service charge if the loan is less than NRs1 million. WEL is provided up to NRs1.5 million. Both receive government interest subsidies. For FY2022, NRs13 billion has been allocated for interest subsidies under these loan schemes. These proved very useful during the first wave of the COVID-19 pandemic.

Of the total number of concessional loans disbursed as of mid-July 2021, 44.2% were CALL loans and 53.4% were provided under WEL. The remaining 2.4% were distributed through the remaining eight schemes.[119] In terms of outstanding loan value, CALL has 66.3% whereas WEL takes 31.6% (Figure 5.9 and Table 5.5).

Since mid-July 2019, there has been rapid growth in concessional loans outstanding and number of beneficiaries under CALL and WEL. For example, number of borrowers under CALL increased by 43.9 % in FY2020 (as of mid-July 2020) and 86.0% for FY2021 (as of mid-July 2021). Outstanding loans for the scheme increased by 68.1% in FY2020 and 97.7% in FY2021. For FY2021, the number of WEL borrowers increased more than 8 times with loans outstanding over 11 times.

Figure 5.9: Concessional Loans

A. Loans Outstanding

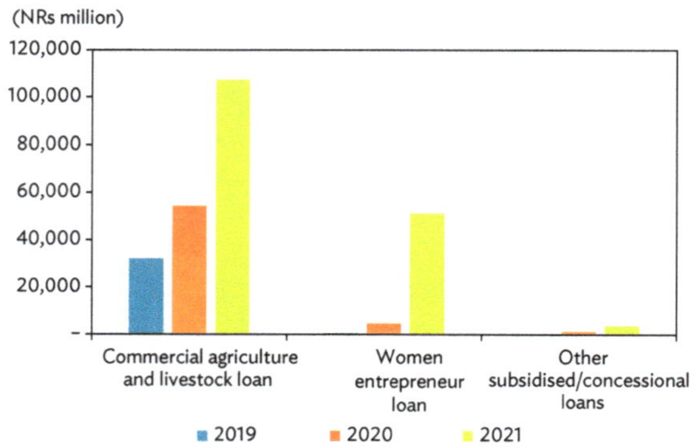

Note: fiscal year data.

Source: ADB Asia SME Monitor 2021 database. Data from Microeconomic and Financial Situation Reports, Nepal Rastra Bank.

B. Number of Borrowers

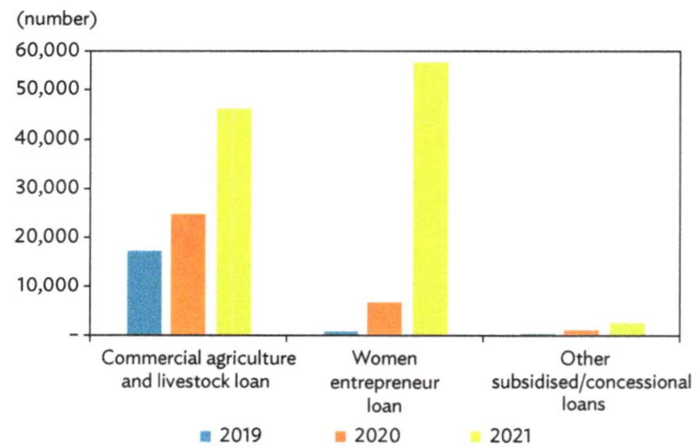

Note: fiscal year data.

Source: ADB Asia SME Monitor 2021 database. Data from Microeconomic and Financial Situation Reports, Nepal Rastra Bank.

119 The loan schemes are the Educated Youth Self-employment Loan; Project Loan for Youth-Returnee Migrant Workers; Dalit Community Business Development Loan; Higher, Technical and Professional Education Loan; Housing Loan for Earthquake Victims; Loan to Textile industries; Loan to training by the Council For Technical Education and Vocational Training-approved institution; and Youth Self-employment Loan.

In addition to the schemes channeled through BFIs, the government provides interest subsidies and removes certain requirements like collateral so more borrowers can avail of the facilities. For example, under CALL, NRs2,190 million in loans were disbursed without collateral as of mid-July 2021.

Concessional commercial loans are also offered to small firms and cottage industries. The central bank prevents BFIs from levying service charges and requires them to complete loan processing within 7 days of receiving an application.

b. Mandatory lending schemes

The government also sets targets for priority sectors. For example, the NRB requires commercial banks to eventually provide 40% of their loans to agriculture (15% by end-July 2023), energy and tourism (10% by end-July 2024), and MSMEs (15% by end-July-2024). MSME lending is defined as loans below NRs10 million. Similarly, development banks must lend 20% and finance companies 15% of their loans to those sectors by 2023. BFIs that miss targets incur penalties according to the amount of lending shortfall.

The NRB also requires BFIs to provide other types of concessional lending. They are required to lend at least 5% of their portfolio to groups such as women, small farmers, craftsmen, and ethnic minorities, with loans up to NRs500,000. This also includes micro-credit of NRs200,000 for renewable energy like home solar power systems, solar fryers, solar pumps, biogas, water mills, and stoves, or collateral-free loans of up to NRs150,000 for those seeking foreign employment.

Figure 5.10: Credit guarantees to MSMEs

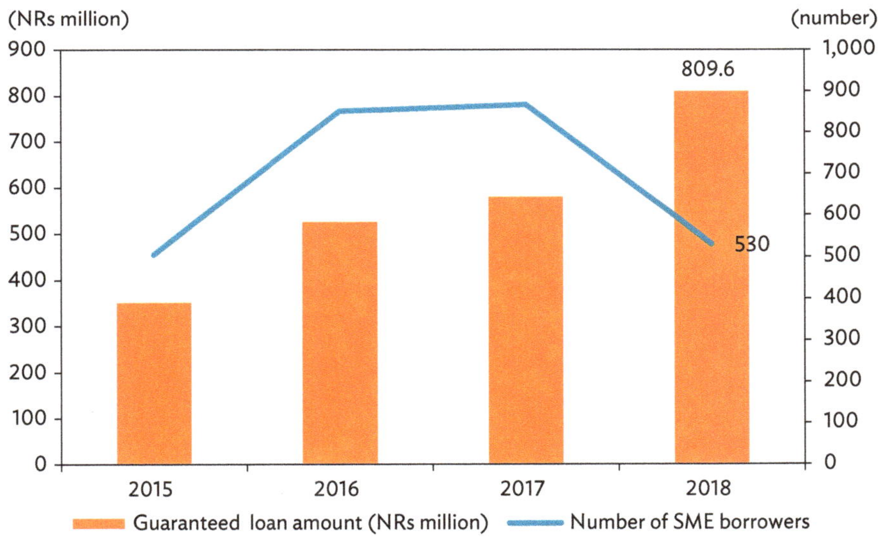

Note: fiscal year data.

MSME = micro, small, and medium-sized enterprise.

Source: ADB Asia SME Monitor 2021 database. Data from SME Financing in Nepal, Nepal Rastra Bank 2019.

c. Credit guarantees

Another important aspect of the MSME financing ecosystem is credit guarantees. The Deposit and Credit Guarantee Fund (DCGF) was established in 2010 and provides guarantees up to NRs300,000 through all NRB-licensed BFIs. It automatically guarantees loans up to NRs10 million disbursed to MSMEs. For loans from NRs10 million to NRs30 million, prior DCGF approval is required (DCGF 2021).[120] The coverage ratio on guaranteed loans up to NRs5 million is 80% of the outstanding balance and from NRs5 million to NRs20 million 70%.

The amount of loans guaranteed has gradually increased (Figure 5.10 and Table 5.5). They grew by an annual 49.3% in FY2016, 10.5% in FY2017, and 40.0% in FY2018 (NRB 2019). However, total guarantees reached just NRs809.6 million in FY2018. The number of MSME borrowers benefitting from credit guarantees increased by 68.5% in FY2016 and 1.9% in FY2017. The number fell by 38.9% in FY2018.

d. Refinancing and consulting services

The NRB also offers refinancing for businesses—including MSMEs—with BFIs refinancing up to NRs1 million at a 3% annual interest rate, lower than the 8.6% average (April 2021). BFIs can access the refinancing facility at 1% annual interest for loans provided to microenterprises. The maximum interest rate BFIs can charge MSMEs is 7%. Also, the NRB has instructed all BFIs to have an "SME Desk" to cater to MSME loan processing.

Box 5.1: Various Funds Created to Support MSMEs

Youth and Self-Employment Fund (YSEF): YSEF was established in 2009 to provide easy and secure commercial loans to promote youth self-employment and small entrepreneurships with traditional skills—including people from marginalized groups. The fund provides NRs200,000 per person (up to NRs5 million for groups) through BFIs and cooperatives at a maximum 8% interest. An interest rebate of up to 60% is provided if borrowers repay on time. To access the loan, borrowers need to hold a skill certificate or have traditional skills for commercial farming, agriculture and forestry, MSMEs, and homestays (tourism), among others. As of February 2021, 77,628 people have benefited from YSEF—34,309 women and 38,480 men (www.ysef.gov.np).

Poverty Alleviation Fund (PAF): Established in 2003 and financed by the government and World Bank, PAF builds awareness through social mobilization and capacity building for poor households and communities to run various income generation activities through skills development, business literacy, technology, access to credit and markets, and building rural community infrastructure such as agricultural roads, trails, culverts, bridges, small irrigation, among others. It is designed "to uplift" livelihoods of the poorest of the poor and should be "replicable." PAF has said it benefited 988,879 households in 60 districts. Yet, the government dismantled the fund citing ineffectiveness (www.pafnepal.org.np) (as of July 2021).

Micro, Cottage, and Small Industries (MCSI) Development Fund: The MCSI Development Fund was established by the Ministry of Industries, Commerce, and Supplies in 2003 to generate employment by promoting entrepreneurship and businesses using local raw materials. Businesses registered as cottage and small industries can apply. The fund also runs various programs to educate and train potential borrowers/entrepreneurs on marketing and financial management, legal and regulatory issues, and intellectual property rights.

continued on next page

[120] DCGF. SME Credit Guarantee. http://www.dcgf.gov.np/en/services/sme-guarantee.

Box 5.1 *continued*

The Challenge Fund: The government's Challenge Fund will provide grants and/or loans to innovative firms and start-ups to create jobs. Selection will be through competition. The fund will promote entrepreneurship and support scaling up MSMEs in priority sectors like agriculture, information and communications technology, and renewable energy, among others. After 5 years, however, it has yet to be formally established. The government plans to provide NRs2.5 million seed money to each firm at a subsidized 1% interest rate against project collateral.

Rural Self-Reliance Fund (RSRF): The Nepal Rastra Bank (NRB) established the RSRF in 1991 to reduce poverty by offering wholesale credit to cooperatives and non government organizations at subsidized interest rates. The objective was to help poor households establish and operate businesses that required long-term capital—like tea and cardamom farming and cold-storage facilities, among others. The government and NRB have contributed NRs793.4 million to 48,379 households through April 2015 (https://www.nrb.org.np/category/rural-self-reliance-fund-rsrf/).

Economic Rehabilitation Fund (ERF): The ERF was created in 2015 after an earthquake devastated businesses in agriculture, tourism, manufacturing, and MSMEs, among others. The fund offers refinancing at concessional rates. ERF is operated by the central bank with funds provided by the government and donor agencies.

Women Entrepreneurship Development Fund (WEDF): In 2015, the Ministry of Industry, Commerce, and Supplies established the WEDF as part of the Industrial Promotion Policy 2011. WEDF provides collateral-free interest-subsidized commercial loans up to NRs500,000 for women entrepreneurs. Borrowers need recommendations from business associations like the Federation of Women Entrepreneurs' Associations of Nepal. Through 2018, NRs332.8 million for 1,888 loans have been approved.

Other Funds: There were several funds either discontinued or replaced by the new funds mentioned above. For example, Production Credit for Rural Women was launched on 30 November 1988; Micro-Credit Project for Women was launched on 15 December 1993; the Third Livestock Development Project was launched in 1997; Poverty Alleviation Project in Western Terai was launched in 1998; and Community Ground Water Irrigation Sector Project was launched in March 1999.

Sources: Nepal Rastra Bank 2019, Poverty Alleviation Fund 2018, Government of Nepal Budget Speech (2017–2018).

Nonbank Financing

Nepal operates various microfinance programs to help the vulnerable and small entrepreneurs with savings, credit, remittances, and micro-insurance to boost self-employment and other income-generating activities. These nonbank finance institutions collect small deposits, provide micro-loans, and practice group-based lending and group savings. In addition, microfinance institutions (MFIs) target remote areas where other financial institutions have low or no penetration. The finance includes diversified use, quick repayment, close monitoring, and simple credit terms/conditions (no collateral in many cases). According to NRB (2013), there are several successfully operated MFIs:

- Classic Grameen model with group-lending for the extremely poor through seed funding for microenterprises.
- BFIs must extend a specified percent of their lending portfolio to vulnerable groups, especially in the rural areas.
- Small farmer cooperatives piloted in 1950s was the first attempt at microfinance. Later, it became the Small Farmers Cooperative Limited, managed by farmers themselves and mobilizing small funds for rural agriculture.

- Financial nongovernment organizations (FINGOs) and savings and credit cooperatives are community-based models; basically they limit their banking services among members.
- Wholesale lending provides fund to cooperatives and banks to on-lend. For example, the Rural Self Reliance Fund lends to the vulnerable through cooperatives and long-term loans through the Agricultural Development Bank.[121,122]

As of January 2021, 76 MFIs were registered and operating nationwide with 4,218 branches (Figure 5.11A). Although the number declined due to a merger and acquisition policy promoted by the NRB since 2015, the number of MFI branches have steadily increased.

Nevertheless, financial institutions reach just about 20% of all households that need credit (ADB 2019).[123] MFIs have thus played an important role in narrowing the gap by providing financial services in rural areas and providing credit in sectors often overlooked by traditional, larger financial institutions.

As of mid-February 2021, MFIs had NRs357.9 billion in loans outstanding, up by 36.2% since July 2020. Year-on-year, consolidated MFI loans outstanding more than doubled from FY2017 to FY2020. They grew by 37.0% in FY2018, 60.4% in FY2019, and 12.2% in FY2020 (Figure 5.11B and Table 5.6).[124]

By sector, in FY2020 agriculture received 42.2% of MFI credit, followed by services (33.8%) (Figure 5.11C). As many loans are wholesale, the agriculture-related share was likely higher.

Of the 84 MFIs in FY2020, 52.4% were national MFIs with nationwide coverage. Some 17.9% of MFIs provided provincial coverage and 29.8% district-level coverage (Figure 5.11D). In general, MFIs work through groups where members collectively borrow and/or receive guarantees. As of January 2021, there were nearly 5 million members associated with over 1 million groups, with 2.8 million borrowers benefitting from MFI credits (Figure 5.11E).

Lending rates charged by the MFIs vary considerably, as the NRB does not regulate interest rates. The reported average annual interest rate by MFIs ranged between 8%–15% as of July 2021.

Before COVID-19, nonperforming loans (NPLs) of MFIs were comparable to other BFIs. However, since the pandemic, NPLs have been steadily rising, reaching 4.2% in January 2021 (Figure 5.11F).

121 Another example is the Rural Micro-finance Development Center (RMD), also a wholesale lending institution.
122 Recently, commercial banks began value-chain financing.
123 Rural Enterprise Finance, Sector Assessment, ADB 2019.
124 Various reports on "Situation of Microfinance Institutions" published by the NRB. https://www.nrb.org.np/category/quarterly-situation-of-mfis/?department=mfd

Figure 5.11: Microfinance Institutions Lending

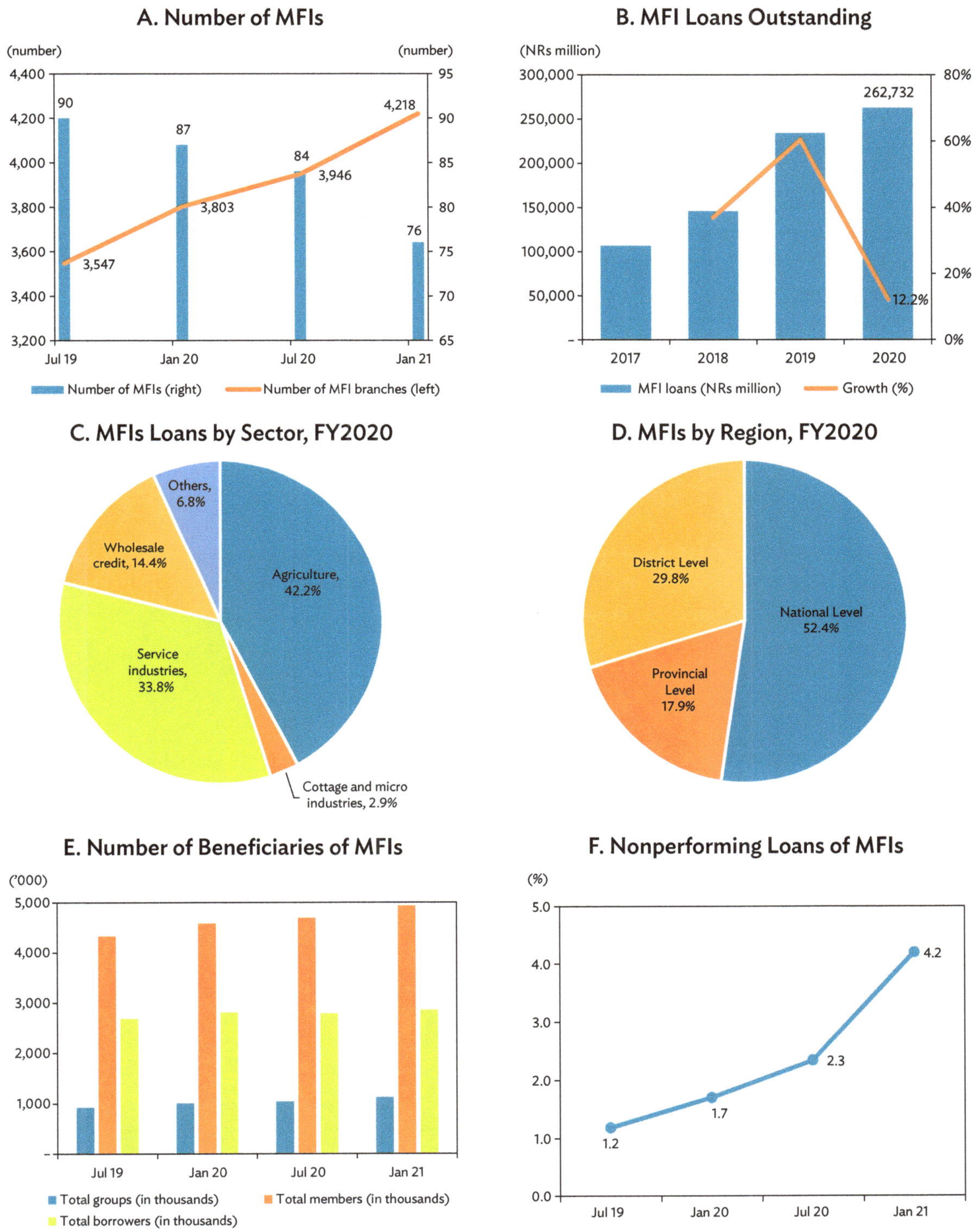

FY = fiscal year, MFI = microfinance institution.

Notes: Fiscal year (Figures 11B, C, and D) and quarterly (Figures 11A, E, and F) data. Figure 11C is based on loans outstanding. Figure 11D is based on the number of MFIs.

Source: ADB Asia SME Monitor 2021 database. Data from Situation of Microfinance Institution Reports, various (January and July 2020 and April 2020), Nepal Rastra Bank.

Digital Financial Services

Mobile banking is the most popular electronic banking service, with more than 13 million registered users, of which 80% were active as of April 2021 (Figure 5.12A and Table 5.7).[125] Use is rising, with nearly 6 million people using debit cards and 0.7 million people accessing internet banking. Low-cost smartphones and expanding internet access are fueling growth. Other services like ticket purchases, utility bill payments, online fund transfers also attract new users. From mid-July 2020 to mid-April 2021, digital financial transactions reached 358 million, valued at NRs26,006 billion (Figure 5.12B).

Besides large corporate online payment platforms like real-time gross settlement (RTGS) services, interbank payments and biller payments are rising. Retail payment systems are mainly operated by the Nepal Clearing House Limited, which provides image-based check clearing and electronic fund transfers. Many national and international private service providers are entering the market as Payment System Operators and offer Quick Response or QR code payments as well as mobile banking services to BFIs. Also, BFIs are introducing online credit processing, account opening, and other advisory services, although at a very early stage.

The NRB regulates and supervises payment institutions. Apart from the Nepal Rastra Bank Act (2002), the Payment and Settlement Act was introduced in 2018 to help regulate the surging number of service providers and array of services provided across the electronic financial service industry. To promote electronic banking, the NRB formulated the Nepal Payments System Development Strategy 2015 as well as a Retail Payment Strategy 2019.

Some commercial banks—like NMB Bank Limited and Standard Chartered Bank—use automated loan processing and a credit rating system for MSMEs. This should expedite loan processing and approvals. Other digital financial platforms and services such as peer-to-peer lending and equity crowdfunding remain unavailable to MSMEs.

Figure 5.12: Electronic Banking

A. Registered and Active Users, 2021

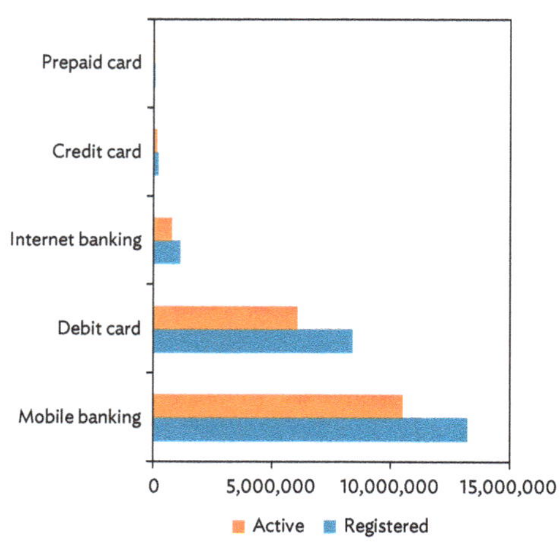

B. Number of Transactions and Value (Mid-July 2020 to Mid-Apr 2021)

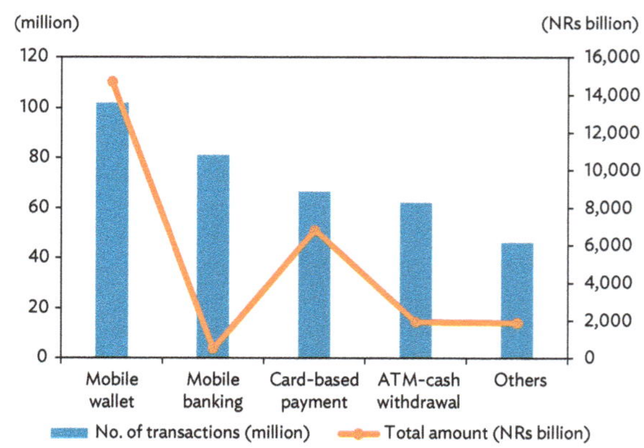

Source: ADB Asia SME Monitor 2021 database. Data from Nepal Rastra Bank, Financial Inclusion Portal (Accessed in April 2021).

[125] Nepal Rastra Bank, Financial Inclusion Portal (https://emap.nrb.org.np/).

Despite the growth of digital banking services, MSMEs and their customers often complain about their high cost, low maximum transaction amounts, security, and the lack of adequate customer service as impediments to their use.[126, 127]

The NRB is mandated to develop a secure, healthy, and efficient payment system. It developed a Nepal Payment System Development Strategy in 2014, which identifies legal, regulatory, technological, and institutional pillars to create a comprehensive wholesale and retail payment system. Since its adoption, the NRB has worked to build a new payment infrastructure—like a RTGS, several e-payment gateways such as IPS Connect—and it has encouraged BFIs to offer digital banking services and digital government payment services.

Capital Markets

Nepal's capital market remains at an early stage of development, although the regulatory and trading infrastructure was created in 1994. As of April 2021, market participants include the Nepal Stock Exchange (NEPSE), Central Depository System and Clearing House, 2 credit rating agencies, 14 mutual funds, 32 merchant bankers, 50 security brokers, 59 "Application Supported by Blocked Amount" members, and 218 listed companies. The Security Exchange Board of Nepal (SEBON) issued a 'letter of intent' in April 2021 to allow five companies to act as private equity and venture capital fund.

As of mid-July 2021, market capitalization was NRs4.0 trillion with total paid-up value of listed shares at NRs573.2 billion (Figure 5.13A and Table 5.8). The secondary market has grown rapidly since FY2006, after the peace process began. It is dominated by financial institutions, owning 66.5% of listed companies as of April 2021—commercial banks (11.9%), development banks (8.3%), finance companies (10.6%), MFIs (22.9%), and insurance companies (12.8%) (Figure 13B). The number of hydropower companies listed increased during the decade from FY2011 to FY2020. The real sector such as hotels (5 firms listed as of April 2021) and trading firms (4) have miniscule market presence.

The SEBON introduced a dematerialized trading system (a paperless computerized system) from mid-January 2016 and made it mandatory for dematerialized accounts for initial public offering applications since mid-July 2016 for the Kathmandu valley and from mid-January 2017 nationwide. The number of dematerialized securities increased significantly, reaching 1.6 million in 2019.

As of May 2021, there was no dedicated SME board. However, the SEBON wants to have a separate SME platform to ease capital market access. The SEBON's Annual Policy and Program 2019–2020 facilitates the establishment of an SME platform at the NEPSE.[128] It has an internal unpublished study on the feasibility of introducing a dedicated SME board.

Alternative financing such as venture capital and private equity investments are a relatively new phenomenon in Nepal. The NRB (2018) SME financing study found only 0.5% of initial financing is sourced from venture capitalists. While only a few venture capital and private equity firms exist, the government created a legal framework in 2019 to regulate their operations—Specialized Investment Fund Rules 2075 (2019). As of May 2021, five firms have submitted expressions of intent to obtain operating licenses.

[126] e-Sewa. Digital Banking and Payment Trend in Nepal: Past, Present, and Future. https://blog.esewa.com.np/digital-banking-and-payment-trend-in-nepal-past-present-and-future/.

[127] A. Dungel and D. Regmi.2019. Digital banking in Nepal: Focus on infrastructure, security. The Himalayan. 20 May. https://thehimalayantimes.com/opinion/digital-banking-in-nepal-focus-on-infrastructure-security.

[128] Security Exchange Board of Nepal. https://www.sebon.gov.np/uploads/uploads/82EzC3ejjKTKc63iWfCtBwKiTOAApveHVERUSr3Y.pdf.

Figure 5.13: Equity Market—Nepal Stock Exchange

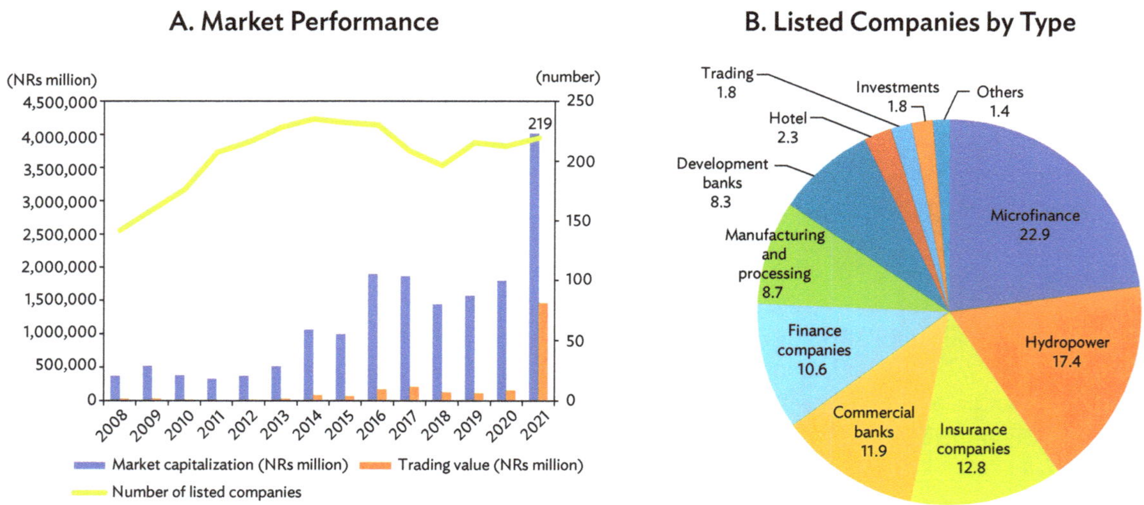

FY = fiscal year.

Note: data as of April 2021.

Source: ADB Asia SME Monitor 2021 database. Data from Nepal Stock Exchange.

Financial Infrastructure

The Credit Information Bureau (CIB) was created in May 1989 to provide adequate, comprehensive, and reliable database of information on BFI borrowers. It was established under the nonprofit Nepal Bankers Association, under the aegis of the NRB. In September 2004, the CIB registered as the limited liability company and began operations in March 2005. As of September 2021, 140 BFIs are CIB members, including 27 commercial banks, 18 development banks, 20 finance companies, 74 MFIs and cooperatives, and 1 infrastructure development bank[129].

The CIB has been instrumental in providing timely, accurate, and credible credit information to BFIs so they can make informed and efficient credit decisions. MSME borrowers have benefited from the system, as it reduces the high-risk perception lenders often have of MSMEs and thus leads to a reduction in borrowing costs. Timely credit information also shortens the time needed to process MSME credit.

Registered borrowers in the CIB database increased by 31.8% in FY2019, 51.5% in FY2018, and 23.8% in FY2017 (Figure 5.14 and Table 5.9). With the database expanding, the number of credit reports generated has also increased considerably. There were 1.4 million credit reports generated in FY2019, up 28.7% from FY2018.

[129] Credit Information Bureau of Nepal. Introduction - Need and Rationale for Credit Information Bureau. https://cibnepal.org.np/introduction.html.

Figure 5.14: Credit Information Bureau Operations

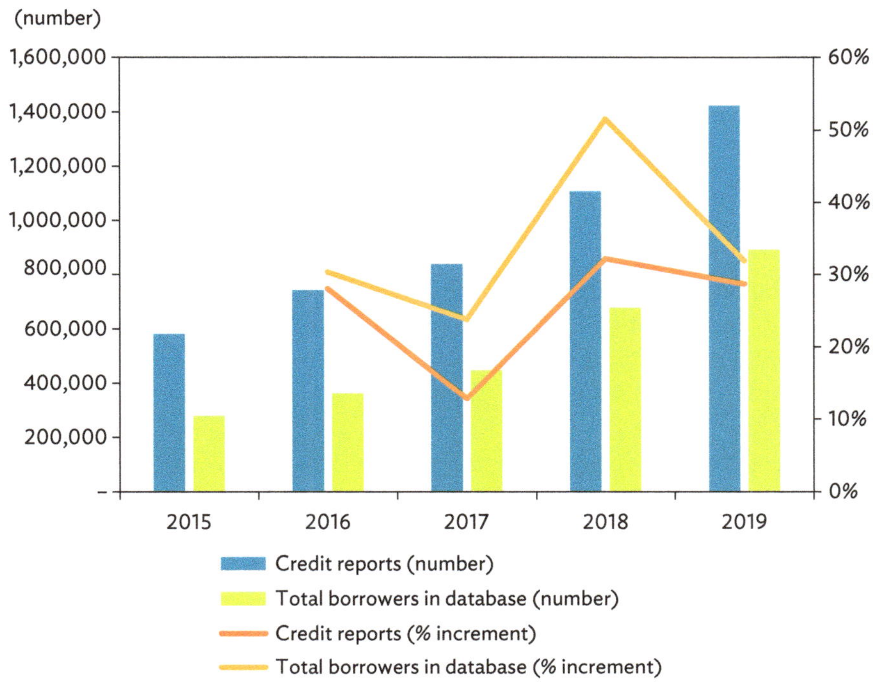

Note: fiscal year data.

Source: ADB Asia SME Monitor 2021 database. Data from Annual Report 2019, Credit Information Bureau.

The government promulgated the Secured Transaction Act in 2006 to "secure obligations with movable and intangible property by making consolidated legal provisions in relation to secured transactions" (Secured Transaction Act 2006).[130] An integral part was to create a central database that contains the details of all claims made on assets of a corporation or individual borrower.

The CIB has operated a Secured Transaction Registry (STR) Service since FY2017. The STR is a repository of movable assets of potential borrowers that allows assets to be prioritized to help BFIs extend credit using those assets as collateral. The STR is "expected to facilitate SME financing by building greater transparency in the financial system, enhancing the rights of creditors and debtors, and thus giving financial institutions greater confidence to lend against movable assets of SMEs who do not often cannot offer fixed assets collateral like real estate, to access loans" (CIB 2019).[131] As of July 2019, 31,000 notices had been registered at the STR and 140,000 reports generated. In 2018, of the total notices registered at the CIB, 66.5% were from MSMEs (NRB 2018).[132]

Credit rating agencies are an integral part of financial sector development. Nepal has two credit rating agencies—ICRA Nepal Limited and CARE Ratings Nepal Limited, both subsidiaries of Indian rating companies. ICRA was established in November 2011 and began operations in October 2012. CARE was established in November 2017. Both provide rating and grading services that include ratings of debt instruments, issuer ratings, bank loan/line of

130 Secured Transaction Act, 2063 (2006). https://www.lawcommission.gov.np/en/wp-content/uploads/2018/10/secured-transaction-act-2063-2006.pdf.

131 CIB Annual Report 2018-19 https://cibnepal.org.np/assets/upload/downloads/annual_report_19.pdf.

132 https://www.nrb.org.np/contents/uploads/2020/04/Study_Reports_2076.pdf.

credit ratings, and ratings of insurance companies. Although these services are not tailored to MSMEs, they could play an important role in narrowing the financing gap faced by MSMEs. However, their high cost keeps MSMEs from using them.

One objective of Nepal's 2017 Financial Sector Development Strategy was "to develop an inclusive financial system to make access to finance easy and comfortable for those with low income and from rural areas and to increase financial literacy in financial services and instruments and to protect the interests of financial consumers." Thus, financial education and literacy has become a priority for financial inclusion by regulators such as the NRB and SEBON.

NRB Act 2002 instructs the bank "to increase the access of the financial service and increase the public confidence towards the banking and financial system" (Section 4 (b)). The NRB included "enhancing financial literacy and financial education" in its Strategic Plan for 2017–2021 as well as in annual monetary policy statements. It has published a Financial Inclusion Roadmap (2017–2022) and Financial Literacy Framework (March 2020).

The NRB conducts various activities to raise awareness and financial literacy by publishing information and communication materials, including books, videos/commercials, even songs. Its flagship program is "NRB with Students."

The SEBON offers education programs for media to enhance their knowledge related to the economy and securities markets. It also regularly conducts an investor literacy program for students, investors, and local businesspeople, among others. For example, it started live conversations with investors to address grievances and questions about capital markets and commodity derivatives markets. The SEBON expects the program "enhances the investor awareness and mitigates investor grievances and strengthens the regulatory mechanism" (SEBON 2020).[133]

4. Policies and Regulations

- The government's MSME policies are guided by the Industrial Promotion Policy (IPP) 2011; 5-year plans, annual budgets, and sector programs from line ministries.
- The Micro Enterprise Development Program (MEDEP) from 1998 to 2018 was a government flagship program for MSME development. It has been integrated with the Micro Enterprise Development Program for Poverty Alleviation (MEDPA).
- The annual national budget FY2020 created the Challenge Fund to provide seed capital to innovative start-ups with growth potential.
- The Financial Inclusion Roadmap for 2017–2022 aims to achieve financial inclusion as described in the NRB's strategic plan.
- A Financial Literacy Framework coordinates currently fragmented financial literacy work for monitoring, evaluation, and policy recommendations.
- The government and central bank have taken several measures to cope with the effect of the COVID-19 pandemic—including relaxing regulations to boost liquidity, allowing debt restructuring, expanding refinancing five fold, and providing subsided loans to BFIs willing to on-lend at concessional rates to priority, MSME, and general borrowers.
- Although there were no special wage subsidies or unemployment benefits, a new NRs50 billion Business Continuity Fund was proposed to provide subsidized lending to MSMEs affected by the pandemic COVID-19 along with tourism and hospitality businesses.

[133] SEBON Annual Report 2019-2020.

MSME Development

There are several government and NRB initiatives that support MSME development (Table 5.10). MSME policies are guided by the Industrial Promotion Policy (IPP) 2011; 5-year periodic plans, annual budgets, and sector programs from line ministries. Similarly, the central bank support comes via monetary policy and periodic directives and circulars.

The IPP aims to develop MSMEs to promote self-employment and create jobs. It created several funds: the Investment Promotion Fund; Technology Development Fund; and the Micro, Cottage, and Small Industries Development Fund—to be operated in collaboration with the private sector and cooperatives. The IPP recommends programs that enhance the competitive capacity of MSMEs for market access and growth. It also seeks to create industrial clusters to make business development services available to production-oriented firms in rural areas. Most of these industrial clusters are in an early stage of development and are small in scale (ADB 2010).[134] Tourism, agriculture, and small-scale manufacturing are potential cluster development sectors.

To implement the IPP, the government initiated several plans and programs to promote and develop MSMEs. The Fifteenth Five Year Plan (FY2020–FY2024) is one example. It promotes entrepreneurship development through MSMEs for job creation and self-employment.

It cites several challenges to MSME development: (i) the lack of an entrepreneurial culture; (ii) inadequate identification of target groups; (iii) inability to link training with industries; (iv) the need to get the Challenge Fund operational; (v) insufficient funds for start-ups; (vi) inadequate access to finance; (vii) the need to institutionalize incubation centers; (viii) need for risk-assessments, (ix) the weak link between entrepreneurs and value chains; (x) inadequate identification of profitable areas based on market demand; and (xi) the inability to harness opportunities created by globalization and new technologies.

The government is trying to address these challenges in several ways: (i) creating an investment-friendly environment; (ii) establishing different types of business-related funds; (iii) business incubation centers; and (iv) providing seed capital for MSMEs. The government aims to add 60,000 jobs annually through the establishment of 15,000 MSMEs each year.

There are various programs that promote microenterprises and cottage industries—such as a ready-made garment promotion program, handmade paper promotion program, ceramic handicraft promotion program, and advance leather products training and promotion program. MOICS has also created a Micro, Cottage, and Small Industries Development Fund. Similarly, there is a Women Entrepreneurship Development Fund.

The Nepal Planning Commission created an Innovation Fund in February 2020 to provide "Seed Capital for Innovative Businesses." The government will provide seed capital up to 50% of the project cost to a maximum NRs5 million to ventures with high growth potential and innovative ideas. These firms are selected from an open call for proposals that opened in May 2020. However, due to the COVID-19 pandemic, progress has stopped (as of July 2021) with the government planning to restart the application process once the situation normalizes.

The government's flagship MSME program was the Micro Enterprise Development Program (MEDEP) that ran from 1998 to 2018. It has been integrated with the Micro Enterprise Development Program for Poverty Alleviation (MEDPA) program.

[134] K. Choe and P. Pradhan. 2010. *Unleashing Economic Growth: Region-Based Urban Development Strategy for Nepal.* Manila: ADB. https://www.adb.org/sites/default/files/publication/27498/unleashing-economic-growth-nepal.pdf.

MEDPA was established in 2010 to increase "employment opportunities and level of income of the people living below the poverty line by developing microenterprises through entrepreneurship development." MEDEP/MEDPA helped create 88,004 micro entrepreneurs from 2010 to 2018, of which more than 70% were women, with the majority from traditionally marginalized communities. Several of these micro entrepreneurs created resilient microenterprises or MSMEs (MOICS 2021).[135]

The national budget for FY2020 created the Challenge Fund to provide seed money to innovative start-ups with growth potential. The government wants local governments to promote microenterprises and expand its microenterprise development program. It targets registering 120 medium-sized enterprises and 40,000 micro and small enterprises, graduate 37,000 microenterprises into SMEs, and create 125,000 new MSME jobs (GON 2021).[136]

Financial Inclusion

The NRB offers various incentives and subsides to support MSMEs access to finance. BFIs are supposed to focus lending on priority sectors and vulnerable groups, provide concessional lending, promote digital banking, and work toward financial inclusion.

The NRB's Strategic Plan (2017–2021) identifies financial inclusion as key pillar of its financial development strategy. It has four core pillars: (i) macroeconomic stability, (ii) financial stability and financial sector development, (iii) external sector stability, and (iv) a sound and effective payments system. Financial inclusion is part of the second pillar for "enhancing financial access and financial inclusion." Specifically, the plan says: "NRB is committed to promote financial inclusion across regions and people, particularly focusing on providing financial services to the disadvantaged segment of the population at affordable costs. NRB will also ensure prompt availability of financial services to the public without any discrimination in terms of cost and access to services."[137]

The Financial Inclusion Roadmap (2017–2022) implements the NRB's strategic plan. It aims to "increase formal financial inclusion in Nepal from 60% to 75% by 2022 and reduce the excluded from 18% to 3% so as to create economic empowerment".[138] The roadmap cites MSMEs as one of six priority market segments for financial inclusion.[139] Specifically, working and investment capital, cost-effective and accessible payment mechanisms, savings products, and viability-based financing were identified as key for improved financial inclusion of MSMEs.

The roadmap recommends several actions: (i) remove barriers to credit and savings markets; (ii) improve payments systems; (iii) bolster risk mitigation capabilities; (iv) enhance and leverage locally based financial service providers; (v) enhance financial inclusion support in national governance; and (vi) strengthen consumer empowerment, protection, and education. It is unclear how progress in these areas is monitored. However, recent monetary policies have enhanced emphasis on expanding financial inclusion. These include capping interest rates charged by MFIs (15%); widening the scope of concessional lending, expanding BFIs and MFIs in all local government districts; promoting digital payment systems and promoting financial literacy, among others.

The NRB issued a Financial Literacy Framework in March 2020 that "aims to enhance and systematize the current fragmented financial literacy activities to facilitate monitoring and evaluation as well as regular assessment through

[135] Government of Nepal. Ministry of Industry, Commerce, and Supplies. Micro Enterprise Development Programme (MEDEP). https://medpa.moics.gov.np/Home/MedepInformation?infoId=1023.

[136] Government of Nepal. Ministry of Finance. https://mof.gov.np/uploads/document/file/Budget%20Speech%20(Final)%20Full_20210530100738.pdf.

[137] NRB. Third Strategic Plan 2017-2021. https://www.nrb.org.np/contents/uploads/2020/01/strategic_plan_2017-2021.pdf.

[138] NRB. Financial Inclusion Roadmap 2017-2022. http://archive.nrb.org.np/mfd/MakingAccessPossible/Financial%20Inclusion%20Roadmap.pdf

[139] The other segments are (i) salaried workers, (ii) remittance recipients, (iii) farmers, (iv) irregular earners, and (v) dependents.

a policy initiation."[140] The framework specifies levels of financial literacy, various delivery channels and mechanisms, expected outcomes, implementation plan, roles and responsibilities, risk mitigation measures, and monitoring and evaluation.

The Financial Literacy Framework categorizes MSMEs with farmers, as they have "seasonal or irregular income flow to their households" and have similar financial literacy needs. The framework identified grievance handling (customer service), digital financial services, household budgets, savings and business plans, and risk management as key competencies for financial literacy. The status of implementation is not readily available.

The NRB adopted a Retail Payment Strategy in 2019. It includes the interoperability of various payment systems, expanding agent networks of payment service operators and payment service providers in both rural and urban areas, the creation of e-money for all types of payments, and to enable e-commerce, among others.

Response to COVID-19

The government has taken several policy measures—financial and non financial—to ease the burden of firms affected by the COVID-19 pandemic as well as to help economic recovery (Table 5.11).

Firms, including MSMEs, were provided tax relief and added subsidies. They include extending filing of value-added tax, income tax, and other service charges; grant subsidies for transporting agriculture products; timely subsidy payments to sugarcane farmers; and customs fee waivers for medical supplies, imported equipment for medicines, health materials, and equipment.

Other support includes discounts on internet, electricity, and water supply; and free online banking. The statutory requirement of submitting company details to the Company Registrar's office or SEBON were also deferred. In addition, the government urged landlords to waive 1 month rent for small businesses and households.

The NRB also took several measures to address the impact of COVID-19 on the national economy. These include debt restructuring and extending loan repayment periods for short-term working capital loans. BFIs were also asked to discount interest rates for on time payments should borrowers choose. The government also shortened administrative processes by instructing banks to approve loans within 5 days, specifically for tourism and transportation, and relaxed the working capital loan ceiling up to 20% of existing working capital.

Several regulatory provisions were also relaxed to boost BFI liquidity, allowing banks to count loans to health facilities for COVID-19 treatment against priority lending requirements, lowering the mandatory cash reserve ratio from 4% to 3%, reducing interest rates on the standing liquidity facility from 6% to 5%, and relaxing the 2% countercyclical capital buffer due in July 2020.[141] The central bank lowered its policy rate from 3.5% to 3.0% and provided additional liquidity through its longer-term repo facility. Also, the limit on total bank loans was raised to 85% (from 80%) of the sum of core credit and deposits.

The refinance facility was expended five fold to provide subsidized interest loans to BFIs willing to on-lend at concessional rates to special group, MSMEs, and general borrowers. Special groups include enterprises run by disabled persons or women or people from disadvantaged communities, export-oriented businesses, and loans to businesses affected by natural disasters, among others. MSME loans up to NRs1.5 million were also eligible for refinancing. General borrowers include businesses not covered by the other two categories. The monetary policy for FY2020 subsidized 1% of interest rates for export-oriented and targeted sectors, 2% for MSME refinancing,

140 NRB. Financial Literacy Framework. https://www.nrb.org.np/contents/uploads/2020/04/Financial-Literacy-Framework_20770114.pdf.

141 Priority sectors includes agriculture, energy, tourism, and MSMEs.

and 3% for general refinancing. Also, decisions on refinancing were decentralized so up to 70% of refinancing facilities can be based on BFI evaluations. Through mid-April 2021, the NRB had provided NRs123.14 billion in refinancing to 48,860 borrowers.

Also, concessional loan schemes with a subsidized interest of 5% were made available "for the operation and continuation of COVID-19 affected businesses including tourism and cottage, small and medium-sized enterprises for payment of salaries to workers and employees of such sectors, and for providing opportunities to develop entrepreneurship to those who have lost jobs in the hard-hit sectors (Monetary Policy 2020-21)." Through mid-April 2021, the NRB provided NRs142.02 billion in concessional loans to 89,879 borrowers.

While no direct employment support was provided in terms of wage subsidies or unemployment benefits, a new NRs50 billion Business Continuity Fund was proposed in November 2020 to provide subsidized lending to COVID-19-affected MSMEs and firms in tourism and hospitality—for paying employee salaries and other operating costs. Businesses categorized as severely affected could receive a maximum NRs100 million, those moderately affected NRs70 million, and those minimally affected NRs50 million. The NRB provided funds to BFIs at 2% interest rate for the first year and 3% for the second year, allowing them to lend at no more than 3% additional interest. To qualify for the facility, borrowers need to have at least five employees, have paid regular salaries through March 2020 via bank accounts, have audited financial records, and tax clearance certification from tax authorities. Through mid-April 2021, the NRB provided NRs420 million in business continuity credit.

Data Tables

Table 5.1: MSME Definition

Item	New Definition based on Industrial Enterprises Act 2020*				Old Definition based on Industrial Enterprises Act 1991		
	Micro	Cottage	Small	Medium	Cottage	Small	Medium
Fixed assets	NRs2 million*	...	Less than NRs150 million	NRs150 million–NRs500 million	...	Up to NRs30 million	NRs30 million–NRs100 million
Employees	9 or less	...	...	...	...	...	...
Annual transaction	NRs10 million	...	...	...	...	...	...
Others	Use of energy up to 20 KW.	Those based on: (i) traditional skills and technology; (ii) specific skills or supply of local raw materials, technologies, arts, and culture; and (iii) use of energy up to 50 KW. Specific Industry list provided by Industrial Enterprise Act 2020.	...	...	Specific Industry list provided by Industrial Enterprise Act 1990.	...	...

* effective 11 February 2020. ** excluding house and land.

KW = kilowatt; MSME = micro, small, and medium-sized enterprise.

Note: Apart from defining microenterprises, the definition is solely based on fixed assets. The act was amended in 2020, but all available data are based on the previous definition. Bank and financial institutions use their own definitions to categorize firms, which differ by bank: some banks use NRs1 million to NRs10 million borrowing limits to define MSME loans, whereas other banks use NRs50 million–NRs200 million.

Source: ADB Asia SME Monitor 2021 database. Data from Industrial Enterprises Act 2020.

Table 5.2: COVID-19 Impact on Businesses

A. Business Operations

Types of Firms	July 2020			December 2020		
	Complete Closure	Partially Operating	Fully Operating	Complete Closure	Partially Operating	Fully Operating
Cottage	63.7	33.6	2.7	16.8	36.6	46.6
Micro	61.8	32.3	5.9	8.1	40.3	51.6
Small	63.7	28.7	7.6	14.1	47.2	38.7
Medium	44.4	50	5.6	12.2	38.8	49
Large	48.3	44.8	6.9	8.3	16.7	75
National average	61	34.9	4.1	9.1	37	54

B. Sales, Employment, and Wages

Types of Firms	Sales/Transaction		Employment Level		Wage Cost	
	July 2020	December 2020	July 2020	December 2020	July 2020	December 2020
Cottage	29.4	46.8	69.5	86.6	57.2	67.5
Micro	26.9	51.8	72.2	95.8	58.2	67.5
Small	26.8	47.5	79	85.1	64.7	75.2
Medium	36.6	49.4	83.1	71.5	71.8	79.7
Large	41.3	50.6	86	86.7	66.6	83.8
National average	28.8	50.5	77.5	87.5	63.4	70.4

Source: ADB Asia SME Monitor 2021 database. Data from Impact of COVID-19 on Economy First Follow-up July 2020; Second Follow-up Dec 2020; Nepal Rastra Bank.

Table 5.3-1: MSME Landscape

*Fiscal year data (15 July)**

Item	2008	2009	2010	2011	2012	2013	2014	2015	2016	2017	2018	2019	2020
NUMBER OF ENTERPRISES													
Number of enterprises, total	...	...	...	...	...	...	...	...	...	...	...	...	...
Number of MSMEs	...	...	156,343	171,004	189,026	204,582	226,711	244,365	268,682	300,721	337,864	390,493	...
Cottage	...	...	...	...	...	...	...	...	...	...	...	...	...
Micro	...	...	...	...	...	...	...	...	...	...	...	43,973	...
Small	...	...	...	...	...	...	...	...	...	...	...	311,430	...
Medium	...	...	...	...	...	...	...	...	...	...	...	...	...
Number of large enterprises	...	...	...	...	...	...	...	...	...	...	...	...	...
MSME to total (%)	...	...	...	...	...	...	...	...	...	...	...	...	...
MSME growth (%)	...	...	...	9.4	10.5	8.2	10.8	7.8	10.0	11.9	12.4	15.6	...
MSMEs by sector (% share)													
Agriculture, forestry, and fisheries	...	...	3.1	3.3	3.8	4.3	5.5	6.9	9.1	11.2	13.6	16.3	...
Manufacturing	...	...	49.2	47.7	46.0	45.0	43.1	41.9	39.9	37.8	35.9	33.2	...
Construction	...	...	5.4	5.0	4.6	4.3	3.9	3.8	3.5	3.3	3.3	3.0	...
Energy based	...	...	0.7	0.7	0.7	0.6	0.6	0.5	0.5	0.5	0.4	0.4	...
Mining and minerals	...	...	0.6	0.6	0.6	0.5	0.5	0.4	0.4	0.4	0.4	0.3	...
Information and technology	...	...	...	...	...	...	...	...	...	0.0	0.1	0.1	...
Tourism	...	...	6.5	7.0	8.0	8.7	9.2	9.4	9.7	10.1	10.2	10.1	...
Other services	...	...	34.5	35.7	36.4	36.6	37.2	37.2	36.8	36.7	36.1	36.6	...
MSMEs by region (% share)													
Capital city (Kathmandu)	...	...	...	...	...	...	...	...	...	...	...	19.5	...
Others	...	...	...	...	...	...	...	...	...	...	...	80.5	...
EMPLOYMENT													
Number of employment, total	...	...	...	...	...	...	...	...	...	...	...	...	...
Number of employment by MSMEs	1,761,863	1,843,908	1,914,469	1,987,387	2,062,497	2,140,706	2,157,744	2,263,363	2,337,373	2,466,992	2,606,086	2,808,052	...
Cottage	...	...	...	...	...	...	...	...	...	...	...	...	...
Micro	...	...	...	...	...	...	...	...	...	...	...	...	...
Small	...	...	...	...	...	...	...	...	...	...	...	...	...
Medium	...	...	...	...	...	...	...	...	...	...	...	...	...
Number of employment by large enterprises	...	...	...	...	...	...	...	...	...	...	...	...	...
MSME employees to total (%)[1]	...	...	...	...	...	...	...	...	...	...	...	...	73.5
MSME employees growth (%)	...	4.7	3.8	3.8	3.8	3.8	0.8	4.9	3.3	5.5	5.6	7.7	...
Share of female employees to total employees (%)	...	...	...	...	...	...	...	...	...	...	...	...	...
Employment by MSME by sector (% share)													
Agriculture, forestry, and fisheries	...	...	...	...	...	...	...	...	...	...	...	...	...
Manufacturing	...	...	...	...	...	...	...	...	...	...	...	...	...
Construction	...	...	...	...	...	...	...	...	...	...	...	...	...
Energy based	...	...	...	...	...	...	...	...	...	...	...	...	...
Mining and minerals	...	...	...	...	...	...	...	...	...	...	...	...	...
Information and technology	...	...	...	...	...	...	...	...	...	...	...	...	...
Tourism	...	...	...	...	...	...	...	...	...	...	...	...	...
Other services	...	...	...	...	...	...	...	...	...	...	...	...	...
Employment by MSMEs by region (% share)													
Capital city (Kathmandu)	...	...	...	...	...	...	...	...	...	...	...	...	...
Others	...	...	...	...	...	...	...	...	...	...	...	...	...
CONTRIBUTION TO GDP													
MSME contribution to GDP (NRs million)	...	...	...	...	...	...	...	...	...	...	...	...	...
MSME contribution to GDP (% share)[2]	...	...	...	...	...	...	...	...	...	...	...	22.0	...
MSME GDP growth (%)	...	...	...	...	...	...	...	...	...	...	...	...	...
MSME GDP by sector (% share)													
Agriculture, forestry, and fisheries	...	...	...	...	...	...	...	...	...	...	...	...	...
Manufacturing	...	...	...	...	...	...	...	...	...	...	...	...	...
Construction	...	...	...	...	...	...	...	...	...	...	...	...	...
Energy-based	...	...	...	...	...	...	...	...	...	...	...	...	...
Mining and minerals	...	...	...	...	...	...	...	...	...	...	...	...	...
Information and technology	...	...	...	...	...	...	...	...	...	...	...	...	...
Tourism	...	...	...	...	...	...	...	...	...	...	...	...	...
Other services	...	...	...	...	...	...	...	...	...	...	...	...	...
MSME GDP by region (% share)													
Capital city (Kathmandu)	...	...	...	...	...	...	...	...	...	...	...	...	...
Others	...	...	...	...	...	...	...	...	...	...	...	...	...
EXPORTS													
Total export value (NRs million)	59,267	67,698	60,824	64,339	74,261	76,917	91,991	85,319	70,117	73,049	81,360	97,110	88,000
Total export growth (%)	...	14.2	(10.2)	5.8	15.4	3.6	19.6	(7.3)	(17.8)	4.2	11.4	19.4	(9.4)
MSME export value (NRs million)	...	...	...	...	...	...	...	...	...	...	...	...	...
MSME export to total export value (%)	...	...	...	...	...	...	...	...	...	...	...	...	...
MSME export growth (%)	...	...	...	...	...	...	...	...	...	...	...	...	...
IMPORTS													
Total import value (NRs million)	221,938	284,470	374,335	396,176	461,668	556,740	714,366	774,684	773,599	990,113	1,245,103	1,418,535	1,148,400
Total import growth (%)	...	28.2	31.6	5.8	16.5	20.6	28.3	8.4	(0.1)	28.0	25.8	13.9	(19.0)
MSME import value (NRs million)	...	...	...	...	...	...	...	...	...	...	...	...	...
MSME import to total import value (%)	...	...	...	...	...	...	...	...	...	...	...	...	...
MSME import growth (%)	...	...	...	...	...	...	...	...	...	...	...	...	...

GDP = gross domestic product; MSME = micro, small, and medium-sized enterprise.

* The fiscal year (FY) of the Government of Nepal ends on 15 July; e.g., FY2020 covers data from 16 July 2019 to 15 July 2020.

[1] Data extracted from Industrial Statistics 2019-20. Small and medium-sized enterprises only.

[2] Data refers to Nepal Rastra Bank (2019): https://www.nrb.org.np/contents/uploads/2020/04/Study_Reports-नेपालमा साना तथा मझौला उद्धयम वत्तिीय साधन परचिालन-2076.pdf.

Source: ADB Asia SME Monitor 2021 database. Data from Micro, Cottage and Small Industries Statistics 2018-19; Department of Industries of the Ministry of Industries, Commerce and Supplies.

Table 5.3-2: MSME Landscape—Registered in Department of Industry

*Fiscal year data (15 July)**

Item	2008	2009	2010	2011	2012	2013	2014	2015	2016	2017	2018	2019	2020
NUMBER OF ENTERPRISES													
Number of enterprises, total	...	...	...	4,552	4,831	5,274	5,646	6,109	6,523	7,031	7,529	7,967	8,247
Number of MSMEs	...	...	...	4,112	4,328	4,660	4,960	5,331	5,667	6,078	6,499	6,855	7,075
Cottage	...	...	...	...	...	...	...	...	...	...	...	...	...
Micro	...	...	...	...	...	...	...	...	...	...	...	...	...
Small	...	...	...	2,999	3,173	3,406	3,630	3,922	4,186	4,516	4,859	5,124	5,219
Medium	...	...	...	1,113	1,155	1,254	1,330	1,409	1,481	1,562	1,640	1,731	1,856
Number of large enterprises	...	...	...	440	503	614	686	778	856	953	1,030	1,112	1,172
MSME to total (%)	...	...	...	90.3	89.6	88.4	87.8	87.3	86.9	86.4	86.3	86.0	85.8
MSME growth (%)	...	...	...	...	5.3	7.7	6.4	7.5	6.3	7.3	6.9	5.5	3.2
MSMEs by sector (% share)													
Agriculture, forestry, and fisheries	...	...	...	4.6	...	...	...	...	...	...	...	...	...
Manufacturing	...	...	...	47.6	...	...	...	...	...	...	...	...	...
Construction	...	...	...	0.7	...	...	...	...	...	...	...	...	...
Energy based	...	...	...	0.4	...	...	...	...	...	...	...	...	...
Mining and minerals	...	...	...	0.8	...	...	...	...	...	...	...	...	...
Information and technology	...	...	...	...	...	...	...	...	...	...	...	...	...
Tourism	...	...	...	17.6	...	...	...	...	...	...	...	...	...
Other services	...	...	...	28.3	...	...	...	...	...	...	...	...	...
EMPLOYMENT													
Number of employment, total	...	...	...	...	...	...	...	...	...	...	...	...	616,502
Number of employment by MSMEs	...	...	...	...	...	...	...	...	...	...	...	...	453,195
Cottage	...	...	...	...	...	...	...	...	...	...	...	...	...
Micro	...	...	...	...	...	...	...	...	...	...	...	...	...
Small	...	...	...	...	...	...	...	...	...	...	...	...	285,713
Medium	...	...	...	...	...	...	...	...	...	...	...	...	167,482
Number of employment by large enterprises	...	...	...	...	...	...	...	...	...	...	...	...	163,307
MSME employees to total (%)	...	...	...	...	...	...	...	...	...	...	...	...	73.5
MSME employees growth (%)	...	...	...	...	...	...	...	...	...	...	...	...	...
Share of female employees to total employees (%)	...	...	...	...	...	...	...	...	...	...	...	...	...

MSME = micro, small, and medium-sized enterprise.

* The fiscal year (FY) of the Government of Nepal ends on 15 July; e.g., FY2020 covers data from 16 July 2019 to 15 July 2020.

Notes: Another statistical report is published by Department of Industries. The report contains annual data on the number of industries that receive approval from the department. However, it does not include enterprises registered elsewhere such as local municipalities. Small-scale industries include only those receiving foreign investment. Enterprises are categorized on small, medium-sized, and large firms only. Disaggregation of 'total' enterprises by sector is available, but not by enterprise 'size' except for FY2011.

Source: ADB Asia SME Monitor 2021 database. Data from Department of Industries of the Ministry of Industries, Commerce and Supplies.

Table 5.3-2a: Number of Small, Medium-Sized, and Large Firms by Region, FY2020

	Number of Enterprises					Share (%) of Enterprises				
Province	Small	Medium	SME	Large	Total	Small	Medium	SME	Large	Total
Province 1	240	336	576	200	776	4.6	18.1	8.1	17.1	9.4
Province 2	184	231	415	136	551	3.5	12.4	5.9	11.6	6.7
Bagmati	4,155	916	5,071	464	5,535	79.6	49.4	71.7	39.6	67.1
Gandaki	388	116	504	175	679	7.4	6.3	7.1	14.9	8.2
Lumbini	167	226	393	158	551	3.2	12.2	5.6	13.5	6.7
Karnali	19	4	23	17	40	0.4	0.2	0.3	1.5	0.5
SudurPaschim	66	27	93	22	115	1.3	1.5	1.3	1.9	1.4
Total	**5,219**	**1,856**	**7,075**	**1,172**	**8,247**	**100.0**	**100.0**	**100.0**	**100.0**	**100.0**

FY = fiscal year.

Source: ADB Asia SME Monitor 2021 database. Data from Industrial Statistics 2019-20, Department of Industries of the Ministry of Industries, Commerce and Supplies (2021).

Table 5.3-2b: Employment by Small, Medium-Sized, and Large Firms by Region, FY2020

Province	Small	Medium	SME	Large	Total	Small	Medium	SME	Large	Total
Province 1	15,903	39,490	55,393	24,833	80,226	5.6%	23.6%	12.2%	15.2%	13.0%
Province 2	10,573	21,459	32,032	24,897	56,929	3.7%	12.8%	7.1%	15.2%	9.2%
Bagmati	233,696	77,388	311,084	60,542	371,626	81.8%	46.2%	68.6%	37.1%	60.3%
Gandaki	11,640	9,261	20,901	17,887	38,788	4.1%	5.5%	4.6%	11.0%	6.3%
Lumbini	9,951	16,642	26,593	29,864	56,457	3.5%	9.9%	5.9%	18.3%	9.2%
Karnali	723	189	912	1,663	2,575	0.3%	0.1%	0.2%	1.0%	0.4%
SudurPaschim	3,227	3,053	6,280	3,621	9,901	1.1%	1.8%	1.4%	2.2%	1.6%
Total	**285,713**	**167,482**	**453,195**	**163,307**	**616,502**	**100.0%**	**100.0%**	**100.0%**	**100.0%**	**100.0%**

FY = fiscal year.

Source: ADB Asia SME Monitor 2021 database. Data from Industrial Statistics 2019-20, Department of Industries of the Ministry of Industries, Commerce and Supplies (2021).

Table 5.3-3: Annual Sales Per Firm, 2018

Types of Enterprises	Total	Registered	Not Registered
Total	3,236,243	6,069,634	508,113
Micro/Cottage (1-9 persons)	2,764,712	3,255,646	1,115,261
Small (10-49 persons)	17,890,418	18,397,511	8,332,185
Medium (50-99 persons)	139,793,094	141,271,466	103,283,176
Large (100 persons and more)	660,591,254	665,423,451	357,780,595

Source: ADB Asia SME Monitor 2021 database. Data from National Report on Revenues/Sales, Expenses, and Profit and Loss National Economic Census 2018; Central Bureau of Statistics.

Table 5.3-4: Industries with Foreign Investments, FY2020

Enterprises	Number of projects	Share of projects (%)	Total foreign investment (NRs million)	Foreign investment per enterprise (NRs million)
Large	314	6.2	207,726	661.5
Medium	525	10.4	51,910	98.9
Small	4,213	83.4	73,421	17.4
Total	5,052	100		

FY = fiscal year.

Source: ADB Asia SME Monitor 2021 database. Data from Industrial Statistics 2019-20, Department of Industries of the Ministry of Industries, Commerce and Supplies (2021).

Table 5.4: Bank Credit

*Fiscal year data (15 July)**

Item	2008	2009	2010	2011	2012	2013	2014	2015	2016	2017	2018	2019	2020
NUMBER OF OPERATING FINANCIAL INSTITUTIONS													
Operating banks, total	173	181	203	218	213	207	204	192	179	149	151	170	154
Commercial banks	25	26	27	31	32	31	30	30	28	28	28	28	27
State-owned banks	3	3	3	3	3	3	3	3	3	3	3	3	3
Private sector banks	22	23	24	28	29	28	27	27	25	25	25	25	24
Specialized banks (development banks)	58	63	79	87	88	86	84	76	67	40	33	29	20
Finance Companies	78	77	79	79	69	59	53	48	42	28	25	23	22
Microfinance banks (microfinance development banks)	12	15	18	21	24	31	37	38	42	53	65	90	85
Saving and credit cooperatives (limited banking activities)	16	16	15	16	16	15	16	15	15	14	14	...	...
NGOs (financial intermediaries)	46	45	45	38	36	31	30	27	25	25	24	...	...
Credit[1]													
Loans outstanding, total (NRs million)	391,538	511,753	620,838	704,025	789,729	955,720	1,129,790	1,361,352	1,681,880	1,994,649	2,422,926	2,911,897	3,266,012
State-owned banks	...	...	...	...	...	...	...	...	...	...	...	...	...
Private sector banks	...	...	...	...	...	...	...	...	...	...	...	...	...
Loans outstanding in domestic currency (NRs million)	...	...	...	...	...	...	...	...	...	...	...	...	...
Loans outstanding in foreign currency (NRs million)	...	...	...	...	...	...	...	...	...	...	...	...	...
Loan growth (%)	34.3	30.7	21.3	86.3	16.6	21.5	18.6	(29.9)	23.5	18.6	21.5	20.2	12.2
Total bank loans to GDP (%)	...	...	...	...	...	...	...	...	74.8	76.7	80.6	84.1	86.9
Lending rate in domestic currency loan (%, annual average)	...	...	...	...	12.1	12.1	10.5	9.6	8.7	11.3	12.5	12.1	10.1
Lending rate in foreign currency loan (%, annual average)	...	...	...	...	...	...	...	...	...	...	...	...	...
Gross nonperforming loans (NPLs) (NRs million)	...	...	...	...	...	...	...	...	...	...	...	...	...
Gross NPLs to total loans (%)	...	...	...	...	...	...	...	...	2.2	1.8	1.6	1.5	1.9
Loans outstanding by sector (% share)[1]													
Agricultural and Forestry	...	...	...	2.4	3.6	4.1	4.3	4.5	4.6	4.4	4.8	5.4	5.8
Fishery	...	...	...	0.3	0.2	0.1	0.2	0.3	0.1	0.1	0.1	0.1	0.2
Mining	...	...	...	0.4	0.3	0.4	0.3	0.3	0.2	0.2	0.2	0.3	0.2
Manufacturing (agri, forestry, and bevarage production)	...	...	...	18.3	19.8	19.9	19.7	18.8	17.6	16.5	17.2	17.5	17.3
Construction	...	...	...	10.7	10.4	10.1	10.5	11.2	10.9	10.7	10.5	10.6	10.6
Electricity, gas, and water	...	...	...	1.3	1.8	2.2	2.3	2.5	2.8	3.2	3.6	4.4	5.0
Metal products, machinary, electronic equipment and assembling	...	...	...	1.3	1.4	1.4	1.2	1.2	1.2	1.3	1.4	1.3	1.4
Transport, communication, and public utilities	...	...	...	5.9	5.0	4.3	3.9	3.6	4.0	3.8	3.4	3.2	3.0
Wholesale and retail trade	...	...	...	20.1	20.2	20.8	21.6	21.8	22.3	21.9	22.0	21.1	20.3
Finance, insurance, and real estate	...	...	...	11.2	10.2	8.9	8.0	7.9	8.0	8.3	8.4	8.0	7.7
Hotel and restaurant	...	...	...	2.6	2.7	2.6	2.9	3.2	3.2	3.4	3.8	4.2	4.6
Other services	...	...	...	4.6	4.9	4.9	4.8	4.7	4.3	4.5	4.4	4.2	4.6
Consumption loans	...	...	...	6.4	6.2	7.3	7.7	7.5	7.2	7.9	6.9	5.6	4.9
Local government	...	...	...	0.3	0.2	0.1	0.1	0.1	0.1	0.1	0.1	0.1	0.1
Others	...	...	...	14.4	13.1	13.1	12.5	12.5	13.6	13.7	13.5	14.0	14.5
Deposits[1]													
Deposits, total (NRs million)	508,906	674,584	788,084	869,951	1,071,394	1,250,062	1,477,833	1,771,946	2,107,503	2,384,807	2,836,930	3,354,428	3,933,738
Deposits in domestic currency (NRs million)	...	...	...	...	...	...	...	...	...	...	...	...	...
Deposits in foreign currency (NRs million)	...	...	...	...	...	...	...	...	...	...	...	...	...
Deposit rate in foreign currency (%, annual average)	...	...	...	...	...	...	...	...	...	...	...	...	...
Deposit rate in domestic currency (%, annual average)	...	...	...	...	6.7	5.3	4.2	3.9	3.9	6.2	6.5	6.6	6.0
MSME LOANS													
MSME loans outstanding, total (NRs million)	...	...	...	...	...	...	...	...	...	...	...	...	...
Commercial banks	...	...	...	...	...	...	...	...	...	...	...	...	...
State-owned banks	...	...	...	...	...	...	...	...	...	...	...	...	...
Private sector banks	...	...	...	...	...	...	...	...	...	...	...	...	...
Specialized banks	...	...	...	...	...	...	...	...	...	...	...	...	...
Microfinance banks	...	...	...	...	...	...	...	...	...	...	...	...	...
Others	...	...	...	...	...	...	...	...	...	...	...	...	...
MSME loans to total loans outstanding (%)[2]	...	...	...	...	...	...	...	...	11.2	11.7	11.5	...	...
MSME loans to GDP (%)	...	...	...	...	...	...	...	...	...	...	...	...	...

continued on next page

Table 5.4 *continued*

Item	2008	2009	2010	2011	2012	2013	2014	2015	2016	2017	2018	2019	2020
MSME loan growth (%)	...	...	...	...	...	...	...	...	...	...	...	...	...
MSME lending rate (%, annual average)[2]	...	...	...	...	...	...	...	...	...	...	...	12.5	...
Nonperforming MSME loans (NPLs) (NRs million)	...	...	...	...	...	...	...	...	...	...	...	...	...
MSME NPLs to total MSME loans (%)	...	...	...	...	...	...	...	...	...	...	...	...	...
Number of MSME loan borrowers	...	...	...	...	...	...	...	...	...	...	...	...	...
MSME loan borrowers to total bank borrowers (%)	...	...	...	...	...	...	...	...	...	...	...	...	...
MSME loan rejection rate (% of total applications)	...	...	...	...	...	...	...	...	...	...	...	...	...
Number of MSME savings account in banks	...	...	...	...	...	...	...	...	...	...	...	...	...
Guaranteed MSME loans (NRs million)	...	...	...	...	...	...	...	...	...	...	...	...	...
Non-collateral MSME loans (NRs million)	...	...	...	...	...	...	...	...	...	...	...	...	...
MSME loans outstanding by sector (% share)													
Agriculture, forestry, and fisheries	...	...	...	...	...	...	...	...	...	...	...	...	...
Manufacturing	...	...	...	...	...	...	...	...	...	...	...	...	...
Transportation and communication	...	...	...	...	...	...	...	...	...	...	...	...	...
Construction	...	...	...	...	...	...	...	...	...	...	...	...	...
Wholesale and retail trade	...	...	...	...	...	...	...	...	...	...	...	...	...
Other services	...	...	...	...	...	...	...	...	...	...	...	...	...
Others	...	...	...	...	...	...	...	...	...	...	...	...	...
MSME loans outstanding by region (% share)													
Capital city (Kathmandu)	...	...	...	...	...	...	...	...	...	...	...	...	...
Others	...	...	...	...	...	...	...	...	...	...	...	...	...
MSME loans outstanding by type of use (% share)													
For working capital	...	...	...	...	...	...	...	...	...	...	...	...	...
For capital investment	...	...	...	...	...	...	...	...	...	...	...	...	...
MSME loans outstanding by tenor (% share)													
Less than 1 year	...	...	...	...	...	...	...	...	...	...	...	...	...
1–5 years	...	...	...	...	...	...	...	...	...	...	...	...	...
More than 5 years	...	...	...	...	...	...	...	...	...	...	...	...	...

GDP = gross domestic product; MSME = micro, small, and medium-sized enterprise; NGO = nongovernment organization; NPL = nonperforming loan.

* The fiscal year (FY) of the Government of Nepal ends on 15 July; e.g., FY2020 covers data from 16 July 2019 to 15 July 2020.

[1] Data based on bank and financial institutions (BFIs).

[2] Data from Nepal Rastra Bank report, SME Financing in Nepal 2019.

Source: ADB Asia SME Monitor 2021 database. Data from Nepal Rastra Bank Monthly Statistics, and Current Macroeconomic and Financial Situation Reports.

Table 5.4a: Source of Initial Financing for MSMEs, 2019

Source of Funds	Share (%)
Inheritance wealth/ancestral properties	33.1
Income/savings	25.8
Bank and financial institutions	16.0
Informal credit	8.0
Remittance income	6.8
Cooperatives	5.9
Others	3.9
Venture capital	0.5
Equity share	0.0

MSME = micro, small, and medium-sized enterprise.

Source: ADB Asia SME Monitor 2021 database. Data from SME Financing in Nepal 2019, Nepal Rastra Bank.

Table 5.4b: Loans Outstanding by Region (NRs million)

Province	Commercial Bank (Class A)	Development Bank (Class B)	Finance Company (Class C)	Total
Province 1	392,581	43,634	10,421	446,637
Province 2	301,331	23,095	8,980	333,406
Bagmati	1,996,115	125,006	39,713	2,160,835
Gandaki	227,941	59,741	6,727	294,408
Lumbini	340,015	78,804	9,894	428,713
Karnali	41,404	4,024	417	45,845
Sudur Paschim	107,681	8,830	1,116	117,627

Source: ADB Asia SME Monitor 2021 database. Data from Financial Inclusion Portal, Nepal Rastra Bank. Accessed in May 2021.

Table 5.4c: Savings and Deposits by Region (NRs million)

Province	Commercial Bank (Class A)	Development Bank (Class B)	Finance Company (Class C)	Total
Province 1	138,835	13,075	4,223	156,133
Province 2	108,637	6,873	4,273	119,783
Bagmati	728,825	35,641	17,051	781,517
Gandaki	111,015	31,099	3,183	145,297
Lumbini	142,785	37,610	2,951	183,346
Karnali	21,828	1,345	92	23,265
Sudur Paschim	46,173	4,438	279	50,890

Source: ADB Asia SME Monitor 2021 database. Data from Financial Inclusion Portal, Nepal Rastra Bank. Accessed in May 2021.

Table 5.5: Public Financing and Guarantees

*Fiscal year data (15 July)**

Item	2015	2016	2017	2018	2019	2020	2021
SUBSIDIZED LOANS TO MSMEs							
Number of funds**	...	...	...	...	...	...	...
Number of subsidized loans (new approval)	...	...	...	8,930	18,295	32,448	104,109
Outstanding of subsidized loans to MSMEs (NRs million)	...	...	...	10,662	32,822	59,563	161,436
Subsidized loans disbursed to MSMEs (NRs million)	...	...	...	...	...	...	...
Number of MSMEs accepted for subsidized loans	...	...	...	...	...	...	...
MSME access to subsidized loans (% of total MSMEs)	...	...	...	...	...	...	...
CREDIT GUARANTEES							
Number of guarantee schemes	...	...	...	...	...	...	...
Guaranteed loans outstanding to MSMEs (NRs million)	350.5	523.4	578.4	809.6	...	...	...
Growth (%)	...	49.3	10.5	40.0	...	...	...
Guaranteed loans approved to MSMEs (NRs million)	...	...	...	...	...	...	...
Guaranteed loans disbursed to MSMEs (NRs million)	...	...	...	...	...	...	...
Number of MSMEs guaranteed	505	851	867	530	...	...	...
Growth (%)	...	68.5	1.9	(38.9)	...	...	...
MSME access to credit guarantees (% of total MSMEs)	...	...	...	...	...	...	...
Guaranteed MSME loans to total MSME loans (%)	...	...	...	...	...	...	...
Nonperforming guaranteed MSME loans to total guaranteed MSME loans (NPL ratio; %)	...	...	...	...	...	...	...

* The fiscal year (FY) of the Government of Nepal ends on 15 July; e.g., FY2021 covers data from 16 July 2020 to 15 July 2021.

** There are 10 types of concessional loans, guided under the Unified Procedure for Interest Subsidy on Concessional Loan of 2017 (Table 5a).

Source: ADB Asia SME Monitor 2021 database. Data from Deposit and Credit Guarantee Fund.

Table 5.5a: Concessional Loan Schemes

*Fiscal year data (15 July)**

		Number of Borrowers**			Loans Outstanding (NRs million)		
Types of Loan		2019	2020	2021	2019	2020	2021
1	Commercial Agriculture and Livestock Loan	17,203	24,763	46,057	32,190	54,114	106,978
2	Educated Youth Self-employment Loan	24	65	140	12	35	64
3	Project Loan for Youth-Returnee Migrant Workers	49	221	839	33	152	598
4	Women Entrepreneur Loan	796	6,682	55,551	512	4,354	50,984
5	Dalit Community Business Development Loan	70	351	965	36	185	573
6	Higher, Technical and Professional Education Loan	60	84	111	15	20	25
7	Housing Loan for Earthquake Victim	93	221	231	25	55	49
8	Loan to Textile industries	...	61	210	...	648	2,162
9	Loan to training by CTEVT-approved institution	...	...	2.0	...	...	0.4
10	Youth Self-employment Loan	...	...	3.0	...	...	1.1
Total		18,295	32,448	104,109	32,822	59,563	161,436

CTVET = Council For Technical Education and Vocational Training; MSME = micro, small, and medium-sized enterprise.

* The fiscal year (FY) of the Government of Nepal ends on 15 July; e.g., FY2021 covers data from 16 July 2020 to 15 July 2021.

** The number of borrowers refers to the number of subsidized loans (new approval).

Note: These schemes are not specially elaborated for MSMEs but applicable to them.

Source: ADB Asia SME Monitor 2021 database. Data from Microeconomic and Financial Situation Reports, Nepal Rastra Bank.

Table 5.6: Nonbank Finance

*Fiscal year data (15 July)**

Item	2008	2009	2010	2011	2012	2013	2014	2015	2016	2017	2018	2019	2020
NUMBER OF NONBANK FINANCE INSTITUTIONS													
Nonbank Finance Institutions, total	...	...	...	...	...	...	...	...	...	...	...	...	...
Microfinance institutions	...	...	...	...	...	...	...	...	...	53	65	90	84
Credit unions/cooperatives	...	...	...	...	...	...	...	...	...	...	34,512	34,737	34,837
Finance companies	...	...	...	...	...	...	...	...	...	...	...	...	...
Pawnshops	...	...	...	...	...	...	...	...	...	...	...	...	...
Leasing companies	...	...	...	...	...	...	...	...	...	...	...	...	...
Factoring companies	...	...	...	...	...	...	...	...	...	...	...	...	...
Insurance companies	...	...	...	...	...	...	...	...	...	...	...	...	...
Others	...	...	...	...	...	...	...	...	...	...	...	...	...
MICROFINANCE INSTITUTIONS													
Financing outstanding, total (NRs million)	...	...	...	...	...	...	...	...	...	106,515	145,952	234,153	262,732
Growth (%)	...	...	...	...	...	...	...	...	...	...	37.0	60.4	12.2
Total financing to GDP (%)	...	...	...	...	...	...	...	...	...	...	...	...	...
Annual lending rate (%, on average)	...	...	...	...	...	...	...	...	...	...	...	...	...
Gross nonperforming loans (NPLs) (NRs million)	...	...	...	...	...	...	...	...	...	...	...	...	...
Gross NPLs to total loans (%)	...	...	...	...	...	...	...	...	0.9	0.8	1.0	1.2	2.3
Savings (NRs million)	...	...	...	...	...	...	...	...	...	...	...	...	...
Number of customers financed, total	...	...	...	...	...	...	...	...	...	...	...	...	...
Financing outstanding by sector (% share)													
Agriculture	...	...	...	...	...	...	...	...	...	...	...	...	42.2
Cottage and Micro Industries	...	...	...	...	...	...	...	...	...	...	...	...	2.9
Service Industries	...	...	...	...	...	...	...	...	...	...	...	...	33.8
Wholesale Credit	...	...	...	...	...	...	...	...	...	...	...	...	14.4
Others	...	...	...	...	...	...	...	...	...	...	...	...	6.8
Financing outstanding by region (% share)													
Capital city (Kathmandu)	...	...	...	...	...	...	...	...	...	...	...	...	...
Others	...	...	...	...	...	...	...	...	...	...	...	...	...
CREDIT UNIONS AND COOPERATIVES													
Financing outstanding, total (NRs million)	...	...	...	...	...	...	...	...	77,240	106,630	145,960	235,150	262,720
Growth (%)	...	...	...	...	...	...	...	...	...	38.1	36.9	61.1	11.7
Total financing to GDP (%)	...	...	...	...	...	...	...	...	...	...	...	...	...
Annual lending rate (%, on average)	...	...	...	...	...	...	...	...	...	...	...	...	...
Gross nonperforming loans (NPLs) (NRs million)	...	...	...	...	...	...	...	...	...	...	...	...	...
Gross NPLs to total loans (%)	...	...	...	...	...	...	...	...	...	...	...	...	...
Number of customers financed, total	...	...	...	...	...	...	...	...	...	...	...	...	...
Financing outstanding by sector (% share)													
Agriculture, forestry, and fisheries	...	...	...	...	...	...	...	...	...	...	...	...	...
Manufacturing	...	...	...	...	...	...	...	...	...	...	...	...	...
Transportation and communication	...	...	...	...	...	...	...	...	...	...	...	...	...
Construction	...	...	...	...	...	...	...	...	...	...	...	...	...
Wholesale and retail trade	...	...	...	...	...	...	...	...	...	...	...	...	...
Other services	...	...	...	...	...	...	...	...	...	...	...	...	...
Others	...	...	...	...	...	...	...	...	...	...	...	...	...
Financing outstanding by region (% share)													
Capital city (Kathmandu)	...	...	...	...	...	...	...	...	...	...	...	...	...
Others	...	...	...	...	...	...	...	...	...	...	...	...	...

GDP = gross domestic product, NPL = nonperforming loan.

* The fiscal year (FY) of the Government of Nepal ends on 15 July; e.g., FY2020 covers data from 16 July 2019 to 15 July 2020.

Note: Credit unions and cooperatives data are not available.

Source: ADB Asia SME Monitor 2021 database. Data from Microfinance Situation Report, Nepal Rastra Bank 2021.

Table 5.7: Electronic Banking

A. Registered and Active Users, 2021

Types of Services	Registered	Active	% of Active Users
Mobile Banking	13,227,302	10,508,322	79.4
Debit Card	8,397,423	6,059,102	72.2
Internet Banking	1,131,547	770,268	68.1
Credit Card	185,628	133,202	71.8
Prepaid Card	56,389	33,357	59.2

B. Number of Transaction and Values (Mid-July 2020 to Mid-April 2021)

Se rvices	Number of Transactions	Total Amount (NRs in billion)
Mobile Wallet	102,115,176	14,736
Mobile Banking	81,066,327	534
Card-Based Payment	66,645,366	6,833
ATM-Cash Withdrawal	62,272,378	1,975
Others	46,244,699	1,927

Source: ADB Asia SME Monitor 2021 database. Data from Financial Inclusion Portal, Nepal Rastra Bank. Accessed in April 2021.

Table 5.8: Capital Markets

*Fiscal year data (15 July)**

Item	2008	2009	2010	2011	2012	2013	2014	2015	2016	2017	2018	2019	2020	2021
EQUITY MARKET														
Main Board - NEPSE														
Index	963.4	749.1	477.7	362.9	389.7	518.3	1,036.1	961.2	1,718.2	1,582.7	1,212.4	1,259.0	1,362.4	2,883.4
Market capitalization (NRs million)	366,248	514,940	376,870	323,484	368,262	514,430	1,057,166	989,404	1,890,130	1,856,829	1,435,138	1,567,499	1,792,763	4,010,958
Growth (%)	96.6	40.6	(26.8)	(14.2)	13.8	39.7	105.5	(6.4)	91.0	(1.8)	(22.7)	9.2	14.4	123.7
Trading value (NRs million)	22,821	21,680	11,850	6,665	10,273	21,553	77,299	65,332	164,652	205,023	121,391	110,075	150,039	1,454,444
Trading volume ('000')	28,600	30,547	26,123	26,240	41,885	81,572	214,144	159,717	303,575	392,881	293,818	387,507	428,522	3,404,514
Number of listed companies	142	159	176	207	216	228	235	232	230	208	196	215	212	219
Number of IPOs	13	...	...	...	...	30	18	18	...	17	...	...	...	...
Number of delisted companies	5	...	...	...	...	...	...	...	...	...	...	...	...	...

IPO = initial public offering, NEPSE = Nepal Stock Exchange.

* The fiscal year (FY) of the Government of Nepal ends on 15 July; e.g., FY2020 covers data from 16 July 2019 to 15 July 2020. Source: ADB Asia SME Monitor 2021 database. Data from Nepal Stock Exchange.

Table 5.9: Credit Information Bureau Operations

Item	2015	2016	2017	2018	2019
Credit reports (number)	579,925	742,302	837,177	1,105,964	1,422,861
Credit reports (% increment)	...	28.0	12.8	32.1	28.7
Total borrowers in database (number)	276,367	360,017	445,614	675,028	889,985
Total borrowers in database (% increment)	...	30.3	23.8	51.5	31.8

* The fiscal year (FY) of the Government of Nepal ends on 15 July; e.g., FY2019 covers data from 16 July 2018 to 15 July 2019. Source: ADB Asia SME Monitor 2021 database. Data from Annual Report 2019, Credit Information Bureau.

Table 5.10: Policies and Regulations

Regulations	
Name	**Outline**
Industrial Enterprises Act, 2020	Define enterprises and group them into micro (including cottage), small, and medium-sized enterprises (MSMEs) and others; stipulate regulatory requirements for establishment and operations (including MSMEs).
Bank and Financial Institution Act, 2017	Regulation on bank and financial institutions.
Secured Transaction Act, 2006	Securing obligations with movable and intangible property by making consolidated legal provisions.
Securities Act, 2007	Regulation on securities markets.

Regulators and Policymakers	
Name	**Responsibility**
Ministry of Finance (MoF)	Provide financial incentives to MSMEs.
Ministry of Industries, Commerce and Supplies (MoICS)	Regulate MSMEs for receiving foreign investments.
Nepal Planning Commission (NPC)	Design national development plans including MSME development strategies.
Nepal Rastra Bank (NRB)	Regulate and supervise banking and nonbank finance sectors; facilitate MSMEs' access to finance, promote digital financial services, and provide financial educations.
Security Exchange Board of Nepal (SEBON)	Regulate and supervise capital markets.

Policies		
Name	**Responsible Entity**	**Outline**
Industrial Promotion Policy 2011	MoICS	1) Provide policy guidelines for development of industrial sectors and enterprises. 2) Create several funds such as the Investment Promotion Fund; Technology Development Fund; and Micro, Cottage and Small Industries Development Fund. 3) Create industrial clusters to make business development services available to the production-oriented industries in rural areas.
15th Five Year Plan 2019/20 - 2023/24	NPC	Provide specific programs/activities to support MSMEs, including access to finance and market. The government aims to add 60,000 jobs annually through the establishment of 15,000 MSMEs each year. 1) Identify major challenges to MSME development. 2) Recommend programs/activities to remove or minimise barriers MSMEs are facing. (i) creation of an investment-friendly environment. (ii) establishment of various types of business-related funds. (iii) business incubation centers. (iv) provision of seed capital for the operation of enterprises.
Annual Program and Policies (Budget)	MoF/MoICS	Provide various incentives and facitlieis to MSMEs such as interest subsidy on credit. 1) Promote the micro and cottage industries through programs such as ready-made garment promotion program, handmade paper promotion program, ceramic handicraft promotion program, and advance leather products training and promotion program. 2) Micro Enterprise Development for Poverty Alleviation (MEDPA) program with the objective of increasing "employment opportunities and level of income of the people living below the poverty line by developing micro enterprises through entrepreneurship development."
Strategic Plan (2017-2021) of NRB	NRB	Provide plans of action for imporving access to finance for enterprises and financial literacy. Financial inclusion is a key pillar of the financial sector development strategy. The enhanced financial access and inclusion is considered as one of the opportunities presented in the financial ecosystem that helps MSMEs access finance. The Plan has four pillars: 1) Macroeconomic stability. 2) Financial stability and financial sector development. 3) External sector stability. 4) Sound and effective payment system.
Financial Inclusion Roadmap (2017-2022)	NRB	The Roadmap implements strategic objectives of achieving financial inclusion as set-out in the strategic plan of NRB. It targets: (i) increasing formal financial inclusion in Nepal from 60% to 75% by 2022 and (ii) reducing the excluded from 18% to 3% to create economic empowerment. 1) Unlock constrained credit and savings markets. 2) Improve payments system. 3) Bolster risk-mitigation capabilities. 4) Enhance and leverage locally based financial service providers. 5) Enhance financial inclusion support in the national governance. 6) Strengthen consumer empowerment, protection, and education.
Financial Literacy Framework (2020)	NRB	Enhance and systematize the current fragmented financial literacy activities to facilitate monitoring and evaluation as well as regular assessment through policy interventions.

Source: ADB Asia SME Monitor 2021 database. Data from various legal/policy documents and program websites of the respective agencies.

Table 5.11: COVID-19 Emergency Measures

Name	Fund Size (NRs billion)	Outline
1. Refinance Fund	n/a,	Refinance is available up to five times the available fund. 1) Special refinancing for designated groups and export-oriented industries provided through the bank and financial institutions (BFIs) at 1% interest. Similalry, micro, small, and medium-sized enterprise (MSME) refinance is to be provided at 2% and general refinance at 3%. 2) The maximum limit per borrower is NRs1.5 million for MSME refinancing and NRs50 million for special and genral refiancing under the lump-sum refinance scheme. 3) NRs200 million for general refiancing to be provided on the basis of customer evaluation.
2. Fund for Business Continuity Loan	50	1) Loan is to be used for the payment of wages of workers and employees of industries and businesses affected by the COVID-19 pandemic. 2) Loans are provided to domestic, small and medium-sized enterprises, and tourism businesses which are affected by the COVID-19. 3) The affected businesses are classified into highly impacted, moderately impacted, and low impacted sectors. 4) The interest rate on the loan is 5% for the first year and 6% for the second year.
Grand Total*	149.17	

* The amount approved for refinance and business continuity loan as of mid-June 2021.

Source: ADB Asia SME Monitor 2021 database. Data from Nepal Rastra Bank.

Country Review

Pakistan

Overview

Pakistan's economy contracted by 0.5% in fiscal year (FY) 2020 (ended 30 June 2020), due to the adverse effects of coronavirus disease (COVID-19) containment measures. These caused supply chain disruptions amid a decreased demand of goods and services, contributing a loss in gross domestic product (GDP) of PRs2.5 trillion, unemployment for 4 to 5 million workers, and a reduction in business earnings.[142] In FY2021, however, the economy rebounded to grow by 3.9%, supported by a strong fiscal and monetary policy responding to the pandemic.[143]

Micro, small, and medium-sized enterprises (MSMEs) are an integral part of the economy. They are therefore prioritized by the government—through its Small and Medium-Sized Enterprise (SME) Policy 2019—and the emphasis on MSMEs within pandemic recovery measures. An estimated 5.2 million MSMEs operated in the country in 2020, contributing nearly 40% to GDP and 25% of exports by value. The labor force was 61.7 million in 2018—a labor force participation rate of 44.3%. Non-agriculture employment reached 38 million, of which 27.3 million (72%) worked for MSMEs.[144]

MSMEs are aided by several measures, including concessional loans for exporters, the implementation of Digital Policy 2018 that supports technology and innovation, along with venture capital and "angel" funding. Nevertheless, barriers to MSME development and growth remain, such as their largely informal status, difficulties in regulatory and trade compliance, limited government support, and access to finance. The number of SME borrowers remained below 200,000 from 2011 to 2020, due to supply-side challenges such as nonperforming loans (NPLs), risk-averseness of lenders, and skewed commercial lending that favors the public sector. Demand-side issues include the lack of documentation and absence of collateral. This leaves many MSMEs ineligible for government refinance schemes or other formal support.

Steps have been taken to enhance financial inclusion, such as promoting the adoption of digital financial services and expanding a digital secured transaction registry for moveable assets. While these are promising, work is needed to strengthen the availability of bank credit, create an enabling regulatory environment, and target business development services for MSMEs to spur economic growth and job creation.

142 Pakistan Economic Survey 2019-20; Small and Medium Enterprise Development Authority; Ministry of Planning, Development, and Special Initiatives. 2020. *Special Survey for Evaluating Socio-Economic Impact of Covid-19 on Wellbeing of People.*

143 Asian Development Bank. 2021. Asian Development Outlook 2021 Update. September.

144 Labor Force Survey 2017–2018.

1. COVID-19 Impact on MSMEs

Pakistan had three waves of COVID-19 infections between March 2020 and May 2021. Its first COVID-19 case was in February 2020, and as the infection numbers increased, the federal and provincial governments applied various containment measures beginning the following month. They included travel restrictions, social distancing, a ban on public gatherings, curbs on commercial activity, and lockdowns to varying extents. To minimize the impact on low-income segments of the population—where workers often rely on daily wages—restrictions were eased beginning in April 2020 with selective economic reopening, such as construction and related activities. In August 2020, restrictions were eased further, as the government established COVID-19 Standard Operating Procedures, including social distancing, limited office occupancy, and the rollout of "smart lockdowns" targeting infection hotspots.[145] A second wave of infections hit beginning October 2020, which forced the government to tighten containment measures (such as an increase in smart lockdowns and curbs on commercial activity, among others). As cases dropped in January 2021, restrictions were once again eased. However, with the onset of a third wave in March 2021—more extreme than previous waves—the government again tightened restrictions, which remained in place until May 2021.

The pandemic devastated Pakistan's economy and economic growth in FY2020. About PRs2.5 trillion in GDP and 20.6 million jobs were lost between April and July 2020.[146] An additional 6.7 million people lost some income. The Pakistan Institute of Development Economics projected job losses to again reach 18.5 million given the impact of the second wave, factoring in earlier structural challenges to the economy related to the power sector and tax generation. Data from the Pakistan Bureau of Statistics (PBS) suggested that after the first wave, 18.4 million people re-commenced work, while over 2 million remained unemployed. Subsequent estimates showed higher job losses—between 4 to 5 million. In addition, economic growth was also affected. The ADB *Asian Development Outlook 2021* estimated the economy contracted by 0.5% in FY2020, which was confirmed by FY results published in the Pakistan Economic Survey 2019–2020.

As the economy gradually reopened after the first wave, exports and remittances began to revive in October 2020. Both remained at more than $2 billion per month until April 2021. Manufacturing also began to recover, with large-scale manufacturing expanding by 4.8% in the first quarter of FY2021 over the previous first quarter level (although from a lower base with growth in selected sectors). Based on these trends, government support packages and policies, and deferments in external debt repayments, the central bank's *State of Pakistan's Economy Report* revised GDP growth to between 1.5% and 2.5% for FY2021. It turns out that the economy rebounded 3.9% growth for FY2021 (footnote 143). This strong recovery was supported by improved fiscal and monetary policy measures responding to the pandemic.

To assess the pandemic's impact on SMEs, the Small and Medium Enterprise Development Authority (SMEDA) conducted a survey in April 2020 among 920 firms.[147] Nearly 95% of the SMEs reported a drop in work due to the pandemic, with 92% reporting supply chain disruptions due to the lockdown. Some 73% temporarily closed, while 27% partially halted operations. Reduced global demand led to a 23% drop in export orders. Overall, 89% of the SMEs reported a fall in revenue, cash flow, credit, or other financial issue. Given weak business performance and

[145] "Smart" lockdowns refer to restrictions in activity and movement in hotspots, which are defined as areas with elevated disease incidence or transmission (i.e., prevalence of infected persons being more than 1.5 per 1,000 persons). Hotspots can be geographically based (i.e., city, town, village, etc.) or temporal locations such as markets or commercial centers. Increased levels of testing, tracing, and quarantining are conducted in identified hotspots.

[146] Ministry of Planning, Development, and Special Initiatives. 2020. *Special Survey for Evaluating Socio-Economic Impact of Covid-19 on Wellbeing of People.*

[147] SMEDA defines SMEs as enterprises with up to 250 employees and turnover up to PRs250 million.

increasing financial challenges, nearly half (48%) had to lay off workers. Services was most affected—the bulk of SMEs—followed by manufacturing.[148]

Another survey was conducted by SMEDA, the Asian Development Bank Institute and the Asian Productivity Organization from August to September 2020.[149] Results showed that SMEs were unprepared to deal with a devastating pandemic and associated lockdowns. While the sample size was limited to 236 SMEs in Pakistan and was conducted online, it still provided useful insights. Following the first wave, SMEs reported losses in earnings, reduced production, cash-flow shortages, and a decrease in domestic demand. Around 81.8% of those surveyed reported lower sales revenue with a similar proportion losing cash flow (often resulting in layoffs). SMEs also said that, on average, five of either their business suppliers or customers had closed operations. Government support went to about 25% of respondents mostly limited to utility payments (electricity, water, and gas)—as many SMEs remain ineligible for other government support due to their informal status or were unaware of the support available. MSME challenges were summarized as credit constraints, supply chain disruptions, decreased consumer demand, and trade logistics.

For economic recovery, to safeguard livelihoods, and mitigate business losses from the pandemic impact, the government unveiled a PRs1.2 trillion COVID-19 Prime Minister's Relief Package in March 2020. The State Bank of Pakistan also implemented a range of measures. These policy support measures (discussed under Policies and Regulations below) contributed to a strong recovery of Pakistan's economy in FY2021.

2. MSME Development

- The SME Policy 2019 was prepared along with an SME Action Plan 2020 to support and expand MSMEs, estimated at 5.2 million in 2020, up from 3.2 million in 2005.
- MSMEs employ a large share of the workforce, estimated at 72% of non-agriculture jobs.
- MSMEs contribute about 40% of GDP, primarily in services.
- MSMEs largely cater to the domestic market, but there are some export-oriented or part of the value chain of larger, export-driven manufacturers. MSMEs contribute about 25% of export value and could expand further through trade compliance and business development.
- Information and communications technology (ICT) is a priority for the government. Connectivity and internet penetration have been growing. In parallel, start-ups have been expanding since 2015, raising an estimated $178 million from local and foreign investors.
- To support the start-up ecosystem, private and public business incubators and accelerators have been growing. National Incubation Centers (NIC) have trained 242 teams from 2017 to 2020, generating an estimated PRs2.9 billion and around 100,000 direct and indirect jobs.

Scale of MSMEs

SMEDA, under the Ministry of Industries and Production, led the preparation of the SME Policy 2019—which upgrades SME Policy 2007—as of June 2021 pending federal government approval. In addition, an SME Action Plan was approved in October 2020. The new policy and action plan provide an inclusive, standardized definition of SMEs—based exclusively on upper thresholds of annual sales turnover.

148 SMEDA. 2020. Survey Report: Impact of COVID-19 on SMEs.

149 Results of the survey were reported in the report titled *Impact of COVID-19 on SMEs, February 2021.*

However, multiple MSME definitions coexist among institutions, based on available data and how they are used. For example, the Pakistan Bureau of Statistics categorizes small firms as those with less than 10 employees (and addresses medium enterprises, which are not defined elsewhere); the central bank—the State Bank of Pakistan (SBP)—defines SMEs as firms employing fewer than 250 employees with an annual turnover of less than PRs800 million; SMEDA categorized SMEs as enterprises with up to 250 employees and turnover up to PRs250 million. As a result, it was critical the Action Plan 2020 agree on a common definition among stakeholders and institutions. The proposed SME Policy 2019 suggests a revised definition based solely on sales turnover instead of a combination of employment or fixed assets (Table 6.1):

- Start-ups are enterprises less than 5 years old with sales turnover as defined below.
- Small enterprises have sales turnover up to PRs150 million.
- Medium enterprises have sales turnover between PRs150 million and PRs800 million.

While this definition awaits formal approval, institutions continue to collect MSME data based on their respective definitions.

The last Census of Economic Establishments (CEE) was conducted by the PBS in 2005. Based on that census, the SME Policy 2007 reported 3.2 million enterprises operating, of which 99.1% were classified as SMEs (firms employing fewer than 10 people). While the census was intended to be conducted every 5 years, the next census took place in 2015–2016 with the data supposed to have been finalized for public release in June 2021.[150] Until it is released, estimates of MSMEs are based on CEE 2005 figures with annual growth rates (for example, real GDP growth and labor growth—based on Labor Force Surveys) are applied. Other estimation models have used data related to electricity connections as a base, aggregating commercial, industrial, and agricultural connections while factoring in the portion of domestic connections (20.0%) estimated to be used for commercial activities.[151] Karandaaz (a special purpose vehicle) and Gallup (polling and research) calculated and summarized results from these models in 2018, estimating the number of MSMEs to be between 4.0 million (based on labor growth), 4.5 million (based on electricity connections), and 4.8 million (based on GDP growth). Discussions with stakeholders during March–April 2021, including PBS and SMEDA, indicated that the actual number of MSMEs was likely higher. Latest estimates from SMEDA based on GDP growth show 5.2 million MSMEs were operating in 2020, accounting for 98.6% of all enterprises (Figure 6.1A and Table 6.2).

Disaggregating CEE 2005 data shows the majority of MSMEs are in services: 53.0% in wholesale and retail trade, followed by 22.0% in other services such as ICT and health (Figure 6.1B). MSMEs in manufacturing totaled 20.0%, while 1.0% are estimated to be in agriculture, forestry, and fisheries. Stakeholder feedback—including PBS and SMEDA—indicated a further increase in MSMEs engaged in services, while the proportion in manufacturing decreased from the 2005 survey.

By geographic spread, in 2005, 65.2% of MSMEs were located in Punjab, 17.8% in Sindh, 14.2% in Khyber Pakhtunkhwa, 2.2% in Balochistan, and 0.6% in the Federal Capital (Islamabad) (Figure 6.1C). Punjab is home to major industrial hubs of large and small-scale manufacturing, focusing on a range of activities from textiles to surgical instruments. The estimates indicate that MSMEs were concentrated around urban centers: the National Electric Power Regulatory Authority said that around 41% of commercial, industrial, and agricultural electricity connections were clustered in Faisalabad, Gujranwala, and Lahore, often referred to as the "golden triangle" of Punjab province.

[150] According to stakeholder consultations held with the Pakistan Bureau of Statistics. As of end-August, new census data have yet to be released.

[151] Based on State of the Industry report by the National Electric Power Regulatory Authority (NEPRA), 2017.

Figure 6.1: Number of MSMEs

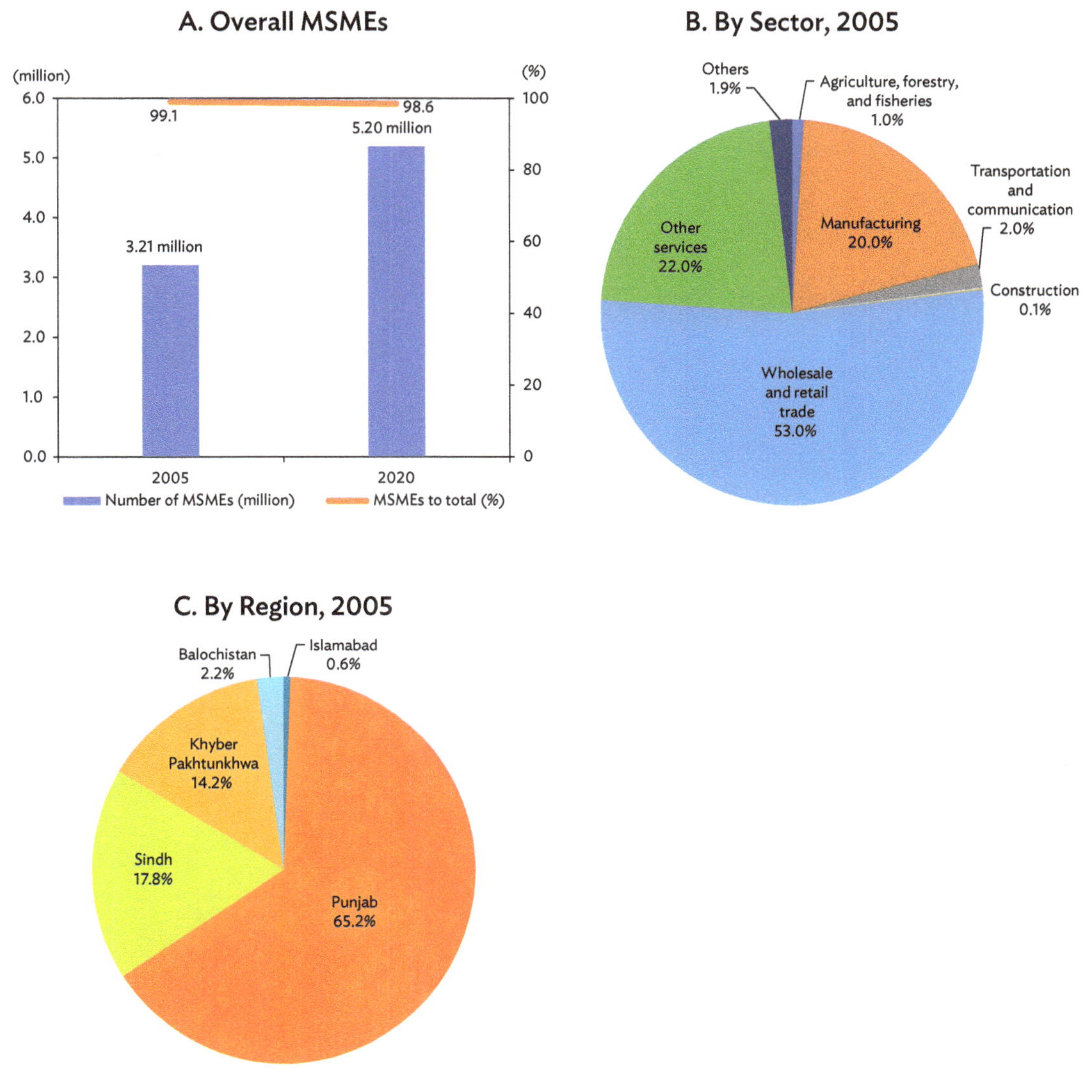

MSME = micro, small, and medium-sized enterprise.

Source: ADB Asia SME Monitor 2021 database. Data from Pakistan Bureau of Statistics, and Small and Medium Enterprise Development Authority.

Employment

Labor Force Survey (LFS) 2017–2018 data show overall employment was 61.7 million, up 4.3 million (7.5%) from the previous 2014–2015 survey. Agriculture accounted for 23.8 million (38.5%), with 38.0 million non-agricultural employment.

Based on the PBS definition of MSMEs (fewer than 10 employees), the LFS categorizes them as "non-agriculture informal economy." They were estimated at 27.3 million (72.0%) in FY2018. The remaining 28.0% were employees of large firms, which the PBS defines as firms with more than 10 employees. MSME employment would have thus increased by 3.2 million from FY2015 to FY2018 (Figure 6.2A).

Figure 6.2: Employment by MSMEs

A. Overall MSMEs

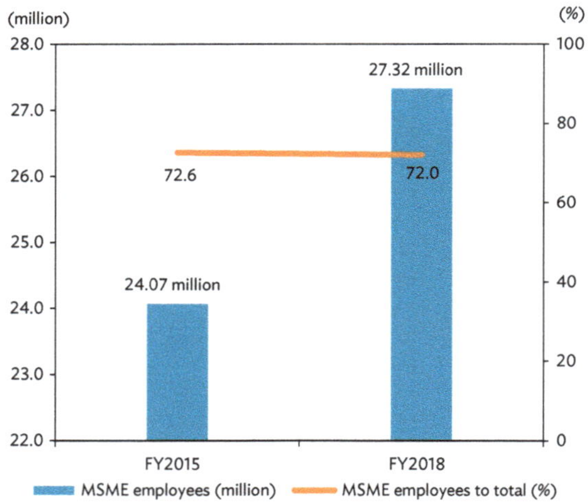

MSME = micro, small, and medium-sized enterprise.

Source: ADB Asia SME Monitor 2021 database. Data from Labor Force Survey 2014-15 and 2017-18.

B. By Sector, FY2018

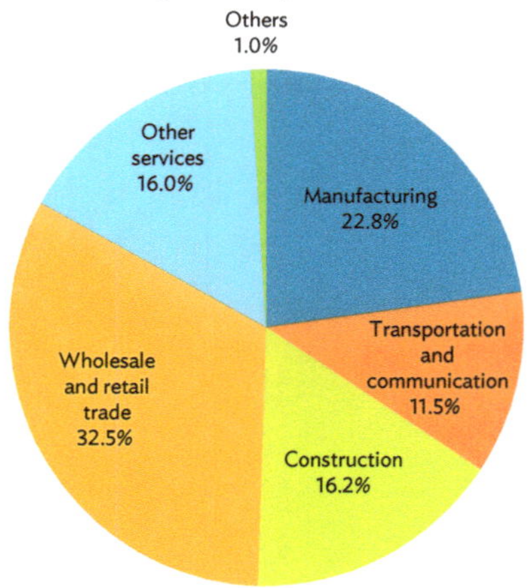

FY = fiscal year; MSME = micro, small, and medium-sized enterprise.

Note: data based on non-agriculture informal economy (as MSMEs).

Source: ADB Asia SME Monitor 2021 database. Data from Labor Force Survey 2017-18.

C. By Region, FY2018

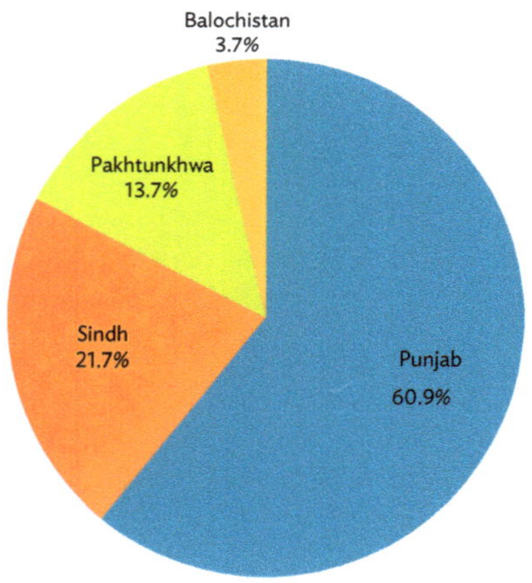

FY = fiscal year; MSME = micro, small, and medium-sized enterprise.

Note: data based on non-agriculture informal economy (as MSMEs), which does not include Islamabad.

Source: ADB Asia SME Monitor 2021 database. Data from Labor Force Survey 2017-18.

By sector, the largest share of MSME employment in FY2018 was wholesale and retail trade (32.5%), followed by manufacturing (22.8%); construction (16.2%); other services such as community, social, and personal services (16.0%); and transport (11.5%) (Figure 6.2B). Between FY2015 and FY2018, there was a small drop in MSME employment in manufacturing (23.2% to 22.8%) as well as wholesale and retail trade (34.1% to 32.5%). On the other hand, there were small increases in other services (14.5% to 16.0%) and transport and communications (10.9% to 11.5%).

In FY2018, MSME employment by region—based on the non-agriculture informal economy (minus Islamabad)—was similar to the MSME geographic spread: most employment was in Punjab (60.9%), followed by Sindh (21.7%), Khyber Pakhtunkhwa (13.7%), and Balochistan (3.7%) (Figure 6.2C).[152] By gender, it was estimated that 22% of MSME workers were female and 78% male, meaning there were relatively few female workers in MSMEs.

Business Productivity

Pakistan's GDP in FY2019 was PRs37,972 billion. Services had the largest share (57.1%), followed by agriculture (23.4%) and manufacturing (19.5%).[153] Due to an economic slowdown, annual growth was just 1.9% in FY2019. It contracted by 0.4% in FY2020 due to the pandemic (by comparison, annual GDP growth was 5.8% in FY2018 and 5.6% in FY2017).

According to the Pakistan Economic Survey 2010-11 (based on SMEDA's MSME definition), MSMEs contributed an estimated 40% to GDP (Table 6.2). The data has not been updated as of July 2021.

The contribution to GDP of MSME manufacturing firms (fewer than 10 employees) was calculated using the PBS dataset. A fixed growth rate was applied using the 2005 Census of Manufacturing Industries as base. Using this approach, manufacturing MSMEs were estimated to have contributed 2.0% to the overall GDP in 2020, similar to recent years—2.0% in 2019, 1.9% in 2018, and 1.8% in 2017 (Figure 6.3). PBS data was only available for MSME manufacturing, which was estimated to have contributed nearly 12.5% of MSME GDP.

Figure 6.3: MSME Contribution to Gross Domestic Product—Small Manufacturing Firms

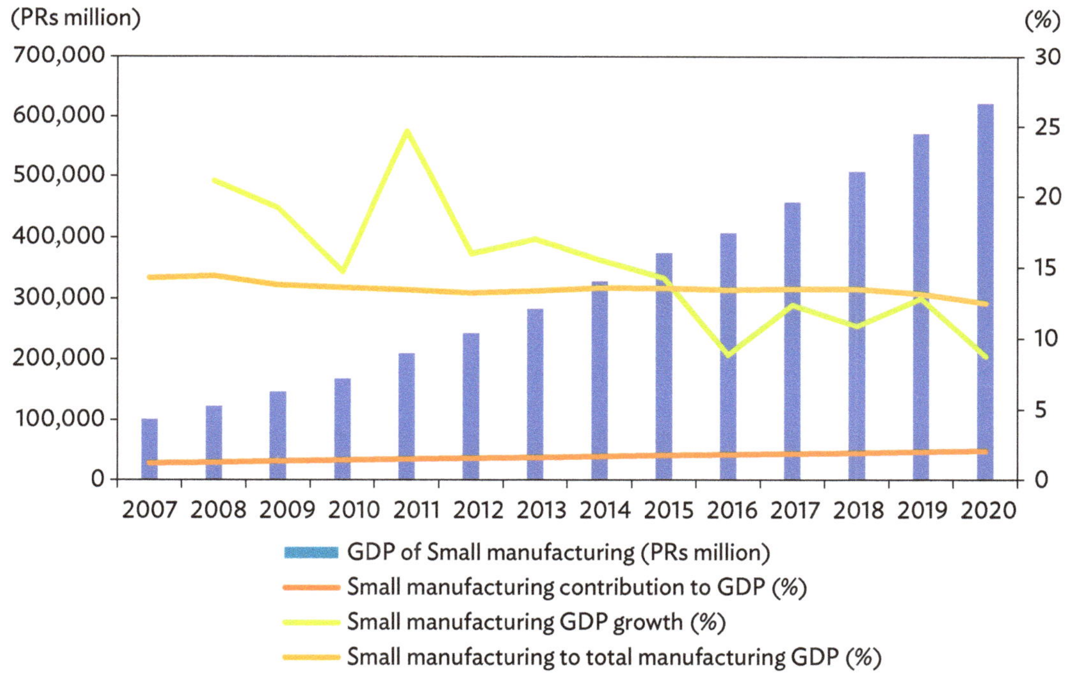

GDP = gross domestic product; MSME = micro, small, and medium-sized enterprise.

Source: ADB Asia SME Monitor 2021 database. Data from Pakistan Bureau of Statistics and Small and Medium Enterprise Development Authority based on Census of Manufacturing Industries, 2005.

152 The Labor Force Survey (LFS) data only provide a provincial breakdown for the four provinces (for employed persons) and does not provide data separately for Islamabad.

153 Pakistan Bureau of Statistics, 2020.

Market Access

MSMEs mainly serve the domestic market. But there are some that are trade-oriented and part of the value chain of larger, export-driven manufacturing firms.

Exports in FY2020 totaled PRs2.7 trillion, according to the Pakistan Economic Survey 2019–2020, down sharply (12.9%) due to the pandemic. By comparison, annual growth was 22.4% in FY2019 and 19.5% in FY2018. Although data has not been updated, the Pakistan Economic Survey 2009–2010 estimated that 25% of export value can be attributed to MSMEs (Table 6.2). The challenges faced by MSMEs in accessing foreign markets include the inability to meet required labor, environmental, social, and international standards, in addition to compliance with complex trading regulations.

Box 6.1: SME Development Authority Support to Sialkot Clusters and Exports

Sialkot is a major export-oriented city from where quality products are manufactured—including sports goods, surgical instruments, leather garments, gloves and accessories, sportswear, and musical instruments. The Small and Medium Enterprise Development Authority (SMEDA) is helping Sialkot's local industries enhance their international market share through initiatives such as the Sports Industries Development Center (SIDC) and Sialkot Business and Commerce Centre (SBCC).

Sports Industry Development Centre (SIDC) offers manufacturing facilities for high-quality sports products. These include bladders, basketballs, thermo balls, volleyballs, American footballs, rubber nozzles, and yarn winding of bladders to small and medium-sized enterprises (SMEs). The center provides laboratory testing, workshop facilities, advisory services, and worker training to sports-related enterprises. It played an innovative role in the manufacturing of thermo balls based on new technology approved by the Federation Internationale de Football Association (FIFA) and International Matchball Standard (IMS). The common facilities have also enabled Sialkot's SMEs to better compete and secure orders for mechanized inflatable balls, among others. SIDC supports sports industry modernization using available (solvent-based auto lamination) and new technology (thermo bonding). SIDC has helped 13 companies establish their own thermo units by forging linkages with equipment importers and building local capacity. The project has generated PRs132 million in revenues by providing services to SMEs and local industries. It has created new jobs for nearly 450 workers directly and trained an additional 200 workers from other firms.

Sialkot Business and Commerce Centre (SBCC) is another SMEDA project that provides marketing support and an infrastructure facility to exporters—especially SMEs—strengthening partnerships with local industries. The center offers 216 stall exposition halls for year-round exhibitions along with 25 Business Incubation Offices for matchmaking and business-to-business meetings, a convention center, management offices, a business facilitation center, and an information technology center. The project will support an estimated 1,000 SMEs annually.

Sources: ADB interview with SMEDA on 5 April 2021; SMEDA.

The current government has focused on promoting exports to generate growth, employment, and foreign reserves. Exports have also been cited as a critical avenue to economic recovery from the pandemic. Several measures have been taken to support exporters, such as the SBP maintaining an Export Finance Scheme (EFS) interest rate of 3.0% and Long-Term Finance Facility (LTFF) of 6.0%. The EFS provides up to 180 day short-term concessional loans through commercial banks to exporters of manufactured goods and services, particularly for value-added goods. The loans can be extended another 90 days. The LTFF offers long-term concessional loans (10 years including a 2-year grace period) for imported or locally manufactured plant and machinery to be used for export production. Also, there are power subsidies for MSMEs and specific intermediate and raw materials that increase product access to export value chains.[154] Together with increasing global demand and greater domestic supply, these measures have helped export values remain above $2 billion per month between October 2020 and April 2021. Exports were driven predominantly by textiles and ready-made garments, with the overall export value estimated at PRs3.5 trillion in 2020.[155]

The United States (US) is the leading destination for Pakistan exports, accounting for $4.0 billion in 2019. Latest data from the PBS further highlights this trend. Exports to the People's Republic of China (PRC) reached $2.0 billion in 2019, with Phase II of the China–Pakistan Free Trade Agreement signed in April 2019, Exports to the United Kingdom ranked third ($1.7 billion in 2019), followed by exports to the European Union, where Pakistan holds a Generalized Scheme of Preferences Plus status. The Association of Southeast Asian Nations (ASEAN) provides favorable market access for 313 export items. The Ministry of Commerce has been encouraging export diversification, such as its "Look Africa Policy Initiative." In 2020, nearly $1.5 billion in goods were exported to Africa.

Pakistan's imports totaled $50.0 billion in 2019. Most goods and services came from the PRC ($12.4 billion), followed by the United Arab Emirates ($6.3 billion) and Saudi Arabia ($2.4 billion). More recently, raw material and intermediate goods imports have increased, along with higher wheat and sugar imports due to domestic shortages.

Technology and Innovation

The government has prioritized ICT as a sector with strong economic and employment growth potential. Digital Policy 2018 was developed to promote digitization through policy reforms, better infrastructure, export promotion, and skills development. ICT contributed 0.9% ($3.5 billion) to GDP in 2019, twice as much as in 2015, and is expected to double again over the next 2 to 4 years.[156] Information technology (IT) exports, driven by software, were valued at an estimated $1.4 billion in 2019—the SBP estimated there was an additional $1.2 billion from unregistered freelancers.

Pakistan Telecommunication Authority data show increased connectivity and penetration levels. As of March 2021, there were 183 million cellular subscribers (or 84.7% tele-density), 98 million 3G/4G subscribers (43.5% penetration), and 101 million broadband subscribers (46.4% penetration). As a result, e-commerce has begun to thrive. An E-commerce Policy was announced by the government at the end of 2019 to create a business-friendly environment for more inclusive and holistic growth. E-commerce (and mobile-commerce) was estimated to have generated $3.9 billion revenue in 2020, benefiting MSMEs, particularly during the lockdowns. E-commerce holds much more potential for MSME growth, but measures such as digital literacy must spread among micro and small-scale entrepreneurs to take advantage of digital platforms.

Pakistan's start-ups raised $77 million in 2020 and nearly $178 million from 2015 to 2020.[157] Airlift ($22 million) and Bykea ($13 million)—start-ups focused on transportation/mobility— were beneficiaries, along with multi-million-dollar investments in e-commerce, such as Cheetay ($9.6 million), which deals with last mile delivery and Bazaar ($7.8 million), an online marketplace linking retailers directly with manufacturers and wholesalers. Innovation (and investments) in other areas—including fintech, edtech, agritech, and healthtech—are also expanding.

[154] Exemption of peak hour charges for 3 years up to 2023; a discount of 50% on additional power usage by SMEs until June 2021; and a discount of 25% for all industries on additional power usage for 3 years as well.

[155] Pakistan Bureau of Statistics dataset.

[156] Ministry of Information Technology.

[157] Based on a Deal Flow Tracker that monitors published investments in start-ups by Invest2Innovate. Invest2Innovate supports the start-up ecosystem through an accelerator program, research and insights, and technical support along with the funding of 121 ventures.

Networking and Support

The Federation of Pakistan Chambers of Commerce and Industry includes 58 chambers of commerce (CCIs) with MSME and large corporate members, including 16 Women's Chambers. Among the oldest of these is the Lahore CCI, founded in 1923 (before the India–Pakistan partition). CCI services vary, but in general, they focus on working with businesses for networking, training, and advocacy. Larger CCIs offer additional help, such as navigating tax issues, export regulations, and utility issues, among others. The Lahore CCI, for instance, has set up a single-window facilitation center with 20 help desks that work with government departments ranging from taxes to electricity. CCI membership is voluntary, and enterprises are often required to pay a nominal fee for annual membership. In a baseline survey conducted by SMEDA, it found that around 40% of MSMEs are members of a CCI.

In addition, there are many sector associations such as the All Pakistan Textile Mills Association (APTMA), Pak Readymade Garment Manufacturers and Exporters Association, Pakistan Sports Goods Manufacturers and Exporters Association, and the Pakistan Software Houses Association (P@SHA), among others. These associations often serve as a useful platform to highlight and discuss specific issues such as energy tariffs, export/import duties, and taxes; and raise them with the government as needed. Examples include successful lobbying by APTMA in 2020–2021 for exemptions on duties on certain raw materials for textile manufacturing to facilitate exports, and P@SHA advocating for the reduction of federal general sales tax on IT services, which was subsequently reduced from 13% to 5%. Where associations are more active, networking is an important service. For instance, P@SHA established a technology incubator called the NEST I/O, which has organized annual conferences since 2017, connecting technology entrepreneurs and investors.

Business incubators and accelerators for start-ups like the NEST I/O have also been established. There are several private sector incubators, such as SEED Ventures and Invest2Innovate, alongside government-backed incubators, known as National Incubation Centers (NICs) and Plan9. The NIC in Islamabad was established on a public-private partnership model (comprising Team-up and the Government of Pakistan, Ministry of Information Technology and Telecommunications along with a private sector telecom operator, Jazz). NICs are also located in other provincial capitals, such as Karachi, Lahore, Peshawar, and Quetta. NICs offer infrastructure and shared facilities for start-ups; customized training; networking between industries, entrepreneurs, and financiers; and facilitating policy development. Collectively, they have trained 242 teams from 2017 to 2020, which have generated an estimated PRs2.9 billion and 100,000 direct and indirect jobs.

3. Access to Finance

- SME bank loans remain small—5.2% of total bank loans outstanding—contracting 1.0% growth in 2020, based on bank data. Limited outreach to SME borrowers (3.5% of total bank borrowers in 2020), and high NPLs (16.9% in 2020) are key challenges.
- The central bank has multiple refinance schemes for MSMEs, with some related to the pandemic. However, many MSMEs are ineligible for bank credit and public financing schemes due to their informal status, and inadequate registration and documentation.
- A Pakistan Credit Guarantee Corporation (PCGC) was established in 2019 but was not yet operational as of April 2021. Microfinance institutions play a critical role in enhancing access to finance for rural MSMEs. Yet NPLs are rising. Venture capital funds are actively providing growth capital to start-ups.

- The government has also introduced several initiatives to support digital financial services. These include Raast and Roshan Development Accounts. There is also an increase in private sector fintech firms that focus on P2P, C2B, and B2B payments. Digital payments have been expanding since 2016, accelerating rapidly since the onset of the COVID-19 pandemic.
- The Growth Enterprise Market (GEM) was established as an alternative to the main exchange board, enabling SMEs and other companies to raise capital through accredited capital market investors with less stringent reporting requirements.
- The financial infrastructure supporting MSMEs continues to evolve. A Digital Secured Transaction Registry was established in 2020, and an e-Credit Information Bureau reduces requirements to include MSMEs in monitoring data.

The SBP is the central bank and is mandated to regulate and supervise the monetary and credit system and to foster its growth to secure monetary stability and better utilize the country's productive resources. The SBP has specific departments catering to SME credit, microfinance, and financial inclusion. The Securities and Exchange Commission of Pakistan (SECP) is responsible for regulating and supervising the nonbank finance industry and securities market. It is responsible for regulating and supervising (i) the corporate sector (business registrations) and capital markets, (ii) insurance companies, (iii) nonbanking finance companies and private pension schemes, and (iv) oversight of various external corporate and financial service providers such as chartered accounts and brokers.

Bank Credit

As of the end of 2020, there were 29 commercial banks in Pakistan. Of these, 20 were privately owned (including 5 Islamic Banks), 5 state-owned, and 4 foreign banks. There were 3 additional specialized banks—the Punjab Provincial Cooperative Bank, SME Bank Limited, and Zarai Taraqiati Bank Limited. Together with 11 microfinance banks, the number of operating banks was 43, slightly down from 47 in 2007.[158]

There are few SME loans in Pakistan. SME loans outstanding (commercial banks and specialized banks) totaled PRs481.8 billion in 2020, a marginal increase of 1.0% from 2019, but a decrease of 6.2% from 2018 (Figure 6.4A and Table 6.3). In 2020, SME loans accounted for 5.2% of total bank loans and 7.3% of total domestic private sector loans. The share of SME loans to GDP has been roughly calculated at less than 2% since 2011, suggesting low levels of available credit to SMEs by formal banks.

The number of SME borrowers from 2011 to 2020 remained below 200,000. The SBP says this is the result of surging NPLs from 2007 to 2012—ranging from 8.5% to 35.9%; thus, banks restricted lending to SMEs. In 2013, the SBP revised regulations to control large numbers of NPLs and encouraged lending to SMEs. Since then, the SME NPL ratio fell moderately to a still high 16.9% in 2020. A revised target of 700,000 SME borrowers was set in the National Financial Inclusion Strategy (NFIS) 2015. However, due to bank risk aversion, SME borrowers were just 179,934 in 2020. Thus, SMEs accounted for just 3.5% of total bank borrowers in 2020.

Concessionary refinancing schemes are available to encourage lending since the COVID-19 outbreak.[159] But their effectiveness has been limited. Access to bank credit remains a challenge for MSMEs. Commercial bank lending is also skewed toward the public sector which offers healthy returns with less risk. Compounding these supply-

158 The SBP has distinct Prudential Regulations for SME financing and microfinance, resulting in separate monitoring. Therefore, SME financing data and microfinance data are not included in the SBP dataset. Thus, only SME financing through commercial banks and specialized banks is analyzed.

159 The end-user rate for SBP refinance schemes ranges from 3% to 6%. The weighted average lending rate of banks on outstanding loans was 8% as of April 2021.

side issues, there were also demand-side challenges. Many MSMEs are informal, and therefore lack the requisite registration and documentation to apply for formal bank loans (or benefit from refinance/formal schemes). Furthermore, weaknesses in contract enforcement are an impediment to lending microenterprises. There is also no program-based lending and value-chain financing for small enterprises that lack collateral.

In 2020, most SME borrowers were in manufacturing (45.7%), followed by wholesale and retail trade (30.0%), transportation and communications (6.2%), other services (5.2%), and construction (2.9%) (Figure 6.4B). Among SME borrowers from commercial and specialized banks, 67.6% used loans for working capital and 23.7% for capital investment. Loans offered to SMEs were largely short term, with the average borrowing rate based on the Karachi Inter Bank Offer Rates (KIBOR) plus 4% to 5%. With the policy rate at 7% since June 2020, this means the average borrowing rate is about 12% (below the 15%–16% pre-pandemic rate). Loans for capital investment tend to have higher borrowing rates. Analyzing SME loans outstanding by tenor in 2020, 64.2% were less than 1 year, 14.5% were between 1 and 3 years, and 21.3% more than 3 years.

Loans provided by microfinance banks to microenterprises (micro loans) totaled PRs60.6 billion at the end of 2020, up a robust 32.2% from 2019. In 2020, microfinance banks financed 217,630 microenterprises.

Figure 6.4: SME Loans

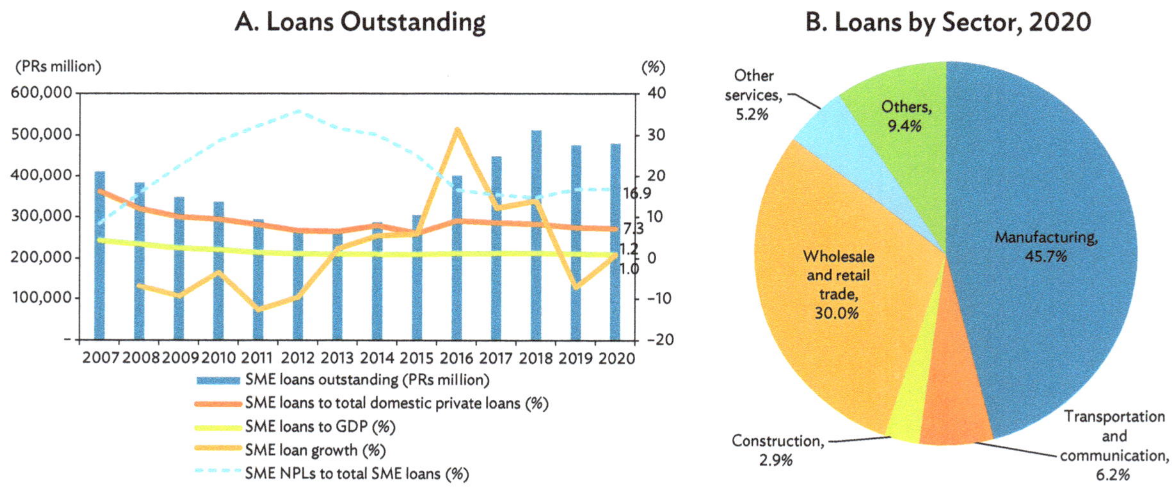

GDP = gross domestic product; NPL = nonperforming loan; SME = small and medium-sized enterprise.

Note: Data refer to SME loans by commercial banks and specialized banks only.

Source: ADB Asia SME Monitor 2021 database. Data from State Bank of Pakistan.

Public Financing and Guarantees

a. Refinancing schemes

The SBP has designed four types of MSME refinance schemes since 2010 (Table 6.4): (i) the Refinance Facility for Modernization of SMEs; (ii) the Refinance and Credit Guarantee Scheme for Women Entrepreneurs; (iii) the Refinance Scheme for Working Capital Financing of Small Enterprises and Low-end Medium-sized Enterprises; and (iv) the Small Enterprise Financing and Credit Guarantee Scheme for Special Persons. They are available through all commercial banks and development finance institutions.

- **Refinance Facility for Modernization of SMEs:** The PRs8.3-billion scheme was launched in June 2010. PRs1.5 billion has been disbursed, benefiting 114 MSMEs. It encourages MSMEs to modernize their equipment and factories and to meet their power requirements by acquiring generators. Loans are available for 10 years with 6.0% annual interest.
- **Refinance and Credit Guarantee Scheme for Women Entrepreneurs:** Launched in 2017, it gives women entrepreneurs better access to finance to expand existing businesses or to set up new ones. The scheme started with PRs2.5 billion. PRs669 million in refinance has been disbursed as of end-2020, benefitting 886 MSMEs. Loan tenor is 5 years with a 5.0% annual interest.
- **Refinance Scheme for Working Capital Financing of Small Enterprises and Low-end Medium-sized Enterprises:** The PRs5.8-billion fund was launched in 2019 for MSMEs operating in eight sectors.[160] It offers 1-year loans at 6% interest. As of end-2020, PRs471 million had been refinanced for 66 MSMEs.
- **Small Enterprise Financing and Credit Guarantee Scheme for Special Persons:** The PRs560-million scheme was announced in 2020 with PRs5 million disbursed among five MSMEs by end-2020. Loan tenor up to 5 years with 5% annual interest.

The government has other finance and refinance facilities to help MSMEs recover from the economic effects of COVID-19. Details are provided under Policies and Regulations.

b. Credit guarantees

The SBP established the Pakistan Credit Guarantee Corporation (PCGC) in 2010 as a partial risk-sharing facility to encourage financial institutions to lend to MSMEs and agricultural firms that lack collateral. It was institutionalized in 2019 and registered with the SECP as a development finance institution. It is funded by the UK's Department for International Development (now known as the Foreign, Commonwealth and Development Office) and the Government of Pakistan under SBP supervision. However, as of April 2021, the PCGC was waiting for shareholder capitalization and therefore, had not conducted any business.

During 2019 and 2020, the PCGC approached commercial and microfinance banks to assess their interest, and received soft commitments from 19 institutions. Once PCGC becomes operational, it will help MSMEs access finance by encouraging commercial and microfinance banks to lend, create awareness among banks and end users, and encourage more collateral-free lending/borrowing. The PCGC would become the main MSME credit guarantee company. Another credit guarantee corporation, InfraZamin, a joint venture between Karandaaz Pakistan and InfraCo Asia Investments Singapore, was established at the end of 2020 for infrastructure-related projects.

[160] Selected sectors include (i) information technology; (ii) furniture; (iii) surgical goods; (iv) data processing; (v) gems and jewelry; (vi) leather; (vii) fruits, vegetables, and food processing; and (viii) printing and packaging.

Nonbank Financing

There were 44 nonbank finance institutions (NBFIs) as of end-2020, with 26 microfinance institutions (MFIs), 12 investment banks, and 6 leasing companies. MFI financing outstanding as of end-2020 was PRs86.4 billion, down by 6.1% from 2019 (Figure 6.5A and Table 6.5). The annual average lending rate for 2020 was 30.0%. Gross NPLs amounted to PRs4.2 billion, 4.9% of loans disbursed. The NPL ratio was higher in 2020 due to the pandemic and the 2019 economic slowdown (the NPL ratio in 2014 was 0.9%, 0.5% in 2017 and 2018, and 1.1% in 2019). Around 42% of outstanding loans went to agriculture, followed by wholesale and retail trade (20%) and other unspecified sectors (19%) (Figure 6.5B). MFIs play an important role in enhancing MSME access to finance, especially rural MSMEs. Outstanding loans grew from PRs13.4 billion in 2011 to PRs92.0 billion in 2019.

Figure 6.5: Nonbank Finance

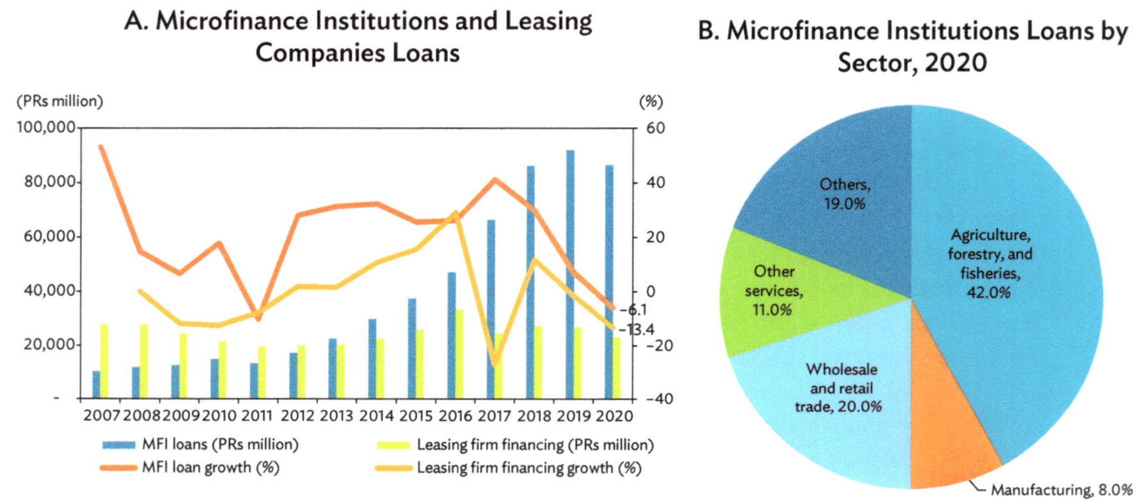

MFI = microfinance institution.

Source: ADB Asia SME Monitor 2021 database. Data from Securities and Exchange Commission of Pakistan.

Outstanding financing from leasing companies totaled PRs23.1 billion in 2020, down by 13.4% from 2019. Gross nonperforming financing (NPF) was PRs2.4 billion, or 10.2% of total financing in 2020. The declining trend in leasing will further hamper access to finance for sub-prime MSME customers. However, investor interest in using NBFIs to provide financial services and as a lending platform for digitizing MSME payments and lending, credit access is expected to improve in the future.

As of end-2020, there were 16 registered venture capital funds, primarily investing in early-stage fintech, e-commerce, mobility, edtech, and healthtech.[161] Local and international venture capital funds held a large share of the estimated $178 million start-up investments from 2015 to July 2020. Of this amount, $91.9 million was invested by international venture capitalists in 23 deals, with $42.4 million invested by local venture capitalists in 42 deals.[162] The second main of funding source for start-ups are local ($4.0 million from 2015 to 2020) and international ($13.4 million) "angels." In the first quarter of 2021 alone, nearly $20 million was raised.

[161] Early-stage investments include seed money (official equity funding after launch of a start-up) to Series A (where start-ups have a track record and raise funds to enhance their user base and/or product offerings).

[162] Invest2Innovate (2021), *Deal Flow Analysis,* https://invest2innovate.com/deal-flow-tracker/

During the 2015–July 2020 period, 30 deals focused on e-commerce start-ups ($76.7 million), 11 deals in transportation/mobility start-ups ($31.5 million), and 10 deals in finance/fintech ($8.6 million).

Taxation and regulatory barriers that restrict funds leaving the country limit additional funds and investment. This often leads local funds to domicile abroad and discourages foreign investors. Also, early-stage start-ups say that investors often hold a disproportionately large amount of equity relative to the funds given.[163] While start-up funding has increased since 2015, the funding gap for early-stage start-ups remains wide.

Digital Financial Services

Digital payments have been growing since 2016 and rapidly accelerated since the COVID-19 pandemic began in 2020. According to the SBP, mobile banking grew 88% year-on-year while internet banking users expanded 31% during 2020, with the number of transactions growing 72%. The combined value of internet and mobile banking transactions in 2020 was PRs4,716 billion compared with PRs2,589 billion in 2019.[164]

Daily online fund transfers grew most. The SBP reported that from 188,000 transactions per day in February 2020, it increased by almost 400% to more than 800,000 by December 2020. On an aggregate basis, mobile phone banking transaction values doubled for the third consecutive year to PRs1.7 trillion by the end of FY2020, due to increased use of smartphone applications to transfer funds, pay utility bills, and retail purchases.

The SBP promotes digital financial services (DFS) by waiving fees for online fund and government-to-person (G2P) transfers, such as under the Ehsaas social welfare program and with Pakistan Customs for duty refunds for businesses. Raast, launched in 2020, is an instant digital payment system. The SBP hopes to use the system to disburse government salaries, pensions, and Ehsaas stipends. In its next phase, the system will expand to allow individual entrepreneurs and small businesses to conduct peer-to-peer (P2P) transactions using a reliable, digital, and approved channel. Thus, individual and business payments can be secured without formal bank accounts. The central bank also launched Roshan Digital Accounts in 2020 through commercial banks, which allows overseas Pakistanis to digitally open bank accounts. Using fintech, it enables financial inclusion for overseas residents/workers to transfer funds, remittances, make payments, or invest.

As digitalization began to take hold in 2010, fintechs from mobile wallet platforms to digital lending and payment systems have begun to flourish. It is expected fintechs will play an increasing role in digitizing financial services from P2P, consumer-to-business (C2B), and business-to-business (B2B) payments. Fintechs can offer school and university fee payment options to major wallet and digital banking channels. The growth in e-commerce has led to a surge in online payments and payment service providers like National Institutional Facilitation Technologies (NIFT), ePay, and PayFast, which aggregate card and direct debit payment options for merchants. Others like bSecure are creating universal checkouts.

For lending, Finja, Tez Financial, and Creditfix have NBFI licenses and offer working capital financing to micro and small enterprises as well as consumer-lending products.

To help start-ups and MSMEs access finance, SECP approved an Equity Crowd Funding Platform as a regulatory sandbox. The platform is being tested with results expected in the first quarter of 2022. Moreover, a draft Equity Investment Policy was approved in 2021 to further support innovation and start-ups.

163 Invest2Innovate (2019) *Pakistan Start-up Ecosystem Report.*

164 State Bank of Pakistan (2020), Annual Performance Review, 2020.

Box 6.2: Innovative MSME Finance Accelerates Financial Inclusion—Karandaaz Pakistan

Karandaaz Pakistan is a nonprofit company set up under Section 42 of the Companies Act to promote access to finance for micro, small, and medium-sized enterprises (MSMEs) using a commercial investment platform. It also promotes financial inclusion for entrepreneurs based on technology-enabled solutions. Karandaaz was established in 2014 with financial and institutional support from the Foreign, Commonwealth and Development Office of the United Kingdom and the Bill and Melinda Gates Foundation—with $316.3 million committed as of April 2020. Since its inception, the company has helped transform the financial landscape for MSMEs in Pakistan through innovative interventions and technical support to the government. It is based on four workstreams.

- Karandaaz Capital offers direct MSME investments between $3 million–$5 million in firms that promise high economic and employment growth. Wholesale investments are allowed in specific product programs, such as finance facilities and financial institutions focusing on specific clusters or segments with large employment potential. Also, strategic investments are channeled into entities that further catalyze investment in specific sectors, such as InfraZamin in 2020, a credit guarantor for infrastructure projects benefiting MSMEs, and the Pakistan Microfinance Investment Company which provides loans to entrepreneurs. The three investment streams provided PRs17.7 billion as of March 2021.
- Karandaz Digital focuses on financial inclusion by supporting regulatory reform and innovation to strengthen digital financial services (DFS). It centers on national payments infrastructure to digitize government payments, providing research, innovation, and incubation to test possible solutions, policies, and regulations that promote DFS—including technical assistance for creating a Regulatory Framework for Digital Banks and Regulatory Framework for Equity Crowdfunding. PRs1.8 billion has been disbursed so far.
- Karandaaz Innovation supports new ways of offering MSME and digital finance through Challenge Funds grants. The Innovation Challenge Fund focuses on overcoming barriers to financial inclusion and entrepreneurship, while the Women Entrepreneurship Challenge invests and provides business support to women. More than PRs100 million has been provided in grants to 10 fintechs and 5 digital pilots, with PRs310 million invested in women-led businesses.
- Karandaaz Knowledge offers in-depth knowledge and data analytics on MSMEs and DFS to promote financial inclusion. It generates evidence-based analysis to help decision-making and define further research.

These have allowed Karandaaz to help spur MSMEs and stimulate job growth. They have created an estimated 800,000 jobs (550,000 for women) through microfinance and have supported 1,973 MSMEs and 52,857 jobs.

Source: ADB's virtual interview with Karandaaz, 17 March 2021.

Capital Markets

The Pakistan Stock Exchange (PSX) had a turbulent year in 2020, but managed to pick up toward the end as macroeconomic indicators improved. At end-2020, market capitalization on its main board was PRs8,035 billion, up by 2.9% from 2019 (Figure 6.6A and Table 6.6). By volume, 113.0 billion shares were traded in 2020, almost twice the 2019 level (60.6 billion). This was also reflected in trading value, which was PRs4,421 billion in 2020 compared with PRs2,270 billion in 2019. The number of listed companies has remained largely the same between 2020 (531) and 2019 (534) (Figure 6.6B). There were four initial public offerings (IPOs) in 2020, while six companies were delisted.[165]

[165] The four IPOs include The Organic Meat Company Limited (meat processing), TPL Trakker (cargo tracking), Agha Steel Industries (steel re-rolling), and Engro Polymer and Chemicals Limited (polymer manufacturing). Two additional IPOs have taken place in 2021 (until June): Panther Tyres Limited (tire manufacturing) and Service Global Footwear Limited (footwear manufacturing).

In March 2020, PSX launched Pakistan's first Exchange Traded Funds (ETFs): United Bank Limited Pakistan Enterprise ETF (UBL-ETF), offered by United Bank Limited Funds; and National Investment Trust Pakistan Gateway ETF (NITG-ETF), offered by National Investment Trust limited. ETFs should allow retail investors to diversify their exposure.

In 2019, the PSX, together with SECP, introduced the Growth Enterprise Market (GEM) to serve growth-oriented firms outside the main board. GEM allows company listings that cannot meet the PSX main board conditions. This allows SMEs and other companies to raise capital from accredited investors through the capital market with reduced reporting compliance (Table 6.7).

Despite multiple awareness sessions conducted by SECP and the PSX, no GEM listings were made as of June 2021. This was often due to incomplete documentation, gaps in financial reporting, or the absence of a basic corporate structure. However, SECP and PSX are using consultants and advisors with the hope of allowing some listings by end-2021. Advisors include securities brokers and scheduled banks, Consultant to the Issue (CTI), along with accounting and auditing firms recognized by the Institute of Chartered Accountants of Pakistan and the Institute of Cost and Management Accountants of Pakistan. SECP has said that only accredited investors—institutional investors and accredited individual investors with a net worth of PRs5 million—are eligible to invest.

Figure 6.6: Equity Market

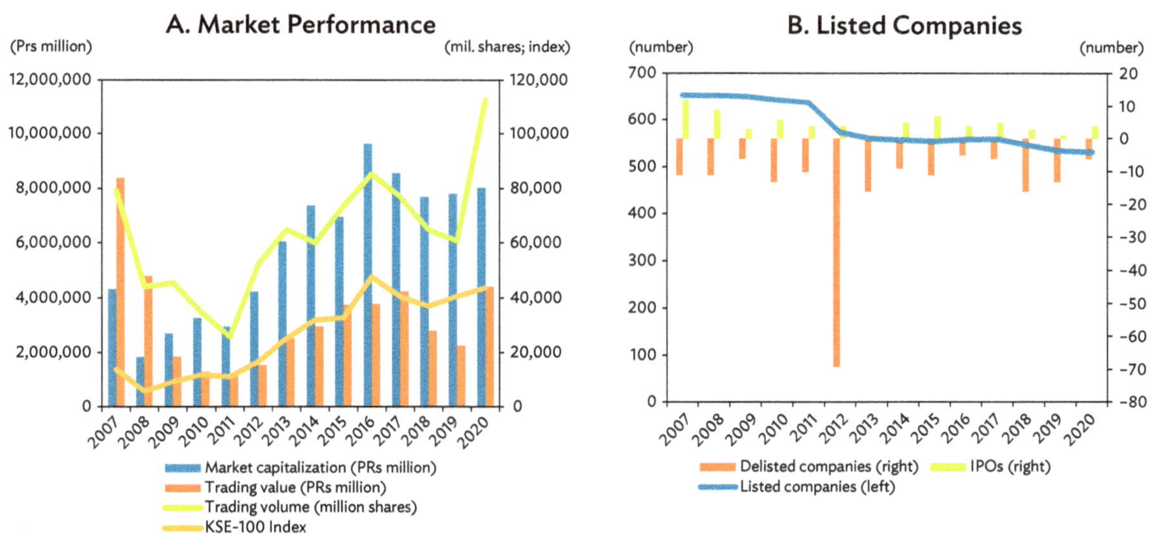

IPO = initial public offering.

Source: ADB Asia SME Monitor 2021 database. Data from Pakistan Stock Exchange.

Financial Infrastructure

As can be seen from the discussions above, the financial infrastructure needed to promote MSME access to finance continues to evolve. There is progress in DFS, the rise in venture capital and business angel investments. Other measures—though nascent—in capital markets such as the GEM Board and the PCGC should ease MSME access to credit.

Additional steps taken include implementing a digital Secured Transaction Registry (STR) by the SECP, backed by the necessary legal framework through the Financial Institutions (Secured Transactions) Act 2016 and e-Financial Institutions (Secured Transactions) (Amendment) Ordinance 2020. The STR allows MSMEs to offer movable assets as collateral for loans from financial institutions, which helps the many MSMEs that do not own property. From its launch in April 2020 through June 2020, over 85,000 charges/security interests had been registered.[166]

An electronic Credit Information Bureau (e-CIB) was established under the SBP in 2005. The requirement of listed borrowers to have a minimum PRs500,000 outstanding was removed to include MSMEs. The SBP reports that e-CIB records have grown from 200,000 borrowers in 2005 to 4 million in 2020.

However, many other barriers to MSME inclusion remain to be addressed. These include a large proportion of informal MSMEs that lack registration and requisite documentation needed for loan processing, high administrative and operational transaction costs for small loans, weaknesses in contract enforcement and judicial delays, absence of program-based lending or value-chain financing, continued information asymmetries between finance providers and MSMEs, generic financial products, and limited financial literacy programs for entrepreneurs or small businesses.

4. Policies and Regulations

- The National SME Policy Action Plan 2020 includes a unified MSME definition, access to finance, business development services, skills and human resources, technology, market access, infrastructure, and entrepreneurship.
- Digital Policy 2018 promotes digitalization across sectors using policy measures, infrastructure, export promotion, and skills development.
- The National Financial Inclusion Strategy (NFIS) promotes inclusive growth and hopes to extend credit to 700,000 MSMEs by 2023. The government launched a *Kamyab Jawan* Program, to provide loans to young people.
- Several digital finance initiatives enhance financial inclusion, with policies and regulations implemented by the SBP and SECP.
- The government unveiled a PRs1.2-million COVID-19 Prime Minister's Relief Package in March 2020 to help the economy recover, safeguard livelihoods, and mitigate business losses from the impact of the pandemic. SBP accommodative measures further support MSMEs.

MSME Development

The SME Policy 2007 was developed under the Ministry of Industries, Production and Special Initiatives (present Ministry of Industries and Production) through the Task Force for SME Policy Development (Table 6.8). It supports economic reforms to enable growth and reduce poverty. MSME-led private sector development was viewed as key to economic progress. The policy focused on four key areas for MSME development: (i) business environment; (ii) access to finance; (iii) support for human resource development, technology upgrading and marketing; and (iv) unifying MSME definitions. It also simplified compliance procedures for MSMEs, increased available credit, improved technological infrastructure, and promoted entrepreneurship.

Led by SMEDA, the SME Policy 2019 was prepared under the Ministry of Industries and Production and is pending federal government approval (as of May 2021). The updates were needed given the 18th constitutional amendment, where provinces have enhanced autonomy over economic and administrative policies. In addition,

[166] SECP (2020) Annual Report, 2020.

the 2007 Pakistan–China Free Trade Agreement and the China–Pakistan Economic Corridor (CPEC) showed economic growth potential. More recently, the digital transformation has powered e-commerce and the rise of fintech and greater entrepreneurship—all addressed in the updated policy. Importantly, it was designed to support the government's goal of creating 10 million jobs and 7% economic growth by 2023.

Policies were designed to address market failures in areas like credit, infrastructure, and skills development, and to reduce the cost of doing business through regulatory reforms. They improved coordination between public investments and private sector growth and along with capacity building where state capacity is weak or non-existent, while creating a supportive environment for innovation and ensuring gender and geographic inclusiveness.

Along with SME Policy 2019, an SME Action Plan 2020 was developed by SMEDA. While still awaiting approval, the plan acknowledges the significance of MSMEs in the economy and helps provide a level playing field for businesses through policies that are favorable for MSMEs. Key recommendations and initiatives proposed under SME Action Plan 2020 include the following:

- revised, unified MSME definition;
- simplified rules, regulations, and taxes;
- increased MSME access to credit;
- simplified procedures for start-ups and existing businesses;
- MSME quotas for public procurement;
- skill development, entrepreneurship, and creating new enterprises;
- promote MSME participation in international fairs and exhibitions at subsidized rates;
- develop an MSME data bank to bridge the information gap.

ICT is a priority for the government to spur economic growth and create jobs. The Digital Policy 2018 was developed to promote digitalization through policies, financial inclusion, infrastructure, export promotion, and skills development.

In 2021, the Board of Investments started work on a Draft Framework Agreement on Industrial Cooperation, aligned with the long-term CPEC Framework. The framework will focus on special economic zones (SEZs) planned as part of CPEC projects. Four SEZs are in "advanced stages of development and colonization"—including Rashakai SEZ (Khyber Pakhtunkhwa), Dhabeji SEZ (Sindh), M-3 Allama Iqbal SEZ (Punjab), and Bostan SEZ (Balochistan). The Board of Investments hopes SEZs will promote local industries including MSMEs, as well as relocate PRC firms and potential public-private partnerships. SEZs should be an avenue for technology transfer, as well as a platform for skills development.

SECP's Annual Report 2020 highlighted the reforms needed for a regulatory environment for businesses that attracts investment and facilitates growth—measures that helped improve the country's ranking on the World Bank's *Ease of Doing Business Index* by 28 points, from 136 to 108 in 2020. Steps were taken to make "starting a business" easier, through a digitized one-stop shop for registration and reducing procedural requirements from 10 to 5, bettering the country's rank from 130 to 72. SECP integrated e-services with the Federal Board of Revenue and the Employees Old Age Benefits Institution together with provincial business registration portals in Punjab and Sindh. The single-window service has also been improved to reduce the time needed to register. In its 2021 outlook, SECP will further review its regulatory framework to reduce over-regulation and remove practical difficulties. It will also leverage its digitized platform and provide new businesses a facility to open bank accounts at the time a company is registered. However, other critical areas remain weak. They include better enforcing contracts and resolving commercial disputes in a timely manner, difficulty in obtaining credit or construction permits, and varying taxation policies and weak enforcement of intellectual property rights.

Financial Inclusion

The 2015 NFIS envisioned universal financial inclusion. It includes a comprehensive action plan and targets for financial inclusion. Indicators of financial inclusion were very low at the time—only 16% of adults had a bank account, financing to priority sectors including MSMEs was minimal, and regional disparities were evident. It includes several targets to be met by 2023:

- Enhance digital payments through 65 million active digital transaction accounts; 20 million held by women.
- Enhance the deposit-to-GDP ratio to 55%.
- Promote MSME finance to 700,000 MSMEs; 17% of private sector credit.
- Increase agricultural finance to serve 6 million farmers digitally; enhance annual disbursements to PRs1.8 trillion.
- Enhance the share of Islamic banking to 25% of the banking industry; increase branches of Islamic banks to 30% of the total.[167]

Specific MSME measures included launching a credit guarantee company, encouraging refinance schemes for tourism and ICT, creating a National SME Policy, doing a census of business enterprises, and creating bank incentives through fiscal measures. Progress has been made via the establishment of PCGC, increased deposits, and the National SME Policy 2019 and SME Action Plan 2020. However, as mentioned above, loans to MSMEs remain stagnant.

The SBP notes progress on DFS—ranging from the accelerated growth in digital payments in both value and volume, creation of Roshan Digital Accounts, and government-to-person (G2P) transfers through Raast, among others. As discussed earlier, the SECP also introduced equity crowdfunding applications under its Regulatory Sandbox Guidelines. And GEM has been set up as a second-tier board at PSX for listing and trading MSME securities as an alternate to the main board.

To promote young entrepreneurs, the government launched *Kamyab Jawan*—a National Youth Development Program. It offers six schemes to help empower youth, ranging from skills development to access to finance. The Youth Entrepreneurship Scheme provides concessionary loans between PRs5 million and PRs25 million to youth in order to support start-ups or existing enterprises. With nearly two-thirds of the population under the age of 30 (40% of the overall labor force is categorized as youth), the government aims to capitalize from this demographic segment.

Response to COVID-19

To help the economy recover, safeguard livelihoods, and mitigate business losses from the pandemic impact, the government unveiled a PRs1.2-trillion COVID-19 Prime Minister's Relief Package in March 2020 (Table 6.9). Measures ranged from relief to daily wage workers, with cash assistance provided to an estimated 6.2 workers who were laid off, to financial support to stores to ensure essential food items were available at subsidized rates.

The package included measures affecting MSMEs, such as the PRs100 billion for accelerated tax refunds to the export industry. Also, PRs100 billion was provided as financial support to agriculture and MSMEs for electricity payment deferments, bank lending, as well as subsidies and tax incentives. The Temporary Economic Refinance Facility 2020 was expanded to allow the purchase of locally manufactured or imported equipment/machinery to

[167] National Financial Inclusion Strategy, 2015.

upgrade replace, expand or create new in electricity payment deferments: up to 3 months for 5-kilowatt (KW) commercial customers, or 70 KW for industrial customers.

The SBP reduced its policy rate from 13.25% at the start of 2020 to 7% by June 2020 to provide stimulus for an economic recovery—the rate has remained as of April 2021. Also, the SBP launched its Refinance Scheme for Payment of Wages and Salaries, the "Rozgar Scheme," in April 2020 to help businesses (large and MSMEs) pay wages and salaries of permanent, contractual, and daily employees to prevent layoffs until September 2020. The interest rate charged was 5% for non tax payers, 4% for taxpayers, and 3% for tax-paying businesses. The SBP says that about half of the beneficiaries were SMEs. In May 2020, the government allocated an additional PRs30 billion under a credit risk-sharing facility to cover the first 40% loss on disbursed loans of lending banks. It applied to SMEs with sales turnover up to PRs800 million and small corporations with sales turnover up to PRs2 billion. In June 2020, coverage was increased to 60%. The SBP reported that as of November 2020, the scheme helped protect 1,677,806 jobs in 2,683 businesses, of which 382,673 belonged to 1,959 SMEs and small corporations.

A Refinance Facility for Combating COVID-19 was implemented with 3% interest to enhance health sector capacity, targeting hospitals, medical centers, and manufacturers of COVID-related items. By June 2021, PRs15.6 billion had been approved under the facility. To encourage export-oriented investment, a PRs90 billion fund was made available under the Long Term Financing Facility (LTFF), with a limit of PRs700 billion allocated under the Export Refinance Scheme (EFS). Beneficiaries, however, have mostly been large enterprises and formal SMEs; many MSMEs have been ineligible due to their informal status and inadequate registration and documentation.

Tax incentives to the construction sector were also extended until the end of 2021. In addition, provincial governments introduced relief packages that included measures such as tax relief for MSMEs along with financial support to MSMEs and economically vulnerable households. The SBP also provided relief to low-income households and microenterprises by allowing microfinance banks to defer payments of principal on loan obligations for 1 year, reschedule or restructure financing for borrowers unable to service interest or need deferment exceeding 1 year. As of April 2021, the SBP reported PRs121 billion of relief was provided to 1.7 million microcredit borrowers through principal deferment and facility rescheduling or restructuring. The SBP also relaxed regulatory requirements of biometric verification for microfinance until the end of 2021 and also raised borrowing limits of microenterprises from microfinance banks from PRs1 million to PRs3 million.

The SBP also introduced temporary regulations to ensure a sound banking system and sustain economic activities. For instance, a capital conversion buffer was reduced by 100 basis points to 1.5%. The regulatory limit was increased on the extension of credit to SMEs by 44% to PRs180. The debt service ratio was relaxed for consumer loans from 50% to 60%. The principal on loan-deferred payments was allowed by banks for 1 year, and bank dividends were suspended for the first half of 2020.[168].

[168] ADB COVID-19 Policy Database.

Data Tables

Table 6.1: MSME Definitions

A. National Definition (to be effective in 2021)

Item	Start-up	Small	Medium
Annual sales turnover	A small or medium-sized enterprise (SME) with operating for up to 5 years from the establishment is considered as start-up SME.	Up to PRs150 million	Above PRs150 million and up to PRs800 million

Source: ADB Asia SME Monitor 2021 database. Data from National SME Policy 2020, Small and Medium Entereprise Development Authority.

B. State Bank of Pakistan Definition

Item	Micro	Small	Medium
Annual sales turnover	...	Up to PRs150 million	Above PRs150 million and up to PRs800 million
Number of employees	Self-employed or the firm employing individuals not exceeding 10 (excluding seasonal labor).	Up to 50	51-250 (manufacturing and services) 51-100 (trading)

Source: ADB Asia SME Monitor 2021 database. Data from State Bank of Pakistan. For microenterprise, Agriculture Credit and Microfinance Department (AC&MFD) Circular No.02 of 2012 and revised Prudential Regulations No.10 and No.11 (updated by circular No.3 of 2014). For small and medium-sized enterprise, Prudential Regulations for Small and Medium Enterprises Financing (updated on 5 April 2021).

C. Definition by Federal Board of Revenue

Item	Small
Paid-up capital	not exceeding PRs50 million
Number of employees	not exceeding 250 any time during the year
Annual sales turnover	not exceeding PRs250 million
Others	Not formed by the splitting up or the reconstitution of business already in existence.

Note: Small company means a company registered on or after the first day of July 2005 under the Companies Ordinance of 1984 (XLVII). Paid-up capital and undistributed reserves increased from PRs25 million to PRs50 million, following the Finance Act of 2015.

Source: ADB Asia SME Monitor 2021 database. Data from Federal Board of Revenue.

D. National Definition as defined in SME Policy 2007

Item	Small and Medium
Paid-up capital	Up to PRs25 million
Number of employees	Up to 250
Annual sales turnover	Up to PRs250 million

MSME = micro, small, and medium-sized enterprise.

Source: ADB Asia SME Monitor 2021 database. Data from SME Policy 2007, Small and Medium Entereprise Development Authority; and Ministry of Industries and Production.

Table 6.2: MSME Landscape

End of period data

Item	2005	2007	2008	2009	2010	2011	2012	2013	2014	2015	2016	2017	2018	2019	2020
NUMBER OF ENTERPRISES[1a]															
Number of enterprises, total	3,249,482	...	...	...	...	...	...	...	...	...	...	...	...	...	...
Number of MSMEs (rounded figure)	3,210,000	...	...	...	...	...	...	...	...	...	...	...	...	...	5,200,000
Micro	...	...	...	...	...	...	...	...	...	...	...	...	...	...	...
Small	...	...	...	...	...	...	...	...	...	...	...	...	...	...	...
Medium	...	...	...	...	...	...	...	...	...	...	...	...	...	...	...
Number of large enterprises	...	...	...	...	...	...	...	...	...	...	...	...	...	...	...
MSME to total (%)	99.1	...	...	...	...	...	...	...	...	...	...	...	...	...	98.6
MSME growth (%)	...	...	...	...	...	...	...	...	...	...	...	...	...	...	...
MSMEs by sector (% share)															
Agriculture, forestry, and fisheries	1.0	...	...	...	...	...	...	...	...	...	...	...	...	...	...
Manufacturing	20.0	...	...	...	...	...	...	...	...	...	...	...	...	...	...
Transportation and communication	2.0	...	...	...	...	...	...	...	...	...	...	...	...	...	...
Construction	0.1	...	...	...	...	...	...	...	...	...	...	...	...	...	...
Wholesale and retail trade	53.0	...	...	...	...	...	...	...	...	...	...	...	...	...	...
Other services	22.0	...	...	...	...	...	...	...	...	...	...	...	...	...	...
Others	1.9	...	...	...	...	...	...	...	...	...	...	...	...	...	...
Number of MSMEs by region (% share)															
Capital city (Islamabad)	0.6	...	...	...	...	...	...	...	...	...	...	...	...	...	...
Others	99.4	...	...	...	...	...	...	...	...	...	...	...	...	...	...
Punjab	65.2	...	...	...	...	...	...	...	...	...	...	...	...	...	...
Sindh	17.8	...	...	...	...	...	...	...	...	...	...	...	...	...	...
Khyber Pakhtunkhwa	14.2	...	...	...	...	...	...	...	...	...	...	...	...	...	...
Balochistan	2.2	...	...	...	...	...	...	...	...	...	...	...	...	...	...
EMPLOYMENT[2b]															
Number of employment, total (million)		48.1	49.5	52.7	54.1	55.2	55.8	56.6	56.5	57.4	...	...	61.7	...	...
Number of employment by MSMEs*		...	...	...	...	...	...	...	...	24.1	...	...	27.3	...	...
Micro		...	...	...	...	...	...	...	...	...	...	...	...	...	...
Small		...	...	...	...	...	...	...	...	...	...	...	...	...	...
Medium		...	...	...	...	...	...	...	...	...	...	...	...	...	...
Number of employment by large enterprises		...	...	...	...	...	...	...	...	...	...	...	...	...	...
MSME employees to total (%)*		...	...	...	...	...	...	...	...	72.6	...	...	72.0	...	...
MSME employees growth (%)		...	...	...	...	...	...	...	...	...	...	...	...	...	...
Share of female employees to total employees (%)		...	...	...	...	...	...	...	...	23.0	...	...	22.0	...	...
Employment by MSME by sector (% share)**															
Agriculture, forestry, and fisheries		...	...	...	...	...	...	...	...	...	...	...	...	...	...
Manufacturing		...	...	...	...	...	...	...	...	23.2	...	...	22.8	...	...
Transportation and communication		...	...	...	...	...	...	...	...	10.9	...	...	11.5	...	...
Construction		...	...	...	...	...	...	...	...	16.4	...	...	16.2	...	...
Wholesale and retail trade		...	...	...	...	...	...	...	...	34.1	...	...	32.5	...	...
Other services (community, social and personal services)		...	...	...	...	...	...	...	...	14.5	...	...	16.0	...	...
Others		...	...	...	...	...	...	...	...	0.8	...	...	1.0	...	...
Employment by MSMEs by region (% share)**															
Capital city (Islamabad)		...	...	...	...	...	...	...	...	...	...	...	...	...	...
Others		...	...	...	...	...	...	...	...	100.0	...	...	100.0	...	...
Punjab		...	...	...	...	...	...	...	...	59.2	...	...	60.9	...	...
Sindh		...	...	...	...	...	...	...	...	22.9	...	...	21.7	...	...
Khyber Pakhtunkhwa		...	...	...	...	...	...	...	...	12.8	...	...	13.7	...	...
Balochistan		...	...	...	...	...	...	...	...	5.1	...	...	3.7	...	...
CONTRIBUTION TO GDP[2c]															
GDP of MSMEs (PRs million)		...	...	...	...	...	...	...	...	...	...	...	...	...	...
MSME contribution to GDP (%)		...	...	...	...	40.0	...	...	...	...	...	...	...	...	...
MSME GDP growth (%)		...	...	...	...	...	...	...	...	...	...	...	...	...	...
CONTRIBUTION TO GDP[1d]															
GDP of small manufacturing (PRs million)		101,162	122,473	145,946	167,383	208,611	241,951	283,107	327,030	373,595	406,648	457,088	506,839	571,951	621,977
Small manufacturing contribution to GDP (%)		1.2	1.2	1.3	1.4	1.5	1.5	1.6	1.7	1.7	1.8	1.8	1.9	2.0	2.0
Small manufacturing GDP growth (%)		...	21.1	19.2	14.7	24.6	16.0	17.0	15.5	14.2	8.8	12.4	10.9	12.8	8.7
MSME GDP by sector (% share)															
Agriculture, forestry, and fisheries		...	...	...	...	...	...	...	...	...	...	...	...	...	...
Manufacturing		14.3	14.4	13.8	13.6	13.5	13.2	13.4	13.6	13.6	13.4	13.5	13.5	13.2	12.5
Transportation and communication		...	...	...	...	...	...	...	...	...	...	...	...	...	...
Construction		...	...	...	...	...	...	...	...	...	...	...	...	...	...
Wholesale and retail trade		...	...	...	...	...	...	...	...	...	...	...	...	...	...
Other services		...	...	...	...	...	...	...	...	...	...	...	...	...	...
Others		...	...	...	...	...	...	...	...	...	...	...	...	...	...

continued on next page

Table 6.2 *continued*

Item	2005	2007	2008	2009	2010	2011	2012	2013	2014	2015	2016	2017	2018	2019	2020
MSME GDP by region (% share)															
Capital city (Islamabad)		...	...	...	...	...	...	...	...	...	...	...	...	...	...
Others		...	...	...	...	...	...	...	...	...	...	...	...	...	...
EXPORTS[2]															
Total export value (PRs million)e		1,029,312	1,196,638	1,383,718	1,617,458	2,120,847	2,110,605	2,366,478	2,583,463	2,397,513	2,166,846	2,138,186	2,555,043	3,128,230	2,725,210
Total export growth (%)e		4.5	16.3	15.6	16.9	31.1	(0.5)	12.1	9.2	(7.2)	(9.6)	(1.3)	19.5	22.4	(12.9)
MSME export value (PRs million)f		...	...	...	404,365	...	...	...	...	...	...	...	...	...	...
MSME export to total export value (%)f		...	...	...	25.0	...	...	...	...	...	...	...	...	...	...
MSME export growth (%)		...	...	...	...	...	...	...	...	...	...	...	...	...	...
IMPORTS[2]															
Total import value (PRs million)e		1,851,806	2,512,072	2,723,570	2,910,975	3,455,287	4,009,093	4,349,880	4,630,521	4,644,152	4,658,749	5,539,721	6,694,897	7,443,253	5,434,524
Total import growth (%)e		8.2	35.7	8.4	6.9	18.7	16.0	8.5	6.5	0.3	0.3	18.9	20.9	11.2	(27.0)
MSME import value (PRs million)		...	...	...	...	...	...	...	...	...	...	...	...	...	...
MSME import to total import value (%)		...	...	...	...	...	...	...	...	...	...	...	...	...	...
MSME import growth (%)		...	...	...	...	...	...	...	...	...	...	...	...	...	...

GDP = gross domestic product, MSME = micro, small, and medium-sized enterprise.

[1] End-of-year data.

[2] Fiscal year data, which ends on 30 June; e.g., FY2020 covers data from 1 July 2019 to 30 June 2020.

[a] Census of Economic Establishments 2005 for data in 2005. Extrapolated from data of Census of Economic Establishments 1988 and 2005 to estimate the number of MSMEs for 2020 (rounded number).

[b] Labor Force Survey 2014-15 and 2017-18. * based on non-agriculture employment. ** based on non-agricultural informal employment or MSMEs.

[c] Pakistan Economic Survey 2010-11.

[d] Data from Pakistan Bureau of Statistics.

[e] Pakistan Economic Survey 2019-20.

[f] Pakistan Economic Survey 2009-10.

Notes: The Census of Establishments 2005 provides the basis for MSME statistical analysis. In Pakistan, there are 3.21 million (rounded figure provided) MSMEs operating in the country, of which 98.66% employ up to 10 employees. The Labor Force Survey 2017-2018 defines the non-agriculture Informal economy as: (i) all household enterprises owned and operated by own-account workers, irrespective of the size of the enterprise (informal own-account enterprises); (ii) enterprises owned and operated by employers with fewer than 10 persons engaged, which includes the owner(s) of the enterprise, the contributing family workers, the employees, whether employed on an occasional or continuous basis, or as an apprentice; and (iii) excluded are all enterprises engaged in agricultural activities or wholly engaged in non-market production.

Source: ADB Asia SME Monitor 2021 database. Data from Small and Medium Enterprise Development Authority; Pakistan Bureau of Statistics.

Table 6.3: Bank Credit

End-of-year data

Item	2007	2008	2009	2010	2011	2012	2013	2014	2015	2016	2017	2018	2019	2020
OPERATING BANKS														
Number of operating banks, total	47	47	47	45	46	47	48	47	45	45	45	45	44	43
Commercial banks	36	36	36	34	34	34	34	33	31	30	30	30	30	29
State-owned banks	4	4	4	5	5	5	5	5	5	5	5	5	5	5
Private sector banks	26	26	25	23	22	22	22	22	22	21	20	20	20	20
Conventional banks	...	...	...	...	...	...	...	...	...	...	15	15	15	15
Islamic banks	...	...	...	...	...	...	...	...	...	...	5	5	5	5
Foreign banks	6	6	7	6	7	7	7	6	4	4	5	5	5	4
Specialized banks	4	4	4	4	4	4	4	4	4	4	4	4	3	3
Microfinance banks	7	7	7	7	8	9	10	10	10	11	11	11	11	11
Credit[1]														
Loans outstanding, total (PRs million)	2,783,154	3,335,561	3,443,788	3,600,353	3,631,440	4,077,474	4,379,794	4,790,098	5,170,688	5,847,085	6,856,940	8,355,797	8,709,390	8,875,962
State-owned banks	527,822	631,587	700,584	716,562	785,014	961,597	964,880	1,023,145	1,039,503	1,189,138	1,365,154	1,674,365	1,782,501	1,826,558
Private sector banks+foreign banks	2,255,889	2,703,974	2,743,204	2,883,791	2,846,426	3,115,877	3,414,914	3,766,953	4,131,184	4,657,947	5,491,785	6,681,432	6,926,889	7,049,404
Loans outstanding in domestic currency	2,395,350	2,998,165	3,132,275	3,218,802	3,234,717	3,646,911	3,800,598	4,154,778	4,555,964	5,193,019	6,248,339	7,728,349	7,962,444	8,226,917
Loans outstanding in foreign currency	387,804	337,397	311,512	381,552	396,723	430,562	579,196	635,321	614,724	654,066	608,600	627,448	746,946	649,045
Loan growth (%)	14.5	19.8	3.2	4.5	0.9	12.3	7.4	9.4	7.9	13.1	17.3	21.9	4.2	1.9
Total bank loans to GDP (%)	...	...	...	...	...	...	...	...	...	...	...	...	...	...
Lending rate (%, annual average)	10.8	12.0	13.0	12.5	12.7	12.1	10.3	10.3	8.6	7.3	7.1	7.8	11.5	9.7
Gross nonperforming loans (NPLs) (PRs million)	181,448	284,515	403,845	515,373	572,548	577,016	553,040	572,155	575,277	568,446	554,602	624,156	706,758	761,693
Gross NPLs to total loans (%)	6.5	8.5	11.7	14.3	15.8	14.2	12.6	11.9	11.1	9.7	8.1	7.5	8.1	8.6
Loans outstanding by sector (% share)[1]														
Chemical and pharmaceuticals	3.3	3.6	3.9	3.9	4.0	3.7	3.4	3.9	4.3	4.3	3.4	3.5	3.6	3.7
Agribusiness	3.5	4.4	4.7	5.9	5.9	6.2	5.3	5.7	6.4	6.8	6.8	6.4	6.4	6.3
Textile	20.4	20.0	19.0	19.5	18.7	17.1	17.7	16.5	14.7	14.5	14.4	13.8	13.8	15.1
Cement	2.8	2.7	2.8	2.6	2.2	1.4	1.2	0.9	1.1	1.2	1.6	2.0	2.2	2.3
Sugar	2.3	2.0	1.8	2.0	2.3	2.6	2.7	2.9	2.8	3.0	3.6	2.8	2.5	2.7

continued on next page

Table 6.3 *continued*

Item	2007	2008	2009	2010	2011	2012	2013	2014	2015	2016	2017	2018	2019	2020
Shoes and leather garments	0.7	0.7	0.6	0.6	0.8	0.6	0.6	0.5	0.5	0.5	0.4	0.4	0.4	0.4
Automobile and transportation equipment	2.0	2.4	1.8	1.3	1.5	1.4	1.4	1.5	1.0	1.6	1.6	1.6	2.0	1.6
Finance	2.4	1.8	1.7	1.2	1.9	2.0	2.8	2.6	2.9	3.1	2.5	2.7	2.9	2.6
Insurance	0.1	0.1	0.0	0.0	0.0	0.0	0.0	0.0	0.0	0.1	0.1	0.0	0.0	0.1
Electronics and electrical appliances	1.4	2.7	2.6	1.7	1.7	1.4	1.3	1.4	1.6	1.3	1.4	1.4	1.4	1.2
Production and transmission of energy	5.0	7.5	8.7	9.7	10.2	12.1	11.3	13.0	13.2	15.3	15.2	17.2	17.1	15.7
Individuals	13.3	11.8	10.9	9.8	9.2	8.1	8.7	9.0	8.8	9.4	9.0	8.8	8.7	9.2
Others	43.0	40.3	41.3	41.5	41.6	43.5	43.6	42.1	42.8	38.9	40.0	39.4	38.8	39.1
Deposits[1]														
Deposits, total (PRs million)	3,838,921	4,203,633	4,769,736	5,432,273	6,220,393	7,282,304	8,295,060	9,195,118	10,343,872	11,727,646	12,930,125	14,201,942	15,895,374	18,457,060
Deposits in domestic currency (PRs million)	3,366,290	3,682,106	4,185,802	4,682,943	5,380,847	6,280,424	7,114,684	7,948,161	8,996,983	10,478,226	11,509,318	12,547,316	13,984,711	16,504,861
Deposits in foreign currency (PRs million)	472,631	521,528	583,934	749,330	839,546	1,001,880	1,180,375	1,246,957	1,346,890	1,249,420	1,420,807	1,654,626	1,910,663	1,952,199
Deposit rate (%, annual average)	4.3	5.2	6.2	5.6	5.8	5.7	4.9	5.0	3.9	3.1	3.0	3.4	5.9	4.8
SME LOANS[2]														
SME loans outstanding, total (PRs million)	411,675	383,698	348,199	336,553	294,306	266,144	272,528	287,881	305,090	401,480	450,384	513,459	477,232	481,780
Commercial banks	403,269	372,538	337,621	326,153	283,970	255,644	262,231	277,672	295,256	390,580	439,601	501,808	465,474	470,166
State-owned banks	55,995	55,311	46,193	45,371	45,936	44,816	57,994	64,761	89,160	101,358	104,923	113,030	100,621	105,406
Private sector banks	347,275	317,227	291,428	280,782	238,034	210,828	204,237	212,912	206,096	289,222	334,678	388,778	364,853	364,760
Specialized banks	8,406	11,161	10,579	10,401	10,336	10,500	10,297	10,209	9,834	10,901	10,783	11,651	11,759	11,613
SME loans to total domestic private loans outstanding (%)	16.2	12.0	10.1	9.6	8.3	6.8	6.5	8.0	6.1	9.2	8.7	8.5	7.6	7.3
SME loans to GDP (%)[3]	4.5	3.6	2.6	2.3	1.6	1.3	1.2	1.1	1.1	1.4	1.4	1.5	1.3	1.2
SME loan growth (%)	...	(6.8)	(9.3)	(3.3)	(12.6)	(9.6)	2.4	5.6	6.0	31.6	12.2	14.0	(7.1)	1.0
SME lending rate (%, annual average)	...	...	...	...	...	...	...	...	...	...	...	...	...	...
Nonperforming SME loans (NPLs) (PRs million)	35,003	60,692	79,141	97,091	95,472	95,440	86,615	87,055	77,170	66,601	69,368	75,440	80,001	81,429
SME NPLs to total SME loans (%)	8.5	15.8	22.7	28.8	32.4	35.9	31.8	30.2	25.3	16.6	15.4	14.7	16.8	16.9
Number of SME loan borrowers	185,292	214,357	212,387	211,419	167,949	134,023	138,843	134,521	158,387	177,595	165,911	180,704	183,606	179,934
SME loan borrowers to total bank borrowers (%)	...	4.8	5.0	5.7	4.6	3.6	4.0	4.3	4.9	5.6	4.7	3.6	3.8	3.5
SME loan rejection rate (% of total applications)	...	...	...	...	...	...	...	...	...	...	...	...	...	...
Number of SME savings account in banks	...	...	...	...	...	...	...	...	...	...	...	...	...	...
Guaranteed SME loans (PRs million)	...	...	...	...	...	...	...	...	...	...	...	...	...	...
Non-collateral SME loans (PRs million)	...	...	...	...	...	...	...	...	...	...	...	...	...	...
SME loans outstanding by sector (% share)														
Agriculture, forestry, and fisheries	...	...	...	...	...	...	...	...	...	...	...	...	0.4	0.5
Manufacturing	...	...	...	...	...	...	...	...	37.2	38.7	40.4	40.9	43.1	45.7
Transportation and communication	...	...	...	...	...	...	...	...	12.9	11.1	10.9	10.9	8.7	6.2
Construction	...	...	...	...	...	...	...	...	2.4	2.3	2.5	2.2	1.9	2.9
Wholesale and retail trade	...	...	...	...	...	...	...	...	30.9	28.8	30.7	30.4	30.0	30.0
Other services	...	...	...	...	...	...	...	...	1.8	1.9	1.9	1.6	4.7	5.2
Others	...	...	...	...	...	...	...	...	14.9	17.2	13.7	14.1	11.1	9.4
SME loans outstanding by region (% share)														
Capital city (Islamabad)	...	...	...	...	...	...	...	...	...	...	...	...	...	...
Others	...	...	...	...	...	...	...	...	...	...	...	...	...	...
SME loan borrowers by type of use (% share)														
For working capital	71.6	75.3	75.6	78.1	80.0	80.1	78.4	73.8	67.4	66.6	68.7	66.5	68.3	67.6
For capital investment	12.0	11.5	11.8	10.8	10.0	10.4	11.9	13.0	23.3	22.4	22.3	24.0	22.9	23.7
For other purposes	16.4	13.2	12.6	11.1	10.0	9.5	9.7	13.1	9.3	10.9	9.1	9.5	8.9	8.8
SME loans outstanding by tenor (% share)														
Less than 1 year	78.5	70.9	76.0	76.2	77.8	68.6	73.2	75.9	67.6	66.9	67.0	66.0	67.7	64.2
1-3 years	11.8	9.8	7.1	8.7	7.6	7.0	3.3	10.3	8.9	8.1	10.0	11.3	14.1	14.5
More than 3 years	9.8	19.3	17.0	15.1	14.6	24.4	23.5	13.8	23.5	25.0	23.0	22.7	18.2	21.3
MICRO LOANS[4]														
Loans outstanding - Microfinance banks (PRs million)	...	1,885	2,295	2,123	2,248	3,510	5,364	7,556	11,806	24,158	34,113	46,435	45,840	60,598
Micro loan growth (%)	...	...	21.8	(7.5)	5.9	56.1	52.8	40.9	56.2	104.6	41.2	36.1	(1.3)	32.2

GDP = gross domestic product, MSME = micro, small, and medium-sized enterprise; NPL = nonperforming loan; SME = small and medium-sized enterprise.

[1] data based on commercial banks.

[2] Data refer to small and medium-sized enterprise (SME) loans by commercial banks and specialized banks only. The State Bank of Pakistan has prudential regulations for SME financing and microfinance, and monitor both data separately.

[3] Calculated based on real GDP (2005-2006 = 100), local currency (Pakistan Bureau of Statistics). SME loans data use end-of-year data, with real GDP data based on end-June data of that year (fiscal year data).

[4] Micro loans (microfinance) data refer to loans by microfinance banks.

Source: ADB Asia SME Monitor 2021 database. Data from State Bank of Pakistan.

Table 6.4: Public Finance—Refinancing Schemes for MSMEs

Name of the Scheme	Year of the launch	Fund Size (PRs million)	Taget Beneficiaries	Amount of Refinance Disbursed (PRs million)	Number of MSMEs Benefited	Status (ongoing/ closed)
Refinance Facility for Modernization of SMEs	June 2010	8,275	...	1,532	114	ongoing
Refinance and Credit Guarantee Scheme for Women Entrepreneurs	August 2017	2,500	...	669	866	ongoing
Refinance Scheme for Working Capital Financing of Small Enterprises and Low-end Medium-sized Enterprises	July 2019	5,832	...	471	66	ongoing
Small Enterprise Financing and Credit Guarantee Scheme for Special Persons	March 2020	560	...	5	5	ongoing
Grand Total (PRs million)		6,392		476	71	

MSME = micro, small, and medium-sized enterprise; SME = small and medium-sized enterprise.

Note: Based on regular schemes. Data as of end-2020.

Source: ADB Asia SME Monitor 2021 database. Data from State Bank of Pakistan.

Table 6.5: Nonbank Finance

End-of-year data

Item	2007	2008	2009	2010	2011	2012	2013	2014	2015	2016	2017	2018	2019	2020
NUMBER OF NONBANK FINANCE INSTITUTIONS														
Nonbank finance companies (NBFCs), total	36	33	36	18	16	15	15	16	17	29	39	42	44	44
Microfinance NBFCs	...	...	...	...	...	...	...	...	...	21*	31*	26	26	26
Investment banks	11	12	11	8	7	7	7	7	8			9	11	12
Housing finance companies	9	5	9	1	...	...	...	...	...	...	...	...	...	...
Leasing companies	16	16	16	9	9	8	8	9	9	8	8	7	7	6
MICROFINANCE INSTITUTIONS														
Financing outstanding, total (PRs million)	10,432	11,951	12,719	14,966	13,411	17,151	22,501	29,744	37,294	47,003	66,330	86,094	92,041	86,422
Growth (%)	53.0	14.6	6.4	17.7	(10.4)	27.9	31.2	32.2	25.4	26.0	41.1	29.8	6.9	(6.1)
Total financing to GDP (%)	0.1	0.1	0.1	0.2	0.1	0.2	0.2	0.3	0.4	0.4	0.6	0.7	0.7	0.7
Annual lending rate (%, on average)	27.4	26.6	24.1	29.4	32.6	30.8	32.8	31.0	30.6	28.9	28.3	32.4	30.9	30.0
Gross nonperforming loans (NPLs) (PRs million)	294	248	662	685	552	1,157	1,096	272	650	926	347	398	972	4,235
Gross NPLs to total loans (%)	2.8	2.1	5.2	4.6	4.1	6.7	4.9	0.9	1.7	2.0	0.5	0.5	1.1	4.9
Savings (PRs million)	...	...	...	...	...	...	...	...	...	...	...	...	...	...
Number of customers financed, total	...	...	...	...	...	...	...	...	...	...	...	...	...	...
Financing outstanding by sector (% share)														
Agriculture, forestry, and fisheries	40.0	40.0	43.0	37.0	38.0	38.0	39.0	39.0	39.0	42.0	42.0	43.0	42.0	42.0
Manufacturing	7.0	7.0	6.0	7.0	9.0	9.0	9.0	9.0	8.0	10.0	10.0	6.0	5.0	8.0
Transportation and communication	...	...	...	...	...	...	...	...	...	...	...	...	...	...
Construction	...	...	...	...	...	...	...	...	...	...	...	...	...	...
Wholesale and retail trade	37.0	31.0	36.0	37.0	38.0	30.0	29.0	29.0	25.0	25.0	20.0	25.0	21.0	20.0
Other services	11.0	7.0	9.0	11.0	7.0	8.0	8.0	8.0	10.0	10.0	10.0	9.0	12.0	11.0
Others	5.0	15.0	6.0	8.0	8.0	15.0	15.0	15.0	18.0	13.0	18.0	17.0	20.0	19.0
Financing outstanding by region (% share)														
Capital city (Islamabad)	0.4	0.3	0.2	0.1	0.1	0.2	0.2	0.2	0.2	0.3	0.3	0.3	0.3	0.4
Others	99.7	99.7	99.8	99.9	99.9	99.9	99.8	99.8	99.8	99.8	99.7	99.7	99.7	99.6
LEASING COMPANIES														
Financing outstanding, total (PRs million)	27,709	27,690	24,402	21,283	19,578	19,911	20,193	22,344	25,803	33,280	24,260	27,099	26,653	23,069
Growth (%)	...	(0.1)	(11.9)	(12.8)	(8.0)	1.7	1.4	10.7	15.5	29.0	(27.1)	11.7	(1.6)	(13.4)
Total financing to GDP (%)	0.3	0.3	0.3	0.2	0.2	0.2	0.2	0.2	0.2	0.3	0.2	0.2	0.2	0.2
Annual financing rate (%, on average)	...	...	...	...	...	...	...	...	...	...	...	...	...	...
Gross nonperforming financing (NPFs) (PRs million)	1,294	1,782	2,199	2,705	2,409	2,155	1,918	1,348	1,524	1,362	1,623	1,711	1,204	2,354
Gross NPFs to total financing (%)	4.7	6.4	9.0	12.7	12.3	10.8	9.5	6.0	5.9	4.1	6.7	6.3	4.5	10.2
Number of customers financed, total	17,970	18,013	15,628	12,528	9,841	8,623	8,191	8,088	8,096	7,822	7,805	7,943	7,714	6,804
Financing outstanding by sector (% share)														
Agriculture, forestry, and fisheries	0.0	0.0	0.0	0.0	0.0	0.0	0.0	0.0	0.0	0.0	1.5	1.6	1.4	1.8
Manufacturing	1.7	1.1	1.1	1.4	1.4	1.3	1.2	0.9	0.3	0.2	0.3	1.2	2.2	2.9
Transportation and communication	11.3	10.8	11.4	12.7	15.7	16.7	18.7	21.7	12.8	16.9	19.0	20.2	24.8	22.4
Construction	3.2	3.4	3.2	3.3	3.0	2.7	2.3	2.4	2.2	2.7	3.7	3.8	3.0	2.8
Wholesale and retail trade	4.4	4.2	3.5	3.7	3.9	4.3	4.4	5.0	5.0	2.4	5.6	5.7	5.4	5.7
Other services	13.2	10.3	10.1	10.2	9.8	10.9	10.7	11.1	12.2	12.4	8.9	8.1	7.1	8.7
Others	66.2	70.1	70.7	68.8	66.1	64.1	62.7	58.9	67.5	65.5	61.0	59.4	56.0	55.7
Financing outstanding by region (% share)														
Capital city (Islamabad)	7.0	7.0	7.0	6.0	5.0	5.0	5.0	5.0	5.0	5.0	5.0	4.0	4.0	5.0
Others	93.0	93.0	93.0	94.0	95.0	95.0	95.0	95.0	95.0	95.0	95.0	96.0	96.0	95.0

* The numbers for 2016 and 2017 include both microfinance and investment finance companies with investment finance service (IFS) licenses.

Source: ADB Asia SME Monitor 2021 database. Data from Securities and Exchange Commission of Pakistan.

Table 6.6: Capital Markets

End-of-year data

Item	2007	2008	2009	2010	2011	2012	2013
Main Board - PSX							
KSE-100 Index	14,076	5,865	9,387	12,022	11,348	16,905	25,261
Market capitalization (PRs million)	4,329,910	1,858,699	2,705,880	3,268,949	2,945,785	4,242,278	6,056,506
Growth (%)	...	(57.1)	45.6	20.8	(9.9)	44.0	42.8
Trading value (PRs million)	8,401,424	4,819,538	1,863,303	1,303,586	1,141,626	1,549,084	2,535,261
Trading volume (million shares)	79,285	44,194	45,842	34,936	25,907	52,575	64,905
Number of listed companies	654	653	651	644	638	573	560
Number of IPOs	12	9	3	6	4	4	1
Number of delisted companies	11	11	6	13	10	69	16

Item	2014	2015	2016	2017	2018	2019	2020
Main Board - PSX							
KSE-100 Index	32,131	32,816	47,807	40,471	37,067	40,735	43,755
Market capitalization (PRs million)	7,380,532	6,947,358	9,628,514	8,570,926	7,692,787	7,811,812	8,035,363
Growth (%)	21.9	(5.9)	38.6	(11.0)	(10.2)	1.5	2.9
Trading value (PRs million)	2,961,012	3,752,654	3,791,335	4,253,250	2,808,125	2,270,207	4,420,926
Trading volume (million shares)	60,022	73,726	85,345	76,982	64,955	60,592	113,016
Number of listed companies	557	554	558	559	546	534	531
Number of IPOs	5	7	4	5	3	1	4
Number of delisted companies	9	11	5	6	16	13	6

IPO = initial public offering, PSX = Pakistan Stock Exchange.

Source: ADB Asia SME Monitor 2021 database. Data from Pakistan Stock Exchange.

Table 6.7: Listing Requirements—Pakistan Stock Exchange

Criteria	Main Board	Growth Enterprise Market (GEM) Board
Type of issuers	All types allowed, even loss making companies and greenfield projects (GFPs).	Aimed at growth companies such as start-ups and greenfield companies (GFCs).
Consultant to the Issue (CTI)/Lead Advisor	Licensed Consultants to the Issue (CTI) can act as Lead Advisors.	Only following can act as Advisor to the Issue: • Licensed CTI • Securities Broker Licensed by the Commission • Scheduled Banks • Accounting and Auditing Firm (Recognized by ICAP or ICMAP)
Paid-up capital	To list, issuer must have a post issue paid-up capital of at least PRs200 million.	To list, issuer must have a post issue paid-up capital of at least PRs25 million. There is no maximum limit to it.
Initial offering	Book Building Portion (BBP): • Issuer must at least receive bids for the total number of shares allocated under BBP. • No. of bids should not be less than 40. • Minimum bid size = PRs1 million. General Public Portion (GPP): • No. of subscribers in IPO should be at least 500. • Minimum amount of subscription required is for 500 shares.	• Initial subscribers should be at least five. • In case of Book Building, the bid size for each initial subscriber shall be PRs100,000.
Method of offering	Fixed Price or Book Building method. In case of Fixed Price method, issue must be completely underwritten.	Fixed Price or Book Building method. In case of Fixed Price method, issue must be completely underwritten.
Eligible investors	BBP: Institutional Investors and HNWIs who can place a minimum bid of PRs1 million. GPP: All Investors.	(i) Institutional investors. (ii) Eligible individual investors registered with the NCCPL having net assets of at least PRs5 million
Market maker (MM)	Market Maker not required.	Growth company may appoint Market Maker (Requirement of MM is optional).

continued on next page

Table 6.7 *continued*

Criteria	Main Board	Growth Enterprise Market (GEM) Board
Trading and settlement	Trading through KATS.	Trading through KATS
Restriction on shares of Sponsors	• 100% to be frozen in Central Depository Company (CDC) for 1 year. • 25% to be frozen in CDC for 3 years.	• 100% to be frozen in CDC for 1 year. • 25% to be frozen in CDC for 3 years.
Minimum free float	As per the PSX Rule 5.4.1, following are the applicable float requirements: **Post Issue Paid up Capital (PIPC)** — **Allocation of Capital to the General Public, excluding Premium Amount and Pre-IPO Placement** Up to PRs2.5 billion. — At-least 10% of PIPC. Provided that the Company shall be required to subsequently enhance the quantum of public shareholding to 25% within next 3 years of its listing. Above PRs2.5 billion and up to PRs5 billion. — At-least 10% of PIPC. Provided that the Company shall be required to subsequently enhance the quantum of public shareholding to 15% within next 3 years of its listing. Above PRs5 billion and up to PRs10 billion. — At-least 10% of PIPC. Above PRs10 billion. — At-least 5% of PIPC.	Minimum free-float requirement is 10% of post issue paid-up capital.
Listing fee	Initial listing fee: capped at PRs1.5 million. Annual listing fee: based on market capitalization, capped at PRs5 million.	• Initial listing fee: capped at PRs50,000. • Annual listing fee based on Paid-up capital, capped at PRs200,000.
Offering document (OD)	Prospectus / Offer for Sale Document is required to be prepared and Published before the Issue.	Instead of a Prospectus, only an IM is required to be prepared and placed on the websites of the Issuer, Advisor and the Exchange.
Vetting of offering document (OD)	Prospectus is vetted by PSX and SECP. However, CTI / Lead Manager / Issuer is responsible for the accuracy / veracity / adequacy of disclosures in the prospectus.	Advisor must do necessary Due Diligence and prepare the IM according to Schedule - I of Chapter 5A. OD shall not be vetted by PSX.
Approval	Listing application and Prospectus is approved by PSX. Prospectus is also approved by SECP.	Listing application is approved by PSX.
Code of corporate governance (CCG)	Compliance with complete CCG is required.	Growth Company (GC) only needs to comply with the following within 2 years of listing: 1. Audit Committee comprising independent directors 2. Female representation on board 4. Minimum number of independent directors should be two or 1/3 of the board, whichever is higher.
Compliance Status	1. Issuer must submit a detailed breakdown of the utilization of the proceeds of the issue in its post issue quarterly / half-yearly and annual accounts till the fulfillment of the commitments mentioned in the prospectus; and also 2. submit: a) half-yearly progress report and; b) annual progress report reviewed by the auditor providing the status of the commitments mentioned in the prospectus to PSX. c) A final report reviewed by auditor after the fulfillment of the commitments written in the Prospectus.	CEO of GC must submit half yearly compliance report to PSX.
Migration	Reverse migration from Main Board to GEM Board is not allowed.	Issuer is allowed to migrate from GEM board to Main Board.
Voluntary Delisting (VD)	VD procedure / process is more stringent.	Easier VD procedure / process.

CDC = Central Depository Company, GEM = Growth Enterprise Market, IPO = initial public offering, KATS = Karachi Automated Trading System, PSX = Pakistan Stock Exchange, SECP = Securities and Exchange Commission of Pakistan.

Source: ADB Asia SME Monitor 2021 database. Data from Pakistan Stock Exchange.

Table 6.8: Policies and Regulations

Regulations	
Name	**Outline**
MSME development	
Business structure/registration	
Companies Act, 2017	Incorporation of a limited liability company.
Limited Liability Partnership Act, 2017	Incorporation of a limited liability partnership. Note: Registration as a limited liability company is not mandatory for starting a business.
Taxation	
Sales Tax Act, 1990	Sales tax registration and sales tax regulation.
Income Tax Ordinance, 2001	National tax number (NTN); income tax applicable on businesses; annual tax returns are required to be filed with FBR by every registered person.
Federal Excise Act, 2005	An act to consolidate and amend the law relating to excise duties.
Customs Act, 1969	Law regulating import and export of goods and services
Labor	
Employees Old Age Benefits Institution (EOBI) Act	Registration for contribution to workers retirement benefits. Act is applicable where 10 or more persons, other than directors, are employed directly or through any other person or were so employed on any day during the last 12 months and shall continue to apply even if the number of persons so employed at any time reduces to 10.
Workers Welfare Ordinance, 1971	Support workers' welfare such as the provision of low-cost residential accommodation and other amenities including education and health facilities.
Industrial Relations Act, 2010	The law allows formation of trade unions in the industry without prescribing any limit as to number of workers for its applicability.
Petroleum and explosives	
Explosives Act, 1884 and The Explosives Rules, 2010	To regulate the manufacture, possession, use, sale, transport, export, and importation of explosives.
Petroleum Act, 1934 and Mineral and Industrial Gases Safety Rules, 2010	License for importation of gas cylinders, storage, filling, sale, and transportation of mineral, compressed, and liquefied petroleum gases.
Pakistan Standards	
Pakistan Standards & Quality Control Authority (PSQCA) Act, 1996	License required for every manufacturer. Manufacturing goods requiring mandatory application of Pakistan standards as notified by the Government of Pakistan. A list of such goods is available at www.psqca.com.pk
Drug Regulations	
Drugs Act, 1976; Drugs (Licensing, Registration, and Administration) Rules, 1976; Drugs (Labeling and Packaging) Rules, 1986; Drugs (import and export) Rules, 1986	Registration and licensing for all firms involved in manufacturing, import and export of drugs in Pakistan.
Access to finance	
Agriculture Credit and Microfinance Department (ACMFD) Circular 1, 4, and 7 of 2020 on regulatory relief to dampen the effect of Covid-19	Treatment of loans threshold as regular was extended until 31 December 2019. Each nonperforming loan (NPL) category extended by 2 months. Earlier the last date for availing benefit was extended until 30 September 2020 to dampen the effect of COVID-19.
ACMFD Circular 2 of 2020 (Revised Prudential Regulations for Micro Finance Banks, R-5 Max loan size and eligibility of borrower, R-6 Max exposure of a borrower)	Maximum size of general loan PRs350,000 with annual income of PRs1,200,000. For housing loans, it is PRs3,000,000 with annual income of up to PRs1,500,000. Loans to microenterprises would be PRs3,000,000. Aggregate exposure against security of gold shall not exceed 35% of gross loan portfolio (GLP).
ACMFD Circular 1 of 2019 on poof of registration card held by Afghan refugees	The Proof of Registration Card of Afghan refugees was given the status of a valid identity document.
ACMFD Circular 2 of 2019 (Revised Prudential Regulation G-2)	The renumeration of non-executive board members for attending the meeting was revised.
ACMFD Circular 4 of 2019 on fit and proper test criteria for Microfinance Bank (MFB)	Revised questionnaire was advised to banks for conducting fit a proper test (FPT).
ACMFD Circular 1 of 2018 on line of credit fund	A line of credit fund was established for onward lending to microfinance borrowers.
ACMFD Circular 1 of 2017 on Micro Credit Guarantee Facility	New guarantees would not be established while the old ones would continue to remain valid.
ACMFD Circular 2 of 2017 on measure to be taken by MFB regarding AML/CFT	Use of biometric technology and other technology based solutions.
ACMFD Circular 3 of 2017 on enhancement of maximum loan size for micro enterprises	Max loan size for up to PRs1 million.
ACMFD Circular 1 of 2015 on amendment in Microcredit Guarantee Facility (MCGF)	Commercial banks and DFIs allowed to lend to tier-2 MFB.
ACMFD Circular 5 of 2015 on FPT for MFB	FPT criteria for MFB notified vide the circular.
ACMFD Circular 3 of 2014 on revised prudential regulation for MFB	Revised set of PRs was issued for MFBs.
SBP Prudential Regulations for Small and Medium Enterprises Financing (updated on 5 April 2021)	Prudential Regulations – General for SME financing are as follows: (i) SME specific credit policy, (ii) electronic Credit Information Bureau (e-CIB) report, (iii) personal guarantees, (iv) limit on clean facility, (v) proper utilization of loan, (vi) restriction on facilities to related parties, (vii) translation of loan documents into Urdu language, (viii) securities and margin requirements, and (ix) general measures (research and development, management information system, customer complaint resolution, database development, etc.)
Chapter 5A of PSX Rule Book on Regulations Governing Listing and Trading of Equity Securities on Growth Enterprise Market (GEM)	This provides regulatory rules on Growth Enterprise Market (GEM) under PSX (listing and trading rules of equity securities), GEM allows SMEs and large cap companies to raise capital from eligible investors.

continued on next page

Table 6.8 *continued*

Regulators and Policymakers	
Name	**Responsibility**
Ministry of Industries and Production (MOIP)	Facilitate industrial development and entrepreneurship through promoting Industrial Parks and Export Processing Zones for investors, skill development of human resources, and socio-economic development with a particular focus on MSME development and traditional crafts.
Small and Medium Enterprise Development Authority (SMEDA)	An autonomous institution under the MoIP, serving as an MSME-policy advisory and implementation body for the government in parallel to facilitating other stakeholders to promote MSME development agendas.
Ministry of Finance (MOF)	Assist formulating and ensuring the effective execution of sound and equitable economic and financial policies.
Ministry of Commerce (MOC)	Promote trade liberalization and facilitation, improving export competitiveness and reducing cost of doing business.
Federal Board of Revenue (FBR)	Federal tax collection agency, promoting compliance with tax and related laws; taxpayer facilitation.
Securities and Exchange Commission of Pakistan (SECP)	Regulate and supervise: (i) corporate sector and capital markets, (ii) insurance companies, (iii) nonbank finance institutions and private pension schemes, and (iv) external service providers to the corporate and financial sectors such as chartered accountants and credit rating agencies.
Employees Old Age Benefits Institution (EOBI)	Provide compulsory social insurance by extending the benefits to insured persons or their survivors on: (i) old-age pension, (ii) survivor's pension, (iii) invalidity pension, (iv) old-age grants.
Pakistan Standards and Quality Control Authority (PSQCA)	Provide product standardization and quality control services.
State Bank of Pakistan (SBP)	Regulate banks for the sound monetary and credit system of Pakistan and foster growth of banks in the best national interest.
Drug Regulatory Authority of Pakistan	Regulate import, export, manufacturing, and sales of drugs in Pakistan.

Policies		
Name	**Responsible Entity**	**Outline**
SME Policy 2007	MOIP; Task Force for SME Policy Development	The first National SME Policy was developed by SMEDA and approved by the Federal Cabinet in 2007. The objective of the policy was to undertake reform initiatives in the following thematic areas: 1. Business environment. 2. Access to finance and related services. 3. Access to resources and services. 4. SME definition, feedback, monitoring and evaluation mechanisms.
National SME Policy Action Plan 2020	MOIP	The National SME Policy Action Plan 2020 focuses on key areas including SME definition, access to finance, business development services, skills and human resource, technology, market access, infrastructure and entrepreneurship, and provides extensive recommendations in each of the aforementioned areas. Key recommendations include: 1. Unified SME definition. 2. Simplification of rules, regulations, and taxation regime. 3. Programs for SME access to credit. 4. Simplification of procedures for start-ups and existing businesses. 5. SME quota in public procurement. 6. Skill development, entrepreneurship and new enterprise creation. 7. Facilitation to participate in international fairs and exhibitions on subsidized rates. 8. Developing SME data bank to bridge information gap.
National Financial Inclusion Strategy 2015	SBP	Target headlines to be achieved by 2023 include: 1. Enhance usage of digital payments (65 million active digital transaction accounts, with gender segregation of 20 million accounts by women) 2. Enhance deposit base (deposit-to-GDP ratio to 55%) 3. Promote MSME finance (extend finance to 700,000 MSMEs; 17% of the private sector credit) 4. Increase agricultural finance (serve 6 million farmers through digitalized solutions; enhance annual disbursement to PRs1.8 trillion) 5. Enhance share of Islamic banking (25% of the banking industry; increase branches of Islamic banks to 30% of the banking industry)

GDP = gross domestic product; MSME = micro, small, and medium-sized enterprise.

Source: ADB Asia SME Monitor 2021 database. Data from Small and Medium Enterprise Development Authority, Securities and Exchange Commission of Pakistan, and State Bank of Pakistan.

Table 6.9: COVID-19 Emergency Measures

Name	Fund Size (PRs billion)	Outline
COVID-19 Prime Minister Relief Package		
SMEDA's Initiatives		
1. Relief to daily wage workers	200	Cash assistance for an estimated 6.2 million daily workers in the formal industrial sector and who had been laid off as a result of COVID-19 pandemic.
2. Cash Transfer to Low Income Families	150	Cash transfers to more than 12 million low-income families through the Ehsaas program.
3. Accelerated Tax Refunds to export Industry	100	Tax refunds available for export-oriented firms.
4. Financial Support to Agriculture sector and SMEs	100	Temporary Economic Refinance Facility (TERF) and its Shariah compliant version to stimulate new investment in manufacturing, managed by State Bank of Pakistan (SBP). The maximum loan size per project is PRs5 billion. The maximum end-user rate is 7% for 10 years. All manufacturing industries, except for the power sector, can access this facility. SBP Initiatives related to Prime Minister's COVID-19 Pandemic Relief Fund 2020: • Increase banks' overall pool of loanable funds. • Ease regulations to extend credit to MSMEs. • Extend borrowing limits for individuals for 1 year. • Defer payment of principal on bank loan obligations. • Relax regulatory criteria for restructuring/rescheduling of loans until 31 March 2021. • Extend relief package to borrowers availing loans under refinance schemes.
5. Accelerated Procurement for Wheat	280	To overcome domestic wheat shortage.
6. Financial Support to Utility Stores	50	Utility stores providing essential food items to the vulnerable segment of society at subsidized rates.
7. Relief in Fuel Prices (PRs 15/liter decline in prices of gasoline and diesel)	70	Fuel prices reduced to provide relief to consumers.
8. Support for Health and Food Supplies	15	Funds for the purchase of health and food supplies.
9. Relief in electricity bill payments	110	The government pays electricity bills for up to 3 months for consumers of 5 kilowatt (commercial customers) or 70 kilowatt (industrial customers) of electricity.
10. Emergency Energy Provision	100	An emergency contingency fund for energy supply.
11. Cash Transfer to National Disaster Management Authority (NDMA)	25	To purchase necessary equipment to deal with pandemic.
Total	1,200	
Other Initiatives		
1. SECP Initiative - Deferred Repayment of Principal Loans		• Securities and Exchange Commission of Pakistan (SECP) allows nonbank finance companies including nonbank microfinance companies to defer repayment of principal loans by their borrowers for 1 year, under the present circumstances owing to the COVID-19 pandemic.
2. Reduction in Different Taxes and Duties on Import and Supply of Different Food Items (COVID-19 Relief Measure)		• Rate of advance tax on the import of different food items was reduced to 0% from 2%. • Individuals and associations of persons providing basic food items to state-owned department stores without a brand name pay 1.5% withholding tax instead of 4.5%. • Additional customs duty at 2% on soya bean oil, canola oil, palm oil, and sunflower oil (also on oil seeds) was exempted.
3. SBP Refinance Scheme to Support Employment and Prevent Layoff of Workers		Provided Refinancing facility at rate of 2% p.a. to finance wages and salaries of all types of workers and employees. Loans to businesses were available to finance 3 months of wages (April to June 2020).
4. SBP Credit Requirements for Exporters and Importers		SBP offers refinance to banks to provide low-cost credit at interest rates that vary between 3% and 6% to exporters for working capital and new projects under the Export Finance Schemes (EFS) and Long Term Financing Facility (LTFF) schemes. • Relaxation in matching amount. • Availing lower-cost credit under EFS is linked to the export. • Extension in time period to meet performance requirements. • Extension in time period to ship goods. • Relaxation in conditions for LTFF. • SBP allows banks to enhance the time period for realization of exports proceeds from existing requirement of 180 days to 270 days on a case by case basis where the delay is related to COVID-19. • Exporters can directly dispatch the shipping documents.
COVID-19 Relief Measures by Provincial Governments		
A. Government of Punjab		
1. Insaaf Imdad package for daily wage workers and labourers		The Punjab government provided relief package worth PRs10 billion to more than 2.5 million marginalized residents of the province.
2. Punjab Rozgar Scheme		The Punjab Provincial Development Working Party approved 'Punjab Rozgar Scheme' with an estimated cost of PRs9500 million to reduce unemployment and drive economic stability by facilitating new micro and small entrepreneurs/startups and existing businesses in Punjab in terms of financial support during the current economic loss due to COVID-19.
3. Tax Relief Package for Businesses		• Punjab Infrastructure Development tax reduced from 0.9% to 0%. • Punjab Sales tax on services on construction services, doctors, private hospitals, marriage halls, catering, laundering, beauty salons, gym, embroidery services, and the services provided by digital platforms reduced from 16% to 0%.

continued on next page

Table 6.9 *continued*

B. Sindh		
1. Paying daily-wage earners through a mobile wallet	Paying daily-wage earners through a mobile wallet.	
2. Tax Relief Package For Businesses	Waived property tax, professional tax, motor vehicle tax, and entertainment duty from 1 April to 30 June 2020.	
3. Relief Measures for SMEs	Exemption from payment of penalty and default surcharge: 1. 1 June 2020 to 15 June 2020: 100% in penalty and 100% in default surcharge. 2. 16 June 2020 to 22 June 2020: 100% in penalty and 95% in default surcharge. 3. 23 June 2020 to 30 June 2020: 100% in penalty and 90% in default surcharge.	
4. Exemption from service tax on commission from EHSAAS Cash Disbursements	Exemption of the Sindh sales tax on the amount of commission (Tariff heading 9819.1300) paid by the banks to their branchless banking retailers in Sindh on account of disbursement of financial assistance under the EHSAAS Emergency Cash Transfer Programme of the Government of Pakistan.	
C. Balochistan		
1. Tax Relief Package	Tax relief package worth more than PRs1.5 billion. • Zero rated Balochistan Infrastructure tax. • Zero rated sales tax on services. • 1% reduction in electricity bills for 3 months.	
2. CM Debt Relief Scheme	Interest-free loans, amount worth PRs10,000 to PRs20,000, were offered to families resident in Quetta, Sibi, Loralai, Pishin, and Gwadar stricken by the virus-induced restrictions.	
D. Khyber Pakhtunkhwa		
1. Tax Relief Package	• Exempted sales tax on all construction and allied services. • Exempted payment of sales tax on such services provided or rendered exclusively by the branchless banking operators (retailers) in respect of distribution of emergency cash assistance under the Ehsaas Emergency Cash Transfer Initiative (EECTI) undertaken in response to the COVID-19 pandemic within the framework of Ehsaas Kafaalat Program (EKP) under Benazir Income Support Programme.	
2. Sales Tax Exemption – Branchless Banking Operators (Retailers) in Respect of Distribution of Emergency Cash	• The banks who have entered into arrangements with the branchless banking operators neither charged nor paid, nor withhold any sales tax on service charges (commission charges) paid or payable to the concerned branchless banking operators for or on account of the relevant service transactions. • Benefits of this notifications were applicable to the banks themselves on the charges or commissions against their banking services provided.	
SBP Initiatives		
Refinance Scheme for Payment of Wages and Salaries (Rozgar Scheme) 2020 for all sectors	Total PRs212 billion disbursed	To support businesses in preventing layoffs during COVID-19. The scheme was available for all sectors for financing 6-month wage bill at 3% p.a. for taxpayers and 5% p.a. for nontax payers. The Government of Pakistan provided 60% risk sharing on first loss basis for SMEs with sales turnover up to PRs800 million and 40% risk sharing for small corporations with sales turnover up to PRs2 billion.
Temporary Economic Refinance Facility (TERF) 2020 for all sectors	Total PRs435.7 billion approved	To stimulate investment in both new and expansion/Balancing, Modernization and Replacement (BMR) of existing units. Financing was available with per project limit of PRs5 billion to all sectors including SMEs except power sector. Financing under the scheme was provided at a maximum end-user rate of 5% for 10 years.
Refinance Facility for Combating COVID-19 (RFCC) for all sectors	Total PRs16.6 billion approved until 17 June 2021	Time-bound Refinance Facility was launched to enhance the capacity of health sector of the country to deal with the COVID-19 health emergency. Financing is available for hospitals/medical centers and manufacturers of COVID-related items like face masks/protective equipment/testing kits/ hospital beds/ventilators, etc. Financing under this scheme is provided for 5 years with maximum end-user rate of 3%. By 17 June 2021, PRs15.6 billion have been approved under the facility.
Other Initiatives - Loan Deferments; Loan Restructuring		SBP introduced a comprehensive relief package for low-income households and microenterprises that allowed microfinance banks (MFBs) to: – defer payment of principal on loan obligations for 1 year; however borrowers will continue to service the interest as per agreed terms and conditions; – reschedule/restructure financing facilities of borrowers who are unable to service interest or need deferment exceeding 1 year (This treatment did not affect borrower's credit history as these facilities were not to be reported as restructured in the credit bureaus' data). As of 16 April 2021, a total of PRs121 billion worth relief was provided to 1.7 million microcredit borrowers in the form of principal deferment and facility rescheduled/restructured. Regulatory requirement of biometric verification has been relaxed for microfinance customers until 31 December 2021. To help mitigate the risk of spread of COVID-19, MFBs have been advised to use NADRA's online Verification System for verification purpose in place of biometric verification. To support post-COVID-19 recovery, limits for housing finance and microenterprise loans have been enhanced up to PRs3 million from the existing limit of PRs1 million for borrowings from MFBs. Likewise, the maximum size of general loans has been enhanced from PRs150,000 to PRs350,000.

Source: ADB Asia SME Monitor 2021 database. Data from Small and Medium Enterprise Development Authority, and State Bank of Pakistan. KPMG. Pakistan - Government and institution measures in response to COVID-19. https://home.kpmg/xx/en/home/insights/2020/04/pakistan-government-and-institution-measures-in-response-to-covid.html; UNESCAP. Pakistan - COVID Country Profile. https://www.unescap.org/sites/default/d8files/2021-03/Pakistan_COVID%20Country%20profile%20230321.pdf; ADB. ADB COVID-19 Policy Database - Pakistan. https://covid19policy.adb.org/policy-measures/PAK; IMF. Policy Responses to COVID-19 - Pakistan. https://www.imf.org/en/Topics/imf-and-covid19/Policy-Responses-to-COVID-19#P; SMEDA. https://smeda.org/index.php?option=com_content&view=article&id=582:prime-minister-s-small-businesses-industries-relief-package&catid=77&Itemid=571; State Bank of Pakistan. https://www.sbp.org.pk/covid/index.html; Khyber Pakhtunkhwa Revenue Authority. https://kpra.gov.pk/; Sindh Revenue Board.

Country Review
Sri Lanka

Overview

The coronavirus disease (COVID-19) pandemic hit an already subdued Sri Lankan economy in 2020. Since 2016, economic growth has fallen due to a series of shocks—such as droughts in 2016 and 2017, a constitutional crisis in 2018 and 2019, and the coordinated Easter Sunday terror attacks of 2019. Economic growth slowed from 5.0% in 2015 to 2.3% in 2019.[169] The pandemic and nationwide lockdown led to a 3.6% contraction in 2020, which severely affected most economic activities, including micro, small, and medium-sized enterprises (MSMEs). In 2021, growth is forecast to recover with gross domestic product (GDP) expanding by 3.4%. Strong fiscal and monetary stimulus contributed, even as risks remain due to COVID-19 variants.

MSMEs comprise 99% of all enterprises and employ 75% of the labor force. They are a key driver of the economy, yet were devastated by the pandemic. Revitalizing operations and their growth is key to building a more resilient economic recovery.

Despite the pandemic, banks still increased lending, with an 11.9% growth in loans outstanding in 2020, primarily due to COVID-19 relief. Nonetheless, the nonperforming loan (NPL) ratio surged to 4.9% during the same period from a low of 2.5% in 2017, suggesting some deterioration in credit quality. MSME loan disbursements increased at a compounded annual growth rate (CAGR) of 12.3% for reporting commercial and specialized banks during 2014–2018. However, MSME access to bank credit remains limited. In 2020, they held 11% of total bank credit, equivalent to 5% of GDP. This remains a serious barrier to MSME growth.

The government and central bank provide concessional loans to unserved or underserved segments, including MSMEs, through various interest rate subsidies and donor-funded refinancing. Nonbank finance is somewhat developed. It finances MSME working capital, yet remains small and has been shrinking recently. While several government-sponsored microfinance programs have expanded—such as Samurdhi poverty alleviation loans—overall private microfinance institution loans have fallen, affected by a 2018 government debt relief program. Market-based financing to businesses has grown gradually, with a new Empower Board open for viable small and medium-sized enterprises (SMEs) to list for growth capital financing.

A national economic development program Vision 2025 cites MSME development as part of its growth framework. It stresses the need for MSMEs to formalize, digitalize, and adopt new technologies. The Enterprise Sri Lanka program supports the creation of new entrepreneurships. The Ministry of Industries is the focal government agency for formulating a national MSME policy framework. Under the 2015 MSME policy, the National Enterprise Development Authority is creating an enabling business environment for MSMEs, boosting market access and their access to finance. The central bank launched a National Financial Inclusion Strategy in 2021, with MSME financing as one of its core pillars.

169 Asian Development Bank. 2021. Asian Development Outlook (ADO) 2021. April; ADO 2021 Update. September.

The pandemic remains a risk that could impede economic recovery and MSME development. The government will need to strengthen its phased recovery approach and differentiate policies by firm size and sector to meet the demand of groups devastated by the pandemic. Digitalizing MSME business is another policy priority, particularly those in the informal sector. Government assistance should help develop entrepreneurship and give viable MSMEs greater access to growth capital. Yet it must do so without impeding national revenue growth or increasing budget deficits.

1. COVID-19 Impact on MSMEs

Economic growth has been slowing since 2016, due to weather, disasters, a constitutional crisis, terror attacks, and recently the pandemic. In 2020, the government acted quickly to contain the pandemic, imposing strict quarantine measures during March and May—social distancing, curfews, and lockdown. People's mobility was restricted and supply chains were disrupted. There was a sharp drop in domestic and foreign demand, which hurt almost all business operations.

The Department of Census and Statistics (under the Ministry of Finance) conducted an MSME survey to assess the initial impact of COVID-19. The survey drew 17,469 responses from MSMEs.[170] It compared their revenue and employment from January to May in 2019 and 2020. It found MSMEs had sharp drops in revenue and employment during the lockdown—a revenue decrease of 40.9% from March 2019 to March 2020, 74.2% for April, and 55.2% for May. The decrease in employment was 38.5% in March, 82.0% in April, and 66.7% in May (Figure 7.1). In April, the lockdown cut mining and quarrying revenues by 90.7%, construction by 89.4%, and services by 87.9%. Employment in these sectors fell by 91.3%, 85.4%, and 85.9%, respectively. Limited business operations or temporary closures lost many MSMEs most of their revenue. Supply chain disruptions also increased costs of keeping businesses operating. Many were forced to temporary cut staffing to save funds to survive the pandemic.

Another survey was conducted by the Federation of Chambers of Commerce and Industry of Sri Lanka (FCCISL) from July to September 2020.[171] The survey involved 300 establishments, 88% of which were MSMEs. Government quarantine measures slowed business operations of 89% of the respondents. By sector, accommodation/food service (tourism) and construction were most affected. The main challenges were retaining sales and accessing additional financing. Those with foreign markets were hit harder than domestic firms, with higher revenue losses, order cancellations, supply chain disruptions, and working-capital shortages. Despite these hardships, surveyed firms managed to keep their businesses functioning by scaling down operations and managing costs flexibly—just 17% reported temporary or permanent closures. The survey found the lockdown transformed several businesses, created new collaborations to mobilize resources, and developed new business opportunities. These included businesses in information and communications technology (ICT), manufacturing, and education. Firms in construction, transport, and storage had higher hurdles to cross.

The International Finance Corporation also interviewed 413 MSMEs in June–July 2020, focused on gender.[172] While the impact was mostly similar regardless of gender ownership, there were some differences for women-owned MSMEs. For example, they were less likely to develop a new digital operating channel and more likely to have borrowed from friends/family, with less access to formal financial services than men-led MSMEs. Some 80% of MSMEs surveyed sought additional funding to cover debt repayments.

170 In the survey, MSMEs are classified as firms with fewer than 200 employees.

171 PwC-FCCISL Business Resurgence Survey Report. March 2021.

172 International Finance Corporation. 2020. Gendered Impacts of COVID-19 on Small and Medium-Sized Enterprises in Sri Lanka.

Figure 7.1: Change of MSME Revenue and Employment in January–May 2019 and 2020

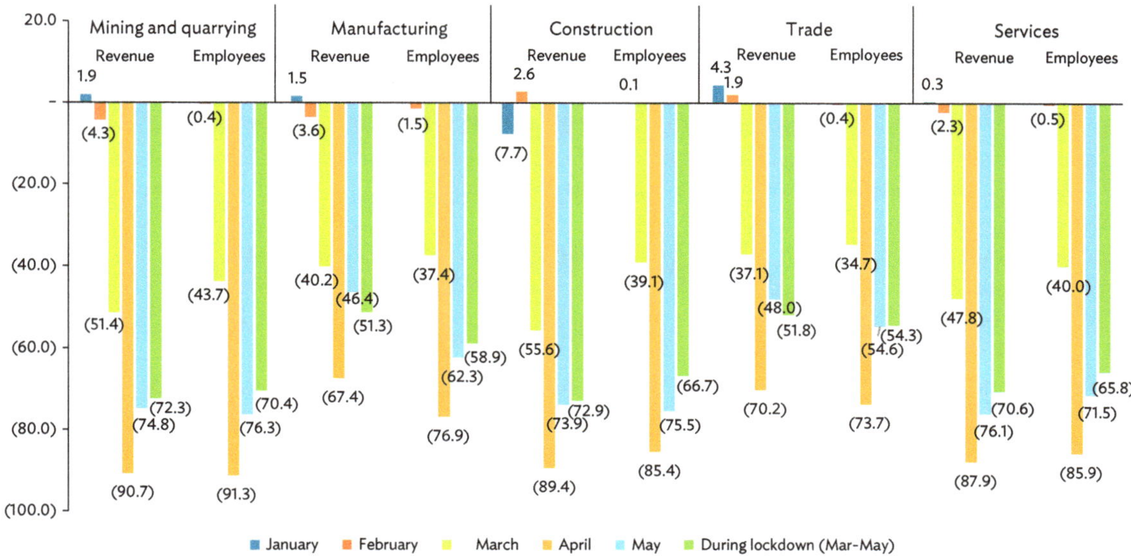

MSME = micro, small, and medium-sized enterprise.

Note: Preliminary survey findings of 17,469 MSMEs (firms with fewer than 200 employees).

Source: Recomposed from preliminary data of the Survey to Assess the Impact of COVID-19 (MSME Sector), Department of Census and Statistics, Ministry of Finance, 20 October 2020.

MSMEs are vulnerable to external or other shocks such as economic crises, natural disasters, or forced changes to the business environment (such as the pandemic response). Typically, they are not sufficiently liquid to keep their businesses running when unexpected events strike. They also lack alternative financing options so rely on retained profits and borrowing from close relatives or informal sources—to cover business costs like office rents and salaries. Thus, timely access to working and growth capital is critical, through diversified financing options.

Government relief measures helped MSMEs raise working capital and reduce debt repayments so they could survive until the first recovery after infections eased. However, a second wave struck in October 2020 with new outbreaks of the delta variant, affecting the Western Province, including the capital Colombo. This disrupted recovery momentum with stricter quarantines. MSMEs had to struggle again.

Limited mobility and supply chain disruptions were characterized by firms hit hardest and those which benefited. Tourism and exporters were hurt most. According to a United Nations report (UN 2020),[173] tourism—with 388,487 employees as of 2018—saw revenues drop from $4.4 billion in 2018 to $3.6 billion in 2019 due to the Easter Sunday terror attacks and faced further drop by travel restrictions under the pandemic. The pandemic largely shut the industry down, as tourist arrivals dropped almost 100% in April 2020. Handicraft trade and gems/jewelry shops (mostly micro and small firms) were also hit hard. The processed food industry, with about 40% MSMEs, benefited from the lockdown due to heightened demand for value-added agricultural products and processed food. The garment industry producing face masks and safety/protective clothing also gained from the lockdown.

The government and central bank introduced several fiscal and monetary policies in March 2020, soon after the COVID-19 outbreak (discussed under Policies and Regulations below).

173 United Nations (DESA/DSDG). 2020. The Impact of COVID-19 on the MSME Sector in Sri Lanka. May.

2. MSME Development

- The National Policy Framework for Small and Medium Enterprise Development 2015 defines MSMEs by annual turnover and number of employees by sector. Latest available MSME statistics are based on the Economic Census 2013 with different employment thresholds from the National SME Policy 2015; there are 1 million MSMEs, or 99.8% of all enterprises. MSME survey data by sector are available through 2018, but annual comparisons are unavailable.
- Most MSMEs are in trade and services, and spread nationwide. A large portion of MSMEs work in agriculture, but they are not included in the data.
- In 2013, MSMEs employed 2.3 million people, or 75% of the workforce. Manufacturing MSMEs absorbed a half of MSME workers, based on survey data.
- Time-series data on MSME contributions to GDP are unavailable; but the National SME Policy 2015 document said they contributed 52% of GDP.
- MSMEs are mostly domestic, with many informal. Export-oriented MSMEs are part of global supply chains as suppliers or lead firms; they were hit hardest by the pandemic with supply disruptions under the lockdown.
- Local B2C e-commerce are mostly MSMEs and have been expanded rapidly. The National SME Policy 2015 cited technology-based MSMEs as a core area for development. A state-owned Industrial Technology Institute supports MSMEs in the transfer, adaptation, and commercialization of technology through advice and capacity building.
- There are several business associations and chambers, such as the FCCISL, NCCSL, Ceylon Chamber of Commerce (CCC), and women-focused WCIC. They support MSMEs through capacity development programs, SME centers, and working with government agencies.

Scale of MSMEs

MSMEs are defined by annual turnover and number of employees by sector, as specified in the National Policy Framework for SME Development 2015 (Table 7.1A). A microenterprise is a firm with fewer than 10 employees and annual turnover of less than SLRs15 million. A small enterprise is a firm with 11–50 employees and annual turnover of SLRs16 million–SLRs250 million. A medium-sized enterprise is a firm with 51–200 for services employees and 51–300 for manufacturing, with annual turnover of SLRs251 million–SLRs750 million. Only medium-sized enterprises have different criteria by sector. If a firm falls under more than one category, the number employed is the determinant.

The latest available MSME statistics are based on the Economic Census 2013 with different employment thresholds from the National Policy Framework 2015. This defines a microenterprise as a firm with up to 4 employees for industry/construction and services (up to 3 for trade); a small enterprise has 5–24 employees for industry/construction (5–15 for services and 4–14 for trade); and a medium-sized enterprise has 25–199 employees for industry/construction (16–74 for services and 15–34 for trade) (Table 7.1B). Based on these definitions, in 2013 there were 1.0 million MSMEs, accounting for 99.8% of all enterprises (91.8% for microenterprises, 7.0% for small enterprises, and 1.0% for medium-sized enterprises) (Figure 7.2A and Table 7.2). There is no annual comparative data on MSMEs from 2014 onward. However, the Department of Census and Statistics compiled sector-based survey data on SMEs up to 2018. Data aggregating manufacturing, trade, and services from these annual surveys are available only for 2015–2017 (Figure 7.2A). These show the number of SMEs expanded by more than 3% annually. The share of SMEs to total firms fell from 94.9% in 2015 to 93.7% in 2017.

In 2013, MSMEs were mostly in trade and services, with 41.1% in wholesale and retail trade, followed by other services—including accommodation and food services (29.2%) and manufacturing (23.6%) (Figure 7.2B). In 2017, sector survey data show 29.9% was in trade, 38.0% in services, and 26.8% in manufacturing, with similar shares during 2015–2017. Agriculture was not counted, even as a large portion of MSMEs operate in the sector.

Figure 7.2: Number of MSMEs

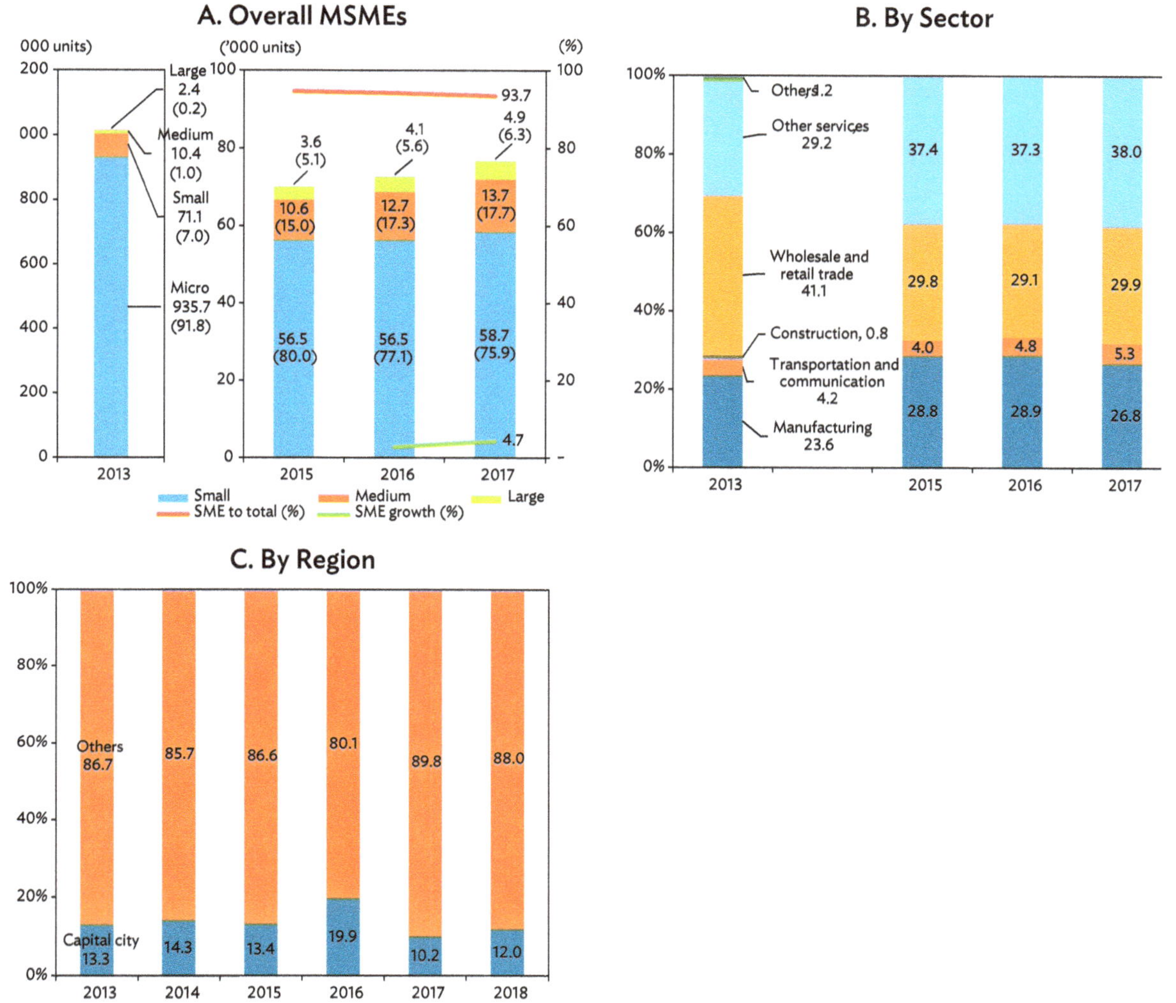

MSME = micro, small, and medium-sized enterprise.

Notes: For Figures 1A and 1B, 2013 data refer to Economic Census 2013. 2015-2017 data refer to the sum of manufacturing, trade, and services (Annual Survey of Industries, Annual Survey of Trade, and Annual Survey of Services). The latter two surveys started in 2016 (reference year 2015). For Figure 1C, Colombo municipal area is taken as the capital city. By-region data from 2014 to 2018 refer to manufacturing only (Annual Survey of Industries).

Source: ADB Asia SME Monitor 2021 Database. Data from Economic Census 2013; Annual Survey of Industries, Annual Survey of Trade, and Annual Survey of Services, Department of Census and Statistics.

MSMEs are spread nationwide. By region, 13.3% were in the Colombo municipal area (capital), while 86.7% were spread across other provinces, based on Census 2013 (Figure 7.2C). There were similar shares for SME manufacturers from 2014 to 2018 (Annual Survey of Industries).

Employment

According to the same data, in 2013 MSMEs employed 2.3 million people, or 75.1% of the total workforce (44.6% for microenterprises, 17.6% for small enterprises, and 12.9% for medium-sized enterprises) (Figure 7.3A). In 2017, aggregate data from sector surveys showed that those employed by SMEs in manufacturing, trade, and services accounted for 37.7% (13.6% for small and 24.1% for medium-sized enterprises) down from 41.6% in 2015 (20.3% for small and 21.4% for medium). The growth in number of SME employees fell from 9.1% in 2016 to 3.2% in 2017.

Figure 7.3: Employment by MSMEs

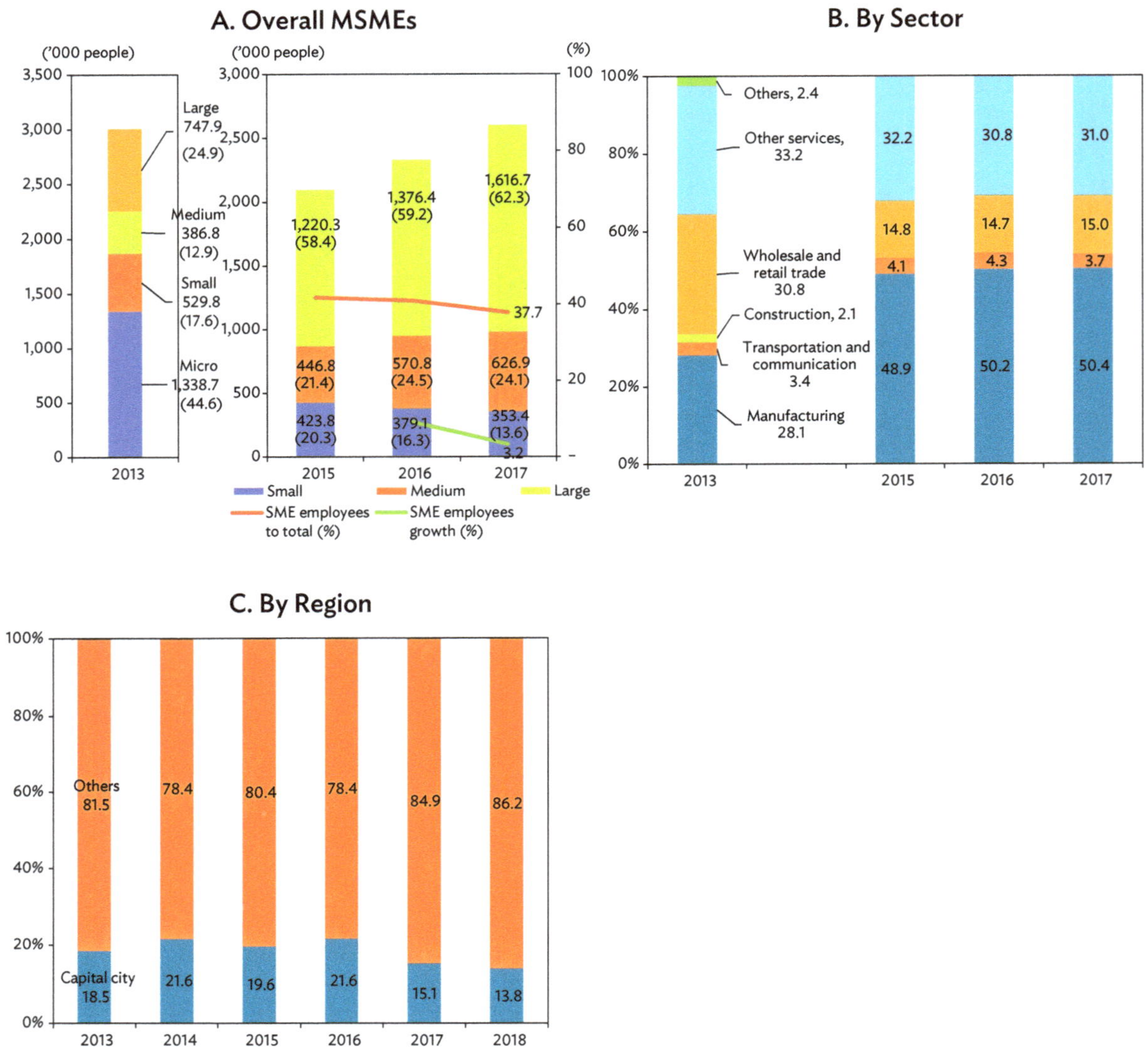

MSME = micro, small, and medium-sized enterprise.

Notes: For Figures 2A and 2B, 2013 data refer to Economic Census 2013. 2015-2017 data refer to the sum of manufacturing, trade, and services (Annual Survey of Industries, Annual Survey of Trade, and Annual Survey of Services). The latter two surveys started in 2016 (reference year 2015). For Figure 2C, Colombo municipal area is taken as the capital city. By-region data from 2014 to 2018 refer to manufacturing only (Annual Survey of Industries).

Source: ADB Asia SME Monitor 2021 Database. Data from Economic Census 2013; Annual Survey of Industries, Annual Survey of Trade, and Annual Survey of Services, Department of Census and Statistics.

In 2013, 28.1% of MSME employees worked in manufacturing, 30.8% in wholesale and retail trade, and 33.2% in other services (Figure 7.3B). Based on the sector survey data, 50.4% of SME employees were in manufacturing, 15.0% in trade, and 31.0% in services. The shares were similar during 2015–2017. Agriculture was not included.

By region, the share of those working in the Colombo municipal area was slightly larger than the overall composition of MSMEs. In 2013, 18.5% of MSME employees worked in the Colombo municipal area, while 81.5% worked in other provinces (Figure 7.3C). Data on SME workers in manufacturing stayed largely the same from 2014 to 2018.

Business Productivity

GDP (at current prices) was SLRs15 trillion in 2020, down by 3.6% due to the pandemic and nationwide lockdown. This exacerbated earlier shocks from drought (2016 and 2017), a constitutional crisis (2018 and 2019), and the coordinated Easter Sunday terror attacks (2019). Growth is forecast to begin recovering by 3.4% in 2021, largely due to government fiscal and monetary stimulus.

Services account for about one-third of GDP, followed by manufacturing (16%) (Figure 7.4). Time-series data on MSME contributions to GDP is unavailable. But given their large share of trade and services, their contribution to GDP remains significant. According to the National SME Policy 2015, SMEs contributed to 52% of GDP.

Figure 7.4: Gross Domestic Product (current prices)

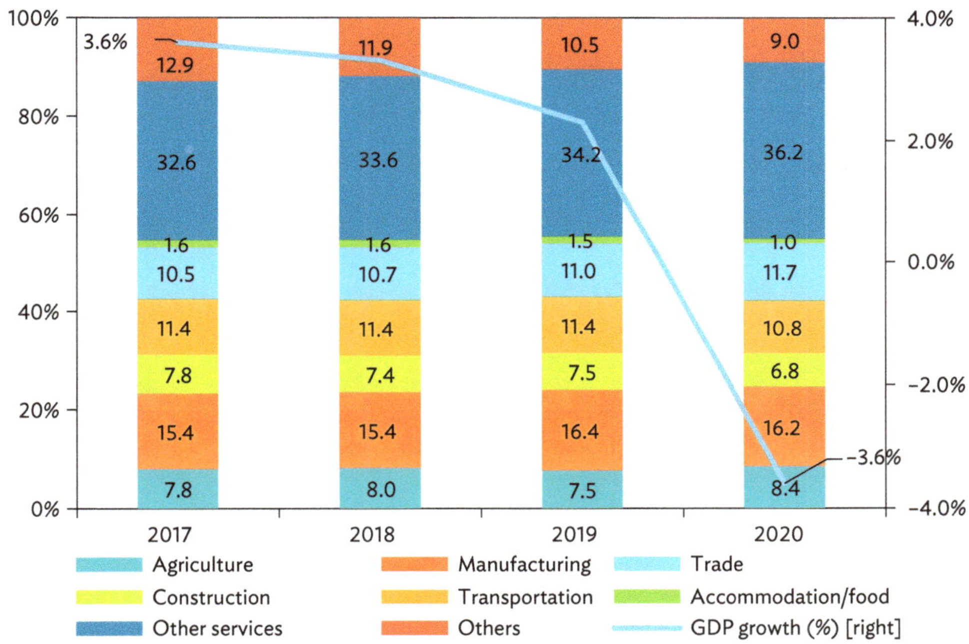

GDP = gross domestic product.

Note: Based on the GDP estimates (base year 2010).

Source: Recomposed from Department of Census and Statistics, Gross Domestic Product by Industrial Origin at Current Market Prices.

Market Access

MSMEs largely supplement domestic markets, with many informal. Market access is one of the core priorities in the National Policy Framework for SME Development 2015. It promotes linkages between MSMEs and larger firms, and assists them in accessing government procurement, e-commerce, and product development/branding. The Vision 2025 national economic development program indicates a growth strategy through integrating MSMEs into the formal sector. MSME business formalization is crucial for the government to effectively assist their market access.

Vision 2025 plans to double exports to $20 billion annually. However, due to reduced foreign demand and supply chain disruptions from the pandemic and lockdown, exports fell from SLRs1,846 million ($10.2 billion) in 2019 to

SLRs1,669 million ($9.0 billion) in 2020, a 9.6% decline (Figure 7.5) (footnote 173).[174] Data is unavailable on MSME exports, yet there are export-oriented MSMEs working as suppliers or lead firms in global supply chains. They were hardest hit by supply disruptions under the lockdown.

Garments are export-oriented, with one-third of its workers employed by MSMEs (UN 2020). Major destinations include the United States (US) and the European Union. Production largely comes from imported fabrics and accessories, mainly from the People's Republic of China (PRC) and India. The lockdown contributed to raw material shortages, which left the industry one of the worst affected.

Figure 7.5: Exports and Imports

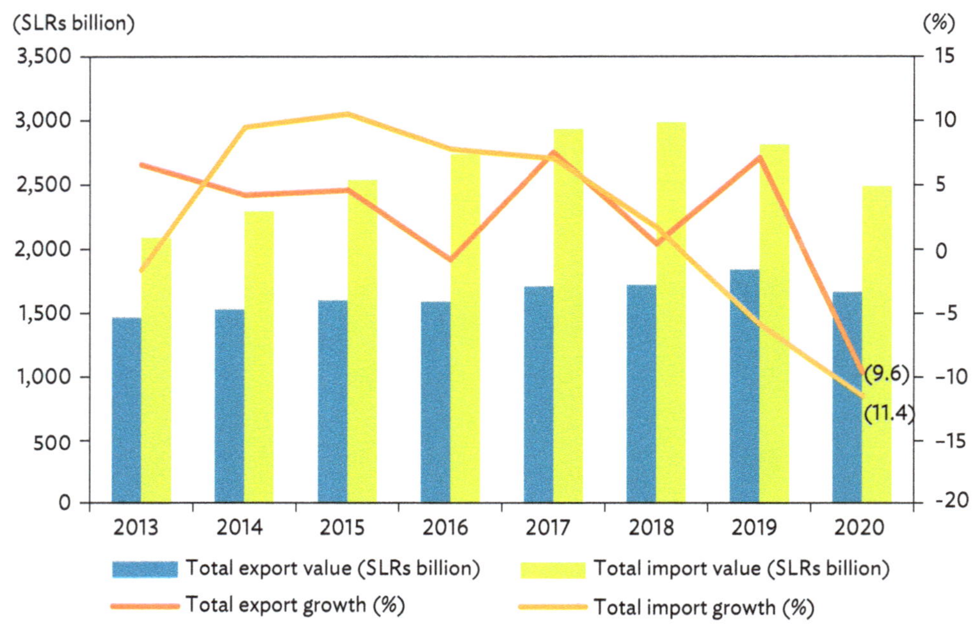

Source: ADB Asia SME Monitor 2021 database. Data from the Department of Census and Statistics.

The Sri Lanka Export Development Board (EDB) supports MSME exporters through advisory services on how to access global markets. The key challenges for MSMEs include (i) a lack of business linkages with large multinationals, (ii) the need for research and development (R&D) to develop and improve products, (iii) limited access to finance, and (iv) a lack of business literacy and capacity. EDB regularly offers capacity development to MSME exporters (through webinars). It has 200 advisors nationwide to train people working at MSMEs.[175]

Technology and Innovation

Internet usage has surged since 2014, from 10.5% of the population to 35% in 2020 (World Development Indicators). Mobile cellular subscriptions reached 29.7 million, or 138.8 per 100 people in 2020. And it continues to grow. E-commerce has thrived as a result. Highly competitive domestic e-commerce businesses have grown rapidly, changing people's lives shifting demand during the pandemic. Online trading, banking, and e-payments in

[174] Exchange rate refers to IMF/IFS, end of period.

[175] Interview with Sri Lanka Export Development Board on 4 March 2021.

commerce, business, and government services have skyrocketed. The Electronic Transactions Act No.19 of 2006, amended in 2017, provides the legal framework for e-commerce transactions.[176]

Major domestic B2C e-commerce companies include Dialog.lk (telecoms), Kapruka.com (gifts), Takas.lk (lifestyle store), Daraz.lk (electronics), Ikman.lk (new and second hand products), Wow.lk (consumer goods), Buyabans.com (consumer goods), Dailcom.lk (electronics), Mydeal.lk (closing), Wishque.com (premium gifts), barclays.lk (electronics), and Mystore.lk (home appliances and gifts). According to an EDB study, of 76 randomly sampled e-commerce providers, most were MSMEs (by employment) (footnote 176). They supplied both domestic and global markets. The study estimated that nearly 58% adopted new technology for sales and marketing. Around 40% use in-house technology platforms for marketing their goods and services. Less than half use online procurement for inputs.

The government views technology and digitalization as a key driver for economic development, as highlighted in Vision 2025, empowering the self-employed and MSMEs. Strategies include promoting private sector investment in digital technology, a national digital identity initiative, ICT-based marketing interfaces (technical support for MSMEs), and innovations in mobile payments and peer-to-peer lending platforms. Promoting technology-based MSMEs is one of the core areas under the National SME Policy 2015. A state-owned Industrial Technology Institute (ITI) supports MSMEs in technology transfer, adaptation, and commercialization through advice and training. ITI established a Techno Centre as a one-stop solution window for businesses, especially MSMEs.

Networking and Support

There are several active business associations and chambers, such as the FCCISL, the National Chamber of Commerce of Sri Lanka (NCCSL), the Ceylon Chamber of Commerce (CCC), and Women's Chamber of Industry and Commerce (WCIC). They support MSME members through capacity building, coaching and advice, establishing SME centers, and collaborating or lobbying with government agencies.

The FCCISL, established in 1973, is the umbrella organization covering 63 chambers of commerce and business associations and monitors over 25,000 businesses, including MSMEs (it conducted a COVID-19 impact survey). It supports trade facilitation for MSMEs, connecting them with domestic and foreign business partners through organized exhibitions, and provides capacity development programs for start-ups. It handles priority sectors such as tea, rubber, construction, information technology, and herbal products, addressing focal groups for assistance such as small manufacturers, start-ups, agribusiness, and exporters/importers. FCCISL works with the government to support MSME development and resolve challenges such as the lack of a centralized MSME database; poor product quality management; complicated procedures on business licenses, permits, registration, taxation; and access to growth capital.[177]

The NCCSL, founded in 1948, promotes domestic and foreign trade with special emphasis on MSMEs and entrepreneurship development. Collaborating with 24 regional chambers, It offers advisory and training services to its 720 active members and holds policy discussions on MSME development. NCCSL has a program for recognizing innovative businesses, which provides incentives to grow for MSMEs and entrepreneurs that contribute national economic development (Box 1).[178]

176 Sri Lanka Export Development Board. 2020. E-commerce Readiness Assessment Report Sri Lanka. March.

177 Interview with FCCISL on 5 March 2021.

178 Interview with NCCSL on 26 March 2021.

Box 7.1: Recovering from the Pandemic through Innovation—Exterminators Ltd.

The National Chamber of Commerce of Sri Lanka (NCCSL), with support from the National Enterprise Development Authority, have run the Western Province Entrepreneur Awards since 2016 to recognize, reward, and motivate innovative businesses and entrepreneurs who contribute to economic development.

The awards for 2020, held in February 2021, were for innovative small businesses and entrepreneurs that survived and recovered from the pandemic and lockdown. Exterminators Ltd. was one of the awardees:

Exterminators is a pioneer in coronavirus disease (COVID-19) disinfection and sanitation services. Originally, it supplied pest control services. After the COVID-19 outbreak, demand for pest control services sharply dropped due to health concerns, especially as people stayed home under the lockdown. Its pest control sales decreased by 12% over 2020. More than 100 service contracts were canceled, and all service renewals were extended 3–6 months. Cash almost ran out soon after the outbreak, making it difficult to manage day-to-day expenses and salary payments. Main suppliers stopped delivering inputs until outstanding invoices were paid. To compensate, the company decided to take the risk of shifting their main business from pest control to disinfection. The company's 'High Risk COVID-19' team of six technicians and four sales/operations staff created a new venture business named "Anti-Microbial Disinfection."

Exterminators restarted its business with specialized anti-microbial disinfection services nationwide. It reversed revenue loss, protected employees, and brought in new pest control contracts during the lockdown/curfew periods through greater brand recognition. Since March 2020, the company disinfected over 10 million square feet of space, travelling thousands of kilometers covering all provinces. It served more than 200 new customers, executed over 1,500 disinfection jobs, and generated 27% of total revenue as of end-March 2021. Exterminators disinfected 71 homes for the elderly, 30 police stations, 15 religious institutions, 13 public places including the 'Lotus Tower & Schools,' travelling over 6,000 kilometers in Colombo, Gampaha, Kalutara, and Kandy districts. Sales increased by 19%; net profits rose by 187%; total assets increased by 67%; and operating cashflows increased by 198% in over the previous fiscal year.

Sources: NCCSL, May 2021; company website.

The CCC, founded in 1839 (the oldest chamber in the country), established a Centre for SMEs as a one-stop shop to assist and guide MSME growth. It provides various business development services for MSMEs, including business consultancies, cloud-based enterprise resource planning solutions, business registration services, e-commerce/online business development advice, social media/website development, tax consultancy, cash flow statement reviews, and evaluates business supply chains. The CCC, in collaboration with the International Trade Centre, has been providing on-the-job coaching services to MSMEs since 2018 (export management).[179]

The WCIC, founded in 1985, aims to leverage women entrepreneurships into the business community. It has 265 active members and offers advisory and training services specially designed for women entrepreneurs. It works for greater access to markets and finance, runs networking through organized events (a Business Book Club, monthly coffee evening, among others), and builds motivation for business development and growth through recognition programs. The WCIC also lobbies with the government. Key challenges for women entrepreneurs include access to finance, childcare in the workplace, development of the care-giving industry to allow women to be more economically productive, procurement opportunities, and post-natal career development.[180]

179 Interview with CCC on 5 March 2021; CCC website: https://www.chamber.lk/the-ceylon-chamber-of-commerce-centre-for-smes
180 Interview with WCIC on 30 March 2021.

3. Access to Finance

- Access to bank credit remains limited, with just 11% of bank loans outstanding in 2020 held by MSMEs—equivalent to 5% of GDP. Half of MSME loans are for manufacturing, a third for services, and 12% for agriculture.
- The government and central bank offer concessional loans to priority groups like MSMEs using interest rate subsidies and refinancing. An independent credit guarantee corporation is being established. Government-sponsored microfinance programs have expanded.
- Although small, nonbank finance is available, helping supply MSME working capital; but it has recently declined due to a series of droughts and the pandemic.
- Digital finance remains the exception, with cash still preferred. The new National Financial Inclusion Strategy 2021–2024 places digital finance and payment services as a core priority.
- Market-based business financing has grown gradually, with a new Empower Board allowing SMEs to tap the capital market.
- The Credit Information Bureau of Sri Lanka provides the core data infrastructure that facilitates MSME to access finance, with a credit information management system and a secured transactions registry system.

The financial system is supervised by the Central Bank of Sri Lanka (CBSL), overseeing commercial and specialized banks, along with deposit-taking financial institutions (licensed finance companies, cooperative rural banks, and thrift and credit cooperative societies); specialized financial institutions (specialized leasing companies, licensed microfinance institutions, primary dealers, stockbrokers, unit trusts/unit trust management companies, market intermediaries [e.g., investment managers, margin providers, underwriters, and credit rating agencies], and venture capital companies); and contractual savings institutions (insurance companies, employee provident funds, employee trust funds, pension and provident funds, and a public service provident fund).

The banking sector held an estimated 72.5% of total financial assets in 2020. Licensed commercial banks held 54.4%. The CBSL regulates and supervises licensed banks and nonbank finance institutions, while the Securities and Exchange Commission of Sri Lanka (SEC) regulates and supervises capital markets.

Bank Credit

There were 24 licensed commercial banks (LCBs) and 6 licensed specialized banks (LSBs) in 2020 (Table 7.3).[181]

The bank credit market has been growing since 2010 or post-civil war at a CAGR of 16.5% during 2010–2020, while NPLs have expanded at a CAGR of 15.7% over the same period. Despite the pandemic, bank loans still grew. Bank loans outstanding reached SLRs9 trillion (up 11.9%) in 2020, mostly from COVID-19 relief measures. The NPL ratio surged to 4.9% from its 2017 low of 2.5%.

MSME loan disbursements rose 12.3% CAGR for commercial and specialized banks from 2014 to 2018 (Figure 7.6A and Table 7.3a).[182] By number of loans, however, they decreased at a CAGR of 2.4%. As a result, average MSME loan size increased from SLRs2.5 million ($19,054) in 2014 to SLRs4.4 million ($23,991) in 2018 (footnote 174).

[181] The six licensed specialized banks are the Housing Development Finance Corporation Bank of Sri Lanka, National Savings Bank (Savings House), Pradeshiya Sanwardhana Bank, Sanasa Development Bank, Sri Lanka Savings Bank, and State Mortgage and Investment Bank (as of September 2021).

[182] Data refer only to reporting commercial and specialized banks. Data is sourced from various editions of Ministry of Finance Annual Reports.

In 2020, MSME loans outstanding totaled SLRs743 billion.[183] LCBs accounted for 90.2%, while LSBs 9.8% (Figure 7.6A). There were 359,349 MSME loans. The average weighted lending rate based on MSME loans outstanding was 10.95% (8.53% based on new MSME lending). LSBs that mostly granted smaller loans offer higher interest rates than LCBs. MSME loans were 11.1% of total bank loans, equivalent to 5.0% of GDP in 2020. MSMEs need greater access to bank credit.

In 2018, one-third of MSME loans disbursed went to services, followed by industry (manufacturing) (22.5%) and agriculture (11.2%) (Figure 7.6B). Based on a 2020 CBSL SME Credit Survey, industry accounted for 50.5% of MSME loans outstanding, followed by services (37.6%) and agriculture (11.9%).[184]

Figure 7.6: MSME Loans

MSME = micro, small, and medium-sized enterprise.

Notes: For 2014-2018, data for loans disbursed. For 2020, data for loans outstanding, where MSME loans are based on the SME Credit Survey in 2020. The survey was based on loans granted by licensed commercial banks and licensed specialized banks, excluding government and central bank refinancing.

Source: ADB Asia SME Monitor 2021 database. Data from various editions of Ministry of Finance Annual Report, Sri Lanka; Central Bank of Sri Lanka.

183 MSME loans based on the 2020 SME Credit Survey refer to rupee loans granted by licensed commercial and specialized banks, excluding government and central bank refinancing schemes.

184 Central Bank of Sri Lanka, Annual Report 2020.

MSME loans outstanding were balanced by tenor, with about one-third short term (less than 1 year), midterm (1–5 years), and long term (more than 5 years) (Figure 7.6C). However, most new lending to MSMEs was short-term, while cash flow disruptions during the pandemic led to the rebalancing (footnote 184).

Public Financing and Guarantees

Finance is pivotal to MSME growth. But limited access remains a huge challenge. Information asymmetry between lenders and borrowers is the prime reason. Public finance and credit enhancement can help narrow the MSME financing gap. The pandemic showed that public finance is critical to support MSMEs vulnerable to unexpected shocks.

The government and central bank offer concessional loans to unserved or underserved segments—including MSMEs—using various interest rate subsidies and donor-funded refinancing. In 2017, these programs, often independently launched, were combined into a single program—Enterprise Sri Lanka—to make public assistance to businesses more effective. It involves 23 programs, with 18 providing subsidized loans; 3 involve donor-funded refinancing (ADB's SME Line of Credit, a Rooftop Solar Power Generation Line of Credit, and JICA's E-Friends Program); while 2 provide institutional support (the planned National Credit Guarantee Institution and a pilot SME Company Formation scheme). CBSL also has a debt relief package to assist MSMEs (both well-performed and contracted firms) access bank credit. Its scope was later extended to self-employed individuals affected by the pandemic. The government also provides several public microfinance programs such as a Samurdhi poverty alleviation loan fund.

a. Subsidized loans

As of end-2019, there were 18 interest subsidy loan schemes operated under the Enterprise Sri Lanka program (Table 7.4a).[185] They target not only MSMEs but also other businesses—those self-employed, the youth, and women entrepreneurs. For instance, *Jaya Isura* targets SMEs engaged in specific sectors (such as agriculture, lite engineering, tourism, handicrafts, apparel, information technology, manufacturing, and renewable energy), with a maximum loan of SLRs50 million for small non-exporters, SLRs100 million for small exporters, SLRs200 million for medium-sized non-exporters, and SLRs400 million for medium-sized exporters. The annual effective interest rate is 13.86% with an on-lending rate of 6.93% (50% interest subsidy) for small enterprises and 10.4% for medium-sized enterprises (25% subsidy) for 7 years (including 1 year grace period). A total of SLRs88,271 million in loans was disbursed by the end of 2019 with paid interest subsidies reaching SLRs2,525 million (Figure 7.7A and Table 7.4).

b. Debt relief

Given the uncertain economic conditions and a series of natural disasters (droughts), in January 2020 CBSL introduced a debt relief package to assist MSMEs access bank credit. It was available to all MSMEs that performed well and affected by drought and the slowing economy. Special concessions include rescheduling existing loans with a 1-year grace period, penalty interest write-offs, doubling loan tenor balances, working capital loans for re-opening businesses.[186] New loans for investment and working capital and a 1-year capital moratorium can be provided for MSMEs who stayed current with their term loans. From March 2020, after the COVID-19 outbreak, the package was extended to cover the self-employed and individuals affected by the pandemic, as well as to allow other financial institutions such as licensed finance companies and specialized leasing companies to join.

185 The 18 are Sonduru Piyasa, Govi Navoda, Ran Aswenna, Riya Shakthi, Rivi Bala Savi, Jaya Isura, Madya Aruna, Green Loan, Erambuma, Home Sweet Home/Middle Income Housing Loan, Diri Saviya, Rekawarana, Singithi Pasala, City Ride, My Future, Sihina Maliga, Working Capital, and Sancharaka Poddo. Source: Ministry of Finance, Sri Lanka, Annual Report 2019.

186 Ministry of Finance, Sri Lanka, Annual Report 2019. Box. 6.1.

c. Refinancing schemes

CBSL had 13 refinancing programs as of end-2020, including a refinance facility (*saubagya, or* Prosperity) to provide working capital for MSMEs. The saubagya was renewed in April 2020 as a COVID-19 Renaissance Facility.

The ADB-funded SME Line of Credit provides financial intermediation targeting MSMEs and women entrepreneurs through participating banks (Table 7.4b).[187] ADB initially allocated $100 million, then added $75 million (additional financing I) plus $165 million (additional financing II). It included an SME Emergency Response Component in response to the pandemic. A new Women Entrepreneur Finance Initiative (We-Fi) grant of $9.5 million was also added. The credit line disbursed 3,491 loans totaling SLRs27.7 billion as of end-March 2020, or 98.1% of allocated loan amounts disbursed to participating banks. The We-Fi grant disbursed SLRs1,092 million for 640 loans, 94.3% of allocated amounts disbursed.

d. Credit guarantees

The independent national credit guarantee corporation has yet to be established. The CBSL provides credit guarantees as part of government assistance programs or loan projects. Since June 2020, the CBSL, under its *Saubagya* COVID-19 Renaissance Facility, offers credit guarantees for subsidized working capital loans to MSMEs. The centralized credit guarantee system will boost access to formal financial services for the traditionally unserved or underserved, including MSMEs. With this perception, the government proposed the establishment of a National Credit Guarantee Institution (NCGI). ADB supported for its seed capital and has provided technical assistance for setting it up ($100 million loan). The legal framework for the independent NCGI was under preparation as of end-2020.

e. Public microfinance programs

Microfinance is a critical financing tool that improves access to finance for low-income households, women, and micro and small firms in rural areas. The government provides concessional micro-loans to low-income groups (including smallholder farmers, the self-employed, and owners of micro and small firms) though its programs or through participating banks. These microfinance programs continue to grow. In 2018, outstanding micro-loans through government programs amounted to SLRs282,248 million, a 7.1% increase from 2017—a CAGR of 9.0% during 2014–2018 (Figure 7.7B and Table 7.4c). The Regional Development Bank provided 48% of micro-loans, the Department of Cooperative Development 25.8%, and the Department of Samurdhi Development 24.2%. Total deposits amounted to SLRs381,745 million in the same period, a 12.8% increase from 2017 and a CAGR of 15.1% during 2014–2018.

The Samurdhi program was launched in 1995 for poverty reduction. The Samurdhi Authority was the implementing agency for financial (microfinance) and non financial (skill training/literacy programs) assistance to low-income families and vulnerable groups including smallholders and micro/small firm owners (such as handicrafts). It was incorporated into the Department of Samurdhi Development in 2014. The Samurdhi microfinance program disbursed SLRs357,497 million in loans with 425,835 newly approved. Loans outstanding totaled SLRs93,736 million in 2020, a 12.2% increase from 2019 (Figure 7.7C and Table 7.4d). Total deposits amounted to SLRs142,043 million with newly approved deposits of 350,174 over the same period, an 8.5% increase from 2019.

187 Participating banks include Bank of Ceylon, People's Bank, Regional Development Bank, DFCC Bank, Sampath Bank, Hatton National Bank, Commercial Bank, National Development Bank, Seylan Bank, and Nations Trust Bank.

Figure 7.7: Public Financing

A. Subsidized Loans

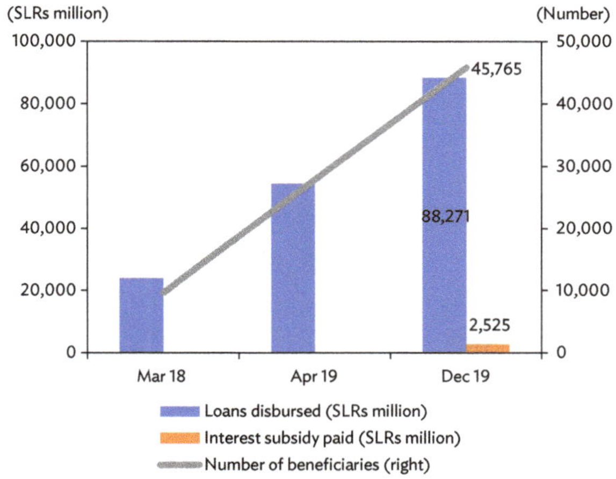

Source: ADB Asia SME Monitor 2021 database. Data from Ministry of Finance, Sri Lanka, Annual Reports 2017, 2018, and 2019.

B. Public Microfinance Programs

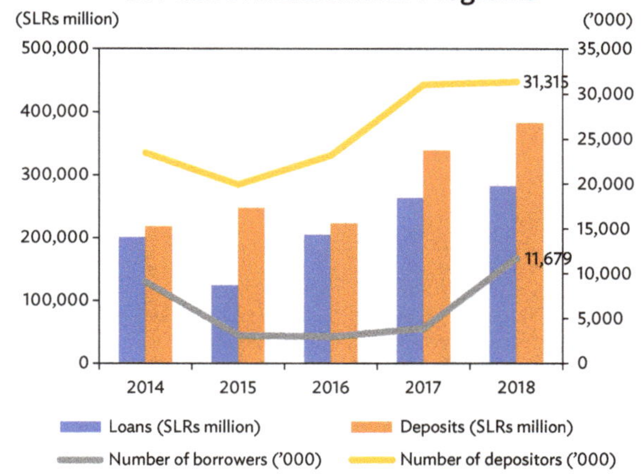

Source: ADB Asia SME Monitor 2021 database. Data from Ministry of Finance, Sri Lanka, Annual Reports 2014-2018.

C. Microfinance Program by Department of Samurdhi Development

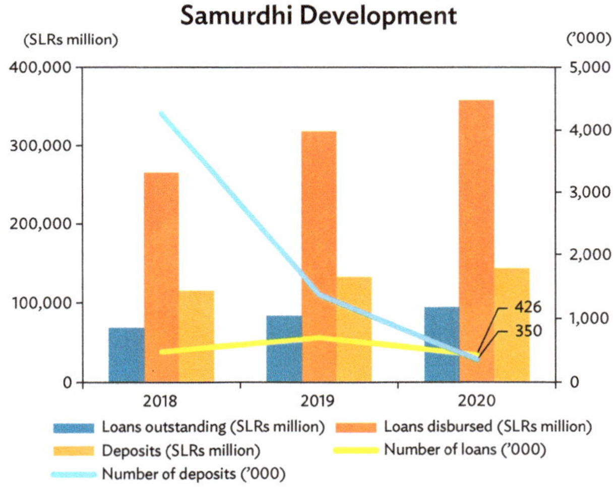

Note: Number of loans and deposits refers to new approval.

Source: ADB Asia SME Monitor 2021 database. Data from Department of Samurdhi Development.

Nonbank Financing

The nonbank finance industry is gradually developing. It supports MSME working capital needs, but it remains small in scale and has recently slowed. As of end-2020, there were 47 nonbank finance institutions regulated by the CBSL, of which 4 were licensed microfinance institutions, 40 were licensed finance companies, and 3 were specialized leasing companies. Their assets were 6.0% of the country's total financial sector assets in 2020 (provisional). Total financing outstanding was SLRs1,164 billion in 2020, 96.7% of which were held by finance companies (Figure 7.8A and Table 7.5). It accounted for 7.8% of GDP, down by 3.0% from 2019, affected by the pandemic and nationwide lockdown.

Figure 7.8: Nonbank Finance

A. Nonbank Finance Institutions Regulated by Central Bank of Sri Lanka

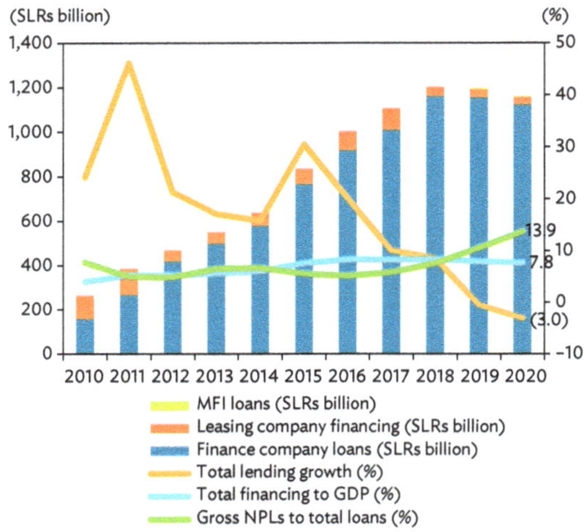

GDP = gross domestic product, MFI = microfinance institution, NPL = nonperforming loan.

Source: ADB Asia SME Monitor 2021 Database. Data from Central Bank of Sri Lanka.

B. Microfinance Institution Loans, excluding Government Programs*

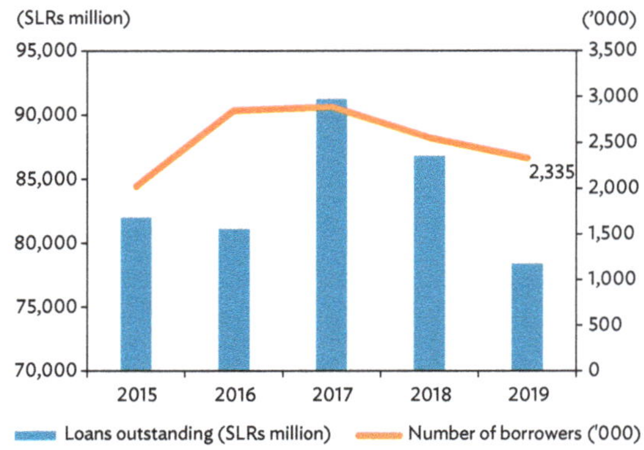

Source: Recomposed from Lanka Microfinance Practitioners' Association. 2019. Microfinance Review, Sri Lanka.

C. Microfinance Institution Loans by Purpose

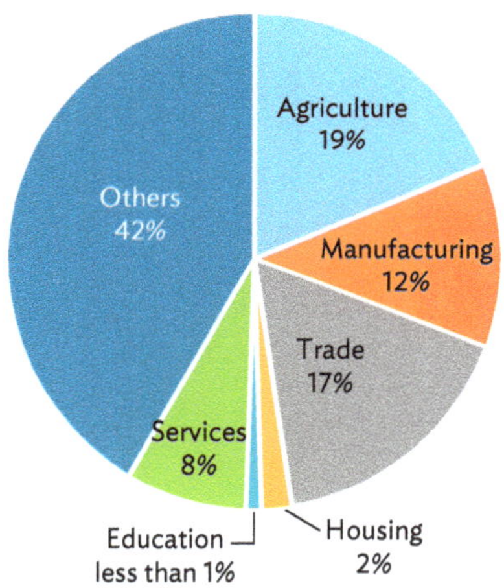

Note: based on 39 microfinance institutions surveyed by Lanka Microfinance Practitioners' Association in 2019.

Source: Recomposed from Lanka Microfinance Practitioners' Association. 2019. Microfinance Review, Sri Lanka.

D. Microfinance Institution Clients by Gender

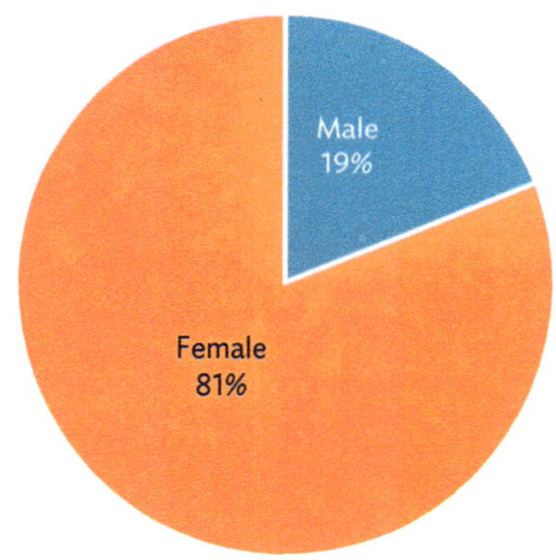

Note: based on 39 microfinance institutions surveyed by Lanka Microfinance Practitioners' Association in 2019.

Source: Recomposed from Lanka Microfinance Practitioners' Association. 2019. Microfinance Review, Sri Lanka.

While several government-sponsored microfinance programs have grown, such as the Samurdhi poverty alleviation loan program, overall private sector microfinance institution (MFI) loans have fallen, affected by the 2018 government debt relief program. Loans outstanding by MFIs, excluding government-sponsored programs and banks' cultivation loans, amounted to SLRs78,448 million in 2019, a 9.7% decrease from 2018 with a CAGR of -1.1% from 2015 to 2019 (Figure 7.8B and Table 7.5a). The number of borrowers fell from 2.6 million in 2018 to 2.3 million in 2019 (an 8.7% decrease).

According to the microfinance review survey conducted by the Lanka Microfinance Practitioners' Association in 2019, 19% of the loan portfolios of MFIs surveyed (39 samples) went to agriculture, followed by trade (17%), manufacturing (12%), and services (8%)—42% were unclassified (Figure 7.8C). Of the surveyed MFIs, 81% of clients were female, with the remaining 19% male (Figure 7.8D). Most loans by those surveyed went to small businesses and women entrepreneurs.[188]

To help borrowers affected by the 2016 and 2017 droughts, the government introduced a debt relief program in 2018, addressing women borrowers. Principal and interest of MFI loans up to SLRs100,000 were written off. While the losses incurred by write-off principal were reimbursed by the government, the loss from write-off interest was borne by the MFIs, which affected their performance. The debt relief program was also applied to licensed finance companies, harming their performance in 2019 and afterwards as well.

Digital Financial Services

Digital financial services offer low-cost financing to traditionally unserved or underserved segments. It is a critical tool to promote inclusive growth nationally. Demand has increased sharply since the outbreak of COVID-19.

Developing and promoting digital finance and payment services is one of the core pillars of the National Financial Inclusion Strategy (NFIS) for Sri Lanka 2021–2024, which was launched in March 2021. Strategies to increase digital financial inclusion were set up in several layers. Cross cutting issues include strengthening (i) financial and digital infrastructure, (ii) an enabling regulatory environment with timely, transparent, and consistent guidance to the market, and (iii) public and private sector commitment and collaboration, with a stronger role played by the National Payments Council and the development of a National Payments Strategy. Supply-side issues include (i) diversifying and facilitating access points, (ii) expanding available payment instruments, and (iii) developing a fintech ecosystem. Demand-side issues include (i) achieving scale through digital social transfers (digitizing government services) and (ii) generating demand to expand use of digital payments.

The NFIS said improving digital finance was needed due to (i) high reliance on cash for daily transactions, (ii) relatively fewer ATMs and point-of-sales terminals, (iii) low acceptance and usage of electronic payment instruments, (iv) low ownership and usage of mobile money accounts, (v) low penetration of online banking, and (vi) low ownership and usage of cards and accounts.

The NFIS was based on the National Financial Inclusion Survey 2018/2019, which is to be conducted every 3 years.[189] According to survey findings, respondents used traditional face-to-face transactions with bank cashiers (85% of respondents) more than ATMs (48%), cash deposit machines (24%), mobile/internet banking (3%), and mobile phone applications (eZ Cash and mCash; e-wallet) (2%). The ownership and usage of ATM/debit cards for payments was low (only 14.8% used payment cards in retail shops). Credit card use was lower (9.7%). Despite relatively high mobile phone penetration (82%), only 2% of adults owned a mobile money account, the main reasons for which were "not seeing the need" and "not knowing how to use it," suggesting the need for strengthening digital finance literacy. It is also a critical benchmark for developing the digital finance industry or tech-based start-ups and more innovative entrepreneurs.

Capital Markets

Market-based financing for businesses has grown gradually. The Colombo Stock Exchange (CSE) is the only stock exchange, with three boards for listing: the Main Board, Diri Savi Board, and Empower Board.

188 Lanka Microfinance Practitioners' Association. 2019. Microfinance Review Sri Lanka – Performance and Analysis Report 2019.

189 Survey samples: 4,800 households (individuals aged 18 and above).

Recent capital market growth has been volatile, affected by the uncertain economic conditions associated with a series of shocks like droughts and terror attacks. However, despite the pandemic, the CSE market showed moderate growth in 2020. The CSE All Share Price Index reached 6,774 by end-2020, a 10.5% increase from 2019 and a CAGR of 1.2% from 2011 to 2020 (Figure 7.9A and Table 7.6). Market capitalization (main board plus Diri Savi Board) amounted to SLRs2,961 billion in 2020, a 3.8% increase from 2019 (a 2011–2020 CAGR of 3.3%). Annual trading value increased by 131.5% and volume by 116.6% respectively in 2020; however, the 2011–2020 CAGR was down 3.5% and 1.5% respectively.

There were 283 listed companies (main board plus Diri Savi Board) as of end-2020, with one initial public offering and 7 delisted companies due to the economic shocks (Table 7.9B).

The Diri Savi Board is an equity financing venue for start-ups and medium-sized firms with fewer listing requirements than the main board. Still, firms listed on the Diri Savi Board are larger than SMEs. The CSE launched the Empower Board in 2018 for viable SMEs that require growth capital.

Figure 7.9: Equity Market

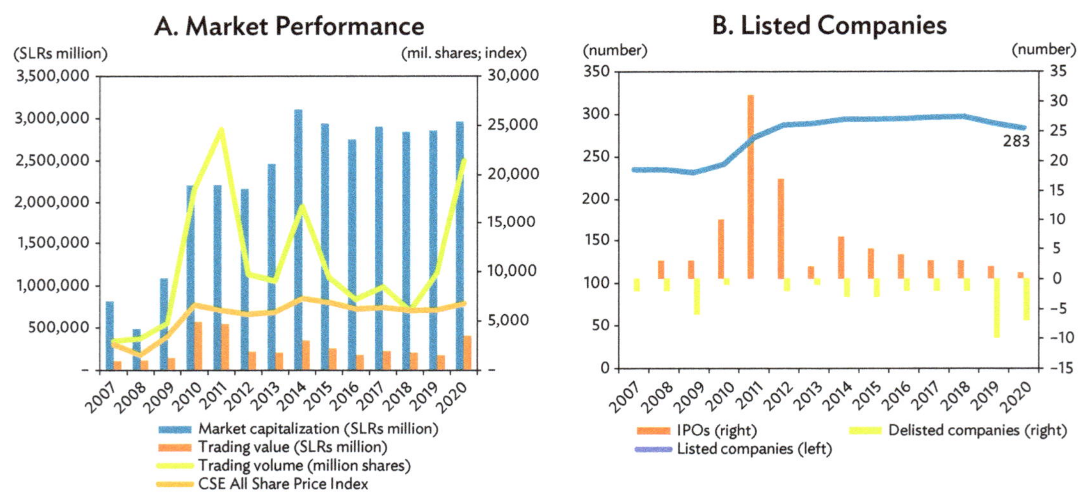

CSE = Colombo Stock Exchange, IPO = initial public offering.

Note: Data include both Main Board and Diri Savi Board. Empower Board was launched in 2018 but no listing as of April 2021.

Source: ADB Asia SME Monitor 2021 database. Data from CSE.

The Empower Board is a sponsor-driven equity market dedicated to SMEs, with various concessional requirements for listing (Table 7.7). Issuers must have stated capital of more than SLRs25 million and less than SLRs100 million at the time of listing. For initial public offerings, required capital should be not less than SLRs10 million at the time of the listing application. The issuer must have positive net assets in audited financial statements for the financial year and at least a 2-year operating history immediately preceding the time of the application. Total assets should be SLRs600 million or less as at the time of the initial listing application.

A unique requirement for listing on the Empower Board is a "sponsor." The application process must be done through a sponsor, which is "a party approved by the CSE as an individual or organization with expertise in the area of listings on the stock exchange and corporate finance" (CSE Empower Board brochure). The sponsor system should help the listing process run smoothly and help ensure quality issuers that can attract a wide range of investors.

However, as of April 2021 there were no listings on the Empower Board. The CSE has been holding several marketing events and seminars nationwide to attract potential SME issuers and to find sponsor institutions.

Financial Infrastructure

The Credit Information Bureau of Sri Lanka (CRIB) provides the core data infrastructure that facilitates MSMEs to access finance. CRIB, established in 1990, has two functions: (i) credit information management and (ii) a secured transactions registry.

The CRIB uses a Credit Information Management System—an advanced information and communication technology-based application—to rapidly provide quality credit information reports to member institutions (banks and financial institutions regulated by the CBSL). Credit reports include (i) credit information reports for member lending institutions (consumer and corporate reports) and (ii) self-inquiry credit reports (iReports) for the general public (individual and corporate reports). They provide details of credit granted to individuals and firms.

CRIB also operates a Secured Transactions Register—"a database, either electronic or in hard copy, in which secured creditors (financial institutions, leasing companies, and private lenders) can give notice of their security interests in the movable goods of an enterprise or individual."[190] The system allows a lender to collateralize a borrower's moveable property. The secured transactions system lets MSMEs access credit by using pledged assets such as personal equipment/goods, harvested crops, account receivables, deposit accounts, licensing rights, intellectual property rights, promissory notes, stock certificates, and warehouse receipts, aside from real estate. The Secured Transactions Act No.49 of 2009 was to help MSMEs access credit.

The NFIS highlights the importance of data infrastructure to boost financial inclusion nationally. It addresses further improvement of the credit information system, secured transactions, and communications infrastructure such as internet coverage and smartphone use.

4. Policies and Regulations

- The National Policy Framework for Small and Medium Enterprise Development 2015 is the benchmark for MSME assistance. The Ministry of Industries is the focal government agency for formulating a national MSME policy framework.
- The National Enterprise Development Authority implements policies under the MSME framework, supporting an enabling business environment for MSMEs, along with access to markets and finance.
- The central bank launched its National Financial Inclusion Strategy in 2021, which includes MSME financing as one of its core pillars.
- The government and central bank acted quickly to contain COVID-19 and curb its impact on the economy using stimulus along with existing and new relief for businesses and individuals.

[190] CRIB website: http://www.crib.lk/en/index.php/our-services/secured-transactions-registery-system

MSME Development

The national economic development program Vision 2025 cited MSME development as part of its growth framework, highlighting the need to formalize, digitalize, and encourage MSMEs to adopt technology. Its targets include (i) increasing per-capita income to $5,000 per year, (ii) creating 1 million new jobs, (iii) increasing foreign direct investment to $5 billion per year, and (iv) doubling export values to $20 billion per year (Table 7.8).

The Enterprise Sri Lanka program supports the creation of new entrepreneurships. It contains both financial (credit) and nonfinancial (technical assistance) support. The program helps both established private enterprises and microenterprises, the self-employed, along with young and women entrepreneurs. It also brought together various independent loan programs under one umbrella.

The Ministry of Industries is the focal government agency for formulating a national MSME policy framework. The ministry promotes domestic industries and strengthens global competitiveness by linking local, regional, and international supply networks through industrial diversification.

The National Policy Framework for Small and Medium Enterprise Development was set up in 2015 under the Ministry of Industries. It includes microenterprises as SMEs. The policy has six core areas for MSME development: (i) an enabling environment (SME friendly laws and regulations); (ii) modern appropriate technology (networking with technology providers, technology transfer and diffusion, and training); (iii) entrepreneurial culture and skills development (women and youth entrepreneurships); (iv) access to finance (expanding SME refinancing schemes, promoting angel/venture capital funds, and concessional bank loans for women and youth entrepreneurships); (v) market facilitation (business linkages with large firms, assisting SMEs access to government procurement, e-commerce, and product development and branding); and (vi) R&D (special fund for SMEs). The policy also addresses two cross-sector areas: (i) regional balance (business development services, new industrial zones and clusters) and (ii) resource efficiency (green technology) in developing SMEs. A May 2016 action plan includes 41 strategies under the six core areas.

The National Enterprise Development Authority implements key policy actions that support an enabling business environment for MSMEs, and their access to markets and finance.

In terms of macroeconomic and financial sector development, the Ministry of Finance also supports MSME development and access to finance. The Department of Development Finance helps provide financial assistance to MSMEs. The Department of Samurdhi Development empowers the disadvantaged and minimizes regional disparities. It offers small loans and microfinancing programs. Similarly, the Department of Cooperative Development under the Ministry of Trade and the Department of Agrarian Development under the Ministry of Agriculture also provide specialized microfinancing programs to the unserved or underserved such as small cooperatives and smallholders.

In addition, several line ministries and government institutions directly or indirectly support MSMEs. The Ministry of Trade plays a critical role in improving market access and promotes a competitive local trade network safeguarding consumer rights. The Sri Lanka Export Development Board under the ministry is responsible for developing and promoting exports, including market access support for MSME exporters. The Industrial Technology Institute, a government-owned institute, supports the development of technology-based MSMEs through advisory and training services on technology transfer, adaptation, and commercialization.

Financial Inclusion

The CBSL, established in 1950, is responsible for maintaining economic and price stability along with a stable financial system. It regulates and supervises banks and nonbank finance institutions through licensing and formulated the National Financial Inclusion Strategy for 2021–2024, which was launched in March 2021 (Table 8).

The strategy has four core pillars for financial inclusion: (i) digital finance and payments; (ii) MSME finance; (iii) consumer protection; and (iv) financial literacy and capacity building. It aims to develop (i) comprehensive and robust data; (ii) strong financial infrastructure (credit bureaus, payment systems, and collateral registries); and (iii) policy tools for an enabling regulatory environment.

There are several bodies implementing the strategy: (i) the National Financial Inclusion Council, (ii) Management Committee, and (iii) Working Groups for the four core pillars. The National Financial Inclusion Council leads policy guidance and strategic direction, co-chaired by the Secretary of the Ministry of Finance and central bank governor. The Management Committee supervises day-to-day implementation of the strategy, comprising senior staff of relevant agencies. The central bank is secretariat of the committee. The Working Groups consult on focal areas for each core pillar. The strategy also has a monitoring and evaluation (M&E) system with four elements: (i) a results framework with key performance indicators, (ii) the mechanics for coordinating and implementing the M&E system, (iii) financial inclusion data, and (iv) evaluating key reforms and programs.

For market-based financing space, the SEC regulates the capital market and supervises the Empower Board of the CSE.

Response to COVID-19

The government and central bank acted quickly to contain COVID-19 and curb its impact on the economy. It strengthened existing relief packages and created new ones for businesses and individuals.

CBSL COVID-19 relief targeted three segments adversely affected by the pandemic and nationwide lockdown: (i) tourism and export-oriented businesses (such as apparel, information technology, tea, spices, plantations, and logistic suppliers); (ii) MSMEs engaged in manufacturing, services, agriculture (including processing), construction, value addition, and trading—including authorized domestic pharmaceutical suppliers with turnover below SLRs1 billion (based on latest available accounts or estimates); and (iii) the self-employed and individuals who lost jobs/income due to the pandemic (Table 7.9).[191]

- **Working capital loans (Saubagya) Phases I–III:** Saubagya COVID-19 Renaissance Facility offered: (i) a new refinancing facility for MSMEs hurt by the COVID-19 outbreak (April 2020 and after); (ii) reduced interest rate applied for sub-loans (June 2020); (iii) a credit guarantee and interest subsidy scheme (June 2020 and afterward); and (iv) extended grace period of 4% working capital loan program from 6 to 9 months (November 2020).
- **Liquidity facility to the construction industry and other government suppliers:** The facility provides funds to commercial banks to satisfy funding needs of government contractors/suppliers in construction, pharmaceuticals, and other sectors. The annual interest rate is 1% from the central bank to commercial banks and 4% from commercial banks to contractors/suppliers. The tenor for commercial banks is 180 days.

[191] CBSL Circular No.5 of 2020.

- **Debt moratorium and financial regulatory measures:** These included deferment of capital and interest payments falling due during the respective concession periods. Self-employed and other individuals who lost their jobs or income due to the COVID-19 outbreak are eligible. A 6-month debt moratorium for affected industries in MSMEs, tourism, apparel, plantations, information technology, and related logistic service providers was also provided.
- **Credit card payments:** This included a debt moratorium on capital and interest, provision of working capital at an annual interest rate of 4%, capping interest rates charged on credit card payments, reducing minimum monthly payments on credit cards, and extending the validity of checks, among others (Circular No.4 of 2020 [March]).
- **Pawnshops:** Licensed banks were instructed to reduce the annual caps on pawnshops to 10% for all new advances and existing facilities that are renewed (Monetary Law Act Order No.02 of 2020 [August]).
- **Payment facilities:** A remittance service provider was granted to provide cash home-delivery services to allow foreign remittances to be delivered to beneficiaries during the period (April 2020). The validity period of checks was extended (May–June 2020).

There were several other COVID-19 policy measures initiated by the CBSL:

- **Measures to reduce interest rates, enhance market liquidity, and finance the government:** The CBSL provided ample liquidity to markets at reduced and concessional interest rates. Large liquidity injections to the banking system enabled banks to provide the support required by businesses and individuals to tide them over during the lockdown.
- **Currency/payments management policy:** The measures allowed the general public to fulfil their currency requirements through bank branches and ATMs even during curfews. The CBSL ensured uninterrupted operations of payments and settlements for both rupee and foreign currency transactions during the pandemic. Several electronic modes of payments were allowed.
- **Public debt management:** The CBSL mobilized large amounts of funds from the domestic money market on behalf of the government to meet its debt service requirements and to meet essential government expenditures.
- **Exchange rate policy, reserve management, and foreign exchange flows:** The CBSL provided all essential services to the economy and financial system during the lockdown.

For capital market, the SEC established a "Taskforce–Better Regulation" to assess the risks emanating from the COVID-19 outbreak. It initiated several measures:

- Issued guidelines on adopting regulatory measures on monitoring credit exposure undertaken by stockbrokers/dealers.
- Relief to public listed companies by granting an extension of time for complying with minimum Public Float requirements and for the submission of Annual Reports.
- Granted a moratorium to clients of all registered margin providers.
- Granted a moratorium to clients of stockbrokers from paying interest on credit.
- Granted relief measures for licensed/registered entities to comply with certain regulatory requirements.
- Extended the timeframe for submitting reports by licensed/registered entities.
- Deferred the SEC's annual licensing/registration fees for 2020 for 1 year.

The Industrial Development Board under the Ministry of Industries also offered several assistance measures:

- Suspended surcharges on industrial park rents over 4 months: Normally, surcharges would be added for late rental payments.
- Conducted trade fairs across the country: It helped industrialists find market opportunities through trade fairs.
- Introduced loan programs to finance MSMEs: it signed a memorandum of understanding with the People's Bank to extend MSME financing.

ADB offered an Emergency Response Facility under the SME Line of Credit Project (December 2020). It provided loans to financial institutions to extend working capital financing to MSMEs.

The prolonged pandemic remains the main risk to economic recovery and MSME development. The government will need to strengthen its phased approach and differentiate policy measures by firm size and sector to help those devastated by the pandemic. The digital transformation of MSMEs is another policy priority, particularly to informal businesses. Government assistance should pay more attention to developing entrepreneurship and creating access to growth capital for viable MSMEs. It needs to find the optimal approach that mobilizes domestic resources and reduces the budgetary burden during the recovery.

Data Tables

Table 7.1: MSME Definition

A. National Definition

Sector	Item	Micro	Small	Medium
Manufacturing	Annual turnover	Less than SLRs15 million	SLRs16 million - SLRs250 million	SLRs251 million - SLRs750 million
	Number of employees	Fewer than 10	11 - 50	51 - 300
Services	Annual turnover	Less than SLRs15 million	SLRs16 million - SLRs250 million	SLRs251 million - SLRs750 million
	Number of employees	Fewer than 10	11 - 50	51 - 200

Source: ADB Asia SME Monitor 2021 Database. Data from National Policy Framework for SME Development, Ministry of Industry and Commerce [present Ministry of Industries], 2015.

B. Definition for Economic Census (2013)

Sector	Item	Micro	Small	Medium
Industry and Construction	Number of persons engaged	1 - 4	5 - 24	25 - 199
Trade	Number of persons engaged	1 - 3	4 - 14	15 - 34
Services	Number of persons engaged	1 - 4	5 - 15	16 - 74

MSME = micro, small, and medium-sized enterprise.

Source: ADB Asia SME Monitor 2021 Database. Data from Economic Census Listing Database, 2013.

Table 7.2: MSME Landscape

End-of-year data

Item	2013[1]	2014[2]	2015[3]	2016[3]	2017[3]	2018[2]	2019	2020
NUMBER OF ENTERPRISES								
Number of enterprises, total	1,019,681	20,325	70,679	73,252	77,290	21,260	...	...
Number of MSMEs	1,017,267	19,251	67,086	69,186	72,407	19,964	...	...
Micro	935,736	...	...	...	...	...	...	...
Small	71,126	14,692	56,516	56,497	58,688	14,890	...	...
Medium	10,405	4,559	10,570	12,689	13,719	5,074	...	...
Number of large enterprises	2,414	1,074	3,592	4,066	4,884	1,296	...	...
MSME to total (%)	99.8	94.7	94.9	94.4	93.7	93.9	...	...
MSME growth (%)	...	...	...	3.13	4.65	...	...	...
MSMEs by sector (% share)								
Agriculture, forestry, and fisheries	...	...	...	...	...	...	...	...
Manufacturing	23.6	...	28.8	28.9	26.8	...	...	...
Transportation and communication	4.2	...	4.0	4.8	5.3	...	...	...
Construction	0.8	...	...	...	...	...	...	...
Wholesale and retail trade	41.1	...	29.8	29.1	29.9	...	...	...
Other services	29.2	...	37.4	37.3	38.0	...	...	...
Others	1.2	...	...	...	...	...	...	...
MSMEs by region (% share)*								
Capital city	13.3	14.3	13.4	19.9	10.2	12.0	...	...
Others	86.7	85.7	86.6	80.1	89.8	88.0	...	...
EMPLOYMENT								
Number of employment, total	3,003,119	1,081,721	2,090,870	2,326,329	2,596,994	1,453,769	...	...
Number of employment by MSMEs	2,255,182	418,432	870,588	949,921	980,332	471,041	...	...
Micro	1,338,675	...	...	...	...	...	...	...
Small	529,751	112,664	423,781	379,127	353,386	114,894	...	...

continued on next page

Table 7.2 *continued*

Item	2013[1]	2014[2]	2015[3]	2016[3]	2017[3]	2018[2]	2019	2020
Medium	386,756	305,769	446,807	570,795	626,945	356,147	...	...
Number of employment by large enterprises	747,937	663,289	1,220,282	1,376,408	1,616,662	982,728	...	...
MSME employees to total (%)	75.1	38.7	41.6	40.8	37.7	32.4	...	...
MSME employees growth (%)	...	...	...	9.11	3.20	...	...	...
Share of female employees to total employees (%)	...	18.6	9.8	10.1	9.5	14.7	...	...
Employment by MSME by sector (% share)								
Agriculture, forestry, and fisheries	...	...	...	...	...	...	...	...
Manufacturing	28.1	...	48.9	50.2	50.4	...	...	...
Transportation and communication	3.4	...	4.1	4.3	3.7	...	...	...
Construction	2.1	...	...	...	...	...	...	...
Wholesale and retail trade	30.8	...	14.8	14.7	15.0	...	...	...
Other services	33.2	...	32.2	30.8	31.0	...	...	...
Others	2.4	...	...	...	...	...	...	...
Employment by MSMEs by region (% share)*								
Capital city	18.5	21.6	19.6	21.6	15.1	13.8	...	...
Others	81.5	78.4	80.4	78.4	84.9	86.2	...	...
CONTRIBUTION TO GDP								
GDP of MSMEs (SLRs million)	...	...	...	...	...	...	...	...
MSME contribution to GDP (% share)	...	...	...	...	...	...	...	...
MSME GDP growth (%)	...	...	...	...	...	...	...	...
MSME GDP by sector (% share)								
Agriculture, forestry, and fisheries	...	...	...	...	...	...	...	...
Manufacturing	...	...	...	...	...	...	...	...
Transportation and communication	...	...	...	...	...	...	...	...
Construction	...	...	...	...	...	...	...	...
Wholesale and retail trade	...	...	...	...	...	...	...	...
Other services	...	...	...	...	...	...	...	...
Others	...	...	...	...	...	...	...	...
MSME GDP by region (% share)								
Capital city	...	...	...	...	...	...	...	...
Others	...	...	...	...	...	...	...	...
EXPORTS								
Total export value (SLRs million)	1,470,967	1,533,668	1,605,147	1,593,234	1,714,147	1,722,275	1,845,686	1,668,855
Total export growth (%)	6.6	4.3	4.7	(0.7)	7.6	0.5	7.2	(9.6)
MSME export value (SLRs million)	...	...	...	...	...	...	...	...
MSME export to total export value (%)	...	...	...	...	...	...	...	...
MSME export growth (%)	...	...	...	...	...	...	...	...
IMPORTS								
Total import value (SLRs million)	2,103,077	2,304,271	2,548,455	2,749,649	2,945,752	2,997,547	2,823,843	2,501,420
Total import growth (%)	(1.5)	9.6	10.6	7.9	7.1	1.8	(5.8)	(11.4)
MSME import value (SLRs million)	...	...	...	...	...	...	...	...
MSME import to total import value (%)	...	...	...	...	...	...	...	...
MSME import growth (%)	...	...	...	...	...	...	...	...

GDP = gross domestic product, MSME = micro, small, and medium-sized enterprise.

1 Data refer to Economic Census 2013.

2 Data refer to manufacturing only (Annual Survey of Industries).

3 Data refer to the sum of manufacturing, trade, and services (Annual Survey of Industries, Annual Survey of Trade, and Annual Survey of Services). The latter two surveys started in 2016 (reference year 2015).

* Colombo municipal area is the capital. By-region data from 2014 to 2018 refer to manufacturing only (Annual Survey of Industries).

Source: ADB Asia SME Monitor 2021 Database. Data from Economic Census 2013; Annual Survey of Industries (for 2014 - 2018), Annual Survey of Trade (for 2015-2017), and Annual Survey of Services (for 2015-2017), Department of Census and Statistics.

Table 7.3: Bank Credit

End-of-year data

Item	2007	2008	2009	2010	2011	2012	2013	2014	2015	2016	2017	2018	2019	2020
OPERATING BANKS														
Number of operating banks, total	37	36	36	31	33	33	33	34	32	32	32	33	32	30
Commercial banks	23	22	22	22	24	24	24	25	25	25	25	26	26	24
Specialized banks	14	14	14	9	9	9	9	9	7	7	7	7	6	6
Credit														
Loans outstanding, total (SLRs million)	1,533,934	1,630,332	1,571,471	1,968,286	2,604,567	3,149,326	3,426,558	3,894,545	4,715,290	5,540,751	6,430,920	7,693,394	8,122,439	9,091,656
Commercial banks	1,365,235	1,453,251	1,382,733	1,760,101	2,335,274	2,830,682	3,079,441	3,453,875	4,258,330	5,007,522	5,791,214	6,980,883	7,362,383	8,289,516
Specialized banks	168,699	177,081	188,738	208,185	269,293	318,644	347,117	440,670	456,961	533,230	639,706	712,511	760,057	802,141
Loans outstanding in domestic currency	...	...	...	...	...	2,590,121	2,803,348	3,077,645	3,777,831	4,535,699	5,253,654	6,156,918	6,487,501	7,291,663
Loans outstanding in foreign currency	...	...	...	...	...	559,205	623,211	816,900	937,460	1,005,053	1,177,266	1,536,476	1,634,938	1,799,993
Loan growth (%)	18.9	6.3	(3.6)	25.3	32.3	20.9	8.8	13.7	21.1	17.5	16.1	19.6	5.6	11.9
Total bank loans to GDP (%)	...	...	...	...	...	...	...	...	...	...	...	...	...	...
Lending rate in domestic currency loan (%, annual average)	...	...	...	...	...	...	...	...	...	...	...	...	...	...
Lending rate in foreign currency loan (%, annual average)	...	...	...	...	...	...	...	...	...	...	...	...	...	...
Gross nonperforming loans (NPLs) (SLRs. million)	77,662	100,727	124,970	104,076	98,306	116,635	191,033	165,474	152,812	142,349	160,672	263,146	381,688	448,062
Gross NPLs to total loans (%)	5.2	6.2	8.0	5.3	3.8	3.7	5.6	4.2	3.2	2.6	2.5	3.4	4.7	4.9
Loans outstanding by sector (% share)														
Agriculture, forestry, and fisheries	4.9	8.9	10.4	13.5	13.0	13.2	12.3	10.4	9.1	8.9	8.6	8.1	7.2	7.7
Manufacturing	16.1	17.2	15.2	12.9	11.9	10.8	11.4	11.4	10.7	10.7	11.2	10.5	9.5	9.5
Transportation and communication[1]	3.5	3.4	2.9	2.6	3.1	2.9	3.9	4.0	4.4	4.4	4.8	3.4	3.3	2.8
Construction	19.1	18.0	17.8	17.8	17.2	18.7	21.0	24.3	25.7	24.9	24.8	23.9	24.4	25.3
Wholesale and retail trade	12.6	12.8	13.3	13.8	11.2	15.2	15.7	15.8	14.9	14.0	14.5	15.0	14.2	12.4
Other services[2]	4.6	5.7	4.7	6.4	6.7	3.3	3.1	3.8	4.6	4.6	4.4	5.1	4.4	5.4
Others	39.1	34.0	35.6	33.1	37.0	35.8	32.6	30.3	30.7	32.5	31.7	33.9	36.9	37.0
Deposits														
Deposits, total (SLRs million)	1,738,900	1,876,664	2,230,815	2,587,093	3,068,669	3,625,374	4,169,520	4,686,306	5,403,131	6,295,559	7,399,006	8,492,427	9,162,264	11,140,932
Deposits in domestic currency (SLRs million)	1,355,237	1,497,168	1,806,130	2,120,843	2,573,601	3,009,996	3,489,550	3,914,396	4,471,076	5,254,085	6,230,629	7,057,748	7,652,090	9,299,197
Deposits in foreign currency (SLRs million)	383,663	379,495	424,685	466,251	495,068	615,378	679,970	771,910	932,055	1,041,474	1,168,377	1,434,679	1,510,174	1,841,735
Deposit rate in foreign currency (%, annual average)	...	...	...	...	...	...	...	...	...	...	...	...	...	...
Deposit rate in domestic currency (%, annual average)	...	...	...	...	...	...	...	...	...	...	...	...	...	...
MSME LOANS*														
MSME loans outstanding, total (SLRs million)	...	...	...	...	...	...	...	...	...	...	...	...	...	743,024
Commercial banks	...	...	...	...	...	...	...	...	...	...	...	...	...	670,463
Specialized banks	...	...	...	...	...	...	...	...	...	...	...	...	...	72,561
MSME loans to total outstanding loans to the private sector (%)[3]	...	...	...	...	...	...	...	...	...	...	...	...	...	11.1
MSME loans to GDP (%)[4]	...	...	...	...	...	...	...	...	...	...	...	...	...	5.0
MSME loan growth (%)	...	...	...	...	...	...	...	...	...	...	...	...	...	...
MSME lending rate - loans outstanding (%, annual average)[5]	...	...	...	...	...	...	...	...	...	...	...	...	...	10.95
MSME lending rate - new loans (%, annual average)[6]	...	...	...	...	...	...	...	...	...	...	...	...	...	8.53
Nonperforming MSME loans (NPLs) (SLRs million)	...	...	...	...	...	...	...	...	...	...	...	...	...	...
MSME NPLs to total MSME loans (%)	...	...	...	...	...	...	...	...	...	...	...	...	...	...
Number of MSME loan borrowers[7]	...	...	...	...	...	...	...	...	...	...	...	...	...	359,349
MSME loan borrowers to total bank borrowers (%)	...	...	...	...	...	...	...	...	...	...	...	...	...	...
MSME loan rejection rate (% of total applications)	...	...	...	...	...	...	...	...	...	...	...	...	...	...
Number of MSME savings account in banks	...	...	...	...	...	...	...	...	...	...	...	...	...	...
Guaranteed MSME loans (SLRs million)	...	...	...	...	...	...	...	...	...	...	...	...	...	...
Non-collateral MSME loans (SLRs million)	...	...	...	...	...	...	...	...	...	...	...	...	...	...
MSME loans outstanding by sector (% share)[8]														
Agriculture	...	...	...	...	...	...	...	...	...	...	...	...	...	11.9
Industry (manufacturing)	...	...	...	...	...	...	...	...	...	...	...	...	...	50.5
Services	...	...	...	...	...	...	...	...	...	...	...	...	...	37.6
MSME loans outstanding by region (% share)														
Capital city	...	...	...	...	...	...	...	...	...	...	...	...	...	...
Others	...	...	...	...	...	...	...	...	...	...	...	...	...	...
MSME loans outstanding by type of use (% share)														
For working capital	...	...	...	...	...	...	...	...	...	...	...	...	...	...
For capital investment	...	...	...	...	...	...	...	...	...	...	...	...	...	...
MSME loans outstanding by tenor (% share)														
Less than 1 year	...	...	...	...	...	...	...	...	...	...	...	...	...	31.0
1-5 years	...	...	...	...	...	...	...	...	...	...	...	...	...	32.6
More than 5 years	...	...	...	...	...	...	...	...	...	...	...	...	...	36.4

GDP = gross domestic product; MSME = micro, small, and medium-sized enterprise.

* Data on MSME loans are based on the SME Credit Survey in 2020. The survey was only based on rupee loans granted by licensed commercial banks (LCBs) and licensed specialized banks (LSBs), excluding refinance schemes of the government and the central bank.

[1] Includes transportation and storage, and information technology and communication servises.

[2] Includes professional, scientific and technical activities and health care, social services and support services.

[3] As a share of total outstanding loans granted to domestic banking units of LCBs and LSBs under the Financial Survey (M4).

[4] Based on provisional GDP at current market prices.

[5] Weighted average interest rate of outstanding loans reported in the SME Credit Survey, by end-2020.

[6] Weighted average interest rate of new loans reported in the SME Credit Survey, by end-2020.

[7] Number of MSME loans.

[8] The SME Credit Survey classified sectors into broad three sectors (agriculture, industry, and services).

Source: ADB Asia SME Monitor 2021 database. Data from Central Bank of Sri Lanka.

Table 7.3a: MSME Loans Disbursed

End-of-year data

Item	2014	2015	2016	2017	2018
MSME loans disbursed, total (SLRs million)	521,385	604,590	719,412	546,024	827,896
MSME loan growth (%)	...	16.0	19.0	(24.1)	51.6
Number of loans, total	208,810	179,074	236,620	141,484	189,321
Average MSME loan size (SLRs)	2,496,935	3,376,202	3,040,369	3,859,263	4,372,975
Average MSME loan size ($)	19,054	23,436	20,296	25,248	23,991
Exchange rate*	131.0	144.1	149.8	152.9	182.3
MSME loans by sector					
Agriculture (SLRs million)	53,075	45,925	55,288	54,010	92,378
Industry (manufacturing) (SLRs million)	100,281	149,787	153,083	139,578	185,955
Services (SLRs million)	232,614	159,293	293,570	76,108	275,809
Others (SLRs million)	135,414	249,585	217,471	276,328	273,753
Agriculture (% share)	10.2	7.6	7.7	9.9	11.2
Industry (manufacturing) (% share)	19.2	24.8	21.3	25.6	22.5
Services (% share)	44.6	26.3	40.8	13.9	33.3
Others (% share)	26.0	41.3	30.2	50.6	33.1

MSME = micro, small, and medium-sized enterprise.

* Exchange rates refer to IMF/IFS, end of period.

Notes: Data for reported commercial and specialized banks only.

For 2018, data from 17 banks: Bank of Ceylon, People's Bank, Regional Development Bank, Lankaputhra Development Bank, Sanasa Development Bank, National Development Bank, DFCC Bank, Commercial Bank of Ceylon, Sampath Bank, Seylan Bank, Hatton National Bank, Standard Chartered Bank, Pan Asia Bank, Cargills, Sri lanka Savings Bank, State Mortgage and Investment Bank, and Amana Bank.

For 2017, data from 14 banks: Bank of Ceylon, People's Bank, Regional Development Bank, Lankaputhra Development Bank, Sanasa Development Bank, National Development Bank, DFCC Bank, Commercial Bank of Ceylon, Sampath Bank, Seylan Bank, Hatton National Bank, Nations Trust Bank, Standard Chartered Bank, and Pan Asia Bank.

For 2016 and 2015, data from 14 banks: Bank of Ceylon, People's Bank, Regional Development Bank, Lankaputhra Development Bank, Sanasa Development Bank, National Development Bank, DFCC Bank, Commercial Bank of Ceylon, Sampath Bank, Seylan Bank, Hatton National Bank, Nations Trust Bank, Standard Chartered Bank, and Union Bank of Colombo.

For 2014, data from 13 banks: Bank of Ceylon, People's Bank, Regional Development Bank, Lankaputhra Development Bank, Sanasa Development Bank, National Development Bank, DFCC Bank, Commercial Bank of Ceylon, Sampath Bank, Seylan Bank, Hatton National Bank, Nations Trust Bank, and Union Bank of Colombo.

Source: ADB Asia SME Monitor 2021 database. Data from various editions of Ministry of Finance Annual Report, Sri Lanka.

Table 7.4: Public Financing

Item	31 Mar 2018	30 Apr 2019	31 Dec 2019
Subsidized Loans			
Number of funds	8	10	18
Number of subsidized loans (new approvals)	...	...	...
Outstanding loans (SLRs million)	...	...	...
Approved loans (SLRs million)	...	...	...
Disbursed loans (SLRs million)	23,885	54,320	88,271
Interest subsidy paid (SLRs million)	...	...	2,525
Number of beneficiaries	9,600	27,850	45,765

Source: ADB Asia SME Monitor 2021 database. Data from Ministry of Finance, Sri Lanka, Annual Reports 2017, 2018, and 2019.

Table 7.4a: Interest Subsidy Loan Schemes

Loan scheme	31 Mar 2018		30 Apr 2019		31 Dec 2019		
	Number of beneficiaries	Amount disbursed (SLRs million)	Number of beneficiaries	Amount disbursed (SLRs million)	Number of beneficiaries	Amount disbursed (SLRs million)	Interest subsidy paid (SLRs million)
Sonduru Piyasa	5,862	1,165	11,831	2,352	21,088	4,199	96.6
Govi Navoda	498	202	2,282	1,744	3,276	2,118	79.3
Ran Aswenna	1,275	3,551	8,824	10,048	12,475	16,645	481.7
Riya Shakthi	537	1,555	802	2,372	914	2,743	188.4
Rivi Bala Savi	390	135	1,070	355	1,307	444	15.8
Jaya Isura	714	17,182	2,200	36,815	2,591	50,162	1,622.2
Madya Aruna	322	96	595	226	737	232	18.4
Green Loan			174	298	326	789	...
Erambuma			58	79	178	235	6.9
Home Sweet Home/ Middle-Income Housing Loan			14	31	678	2,341	...
Diri Saviya	2	1			447	315	1.1
Rekawarana					7	31	...
Singithi Pasala					34	32	0.0
City Ride					7	42	0.3
My Future					275	241	0.0
Sihina Maliga					91	518	...
Working Capital					109	6,634	9.1
Sancharaka Poddo					1,225	552	5.5
Total	9,600	23,885	27,850	54,320	45,765	88,271	2,525.2

Source: Recomposed from Ministry of Finance, Sri Lanka, Annual Reports 2017, 2018, and 2019.

Table 7.4b: Refinancing Scheme—ADB (SME Line of Credit), end-March 2020

Name of PFI	Loan amount allocated (SLRs million)	Loans disbursed		% disbursed	We-Fi grant allocated (SLRs million)	We-Fi grant disbursed		% disbursed
		Number of loans	Amount (SLRs million)			Number of loans	Amount (SLRs million)	
Bank of Ceylon	2,785	596	2,785	100.0	169	194	169	100.0
People's Bank	2,015	284	2,015	100.0	36	20	36	100.0
Regional Development Bank	2,785	1,185	2,764	99.2	117	209	117	100.0
DFCC Bank	3,410	244	3,371	98.8	126	34	121	96.1
Sampath Bank	2,771	158	2,725	98.4	143	33	140	97.9
Hatton National Bank	3,410	257	3,382	99.2	81	28	70	86.4
Commercial Bank	2,785	186	2,780	99.8	156	42	156	100.0
National Development Bank	4,607	386	4,414	95.8	178	51	137	77.0
Seylan Bank	1,637	93	1,637	100.0	127	23	127	100.0
Nations Trust Bank	2,015	102	1,811	89.9	27	6	21	75.9
Total	28,220	3,491	27,682	98.1	1,158	640	1,092	94.3

PFI = participating financial institution, We-Fi = Women Entrepreneur Finance Initiative.

Source: Citation from Ministry of Finance, Sri Lanka, Annual Report 2019.

Table 7.4c: Public Microfinance Programs

Item		2014	2015	2016	2017	2018
Department of Samurdhi Development	Loans outstanding (SLRs million)	128,026	38,320	42,982	54,547	68,206
	Deposits (SLRs million)	54,479	65,034	76,961	87,407	113,993
	Number of borrowers	6,618,730	1,599,058	1,272,504	1,314,357	8,868,512
Department of Cooperative Development	Number of depositors	9,104,024	4,234,029	7,417,540	14,060,141	14,540,246
	Loans outstanding (SLRs million)	37,757	39,406	49,722	75,281	72,788
	Deposits (SLRs million)	89,634	94,685	101,225	113,387	140,434
	Number of borrowers	1,454,695	569,376	548,910	1,347,237	1,193,561
	Number of depositors	8,743,625	9,631,080	9,394,710	9,868,445	9,254,618
Department of Agrarian Development	Loans outstanding (SLRs million)	5,826	976	1,207	1,452	2,122
	Deposits (SLRs million)	328	350	323	680	827
	Number of borrowers	483,250	62,009	571,384	630,806	695,741
	Number of depositors	272,023	253,370	521,101	697,977	802,454
Regional Development Bank	Loans outstanding (SLRs million)	25,881	41,276	106,802	128,343	135,442
	Deposits (SLRs million)	72,544	86,340	43,792	136,582	126,193
	Number of borrowers	466,106	839,664	564,080	576,293	915,720
	Number of depositors	5,228,002	5,676,619	5,730,651	6,263,479	6,653,368
Lankaputhra Development Bank	Loans outstanding (SLRs million)	2,768	3,371	3,740	3,965	3,690
	Deposits (SLRs million)	354	500	396	375	298
	Number of borrowers	7,677	8,555	8,848	8,899	5,565
	Number of depositors	40,244	56,145	63,987	64,530	64,511
Total	Loans outstanding (SLRs million)	200,258	123,349	204,453	263,588	282,248
	Deposits (SLRs million)	217,339	246,909	222,697	338,431	381,745
	Number of borrowers	9,030,458	3,078,662	2,965,726	3,877,592	11,679,099
	Number of depositors	23,387,918	19,851,243	23,127,989	30,954,572	31,315,197

Source: ADB Asia SME Monitor 2021 database. Data from Ministry of Finance, Sri Lanka, Annual Reports 2014-2018.

Table 7.4d: Microfinance Program by Department of Samurdhi Development

Item	2018	2019	2020
Loans outstanding (SLRs million)	68,206	83,555	93,736
Loans disbursed (SLRs million)	264,519	317,915	357,497
Number of loans (new approval)	477,624	693,551	425,835
Total deposits (SLRs million)	113,994	130,918	142,043
Number of deposits (new approval)	4,265,090	1,367,864	350,174

Source: ADB Asia SME Monitor 2021 database. Data from Department of Samurdhi Development.

Table 7.5: Nonbank Finance

End-of-year data

Item	2007	2008	2009	2010	2011	2012	2013	2014	2015	2016	2017	2018	2019	2020
NUMBER OF NONBANK FINANCE INSTITUTIONS														
Financial Institutions regulated by CBSL	52	56	56	58	55	60	58	56	53	53	51	48	49	47
Microfinance institutions	...	...	...	...	...	...	...	...	...	...	...	...	3	4
Finance companies	32	34	35	37	39	47	48	48	46	46	45	43	42	40
Leasing companies	20	22	21	21	16	13	10	8	7	7	6	5	4	3
FINANCIAL INSTITUTIONS REGULATED BY CBSL														
Financing outstanding, total (SLRs billion)	106	128	213	265	388	472	553	641	838	1,006	1,109	1,205	1,200	1,164
Growth (%)	...	20.9	66.2	24.4	46.3	21.4	17.3	16.0	30.6	20.1	10.2	8.7	(0.4)	(3.0)
Total financing to GDP (%)	3.0	2.9	4.4	4.1	5.4	5.4	5.8	6.2	7.6	8.4	8.3	8.4	8.0	7.8
Annual lending rate (%, on average)	...	...	...	...	...	...	...	...	...	...	...	...	...	...
Gross nonperforming financing (NPFs) (SLRs billion)	...	...	6.1	20.9	19.9	23.6	37.0	44.1	47.4	53.0	65.9	93.0	127.6	161.6
Gross NPFs to total loans (%)	...	...	2.8	7.9	5.1	5.0	6.7	6.9	5.7	5.3	5.9	7.7	10.6	13.9
Number of customers financed, total	...	...	...	...	...	...	...	...	...	...	...	...	...	...
MICROFINANCE INSTITUTIONS														
Financing outstanding, total (SLRs billion)	...	...	...	...	...	...	...	...	...	...	...	...	5.6	5.7
Growth (%)	...	...	...	...	...	...	...	...	...	...	...	...	...	1.3
Total financing to GDP (%)	...	...	...	...	...	...	...	...	...	...	...	...	0.04	0.04
Annual lending rate (%, on average)	...	...	...	...	...	...	...	...	...	...	...	...	23.8	22.0
Gross nonperforming loans (NPLs) (SLRs billion)	...	...	...	...	...	...	...	...	...	...	...	...	0.01	0.53
Gross NPLs to total loans (%)	...	...	...	...	...	...	...	...	...	...	...	...	9.8	9.3
Number of customers financed, total	...	...	...	...	...	...	...	...	...	...	...	...	173,131	161,396
FINANCE COMPANIES														
Financing outstanding, total (SLRs billion)	106	128	133	160	271	422	501	580	768	921	1,012	1,163	1,157	1,126
Growth (%)	...	20.9	3.9	19.9	69.1	55.9	18.8	15.7	32.5	19.9	10.0	14.9	(0.5)	(2.7)
Total financing to GDP (%)	3.0	2.9	2.8	2.5	3.7	4.8	5.2	5.6	7.0	7.7	7.6	8.1	7.7	7.5
Annual lending rate (%, on average)	...	...	...	...	...	...	18.4	16.1	18.0	21.0	21.8	19.7	17.6	13.8
Gross nonperforming loans (NPLs) (SLRs billion)	...	...	...	15.6	16.0	21.6	34.2	41.6	46.1	51.7	63.9	91.5	125.8	156.7
Gross NPLs to total loans (%)	...	...	...	9.7	5.9	5.1	6.8	7.2	6.0	5.6	6.3	7.9	10.9	13.9
Number of customers financed, total	...	...	...	...	...	...	...	...	...	...	...	...	...	...
LEASING COMPANIES														
Financing outstanding, total (SLRs billion)	...	...	80	105	118	50	52	62	70	86	96	42	38	33
Growth (%)	...	...	...	31.9	11.8	(57.7)	4.6	18.5	13.1	22.8	12.5	(56.5)	(9.9)	(12.6)
Total financing to GDP (%)	...	...	1.7	1.6	1.6	0.6	0.5	0.6	0.6	0.7	0.7	0.3	0.3	0.2
Annual lending rate (%, on average)	...	...	...	...	...	...	...	...	...	...	...	...	...	...
Gross nonperforming financing (NPFs) (SLRs billion)	...	...	6.1	5.4	3.9	2.0	2.9	2.5	1.4	1.3	2.0	1.5	1.8	4.4
Gross NPFs to total financing (%)	...	...	7.6	5.1	3.3	4.0	5.5	4.0	1.9	1.5	2.1	3.7	4.9	13.3
Number of customers financed, total	...	...	...	...	...	...	...	...	...	...	...	...	...	...

GDP = gross domestic product.

Note: By sector and region data are not available.

Source: ADB Asia SME Monitor 2021 Database. Data from Central Bank of Sri Lanka (CBSL).

Table 7.5a: Microfinance Institutions Loans, Excluding Government Programs*

End-of-year data

Item	2015	2016	2017	2018	2019
Loans outstanding (SLRs million)	82,008	81,144	91,265	86,863	78,448
Growth (%)	...	(1.1)	12.5	(4.8)	(9.7)
Number of borrowers ('000)	2,028	2,860	2,897	2,559	2,335

* excludes government-sponsored programs such as Samurdhi and cultivation loan schemes operated by banks.

Source: Recomposed from Lanka Microfinance Practitioners' Association. 2019. Microfinance Review, Sri Lanka.

Table 7.6: Capital Markets

End-of-year data

Item	2007	2008	2009	2010	2011	2012	2013	2014	2015	2016	2017	2018	2019	2020
EQUITY MARKET														
Main Board - CSE*														
Index [CSE All Share Price Index]	2,540.99	1,503.02	3,385.55	6,635.87	6,074.42	5,643.00	5,912.78	7,298.95	6,894.50	6,228.26	6,369.26	6,052.37	6,129.21	6,774.22
Market capitalization (SLRs million)	820,652	488,813	1,092,138	2,210,452	2,213,873	2,167,581	2,459,897	3,104,864	2,937,998	2,745,406	2,899,291	2,839,446	2,851,313	2,960,648
Growth (%)	...	(40.4)	123.4	102.4	0.2	(2.1)	13.5	26.2	(5.4)	(6.6)	5.6	(2.1)	0.4	3.8
Trading value (SLRs million)	104,985	110,454	142,463	570,327	546,256	213,827	200,468	340,917	253,251	176,935	220,591	200,069	171,408	396,882
Trading volume (million shares)	2,887	3,155	4,763	18,489	24,544	9,691	9,054	16,722	9,415	7,196	8,468	6,001	9,855	21,349
Number of listed companies	235	235	231	241	272	287	289	294	294	295	296	297	289	283
Number of IPOs	0	3	3	10	31	17	2	7	5	4	3	3	2	1
Number of delisted companies	2	2	6	1	0	2	1	3	3	2	2	2	10	7

IPO = initial public offering.

* Data include both Main Board and Diri Savi Board. Empower Board was launched in 2018 but no listing as of April 2021.

Source: ADB Asia SME Monitor 2021 database. Data from Colombo Stock Exchange (CSE).

Table 7.7: Listing Requirements—Colombo Stock Exchange

<table>
<tr><th rowspan="2">Criteria</th><th colspan="3">Stock Trading Boards</th></tr>
<tr><th>Main Board</th><th>Diri Savi Board</th><th>Empower Board</th></tr>
<tr><td></td><td colspan="2">Fully paid, freely transferable, and issued for cash only (for offer of subscription and offer for sale).</td><td></td></tr>
<tr><td>Capital requirement (stated capital)</td><td>Minimum of SLRs500 milion at the point of listing.</td><td>Minimum of SLRs100 milion at the point of listing.</td><td>Above SLRs23 milion and below SLRs200 milion at the time of listing. In the event of an initial public offering, the applicant entity shall have a stated capital of not less than SLRs10 million as at the date of listing application.</td></tr>
<tr><td rowspan="4">Tests</td><td colspan="2">The applicant entity shall satisfy any one of the following tests:</td><td></td></tr>
<tr><td>Profit and net assets test:
1. Net profit after tax as per the audited financial statements of the entity for the three (3) consecutive financial years immediately preceding the date of the initial listing application to the exchange; or

Aggregate net profit after tax as per the audited financial statements of the entity for the three (3) consecutive financial years immediately preceding the date of the initial listing application to the exchange; and
2. Positive net assets as per the audited financial statements of the entity for the last two (2) financial years immediately preceding the date of the initial listing application to the exchange.</td><td>Positive net assets test as per the audited financial statements of the entity for the financial year immediately preceding the date of the initial listing application to the exchange.</td><td>Positive net assets:
• As per the audited financial statements for the financial year immediately preceding the date of application.
• In the event the applicant entity is a parent entity, positive net assets as per the consolidated audited financial statements for the financial year immediately preceding the date of application.</td></tr>
<tr><td>Revenue and market capitalization test:
1. Aggregate revenue of SLRs3 billion as per the audited financial statements of the entity for the three (3) financial years immediately preceding the date of the initial listing application to the exchange; and
2. Market capitalization of SLRs5 billion at time of listing.</td><td>Revenue and market capitalization test:
1. Revenue of SLRs350 million as per the audited financial statements of the entity for the financial year immediately preceding the date of the initial listing application to the exchange; and
2. Market capitalization of SLRs2 billion at the time of listing.</td><td rowspan="2"></td></tr>
<tr><td>Positive operating cash flow (after adjustment for working capital) and market capitalization test:
1. Positive operating cash flow (after adjustment for working capital) as per the audited financial statements of the entity for the two (2) consecutive financial years immediately preceding the date of the initial listing application to the exchange; and
2. Market capitalization of SLRs5 billion at the time of listing.</td><td></td></tr>
<tr><td>Minimum public holding requirement</td><td><table><tr><th>Option</th><th>Float adjusted market capitalization</th><th>Public holding percentage</th><th>Number of public shareholdings</th></tr><tr><td>1</td><td>SLRs10.0 billion</td><td>...</td><td>500</td></tr><tr><td>2</td><td>SLRs7.5 billion</td><td>5%</td><td>500</td></tr><tr><td>3</td><td>SLRs5.0 billion</td><td>7.5%</td><td>500</td></tr><tr><td>4</td><td>SLRs2.5 billion</td><td>10%</td><td>500</td></tr><tr><td>5</td><td>Less than SLRs2.5 billion</td><td>20%</td><td>500</td></tr></table></td><td><table><tr><th>Option</th><th>Float adjusted market capitalization</th><th>Public holding percentage</th><th>Number of public shareholdings</th></tr><tr><td>1</td><td>SLRs1 billion</td><td>7.5%</td><td>200</td></tr><tr><td>2</td><td>Less than SLRs1 billion</td><td>10%</td><td>200</td></tr></table></td><td></td></tr>
<tr><td>Independent auditor's report</td><td colspan="2">The independent auditor's report in the audited financial statements of the entity for the financial year immeidately preceding the date of the initial listing application to the exchange shall not contain an emphasis of matter on going concern.</td><td>An unmodified audit opinion for the financial year immediately preceding the date of the initial listing application or an audit opinion which does not contain an emphasis of matter on "going concern" as set out in the independent auditor's report of audited financial statements contained in the annual report of the entity.</td></tr>
<tr><td>Others</td><td></td><td>In the event the entity is seeking a listing on the exchange by way of an introduction, the entity should ensure that not more than 50% of the shares in the hands of the public shareholders are held by the 3 largest public shareholders of the entity at the time of listing.</td><td>Operating history: At least 2 years immediately preceding the date of application.
Total assets: Of or below SLRs600 million as at the date of the initial listing application.
Sponsor: The application to list securities shall be made through a 'Sponsor' approved by with CSE.</td></tr>
</table>

Source: ADB Asia SME Monitor 2021 database. Data from Colombo Stock Exchange (CSE).For Futher Details:
https://www.cse.lk/pages/main-dirisavi-board/main-dirisavi-board.component.html
https://www.cse.lk/pages/empower-board/empower-board.component.html

Table 7.8: Policies and Regulations

Regulations		
Name	**Outline**	
Industrial Promotion Act, No.46 of 1990	Establish an industrialization commission, set up an advisory council of industry, and set up regional industry service committees, through providing incentives, infrastructure, and the creation of a suiatable environment for the promotion and development of industries, especially export industries.	
National Enterprise Development Authority Act, No.17 of 2006	Stipulate National Enterprise Development Authority activities and promote MSME development in Sri Lanka.	
Sri Lanka Export Development Board Act, No.40 of 1979	Regulate Sri Lanka export business including MSME exporters.	
Co-operative Wholesale Establishment Act, No.44 of 1949	Regulate cooperatives and businesses as exporters/importers and wholesale and retail dealers in goods.	
Co-operative Societies Act, No.5 of 1972	Regulate cooperatives.	
Agrarian Development Act, No.46 of 2000	Stipurate activities of the Department of Agrarian Development.	
Tea Small Holdings Development Act, No.35 of 1975	Establish the Tea Small Holdings Development Authority and regulate its activities.	
Science and Technology Development Act, No.11 of 1994	Promote technology transfer, adaptation of technologies, and the development of new technologies.	
Divineguma Act, No.01 of 2013	Establish a department of divineguma development by amalgamating the Samurdhi Authority, Southern Development Authority, and the Udarata Development Authority. Promote the Samurdhi Program to reduce poverty in Sri Lanka, administered by the Department of Samurdhi Development.	
Microfinance Act, No.6 of 2016	Provide for licensing, regulation, and supervision of microfinance institutions. Registration and regulation of microfinance nongovernment organizations (NGO-MFIs) with limited savings deposits.	
Banking Act, No.30 of 1988	Provide for licensing, regulation, and supervision of banking business. Under the Banking Act, several regulations on MSME bank credit have been set, e.g., maximum credit exposure of lending to MSMEs.	
Securities and Exchange Commission of Sri Lanka Act, No.36 of 1987	Establish the Securities and Exchange Commission of Sri Lanka for the purpose of regulating the securities market.	
Secured Transactions Act No.49 of 2009	Security over movable assets and registry, improve MSME access to credit.	
Regulators and Policymakers		
Name	**Responsibility**	
Ministry of Industries (MOI)	Promote local industry and strengthen global competitiveness by establishing links with local, regional, and international supply networks by diversifying industries. Formulate MSME development policies and funds.	
National Enterprise Development Authority	Promote, support, encourage, and facilitate enterprise development, addressing MSME development.	
Ministry of Trade	Promote a competitive local trade network safeguarding the consumer rights.	
Sri Lanka Export Development Board	Develop and promote exports, including market access support for MSME exporters.	
Cooperative Wholesale Establishment	Supervise cooperative wholesellers and wholesale/retail businesses.	
Department of Cooperative Development	Registrar of cooperatives. Provide microfinancing programs.	
Ministry of Agriculture	Promote agri-business adopting modern technology.	
Department of Agrarian Development	Provide necessary facilities to farmer communities and microfinancing programs.	
Ministry of Plantation	Re-orient the overall plantation industry to open export markets by diversifying value-added production.	
Tea Small Holdings Development Authority	Registrar of tea small holder societies.	
Minister of Education	Promote skills development, vocational education, and research and innovation to creat a skillful society. Priorities include establishing information technology entrepreneurship and making Sri Lanka an innovation hub.	
Industrial Technology Institute	A wholly government-owned institute to elevate the level of technology to that required for rapid industrialization.	
Ministry of Finance	Responsible for macroeconomic policies, annual budget, public financial management, local/foreign savings and investments, public debt, banking, finance and insurance activities, international financial cooperation, and directing social security and economic development activities.	
Department of Development Finance	Responsible for treasury affairs including the facilitation of financial assistance to MSMEs.	
Department of Samurdhi Development	Promote economic development through building up a poverty free prosperous country by empowering disadvantaged people and minimizing regional disparities. Provide small loans and microfinancing programs.	
Central Bank of Sri Lanka (CBSL)	Overseas the financial sector, established in 1950 with responsibility for maintaining economic and price stability and financial system stability. Regulate and supervise banks and nonbank finance institutions. Lead the formulation and implementation of the National Financial Inclusion Strategy including the improvement of MSME financing as one of its four core pillars.	
Security and Exchange Commission of Sri Lanka	Promote, develop, and maintain a capital market that is fair, efficient, orderly, and transparent. Regulate and supervise securities markets, including the Empower Board of the Colombo Stock Exchange.	
Policies		
Name	**Responsible Entity**	**Outline**
Vision 2025: A Country Enriched	Government of Sri Lanka	A national economic development program, with targets of (i) per-capita income to $5,000 per year, (ii) creation of 1 million new jobs, (iii) increase of foreign direct investment (FDI) to $5 billion per year, and (iv) double of export values to $20 billion per year. (a) Strengthening the macroeconomic framework. (b) Strengthening the growth framework (empower the private sector): - integrate SMEs into the formal sector. - establish a conducive institutional framework for SMEs in the tourism industry to flourish.

continued on next page

Table 7.8 *continued*

		(c) Reforms in land, labor, and capital markets. (d) Economic and social infrastructure (education and skills development; empowering the youth). (e) Technology and digitalization (enhanced digital ecosystems, empowering the self-employed and SMEs): - promote private sector investment in digital technology. - continue the national digital identity initiative. - strengthen ICT-based marketing interfaces (technical support for SMEs). - encourage innovations in mobile payment systems and peer-to-peer lending platforms. (f) Social safety nets. (g) Agriculture and sustainable development: - help smallholders in the tea, rubber, and non-traditional exports. - promote a Smallholder Agribusiness Partnership (SAP) project to enhance competitiveness. - establish a new development bank (particularly for SMEs). - establish regional technology centers (improving SME access to new technology). - implement strategies for financial inclusion (soft loan programs for SMEs; SME credit guarantees). (h) Governance and accountability. (i) Strengthen coordination and monitor implementation.
Enterprise Sri Lanka (2017)	Government of Sri Lanka	A program to revitalize the latent entrepreneurship capacities of Sri Lankans containing both financial support via credit schemes and non financial support via technical assistance. The program facilitates not only the established private sector enterprises but also microenterprises, the self-employed, young entrepreneurs, women entrepreneurs, and disabled entrepreneurs. Various independent loan programs have been unified under the "Enterprise Sri Lanka" theme: 23 programs including 18 interest subsidies, 3 donor-funded refinancing programs, and 2 financial plus nonfinancial support programs (as of 2018).
National Policy Framework for Small and Medium Enterprise Development (2015)	MOI	Six core areas for MSME development: (i) Enabling environment (SME friendly laws and regulations). (ii) Modern appropriate technology (networking with technology providers; technology transfer/diffusion; training). (iii) Entrepreneurial culture and skills development (women and youth entrepreneurship development). (iv) Access to finance (expanding SME refinancing schemes; promoting angel/venture capital funds; concessional bank loans for women and youth entrepreneurships). (v) Market facilitation (business linkages with large firms; assisting SMEs access to government procurement; e-commerce; product development/branding). (vi) Research and development (special fund to SMEs). Two cross-sector areas: (a) Regional balance (business development services; new industrial zones/clusters). (b) Resource efficiency (green technology) in developing SMEs. Action plan was formulated in May 2016: 6 core areas and 41 strategies.
National Financial Inclusion Strategy for Sri Lanka 2021-2024 (March 2021)	CBSL	Four core pillars for financial inclusion: (i) Digital finance and payments. (ii) MSME finance. (iii) Consumer protection. (iv) Financial literacy and capacity building. Three core enablers: (i) Comprehensive and robust data. (ii) Strong financial infrastructure (credit bureaus; payment systems; collateral registries). (iii) Policy tools and an enabling regulatory environment. Coordination mechanism: (a) National Financial Inclusion Council; Management Committee; 4 Working Groups (each core pillar). (b) Management Committee (Secretariat: CBSL). (c) Four Working Groups (for each core pillar).

( ) = year when the program/initiative was launched.

Source: ADB Asia SME Monitor 2021 database. Data from the Gazette of the Democratic Socialist Republic of Sri Lanka (October 2020); Ministry of Industries; Central Bank of Sri Lanka; Ministry of Finance Annual Reports (2017 and 2018).

Table 7.9: COVID-19 Emergency Measures

Name	Fund Size (SLRs billion)	Outline
Central Bank of Sri Lanka (CBSL)		
A. COVID-19 Relief Measures		Eligible for MSMEs engaged in business sectors such as manufacturing, services, agriculture (including processing), construction, value addition, and trading businesses including authorized domestic pharmaceutical suppliers with turnover below SLRs1 billion (for this annual turnover is considered based on the latest available accounts or estimates).
(a) Working capital loans (Saubagya) Phases I - III	176	Saubagya (Prosperity) COVID-19 Renaissance Facility:
		(i) a new refinancing facility for MSMEs adversely affected by the COVID-19 outbreak (April 2020 -).
		(ii) reduced interest rate applied for sub-loans (June 2020).
		(iii) a credit guarantee and interest subsidy scheme (June 2020 -)
		(iv) extended grace period of 4% working capital loan scheme from 6 to 9 months (November 2020).
(b) Liquidity facility to the construction sector and other suppliers of the government	...	Provide funds to commercial banks to satisfy funding needs of contractors/suppliers of the government in construction, pharmaceuticals, and other sectors. Annual interest rate: 1% from central bank to commercial banks; 4% from commercial banks to contractors/suppliers. Duration of liquidity facility to commercial banks: 180 days.
(c) Debt moratorium and financial sector regulatory measures	...	Deferment of capital/interest payments which fall due within respective concession periods. Eligible for self-employed and other individuals who have lost jobs or income due to the COVID-19 outbreak. A 6-month debt moratorium for affected industries in MSMEs, tourism, apparel, plantation, information technology, and related logistic service providers.
(d) Credit card payments	...	Included a debt moratorium on capital and interest, provision of working capital at an annual interest rate of 4%, capping of interest rates charged on credit card payments, reducing minimum monthly payment dues on credit cards, extended check validity, etc. (Circular No.4 of 2020 [March]).
(e) Pawning facilities	...	Licensed banks were instructed to reduce the annual caps on pawnshops and other facilities to 10% for all new pawn advances and existing pawnshop facilities that are renewed. (Monetary Law Act Order No.02 of 2020 [August]).
(f) Payment facilities	...	A remittance service provider provides cash home-delivery services allowing disbursement of foreign remittances to be delivered to beneficiaries during the period (April 2020). Validity period of checks extended (May-June 2020).
B. COVID-19 Policy Measures		
(a) Measures to reduce interest rates, enhance market liquidity, and finance the government.	...	CBSL provided ample market liquidity at reduced and concessional interest rates. Large liquidity injections to the banking system enabled banks to provide the support required by businesses and individuals to tide them during the lockdown period.
(b) Currency/payments management policy	...	The measures allowed the general public to fulfil their currency requirements through bank branches and automated teller machines (ATMs) even during curfews. The CBSL ensured uninterrupted operation of payments and settlements for both rupee and foreign currency transactions during the pandemic. Several electronic modes of payments were promoted and facilitated.
(c) Public debt management	...	CBSL mobilized a large amount of funds from the domestic money market on behalf of the government to meet debt service requirements and to meet essential government expenditures.
(d) Exchange rate policy, reserve management, and foreign-exchange flows	...	CBSL provided its full scope of essential services to the economy and the financial system during the lockdown.
Securities and Exchange Commission of Sri Lanka (SEC)		
The SEC has set up a "Taskforce – Better Regulation" (TFBR) to assess the risks emanating from the COVID-19 outbreak.		
(a) Issued guidelines on adopting regulatory measures on monitoring credit exposure undertaken by stockbrokers/dealers.		
(b) Relief to public listed companies by granting an extension of time for complying with minimum Public Float requirements and for the submission of Annual Reports.		
(c) Granted a moratorium to clients of all registered margin providers.		
(d) Granted a moratorium to clients of stockbrokers from the payment of interest on credit.		
(e) Granted relief measures taking into consideration the constraints and administrative challenges faced by the licensed/registered entities in complying with certain regulatory requirements.		
(f) The timeframe for submission of reports by licensed/registered entities was extended.		
(g) A deferment of the SEC's annual licensing/registration fees for the year 2020 was granted on the core-regulated activity of all licensed/registered entities for 1 year.		
Industrial Development Board (IDB), Ministry of Industries		
(a) Suspended surcharge on industrial park's rental payment over 4 months.	...	Normally, a surcharge is added to the rents of industries located in the industrial estate for late payment.
(b) Conducting trade fairs covering all the districts of the country.	...	Facilitate industrialists to find market opportunities by holding trade fairs.
(c) Introducing loan scheme to finance MSMEs	...	IDB has signed a memorandum of understanding (MOU) with the People's Bank to extend financing to MSMEs.
Donor financial assistance (Asian Development Bank)		
Emergency Response Facility under the SME Line of Credit Project (December 2020)	20 (approximately)	Provide loans to financial institutions to extend working capital financing to MSMEs.

MSME = micro, small, and medium-sized enterprise.

Source: ADB Asia SME Monitor 2021 database. Data from Central Bank of Sri Lanka website (https://www.cbsl.gov.lk/en/covid-19-measures), Securities and Exchange Commission of Sri Lanka website (https://www.sec.gov.lk/index.php/sec-covid-19-response/), Industrial Development Board, and Department of Development Finance.

Appendix: Regional Data Tables

A. MSME Landscape

A1. Number of MSMEs

Country	2003	2004	2005	2006	2007	2008	2009	2010	2011	2012	2013	2014	2015	2016	2017	2018	2019	2020
Southeast Asia																		
Brunei Darussalam	...	...	...	...	...	...	...	5,427	...	...	...	...	5,248	5,721	5,876	5,913	5,990	...
Cambodia	...	...	...	...	...	...	376,069	...	462,582	...	...	512,870	...	...	...	...	...	...
Indonesia	...	...	...	...	...	...	...	52,764,750	54,114,821	55,206,444	56,534,592	57,895,721	59,262,772	61,651,177	62,922,617	64,194,057	65,465,497	...
Lao People's Democratic Republic	...	...	...	126,717	...	...	...	...	...	...	124,510	...	...	...	...	124,567	...	133,721
Malaysia	548,267	...	...	...	...	...	...	638,790	...	...	...	...	907,065	...	...	...	...	1,151,339
Myanmar*	...	...	...	39,949	40,811	40,529	40,396	39,272	38,978	38,590	38,654	39,062	39,162	59,694	61,949	71,290	75,116	...
Philippines	...	...	...	780,469	781,201	758,436	777,357	774,664	816,759	940,886	937,327	942,925	896,839	911,768	920,677	998,342	995,745	996,701
Singapore	...	...	...	...	...	...	...	...	...	...	...	242,800	246,200	247,800	254,100	262,400	272,000	279,700
Thailand	...	...	...	...	2,366,227	2,827,633	2,896,106	2,913,167	2,646,549	2,730,591	2,763,997	2,736,744	2,765,986	3,004,679	3,046,790	3,077,822	3,105,096	3,134,442
Viet Nam	...	...	...	...	143,622	186,379	230,365	272,283	316,941	338,916	365,181	393,915	433,453	495,010	544,212	593,865	651,138	...
South Asia																		
Bangladesh	...	...	...	...	...	...	...	...	...	...	7,813,315	...	...	...	...	...	...	...
India*	...	...	...	...	...	36,176,000	37,736,000	39,370,000	41,080,000	42,873,000	44,764,000	46,754,000	48,846,000	51,057,000	51,299,000	63,387,673	...	...
Nepal*	...	...	...	...	...	...	...	156,343	171,004	189,026	204,582	226,711	244,365	268,682	300,721	337,864	390,493	...
Pakistan	...	...	3,210,000	...	...	...	...	...	...	...	...	...	...	...	...	...	...	5,200,000
Sri Lanka	...	...	...	...	...	...	...	...	...	...	1,017,267	...	...	...	...	...	...	...

MSME = micro, small, and medium-sized enterprise.

Note: End-of-year data except * fiscal year data (ended 31 March in India and Myanmar, and 15 July in Nepal).

.A2. MSMEs to Total (%)

Country	2003	2004	2005	2006	2007	2008	2009	2010	2011	2012	2013	2014	2015	2016	2017	2018	2019	2020
Southeast Asia																		
Brunei Darussalam	...	...	...	...	...	...	...	97.5	...	...	...	...	96.6	97.0	97.2	97.3	97.3	...
Cambodia	...	...	...	...	...	...	99.8	...	99.8	...	...	99.8	...	...	...	...	...	...
Indonesia	...	...	...	...	...	...	...	99.99	99.99	99.99	99.99	99.99	99.99	99.99	99.99	99.99	99.99	...
Lao People's Democratic Republic	...	...	...	99.8	...	...	...	...	...	...	99.8	...	...	...	...	99.8	...	99.8
Malaysia	99.2	...	...	...	...	...	...	98.5	...	...	...	...	98.5	...	...	...	...	97.2
Myanmar*	...	...	...	92.0	92.0	91.8	91.6	90.3	89.1	88.4	87.9	87.4	87.1	90.2	89.6	90.1	89.9	...
Philippines	...	...	...	99.7	99.7	99.6	99.6	99.6	99.6	99.6	99.6	99.6	99.5	99.6	99.6	99.5	99.5	99.5
Singapore	...	...	...	...	...	...	...	...	...	...	...	99.5	99.4	99.5	99.5	99.5	99.5	99.5
Thailand	...	...	...	...	99.6	99.7	99.8	99.6	99.8	97.2	97.2	99.7	99.7	99.7	99.8	99.8	99.5	99.5
Viet Nam	...	...	...	...	96.3	97.0	97.4	97.5	97.6	97.7	97.8	97.9	98.0	98.0	97.1	97.2	97.4	...
South Asia																		
Bangladesh	...	...	...	...	...	...	...	...	...	...	99.97	...	...	...	...	...	...	...
India	...	...	...	...	...	...	...	...	...	...	...	...	...	99.9	...	...	...	...
Nepal	...	...	...	...	...	...	...	...	...	...	...	...	...	...	...	...	...	...
Pakistan	...	...	99.1	...	...	...	...	...	...	...	...	...	...	...	...	...	...	98.6
Sri Lanka	...	...	...	...	...	...	...	...	...	...	99.8	...	...	...	...	...	...	...

MSME = micro, small, and medium-sized enterprise.

Note: End-of-year data except * fiscal year data (ended 31 March in Myanmar).

A3. MSMEs by Sector (% share, latest available year)

Item / Southeast Asia	Brunei Darussalam	Cambodia	Indonesia	Lao People's Democratic Republic	Malaysia	Myanmar	Philippines	Singapore	Thailand	Viet Nam
Agriculture	2.8	...	...	1.4	1.7	...	0.9	...	1.8	1.1
Manufacturing	10.7	13.9	16.7	14.7	5.1	...	11.6	...	17.0	15.7
Transportation and communication	5.5	...	7.3	3.0	...	...	...	...	...	7.9
Construction	9.9	...	0.9	1.7	7.4	...	...	...	...	13.7
Wholesale and retail trade	34.7	59.6	63.5	61.2	85.5	...	46.4	...	41.1	37.5
Other services	35.1	26.5	10.7	3.2	...	...	40.4	...	40.1	22.8
Others	1.3	...	0.9	14.8	0.3	...	0.7	...	...	1.2
Year	2019	2014	2016	2020	2020		2020		2020	2019

Item / South Asia	Bangladesh	India*	Nepal*	Pakistan	Sri Lanka
Agriculture	...	...	16.3	1.0	...
Manufacturing	11.1	31.0	33.2	20.0	23.6
Transportation and communication	16.9	...	...	2.0	4.2
Construction	0.1	...	3.0	0.1	0.8
Wholesale and retail trade	45.9	36.3	...	53.0	41.1
Other services	25.7	32.6	46.7	22.0	29.2
Others	0.3	0.01	0.7	1.9	1.2
Year	2013	FY 2018	FY 2019	2005	2013

MSME = micro, small, and medium-sized enterprise.

Notes: End-of-year data except * fiscal year (FY) data (ended 31 March in India and 15 July in Nepal). For Malaysia, "Wholesale and retail trade" includes transportation and storage, telecommunication, and real estate. For Nepal, "Others" include energy-based, mining and minerals; other services include information and technology, and tourism.

A4. MSMEs by Region (% share, latest available year)

Item / Southeast Asia	Brunei Darussalam	Cambodia	Indonesia	Lao People's Democratic Republic	Malaysia	Myanmar*	Philippines	Singapore	Thailand	Viet Nam
Capital city	...	18.8	...	22.3	14.7	15.3	20.3	...	18.0	...
Other areas	...	81.2	...	77.7	85.3	84.7	79.7	...	82.0	...
Year		2014		2020	2015	FY2019	2020		2020	

Item / South Asia	Bangladesh	India*	Nepal*	Pakistan	Sri Lanka
Capital city	28.5	48.8	19.5	0.6	13.3
Other areas	71.5	51.3	80.5	99.4	86.7
Year	2013	FY 2018	FY 2019	2005	2013

MSME = micro, small, and medium-sized enterprise.

Notes: End-of-year data except * fiscal year (FY) data (ended 31 March in India and Myanmar, and 15 July in Nepal). Capital city: Phnom Penh in Cambodia, Vientiane in Lao People's Democratic Republic, Kuala Lumpur in Malaysia, Yangon in Myanmar, National Capital Region in the Philippines, Bangkok in Thailand, Kathmandu in Nepal, Islamabad in Pakistan, Colombo in Sri Lanka. For Bangladesh and India, Urban/Rural.

A5. Number of Employees by MSMEs

Country	2003	2004	2005	2006	2007	2008	2009	2010	2011	2012	2013	2014	2015	2016	2017	2018	2019	2020
Southeast Asia																		
Brunei Darussalam	...	...	...	...	...	...	...	59,179	...	...	...	...	64,722	65,486	66,123	64,392	64,517	...
Cambodia	...	...	...	...	...	...	1,099,647	...	1,158,871	...	...	1,345,100	...	...	...	...	...	...
Indonesia	...	...	...	...	...	...	...	96,193,623	98,238,913	101,722,458	107,657,509	114,144,082	123,229,386	112,828,610	116,431,224	116,978,631	119,562,843	...
Lao People's Democratic Republic	...	...	...	238,703	...	...	...	...	...	...	472,231	...	...	...	...	472,529	...	...
Malaysia	...	...	...	...	...	...	...	...	...	...	...	...	6,527,000	6,663,000	6,889,000	7,108,000	7,319,000	7,253,000
Myanmar	...	...	...	...	...	...	...	...	...	...	...	...	...	...	...	...	...	...
Philippines	...	...	...	3,327,855	3,355,742	3,395,505	3,595,641	3,532,935	3,872,406	4,930,851	4,770,445	4,891,836	4,784,870	4,879,179	4,922,251	5,714,262	5,510,760	5,525,497
Singapore	...	...	...	...	...	...	...	...	...	...	...	2,450,000	2,470,000	2,480,000	2,470,000	2,480,000	2,520,000	2,360,000
Thailand	...	...	...	...	8,900,567	...	9,701,354	10,507,507	10,995,977	11,783,143	11,414,702	10,501,166	10,749,735	11,747,093	13,088,802	13,950,241	12,060,369	12,714,916
Viet Nam	...	...	...	...	2,834,950	3,347,883	3,872,711	4,394,037	5,060,430	5,107,958	5,179,702	5,321,882	5,682,980	6,205,320	5,538,134	5,627,952	5,681,518	...
South Asia																		
Bangladesh	...	...	...	...	...	...	...	...	...	...	21,033,994	...	...	...	...	...	...	...
India*	...	...	...	...	...	80,523,000	84,200,000	88,084,000	92,179,000	96,515,000	101,169,000	106,140,000	111,429,000	117,132,000	111,228,000	110,989,000.0	...	...
Nepal*	...	...	...	...	...	1,761,863	1,843,908	1,914,469	1,987,387	2,062,497	2,140,706	2,157,744	2,263,363	2,337,373	2,466,992	2,606,086	2,808,052	...
Pakistan*	...	...	...	...	...	...	...	...	...	...	...	...	24,066,900	...	...	27,324,000	...	...
Sri Lanka	...	...	...	...	...	...	...	...	...	...	2,255,182	...	...	...	...	...	...	...

MSME = micro, small, and medium-sized enterprise.

Note: End-of-year data except * fiscal year data (ended 31 March in India, 15 July in Nepal, and 30 June in Pakistan).

A6. MSME Employees to Total (%)

Country	2003	2004	2005	2006	2007	2008	2009	2010	2011	2012	2013	2014	2015	2016	2017	2018	2019	2020
Southeast Asia																		
Brunei Darussalam	...	...	...	...	...	...	...	59.4	...	...	...	...	55.1	56.5	57.3	57.7	55.6	...
Cambodia	...	...	...	...	...	...	74.8	...	72.0	...	...	71.8	...	...	...	...	...	...
Indonesia	...	...	...	...	...	...	...	97.3	97.3	97.2	97.2	97.0	96.7	97.0	96.8	97.0	96.9	...
Lao People's Democratic Republic	...	...	...	87.4	...	...	...	...	...	...	82.9	...	...	...	...	82.4	...	...
Malaysia	56.4	56.6	56.8	56.9	58.2	58.9	58.0	55.5	57.3	57.2	57.5	63.8	46.6	47.0	47.6	48.0	48.4	48.0
Myanmar	...	...	...	...	...	...	...	...	...	...	...	...	...	...	...	...	...	...
Philippines	...	...	...	66.8	64.7	61.2	63.2	62.3	61.0	64.9	63.7	62.8	61.6	63.3	62.8	63.2	62.4	62.8
Singapore	...	...	...	...	...	...	...	...	...	...	...	72.1	72.2	72.3	72.2	71.7	71.6	70.4
Thailand	...	...	...	...	76.0	--	78.2	77.9	83.9	81.0	81.0	80.3	80.4	78.5	82.2	85.5	69.5	71.7
Viet Nam	...	...	...	...	39.2	42.1	44.4	45.1	46.8	46.4	45.2	44.2	44.2	44.3	38.1	38.0	37.5	...
South Asia																		
Bangladesh	...	...	...	...	...	...	...	...	...	...	85.9	...	...	...	...	...	...	...
India*	...	...	...	...	...	...	...	...	...	...	...	...	...	...	...	...	...	...
Nepal*	...	...	...	...	...	...	...	...	...	...	...	...	...	...	...	...	...	73.5
Pakistan*	...	...	...	...	...	...	...	...	...	...	...	...	72.6	...	...	72.0	...	...
Sri Lanka	...	...	...	...	...	...	...	...	...	...	75.1	...	...	...	...	...	...	...

MSME = micro, small, and medium-sized enterprise.

Notes: End-of-year data except * fiscal year data (ended 31 March in India, 15 July in Nepal, and 30 June in Pakistan). Notes: For Malaysia, data in 2015-2019 was revised based on a methodology change. Revised data include the government, informal sector excluding agriculture, unregistered businesses in agriculture, and outsourcing activities in computing the overall employment which signified as denominator. For Nepal, data was extracted from the Industrial Statistics 2019-2020, and small and medium-sized enterprises only.

A7. MSME Employees by Sector (% share, latest available year)

Item/Southeast Asia	Brunei Darussalam	Cambodia	Indonesia	Lao People's Democratic Republic	Malaysia	Myanmar	Philippines	Singapore	Thailand	Viet Nam
Agriculture	1.5	...	...	2.1	10.7	...	1.9	...	0.5	1.5
Manufacturing	10.4	15.2	20.5	22.5	16.4	...	13.5	...	22.5	25.4
Transportation and communication	5.8	...	4.7	3.1	...	...	...	...	...	8.3
Construction	15.3	...	...	2.8	9.3	...	...	...	...	17.3
Wholesale and retail trade	30.9	46.7	54.4	46.6	63.3	...	36.1	...	33.4	24.2
Other services	33.2	38.1	19.5	1.8	...	...	45.4	...	43.7	21.6
Others	2.8	...	0.9	21.1	0.3	...	3.0	...	...	1.7
Year	2019	2014	2016	2020	2020		2020		2020	2019
Item / South Asia	**Bangladesh**	**India***	**Nepal**	**Pakistan***	**Sri Lanka**					
Agriculture	...	...	...	...	...					
Manufacturing	20.3	32.5	...	22.8	28.1					
Transportation and communication	9.4	...	...	11.5	3.4					
Construction	0.2	...	...	16.2	2.1					
Wholesale and retail trade	39.9	34.9	...	32.5	30.8					
Other services	29.9	32.6	...	16.0	33.2					
Others	0.4	0.01	...	1.0	2.4					
Year	2013	FY 2018		FY 2018	2013					

MSME = micro, small, and medium-sized enterprise.

Notes: End-of-year data except * fiscal year (FY) data (ended 31 March in India and 30 June in Pakistan). For Malaysia, "Wholesale and retail trade" includes transportation and storage, telecommunication, and real estate.

A8. MSME Employees by Region (% share, latest available year)

Item/Southeast Asia	Brunei Darussalam	Cambodia	Indonesia	Lao People's Democratic Republic	Malaysia	Myanmar	Philippines	Singapore	Thailand	Viet Nam
Capital city	...	20.0	...	...	15.7	...	27.8	...	28.3	...
Other areas	...	80.0	...	...	84.3	...	72.2	...	71.7	...
Year		2014			2015		2020		2020	
Item / South Asia	**Bangladesh**	**India***	**Nepal**	**Pakistan**	**Sri Lanka**					
Capital city	34.4	44.9	...	...	18.5					
Other areas	65.6	55.2	...	...	81.5					
Year	2013	FY 2018			2013					

MSME = micro, small, and medium-sized enterprise.

Notes: End-of-year data except * fiscal year (FY) data (ended 31 March in India). Capital city: Phnom Penh in Cambodia, Kuala Lumpur in Malaysia, National Capital Region (NCR) in the Philippines, Bangkok in Thailand, Colombo in Sri Lanka. For Bangladesh and India, Urban/Rural.

A9-1. GDP of MSMEs (local currency)

Country	2003	2004	2005	2006	2007	2008	2009	2010	2011	2012	2013	2014	2015	2016	2017	2018	2019	2020
Southeast Asia																		
Brunei Darussalam	...	...	...	...	...	...	...	3,233	3,472	3,808	3,984	...	3,612	5,399	5,323	5,129	4,956	...
Cambodia	...	...	...	...	...	...	...	...	...	...	...	...	...	...	...	...	...	...
Indonesia	...	...	...	...	...	...	...	2,969,346	3,411,575	4,321,830	4,869,568	5,440,008	6,228,285	7,009,283	7,820,283	8,573,895	9,580,763	...
Lao People's Democratic Republic	...	...	...	...	...	...	...	...	...	...	...	...	...	...	...	...	...	...
Malaysia	190,199	205,999	220,213	234,359	257,883	274,766	275,324	298,180	319,832	339,121	360,916	409,776	435,072	458,686	491,568	522,415	553,458	512,798
Myanmar	...	...	...	...	...	...	...	...	...	...	...	...	...	...	...	...	...	...
Philippines	...	...	...	751,943	...	...	...	...	...	...	...	...	...	...	...	...	...	...
Singapore	...	...	...	...	...	...	...	...	...	...	...	180	181	191	201	204	201	183
Thailand	...	...	...	...	3,758,130	3,863,743	3,858,146	4,258,542	4,445,932	4,831,990	5,044,252	5,261,090	5,631,426	6,099,185	6,557,750	7,013,971	5,963,156	5,376,066
Viet Nam	...	...	...	...	...	...	...	...	...	...	...	...	...	...	...	...	...	...
South Asia																		
Bangladesh*	...	...	...	...	...	...	...	...	...	225,691	245,579	261,131	283,426	309,094	339,458	370,864	411,480	443,476
India*	...	...	...	...	...	24,366	25,621	27,582	30,457	25,833	27,584	29,169	30,888	33,517	36,001	39,196	42,322	...
Nepal	...	...	...	...	...	...	...	...	...	...	...	...	...	...	...	...	...	...
Pakistan	...	...	...	...	101,162	122,473	145,946	167,383	208,611	241,951	283,107	327,030	373,595	406,648	457,088	506,839	571,951	621,977
Sri Lanka	...	...	...	...	...	...	...	...	...	...	...	...	...	...	...	...	...	...

GDP = gross domestic product; MSME = micro, small, and medium-sized enterprise.

Notes: End-of-year data except * fiscal year data (ended 30 June in Bangladesh and 31 March in India). For Malaysia, real GDP data. For Singapore, nominal value added of SMEs. For Bangladesh, manufacturing gross value added of cottage and small enterprises. For Pakistan, GDP of small manufacturing only. Brunei Darussalam: B$ million; Indonesia: Rp billion; Malaysia: RM million; Philippines: P million; Singapore: S$ billion; Thailand: B million; Bangladesh: Tk million; India: Rs billion; Pakistan: PRs million.

A9-2. GDP of MSMEs ($ million)

Country	2003	2004	2005	2006	2007	2008	2009	2010	2011	2012	2013	2014	2015	2016	2017	2018	2019	2020
Southeast Asia																		
Brunei Darussalam	...	...	...	...	...	...	...	2,503	2,669	3,113	3,139	...	2,555	3,733	3,982	3,748	3,672	...
Cambodia	...	...	...	...	...	...	...	...	...	...	...	...	...	...	...	...	...	...
Indonesia	...	...	...	...	...	...	...	330,258	376,221	446,932	399,505	437,300	451,489	521,679	577,228	592,079	689,214	...
Lao People's Democratic epublic	...	...	...	...	...	...	...	...	...	...	...	...	...	...	...	...	...	...
Malaysia	50,052	54,210	58,257	66,362	77,993	79,320	80,398	96,702	100,671	110,887	109,985	117,246	101,368	102,248	121,016	126,233	135,237	127,784
Myanmar	...	...	...	...	...	...	...	...	...	...	...	...	...	...	...	...	...	...
Philippines	...	...	...	15,305	...	...	...	...	...	...	...	...	...	...	...	...	...	...
Singapore	...	...	...	...	...	...	...	...	...	...	...	136,229	128,015	130,678	149,633	149,472	149,198	138,416
Thailand	...	...	...	...	111,456	110,716	115,792	141,239	140,289	157,745	153,724	159,606	156,044	170,222	200,660	216,148	197,757	178,981
Viet Nam	...	...	...	...	...	...	...	...	...	...	...	...	...	...	...	...	...	...
South Asia																		
Bangladesh*	...	...	...	...	...	...	...	...	...	2,826	3,159	3,350	3,611	3,927	4,105	4,420	4,847	5,230
India*	...	...	...	...	...	502,851	548,873	615,535	571,859	471,606	445,640	460,575	465,703	493,230	563,163	561,611	593,790	...
Nepal	...	...	...	...	...	...	...	...	...	...	...	...	...	...	...	...	...	...
Pakistan	...	...	...	...	1,652	1,548	1,732	1,953	2,319	2,491	2,679	3,255	3,563	3,880	4,139	3,652	3,693	3,897
Sri Lanka	...	...	...	...	...	...	...	...	...	...	...	...	...	...	...	...	...	...

GDP = gross domestic product; MSME = micro, small, and medium-sized enterprise.

Notes: End-of-year data except * fiscal year data (ended 30 June in Bangladesh and 31 March in India). Exchange rates of local currency to US dollar refer to end-of-year currency rates from the International Monetary Fund (IMF) International Financial Statistics in designated years.

A10. MSME Contribution to GDP (%)

Country	2003	2004	2005	2006	2007	2008	2009	2010	2011	2012	2013	2014	2015	2016	2017	2018	2019	2020
Southeast Asia																		
Brunei Darussalam	...	...	...	...	...	...	...	17.3	14.9	16.0	17.6	...	20.3	34.3	31.8	28.0	27.0	...
Cambodia	...	...	...	...	...	...	...	...	...	...	...	...	...	...	...	...	...	...
Indonesia	...	...	...	...	...	...	...	56.2	56.2	58.0	59.1	60.3	61.4	59.8	60.9	61.1	60.5	...
Lao People's Democratic Republic	...	...	...	...	...	...	...	...	...	...	...	...	...	...	...	...	...	...
Malaysia	29.3	29.7	30.2	30.4	31.5	32.0	32.6	32.8	33.4	33.6	34.2	36.6	37.0	37.3	37.8	38.3	38.9	38.2
Myanmar	...	...	...	...	...	...	...	...	...	...	...	...	...	...	...	...	...	...
Philippines	...	...	...	35.7	...	...	...	...	...	...	...	...	...	...	...	...	...	...
Singapore	...	...	...	...	...	...	...	...	...	...	...	50.1	47.5	48.2	47.0	44.1	43.1	42.8
Thailand	...	...	...	...	41.4	39.8	39.9	39.4	39.3	39.1	39.1	39.8	41.0	41.9	42.4	43.0	35.3	34.2
Viet Nam	...	...	...	...	...	...	...	...	...	...	...	...	...	...	...	...	...	...
South Asia																		
Bangladesh*	...	...	...	...	...	...	...	...	...	18.7	18.5	18.1	17.8	17.3	17.2	16.5	16.1	16.4
India*	...	...	...	...	...	35.4	36.1	36.1	36.7	29.6	29.9	29.8	29.3	29.5	29.3	29.8	30.3	...
Nepal	...	...	...	...	...	...	...	...	...	...	...	...	...	...	...	...	22.0	...
Pakistan	...	...	...	...	1.2	1.2	1.3	1.4	1.5	1.5	1.6	1.7	1.7	1.8	1.8	1.9	2.0	2.0
Sri Lanka	...	...	...	...	...	...	...	...	...	...	...	...	...	...	...	...	...	...

GDP = gross domestic product; MSME = micro, small, and medium-sized enterprise.

Notes: End-of-year data except * fiscal year data (ended 30 June in Bangladesh and 31 March in India). For Malaysia, real GDP data. For Singapore, nominal value added of SMEs. For Bangladesh, contribution of cottage and small enterprises to manufacturing gross value added. For Nepal, data cited from the 2019 Nepal Rastra Bank Report. For Pakistan, small manufacturing contribution to GDP.

A11. MSME GDP by Sector (% share, latest available year)

Item/Southeast Asia	Brunei Darussalam	Cambodia	Indonesia	Lao People's Democratic Republic	Malaysia	Myanmar	Philippines	Singapore	Thailand	Viet Nam
Agriculture	...	...	...	...	10.5	...	1.0	...	0.3	...
Manufacturing	...	...	26.8	...	20.7	...	19.3	...	32.0	...
Transportation and communication	...	...	4.8	...	...	...	...	...	...	...
Construction	...	...	...	...	5.1	...	...	...	4.0	...
Wholesale and retail trade	...	...	47.8	...	62.1	...	18.4	...	21.6	...
Other services	...	...	20.6	...	...	...	41.9	...	40.5	...
Others	...	...	...	...	1.7	...	19.3	...	1.6	...
Year			2016		2020		2006		2020	

Item / South Asia	Bangladesh	India	Nepal	Pakistan	Sri Lanka
Agriculture	...	...	...	...	...
Manufacturing	...	...	...	12.5	...
Transportation and communication	...	...	...	...	...
Construction	...	...	...	...	...
Wholesale and retail trade	...	...	...	...	...
Other services	...	...	...	...	...
Others	...	...	...	...	...
Year				2020	

GDP = gross domestic product; MSME = micro, small, and medium-sized enterprise.

Notes: End-of-year data. For Malaysia, real GDP data, and "Wholesale and retail trade" includes transportation and storage, telecommunication, and real estate. For Pakistan, GDP of small manufacturing only.

A12. MSME GDP by Region (% share, latest available year)

Item/Southeast Asia	Brunei Darussalam	Cambodia	Indonesia	Lao People's Democratic Republic	Malaysia	Myanmar	Philippines	Singapore	Thailand	Viet Nam
Capital city	...	...	...	...	23.0	...	...	...	...	...
Other areas	...	...	...	...	77.0	...	...	...	...	...
Year					2015					
Item / South Asia	**Bangladesh**	**India**	**Nepal**	**Pakistan**	**Sri Lanka**					
Capital city	...	...	...	...	...					
Other areas	...	...	...	...	...					

GDP = gross domestic product; MSME = micro, small, and medium-sized enterprise.

Notes: End-of-year data. For Malaysia, real GDP data. Capital city: Kuala Lumpur in Malaysia.

A13-1. MSME Export Value (local currency)

Country	2003	2004	2005	2006	2007	2008	2009	2010	2011	2012	2013	2014	2015	2016	2017	2018	2019	2020
Southeast Asia																		
Brunei Darussalam	...	...	...	...	...	...	...	...	...	...	...	...	...	...	...	...	...	...
Cambodia	...	...	...	...	...	...	...	...	...	...	...	...	...	...	...	...	...	...
Indonesia	...	...	...	...	...	...	...	162,255	175,895	187,442	166,627	182,113	185,975	255,126	301,630	293,841	339,191	...
Lao People's Democratic Republic	...	...	...	...	...	...	...	...	...	...	...	1,238	...	...	...	...	...	...
Malaysia	...	...	...	...	...	...	...	116,800	131,000	134,700	136,900	145,200	145,000	155,100	166,200	171,800	176,300	117,800
Myanmar	...	...	...	...	...	...	...	...	...	...	...	...	...	...	...	...	...	...
Philippines	...	...	...	...	...	...	...	...	...	...	...	...	...	...	...	...	...	...
Singapore	...	...	...	...	...	...	...	...	...	...	...	...	...	...	...	...	...	...
Thailand	...	...	...	...	1,576,000	1,691,000	1,564,000	1,669,000	1,971,000	2,065,460	1,761,800	1,922,500	1,978,300	2,190,500	1,990,420	2,325,852	1,023,713	839,750
Viet Nam	...	...	...	...	...	...	...	...	...	...	...	...	...	...	...	...	...	...
South Asia																		
Bangladesh	...	...	...	...	...	...	...	...	...	...	...	...	...	...	...	...	...	...
India*	...	...	...	...	...	...	...	...	...	...	7,922,321	8,442,912	9,212,416	8,886,300	8,762,387	10,286,693	11,345,380	11,308,805
Nepal	...	...	...	...	...	...	...	...	...	...	...	...	...	...	...	...	...	...
Pakistan	...	...	...	...	...	...	...	404,365	...	...	...	...	...	...	...	...	...	...
Sri Lanka	...	...	...	...	...	...	...	...	...	...	...	...	...	...	...	...	...	...

MSME = micro, small, and medium-sized enterprise.

Notes: End-of-year data except * fiscal year data (ended 31 March in India). For Pakistan, data from Pakistan Economic Survey 2009-10. Indonesia: Rp billion; Lao People's Democratic Republic: KN million; Malaysia: RM million; Thailand: B million; India: Rs million; Pakistan: PRs million.

A13-2. MSME Export Value ($ million)

Country	2003	2004	2005	2006	2007	2008	2009	2010	2011	2012	2013	2014	2015	2016	2017	2018	2019	2020
Southeast Asia																		
Brunei Darussalam	...	...	...	...	...	...	...	...	...	...	...	...	...	...	...	...	...	...
Cambodia	...	...	...	...	...	...	...	...	...	...	...	...	...	...	...	...	...	...
Indonesia	...	...	...	...	...	...	...	18,046	19,397	19,384	13,670	14,639	13,481	18,988	22,264	20,291	24,400	...
Lao People's Democratic Republic	...	...	...	...	...	...	...	...	...	...	...	0	...	...	...	...	...	...
Malaysia	...	...	...	...	...	...	...	37,879	41,234	44,045	41,719	41,545	33,784	34,574	40,916	41,513	43,079	29,355
Myanmar	...	...	...	...	...	...	...	...	...	...	...	...	...	...	...	...	...	...
Philippines	...	...	...	...	...	...	...	...	...	...	...	...	...	...	...	...	...	...
Singapore	...	...	...	...	...	...	...	...	...	...	...	...	...	...	...	...	...	...
Thailand	...	...	...	...	46,740	48,456	46,939	55,354	62,194	67,429	53,691	58,323	54,818	61,135	60,905	71,675	33,949	27,957
Viet Nam	...	...	...	...	...	...	...	...	...	...	...	...	...	...	...	...	...	...
South Asia																		
Bangladesh	...	...	...	...	...	...	...	...	...	...	...	...	...	...	...	...	...	...
India*	...	...	...	...	...	...	...	...	...	...	127,992	133,313	138,896	130,768	137,068	147,390	159,180	154,801
Nepal	...	...	...	...	...	...	...	...	...	...	...	...	...	...	...	...	...	...
Pakistan	...	...	...	...	...	...	...	4,718	...	...	...	...	...	...	...	...	...	...
Sri Lanka	...	...	...	...	...	...	...	...	...	...	...	...	...	...	...	...	...	...

MSME = micro, small, and medium-sized enterprise.

Notes: End-of-year data except * fiscal year data (ended 31 March in India). For Pakistan, data from Pakistan Economic Survey 2009-10. Exchange rates of local currency to US dollar refer to end-of-year currency rates from the International Monetary Fund (IMF) International Financial Statistics in designated years.

A14. MSME Exports to Total (%)

Country	2003	2004	2005	2006	2007	2008	2009	2010	2011	2012	2013	2014	2015	2016	2017	2018	2019	2020
Southeast Asia																		
Brunei Darussalam	...	...	...	...	...	...	...	...	...	...	...	...	...	...	...	...	...	...
Cambodia	...	...	...	...	...	...	...	...	...	...	...	...	...	...	...	...	...	...
Indonesia	...	...	...	...	...	...	...	17.0	15.8	16.4	14.1	15.7	15.7	14.4	14.5	14.4	15.7	...
Lao People's Democratic Republic	...	...	...	...	...	...	...	...	...	...	...	...	...	...	...	...	...	...
Malaysia	...	...	...	...	...	...	...	16.4	16.9	17.5	17.8	17.8	17.7	18.6	17.3	17.3	17.9	13.5
Myanmar	...	...	...	...	...	...	...	...	...	...	...	...	...	...	...	...	...	...
Philippines	...	...	...	...	...	...	...	...	...	...	...	...	...	...	...	...	...	...
Singapore	...	...	...	...	...	...	...	...	...	...	...	...	...	...	...	...	...	...
Thailand	...	...	...	...	30.1	28.9	30.1	27.3	29.4	29.9	25.5	27.9	28.2	29.0	28.9	28.7	13.4	11.7
Viet Nam	...	...	...	...	...	...	...	...	...	...	...	...	...	...	...	...	...	...
South Asia																		
Bangladesh	...	...	...	...	...	...	...	...	...	...	...	...	...	...	...	...	...	...
India*	...	...	...	...	...	...	...	...	...	...	42.6	42.4	44.8	49.9	49.7	48.6	48.1	49.8
Nepal	...	...	...	...	...	...	...	...	...	...	...	...	...	...	...	...	...	...
Pakistan	...	...	...	...	...	...	...	25.0	...	...	...	...	...	...	...	...	...	...
Sri Lanka	...	...	...	...	...	...	...	...	...	...	...	...	...	...	...	...	...	...

MSME = micro, small, and medium-sized enterprise.

Notes: End-of-year data except * fiscal year data (ended 31 March in India). For Pakistan, data from Pakistan Economic Survey 2009-10.

B. MSME Access to Finance (Banking)

B1-1. MSME Bank Loans Outstanding (local currency)

Country	2003	2004	2005	2006	2007	2008	2009	2010	2011	2012	2013	2014	2015	2016	2017	2018	2019	2020
Southeast Asia																		
Brunei Darussalam	...	...	...	...	...	...	...	...	...	...	...	...	...	...	...	3,304,913	8,996,023	...
Cambodia	...	...	...	...	...	...	...	...	...	...	...	...	...	...	...	...	...	...
Indonesia	...	...	...	...	...	...	...	...	458,164	526,397	608,823	763,307	790,467	856,997	942,388	1,032,643	1,111,340	1,091,232
Lao People's Democratic Republic	...	...	...	...	...	...	...	...	...	...	...	...	14,919	13,997	15,939	14,241	14,104	15,731
Malaysia	...	...	...	...	127,984	138,859	141,608	141,159	165,316	187,039	211,038	243,708	274,412	299,733	315,660	297,615	278,355	305,064
Myanmar*	...	...	...	...	...	...	...	...	...	...	...	...	...	...	733,235	896,840	1,131,665	...
Philippines	...	...	...	...	...	270,526	257,894	311,452	351,693	384,082	395,031	425,155	461,650	496,863	532,198	577,719	588,837	494,977
Singapore	...	...	...	...	...	...	...	46,424	56,869	60,497	66,752	74,190	76,018	77,983	80,667	78,204	86,242	90,429
Thailand	...	...	...	...	2,688	2,768	2,585	3,594	4,272	4,627	5,123	5,460	5,974	6,096	6,288	6,560	6,581	5,073
Viet Nam	...	...	...	...	...	...	...	...	...	...	...	...	...	...	...	...	...	1,818,223
South Asia																		
Bangladesh	...	...	...	...	...	...	...	671	785	977	1,123	1,318	1,433	1,655	1,926	1,785	2,092	2,273
India	...	...	...	...	52,833	68,723	79,685	170,155	217,022	242,539	269,069	287,208	12,368,744	12,377,008	13,924,802	16,208,160	17,419,130	18,700,493
Nepal	...	...	...	...	...	...	...	...	...	...	...	...	...	...	...	...	...	...
Pakistan	...	...	...	...	411,675	383,698	348,199	336,553	294,306	266,144	272,528	287,881	305,090	401,480	450,384	513,459	477,232	481,780
Sri Lanka	...	...	...	...	...	...	...	...	...	...	...	...	...	...	...	...	...	743,024

MSME = micro, small, and medium-sized enterprise.

Notes: End-of-year data except * fiscal year data (ended 31 March in Myanmar). For India, urban cooperative banks only for 2007-2014; urban cooperative banks plus commercial banks for 2015-2020. Brunei Darussalam: B$; Indonesia: Rp billion; Lao People's Democratic Republic: KN billion; Malaysia: RM million; Myanmar: MK million; Philippines: P million; Singapore: S$ million; Thailand: B billion; Viet Nam: D billion. Bangladesh: Tk billion; India: Rs million: Pakistan: PRs million; Sri Lanka: SLRs million.

B1-2. MSME Bank Loans Outstanding ($ million)

Country	2003	2004	2005	2006	2007	2008	2009	2010	2011	2012	2013	2014	2015	2016	2017	2018	2019	2020
Southeast Asia																		
Brunei Darussalam	...	...	...	...	...	...	...	...	...	...	...	...	...	...	...	2.4	6.7	...
Cambodia	...	...	...	...	...	...	...	...	...	...	...	...	...	...	...	...	...	...
Indonesia	...	...	...	...	...	...	...	...	50,525	54,436	49,949	61,359	57,301	63,784	69,559	71,310	79,947	77,365
Lao People's Democratic Republic	...	...	...	...	...	...	...	...	...	...	...	...	1,831	1,710	1,922	1,669	1,592	1,696
Malaysia	...	...	...	...	37,231	41,626	40,178	43,823	54,025	60,554	66,977	74,463	70,263	72,254	73,402	73,756	67,195	76,019
Myanmar*	...	...	...	...	...	...	...	...	...	...	...	...	...	...	538	579	772	...
Philippines	...	...	...	...	...	5,697	5,563	7,097	8,006	9,324	8,894	9,529	9,788	9,975	10,660	10,957	11,604	10,304.3
Singapore	...	...	...	...	...	...	...	36,057	43,722	49,446	52,756	56,149	53,765	53,919	60,352	57,301	64,016	68,398
Thailand	...	...	...	...	77,867	83,091	75,400	113,428	140,105	148,846	166,745	168,090	174,449	172,698	185,278	203,029	211,978	168,892
Viet Nam	...	...	...	...	...	...	...	...	...	...	...	...	...	...	...	...	...	78,605
South Asia																		
Bangladesh	...	...	...	...	...	...	...	9,478	9,594	12,237	14,445	16,904	18,260	21,024	23,295	21,273	24,638	26,802
India	...	...	...	...	1,340	1,418	1,707	3,797	4,075	4,428	4,347	4,535	186,484	182,136	217,822	232,234	244,397	255,983
Nepal	...	...	...	...	...	...	...	...	...	...	...	...	...	...	...	...	...	...
Pakistan	...	...	...	...	6,724	4,851	4,132	3,927	3,271	2,740	2,579	2,866	2,909	3,830	4,078	3,699	3,082	3,019
Sri Lanka	...	...	...	...	...	...	...	...	...	...	...	...	...	...	...	...	...	3,986

MSME = micro, small, and medium-sized enterprise.

Notes: End-of-year data except * fiscal year data (ended 31 March in Myanmar). Exchange rates of local currency to US dollar refer to end-of-year currency rates from the International Monetary Fund (IMF) International Financial Statistics in designated years.

B2. MSME Bank Loans to Total (%)

Country	2003	2004	2005	2006	2007	2008	2009	2010	2011	2012	2013	2014	2015	2016	2017	2018	2019	2020
Southeast Asia																		
Brunei Darussalam	...	...	...	...	...	...	...	...	...	...	...	...	...	...	...	0.1	0.2	...
Cambodia	...	...	...	...	...	...	...	...	...	...	...	...	...	...	...	...	...	...
Indonesia	...	...	...	...	...	...	...	...	20.8	19.4	18.5	20.4	19.3	19.4	19.7	19.3	19.6	19.7
Lao People's Democratic Republic	...	...	...	...	...	...	...	...	...	...	...	...	30.9	23.4	23.8	20.6	19.8	17.1
Malaysia	...	...	...	...	19.9	19.1	18.1	16.0	16.5	16.9	17.2	18.2	19.0	19.7	19.9	17.4	15.8	16.7
Myanmar*	...	...	...	...	...	...	...	...	...	...	...	...	...	...	4.5	4.6	4.8	...
Philippines	...	...	...	...	...	11.6	10.6	11.7	11.0	10.6	9.3	8.3	7.9	7.2	6.6	6.2	6.1	5.1
Singapore	...	...	...	...	...	...	...	7.2	7.1	6.9	6.3	6.5	6.6	6.7	6.5	6.0	6.3	6.7
Thailand	...	...	...	...	33.6	29.1	25.4	30.9	32.3	30.9	31.3	32.1	33.5	32.9	31.5	31.8	30.9	22.4
Viet Nam	...	...	...	...	...	...	...	...	...	...	...	...	...	...	...	...	...	21.5
South Asia																		
Bangladesh	...	...	...	...	...	...	...	...	...	...	...	...	23.7	23.7	23.4	19.0	20.1	20.2
India	...	...	...	...	...	...	...	...	...	...	...	...	17.2	16.6	17.0	17.3	17.4	17.6
Nepal*	...	...	...	...	...	...	...	...	...	...	...	...	11.2	11.7	11.5	...	...	...
Pakistan	...	...	...	...	16.2	12.0	10.1	9.6	8.3	6.8	6.5	8.0	6.1	9.2	8.7	8.5	7.6	7.3
Sri Lanka	...	...	...	...	--	...	...	...	...	...	...	...	...	...	...	...	...	11.1

MSME = micro, small, and medium-sized enterprise.

Notes: End-of-year data except * fiscal year data (ended 31 March in Myanmar and 15 July in Nepal). For Bangladesh, commercial banks' MSME loans outstanding divided by total loans outstanding of all operating banks; actual percentage share of MSME loans to total loans outstanding in commercial banks would be higher. For India, commercial banks only. For Nepal, data from NRB Report, SME Financing in Nepal 2019. For Pakistan, SME loans to total domestic private loans outstanding. For Sri Lanka, MSME loans to total outstanding loans to the private sector.

B3. MSME Bank Loans to GDP (%)

Country	2003	2004	2005	2006	2007	2008	2009	2010	2011	2012	2013	2014	2015	2016	2017	2018	2019	2020
Southeast Asia																		
Brunei Darussalam	...	...	...	...	...	...	...	...	...	...	...	...	...	...	...	0.0	0.1	...
Cambodia	...	...	...	...	...	...	...	...	...	...	...	...	...	...	...	...	...	...
Indonesia	...	...	...	...	...	...	...	...	6.2	6.4	6.7	7.2	6.9	6.9	6.9	7.0	7.0	7.1
Lao People's Democratic Republic	...	...	...	...	...	...	...	...	...	...	...	...	12.7	10.8	11.3	9.3	8.5	9.1
Malaysia	...	...	...	...	19.3	18.0	19.9	17.2	18.1	19.3	20.7	22.0	23.3	24.0	23.0	22.1	18.5	21.6
Myanmar*	...	...	...	...	...	...	...	...	...	...	...	...	...	...	0.9	1.0	...	...
Philippines	...	...	...	...	...	3.5	3.2	3.5	3.6	3.6	3.4	3.4	3.5	3.4	3.4	3.3	3.2	5.8
Singapore	...	...	...	...	...	...	...	14.2	15.8	14.7	16.8	17.6	17.2	16.2	15.9	15.1	...	...
Thailand	...	...	...	...	29.6	28.5	26.8	25.9	28.6	29.0	31.8	33.2	33.7	32.3	32.3	31.6	30.3	...
Viet Nam	...	...	...	...	...	...	...	...	...	...	...	...	...	...	...	...	...	...
South Asia																		
Bangladesh	...	...	...	...	...	...	...	8.4	8.6	9.3	9.4	9.8	9.5	9.5	9.8	7.9	8.2	8.1
India	...	...	...	...	...	...	...	...	...	...	...	...	10.6	9.8	10.3	11.3	11.7	...
Nepal	...	...	...	...	...	...	...	...	...	...	...	...	...	...	...	...	...	...
Pakistan	...	...	...	...	4.5	3.6	2.6	2.3	1.6	1.3	1.2	1.1	1.1	1.4	1.4	1.5	1.3	1.2
Sri Lanka	...	...	...	...	...	...	...	...	...	...	...	...	...	...	...	...	...	5.0

GDP = gross domestic product; MSME = micro, small, and medium-sized enterprise.

Notes: End-of-year data except * fiscal year data (ended 31 March in Myanmar). For India, data for commercial banks only.

B4. MSME Bank Loans by Sector (% share, latest available year)

Item	Brunei Darussalam	Cambodia	Indonesia	Lao People's Democratic Republic	Malaysia	Myanmar*	Philippines	Singapore	Thailand	Viet Nam
Agriculture	12.2	...	11.9	3.8	4.7	1.0	...	0.4	2.0	3.2
Manufacturing	30.2	...	10.3	7.9	15.5	18.9	...	7.4	20.3	...
Transportation and communication	0.4	...	3.9	1.1	...	3.4	...	8.0	2.9	...
Construction	1.2	...	5.4	20.7	12.8	1.5	...	40.2	4.8	40.0
Wholesale and retail trade	24.6	...	48.6	37.0	66.1	45.6	...	23.9	33.0	56.8
Other services	27.9	...	17.5	18.6	...	11.4	...	13.6	32.5	...
Others	3.5	...	2.3	11.0	0.4	18.3	...	6.6	4.6	...
Year	2019		2020	2019	2020	FY2019		2020	2020	2020

Item	Bangladesh	India	Nepal	Pakistan	Sri Lanka
Agriculture	...	...	...	0.5	11.9
Manufacturing	40.0	...	...	45.7	50.5
Transportation and communication	...	...	...	6.2	...
Construction	...	...	...	2.9	...
Wholesale and retail trade	41.0	...	...	30.0	...
Other services	19.0	...	...	5.2	37.6
Others	...	...	...	9.4	...
Year	2020			2020	2020

MSME = micro, small, and medium-sized enterprise.

Notes: End-of-year data except * fiscal year (FY) data (ended 31 March in Myanmar). For Malaysia, "Wholesale and retail trade" includes transportation and storage, telecommunication, and real estate. For Viet Nam, "Wholesale and retail trade" refers to commercial services. Data for Brunei Darussalam refers to SME Bank data only.

B5. MSME Bank Loans by Region (% share, latest available year)

Item	Brunei Darussalam	Cambodia	Indonesia	Lao People's Democratic Republic	Malaysia	Myanmar	Philippines	Singapore	Thailand	Viet Nam
Capital city	96.0	...	...	...	...	...	...	...	...	26.9
Other areas	4.0	...	...	...	...	...	...	...	...	73.1
Year	2019									2020

Item	Bangladesh	India	Nepal	Pakistan	Sri Lanka
Capital city	84.2	...	...	...	...
Other areas	15.8	...	...	...	...
Year	2020				

MSME = micro, small, and medium-sized enterprise.

Notes: End-of-year data. Data for Brunei Darussalam refers to SME Bank data only. Capital city: Bandar Seri Begawan in Brunei Darussalam; Viet Nam: Hanoi. For Bangladesh, Urban/Rural.

B6-1. Nonperforming MSME Bank Loans (local currency)

Country	2003	2004	2005	2006	2007	2008	2009	2010	2011	2012	2013	2014	2015	2016	2017	2018	2019	2020
Southeast Asia																		
Brunei Darussalam	...	...	...	...	...	...	...	...	...	...	...	...	...	...	...	...	...	...
Cambodia	...	...	...	...	...	...	...	...	...	...	...	...	...	...	...	...	...	...
Indonesia	...	...	...	...	...	...	...	...	15,674	17,011	19,515	31,560	33,208	35,597	38,520	35,504	40,089	43,110
Lao People's Democratic Republic	...	...	...	...	...	...	...	...	...	...	...	...	...	...	...	...	...	...
Malaysia	...	...	...	...	12,083	9,882	8,895	10,590	9,552	8,574	8,216	8,553	8,880	8,874	10,065	10,261	10,399	9,798
Myanmar	...	...	...	...	...	...	...	...	...	...	...	...	...	...	...	...	...	...
Philippines	...	...	...	...	...	...	...	23,656	26,078	25,347	25,512	25,097	25,209	26,217	25,989	30,030	32,306	34,979
Singapore	...	...	...	...	...	...	...	696	783	612	561	627	1,458	2,330	4,018	4,267	3,591	3,896
Thailand	...	...	...	...	...	...	184	153	130	125	136	137	164	205	220	230	231	238
Viet Nam	...	...	...	...	...	...	...	...	...	...	...	...	...	...	...	...	...	...
South Asia																		
Bangladesh	...	...	...	...	...	...	...	...	...	...	...	...	...	...	...	...	...	...
India	...	...	...	...	...	...	...	...	...	...	...	...	1,156,321	1,246,214	1,482,100	1,637,547	1,545,805	1,366,862
Nepal	...	...	...	...	...	...	...	...	...	...	...	...	...	...	...	...	...	...
Pakistan	...	...	...	...	35,003	60,692	79,141	97,091	95,472	95,440	86,615	87,055	77,170	66,601	69,368	75,440	80,001	81,429
Sri Lanka	...	...	...	...	...	...	...	...	...	...	...	...	...	...	...	...	...	...

MSME = micro, small, and medium-sized enterprise.

Notes: End-of-year data. For India, data for commercial banks only. Indonesia: Rp billion; Malaysia: RM million; Philippines: P million; Singapore: S$ million; Thailand: B billion; India: Rs million; Pakistan: PRs million.

B6-2. Nonperforming MSME Bank Loans ($ million)

Country	2003	2004	2005	2006	2007	2008	2009	2010	2011	2012	2013	2014	2015	2016	2017	2018	2019	2020
Southeast Asia																		
Brunei Darussalam	...	...	...	...	...	...	...	...	...	...	...	...	...	...	...	...	...	...
Cambodia	...	...	...	...	...	...	...	...	...	...	...	...	...	...	...	...	...	...
Indonesia	...	...	...	...	...	...	...	...	1,728	1,759	1,601	2,537	2,407	2,649	2,843	2,452	2,884	3,056
Lao People's Democratic Republic	...	...	...	...	...	...	...	...	...	...	...	...	...	...	...	...	...	...
Malaysia	...	...	...	...	3,515	2,962	2,524	3,288	3,121	2,776	2,608	2,613	2,274	2,139	2,340	2,543	2,510	2,442
Myanmar	...	...	...	...	...	...	...	...	...	...	...	...	...	...	...	...	...	...
Philippines	...	...	...	...	...	...	...	539	594	615	574	562	534	526	521	570	624	728
Singapore	...	...	...	...	...	...	...	541	602	500	443	474	1,031	1,611	3,006	3,126	2,666	2,947
Thailand	...	...	...	...	...	...	5,374	4,815	4,252	4,019	4,431	4,226	4,779	5,814	6,472	7,106	7,447	7,938
Viet Nam	...	...	...	...	...	...	...	...	...	...	...	...	...	...	...	...	...	...
South Asia																		
Bangladesh	...	...	...	...	...	...	...	...	...	...	...	...	...	...	...	...	...	...
India	...	...	...	...	...	...	...	...	...	...	...	...	17,434	18,339	23,184	23,463	21,688	18,710
Nepal	...	...	...	...	...	...	...	...	...	...	...	...	...	...	...	...	...	...
Pakistan	...	...	...	...	572	767	939	1,133	1,061	983	820	867	736	635	628	544	517	510
Sri Lanka	...	...	...	...	...	...	...	...	...	...	...	...	...	...	...	...	...	...

MSME = micro, small, and medium-sized enterprise.
Notes: End-of-year data. Exchange rates of local currency to US dollar refer to end-of-year currency rates from the International Monetary Fund (IMF) International Financial Statistics in designated years.

B7. MSME NPL to Total MSME Bank Loans (%)

Country	2003	2004	2005	2006	2007	2008	2009	2010	2011	2012	2013	2014	2015	2016	2017	2018	2019	2020
Southeast Asia																		
Brunei Darussalam	...	...	...	...	...	...	...	...	...	...	...	...	...	...	...	...	...	...
Cambodia	...	...	...	...	...	...	...	...	...	...	...	...	...	...	...	...	...	...
Indonesia	...	...	...	...	...	...	...	...	3.4	3.2	3.2	4.1	4.2	4.2	4.1	3.4	3.6	4.0
Lao People's Democratic Republic	...	...	...	...	...	...	...	...	...	...	...	...	...	...	...	...	...	...
Malaysia	...	...	...	...	9.4	7.1	6.3	7.5	5.8	4.6	3.9	3.5	3.2	3.0	3.2	3.4	3.7	3.2
Myanmar	...	...	...	...	...	...	...	...	...	...	...	...	...	...	...	...	...	...
Philippines	...	...	...	...	...	...	...	7.6	7.4	6.6	6.5	5.9	5.5	5.3	4.9	5.2	5.5	6.7
Singapore	...	...	...	...	...	...	...	1.5	1.4	1.0	0.8	0.8	1.9	3.0	5.0	5.5	4.2	4.3
Thailand	...	...	...	...	...	...	7.1	5.4	4.0	3.5	3.3	3.1	3.5	4.4	4.5	4.6	4.7	7.0
Viet Nam	...	...	...	...	...	...	...	...	...	...	...	...	...	...	...	...	...	...
South Asia																		
Bangladesh	...	...	...	...	...	...	...	3.6	3.6	6.4	7.9	11.8	...	...	...	...	...	...
India	...	...	...	...	...	...	...	...	...	...	...	...	9.6	10.3	10.9	10.4	9.1	7.5
Nepal	...	...	...	...	...	...	...	...	...	...	...	...	...	...	...	...	...	...
Pakistan	...	...	...	...	8.5	15.8	22.7	28.8	32.4	35.9	31.8	30.2	25.3	16.6	15.4	14.7	16.8	16.9
Sri Lanka	...	...	...	...	...	...	...	...	...	...	...	...	...	...	...	...	...	...

MSME = micro, small, and medium-sized enterprise; NPL = nonperforming loan.

Notes: End-of-year data. For India, data for commercial banks only.

B8-1. Outstanding Guaranteed Loans (local currency)

Country	2003	2004	2005	2006	2007	2008	2009	2010	2011	2012	2013	2014	2015	2016	2017	2018	2019	2020
Southeast Asia																		
Brunei Darussalam	...	...	...	...	...	...	...	...	...	...	...	...	...	...	...	...	...	...
Cambodia	...	...	...	...	...	...	...	...	...	...	...	...	...	...	...	...	...	...
Indonesia	...	...	...	...	...	...	8,154	5,010	30,486	40,760	47,422	49,546	22,757	70,669	75,004	125,912	163,722	178,067
Lao People's Democratic Republic	...	...	...	...	...	...	...	...	...	...	...	...	...	...	...	...	...	...
Malaysia	...	...	...	...	39	42	45	47	50	51	53	56	60	64	67	71	75	81
Myanmar	...	...	...	...	...	...	...	...	...	...	...	...	...	...	...	...	...	...
Philippines	...	...	...	215	131	108	58	67	26	126	80	175	230	123	595	185	78	324
Singapore	...	...	...	...	...	...	...	...	...	...	...	...	...	...	...	...	...	...
Thailand	...	...	...	...	22	22	40	73	113	180	244	270	309	331	354	374	389	451
Viet Nam	...	...	...	...	...	...	...	...	...	...	...	...	...	...	...	...	...	...
South Asia																		
Bangladesh	...	...	...	...	...	...	...	...	...	...	...	...	...	...	...	...	...	...
India*	...	...	...	...	...	10,560	21,990	68,750	125,890	137,840	160,620	181,880	212,750	199,490	199,310	190,660	301,680	458,510
Nepal*	...	...	...	...	...	...	...	...	...	...	...	...	350	523	578	810	...	...
Pakistan	...	...	...	...	...	...	...	...	...	...	...	...	...	...	...	...	...	...
Sri Lanka	...	...	...	...	...	...	...	...	...	...	...	...	...	...	...	...	...	...

Notes: End-of-year data except * fiscal year data (ended 31 March in India and 15 July in Nepal). For Malaysia, data from Credit Guarantee Corporation. For the Philippines, approved guaranteed loans data from Small Business Corporation until August 2019; outstanding guaranteed loan from PhilGuarantee for 2020. For India, guaranteed loans approved to MSMEs (CGTMSE). For Nepal, data from Deposit and Credit Guarantee Fund. Indonesia: Rp billion; Malaysia: RM million; Philippines: P million; Thailand: B billion; India: Rs million; Nepal: NRs million.

B8-2. Outstanding Guaranteed Loans ($ million)

Country	2003	2004	2005	2006	2007	2008	2009	2010	2011	2012	2013	2014	2015	2016	2017	2018	2019	2020
Southeast Asia																		
Brunei Darussalam	...	...	...	...	...	...	...	...	...	...	...	...	...	...	...	...	...	...
Cambodia	...	...	...	...	...	...	...	...	...	...	...	...	...	...	...	...	...	...
Indonesia	...	...	...	...	...	...	867	557	3,362	4,215	3,891	3,983	1,650	5,260	5,536	8,695	11,778	12,624
Lao People's Democratic Republic	...	...	...	...	...	...	...	...	...	...	...	...	...	...	...	...	...	...
Malaysia	...	...	...	...	11,287	12,531	12,739	14,714	16,424	16,641	16,789	17,141	15,235	15,356	15,598	17,537	18,057	20,115
Myanmar	...	...	...	...	...	...	...	...	...	...	...	...	...	...	...	...	...	...
Philippines	...	...	...	4.2	2.8	2.4	1.2	1.5	0.6	3.0	1.9	3.9	5.0	2.6	11.8	3.5	1.5	6.7
Singapore	...	...	...	...	...	...	...	...	...	...	...	...	...	...	...	...	...	...
Thailand	...	...	...	...	645	656	1,163	2,301	3,707	5,806	7,929	8,299	9,021	9,378	10,426	11,570	12,519	15,027
Viet Nam	...	...	...	...	...	...	...	...	...	...	...	...	...	...	...	...	...	...
South Asia																		
Bangladesh	...	...	...	...	...	...	...	...	...	...	...	...	...	...	...	...	...	...
India*	...	...	...	...	...	218	471	1,534	2,364	2,516	2,595	2,872	3,208	2,936	3,118	2,732	4,233	6,276
Nepal*	...	...	...	...	...	...	...	...	...	...	...	...	3.3	4.8	5.6	7.0	...	...
Pakistan	...	...	...	...	...	...	...	...	...	...	...	...	...	...	...	...	...	...
Sri Lanka	...	...	...	...	...	...	...	...	...	...	...	...	...	...	...	...	...	...

Notes: End-of-year data except * fiscal year data (ended 31 March in India and 15 July in Nepal). Exchange rates of local currency to US dollar refer to end-of-year currency rates from the International Monetary Fund (IMF) International Financial Statistics in designated years.

B8-3. Number of MSMEs Guaranteed

Country	2003	2004	2005	2006	2007	2008	2009	2010	2011	2012	2013	2014	2015	2016	2017	2018	2019	2020
Southeast Asia																		
Brunei Darussalam	...	...	...	...	...	...	...	...	...	...	...	...	...	...	...	...	...	...
Cambodia	...	...	...	...	...	...	...	...	...	...	...	...	...	...	...	...	...	...
Indonesia	...	...	...	...	3,623	1,652,965	718,320	1,437,650	1,909,912	1,962,121	2,347,429	2,443,907	722,621	4,362,599	4,086,971	4,440,028	4,728,330	6,112,058
Lao People's Democratic Republic	...	...	...	...	...	...	...	...	...	...	...	...	...	...	...	...	...	...
Malaysia	...	...	...	...	13,004	10,368	14,073	7,670	7,504	2,152	2,368	6,839	8,225	7,568	8,637	8,999	10,827	13,472
Myanmar	...	...	...	...	...	...	...	...	...	...	...	...	...	...	...	...	...	...
Philippines	...	...	...	64	43	36	17	10	9	44	22	91	142	181	14,799	327	80	2,923
Singapore	...	...	...	...	...	...	...	...	...	...	...	...	...	...	...	...	...	...
Thailand	...	...	...	...	...	...	...	...	...	...	...	...	...	...	...	...	...	...
Viet Nam	...	...	...	...	...	...	...	...	...	...	...	...	...	...	...	...	...	...
South Asia																		
Bangladesh	...	...	...	...	...	...	...	...	...	...	...	...	...	...	...	...	...	...
India	...	...	...	...	...	...	...	...	...	...	...	...	...	...	...	...	...	...
Nepal*	...	...	...	...	...	...	...	...	...	...	...	...	505	851	867	530	...	...
Pakistan	...	...	...	...	...	...	...	...	...	...	...	...	...	...	...	...	...	...
Sri Lanka	...	...	...	...	...	...	...	...	...	...	...	...	...	...	...	...	...	...

MSME = micro, small, and medium-sized enterprise.

Note: End-of-year data except * fiscal year data (ended 15 July in Nepal).

C. MSME Access to Finance (Nonbanking)

C1-1. NBFI Financing, Total (local currency)

Country	2003	2004	2005	2006	2007	2008	2009	2010	2011	2012	2013	2014	2015	2016	2017	2018	2019	2020
Southeast Asia																		
Brunei Darussalam	...	...	...	...	...	...	...	1,415	1,562	1,716	1,815	2,023	1,881	1,677	1,570	1,552	1,537	1,576
Cambodia	...	...	...	...	617,271	1,130,585	1,244,970	1,724,841	2,591,263	3,538,889	5,261,752	7,299,407	12,589,330	13,146,529	17,761,787	22,527,051	30,527,095	28,877,763
Indonesia	...	...	...	...	...	...	...	...	...	...	...	...	...	423,126	452,048	477,590	503,198	427,983
Lao People's Democratic Republic	...	...	...	...	...	...	...	49,209	93,042	103,110	459,065	430,988	835,488	1,461,276	2,196,508	4,808,287	6,075,379	5,405,244
Malaysia	...	...	...	...	2,479	2,277	2,097	553	953	1,130	1,364	1,487	1,392	1,641	1,245	1,386	1,503	1,312
Myanmar*	...	...	...	...	...	...	...	...	...	49,194	67,245	110,069	169,293	260,948	426,016	793,197	1,800,232	...
Philippines	...	...	...	...	...	...	6,544	5,947	7,711	8,876	8,538	130,201	310,467	382,749	403,599	527,932	610,164	234,241
Singapore	...	...	...	...	...	...	...	8,058	9,460	11,312	11,654	12,385	13,252	12,547	12,849	13,254	14,712	14,080
Thailand	...	...	...	...	...	...	...	...	...	...	...	...	...	...	...	...	...	...
Viet Nam	...	...	...	...	...	...	...	23,708,082	29,076,880	36,450,034	45,557,772	53,221,190	61,880,958	71,700,966	84,896,048	96,140,373	75,707,125	92,405,581
South Asia																		
Bangladesh	...	...	...	...	...	...	...	...	...	268,628	344,538	407,375	448,478	530,724	615,962	662,449	671,768	669,232
India	...	...	...	...	...	...	...	...	...	...	...	...	574,766	755,150	1,108,210	1,282,338	1,257,732	1,503,208
Nepal*	...	...	...	...	...	...	...	...	...	...	...	...	...	...	106,515	145,952	234,153	262,732
Pakistan	...	...	...	...	38,141	39,641	37,121	36,249	32,989	37,062	42,694	52,088	63,097	80,283	90,590	113,193	118,694	109,491
Sri Lanka	...	...	...	...	106,211	128,378	213,397	265,456	388,416	471,698	553,085	641,349	837,672	1,006,306	1,108,691	1,205,002	1,200,314	1,164,440

MSME = micro, small, and medium-sized enterprise; NBFI = nonbank finance institution.

Notes: End-of-year data except * fiscal year data (ended 15 July in Nepal and 31 March in Myanmar). Brunei Darussalam: B$ million (finance companies and pawnbrokers); Cambodia: KR million (microfinance institutions and leasing companies); Indonesia: Rp billion (finance companies, microfinance institutions, and government pawnshops); Lao People's Democratic Republic: KN million (microfinance institutions, pawnshops, and leasing companies); Malaysia: RM million (private equity, venture capital, factoring, and leasing companies); Myanmar: MK million (microfinance institutions); Philippines: P million (credit unions and cooperatives [2015-2018], pawnshops [2009-2018], and nonstock savings and loans associations [NSSLAs; 2014-2020]); Singapore: S$ million (finance companies); Viet Nam: D million (People's Credit Funds and microfinance institutions); Bangladesh: Tk million (nonbank finance institutions regulated by Bangladesh Bank); India: Rs million (nonbank finance institutions regulated by Reserve Bank of India; MSME financing only); Nepal: NRs million (microfinance institutions); Pakistan: PRs million (microfinance institutions and leasing companies); Sri Lanka: SLRs million (nonbank finance institutions regulated by Central Bank of Sri Lanka).

C1-2. NBFI Financing, Total ($ million)

Country	2003	2004	2005	2006	2007	2008	2009	2010	2011	2012	2013	2014	2015	2016	2017	2018	2019	2020
Southeast Asia																		
Brunei Darussalam	...	...	...	...	...	...	...	1,095	1,201	1,402	1,430	1,531	1,331	1,159	1,174	1,134	1,139	1,180
Cambodia	...	...	...	...	154	277	299	426	642	886	1,317	1,791	3,107	3,250	4,395	5,586	7,475	7,084
Indonesia	...	...	...	...	...	...	...	...	...	...	...	...	...	31,492	33,366	32,980	36,199	30,343
Lao People's Democratic Republic	...	...	...	...	...	...	...	6	12	13	57	53	103	179	265	564	686	583
Malaysia	...	...	...	...	750	657	612	179	300	369	416	425	324	366	306	335	367	327
Myanmar*	...	...	...	...	...	...	...	...	...	58	68	107	130	192	313	512	1,228	...
Philippines	...	...	...	...	...	...	141	136	176	215	192	2,918	6,582	7,684	8,084	10,013	12,024	4,876
Singapore	...	...	...	...	...	...	...	6,259	7,273	9,245	9,210	9,374	9,372	8,675	9,613	9,712	10,921	10,650
Thailand	...	...	...	...	...	...	...	...	...	...	...	...	...	...	...	...	...	...
Viet Nam	...	...	...	...	...	...	...	1,252	1,396	1,750	2,166	2,505	2,827	3,236	3,786	4,212	3,270	3,995
South Asia																		
Bangladesh	...	...	...	...	...	...	...	...	...	3,364	4,431	5,226	5,713	6,743	7,448	7,896	7,912	7,892
India	...	...	...	...	...	...	...	...	...	...	...	...	8,666	11,113	17,335	18,374	17,646	20,577
Nepal*	...	...	...	...	...	...	...	...	...	...	...	...	...	...	1,035	1,269	2,067	2,230
Pakistan	...	...	...	...	623	501	441	423	367	382	404	519	602	766	820	816	766	686
Sri Lanka	...	...	...	...	977	1,135	1,866	2,393	3,410	3,709	4,230	4,894	5,815	6,718	7,253	6,611	6,608	6,247

NBFI = nonbank finance institution.

Notes: End-of-year data except * fiscal year data (ended 15 July in Nepal and 31 March in Myanmar). Exchange rates of local currency to US dollar refer to end-of-year currency rates from the International Monetary Fund (IMF) International Financial Statistics in designated years.

C2. NBFI Financing to Bank Loans (%)

Country	2003	2004	2005	2006	2007	2008	2009	2010	2011	2012	2013	2014	2015	2016	2017	2018	2019	2020
Southeast Asia																		
Brunei Darussalam	...	...	...	...	...	...	...	27.3	30.7	33.0	32.3	35.4	30.8	31.0	30.6	28.3	27.9	...
Cambodia	...	...	...	...	9.7	11.5	11.9	13.1	14.8	15.2	17.9	19.2	27.0	23.5	27.1	27.7	29.8	23.0
Indonesia	...	...	...	...	...	...	...	...	...	...	...	...	...	9.2	9.0	9.5	11.3	...
Lao People's Democratic Republic	...	...	...	...	...	...	...	0.4	0.5	0.4	1.3	1.1	1.7	2.4	3.3	7.0	8.5	6.9
Malaysia	...	...	...	...	0.38	0.31	0.27	0.06	0.09	0.10	0.11	0.11	0.10	0.11	0.08	0.08	0.09	0.07
Myanmar*	...	...	...	...	...	...	...	...	...	1.7	1.6	1.7	1.9	2.1	2.6	4.1	7.7	...
Philippines	...	...	...	...	...	...	...	...	...	0.2	0.2	2.5	5.3	5.6	5.0	5.7	6.3	2.4
Singapore	...	...	...	...	...	...	...	1.3	1.2	1.3	1.1	1.1	1.2	1.1	1.0	1.0	1.1	1.0
Thailand	...	...	...	...	...	...	...	...	...	...	...	...	...	...	...	...	...	...
Viet Nam	...	...	...	...	...	...	...	...	...	1.2	1.3	1.3	1.3	1.3	1.3	1.3	0.9	1.0
South Asia																		
Bangladesh	...	...	...	...	...	...	...	...	...	...	...	...	7.4	7.6	7.5	7.1	6.5	5.9
India	...	...	...	...	...	...	...	...	...	...	...	...	0.8	1.0	1.4	1.4	1.3	1.5
Nepal*	...	...	...	...	...	...	...	...	...	...	...	...	...	...	5.3	6.0	8.0	8.0
Pakistan	...	...	...	...	1.4	1.2	1.1	1.0	0.9	0.9	1.0	1.1	1.2	1.4	1.3	1.4	1.4	1.2
Sri Lanka	...	...	...	...	6.9	7.9	13.6	13.5	14.9	15.0	16.1	16.5	17.8	18.2	17.2	15.7	14.8	12.8

NBFI = nonbank finance institution.

Note: End-of-year data except * fiscal year data (ended 15 July in Nepal and 31 March in Myanmar).

C3. NBFI Financing to GDP (%)

Country	2003	2004	2005	2006	2007	2008	2009	2010	2011	2012	2013	2014	2015	2016	2017	2018	2019	2020
Southeast Asia																		
Brunei Darussalam	...	...	...	...	...	...	...	7.6	6.7	7.2	8.0	9.3	10.6	10.6	9.4	8.5	8.4	9.5
Cambodia	...	...	...	...	1.8	2.7	2.9	3.7	5.0	6.2	8.6	10.8	17.1	16.2	19.8	22.6	27.7	27.9
Indonesia	...	...	...	...	...	...	...	...	...	...	...	...	...	3.4	3.3	3.2	3.2	2.8
Lao People's Democratic Republic	...	...	...	...	...	...	...	0.1	0.1	0.1	0.5	0.4	0.7	1.1	1.6	3.2	3.7	3.1
Malaysia	...	...	...	...	0.37	0.30	0.29	0.07	0.10	0.12	0.13	0.13	0.12	0.13	0.09	0.10	0.10	0.09
Myanmar*	...	...	...	...	...	...	...	...	...	0.1	0.1	0.2	0.2	0.3	0.5	2.4	...	...
Philippines	...	...	...	...	...	...	0.1	0.1	0.1	0.1	0.1	1.0	2.2	2.5	2.4	2.9	3.1	1.3
Singapore	...	...	...	...	...	...	...	2.5	2.7	3.1	3.0	3.1	3.1	2.9	2.7	2.6	2.9	3.0
Thailand	...	...	...	...	...	...	...	...	...	...	...	...	...	...	...	...	...	...
Viet Nam	...	...	...	...	...	...	...	...	...	1.1	1.3	1.4	1.5	1.6	1.7	1.7	1.3	1.5
South Asia																		
Bangladesh	...	...	...	...	...	...	...	...	...	2.5	2.9	3.0	3.0	3.1	3.1	2.9	2.6	2.4
India	...	...	...	...	...	...	...	...	...	...	...	...	0.4	0.5	0.6	0.7	0.6	0.8
Nepal*	...	...	...	...	...	...	...	...	...	...	...	...	...	...	3.5	4.2	6.1	6.7
Pakistan	...	...	...	...	0.4	0.4	0.3	0.2	0.2	0.2	0.2	0.2	0.2	0.3	0.3	0.3	0.3	0.3
Sri Lanka	...	...	...	...	3.0	2.9	4.4	4.1	5.4	5.4	5.8	6.2	7.6	8.4	8.3	8.4	8.0	7.8

GDP = gross domestic product, NBFI = nonbank finance institution.

Note: End-of-year data except * fiscal year data (ended 15 July in Nepal and 31 March in Myanmar).

C4-1. Nonperforming NBFI Financing (local currency)

Country	2003	2004	2005	2006	2007	2008	2009	2010	2011	2012	2013	2014	2015	2016	2017	2018	2019	2020
Southeast Asia																		
Brunei Darussalam	...	...	...	...	...	...	...	13	13	19	20	24	20	19	20	15	17	35
Cambodia	...	...	...	...	1,171	4,719	34,847	20,361	5,753	10,284	30,880	52,119	94,788	210,885	298,210	335,399	262,692	563,564
Indonesia	...	...	...	...	...	...	...	...	...	...	...	...	...	12,644	12,260	11,810	10,864	...
Lao People's Democratic Republic	...	...	...	...	...	...	...	...	...	...	...	...	...	...	...	...	...	...
Malaysia	...	...	...	...	...	...	...	...	...	...	...	...	...	...	...	...	...	...
Myanmar*	...	...	...	...	...	...	...	...	...	42	41	68	258	1,645	2,769	9,085	14,376	...
Philippines	...	...	...	...	...	...	...	...	...	...	...	...	20,356	32,840	24,868	29,302	38,268	...
Singapore	...	...	...	...	...	...	...	...	...	...	...	...	...	...	...	...	...	...
Thailand	...	...	...	...	...	...	...	...	...	...	...	...	...	...	...	...	...	...
Viet Nam	...	...	...	...	...	...	...	...	84	912	140	87	115	554	16,319	18,669	644,466	705,880
South Asia																		
Bangladesh	...	...	...	...	...	...	...	...	...	13,871	18,064	20,223	40,012	38,693	45,232	54,394	63,988	100,536
India	...	...	...	...	...	...	...	...	...	...	...	...	467,032	606,742	867,226	1,530,874	1,540,101	1,265,910
Nepal	...	...	...	...	...	...	...	...	...	...	...	...	...	...	...	...	...	...
Pakistan	...	...	...	...	1,589	2,031	2,862	3,390	2,961	3,312	3,014	1,620	2,174	2,288	1,970	2,109	2,176	6,589
Sri Lanka	...	...	...	...	...	...	6,053	20,911	19,904	23,627	37,024	44,095	47,429	52,973	65,895	93,010	127,626	161,602

NBFI = nonbank finance institution.

Notes: End-of-year data except * fiscal year data (ended 31 March in Myanmar). Brunei Darussalam: B$ million (finance companies only for 2010–2011; finance companies and pawnbrokers for 2012–2020); Cambodia: KR million (microfinance institutions and leasing companies); Indonesia: Rp billion (data from 2016 to 2019 based on New Business Activities (POJK 35/POJK.05/2018) and New Economy Sector (SEOJK 3/SEOJK.05/2016); data from 2007 to 2015 based on the old classification; excludes microfinance institutions and government pawnshops because of no nonperforming financing data); Myanmar: MK million (microfinance institutions); Philippines: P million (credit unions and cooperatives only); Viet Nam: D million (microfinance institutions only for 2011–2018; microfinance institutions and People's Credit Funds for 2019–2020); Bangladesh Tk million (nonbank finance institutions regulated by Bangladesh Bank); India: Rs million (nonbank finance institutions regulated by Reserve Bank of India); Pakistan: PRs million (microfinance institutions and leasing companies); Sri Lanka: SLRs million (nonbank finance institutions regulated by Central Bank of Sri Lanka).

C4-2. Nonperforming NBFI Financing ($ million)

Country	2003	2004	2005	2006	2007	2008	2009	2010	2011	2012	2013	2014	2015	2016	2017	2018	2019	2020
Southeast Asia																		
Brunei Darussalam	...	...	...	...	...	...	...	10.0	10.1	15.5	16.0	17.8	14.4	13.2	15.1	11.0	12.8	26.1
Cambodia	...	...	...	...	0.3	1.2	8.4	5.0	1.4	2.6	7.7	12.8	23.4	52.1	73.8	83.2	64.3	138.2
Indonesia	...	...	...	...	...	...	...	...	...	...	...	...	...	941.0	904.9	815.6	781.5	...
Lao People's Democratic Republic	...	...	...	...	...	...	...	...	...	...	...	...	...	...	...	...	...	...
Malaysia	...	...	...	...	...	...	...	...	...	...	...	...	...	...	...	...	...	...
Myanmar*	...	...	...	...	...	...	...	...	...	0.05	0.04	0.07	0.20	1.21	2.03	5.86	9.81	...
Philippines	...	...	...	...	...	...	...	...	...	...	...	...	431.6	659.3	498.1	555.8	754.1	...
Singapore	...	...	...	...	...	...	...	...	...	...	...	...	...	...	...	...	...	...
Thailand	...	...	...	...	...	...	...	...	...	...	...	...	...	...	...	...	...	...
Viet Nam	...	...	...	...	...	...	...	...	0.004	0.044	0.007	0.004	0.005	0.025	0.728	0.8	27.8	30.5
South Asia																		
Bangladesh	...	...	...	...	...	...	...	...	...	173.7	232.3	259.4	509.7	491.6	546.9	648.3	753.7	1,185.5
India	...	...	...	...	...	...	...	...	...	...	...	...	7,041.5	8,928.6	13,565.8	21,934.7	21,608.2	17,328.5
Nepal	...	...	...	...	...	...	...	...	...	...	...	...	...	...	...	...	...	...
Pakistan	...	...	...	...	26.0	25.7	34.0	39.6	32.9	34.1	28.5	16.1	20.7	21.8	17.8	15.2	14.1	41.3
Sri Lanka	...	...	...	...	...	...	52.9	188.5	174.8	185.8	283.2	336.5	329.2	353.6	431.1	510.3	702.7	866.9

NBFI = nonbank finance institution.

Notes: End-of-year data except * fiscal year data (ended 31 March in Myanmar). Exchange rates of local currency to US dollar refer to end-of-year currency rates from the International Monetary Fund (IMF) International Financial Statistics in designated years.

C5. NBFI NPF to Total Financing (%)

Country	2003	2004	2005	2006	2007	2008	2009	2010	2011	2012	2013	2014	2015	2016	2017	2018	2019	2020
Southeast Asia																		
Brunei Darussalam	...	...	...	...	...	...	...	0.91	0.84	1.10	1.12	1.16	1.08	1.14	1.28	0.97	1.12	0.95
Cambodia	...	...	...	...	0.19	0.42	2.80	1.18	0.22	0.29	0.59	0.71	0.75	1.60	1.68	1.49	0.86	1.95
Indonesia	...	...	...	...	...	...	...	...	...	...	...	...	...	3.3	3.0	2.7	2.4	4.0
Lao People's Democratic Republic	...	...	...	...	...	...	...	...	...	...	...	...	...	...	...	...	...	...
Malaysia	...	...	...	...	...	...	...	...	...	...	...	...	...	...	...	...	...	...
Myanmar*	...	...	...	...	...	...	...	...	...	0.09	0.06	0.06	0.15	0.63	0.65	1.15	0.80	...
Philippines	...	...	...	...	...	...	...	...	...	...	...	...	...	...	...	...	...	...
Singapore	...	...	...	...	...	...	...	...	...	...	...	...	...	...	...	...	...	...
Thailand	...	...	...	...	...	...	...	...	...	...	...	...	...	...	...	...	...	...
Viet Nam	...	...	...	...	...	...	...	...	0.000	0.003	0.000	0.000	0.000	0.001	0.019	0.019	0.851	0.764
South Asia																		
Bangladesh	...	...	...	...	...	...	...	...	...	5.2	5.2	5.0	8.9	7.3	7.3	8.2	9.5	15.0
India	...	...	...	...	...	...	...	...	...	...	...	...	3.7	3.9	4.8	7.1	6.4	5.8
Nepal*	...	...	...	...	...	...	...	...	...	...	...	...	...	0.9	0.8	1.0	1.2	2.3
Pakistan	...	...	...	...	4.2	5.1	7.7	9.4	9.0	8.9	7.1	3.1	3.4	2.9	2.2	1.9	1.8	6.0
Sri Lanka	...	...	...	...	...	...	2.8	7.9	5.1	5.0	6.7	6.9	5.7	5.3	5.9	7.7	10.6	13.9

NBFI = nonbank finance institution, NPF = nonperforming financing.

Note: End-of-year data except * fiscal year data (ended 15 July in Nepal and 31 March in Myanmar).

C6. NBFI Financing by Sector (% share, latest available year)

Item	Brunei Darussalam	Cambodia	Indonesia	Lao People's Democratic Republic	Malaysia	Myanmar	Philippines	Singapore	Thailand	Viet Nam
Agriculture	...	19.2	4.9	7.4	...	30.8	...	...	...	...
Manufacturing	...	1.0	10.0	0.4	...	10.5	...	...	...	...
Transportation and communication	97.2	5.9	7.3	0.1	...	...	...	...	...	...
Construction	...	3.8	3.5	3.0	...	...	...	...	...	...
Wholesale and retail trade	...	20.9	22.4	21.0	...	33.2	...	...	...	...
Other services	...	15.9	43.0	2.5	72.4	25.6	...	...	...	...
Others	2.8	33.3	8.9	65.7	27.6	...	...	...	...	...
Year	2020	2020	2020	2020	2020	September 2019				

Item	Bangladesh	India*	Nepal*	Pakistan	Sri Lanka
Agriculture	2.5	2.6	42.2	42.0	...
Manufacturing	43.6	53.6	...	8.0	...
Transportation and communication	3.9	...	...	...	...
Construction	18.9	...	...	...	...
Wholesale and retail trade	13.6	23.3	...	20.0	...
Other services	...	15.8	33.8	11.0	...
Others	17.5	4.7	24.1	19.0	...
Year	2020	FY2020	FY 2020	2020	

NBFI = nonbank finance institution.

Notes: End-of-year data except * fiscal year (FY) data (ended 31 March in India and 15 July in Nepal) and September 2019 data in Myanmar. For Brunei Darussalam, finance companies only. For Cambodia and the Lao People's Democratic Republic, microfinance institutions only. For Indonesia, NBFI financing based on new economic sector (SEOJK 3/SEOJK.05/2016). For Malaysia, "Other services" include life sciences and information and communication technology. For Bangladesh, nonbank finance institutions regulated by Bangladesh Bank. For Nepal, microfinance institutions only; "Others" includes wholesale credit, and cottage and micro industries. For Pakistan, microfinance institutions only.

C7. NBFI Financing by Region (% share, latest available year)

Item	Brunei Darussalam	Cambodia	Indonesia	Lao People's Democratic Republic	Malaysia	Myanmar	Philippines	Singapore	Thailand	Viet Nam
Capital city	...	11.3	...	...	...	99.3	36.5	...	...	...
Other areas	...	88.8	...	...	...	0.7	63.5	...	...	...
Year		2020				September 2019	2019			

Item	Bangladesh	India	Nepal	Pakistan	Sri Lanka
Capital city	...	...	...	0.4	...
Other areas	...	...	...	99.6	...
Year				2020	

NBFI = nonbank finance institution.

Notes: For Cambodia, Myanmar, and Pakistan, microfinance institutions only. For the Philippines, credit unions and cooperatives only.

C8-1. Market Capitalization (local currency)

Country	2003	2004	2005	2006	2007	2008	2009	2010	2011	2012	2013	2014	2015	2016	2017	2018	2019	2020
Southeast Asia																		
BRU (no exchange market)	...	...	...	...	...	...	...	...	...	...	...	...	...	...	...	...	...	...
CAM - Main board	...	...	...	...	...	...	...	...	...	539,234	466,176	658,682	716,387	804,539	1,230,678	1,771,677	2,805,807	9,827,745
INO - Main board	...	...	...	...	1,988,326	1,076,491	2,019,375	3,247,097	3,537,294	4,126,995	4,219,020	5,228,043	4,872,702	5,753,613	7,052,389	7,023,497	7,265,016	6,970,010
INO - Acceleration Board	...	...	...	...	...	...	...	...	...	...	...	...	...	...	...	...	...	1,068
LAO - Main board	...	...	...	...	...	...	...	...	4,638,300	8,136,540	8,826,800	10,968,690	12,047,100	10,414,100	11,352,400	9,868,000	9,618,492	7,908,931
MAL - ACE	...	...	...	...	...	...	5,293	5,761	6,415	6,935	9,865	9,665	11,853	9,956	15,646	12,141	18,829	35,590
MAL - LEAP	...	...	...	...	...	...	...	...	...	...	...	...	...	...	213	920	2,435	3,146
MYA - Main board	...	...	...	...	...	...	...	...	...	...	...	...	...	583,957	578,721	554,599	627,449	...
PHI - SME board	...	263	290	322	4,509	2,226	335	549	713	586	871	34,470	28,513	17,029	20,657	11,308	11,587	58,431
SIN - Catalist	...	...	...	...	...	3,562	5,325	6,462	5,347	6,782	9,326	10,791	9,521	9,233	12,819	10,534	9,809	10,975
THA - mai	...	...	...	...	38	22	39	55	77	133	177	383	323	425	339	241	215	235
VIE - UPCoM	...	...	...	...	...	...	4,259,814	16,237,680	22,663,598	28,868,424	25,745,000	37,169,559	61,033,252	303,359,258	677,705,000	893,777,000	911,940,645	1,000,696,230
South Asia																		
BAN - CSE*	...	...	...	...	399,268	777,743	974,948	1,538,393	2,237,585	1,878,171	1,919,891	2,286,679	2,370,421	2,496,849	3,113,243	3,123,522	3,293,303	2,447,567
BAN - DSE*	...	...	...	...	475,855	931,025	1,241,339	2,700,745	2,853,892	2,491,613	2,530,246	2,943,202	3,247,306	3,185,749	3,801,001	3,847,348	3,998,164	3,119,670
IND - BSE SME Exchange	...	...	...	...	...	...	...	...	...	2,871	30,124	90,699	89,577	188,444	215,740	186,110	183,489	212,795
IND - NSE Emerge	...	...	...	...	...	...	...	...	...	1,490	2,746	4,292	5,174	14,105	105,207	126,396	79,942	56,048
NEP - NPSE*	...	...	...	...	...	366,248	514,940	376,870	323,484	368,262	514,430	1,057,166	989,404	1,890,130	1,856,829	1,435,138	1,567,499	1,792,763
PAK - PSX	...	...	...	...	4,329,910	1,858,699	2,705,880	3,268,949	2,945,785	4,242,278	6,051,696	7,380,532	6,947,358	9,628,514	8,570,926	7,692,787	7,811,812	8,035,363
SRI - Colombo Stock Exchange	...	...	...	...	820,652	488,813	1,092,138	2,210,452	2,213,873	2,167,581	2,459,897	3,104,864	2,937,998	2,745,406	2,899,291	2,839,446	2,851,313	2,960,648

BAN = Bangladesh; BRU = Brunei Darussalam; BSE = Bombay Stock Exchange; CAM = Cambodia; CSE = Chittagong Stock Exchange; DSE = Dhaka Stock Exchange; INO = Indonesia; LAO = Lao People's Democratic Republic; MAL = Malaysia; MYA = Myanmar; NEP = Nepal; NPSE = Nepal Stock Exchange; NSE = National Stock Exchange; PAK = Pakistan; PHI = Philippines; PSX = Pakistan Stock Exchange; SIN = Singapore; SME = small and medium-sized enterprise; SRI = Sri Lanka; THA = Thailand; VIE = Viet Nam.

Notes: End-of-year data except * fiscal year data (ended 30 June in Bangladesh and 15 July in Nepal). Cambodia: KR million; Indonesia: Rp billion; Lao People's Democratic Republic: KN million; Malaysia: RM million; Myanmar: MK million; Philippines: P million; Singapore: S$ million; Thailand: B billion; Viet Nam: D million; Bangladesh: Tk million; India: Rs million; Nepal: NRs million; Pakistan: PRs million; Sri Lanka: SLRs million.

C8-2. Market Capitalization ($ million)

Country	2003	2004	2005	2006	2007	2008	2009	2010	2011	2012	2013	2014	2015	2016	2017	2018	2019	2020
Southeast Asia																		
BRU (no exchange market)	...	...	...	...	...	...	...	...	...	...	...	...	...	...	...	...	...	...
CAM - Main board	...	...	...	...	...	...	...	...	...	135	117	162	177	199	305	439	687	2,411
INO - Main board	...	...	...	...	211,097	98,310	214,827	361,150	390,085	426,783	346,133	420,261	353,222	428,224	520,548	485,015	522,625	494,152
INO - Acceleration Board	...	...	...	...	...	...	...	...	...	...	...	...	...	...	...	...	...	76
LAO - Main board	...	...	...	...	...	...	...	...	578	1,019	1,100	1,357	1,479	1,272	1,369	1,157	1,085	853
MAL - ACE	...	...	...	...	...	...	1,546	1,868	2,019	2,268	3,006	2,765	2,762	2,219	3,852	2,934	4,601	8,869
MAL - LEAP	...	...	...	...	...	...	...	...	...	...	...	...	...	...	52	222	595	784
MYA - Main board	...	...	...	...	...	...	...	...	...	...	...	...	...	430	425	358	428	...
PHI - SME board	...	4.7	5.5	6.5	108.9	46.9	7.2	12.5	16.2	14.2	19.6	773	605	342	414	214	228	1,216
SIN - Catalist	...	...	...	...	...	2,475	3,795	5,019	4,111	5,543	7,371	8,167	6,734	6,384	9,591	7,718	7,281	8,301
THA - mai	...	...	...	...	1,135	635	1,174	1,828	2,439	4,342	5,405	11,621	8,963	11,872	10,368	7,421	7,135	7,825
VIE - UPCoM	...	...	...	...	...	...	237	858	1,088	1,386	1,224	1,749	2,788	13,690	30,221	39,158	39,384	43,262
South Asia																		
BAN - CSE*	...	...	...	...	5,822	11,285	14,075	21,744	27,337	23,521	24,693	29,335	30,196	31,725	37,645	37,229	38,790	28,862
BAN - DSE*	...	...	...	...	6,939	13,509	17,921	38,173	34,866	31,204	32,543	37,758	41,367	40,479	45,961	45,856	47,093	36,788
IND - BSE SME Exchange	...	...	...	...	...	...	...	...	...	52	487	1,432	1,351	2,773	3,375	2,667	2,574	2,913
IND - NSE Emerge	...	...	...	...	...	...	...	...	...	27	44	68	78	208	1,646	1,811	1,122	767
NEP - NPSE*	...	...	...	...	...	4,717	6,918	5,260	3,783	4,237	5,175	10,607	9,221	17,501	18,036	12,475	13,835	15,215
PAK - PSX	...	...	...	...	70,726	23,499	32,112	38,139	32,743	43,674	57,265	73,468	66,250	91,864	77,612	55,427	50,443	50,349
SRI - Colombo Stock Exchange	...	...	...	...	7,548	4,320	9,548	19,922	19,437	17,046	18,813	23,692	20,394	18,327	18,968	15,578	15,698	15,883

BAN = Bangladesh; BRU = Brunei Darussalam; BSE = Bombay Stock Exchange; CAM = Cambodia; CSE = Chittagong Stock Exchange; DSE = Dhaka Stock Exchange; INO = Indonesia; LAO = Lao People's Democratic Republic; MAL = Malaysia; MYA = Myanmar; NEP = Nepal; NPSE = Nepal Stock Exchange; NSE = National Stock Exchange; PAK = Pakistan; PHI = Philippines; PSX = Pakistan Stock Exchange; SIN = Singapore; SME = small and medium-sized enterprise; SRI = Sri Lanka; THA = Thailand; VIE = Viet Nam.

Notes: End-of-year data except * fiscal year data (ended 30 June in Bangladesh and 15 July in Nepal). Exchange rates of local currency to US dollar refer to end-of-year currency rates from the International Monetary Fund (IMF) International Financial Statistics in designated years.

C8-3.Market Capitalization to GDP (%)

Country	2003	2004	2005	2006	2007	2008	2009	2010	2011	2012	2013	2014	2015	2016	2017	2018	2019	2020
Southeast Asia																		
BRU (no exchange market)	...	...	...	...	...	...	...	...	...	...	...	...	...	...	...	...	...	...
CAM - Main board	...	...	...	...	...	...	...	...	...	1.0	0.8	1.0	1.0	1.0	1.4	1.8	2.6	9.5
INO-Main board	...	...	...	...	50.3	21.8	36.0	47.3	45.2	47.9	44.2	49.5	42.3	46.4	51.9	47.3	45.9	45.2
INO - Acceleration Board	...	...	...	...	...	...	...	...	...	...	...	...	...	...	...	...	...	0.01
LAO- Main board	...	...	...	...	...	...	...	...	7.2	10.0	9.4	10.3	10.3	8.1	8.1	6.5	5.9	4.6
MAL-ACE	...	...	...	...	...	...	0.7	0.7	0.7	0.7	1.0	0.9	1.0	0.8	1.1	0.8	1.2	2.5
MAL-LEAP	...	...	...	...	...	...	...	...	...	...	...	...	...	...	0.0	0.1	0.2	0.2
MYA-Main board	...	...	...	...	...	...	...	...	...	...	...	...	...	0.7	0.6	1.7	...	...
PHI-SME board	...	0.005	0.005	0.005	0.065	0.029	0.004	0.006	0.007	0.005	0.007	0.261	0.204	0.113	0.125	0.062	0.059	0.326
SIN-Catalist	...	...	...	...	...	...	...	2.0	1.5	1.8	2.4	2.7	2.2	2.1	2.7	2.1	1.9	2.3
THA-mai	...	...	...	...	0.4	0.2	0.4	0.5	0.7	1.1	1.4	2.9	2.4	2.9	2.2	1.5	1.3	1.5
VIE-UPCoM	...	...	...	...	...	...	...	0.2	0.6	0.7	0.8	0.7	0.9	1.4	6.1	12.2	14.8	15.9
South Asia																		
BAN - CSE*	...	...	...	...	7.3	12.4	13.8	19.3	24.4	17.8	16.0	17.0	15.6	14.4	15.8	13.9	13.0	8.8
BAN - DSE*	...	...	...	...	8.7	14.8	17.6	33.9	31.2	23.6	21.1	21.9	21.4	18.4	19.2	17.1	15.7	11.2
IND - BSE SME Exchange	...	...	...	...	...	...	...	...	...	0.003	0.027	0.073	0.065	0.122	0.126	0.099	0.090	0.108
IND - NSE Emerge	...	...	...	...	...	...	...	...	...	0.001	0.002	0.003	0.004	0.009	0.062	0.067	0.039	0.028
NEP - NPSE*	...	...	...	...	...	44.9	52.1	31.6	20.7	20.9	26.4	47.4	40.8	72.5	60.3	41.5	40.6	45.8
PAK - PSX	...	...	...	...	46.9	17.5	20.5	22.0	16.1	21.2	27.0	29.3	25.3	33.1	26.8	22.2	20.5	19.3
SRI - Colombo Stock Exchange	...	...	...	...	22.9	11.1	22.6	34.5	30.7	24.8	25.6	30.0	26.8	22.9	21.8	19.9	19.0	19.8

BAN = Bangladesh; BRU = Brunei Darussalam; BSE = Bombay Stock Exchange; CAM = Cambodia; CSE = Chittagong Stock Exchange; DSE = Dhaka Stock Exchange; GDP = gross domestic product; INO = Indonesia; LAO = Lao People's Democratic Republic; MAL = Malaysia; MYA = Myanmar; NEP = Nepal; NPSE = Nepal Stock Exchange; NSE = National Stock Exchange; PAK = Pakistan; PHI = Philippines; PSX = Pakistan Stock Exchange; SIN = Singapore; SME = small and medium-sized enterprise; SRI = Sri Lanka; THA = Thailand; VIE = Viet Nam.

Note: End-of-year data except * fiscal year data (ended 30 June in Bangladesh and 15 July in Nepal).

C8-4. Number of Listed Companies

Country	2003	2004	2005	2006	2007	2008	2009	2010	2011	2012	2013	2014	2015	2016	2017	2018	2019	2020
Southeast Asia																		
BRU (no exchange market)	...	...	...	...	...	...	...	...	...	...	...	...	...	...	...	...	...	...
CAM - Main board	...	...	...	...	...	...	...	...	...	1	1	2	3	4	5	5	5	7
INO - Main board	...	...	...	...	383	396	398	420	440	459	483	506	521	537	566	619	668	713
INO - Acceleration Board	...	...	...	...	...	...	...	...	...	...	...	...	...	...	...	...	...	5
LAO - Main board	...	...	...	...	...	...	...	...	2	2	3	4	5	5	6	9	11	11
MAL - ACE	...	...	...	...	...	...	116	113	119	112	109	107	109	113	115	119	129	135
MAL - LEAP	...	...	...	...	...	...	...	...	...	...	...	...	...	...	2	13	28	34
MYA - Main board	...	...	...	...	...	...	...	...	...	...	...	...	...	3	4	5	5	...
PHI - SME board	...	3	3	3	2	2	2	2	2	2	2	4	4	4	4	4	5	7
SIN - Catalist	...	...	...	...	...	133	134	133	136	139	139	155	172	185	200	214	216	217
THA - mai	...	...	...	...	48	49	60	66	73	81	95	111	122	134	150	159	169	175
VIE - UPCoM	...	...	...	...	...	...	34	109	131	132	142	169	256	417	690	810	872	910
South Asia																		
BAN - CSE*	...	...	...	...	204	...	228	204	200	207	220	232	252	261	266	274	288	293
BAN - DSE*	...	...	...	...	259	...	282	243	232	238	251	263	283	292	297	305	317	321
IND - BSE SME Exchange	...	...	...	...	...	...	...	...	...	11	43	82	119	162	216	281	314	331
IND - NSE Emerge	...	...	...	...	...	...	...	...	...	2	4	6	11	33	111	192	206	214
NEP - NPSE*	...	...	...	...	...	142	159	176	207	216	228	235	232	230	208	196	215	212
PAK - PSX	...	...	...	...	654	653	651	644	638	573	560	557	554	558	559	546	534	531
SRI - Colombo Stock Exchange	...	...	...	...	235	235	231	241	272	287	289	294	294	295	296	297	289	283

BAN = Bangladesh; BRU = Brunei Darussalam; BSE = Bombay Stock Exchange; CAM = Cambodia; CSE = Chittagong Stock Exchange; DSE = Dhaka Stock Exchange; INO = Indonesia; LAO = Lao People's Democratic Republic; MAL = Malaysia; MYA = Myanmar; NEP = Nepal; NPSE = Nepal Stock Exchange; NSE = National Stock Exchange; PAK = Pakistan; PHI = Philippines; PSX = Pakistan Stock Exchange; SIN = Singapore; SME = small and medium-sized enterprise; SRI = Sri Lanka; THA = Thailand; VIE = Viet Nam.

Note: End-of-year data except * fiscal year data (ended 30 June in Bangladesh and 15 July in Nepal).

www.ingramcontent.com/pod-product-compliance
Lightning Source LLC
Chambersburg PA
CBHW041753220926
51847CB00014B/191
9789292691745